W9-BKS-065

·THE·
·ROMAN·WORLD·

1.1 Frontispiece   Rome: the Eternal City

·THE·
·ROMAN·WORLD·

EDITED BY
JOHN WACHER

Emeritus Professor of Archaeology
University of Leicester

Volume I

LONDON AND NEW YORK

RARITAN VALLEY COMMUNITY COLLEGE
EVELYN S. FIELD LIBRARY

First published 1987 by Routledge & Kegan Paul Ltd

First published in paperback 1990
by Routledge
11 New Fetter Lane, London EC4P 4EE

Simultaneously published in the USA and Canada
by Routledge
29 West 35th Street, New York, NY 10001

Reissued in paperback 2002

Routledge is an imprint of the Taylor & Francis Group

© Routledge 1987, 1990, 2002

Printed and bound in Great Britain by
TJ International Ltd, Padstow, Cornwall

All rights reserved. No part of this book may be reprinted or reproduced or utilised in any form
or by any electronic, mechanical, or other means, now known or hereafter invented, including
photocopying and recording, or in any information storage or retrieval system, without
permission in writing from the publishers.

British Library Cataloguing in Publication Data
A catalogue record for this book is available from the British Library

Library of Congress Cataloging in Publication Data
A catalog record for this book has been requested

ISBN 0-415-26315-8 (Volume I)
ISBN 0-415-26316-6 (Volume II)
ISBN 0-415-26314-X (Set)

·CONTENTS·

VOLUME I

Editor's preface   xxii   Acknowledgments   xxxii
Preface to the reissued edition   xxiii   Chronological table   xxxiv
Contributors   xxiv   Glossary   xlv
General bibliography and principal
abbreviations used in the text   xxvi

PART 1

1   **Introduction**
     John Wacher   3

PART 2
·THE·RISE·OF·THE·EMPIRE·

2   **Celtic Europe before the Romans**   **4**   **The legacy of the Republic**
     John Collis   15   *David C. Braund*   55
3   **Hellenistic influence on the**   Bibliography for Part 2   69
     Roman world
     Keith Branigan   38

PART 3
·THE·ARMY·

5   **The army of the Republic**   **7**   **The army of the Late Empire**
     G. R. Watson   75   *R. S. O. Tomlin*   107
6   **The imperial army**   Bibliography for Part 3   134
     Alistair Scott Anderson   89

PART 4
·THE·FRONTIERS·

8	**Mainland Europe**	11	**The East**
	Valerie A. Maxfield 139		*David Kennedy* 266
9	**Britain**		Bibliography for Part 4 309
	David J. Breeze 198		
10	**Africa**		
	Charles Daniels 223		

PART 5
·CITIES·TOWNS·AND·VILLAGES·

12	**Urbanization in the Eastern Empire**	14	**Townships and villages**
	Barbara Levick 329		*Andrew Poulter* 388
13	**Urbanization in Italy and the Western Empire**		Bibliography for Part 5 412
	J. F. Drinkwater 345		

PART 6
·GOVERNMENT·AND·LAW·

15	**Government and the provinces**	17	**Government and administration in the Late Empire**
	Graham Burton 423		*J. H. W. G. Liebeschuetz* 455
16	**Law and the legal system in the Principate**		Bibliography for Part 6 470
	Elizabeth Green 440		

VOLUME II

PART 7
·RURAL·LIFE·

18	**Agriculture and horticulture**	20	**The villa in Italy and the provinces**
	Sian Rees 481		*John Percival* 527
19	**Animal husbandry**		Bibliography for Part 7 548
	Shimon Applebaum 504		

CONTENTS

PART 8
·THE·ECONOMY·

21 Imperial estates
    Dorothy J. Thompson   555
22 The monetary system
    John Kent   568
23 Industrial growth
    W. H. Manning   586
24 Mining
    Ann Woods   611

25 Trade within the Empire and
    beyond the frontiers
    A. J. Parker   635
26 Transport by land and water
    Alan McWhirr   658
    Bibliography for Part 8   671

PART 9
·SOCIETY·

27 Romans and non-Romans
    Mark Hassall   685
28 Labour
    P. A. Brunt   701

29 Society and the artist
    T. F. C. Blagg   717
    Bibliography for Part 9   743

PART 10
·RELIGION·AND·BURIAL·

30 Classical religions
    John Ferguson   749
31 Ruler-worship
    John Ferguson   766
32 Provincial cults
    Miranda J. Green   785

33 The rise of Christianity
    Jill Harries   796
34 Burial customs of Rome and the
    provinces
    Richard Jones   812
    Bibliography for Part 10   838

PART 11
·POST-SCRIPT·

35 Post-script
    John Wacher   847
    Index   850

vii

·PLATES·

VOLUME I

1.1   Frontispiece: Rome: the Eternal City (*Istituto Italiano di Cultura, London*)

pages

3.1   Sculptured Etruscan sarcophagus (*Scala*)   51

3.2   The François Vase, Florence Museum (*Scala*)   51

3.3   Bust of Cicero (*Uffizi Gallery, Florence*)   52

3.4   The 'Boxer' of Apollonios (*Museo delle Terme, Rome*)   52

3.5   Greek comedy illustrated on a relief from Pompeii   53
    (*National Museum of Pompeii*)   53

3.6   Bust of Epicurus (*Metropolitan Museum of Art, New York*)   53

3.7   Bust of Zeno (*National Museum, Naples*)   53

3.8   Statue of Cato (*Vatican Museum*)   54

7.1   Diocletian and his colleagues (*Scala*)   121

7.2   Arch of Galerius, Thessalonika (*Deutsches Archäologisches Institut, Athens*)   121

7.3   Cavalry helmet, *c.* 320, of iron and silver-gilt (*Rijksmuseum van Oudheden te Leiden*)   122

7.4   *Notitia Dignitatum*: insignia of the Master of the Offices (*Bodleian Library,* and R. *Goodburn*)   123

7.5   *Notitia Dignitatum*: insignia of the Count of the Sacred Largesses (*Bodleian Library,* and R. *Goodburn*)   124

7.6   The accession donative of five *solidi* of Valens, Valentinian I and Gratian, and a pound of silver (*The British Museum*)   125

7.7   Silver and silver-gilt dish of Constantius II (*The British Museum*)   126
7.8   Snake (*draco*) battle-standard of gilded bronze (*Römisches-Germanisches Zentralmuseum, Mainz*)   126
7.9   Ivory diptych, *c.* 396, of Stilicho in uniform as *magister peditum praesentalis* (*Monza, Cathedral Treasury*)   127
7.10 Glass beaker from Cologne (*Römisches-Germanisches Museum, Cologne*)   128
7.11 Fourth–fifth-century Christian cemetery at Concordia   128
7.12 Silver donative dish from Geneva (*Musée d'Art et d'Histoire, Geneva*)   129
7.13 Letter-book from Panopolis (*Chester Beatty Library, Dublin*)   129
7.14 Silver donative dish of Theodosius (*Academia de la Historia, Madrid*)   130
7.15 Honorius in battle-dress on an ivory diptych dated to 406 (*Aosta Cathedral Treasury*)   131
7.16 Part of the tombstone from Phrygia on which a retired NCO of Diocletian's mobile army recorded his travels   132
7.17 Ténès hoard (*Musée St. Gsell*)   133

8.1   Aerial view of the Lorenzberg (*Otto Braasch*)   194
8.2   View along the *limes* in the Taunus region of Upper Germany   195
8.3   The Danube at the Kazan Gorge   195
8.4   Trajan's column: towers on the bank of the Danube (*Peter Connolly*)   196
8.5   The insignia of the *comes Italiae* from the *Notitia Dignitatum* (*Bodleian Library, Oxford*)   197

9.1   Milecastle 42 (Cawfields) on Hadrian's Wall (*Crown Copyright*)   218
9.2   Turret 48a (Willowford east) on Hadrian's Wall   218
9.3   Aerial view of Hadrian's Wall looking east (*Copyright: Committee for Aerial Photography, University of Cambridge*)   219
9.4   The fort at Housesteads on Hadrian's Wall from the air (*Copyright: Committee for Aerial Photography, University of Cambridge*)   219
9.5   Aerial view of the Antonine Wall at Croy Hill looking east (*Crown Copyright*)   220
9.6   Aerial view of the fort at Rough Castle on the Antonine Wall looking north (*Crown Copyright*)   221
9.7   The Bridgeness Distance Slab from the eastern end of the Antonine Wall (*National Museums of Scotland*)   221
9.8   The Roman fort at Ardoch from the air (*Crown Copyright*)   222
9.9   The Saxon Shore fort at Portchester from the air (*Copyright: Committee for Aerial Photography, University of Cambridge*)   222

11.1 Aerial view of the Euphrates at Samosata, looking east (*Aerial Photographic Archive*) 301

11.2 (a–d) Discharge diploma of 7th November, 88 for Syria (*J. Paul Getty Museum, Sta Monica*) 302–3

11.3 Aerial view of Sura, Syria (*A. Poidebard*) 304

11.4 A dedication to Good Fortune set up by Ti. Claudius Subatianus Aquila (*British Institute of Archaeology at Ankara*) 304

11.5 Wall and road apparently of Roman origin at Zairwan, Iraq (*Aerial Photographic Archive for Archaeology in the Middle East*) 305

11.6 Aerial view of Hatra (*Aerial Photographic Archive for Archaeology in the Middle East*) 305

11.7 Aerial view of Dura-Europus, Syria (*A. Poidebard*) 306

11.8 Aerial view of Palmyra, Syria (*A. Poidebard*) 306

11.9 Aerial view of Qasr el-Azraq, Jordan (R. *Wilkins and the Crawford Collection, Oxford*) 307

11.10 Qasr el-Hallabat, Jordan (R. *Wilkins and the Crawford Collection, Oxford*) 307

11.11 Aerial view of Lejjun, Jordan (*The University Museum, Philadelphia*) 308

11.12 El-Ula Oasis, ancient Dedan in the Hedjaz, Saudi Arabia (*Jaussen and Savignac*) 308

13.1 Aerial view of Timgad, Algeria (*Dept of Antiquities, Algeria*) 380

13.2 The 'Maison Carrée', Nîmes, France 381

13.3 Model of a rich road-side cemetery, Bonn, Germany (*Rheinisches Landesmuseum, Bonn*) 381

13.4 Arles, France 382

13.5 The *castellum divisorum*, Nîmes 382

13.6 Traces of four parallel wooden water-pipes show as dark stains in the surrounding soil at Colchester, Britain (*Colchester Archaeological Trust*) 383

13.7 Triumphal arch at Orange 383

13.8 Aerial view of Cuicul, Algeria (*Dept of Antiquities, Algeria*) 384

13.9 Aerial view of Lepcis Magna (*The British School at Rome*) 385

13.10 The Pantheon, Rome (*M. Greenhalgh*) 385

13.11 School scene from Neumagen, Germany (*Rheiniches Landesmuseum, Trier*) 386

13.12 Heavy transport of woollen cloth by road: the Igel monument, Germany (*Rheiniches Landesmuseum, Trier*) 386

13.13 Heavy transport of woollen cloth by river: the Igel monument, Germany (*Rheiniches Landesmuseum, Trier*) 387

13.14 Relief of a draper's shop from Arlon, Belgium 387

14.1 Aerial view of Water Newton (Durobrivae) Britain (*Copyright: Committee for Aerial Photography, University of Cambridge*) 410

14.2 Aerial view of part of the interior of Water Newton (*Copyright: Committee for Aerial Photography, University of Cambridge*) 410

14.3 Schwarzenaker from the air (*Staatliches Konservaforaent, Saarbrucken*) 411

VOLUME II

18.1 Reconstructed hafting of a copy of a Roman scythe from Great Chesterford (*Museum of English Rural Life, Reading*) 501

18.2 A harvesting machine shown on a relief from Montaubon (*Musée Gaumais, Virton*) 501

18.3 Animals used on a modern threshing-floor at Santorini 502

18.4 Representations of olive and grape harvests on a mosaic from St-Romain-en-Gal (*Museum, St-Romain-en-Laye*) 503

19.1 Transport by ox-waggon in Asia; a sculptured frieze from Ephesus (*The British Museum*) 521

19.2 A group of bronze figurines from Città Castellana, Italy (*Metropolitan Museum of Art, New York*) 521

19.3 Part of a large sarcophagus from Rome showing a road scene with an ox-cart, horse and rider, and a dog (*Museo delle Terme, Rome*) 522

19.4 Sheep illustrated on the column of Marcus Aurelius, Rome (*Deutsches Archäologisches Institut, Rome*) 522

19.5 A shepherd with his flock; the tombstone of the freedman Iucundus, from Mainz (*Römisches-Germanisches Zentralmuseum, Mainz*) 523

19.6 Pack-horses carrying loads over a hill; the Igel monument, Trier (*Rheinisches Landesmuseum, Trier*) 523

19.7 A relief from Langres showing the transport of wine in bulk on a waggon drawn by a pair of mules (*Musée de Langres*) 523

19.8 Bronze statuette from Syria of a donkey with panniers (*The British Museum*) 524

19.9 Terracotta statuette from Aphrodisias, Asia, of a camel carrying *amphorae* (*The Louvre*) 524

19.10 Mosaic from a villa near Zliten, Tripolitania, showing grain being threshed by horses and oxen (*Deutsches Archäologisches Institut, Rome*) 525

19.11 Mosaic from a villa near Oudna in Tunisia showing livestock on an estate (*Deutches Archäologisches Institut, Rome*) 525

19.12 The equestrian statue of Marcus Aurelius, Rome (*M. Greenhalgh, Leicester*) 526

20.1	Aerial view of the villa at Vieux-Rouen-sur-Bresle, France (*Photo: R. Agache*)	547
20.2	Aerial view of the villa at Grivesnes, France (*Photo: R. Agache*)	547
22.1	Coins of the Republic and Empire discussed in the text (pp. 568–74)	584
22.2	Coins of the Empire discussed in the text (pp. 575–83)	585
23.1	(a) The first face of the funerary relief of L. Cornelius Atimetus, showing the forge on one side	606
	(b) The second face of the funerary relief of L. Cornelius Atimetus, showing the shop on the other (*Deutsches Archäologisches Institut, Rome*)	607
23.2	Pompeiian bakery with millstones	608
23.3	Relief from Rome of a donkey-powered flour mill (*Vatican Museum*)	608
23.4	Relief from the monument of the Haterii, Rome, depicting a building under construction with a crane (*Vatican Museum*)	608
23.5	Frescoes from the *triclinium* of the House of the Vettii, Pompeii, showing cupids acting as (a) perfumers; (b) goldsmiths; (c) fullers (*A. Wallace-Hadrill and Soprintendenza Archeologica Pompei*)	609
23.6	Arretine crater by M. Perennius Tigranus (*The Ashmolean Museum*)	610
23.7	The sequence of water-mills at the Barbegal, near Arles, France	610
25.1	(a) and (b) The shipwreck at Madrague de Giens, southern France, with its cargo of *amphorae* (*A. Tchernia and Centre Camille Julian*)	654
25.2	Glass jug from the workshop of Ennion (*Bristol City Museum and Art Gallery*)	655
25.3	Glass jug found at Enfield (Middx.), Britain (*Forty Hall Museum, Enfield*)	656
25.4	The Pantheon, Rome, showing the size of the columns in the portico (*M. Greenhalgh*)	657
26.1	Roman bridge at Rimini (*Fototeca dell'Unione, Rome*)	668
26.2	South-west corner of the late first-century timber quay and possible abutment of the contemporary bridge over the Thames, at Pudding Lane, London (*Museum of London*)	668
26.3	Late first-century timber quay backed by an open-fronted warehouse, Pudding Lane, London (*Museum of London*)	669
26.4	The *pharos* at Dover (*Crown Copyright*)	670
26.5	Mosaic from the Piazzale delle Corporazioni, Ostia, showing a grain ship from Sicily (*Soprintendenza Acheologica Ostia*)	670

27.1 (a) Inner faces of the *diploma* of AD 122 (*CIL* XVI 69) granting
Roman citizenship to a Pannonian, Gemellus 699

(b) Outer faces of the same *diploma* (*Photos: S. Laidlaw*) 699

27.2 Dedicatory inscription from Walldürn on the *limes* in southern
Germany (*ILS* 9184) (*Photo: M. M. Roxan*) 700

29.1 *Aureus* of Nero (*The British Museum*) 733

29.2 Bronze statue of Aulus Metellus (*Archaeological Museum, Florence*) 733

29.3 Portrait of a Roman patrician, Rome (*Museo Torlonia*) 733

29.4 Marble statues: 'Orestes and Electra' from the school of Pasiteles
(*Museo Nazionale, Naples*) 734

29.5 Caryatids from the Forum of Augustus, Rome (*Comune di Roma
Ripartizione X*) 735

29.6 Garden of the House of M. Lucretius, Pompeii (*Soprintendenza
Archeologica Pompei*) 735

29.7 Procession of the Imperial Family on the Ara Pacis, Rome
(*M. Greenhalgh*) 736

29.8 *Aureus* of Claudius with a triumphal arch inscribed DE BRITANN
(*The British Museum*) 736

29.9 The Arch of Titus, Rome. Relief showing the triumphal procession
(*M. Greenhalgh*) 737

29.10 Relief carving from Aphrodisias showing Claudius overcoming
Britannia (*Photo: M. Ali Doğenei. Copyright Aphrodisias Excavations and
the Roman Society*) 737

29.11 Follis of Diocletian (*The British Museum*) 738

29.12 Septimius Severus and Julia Domna in a relief on the Arch of the
Argentarii, Rome (*M. Greenhalgh*) 738

29.13 Tombstone of Regina from South Shields, Britain (*The University
Museum, Newcastle and the National Museum of Wales*) 739

29.14 Shipbuilding scene from the tombstone of P. Longidienus, Ravenna
(*T. F. C. Blagg*) 740

29.15 Scene showing payment and accounting from a tomb at Neumagen,
Germany (*Rheiniches Landesmuseum Trier*) 740

29.16 Landscape painting from the House of the Small Fountain, Pompeii
(*Soprintendenza Archeologica Pompei*) 741

29.17 Cornelian intaglio, showing a Trojan scene, and signed by
Dioskourides (*Chatsworth, Collection of the Duke of Devonshire*) 741

29.18 Tombstone of the sculptor M. Se . . . Amabilis from Bordeaux
(*J. M. Arnaud, Musée d'Aquitaine, Bordeaux*) 742

30.1   A sacrificial procession of a bull, sheep and pig (*The Louvre*)   761
30.2   The temple of Saturn, Rome (*Fototeca dell' Unione*)   761
30.3   The Villa of the Mysteries, Pompeii (*Mansell/Alinari*)   762
30.4   A vessel from Boscoreale depicting the sacrifice of a bull in front of
        an altar (*The Louvre*)   763
30.5   Bronze statuette of a *lar* (*Alinari*)   764
30.6   Stucco relief of a sacro-idyllic landscape from the Farnesina House,
        Rome (*Museo Nazionale, Rome*)   764
30.7   The Mithraeum under the church of St Clemente, Rome (*Mansell-
        Alinari*)   765
30.8   An early fourth-century mosaic under St Peter's, Rome, portraying
        Christ sweeping across the heavens in a sun-god's chariot (*The Vatican
        Museum*)   765

31.1   The apotheosis of Germanicus on a cameo now in the Bibliothèque
        Nationale, Paris (*Bibliothèque Nationale*)   780
31.2   The apotheosis of Trajan on the Arch of Trajan, Benevento, dating
        to AD 115 (*M. Greenhalgh*)   781
31.3   The apotheosis of Antoninus Pius and Faustina (*The Vatican Museum*)   781
31.4   A *sestertius* of Antoninus Pius depicting the temple of Faustina (*Fototeca
        dell'Unione*)   782
31.5   The apotheosis of Antoninus Pius and Faustina portrayed on an ivory
        diptych (*The British Museum*)   783
31.6   A statue of Commodus as Hercules, his favourite identity (*Museo dei
        Conservatori, Rome*)   784
31.7   Coin of Claudius II: *obv.* DIVO CLAUDIO; *rev.* an eagle and CONSECRATIO
        (*Barber Institute of Fine Arts, Birmingham*)   784

32.1   The temple Kasr-el-Bint at Petra (*Ian Browning*)   793
32.2   Early fourth-century relief of the Genius or Spirit of Salona (*Split
        Archaeological Museum, by courtesy of J. J. Wilkes*)   793
32.3   Statue of Isis Noreia from Virunum (*M. Leischner*)   794
32.4. A lead plaque from Romula depicting the Danubian rider deity in
        duplicate (*D. Tudor*)   794
32.5   The temple of Baal Shamin at Palmyra (*Ian Browning*)   795
32.6   Relief of *Genii Cucullati* from Cirencester (*Corinium Museum*)   795

34.1   Relief of a dead girl on a couch (*Musée de Cluny, Paris*)   832
34.2   Relief of a funeral procession from Amiternum, Italy (*Mansell/Alinari*)   832
34.3   Street of the tombs, Pompeii (*Mansell/Alinari*)   833

34.4   Cremation groups *in situ* at Chichester, Britain (*Chichester Excavation Committee*)   833

34.5   The Simpelveld Sarcophagus, Holland (*Museum of Antiquities, Leiden*)   834

34.6   Monument of the Julii at Glanum (St-Rémy-de-Provence) (*Jones*)   834

34.7   Mausoleum at Centcelles, near Tarragona, Spain (*Jones*)   835

34.8   The Bartlow Hills, Essex (*Copyright: Committee for Aerial Photography, University of Cambridge*)   835

34.9   Tomb of the Scipios, near Tarragona, Spain (*Jones*)   836

34.10   Poundbury cemetery, Dorchester (*C. J. S. Green*)   836

34.11   Collective grave at Lynch Farm, near Peterborough, Britain (*Jones*)   837

·FIGURES·

VOLUME I

		pages
1.1	The Empire under Augustus	4
1.2	The Empire under Hadrian	6
1.3	The Empire under Severus	7
1.4	The Empire at the beginning of the fourth century	9
1.5	The collapse of the Empire in the west	10
1.6	The Empire beyond the frontiers	11
2.1	Chronological and cultural table	16
2.2	Settlement development of Levroux (Indre), France	19
2.3	Examples of house plans from Manching, Bavaria	20
2.4	Distribution of flat, inhumation cemeteries of La Tène BC	21
2.5	Distribution of iron smelting sites around Manching	24
2.6	The *oppidum* of Kelheim, Bavaria	24
2.7	Cooking pot of *Graphittonkeramik* from Manching	25
2.8	Examples of late La Tène painted pottery	25
2.9	Manching: distribution of objects connected with weaving and leatherworking	26
2.10	Manching: distribution of objects connected with bronzeworking and coin manufacture	27
2.11	Generalized map showing the intensity of trade contact with the Mediterranean world	30
2.12	Dressel Ia *amphora* (*c.* 150–50 BC) and Dressel Ib (*c.* 60–10 BC)	31
2.13	Towns mentioned on inscriptions from the traders' quarters on the Magdalensberg, Austria	32
2.14	Distribution map of *Graphittonkeramik*	33
2.15	Development of Holzhausen	35
6.1	Plan of a Hyginian camp	98

xvi

8.1   Rhine and Danube provinces in the mid-second century   141
8.2   Pre-Flavian military sites in the upper Rhine and Danube regions   142
8.3   Augustan and Tiberian military sites in the area of the lower Rhine   144
8.4   The Lower German *limes* in the mid-second century   146
8.5   The development of the Upper German–Raetian *limes*   150–1
8.6   Saalburg: forts, fortlets and civil settlement   152
8.7   The Upper German *limes* between towers 4/9 and 4/11   153
8.8   Upper German *limes* in the area of towers 4/33 and 4/34   154
8.9   Odenwald *limes*: timber tower on a dry-stone base   155
8.10   The *numerus* fort at Hesselbach   156
8.11   Profiles of the Upper German palisade trench   158
8.12   Restored profile of the Sibyllenspur   159
8.13   Hypothetical section through a stone tower   160
8.14   Upper German *limes* at watchtowers 1/59 and 3/61   161
8.15   Upper German *limes* in its final form   163
8.16   The four building phases of the Upper German *limes*   164
8.17   The four building phases of the Raetian *limes*   165
8.18   The Raetian *limes* in its final form   166
8.19   The crossing through the Raetian *limes* at Dalkingen   167
8.20   The Raetian *limes* by towers 14/15 and 14/17   168
8.21   The late-Roman *limes* on the Danube–Iller–Rhine   169
8.22   Late-Roman fortifications on the lower and middle Rhine   170
8.23   The Danubian provinces: military sites of the Julio-Claudian period   173
8.24   The Danubian *limes* in the late-Flavian period   177
8.25   Trajan's canal at the Iron Gate   180
8.26   Dacia: military sites   181
8.27   The *limes Porolissensis*   183
8.28   Sections across the *limes Porolissensis*   185
8.29   The fortlets at Brebi on the *limes Porolissensis*   186
8.30   Late-Roman fortifications on the Danube   189
8.31   Late-Roman defences in the Danube gorge area   190
8.32   The *claustra Alpium Iuliarum*   191

9.1   Military dispositions in Britain under Agricola   200
9.2   The Gask Ridge frontier arrangements   202
9.3   Reconstruction drawing of a Gask Ridge watchtower   203
9.4   Hadrian's Wall   206
9.5   Reconstruction drawing of a turret and milecastle on Hadrian's Wall   207
9.6   The Antonine Wall   209
9.7   Reconstruction drawing of a fortlet and 'beacon platform' on the
           Antonine Wall   210

9.8	Saxon Shore forts and other fourth-century defences in Britain	215
10.1	Egypt	224
10.2	Late-Roman forts in Egypt	228
10.3	Cyrenaica to Egypt: provinces, principal sites, regions, geographical features and transhumance routes	231
10.4	Cyrenaica to Tripolitania: sites, roads and rainfall	232
10.5	Tripolitania to Tingitana: provinces, principal sites, regions, geographical features and transhumance routes	234
10.6	Numidia and Proconsular Africa: sites and roads	237
10.7	Tingitana: sites, roads and rainfall	240
10.8	Caesariensis: sites and roads	241
10.9	Legionary fortresses	243
10.10	Frontier works	245
10.11	Auxiliary forts	247
10.12	Frontier works	251
10.13	Tripolitania: sites and roads	252
10.14	Numidia and the frontier command of Anicius Faustus	253
10.15	Forts and settlements	258
10.16	Forts and settlements	259
10.17	Small *centenaria, burgi* and towers	261
10.18	The dioceses and provinces of north Africa in the late Empire	262
10.19	Late forts	263
10.20	Sketch of two fortified structures	264
11.1	Distribution of frontier forces *c.* 150	269
11.2	The physical geography of the eastern frontier region	271
11.3	The eastern frontier area of the Roman Empire	272
11.4	Alexander's Empire, *c.* 323 BC	273
11.5	Achaemenid Empire (fourth century BC)	275
11.6	Eastern frontier provinces at the death of Augustus (AD 14)	276
11.7	Eastern legionary fortresses	278
11.8	Forts of the eastern frontier	281
11.9	Eastern frontier provinces at the death of Severus (AD 211)	284
11.10	Dura-Europus, Syria	285
11.11	Sasanian Empire	287
11.12	Forts of the eastern frontier	289
11.13	Dioceses and provinces according to the *Notitia Dignitatum*	293
11.14	Eastern frontier provinces at the death of Arcadius (AD 408)	296
11.15	Pre-Severan survivals in the *Notitia Dignitatum*	297

9.8	Saxon Shore forts and other fourth-century defences in Britain	215
10.1	Egypt	224
10.2	Late-Roman forts in Egypt	228
10.3	Cyrenaica to Egypt: provinces, principal sites, regions, geographical features and transhumance routes	231
10.4	Cyrenaica to Tripolitania: sites, roads and rainfall	232
10.5	Tripolitania to Tingitana: provinces, principal sites, regions, geographical features and transhumance routes	234
10.6	Numidia and Proconsular Africa: sites and roads	237
10.7	Tingitana: sites, roads and rainfall	240
10.8	Caesariensis: sites and roads	241
10.9	Legionary fortresses	243
10.10	Frontier works	245
10.11	Auxiliary forts	247
10.12	Frontier works	251
10.13	Tripolitania: sites and roads	252
10.14	Numidia and the frontier command of Anicius Faustus	253
10.15	Forts and settlements	258
10.16	Forts and settlements	259
10.17	Small *centenaria, burgi* and towers	261
10.18	The dioceses and provinces of north Africa in the late Empire	262
10.19	Late forts	263
10.20	Sketch of two fortified structures	264
11.1	Distribution of frontier forces *c.* 150	269
11.2	The physical geography of the eastern frontier region	271
11.3	The eastern frontier area of the Roman Empire	272
11.4	Alexander's Empire, *c.* 323 BC	273
11.5	Achaemenid Empire (fourth century BC)	275
11.6	Eastern frontier provinces at the death of Augustus (AD 14)	276
11.7	Eastern legionary fortresses	278
11.8	Forts of the eastern frontier	281
11.9	Eastern frontier provinces at the death of Severus (AD 211)	284
11.10	Dura-Europus, Syria	285
11.11	Sasanian Empire	287
11.12	Forts of the eastern frontier	289
11.13	Dioceses and provinces according to the *Notitia Dignitatum*	293
11.14	Eastern frontier provinces at the death of Arcadius (AD 408)	296
11.15	Pre-Severan survivals in the *Notitia Dignitatum*	297

14.3	Plan of Houses 1–6, Schwarzenaker, G.D. Luxemburg	402
14.4	Reconstruction of a street with portico, Schwarzenaker	403
14.5	Plan of the eastern quarter of the village at Karanis, Egypt	406
14.6	Elevation of the state granary, Karanis, Egypt	407
14.7	Plan of Beḥyo, Syria	408

VOLUME II

18.1	Roman ploughs	489
18.2	Romano-British ploughshares and coulters	491
18.3	Roman spades and hoes	492
18.4	Roman sickles, hooks and scythes	493
18.5	Roman mills and presses	494
20.1	Mayen	528
20.2	Eccles	530
20.3	(A) Hambledon; (B) Noyers-sur-Serain; (C) Great Staughton; (D) La Cocosa, Badajoz; (E) Winterton	532
20.4	(A) Francolise; (B) North Leigh; (C) Gragnano; (D) St Ulrich; (E) Frocester	533
20.5	(A) Hosté; (B) Selvasecca; (C) Brixworth; (D) Huntsham; (E) Sette Finestre; (F) Woodchester	535
20.6	Vieux-Rouen-sur-Bresle	536
20.7	Restoration drawing of the villa at Whitton	537
21.1	The resources of the Roman Empire	552
22.1	Comparative values of Roman coinage	570
22.2	Map of the Roman Empire showing the distribution of mints	571
23.1	Plan of the villa at Boscoreale	591
23.2	Tombstones from Sens	599
23.3	Reconstruction drawing of a water-mill for grinding cereals, as proposed by Vitruvius	604
24.1	Spain, showing provincial boundaries and principal mining sites mentioned in the text	614
24.2	Fire-setting as depicted by Agricola	616
24.3	Archimedean screw-pump used for drainage at Centenillo	620
24.4	Eight pairs of water-wheels used to drain one mine at Rio Tinto	621

24.5	Water-wheels used to raise water to a higher level at the Terme del Mithra, Ostia	622
24.6	Section of the rim of a water-wheel	623
24.7	Reconstruction of the method used to work pairs of wheels	624
24.8	Castropodame	627
24.9	Braña la Folgueirosa	628
24.10	Plan of la Leitosa	630
24.11	Ground sluicing in the Duerna valley	631
24.12	Plan of Fucochicos	632
24.13	Montefurado	633
24.14	Wooden sluice boxes as employed in modern mining	634
24.15	Another type of washing table used in modern mining	634
25.1	Olive-oil *amphora* found in a shipwreck off the south of France	641
25.2	Map showing the development of samian factories	644
25.3	*Mortarium* manufactured at Ras el-Basit, Syria	646
25.4	Distribution map of tiles stamped TPF in Britain	648
25.5	Quarry inscription on the underside of the Column of Antoninus Pius	649
25.6	Marketing of late Roman pottery	652
26.1	The principal land and sea routes of the Roman Empire	659
26.2	Plan of the harbour area at Carthage	664
26.3	The harbour at Ostia	665
34.1	Trier with cemetery areas	814
34.2	Canterbury with cemetery areas	815
34.3	Histogram of cremation and inhumation cemeteries in northern Gaul	817
34.4	Plan of the villa and mausoleum at Newel, near Trier	818
34.5	Plan of the cemetery at Carmona	819
34.6	Plan of the cemeteries at Ampurias	820
34.7	Rich and poor cemetery areas at Ampurias	821
34.8	Ampurias: grave types in inhumation cemeteries	822
34.9	Ampurias: grave types in mixed rite and all-inhumation cemeteries	823
34.10	Ampurias: grave types related to children and adults	823
34.11	Cemeteries and settlements at York	824
34.12	Plan of the Trentholme Drive cemetery at York	825
34.13	Plan of the cemetery at Lankhills, Winchester	826
34.14	Urban development at Tours	827
34.15	Plan of the cemetery at Owslebury	828
34.16	Plan of the cemetery at Lynch Farm	829
34.17	Inhumation in a wooden coffin at Lynch Farm	830

·PREFACE·

This book has been designed to bring together the best of both ancient historians and archaeologists on the Roman Empire. All contributors were allowed complete freedom, within only the broadest set limits, to treat their subjects as they wished; editorial action was restricted to the minimum required to produce some degree of uniformity in presentation. Consequently, each contribution has retained its individuality while no attempts have been made to remove overlaps of subject interest between them. Equally, some contributors required few or no illustrations while others asked for the maximum number, so that their distribution, although uneven, is intentional; some subjects needed such support for their proper understanding, while others did not. It was also decided that, for the sake of brevity and to avoid numerous repetitions, consolidated bibliographies would be provided for each part and not for each chapter.

The editor wishes to state, though, that all opinions expressed are those of individual contributors, with which he may, or may not, agree.

JOHN WACHER

· PREFACE TO THE REISSUED EDITION·

Fourteen years have passed since these two volumes were first published; fourteen years during which the tide of fieldwork and excavations has grown ever greater, adding immeasurably to our knowledge and understanding of the Roman Empire. This has been matched by an increasing number of books and other publications, some on aspects which had never before been attempted. But this must be placed against a background of the modern political situation, rendering some sites and areas more accessible, and unfortunately others less so.

Yet many of the fundamental truths about the Empire have remains unchanged and any attempt to update a work of this nature would largely have been a matter of detail, important though it might be. Consequently, after careful thought, it was decided to reissue the volumes as they stood, since updating, even of detail, would have been a Herculean task, rendered more difficult by the fact that four of the contributors are sadly no longer with us, while others have retired; a small number have even drifted away from archaeology and ancient history to seek other occupations or interests.

Therefore the volumes remain the same, and the original preface states their aims. If some aspects of the Roman World were omitted, as one reviewer pointed out, I must plead that, to have included them, would have produced volumes with an even more 'eye-watering price'.

JOHN WACHER
Hayle, March 2001

· CONTRIBUTORS·

Anderson, Alistair Scott, MA: Depart of Archaeology, University of Leicester.
Applebaum, Shimon, BLitt DPhill: Emeritus Professor of Classical Archaeology, Ancient History and Jewish History, University of Tel Aviv.
Blagg, T. F. C., MA, PhD, FSA: Lecturer in Archaeology, School of Continuing Education, University of Kent.
Branigan, Keith, BA, PhD, FSA: Professor of Prehistory and Archaeology, University of Sheffield.
Braund, David C., MA, PhD: Dept of Classics, University of Exeter.
Breeze, David J., BA, PhD, FSA: Inspector of Ancient Monuments, Historic Buildings and Monuments Directorate, Scottish Development Department.
Brunt, P. A.: formerly Camden Professor of Ancient History, University of Oxford.
Burton, Graham, BA, DPhill: Lecturer in History, University of Manchester.
Collis, John, MA, PhD: Reader, Dept of Archaeology and Prehistory, University of Sheffield.
Daniels, Charles, MA, FSA: Senior Lecturer, Dept of Archaeology, University of Newcastle-upon-Tyne.
Drinkwater, J. F., MA, DPhill: Lecturer in Dept of Ancient History and Classical Archaeology, University of Sheffield.
Ferguson, John, MA, BD, FIAL: President, Selly Oak Colleges, Birmingham.
Green, Elizabeth, BA: sometime Lecturer in Ancient History, University of St Andrews and University of Leicester.
Green, Miranda, J., MLitt, PhD, FSA: Tutor in Roman Studies, Open University; Tutors' Administrator, Open University in Wales.
Harries, Jill, MA, DPhill: Lecturer in Ancient History, University of St Andrews.
Hassall, Mark, MA, FSA: Lecturer, Institute of Archaeology, University of London.
Jones, Richard, BA, PhD, MIFA: Lecturer in Archaeology, School of Archaeological Sciences, University of Bradford.
Kennedy, David, BA, DPhill: Lecturer in Dept of Ancient History and Classical Archaeology, University of Sheffield.
Kent, John, BA, PhD, FSA: Keeper, Dept of Coins and Medals, British Museum.
Levick, Barbara: Fellow and Tutor in Literae Humaniores, St Hilda's ollege, University of Oxford.
Liebeschuetz, J. H. W. G., BA, PhD: Professor and Head of Dept of Classical and Archaeological Studies, University of Nottingham.
McWhirr, Alan, BSC, MA, PhD, MIFA: Senior Lecturer in the School of Humanities, Leicester Polytechnic.
Manning, WE. H., BSC, PhD, FSA: Professor and Head of Dept of Archaeology, University College, Cardiff.
Maxfield, Valerie A., BA, PhD, FSA: Lecturer in Roman Archaeology, University of Exeter.
Parker, A. J., MA, DPhil: Lecturer in Roman Archaeology, University of Bristol.
Percival, John, MA, DPhil: Professor of Classics, University College, Cardiff.
Poulter, Andrew, BA, MA, PhD: Lecturer in Roman Archaeology, University of Nottingham.
Rees, Sian, PhD, FSA: Inspector of Ancient Monuments, CADW.
Thompson, Dorothy J., MA, PhD: Senior Tutor, Girton College, University of Cambridge.
Tomlin, R. S. O., MA, DPhil, FSA: Lecturer in late-Roman History, University of Oxford.
Wacher, John, BSC, FSA, MIFA: Professor of Archaeology, University of Leicester.
Watson, G R., BA, MLitt: sometime SDenior Lecturer in Classics, University of Nottingham.
Woods, Ann, BA, Dip Cons: Tutor, Dept of Archaeology, University of Leicester.

·GENERAL·BIBLIOGRAPHY· ·AND·PRINCIPAL· ·ABBREVIATIONS·

1 ANCIENT SOURCES

Ammianus Marcellinus	*Res Gestae*
Apuleius	*Metamorphoses*
Aurelius Victor	*Caesares* *De Viris Illustribus*
Ausonius	*Mosella*
BGU	*Berliner Griechische Urkunden (Agyptische Urkunden aus den Kgl.* *Museen zu Berlin)*, 1895–
Caesar, C. Julius	*Bellum Gallicum*
Cassius Dio	*Histories*
Cato	*De Agricultura* *De Re Rustica Origines*
Codex Iustinianus	*Corpus Iuris Civilis* ed. P. Krüger, 1954
Codex Theodosianus	(trans. E. Pharr)

Columella   *De re rustica*

Diodorus Siculus   *Bibliotheca Historica*

Eunapius   *Vitae Sophistarum*

Eusebius   *Historia Ecclesiastica*

Frontinus   *De Aquae Ducta Urbis Romae Strategemata*

Gaius   *Institutiones*

Galen   *On the Natural Faculties*

It.Ant.   *Itineraria Antonini Augusti*

Josephus   *Bellum Judaicum*

Libanius   *Julianic Orations*

Livy   *Epitomae*

Not. Dig.   *Notitia Dignitatum in partibus occidentis orientis*, ed. O. Seeck, Frankfurt, 1962

Palladius   *De Re Rustica*

P. Cairo Goodspeed   *Greek Papyri from the Cairo Museum, together with Papyri of Roman Egypt from American Collections*, ed. E. J. Goodspeed, Chicago, 1902

P. Chic. (=SB/Bh)   *Papyri from Karanis in the Chicago Museum*, ed. E. J. Goodspeed, Chicago, 1902 (=ed. F. Preisigke, *Sammelbuck gr. Urkunden aus Ägypten*, 1915–   )

P. Mich.   *Papyri in the University of Michigan Collection: Miscellaneous Papyri*, ed. J. G. Winter, Ann Arbor, 1936

P. Oxy.   *Oxyrhynchus Papyri*, eds B. P. Grenfell and A. S. Hunt, 1898–

P. Petaus	*Papyrologica Colonensia, Vol. IV. Das Archiv des Petaus,* eds U. and D. Hagedorn, L. and H. C. Youtie, Cologne, 1969
P. Ryl.	*Catalogue of Greek Papyri in the John Rylands Library at Manchester, 1911–*
Pausanias	*Graeciae Descriptio*
Pliny (the Elder)	*Naturalis Historia*
Rav. Cosm.	*Cosmographia Anonymi Ravennatis*
Sallust	*Catalina, Iugurtha, Fragmenta Ampliora*
S.H.A.	*Scriptores Historiae Augustae*
Statius	*Silvae* *Thebaid*
Strabo	*Geographica*
Suetonius	*Vitae Caesarum*
Tacitus	*Agricola* *Annales* *Germania* *Historiae*
Varro	*De Re Rustica*
Vegetius	*De re militari,* trans. Lt. John Clark, ed. Brig. T. R. Phillips, Harrisburgh, Penn., 1944
Vitruvius	*De Architectura*
W. Chrest.	*Grundzüge und Chrestomathie der Papyruskunde, Historischer Teil* 1 and 2, ed. U. Wilcken, Leipzig, 1912
Zosimus	*New History of Rome*

2 GENERAL BIBLIOGRAPHY

AE   *L'Année Epigraphique*

ARS   *Ancient Roman Statutes*, eds A. C. Johnson, P. R. Coleman-Norton, F. C. Bourne, Austin, Texas, 1961

CAH   *Cambridge Ancient History*, 1923–39

CIG   *Corpus Inscriptionum Graecorum*

CIL   *Corpus Inscriptionum Latinarum*

CMH   *Cambridge Medieval History*

Dessau   see *ILS*

Diehl, E.   *Inscriptiones Latinae Christianae Veteres*

EE   *Ephemeris Epigraphica, Corporis Inscriptionum Latinarum Supplementum*, Berlin, 1872–

Tenny Frank, (ed.) *An Economic Survey of Ancient Rome*, I–V, USA, 1933–40

IGBulg.   *Inscriptiones Graecae in Bulgaria repertae*, I–IV, ed. G. Mihailov, Sofia, 1956–71

IGRR   *Inscriptiones Graecae ad Res Romanas pertinentes*, I, III, IV, eds R. Cagnat, J. Toutain, G. Lafaye, Paris, 1906–27

ILAfr.   *Inscriptiones latines d'Afrique*, ed. R. Cagnat *et al.*, Paris, 1923

ILAlg.   *Inscriptions latines de l'Algérie*, 2 vols, ed. S. Gsell *et al.*, Paris, 1922, 1957

ILS   *Inscriptiones Latinae Selectae*, I–V, ed. H. Dessau, Berlin, 1892–1914

ILTun.   *Inscriptions latines de la Tunisie*, ed. A. Merlin, Paris, 1944

Insc.It.	*Inscriptiones Italiae*
ISM	*Inscriptiile din Scythia Minor*, I, V, eds D. M. Pippidi and E. Doruţiu-Boilă, 1980 and 1983
Lewis and Reinhold	*Roman Civilization Sourcebook I: The Republic,* 1951; *Roman Civilization Sourcebook II: The Empire*, New York, 1955
Limes Congress (1952–)	*The Proceedings of the International Congress of Roman Frontier Studies* as follows:

    1 Durham, 1948, ed. Eric Birley, Durham, 1952.
    2 Carnuntum, 1955, ed. Eric Swoboda, Graz-Köln, 1956.
    3 Basle, 1957, ed. R. Laur-Belart, Basel, 1959.
    4 Durham, 1959, unpublished.
    5 Yugoslavia, 1963, ed. Grga Novak, Zagreb, 1964.
    6 Suddeutschland, 1964, ed. H. Schönberger, Koln Graz, 1967.
    7 Tel Aviv, 1967, ed. S. Applebaum, Tel Aviv, 1971.
    8 Cardiff, 1969, eds Eric Birley, Brian Dobson and Michael Jarrett, Cardiff, 1974.
    9 Mamaia, 1972, ed. D. M. Pippidi, Bucarest, 1974.
    10 Lower Germany, 1974, eds Dorothea Haupt and Heinz Günther Hörn, Köln, 1977.
    11 Székesfehévár, 1976, eds J. Fitz, Budapest, 1977.
    12 Stirling, 1979, eds W. S. Hanson and L. J. F. Keppie, Oxford, 1980.
    13 Aalen, 1983, eds D. Planck and D. Unz, Stuttgart, 1985.

MAMA	*Monumenta Asiae Minoris Antiqua*, I–VIII, eds W. M. Calder and J. M. R. Cormack, Manchester, 1928–62
OCD	*Oxford Classical Dictionary*, second edition, 1970
OGIS	*Orientis Graeci Inscriptiones Selectae*, ed. W. Dittenberger, Leipzig, 1902–5
ORL	*Der obergermanisch-raetische Limes des Romerreichs*, Berlin, 1894–1937

Real-Encyclopädie	*Real-Encyclopädie d.klassischen Altertumswissenschaft*, eds A. Pauly, G. Wissowa and W. Kroll, Berlin, 1894–
RIB	*The Roman Inscriptions of Britain, Vol. I: inscriptions on stone*, eds R. G. Collingwood and R. P. Wright, Oxford, 1965
RIU	*Die romischen Inschriften Ungarns*, eds L. Barkóczi and A. Móscy, Budapest, 1976
RLO	*Der römische Limes in Osterreich*, Vienna, 1900–
RMD	*Roman Military Diplomas*, I and II, ed. M. Roxan, London, 1978
Rostovtzeff, M.	*The Social and Economic History of the Roman Empire*, second edition, Oxford, 1957
SEG	*Supplementum epigraphica Graecum*, 1923–
SNG	*Sylloge Nummorum Graecorum*, London, 1931–
Stillwell, R., MacDonald, W. L. and McAllister, M. H.	*The Princeton Encyclopedia of Classical Sites*, Princeton, 1976
Syll.	*Sylloge Inscriptionum Graecarum*, ed. W. Ditenberger, Leipzig, 1915–24
Tab. Vindol.	*Vindolanda: the Latin Writing Tablets*, eds A. K. Bowman and J. D. Thomas, Britannia Monograph, 4, London, 1983

·ACKNOWLEDGMENTS·

The editor and contributors are grateful for the help of the following people and institutions in obtaining illustrations and for giving permission for their publication:

Academia de la Historia, Madrid, pl. 7.14; R. Agache, pls 20.1 and 20.2; Aosta Cathedral Treasury, pl. 7.15; Aphrodisias Excavations (Prof. K. T. Erim) pl. 29.10; Archaeological Museum, Florence, pl. 29.10, J. M. Arnaud and the Musée d'Aquitaine, Bordeaux, pl. 29.18; Ashmolean Museum, pl. 23.6; Barber Institute of Fine Arts, Birmingham, pl. 31.7; Bibliothéque Nationale, pl. 31.1; the Bodleian, Oxford, pls 7.4, 7.5 and 8.5; O. Braasch, pl. 8.1; Bristol City Museum and Art Gallery, pl. 25.2; British Institute of Archaeology, Ankara, pl. 11.4; the British Museum, pls 7.6, 7.7, 19.1, 19.8, 29.1, 29.8, 29.11, and 31.5; Ian Browning, pls 32.1 and 32.5; Chatsworth Collection of the Duke of Devonshire, pl. 29.17; Chester Beatty Library, Dublin, pl. 7.13; Chichester Excavation Committee, pl. 34.4; Colchester Archaeological Trust, pl. 13.6; Comune di Roma Ripartizione X, pl. 29.5; Committee for Aerial Photography, University of Cambridge, pls 9.3, 9.4, 9.9, 14.1, 14.2 and 34.8; P. Connolly, pl. 8.4; Corinium Museum, pl. 32.6; Crawford Collection, Oxford, pls 11.9 and 11.10; Department of Antiquities, Algeria, pls 13.1 and 13.8; Department of Antiquities, Libya, pl. 13.9; Department of the Environment, pls 9.1 and 26.4; Deutsches Archäologisches Institut, Athens, pl. 7.2; Deutsches Archäologisches Institut, Rome, pls 19.4, 19.10, 19.11 and 23.4; Forty Hall Museum, Enfield, pl. 25.3; Fototeca dell'Unione, Rome, pls 26.1, 30.2 and 31.4; R. Goodburn, pls 7.4 and 7.5; C. J. S. Green, pl. 34.10; M. Greenhalgh, pls 13.10, 19.12, 25.4, 29.7, 29.9, 29.12 and 31.2; Institutio Italiano di Cultura, London, pl. 1.1; S. Laidlaw, pl. 27.1; M. Leischner, pl. 32.3; The Louvre, pls 19.9, 30.1 and 30.4; Mansell/Alinari, pls 30.3, 30.5, 30.7, 34.2 and 34.3; Metropolitan Museum of Art, New York, pls 3.6 and 19.2; Monza Cathedral Treasury, pl. 7.9; Musée d'Art et d'Histoire, Geneva, pl. 7.12; Musée de Cluny, Paris, pl. 34.1; Musée Gaumais, Virton, pl. 18.2; Musée St.

Gsell, pl. 7.17; Museo Nazionale, Rome, pl. 30.6; Museo delle Terme, Rome, pls 3.4 and 19.3; Museo dei Conservatore, Rome, pl. 31.6; Museo Torlonia, pl. 29.3; Museum of English Rural Life, Reading, pl. 18.1; Musée de Langres, pl. 19.7; Museum of London, pls 26.2 and 26.3; Musée de St Romain-en-Laye, pl. 18.4; National Museums of Scotland, pl. 9.7; National Museum, Naples, pls 3.7 and 29.4; National Museum of Pompeii, pl. 3.5; J. Paul Getty Museum, Santa Monica, pl. 11.2; Rheinisches Landsmuseum, Bonn, pl. 13.3; Rheinisches Landsmuseum, Trier, pls 13.11, 13.12, 13.13, 19.6 and 29.15; Rijksmuseum van Oudheden te Leiden, pls 7.3 and 34.5; the Roman Society and A. Doğenci, pl. 29.10; Römisches-Germanisches Museum, Cologne, pl. 7.10; Römisches-Germanisches Zentralmuseum, Mainz, pls 7.8 and 19.5; M. M. Roxan, pl. 27.2; Scala, pls 3.1, 3.2 and 7.2; Scottish Development Department, Historic Buildings and Monuments Directorate, pls 9.5, 9.6 and 9.8; Sheffield Aerial Photographic Archive, pls 11.1, 11.5 and 11.6; Soprintendenza Archeologica Ostia, pl. 26.5; Soprintendenza Archeologica Pompei, pls 23.5, 29.6 and 29.16; Split Archaeological Museum and J. J. Wilkes, pl. 32.2; Staatliches Konservaforaent, Saarbrucken, pl. 14.3; A. Tchernia and the Centre Camille Julian, pl. 25.1; D. Tudor, pl. 32.4; Uffizi Gallery, Florence, pl. 3.3; University Museum, Newcastle-upon-Tyne, and the National Museum of Wales, pl. 29.13; the University Museum, Philadelphia, pl. 11.11; the Vatican Museum, pls 3.8, 23.2, 23.3, 30.8 and 31.3; A. Wallace-Hadrill, pl. 23.5.

The editor would also like to offer his unbounded gratitude to the following for their help in various editorial processes: Susan Semmens for preparing the bibliographical references and David Parsons for his assistance in checking them; Andy Clarke, Lorna Smith and Michael Rouillard for preparing 192 separate pages of drawings, often from difficult material; Marius Cooke for photographic services. Cheryl McCormick was responsible for the huge task of typing the main contributions and the glossary, virtually without error; Dorothy Tudor typed the bibliographies and Pam Thornett the prelims. All have contributed in their own ways to the ultimate successful production.

·CHRONOLOGICAL·TABLE·

	55	50	45	40	35	30	25	20	15	10	5	BC
							27 **Augustus**					
Italy and Africa		49 Caesar crosses Rubicon					27 Octavian becomes Augustus Reorganization of the Provinces					
			48 Caesar in Egypt									
			46 Battle of Thapsus			30 Death of Antony						
				44 Caesar assassinated		33 Juba I in Numidia			12 Death of Agrippa			
							29 Campaign against Ethiopa					
Greece, Balkans and Middle Danube		49 Pompey in Greece							12 Pannonian revolt suppressed by Tiberius			
			48 Battle of Pharsalus Death of Pompey									
				42 Battle of Philippi								
						31 Battle of Actium						
							29 Lower Danube reached					
Gaul and Germany		52 Vercingetorix defeated at Alesia						16–13 Augustus in Gaul				
		49 Massilia falls to Caesar							12–9 Drusus campaigns on the Rhine			
				38 Agrippa suppresses Aquitanian revolt					8 Tiberius campaigns in Germany			
The East	53 Disaster at Carrhae						24 Aelius Gallus in Aden					
								20 Cliency in Armenia Reduction of client kingdoms				
Spain			46 Caesar in Spain									
			45 Battle of Munda									
							27 Provincial reorganization					
							26 Augustus campaigns against Cantabri					
								19 Agrippa subdues Cantabri				
Britain		51 Flight of Commius to Britain										
							Growing strength of Catuvellauni (Tasciovanus)					

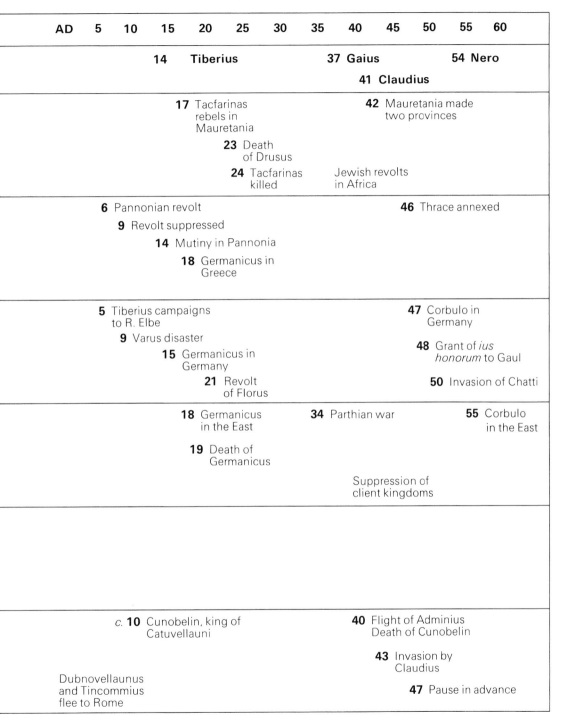

AD	5	10	15	20	25	30	35	40	45	50	55	60

14 Tiberius **37 Gaius** **54 Nero**

41 Claudius

17 Tacfarinas
rebels in
Mauretania

42 Mauretania made
two provinces

23 Death
of Drusus

24 Tacfarinas
killed

Jewish revolts
in Africa

6 Pannonian revolt

46 Thrace annexed

9 Revolt suppressed

14 Mutiny in Pannonia

18 Germanicus in
Greece

5 Tiberius campaigns
to R. Elbe

47 Corbulo in
Germany

9 Varus disaster

48 Grant of *ius
honorum* to Gaul

15 Germanicus in
Germany

21 Revolt
of Florus

50 Invasion of Chatti

18 Germanicus
in the East

34 Parthian war

55 Corbulo
in the East

19 Death of
Germanicus

Suppression of
client kingdoms

c. **10** Cunobelin, king of
Catuvellauni

40 Flight of Adminius
Death of Cunobelin

43 Invasion by
Claudius

Dubnovellaunus
and Tincommius
flee to Rome

47 Pause in advance

	60	65	70	75	80	85	90	95	100	105	110
			69 Vespasian		**81 Domitian**			**96**	**98 Trajan**		
					79/81			**Nerva**			
					Titus						
Italy and Africa		**64** Rome burnt			**79** Eruption of Vesuvius						
		69 Civil war: Year of the Four Emperors: Galba, Otho, Vitellius, Vespasian									
			Battle of Cremona								
Greece, Balkans and Middle Danube		**66** Nero in Greece			**86** Dacian war against Decebalus			**101** Dacian war: battle of Tapae II			
		69 Roxolani invade			**88** Battle of Tapae I		**98** Trajan on the Danube				
			73 Frontier on the Danube			**92** Pannonia invaded		**105** Second Dacian war death of Decebalus			
				85 Moesia divided							
Gaul and Germany		**68** Revolt of Vindex		Germany two provinces							
		69 Revolt of Civilis									
			74 Creation of *agri decumates*		**88** Revolt of Saturninus						
				82 Chattan war Limes in Upper Germany begun							
The East		**66** Vespasian in the East: Jewish revolt							**106** Arabia annexed		
			70 Fall of Jerusalem the Diaspora								
Spain				**74** Grant of *ius latium* to all Spain							
Britain	**60** Boudican rebellion		**71** Cerealis campaigns in Brigantia							**105** Withdrawal from Scotland	
			74 Frontinus in Wales								
				78 Agricola Battle of Mons Graupius							

115	120	125	130	135	140	145	150	155	160	165

117 Hadrian   **138 Antoninus Pius**   **161 Marcus Aurelius**

---

115 Jewish/Moorish
revolts
    122 War in Mauretania
        128 Hadrian in Africa
        ? Limes in Numidia
        130 Hadrian in Egypt

---

118 Roxolani
threaten
    124 Hadrian in
Greece
      128 Hadrian in
Greece

---

121 Hadrian in Gaul
and Germany:
construction of
palisade in Upper Germany
and Raetia
          140– Advance of Upper
German and Raetian
limes

---

115 Parthian war begins   **162** Armenia invaded
116 Jewish revolts **128** Hadrian in the East   by Parthia
117 Trajan's conquests   Antioch threatened
abandoned
      123 Hadrian in the East
         132 Jewish revolt
         Hadrian returns

122 Hadrian in Spain

---

117 Revolt in the North   **143** Antonine Wall
    121 Hadrian in Britain   Reoccupation
      122 Hadrian's Wall   of Scotland
                                ?154 Brigantian
rebellion
                                      ?163 Antonine Wall
abandoned

	165	170	175	180	185	190	195	200	205	210
		Marcus Aurelius		180 Commodus			192/193 Sept. Severus Pertinax			211 Caracalla
Italy and Africa		167 Epidemic in Italy N. Italy threatened by invasion 173 War with Mauri					Civil war Limes in Africa strengthened Municipal autonomy granted in Egypt			211 *Constitutio Antoniniana* 212 Geta murdered
Greece, Balkans and Middle Danube		167 Marcomannic wars 172 Barbarian settlements on Danube 174 Sarmatian war Peace made with Sarmatians					193 Severus proclaimed Emperor in Pannonia			
Gaul and Germany				Disturbance caused by Maternus			196 Albinus defeated in Gaul at Lyon 'Pfahlgraben' and ? Raetian wall			
The East	166 War ended by epidemic						194 Severus defeats Niger 197 Severus in the East Mesopotamia a province Syria two provinces			
Spain			173 Invasion by Mauri in Baetica		Disturbance caused by Maternus	Tarraconensis sides with Albinus				
Britain				181 Revolt in North Army mutiny		193 Albinus as Caesar			208 Severus restores Britain Britain two provinces	

215	220	225	230	235	240	245	250	255	260	265

217 Elegabalus **222 Severus Alexander** **235** ←———— Fifteen emperors between 235–70 ————→ in a period of anarchy

238 Revolts in Africa Leg III Aug cashiered

258 Italy invaded

Beginning of reforms in the army

Danube campaigns Gothic invasions
251 Decius defeated and killed
245 Invasions across Danube
248 Rebellion: Goths invade
258 Gallienus checks barbarians

233 Attacks by Alamanni Army mutiny
253 Alamannic invasions
260 Gallic Empire of Postumus

215 Caracalla in the East
242 War with Persia
260 Valerian and army captured by Persians
225 Rise of Persia
Pretenders in the East
230 Mesopotamia over-run and recovered: army mutiny
250 Mesopotamia falls to Persians Epidemic disease

Tarragona sacked by Franks
258 Frankish invasions
260 Part of Gallic empire

260 Part of Gallic empire

	265	270	275	280	285	290	295	300	305	310
	⟶ **270** Aurelian				**284** Diocletian				**305**	
			275 Probus				**293** Constantius I		**306**	
Italy and Africa		Rome walled				Revolts in Egypt				Four Western Augusti
			274 Empire reunited							
						The Tetrarchy Diocletian reforms the Empire: subdivision of provinces				Civil wars
Greece, Balkans and Middle Danube		Pannonia invaded				**289** Diocletian defeats Sarmatians				
		269 Claudius II pacifies Danube frontier								
			Dacia abandoned							
Gaul and Germany			**274** Rejoined to Empire	*Agri decumates* abandoned						
			276 Alamannic invasions	Fighting on the Rhine						
The East	**267** Kingdom of Palmyra									Two Eastern Augusti
			273 Aurelian recovers Eastern provinces							
							296 Galerius defeats Persia			
Spain			**274** Rejoined to Empire							
Britain			**274** Rejoined to Empire			**296** Allectus defeated Provinces reunited with Empire Northern frontier over-run				
					285 Carausius defects					
						294 Carausius murdered by Allectus				

315	320	325	330	335	340	345	350	355	360	365

	Constantine I			**337**		**Constans**	**350**		**361 363**	**Valentinian I**
										Julian
		333				**Constantius II**				

312 Battle of
Milvian Bridge

Constantine converted
to Christianity

313 Edict of Milan

Succession of palace revolutions

---

322 Sarmatian
invasion

324 Foundation of
Constantinople

324 Battle of Adrianople
Constantine sole Emperor

---

314 Council of Arles

Alamannic
invasions

354 Alamannic
invasions

357 Valentinian
at Trier

Franks settle
in Gaul

---

314 Licinius Emperor
in the East

338–350 Successive
sieges of
Nsibis

360 Amida captured

363 Julian in the
East

Provinces
surrendered

---

342 Constans visits
Britain

	365	370	375	380	385	390	395	400	405	410
	Valentinian I 375			Valentinian II			392	Honorius (West) Arcadius (East)		408
	367 Gratian			378	Theodosius I		395			
Italy and Africa							Moorish revolt in Africa		**410** Alaric takes Rome
								402 Visigoths invade Italy	
								405 Germans invade Italy	
Greece, Balkans and Middle Danube			Visigoths settled in Thrace				**398** Visigoths settled in Epirus		
				378 Battle of Adrianople					
Gaul and Germany									**406** Marcomanni, Quadi, Alans and Vandals invade Gaul
									410 Visigoths settle in S. Gaul
The East	**368** Further war								
Spain									**409** Alans, Vandals in Spain
Britain	**367** Barbarian conspiracy					**395** Stilicho in Britain			**410** Rescript of Honorius
	369 Theodosius restores Britain							**405** Marcus Gratian Constantine III	
				383 Revolt of Magnus Maximus					

415	420	425	430	435	440	445	450	455	460	465	470	475

| | **423** **Valentinian III** | | | | | | **450** | **455** **Various (East and West)** | | | | |
| | **Theodosius II (East)** | | | | | | | | | | | |

Vandals settle in Africa					**455** Vandals sack Rome							**476** Deposition of last Western Emperor: Romulus Augustulus
				Huns invade Italy								
				Vandal kingdom								

				438 Theodosian code			Vandals ravage Illyricum					Vandal kingdom recognized
				Attila crosses the Danube								
						Huns in Eastern Empire						

| | | | | | | | **451** Attila invades Gaul | | | | | |
| | | | | | | | Visigothic kingdom in S. Gaul | | | | | |

| | | | | | **440** Persia invades Armenia | | | | | | | |

| **417** Visigoths in Spain | | | | | | | Visigothic kingdom | | | | | |

		429 Visit of St Germanus										
			Jutes, Angles and Saxons									
						'The Groans of the Britons'						

·GLOSSARY·

Acropolis
the citadel of Athens.

aediles
magistrates with powers of minor jurisdiction. They were normally responsible for public buildings and works, such as the aqueducts and markets.

aedituus
the keeper of the consecrated building.

agora
the *forum* (q.v.) or civic centre of a Greek city, usually consisting of an open space surrounded by colonnades and public buildings.

annona
originally the corn supply of Rome. Hence the *annona militaris*, a tax in kind imposed on Italy and the provinces, at first exceptionally, but later regularly, intended to supply the army.

apolusinoi
demobilized soldiers.

Ara Pacis
a monument erected in 9 BC, in the Campus Martius to commemorate Augustus' safe return from Gaul and Spain.

archon
originally office holders in a state in Greece. Later the chief magistrate of a city in the Greek part of the Empire.

atrium
the forecourt or entrance hall of a Roman house.

auctoritas
the authority vested in prominent men by virtue of the high office they had held: that of an elder statesman.

ballista
an artillery piece, actuated by some form of torsion, to fire an iron bolt or small rock.

basilica
a large, multi-purpose public hall, normally attached to the *fora* of towns in the western Empire; later applied to domestic and commercial buildings of similar architectural form, and also to early churches.

birrus Britannicus
a long, sleeveless hooded cape, probably made of hard-wearing

wool; the nap was probably left long to repel rain. The garment most likely originated in Gaul and was listed in the Edict of Prices of Diocletian.

boule the council of a self-governing community in the Greek world, originally formed to advise the king of a city-state.

bustum the place where the bodies of the dead were cremated and buried; also a tomb (q.v. *ustrinum*).

capitolium the principal temple of a city, dedicated to Jupiter, Juno and Minerva – the Capitoline Triad, after the temple on the Capitoline Hill in Rome.

centonarii dealers in rags; makers of patchwork.

cheiristai men of lowest degree.

cives a citizen.

civitas primarily citizenship of any type; but also used to describe a self-governing community of citizens – usually urban – of any origin.

clipeus a shield, usually round and of bronze, occasionally used to carry a bust or other representation of a deity.

collegium an association or club, usually formed for religious (e.g. burial, priestly) or trade (e.g. blacksmiths, carpenters, etc.) purposes. The membership and constitution would be fixed by statute.

colonus a member of a *colonia*; also a tenant farmer on public land, or on an imperial or private estate.

comes a title bestowed on leading military and civil officers of state in the late Empire.

comitatus an escort or retinue, usually associated with an emperor.

comitia assemblies, usually of Rome, but also of chartered cities.

concilium any assembly, originally of Rome (cf. Plebeian Assembly), later of the provinces, composed of delegates from the constituent self-governing communities.

conductor a contractor who either carried out work for a private person or who leased agricultural and/or industrial property, either on behalf of a third party or himself.

curia the Senate House of Rome; also the name given to the places of assembly of municipal councils in the provinces; in many places attached to the *basilica* (q.v.).

demiourgoi craftsmen and 'professional' men of independent means; later forming small advisory councils in states, in the Greek parts of the Empire, with varying functions.

dignitas a concept implying a dignified rank, bearing or authority.

di Manes the gods of the underworld.

di Superi	the gods of the upper world.
Domus Divinae	the 'divine house' of deified emperors and past dynasties; sometimes invoked in dedications to the imperial cult.
duumvir	a senior municipal magistrate.
dux	a military commander acting above his substantive rank; in the Late Empire the title of a military commander in some frontier areas.
eques	a horseman; commonly a term used for a cavalry trooper.
equites	cavalry; also used to describe the social class (equestrian) below that of the senatorial order. Most military prefects and tribunes, as well as procurators, were recruited from this class.
exedra	a hall.
fabri	literally armourers (military); also blacksmiths. *Praefectus fabrum*, originally the commander of the above, became an honorary title used to describe a general's principal staff officer.
fellahin	the peasant class in Egypt.
flamen Dialis	the priest assigned to the cult of Jupiter.
foederatus	an ally, confederate.
foedus	a treaty.
forum	an open space, usually in the centre of a town or city, used for political gatherings and, in most cases, for markets. Most were also surrounded by colonnades linked with other public buildings, one of which was frequently the *basilica* (q.v.).
fustuarium	normally a military punishment, whereby the defaulter was cudgelled to death.
Gaea	the Earth Goddess.
gene	organized corporations devoted to ancestor worship in Greece.
genius loci	a nameless spirit thought to inhabit a specific place.
Gottkönigtum	theocratic monarchy; the divine nature of kingship.
grammateis	a secretary, normally of public bodies in the Greek parts of the Empire.
hasta	a spear, used as a badge of distinction.
hastatus	literally a spearman; also used to describe the companies in the first line of battle in the Roman army, and the commanders of these companies.
Hippodamian grid	the adaptation of a town-planning system by the architect Hippodamus of Miletus.
honestiores	a social, and legally undefined, distinction applied to the upper class (q.v. *humiliores*).
humiliores	the lower social class (q.v. *honestiores*).

imagines	representations, statues or pictures (e.g. of an emperor).
imaginifer	a soldier who carried the emperor's image as a standard.
imperium	the highest power of the principal magistrates and pro-magistrates of Rome, which conferred on the recipient the ability to command an army and administer the most extreme penalties of the law.
inquilinus	an inhabitant of a place in which he had not been born; also a tenant.
iugerum	an area of land measuring 73 by 36.5 m (80 by 40 yd).
iurisprudentes	jurists.
ius gentium	'international' law open to both Roman and non-Roman.
ius Italicum	the legal status of Roman land in Italy, exempt from certain taxes, in contrast to the provinces. It was later granted to some provincial municipalities.
ius Latii	the so-called Latin rights, which became an intermediate stage in the promotion of non-Roman communities to full Roman status.
koinon	common assembly.
lar familiaris	spiritual guardians, especially of servants, of a household, which seem to have originated on farms. Usually depicted as small statuettes of bronze or terracotta, placed in the house.
latifundium	an exceptionally large estate.
legatus	normally the commander of a legion (when *legionis*) or a governor of an imperial province (when *Augusti pro praetore*) also used for some other imperial appointments.
leges	binding agreements between two or more parties, one of which might be the state, broadly divided between *leges rogata* and *leges datae*. The latter were issued, with the approval of the Senate, by a Roman magistrate and were mainly concerned with the provinces; from the end of the first century they were replaced by imperial constitutions.
lex provinciarum	the constitution by which a governor administered his province.
liberalitas	of a noble, kind or friendly disposition; generosity or gifts.
libertus	an emancipated slave.
limes	originally a road leading into unoccupied territory; finally adapted to describe a complete system of frontier works.
locus consecratus	a sacred place.
Magna Graecia	the collective name for the Greek cities of southern Italy.
manumission	the act of granting freedom to a slave.
mercator	a merchant, especially a wholesale dealer (see *negotiator*).

metropolis   an honorary title usually granted to provincial capitals in the Greek part of the empire.

negotiator   a trader, wholesaler, business agent or manager (see *mercator*).

neocorate   the body to which *neokoroi* (q.v.) belonged.

neokoroi   persons in charge of a temple; supervisors of sacrifices.

nome   the Greek name for the administrative districts of Egypt, and some other neighbouring eastern provinces.

numen   the divine will of a deity; the spiritual power of an emperor.

nymphaeum   a fountain or spring consecrated to the nymphs.

obaeratus   debt bondage.

odeum   a small theatre or covered hall, used especially for music competitions and recitations.

officina   a workshop or factory.

oppidum   a town; urban settlement; also used to describe Iron Age hill-forts and fortified valley settlements.

optio   rank in the Roman army below that of centurion.

ordo   the council of decurions in a municipal or similar local government institution.

paean   a religious or festive hymn, often of triumph.

parens patriae   an alternative version of *pater patriae*, 'father of the country', a title adopted by some emperors.

parilis   equal.

patera   a bowl or dish used for making offering and libations.

pax Romana   the peace which supposedly came about as the result of the expansion of Roman influence; a political concept used to proclaim the benefits of Roman rule.

peculium   money, goods, land, etc. which a slave was allowed to accumulate with the full knowledge of his master. It was often used to purchase freedom.

pedites   infantry.

peristyle   an enclosed court in a building surrounded by columns.

phrontistes   a philosopher.

pilum   a throwing spear used by legionaries, with a soft iron shank which bent on impact, causing the weapon to become attached to the object it had struck.

plebiscitum   a resolution of a plebeian tribal assembly presided over by a plebeian magistrate.

polis   the Greek city-state; under the Empire it came to be used generally to mean a city.

pontifex   a priest normally connected with the official cults of the state;

pontifex maximus was a title assumed by most emperors.

praefectus praetorio a prefect of the Praetorian Guard.

praeses a term which, in the Late Empire, came to be used generally for officers of gubernatorial status.

praetor a senior magistrate of Rome, next in seniority to the consuls; the number varied. In the early Republic they were connected with military affairs; it eventually became an honorary title.

primicerius notariorum the head of the public record office in the Late Empire.

principes originally the second line of an army in battle order, lying between the *hastati* (q.v.) and *triarii*; in the imperial army it was used to describe the centurions of a first legionary cohort.

providentia foresight, providence, later personified as a deity.

quaestor the lowest of the regular magistrates in Rome. Under the principate, they were attached to emperors and provincial governors as staff officers; they also appear as municipal magistrates and in *collegia* (q.v.). In most cases, they were normally connected with financial matters.

rector sometimes used to describe a provincial governor.

regiones the divisions of the city of Rome; districts in provinces overseen by a *regionarius*, usually a legionary centurion.

res privata one of the three divisions of the imperial treasury in the Late Empire which dealt primarily with imperial property.

rex sacrorum a priest, subordinate to the *pontifex maximum* (q.v.), who assumed the sacral functions of the kings after their expulsion from Rome.

sacrae largitiones one of the three divisions of the imperial treasury in the Late Empire which dealt with mines, mints and state factories and also collected taxes in cash.

scutum a rectangular shield, normally used by legionaries.

Senatus Consultum the advice of the Senate to the magistrates; later *consulta* often had the force of law.

sicarii assassins, bandits.

stategos the governor of an Egyptian district (q.v. *nome*) and the regular Greek equivalent for the Latin *praetor* (q.v.).

stephanophoroi certain magistrates in Greek states, who had the right to wear a crown or wreath.

stipendarii those receiving pay, e.g. soldiers.

sufes the chief Carthaginian magistrate corresponding to the Roman consul.

suovetaurilia a sacrifice consisting of a pig, a ram and a bull.

synoecism the joining of several communities into one city-state.

tabularium various types of record office, often connected with taxation in a civilian context.

temenos the consecrated and enclosed precinct of a temple.

toga virilis the *toga* assumed by boys on reaching manhood.

togata native Italian comedy based on the Greek New Comedy.

tractus territory, district or region.

tria nomina the three names of a Roman citizen, *praenomen, nomen* and *cognomen*.

tribuni militum in the Republican army the senior officers of legions. With the decline of their importance, they were divided into two classes, the *laticlavii* of senatorial, and the *angusticlavii* of equestrian, descent.

tribunicia potestas in the Republic the power of the officers of the plebs; later assumed by most emperors annually, while the office also remained a step in the senatorial career.

truss a support for a roof or bridge.

turma a troop of a cavalry regiment.

ustrinum a place for the cremation of the dead (see *bustum*).

vallum an earth wall or rampart, sometimes incorporating palisades. Incorrectly used to describe the embanked ditch to the rear of Hadrian's Wall.

velites lightly-armed soldiers of the Republican army.

vergobret the title of the chief magistrate of the Gallic tribe of the Aedui.

verutum a type of javelin.

viereckschanze a square, ditched enclosure characteristic of the Celtic Iron Age in Britain and Europe, often associated with a religious function and containing a totem and/or temple.

PART 1

·INTRODUCTION·

CHAPTER 1

·INTRODUCTION·

John Wacher

The influence of the Roman world in antiquity was immense, stretching far beyond the Empire's boundaries. The latter, at their greatest extent, included the entire Mediterranean basin from the fringes of the Sahara in the south to beyond the Rhine and Danube in the north, eastwards to the head of the Persian Gulf, Syrian and Arabian deserts, and westwards to the Atlantic and North and Irish Seas. Beyond lay contacts, mainly through trade, with China and India, east Africa and trans-Saharan tribes, central Europe up to the Baltic, Scotland and Ireland; Roman coins have reputedly been found in Manchuria.

It took time to grow and was not constant; it had its roots in the Roman Republic, Hellenistic East, Carthaginian Africa and Celtic Europe (Part 2). The principal agency for the expansion from city-state to world-wide empire was the army (Part 3), which both followed and was followed by traders and merchants. The Roman army began as a citizen army under the Republic which was called out when need arose. As the needs grew and service lengthened, it developed into a permanent, professional army, trained and organized to a very high standard; providing it could choose its battleground, there were few other contemporary forces which could withstand its onslaught. Yet despite the extent of the Empire, the army never possessed more than thirty legions, although this number was considerably augmented with, at first non-citizen, auxiliaries of infantry and cavalry; even then its total manpower, at the height of the Principate, probably never exceeded much more than 350,000 men. At that same time, the frontiers, where almost all the army was ultimately stationed, stretched for nearly 10,000 km (6,000 miles), which, averaging out at about thirty-five men per kilometre, was no great concentration, especially since there was no central reserve; if one area was threatened, it could only be reinforced from another which was peaceful. Consequently, the chief external danger to the empire lay in one or more simultaneous attacks, which happened

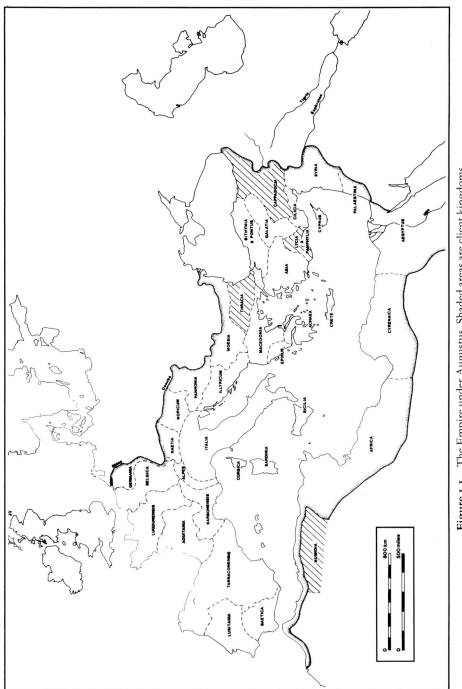

Figure 1.1 The Empire under Augustus. Shaded areas are client kingdoms

with increasing frequency in the fourth and fifth centuries, and led to marked changes in strategy and organization.

But even the frontiers (Part 4) were slow to develop and subsequently to decline. The concept of a fortified, linear barrier was at first anathema to the Roman ideal of unlimited conquest. But gradually, as the ideal lost its momentum, caused by setbacks and the increasing strains which its pursuit placed upon the Empire's reserves of manpower, a more pragmatic approach was adopted by successive emperors towards the boundaries. This led ultimately to the construction of linear barriers to supplement natural features such as rivers, mountains or deserts, with garrisons strung out along them. A great deal of argument has been caused by the remarkable diversity presented by these barriers, which range in type from little more than a stout fence in parts of Germany, through modest walls in Numidia to the massive structure of Hadrian's Wall, with its implied degree of 'overkill'. Only in the east, where Rome faced a potential enemy of approximately equal strength, were little or no supplementary barriers erected, so providing an important clue to the solution of the problem argued by many that there was no such thing as a Roman frontier policy. The inherent weaknesses of all such barriers were twofold: they were only as strong as the fighting garrisons made them, and, once punctured, there was nothing then left to hold an advancing enemy. Hence the uselessness of providing any real barriers in the east against a power of equivalent strength: Parthia. Once this is appreciated, it can then be argued that the nature of the barriers, upon erection, was in each case nicely adjusted to meet the specific needs, at a certain time and at any given point, on the imperial boundaries. The nature of the needs and threats changed with the times, and it is not surprising therefore to find that the Late Empire required defences of a very different character from those deemed adequate in the second century.

The core of the Empire had for long been familiar with all levels of urban development, inheriting and adapting ideas from Greece, the East and from Africa (Part 5). But in the north and west lay areas which were either in a state of urban infancy, or altogether unfamiliar with its way of life. Into these areas marched the army, bringing with it, even if diluted, all forms of Roman cultural achievement, which included the urban ideal. It founded fortresses and forts, which, because of the spending power wielded by each soldier, attracted local, and sometimes not-so-local, traders. In time, they tended to settle down in nucleated settlements outside the forts, and indeed were often encouraged to do so by the military authorities. In time also many of these settlements grew and developed the full functions of urban centres, which were further augmented by the Roman policy of settling retired legionaries in model towns, or *coloniae*. Some native settlements, though, did not grow to this level, usually for economic reasons, and so provided a whole range of villages to match those in other, more developed parts of the Empire, where similar forces prevailed.

Binding all together within the provincial system were the forces of the law. The

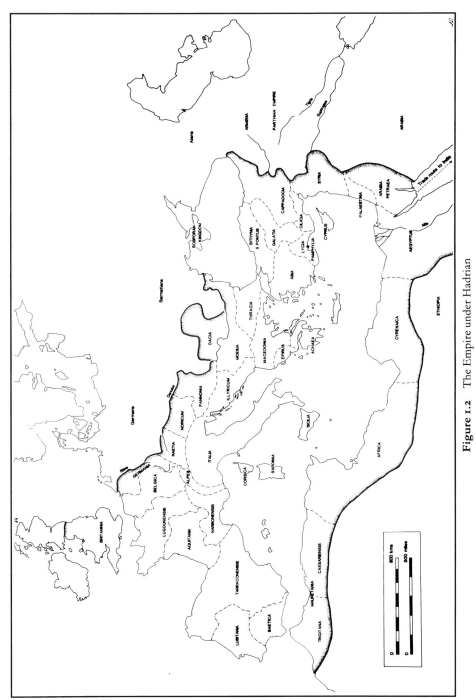

Figure 1.2   The Empire under Hadrian

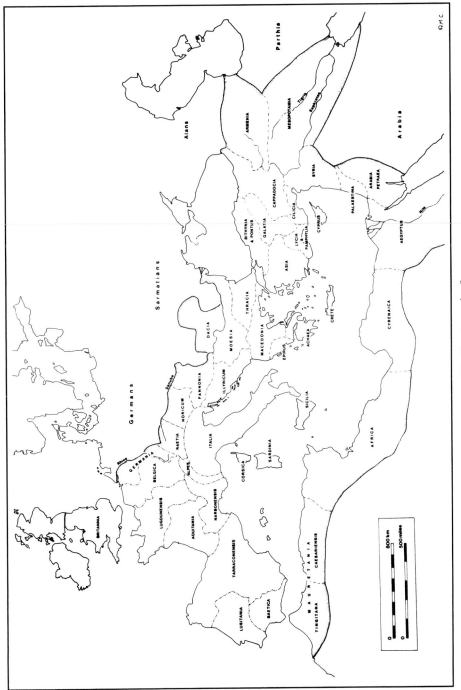

Figure 1.3   The Empire under Severus

central laws of the Empire, as with so many of its aspects, were firmly rooted in the Republic, and produced in time a system where much of the burden of administration was placed on the shoulders of local leaders, and interference by, or recourse to, the provincial governors, must at first have been the exception rather than the norm (Part 6); the path was eased by allowing acceptable local native law to continue in existence alongside Roman law in many provinces. Gradually, though, changes brought about by the difficulties of the Late Empire tied more and more people ever more tightly to the state, as it interfered, for good or ill, in their affairs. Taxes increased, as did the number of civil servants or those dependent on the bounty of the government. Indeed it has been suggested that the increase in the official class was so enormous that the receivers of public money seemed to outnumber the tax payers, while, in the end, tax-collectors were demanding the means for an administration which ruled but could no longer protect.

Despite the growth of urban and semi-urban settlements throughout the Empire, it is probably true to say that by far and away the greater proportion of the population dwelt in the country and engaged in rural activities (Part 7). The Empire's economy was firmly linked to agriculture and the provision of food for the army and for the inhabitants of the cities always remained a prime objective. The existence of a permanent and profitable food market enabled many landowners, whose earliest interests had lain almost entirely in subsistence farming, to increase their holdings and to build substantial residences. Agricultural methods were also improved – up to a point; some occurred in both farm animals and cultivated crops, by selective breeding, while many of the outlying provinces gained by the introduction of better implement technology. Primarily the Empire depended on adequate grain production, but wine, olive oil, wool, leather and meat were all important to the economy.

But the economy of the Empire depended on more than just agricultural produce, important though it was (Part 8). One of the principal benefits which the Empire conferred upon its inhabitants was a comparatively stable monetary system of a trimetallic nature with ample low-value coins for small change, so that even the meanest transactions could take place. The monetary system in turn depended on the supply of necessary metals, gold, silver and copper, while iron and tin also formed part of the mining economy, which was vital for the Empire's survival. Exhaustion of many of the primary metal sources in the Late Empire was to cause a crippling inflation. It was not only a common and convenient currency throughout the Empire which facilitated trade, but also the establishment of better means of communication. Roads, rivers and the sea, augmented in a few places by canals, provided the arteries down which flowed, not only the necessary supplies to the army, but also a greatly increased volume of trade. It was in this that the Roman world reached out to its fullest extent, sending its manufactured goods far beyond the frontiers and receiving raw materials often of an exotic nature in return. Ideas travelled with the goods, bringing new religions which mingled

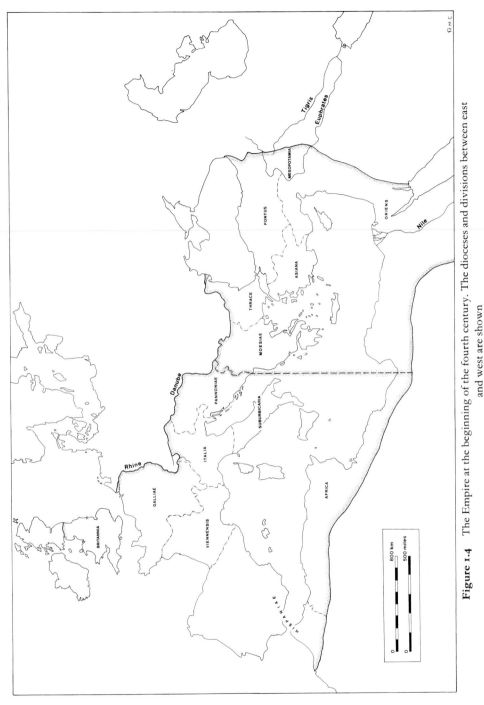

Figure 1.4 The Empire at the beginning of the fourth century. The dioceses and divisions between east and west are shown

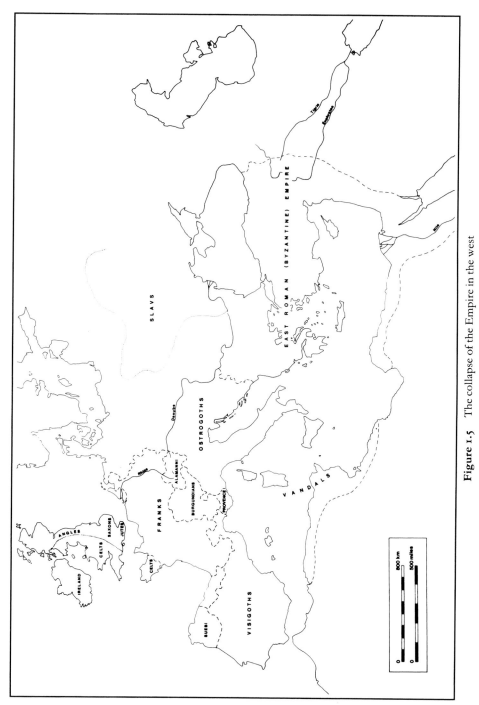

Figure 1.5 The collapse of the Empire in the west

with the cults of the Empire (Part 10); in most cases, the inhabitants were far too superstitious to ignore them, and, by means of the *interpretatio Romana*, gave many a place in the pantheon of Roman deities.

The society which made up the Empire was diverse, cosmopolitan, often much-travelled and multi-lingual (Part 9); Greeks and Syrians are found in northern Britain, while Britons served in the army and retired in Dacia and Germany. Undoubtedly troop movements stirred the mixture. There were divisions between social classes, primarily between Roman citizen and non-citizen, just as there were between freeborn, freedman and slave. Equally there was a good deal of social mobility: the non-citizen aspired to the citizenship, as a slave did to his freedom; the son of a freedman might be freeborn and so heir to much that had passed by his father. The extension of the citizenship to all freeborn in the early third century removed some of these divisions, but at the same time caused others to be created. It is important, though, to remember that, as a slave-owning society, there was normally an abundance of cheap labour, supplemented by condemned criminals for the really nasty jobs, such as mining and sewer-cleaning. The number of slaves probably increased in the later Empire, and there must also have been a rise in the number of freeborn 'peasant' class, bound to the land they worked by their tenancy agreements, and so little better than slaves. Society was also reflected by its art, from the rich patrons to the practitioners who executed their commissions.

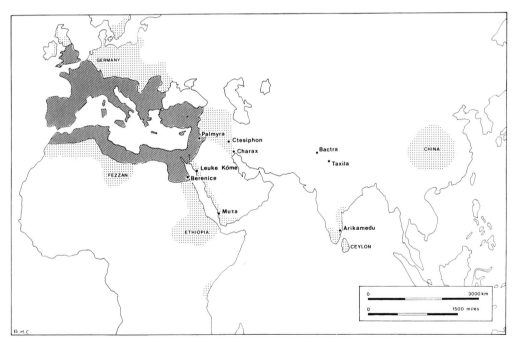

Figure 1.6 The Empire beyond the frontiers

As with many other things in the Empire, some remarkable fusions took place between the different artistic styles of its component parts.

The endurance of the Roman Empire for five hundred years is one of the success stories of history. That it survived so long is a sign of its principal achievement, whereby a heterogeneous mixture of races and creeds were induced to settle down together in a more or less peaceful way under the *Pax Romana*.

PART 2

·THE·RISE·OF·THE·EMPIRE·

CHAPTER 2

·CELTIC·EUROPE·BEFORE· ·THE·ROMANS·

John Collis

Introduction

Within temperate Europe, the zone north of the Alps but south of the North European Plain, there was a main stream of development which presented a fairly homogeneous picture in terms of social and economic development, and in material culture. This will form the main theme of this brief study. On its periphery, in the German Mittelgebirge, the Alpine valleys, the Atlantic coast of France, and western Britain, there was a number of more disparate groups, varied in material culture, and with social and economic trajectories that differed considerably from that of the main zone. Because of their lack of homogeneity, these societies are dealt with only in passing, or not at all. Space precludes any other approach, even though they formed an integral part of iron age society, being the source of major raw materials such as metals and salt, and even though at the time of the Roman conquest, they played a disproportionate role in military events, as their low level of social organization and often mountainous environment made permanent conquest difficult.

The nomenclature used here is that developed by German scholars, based on the system devised by Reinecke earlier this century. Figure 2.1 shows the approximate relationship with the Déchelette/Viollier system, which may be more familiar to British readers, and also some approximate dates are suggested. The bibliography has been kept brief, and those interested in following up any points are referred to the contributor's two recent books, *The European Iron Age*, which gives a general background to the period, and *Oppida: earliest towns north of the Alps* which deals in depth with the period covered in this essay. Cunliffe's book *Iron Age Communities in Britain* provides an excellent introduction to the British Iron Age.

By the third century BC a broadly homogeneous group of societies had developed

Tischler	Reinecke	Déchelette	date
	Hallstatt C1	Hallstatt I	700
	Hallstatt C2		600
	Hallstatt D1 Hallstatt D2	Hallstatt II	
	Hallstatt D3		475
Early La Tène	La Tène A	La Tène Ia	400
	La Tène B1	La Tène Ib	
	La Tène B2	La Tène Ic	250
Middle La Tène	La Tène C1	La Tène IIa	
	La Tène C2	La Tène IIb	100
	La Tène D1	La Tène III	50
Late La Tène	La Tène D2	Gallo-Romaine précoce	
	La Tène D3		20
	Augustan	Augustan	

Figure 2.1 Chronological and cultural table

in the zone from Romania in the east to south-eastern Britain in the west, and from the central Alps to the highland belt that runs from the Carpathians, through the German Mittelgebirge, and into Belgium. There was a general, simple level of social organization with no marked social differentiation, no major centres or hill-forts and a relatively non-specialized organization of production and industry. Trade was localized, and few, if any, goods from the classical world found their way into the area. Though traditionally this culture is referred to as 'Celtic', ethnically and linguistically it was probably varied, as almost everywhere there can be seen continuity from the preceding Hallstatt period, and, as in Britain, La Tène material culture, brooches, weapon types, and above all, the abstract art style which flourished on ornaments and sword scabbards, was gradually absorbed by the indigenous society.

By the second century, and increasingly into the first century BC, this homogeneity disappeared. Trade with the Mediterranean encouraged social differentiation, conflict for resources led to more developed levels of social organization, and eventually to patterns of settlement nucleated for defence. With nucleation came industrialization and urbanization. Ethnically too the situation became more complex, especially with the gradual absorption of the areas north of the Danube into the Germanic cultural sphere during the first century BC.

Social and political organization

Direct evidence on the level of social and political organization is contained in meagre Latin and Greek texts, but it is clear that at one extreme were state organizations closely comparable with those of the classical world, at the other fairly simple tribal organizations, such as Caesar encountered in northern Gaul, or among the tribes of northern and western Britain in which some form of lineage or clan predominated. At the state level the best information exists on the tribe of the Aedui, who elected an annual chief magistrate, the *vergobret*. There were rules which did not allow for re-election, or for a close relative to be elected during the lifetime of an ex-*vergobret*. These are clear attempts by the ruling oligarchy to prevent any one individual or family dominating, and so establishing dynastic monarchy. Such states were however vulnerable to individuals' ambitions, as the histories of Dumnorix of the Aedui or Orgetorix of the Helvetii show. Occasionally kings did emerge, though often like Commius of the Atrebates, it may have been due to Roman support. Otherwise it was through some form of monopoly control – military (Ariovistus), collection of river tolls (Dumnorix), or external trade (Cunobelin?). The Aedui also had a 'senate' which met at their chief town, Mont Beuvray (Bibracte), and the state could also raise funds, for instance by auctioning the right to collect river tolls.

Unlike the Mediterranean region, these states were based on tribal groupings rather than cities, as urbanization came later than the state, and it is perhaps not without significance that it is not the city name but the tribe's which tends to survive in modern place names: Paris (Lutetia Parisiorum), Rheims (Durocortorum Remorum), Bourges (Avaricum Biturigum), but such was their political and social organization that these states were readily absorbed into the Roman administrative system. Less is known of the simpler societies. The lack of any centralized organization is usually implied by the Roman sources rather than described. Also these societies are only encountered under periods of stress, when temporary war leaders might be appointed to co-ordinate and unify a tribe which under normal circumstances might be in a state of internal conflict of feud and vendetta. Thus individuals such as Cassivellaunus are given greater prominence than they deserve and their power may have been as short-lived as the crisis that brought them to the top. Other societies may not have achieved even this level of unity; Vespasian's conquest of the Durotriges in Dorset seems to have been a piecemeal affair, with each hill-fort organizing its own defence. Group identity in the form of a tribal name did not guarantee co-operation.

Settlement pattern

The second and first centuries BC saw fundamental changes in settlement pattern with the appearance of nucleated defended '*oppida*' which have been claimed as the earliest urban settlements in temperate Europe (Collis, 1984b). In the immediately preceding centuries over much of temperate Europe the small hamlet or agricultural village had been the norm, and even hill-forts were a rare phenomenon, confined largely to the Atlantic Coast, in Brittany and western Britain. The farming settlement at Manching in Bavaria started to increase in size in the third century BC and by the second it had achieved urban proportions, but at present it stands alone. Elsewhere the most complex settlements encountered are 'industrial villages' such as Mšecké Žehrovice in Bohemia or Aulnat in central France. The former was working iron and producing sapropelite bracelets and had a double *Viereckschanze*, the latter was working gold, silver, bronze, iron, glass, textiles and bone, but was by no stretch of the imagination urban.

In the second half of the second century larger open settlements were appearing in western Europe: Breisach and Basel on the Rhine, Levroux in central France (fig. 2.2), the latter being about 12 ha (30 acres) in size. Trade, including contact with the Mediterranean world, was one factor that led to their development, and similar sites are now beginning to be found on the Rhône and Saône, the major routes to the Mediterranean. However this is not the case in central Europe, in Czechoslovakia and the German Mittelgebirge, where the earliest *oppida* appear in La Tène C2. At present ignorance must be confessed of what preceded them or caused them to come into existence; pressure from German expansion in northern Europe still appears the best explanation. During La Tène D, at the end of the second and beginning of the first centuries BC, *oppida* appear in western Europe as well. Formerly open settlements such as Manching were enclosed, and other settlements were abandoned for new defensive positions on hill-tops at Levroux (fig. 2.2), Basel and Breisach. In these latter cases the defended *oppidum* is about the same size as the preceding settlement, but with the larger *oppida* we are clearly dealing with a number of different settlements joining together. Aulnat 7 ha (17 acres) was abandoned when Gergovie 150 ha (370 acres) was founded. In many cases the new site developed rapidly to become a major centre of population (Gergovie, Mont Beuvray, Alise-Ste-Reine), others were soon abandoned or only possessed a small population (Staffelberg, Heidengraben bei Grabenstetten). What impact these new sites had on the total settlement pattern is unclear. In some cases it may be that there was a total nucleation of the population and complete abandonment of the countryside, but more normally it seems that the developing artisan class and social élite formed the population of the new towns, while the farmers returned to the countryside.

Excavations on the *oppida* have shown they are complex in both their social and economic organization. Large fenced areas (palisade enclosures up to a hectare in size) surround large timber buildings and other ancillary buildings, and they may be the

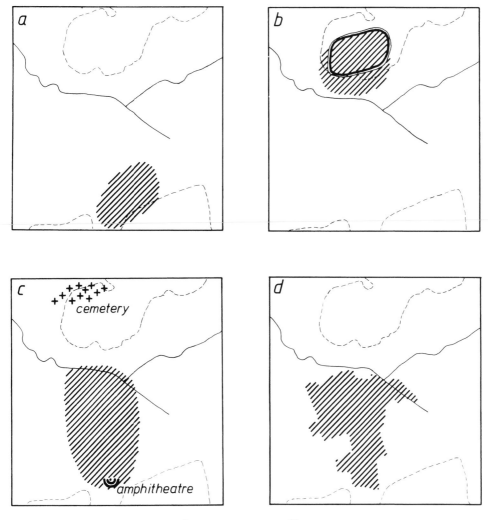

Figure 2.2   Settlement development of Levroux (Indre), France (*Collis 1984b*)

equivalents of courtyard houses on classical Greek and Roman sites. At the other end of the spectrum are the small timber houses (fig. 2.3) which cluster along the major east–west road at Manching, or along the terraces on a number of Czech sites. These are generally associated with industrial activity, and seem to be the residences of an artisan class specializing in the production of metal objects, textiles and other commodities (figs 2.9 and 2.10). But at Manching there are other sorts of buildings whose function is still unknown, such as the 'warehouses', structures up to 30 m (100 ft) long.

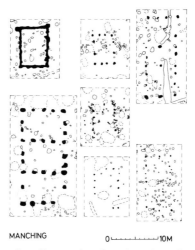

MANCHING   0 ⎣_____⎦ 10M

Figure 2.3   Examples of house plans from Manching, Bavaria (*Collis 1984b*)

Britain at the time of the Roman conquest presented a rather different picture. There are *oppida* in the east but, unlike their continental counterparts, they are in low-lying, non-defensive situations defined by vast linear dykes. They also enclose much larger, but only partly occupied, areas: 2,000 ha (5,000 acres) at Colchester, 350 ha (860 acres) at Stanwick, although this may include, as on the Sheepen site at Colchester, an area with an industrial character. At Stanwick the monumental earthworks in places follow pre-existing land boundaries; one interpretation would see these as royal estates controlling key areas, and deliberately imposing in their public works to demonstrate the power of the newly-emerged royal class. In western Britain the hill-forts still predominated. Though they were clearly centres of defence in times of need, as the cemetery of defenders at Maiden Castle demonstrates, it is still a matter of argument to what extent they played a role as 'central places' (for conflicting views see Cunliffe, 1983, 1984; and Collis, 1981). They clearly had central storage facilities for grain, and a permanent population, but evidence for industrial activity is limited and occurs on minor farming settlements and villages as well. There is no evidence that the hill-forts' inhabitants were any wealthier than those on the surrounding farms, if anything the opposite seems to be the case.

These are only a few of the settlement patterns which may have existed at the time of the Roman conquest. It is clear that there was an enormous range, from societies based on small farming settlements with no nucleation (e.g. the Yorkshire Wolds, Dent, 1983) to highly urbanized systems as in central France, though in the latter case the large size of some of the sites, in comparison with their Roman successors, suggests a fairly undeveloped system with urban sites exercising a monopoly, rather than a more competitive system with secondary and tertiary tiers of urban sites such as are found in the Roman period.

Burial practice and social structure

Up to the middle of the second century BC the dominant burial rite had been inhumation in 'flat' cemeteries (fig. 2.4), though the systematic layout of some cemeteries shows that markers, presumably low mounds, were employed. This burial rite is found from Slovakia and the Hungarian Plain in the east, to Champagne and central France in the west. The women were buried with their jewellery – torc, brooches, bracelets, armlets, finger-rings, belt chain and anklets – although there was considerable regional variation (for instance the presence or absence of a torc, the number of bracelets, and also in the number of grave-goods per grave within a single cemetery). Universally these ornaments were of bronze (only finger-rings might be of gold), and occasionally bracelets of shale (sapropelite) or glass, and beads or inlays of coral or amber. The male graves were usually accompanied by an iron brooch, an armlet, and more rarely by weapons. About a fifth of the male graves had a fairly complete set of weapons: spear, sword, shield, and sometimes a helmet. In absolute terms of wealth the burials are poorer than those of the sixth and fifth centuries, and imply a less socially differentiated society.

In the second century this burial rite starts to disappear, initially in central Europe

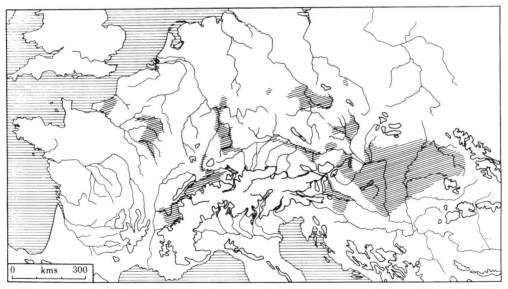

Figure 2.4 Distribution of flat, inhumation cemeteries of La Tène B-C (fourth–second centuries BC)
(*Collis 1984b*)

(in La Tène C1) and later in western Europe (La Tène C2). At the long-lived cemetery of Münsingen in Switzerland the graves become notably shallower and grave-goods rarer in C2. At Basel, one of the few sites of La Tène D in Switzerland to produce any burials, the cemetery showed little sign of formal layout. Graves often cut one another, and the few grave-goods (brooches and pendants) could only with difficulty be assigned to individual graves. The general pattern, however, from Central Europe to France, is for burial evidence to disappear in La Tène D, and virtually nothing is known of how, for instance, the inhabitants of Manching normally disposed of their dead. This contrasts with what Caesar tells us of the lavish funerals accorded to individuals of rank in Gallic society, and he mentions the burning of letters on pyres, implying that cremation was the norm.

The one exception to this lack of burial evidence is in an east–west zone extending from the central Rhine, through northern France to south-east Britain (Collis, 1977). Here cremation was the normal burial rite, in cemeteries which could number several hundreds of burials, as at Wederath or St Albans, though every settlement, both large or small, had its own cemetery. The emphasis in grave-goods was in pottery vessels, and metalwork (brooches, bracelets), and glass bracelets and pendants are rare. Weapons also appear, but are generally confined to continental cemeteries; in Britain only defensive weapons such as shields and corselets are known. Some at least of the continental weapon-graves post-date the Roman conquest when the right to bear weapons became an indication of status.

A small number of graves are much richer. This wealth appears not only in the number of local grave-goods, especially large numbers of pottery vessels, but also in terms of imported objects – wine *amphorae*, imported Italian pottery, bronze and silver vessels, and occasionally glass. Local prestige goods may include a wagon, silver brooches, a mirror, bronze-bound wooden buckets, and, in two recorded cases, the body was draped in a bearskin. In Britain these burials are associated with the rise of the Catuvellaunian state, and the richest graves from Lexden at Colchester are probably of members of the royal family. Both in Britain and on the continent these rich graves continue after the Roman conquest – for instance Goeblingen-Nospelt in Luxembourg and Stanfordbury in Northamptonshire. Indeed it is often difficult among the poorer graves to distinguish between pre- and post-conquest. With only subtle changes in the character of the grave-goods, for example the appearance of flagons, platters, samian and other artefacts, this burial rite becomes the norm in early Roman times in the northern provinces, and many cemeteries show continuity into the Roman period.

There are dangers in comparing and contrasting the burial rites in two different areas (for example Switzerland with western Germany). Ideology certainly plays a role in the gradual downgrading of the burial in the later phases of such cemeteries as Münsingen; the sword is more rarely disposed of in the funereal context, but more commonly on ritual sites such as the site of La Tène itself. None the less, the burial and settlement evidence combined suggests that social differentiation was becoming more marked during La Tène C and D, a process which did not necessarily halt with the Roman conquest. The royal family of the Catuvellauni may have disappeared, but that of the Iceni and the Atrebates did not. The increasing wealth of the rich burials of the Treveri at Goeblingen-Nospelt in Luxembourg also indicates Roman support for the native élite class in Gaul. The other end of the social spectrum however is less easy to study, and only the documentary evidence suggests that the rise of the élite was accompanied by a suppression of the lower classes, rather than a general rise in material wealth throughout society as a whole.

Production

Between La Tène C and La Tène D there are no obvious technological breakthroughs, either in iron or bronze production, in ceramics, or in any other crafts. In quantitative terms however, there seems to have been an industrial revolution, most clearly detectable in iron production, as the tons of iron needed for the spikes used in the *murus gallicus* defences, or the quantities of discarded iron tools and nails littering such sites as Manching, eloquently testify. The foundation of the *oppida*, and the nucleation of artisan production paved the way for permanent changes in the mode of production, with the proliferation of full-time craftsmen who were beginning to exercise the freedom of an independent class.

This process is most clearly visible in iron production. From late Hallstatt times raw iron had been traded in the form of 'currency bars', which were turned into finished objects on each settlement. Every hamlet seems to have possessed at least a part-time blacksmith; specialist master craftsmen, however, existed at least for the production of weapons. Although some swords bent on impact, as Polybius sneeringly relates, Livy, Pliny and others tacitly imply that the Mediterranean world had much to learn from the Celtic world, and this finds support in the archaeological record. Already by La Tène C production of swords had begun in Switzerland, by welding thin bars of steel to form composite forged blades the strength and flexibility of which were perhaps only surpassed with the advent of the pattern-welded sword. The blades were etched to show the structure, and stamped as a sign of quality. These stamped swords are widely distributed in Europe, including Britain, though whether through trade or local production is unclear.

In La Tène D the currency bar disappears and the production of finished articles is concentrated on the *oppida*. Some sites, such as the Titelberg in Luxembourg, and some in Czechoslovakia, are sited near, if not actually on, major sources of good quality iron ore. Others such as Manching (fig. 2.5) made use of poor quality sources such as bog iron, or were importing ore for smelting. Fifty kilometres (30 miles) downstream

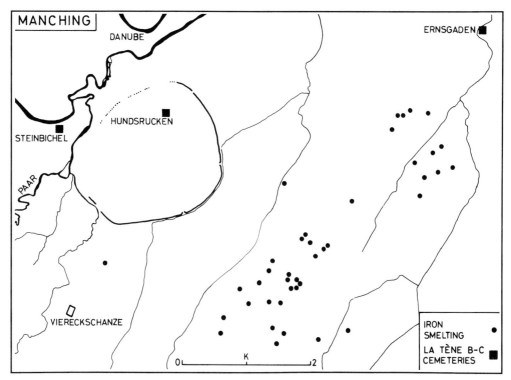

Figure 2.5 Distribution of iron smelting sites around Manching (*Collis 1984b*)

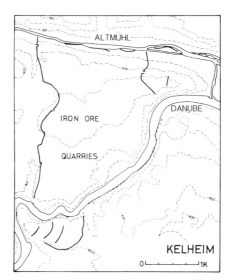

Figure 2.6 The *oppidum* of Kelheim, Bavaria, showing areas of iron quarrying (*Collis 1984b*)

Figure 2.7   Cooking pot of *Graphittonkeramik* from Manching. Scale 1:4 (*Collis 1984b*)

from Manching is the huge *oppidum* of Kelheim (fig. 2.6) which seems to have had only a small population, although its interior is riddled with pits for the extraction of ore, which was presumably exported up river to its more populous neighbour.

Manching was also importing graphite clay for its pottery industry, in this case from some 200 km (125 miles) down the Danube at Passau (fig. 2.14). Although sites like Manching, Stradonice or Budapest were producing specialist wares, such as the *Graphittonkeramik* cooking pots (fig. 2.7) or painted wares, both for their hinterland and for other *oppida*, each major settlement may have still been largely self-sufficient in more mundane wares. Plain cordoned wares are common at Manching for jars and eating bowls, but 20 to 25 per cent of the pottery was still hand-made. Some centres may have specialized in fine ware production, such as Roanne which produced painted wares with exciting geometric and zoomorphic designs (fig. 2.8) and later samian production sites such as La Graufesenque and Lezoux started initially with painted wares. One settlement at least, Sissach in Switzerland, was almost wholly dependent on pottery production. In Britain the producers of Gallo-Belgic wares were among the literate class, and were obviously highly-specialized full-time artisans, but entrepreneurial activity and

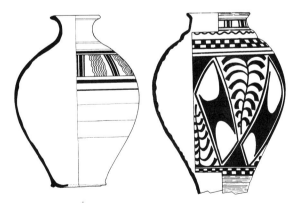

Figure 2.8   Examples of late La Tène painted pottery from: (1) Manching; (2) Aulnat. Scale 1:4 (*Collis 1984b*)

25

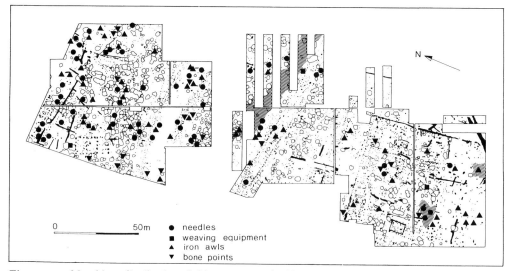

Figure 2.9 Manching: distribution of objects connected with weaving and leatherworking (*Collis 1984b*)

factory production does not appear until the Roman period.

At Manching the enormous range of iron tools indicates the presence of cart-wrights, wheelwrights, leather workers, coopers and specialist metalworkers, and even the traditionally domestic craft of weaving was becoming artisan-based. Indeed the concentration of objects associated with weaving – needles, bone bodkins and occasional shuttles – in the excavated area was centred on the small houses fronting the main street (fig. 2.9). The normally ubiquitous debris from metalworking was notable by its absence in this zone, while industries such as potting were poorly represented in the whole of the excavated area. This hints at a zoning at Manching according to craft specialism, a phenomenon which was often linked with the presence of craft-guilds. Though some production, for instance of coins (fig. 2.10), was concentrated inside the 'palisaded enclosures', implying direct control by an élite, the artisan class seemed already to have established its freedom.

On the continent local production concentrated mainly on normal domestic needs: tools and utensils in the case of iron, and simple personal ornaments, such as belt fittings and brooches, and harness. Most was mass-produced, stereotyped and artistically mundane. Production of prestige metalwork, other than weapons, wagon fittings and hearth furniture was non-existent, as though no élite market existed. From the evidence of burials it was the imported Mediterranean goods which largely performed the role of prestige goods. Except for the occasional gold torc or silver brooch, precious metals were virtually exclusively reserved for coin production.

In this respect Britain forms a contrast. Even though Mediterranean goods were available, and appear in the rich graves, prestige items of high artistic merit were still

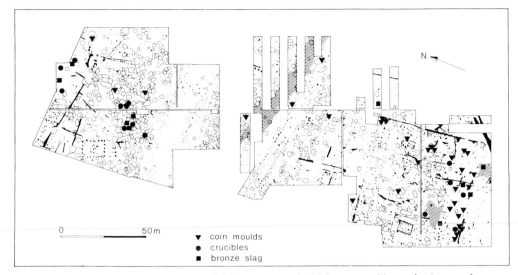

Figure 2.10   Manching: distribution of objects connected with bronzeworking and coin manufacture
(*Collis 1984b*)

being produced, not only in the less industrially developed areas of western and northern Britain, but also in the south-east where mass-production in continental style might be expected, and it can only be conjectured that this may be connected with more direct royal involvement in production, from which may also have come the encouragement of Gallo-Belgic potters to move to Britain. The products of the bronze- and goldsmiths of the first century BC/AD represent the climax of prehistoric art in Britain: the whole range of engraved bronze mirrors, the harness and the chariot fittings (all of which types were on occasion exported to the continent), the Battersea shield, the Waterloo Bridge helmet, the gold torcs from Ipswich and Snettisham. Production did not cease at the Roman conquest, as items such as the Aesica brooch demonstrate, but slowly the market dwindled as wealth was turned into bricks and mortar, or into aping or importing Mediterranean tastes.

Coinage

The earliest coins of temperate Europe imitate Greek prototypes (Allen, 1980), in the early phase mainly those of Philip of Macedon: his gold stater in the west and his silver tetradrachm in the east. Later it was the Greek colonies: Rhode, which provided the source of the *monnaies à la croix* of south-western France, and Marseilles, whose 'charging bull' was used for a large series of lower-value coins in France and Britain. Only rarely, mainly after the Roman conquest of Gaul, were Roman coins imitated. Local designs were also invented, like the *Rolltier* in southern Germany, but these represent a minority.

Early coins are virtually unknown from archaeological contexts, and estimates of the date of their appearance have varied from the fourth to the end of the second century BC, though the consensus is now for an early date contemporary with the originals. The mechanism of their introduction is also a problem. Although coins appear in an economic context in which standardization was increasingly important (for example the production of iron bars in standard sizes), they arrived at a time when trade contact with the Mediterranean was at a minimum. Mercenaries returning from Greek service have been invoked, but this does not explain the transfer of technological skill, as the earliest copies in terms of design and striking are of high technical quality. Economically these early coins would have had little impact; they would have taken their place alongside other prestige goods which were circulating through social and political channels. They seem, however, largely to have ousted other items of gold, such as brooches and finger-rings, and only torcs seem to survive, possibly representing a multiple of the coin, as the two are often found together in hoards.

The next major change was the advent of lower-value coins in the form of silver minims, struck or cast bronze, or cast potin (bronze with up to 25 per cent tin). The date when this happened is also disputed. Archaeological evidence might suggest one as early as the late second century, although, on historical grounds, some numismatists would suggest the Caesarian conquest; certainly the vast majority were produced in the decades after 50 BC. Some are inscribed, though usually with the names of individuals otherwise unknown, so whether these were produced by private nobles as a means of personal prestige, or by magistrates acting on behalf of a state is unclear. Certainly the more common types have distributions which cross tribal boundaries or are equally common in several different tribal areas. Both the reason for their production and their subsequent use remain obscure. They occur commonly on many, though not all, the major *oppida*, suggesting they may have been used in local exchange, perhaps in a market context, a process of economic development which can be charted in Athens on the strength of documentary evidence. To what extent the countryside was using this coinage is also hotly disputed, though the level of coin usage clearly varied from one community to another, and gold and bronze may well have operated in different spheres of exchange.

Inscribed coins, other than those with imitations of Greek inscriptions, are also a late adoption; indeed in some areas they never appeared. In some cases, especially where two names occur, we may be dealing with tribal magistrates. Individuals such as Vercingetorix are known from the writings of Caesar, but his estimation of a person's importance does not seem to equate with the numbers of coins inscribed with their names. Inscriptions became more common after the Roman conquest, and local Gallic coinage was in extensive production and use until ousted by the official bronze coinage of Augustus after 30 BC.

In the cases where we can recognize kings in the inscriptions we are clearly dealing with official state production, for instance in the kingdom of Noricum. The best example is the latest coinage of south-east Britain where Allen (1944) was able to build up a plausible dynastic relationship between various rulers, and to define their respective spheres of influence. But to impose this interpretation on early uninscribed, and even the earlier inscribed, coins when the state and kingship was less developed, is a doubtful procedure.

External trade

After the great climax of trade with the Mediterranean world in Hallstatt D and La Tène A, from 600 to about 350 BC, there is a major hiatus in the occurrence of Mediterranean goods in central Europe, due in part to a shift in Greek trading to the east, and in part to the Gallic incursions into northern Gaul which affected Italian production. This also made the traditional contact with northern Italy less detectable as both there and in central Europe the material culture was very similar, including, for instance, prestige goods decorated in Wadalgesheim style.

The renewal of contact in the second century is not as yet readily detectable. This is partly because burial rites were placing less emphasis on grave-goods, partly due to a lack of settlement archaeology for this period, and partly because it is still not possible to distinguish and date early imports. The introduction of coinage shows that contact existed, but so far it is only at Aulnat that early second century imports can be identified, with black slipped 'campanian' pottery and cream *mortaria* turning up in association with a relatively early gold coin.

The next phase lasted until the Caesarian conquest of Gaul. The dominant import, the Dressel Ia wine *amphora* (fig. 2.12), was in vogue for about a century, and at present we cannot distinguish between early and late varieties. The fine black-slipped plates and dishes that accompany it are equally insusceptible to precise dating, so the impact of the Roman conquest of southern France, for instance, cannot be judged, nor the stimulus this may have had on trade. Certainly the Romans extended their territory along the major through routes, the Carcassonne gap, over to the headwaters of the Garonne at Toulouse, and along the Rhône to Vienne and Geneva. Strabo tells us that Vienne developed from a village to a metropolis, and, on the borders of the Roman province from 125 to 58 BC, it controlled the routes to the north and north-east along the Rhône and Saône, the land route to the headwaters of the Loire, and so to the Atlantic coast.

During this period the trade grew prodigiously (fig. 2.11). Most sites in central and eastern France produce large quantities of *amphorae*, and the Palais d'Essalois on the Loire, at the end of the land route to Vienne, is littered with fragments. They were

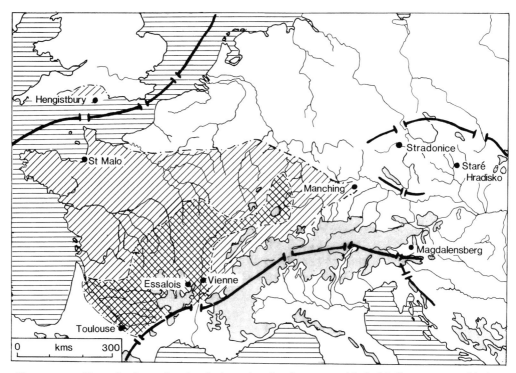

Figure 2.11 Generalized map showing the intensity of trade contact with the Mediterranean world, sites exceptionally rich within their zones, and some physical restrictions to trade routes (*Collis 1984b*)

reaching northern France and western Germany in some quantity, as well as southern Britain, and more rarely central Europe. Both these *amphorae* and the fine wares were products of the west coast of Italy, and some of the *amphorae* were being manufactured near Pompeii and near Cosa, the two major ports involved in this trade.

The third main category of Italian exports was bronze vessels, mainly pans and jugs. These have an even wider distribution, occurring in burials in Poland, northern Germany, Britain, and occasionally in Denmark. They are also more common in central Europe, due to the greater ease with which they could be carried over the Alps in comparison with *amphorae*. Some of these finds perhaps date to before 50 BC, but most belong to the period up to 10 BC. This phase is characterized by a larger wine *amphora*, Dressel Ib (fig. 2.12), whose source and distribution is much the same as Ia, except in Britain, where it has a more easterly distribution, due to the decline of Hengistbury Head, and the rise of the East Anglia–Rhine route.

Mediterranean trade seems to have been largely in the hands of Italian merchants, who are mentioned by both Posidonius and Caesar as active in central France and beyond the Rhine, and it is doubtful if any indigenous trading class existed as such at this period. Caesar also notes the presence of Roman commissariats at Orléans (Cenabum) and

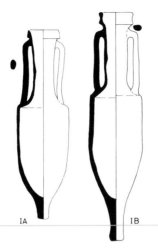

IA   IB

Figure 2.12   Dressel Ia *amphora* (*c.* 150–50 BC) and Dressel Ib (*c.* 60–10 BC). Scale 1:10 (*Collis 1984b*)

Châlons-sur-Saône (Cabillonum). On the Magdalensberg in Austria, perhaps the ancient Noreia, capital of the kingdom of Noricum, one of the lower terraces formed an Italian merchants' quarter. Their accounts, scribbled on the plaster of their walls, tell of their trading partners and connections in Italy, and in one case, in Volubilis in Mauretania (fig. 2.13). The main product traded from Noricum was iron, which was of superior quality to that made in Italy, and the Norican smiths were able to produce steel of a consistently high standard. Elsewhere it is the predictable range of products required by a higher civilization from peripheral areas: raw metals, corn and slaves, and Posidonius tells us that an *amphora* of wine could be changed for a slave in central France. In this context the almost annual conflicts, mentioned by Caesar, between the Gallic tribes for control of the trade routes and of the goods to trade become understandable.

Internal trade

The material culture of late La Tène in temperate Europe is very homogeneous, which on the one hand might mean that local self-sufficiency in finished products obviated the need for trade, but on the other that continuous contact existed through which ideas could spread. Traded objects are difficult to identify. Some brooches of foreign types occur at Manching, and central European brooches occur in a burial at Wilanów near Warsaw, but in these cases it is likely that the women who owned them moved with their possessions, and inter-regional marriages are historically documented among the upper classes. Occasionally coins travelled; Gallic coins occur in central Europe and Britain, but not in sufficient quantities to suggest they were more than curiosities,

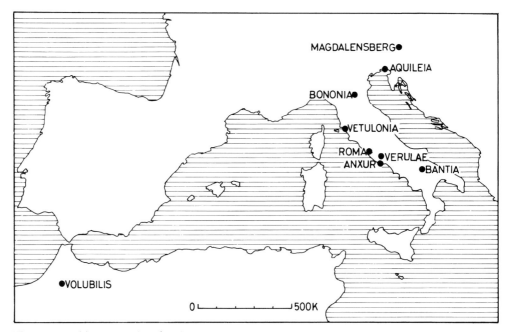

Figure 2.13 Towns mentioned on inscriptions from the traders' quarters on the Magdalensberg, Austria (*Collis 1984b*)

and they certainly played no part in long-distance trade. Most traded goods, however, were probably raw materials such as good-quality iron, bronze and salt, and Strabo lists other archaeologically intangible items such as linen and salted pork.

Pottery was certainly traded, but is poorly documented due in part to the limited research programmes of the German and central European schools of archaeology. The one distinctive product on which we have information is the *Graphittonkeramik* cooking pots whose clay was chosen for its high conductivity and its heat resistance (fig. 2.7). The sources are limited: around Passau on the German/Austrian border, near Český Budějovice in southern Bohemia, and a number of small deposits in Moravia. Centres such as Budapest, Manching and Hallstatt were importing the raw clay and manufacturing cooking pots, which commonly reached as far as the German Mittelgebirge, southern Poland and Romania, and individual vessels could move several hundred kilometres, to Aquileia on the Adriatic or Aulnat in central France (fig. 2.14).

Whether other specialized wares like the painted pottery travelled similar distances we do not know. If Stradonice was the only production centre in Bohemia, its products were travelling up to 100 km (60 miles), but not in any great quantities. In Britain fine decorated pottery made from the gabbroic clays on the Lizard was moving greater distances, up to 150 km (95 miles), but neolithic pottery from the same source had had a similar distribution three millennia before. Unfortunately the one case of distinctive

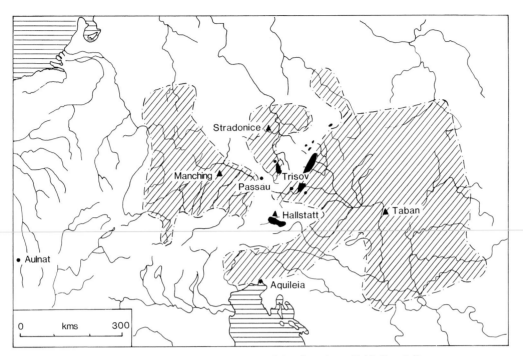

Figure 2.14 Distribution map of *Graphittonkeramik* (*Collis 1984b*)

pottery manufactured in Britain, the butt beakers and other Gallo-Belgic wares produced at Colchester, are at present impossible to distinguish from their Roman successors, though possibly pre-conquest finds come from the Humber estuary and central Hampshire.

The Colchester trade network is informative because we have a number of goods which have a source definitely in the area. The bronze coins struck there are mainly found in the *oppidum* itself, and only form a small percentage of the coins found at other sites such as St Albans. A second zone can be defined in which Roman imports occur such as amphorae, samian and other luxury items which presumably reached Britain through Colchester. They have a radius of about 60–70 km (35–45 miles). Gold coins from Colchester also circulated in this area, but also beyond in an arc of 140–150 km (85–95 miles) in the Thames valley. A further zone is defined by the fine Gallo-Belgic pottery already discussed. Both the zoning and the contexts in which these goods appear (for example the imports in rich burials) imply different trade mechanisms. Some are clearly upper-class luxuries which were obtained by direct personal contact with the centre; the fine pottery indicates indirect contact, perhaps 'down-the-line', or redistribution from sites on the periphery of the main area of Colchester's influence. Goods in the *oppidum* itself may in part have circulated through some limited form of market exchange. Certainly the system was complex, but was probably less developed than those of central France which have still to be analysed.

Religious and ceremonial sites

The construction of special sites and buildings for cult or ceremonial purposes had been a major feature of the neolithic and early bronze age, but in the millennium or so up to the second century BC such sites have rarely been identified and they seem generally to have had no role to play within late bronze age and early iron age society. In certain areas the increase of hoards and river finds may indicate deliberate destruction of wealth in either a social (such as potlatch) or religious context, but most ritual probably took place in the everyday settlement context, which only large-scale excavations might start to identify. The rare exceptions, such as Dun Ailinne, the Navan Fort, the Goloring and Libenice, prove the rule.

The first widespread appearance of cult sites is in the second century BC: the so-called *Viereckschanzen* of southern Germany. The most extensively excavated is Holzhausen in Bavaria (fig. 2.15). The basic characteristics are a small square wooden temple in one corner of a square enclosure with wooden palisade, later replaced by a bank and ditch. A number of shafts up to 30 m (100 ft) deep were found cut into the loose gravel, two with standing posts at the bottom, surrounded by organic deposits, perhaps from meat and plant offerings. At various places in the interior fires had been built. Ritual shafts have also been found at Tomerdingen and Fellbach-Schmiden, the latter containing wooden cult figures. In Bavaria the density of sites suggests virtually every settlement possessed a *Viereckschanze*, though they were apparently constructed in woodland away from occupation areas. However, elsewhere in Bohemia for instance, they form part of a settlement, although only a few sites had enclosures. The later *Viereckschanze* at Gosbecks Farm, within the dyked enclosures at Colchester, was more of a tribal focus.

In Britain small square or rectangular buildings like those at Holzhausen are known on several settlement sites, in hill forts such as South Cadbury and Danebury, or in open settlements like Heath Row, perhaps appearing as early as the fifth century BC. In all these cases it is mainly the contrast of the ground plan with the normal domestic round-houses that distinguishes them, rather than any associated finds, and it is not surprising that continental equivalents, for instance in the urban *oppida* where rectangular houses are the norm, have not been identified. In France and Britain there are rural sites which continued in use into Roman times when formal stone buildings, sculptures and inscriptions appear. In some cases wooden buildings preceded those of stone, as at Hayling Island, and Tremblois; in others there are only spreads of offerings such as coins and personal ornaments as at Allones and Harlow, but no environmental work

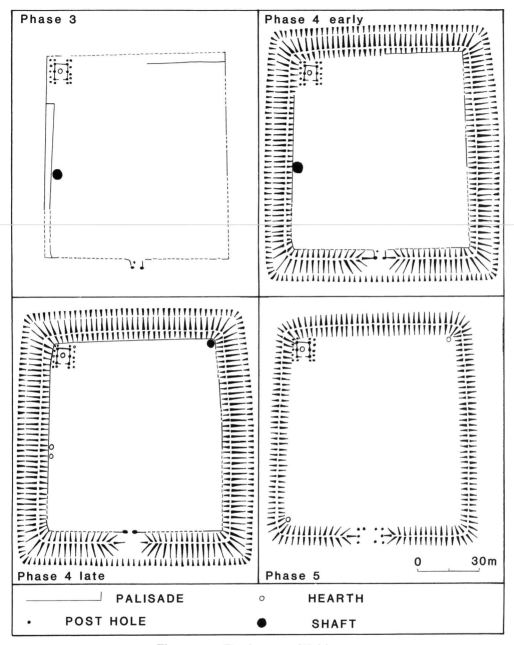

Figure 2.15 Development of Holzhausen

has been attempted to show, for instance, if there were groves of trees. Votive offerings could include weapons, as at Gournay-sur-Aronde, or miniature shields and swords, at Frilford and Worth, and river or marsh deposits of weapons are encountered, such as at La Tène, Hjortsprung, Llyn Cerrig Bach, or the historically documented Toulouse. At Gournay there were also human and animal bones while, beneath the great Gallo-Roman temple complex of Ribemont-sur-Ancre, there was a timber-framed enclosure retaining a heap of some 500 human femurs.

Why the second to first centuries BC should see this upsurge in formal religious sites is unclear, but it laid the foundation for religious practice in the western Roman provinces. It seems not to be connected with producing tribal or state cohesiveness (Gournay and Ribemont may be exceptions). The meagre historical sources and Roman activity suggest it was a personal, individual matter, but also the mention by Caesar of national convocations of the druids shows that religion could transcend state and tribal organization as did religion in the Greek world.

Epilogue

Even before the Roman Empire expanded to incorporate the Celtic societies here described, they were already under threat, if not exterminated. By the time Tiberius conquered southern Germany in 15–14 BC, Manching had been deserted for a generation or more, though how and precisely when this happened is still unclear. What little archaeology we have from the area to fill the gap between Manching and the Roman period suggests a culture of more northern origin. Certainly, at about the middle of the first century BC, burials of Germanic type had appeared fleetingly in Hesse, to return in force by the end of the century. By the decade 20–10 BC the last of the *oppida* in the Mittelgebirge had disappeared, and about the same time, possibly even earlier, the Czech sites were abandoned, in two cases, Hrazany and Závist, after their gates had been hurriedly reinforced and then burnt. Urban life was receding north of the Danube and east of the Rhine. By the time of Tacitus all these areas were inhabited by the Germani, who possessed no towns.

In the areas conquered by Rome, native life was often undisturbed for a generation or two after the conquest, indeed archaeologically it is often difficult to detect the conquest on native sites. The traditional division between Iron Age and Roman is in fact meaningless. Subsequent Roman developments throw much light on the less well documented Iron Age, while the Roman period is incomprehensible without an understanding of native society. It is not a question of whether one tribe or another was pro- or anti-Roman at the time of the conquest. What happened subsequently, and how quickly an area became romanized, is more connected with the pre-existing social structure, political and economic organization, and systems of land tenure. It has even been suggested that it was the structure of native society in adjacent areas, rather than the failings of the Roman army, which finally defined the limits of the Roman Empire, due to the inability of simple social systems to adapt to the Mediterranean model imposed by Rome.

CHAPTER 3

·HELLENISTIC·
·INFLUENCE·ON·
·THE·ROMAN·WORLD·

Keith Branigan

When Heraclides Ponticus described the Rome captured by the Gauls in 390 BC as a 'Greek' city, he probably raised far fewer eyebrows amongst his contemporaries than he does amongst ancient historians and archaeologists today. By the beginning of the fourth century, Rome had been subjected for some three centuries to the influences of Greek culture. Situated between Magna Graecia – the Greek colonial city states of southern Italy and Sicily – and the Etruscan cities to the north, Rome had inevitably received the impulses of both the truly Greek culture of the colonial cities and of the much modified and adapted Greek influences found in the Etruscan cities. The Etruscans exercised the greater and more immediate influence, by reason both of the proximity of the Etruscan heartland and the political domination which they exercised over affairs in Etruria and Latium, even after their kings were driven from Rome at the end of the fifth century BC.

The Etruscans acquired Greek vases and bronzes, and certainly employed Greek painters in cities such as Cerveteri in the sixth century BC. At the Etruscan port of Gravisca, Etruscans and Greek colonists lived alongside one another throughout the sixth century. The effect of both imported goods and imported artists and traders can be seen on contemporary Etruscan statuary, sculptured sarcophagi (pl. 3.1) and the repertoire of the Etruscan tomb painters. Though still little is known of Rome in the sixth and fifth centuries, it is certain that these modified artistic influences reached into the city, and indeed the last Etruscan king of Rome, Tarquinius Superbus, is known to have brought artists from Veii to decorate the temple of Jupiter on the Capitol. In the long term, however, the more significant contributions of the Etruscans in introducing Greek ways to the Romans may be judged to be the growing of vines and olives (Potter, 1979, 126), and the use of the alphabet. Though they are of no concern here, it should not be forgotten either that Rome benefited from Etruscan skills, such as hydraulic engineering, which owed little or nothing to the Greeks.

Although the Greek colonies of southern Italy and Sicily were mostly founded between the eighth and the sixth centuries BC, their influences on Rome were probably only directly felt after the eclipse of Etruscan power further north in the fifth century BC. Vast quantities of imported vases (pl. 3.2), bronzes and other goods from Greece found their way into Etruscan cities, and in small quantities perhaps into Rome itself, but initially there was little direct contact between the city-states and Rome. Only as Rome began to exert control over the country to the south of it, and the Greek colonies began to feel the threat of the hill peoples from the Apennines, did mutual interests drive Greeks and Romans into closer contacts. In the course of the fourth century, the Romans came to know cities such as Naples (Neapolis), Paestum (Poseidonia), and Heraclea, with their orthogonal planning which was to be developed in modified form in early Roman colonies such as Cosa founded in 273 BC. In these and other cities they came into contact not only with imported Greek works of art, and locally-produced ones too, but with Greek ideas and ideals. These same cities had spawned their own philosophers and poets from an early period of their history but from the fifth century onwards Greek philosophers, poets, historians and authors from Greece itself, had been frequent visitors to the cities of Magna Graecia. Aeschylus had died at Gela, Herodotus had been amongst the founders of Thurii, and Plato made several visits to both Sicily and the peninsula. The cities of Magna Graecia were an integral part of the Greek world, and in establishing relations with those cities, Rome was entering that world herself.

But she was entering it at a time when the nature of that world was itself about to change dramatically. The Greek influences exerted on the Etruscans, and through them on Rome, had been the influences of classical Greece. By the end of the fourth century, not only Magna Graecia but the whole of the central and east Mediterranean had been dragged into the very different world of Hellenistic Greece by the conquests of Philip of Macedon and his son, Alexander the Great. In particular, the conquest of the east by Alexander had opened up Greek culture itself to new and vital impulses from the near east, which were first assimilated and then soon passed on to the Greek colonies of southern Italy. Thus, the Greek influences which exerted themselves so strongly on republican Rome in the third to first centuries BC were quite different from those which had been felt much more weakly in the preceding three centuries. They were the influences of Hellenistic Greece, and they were at once more vigorous and more moribund than those of the classical era. To understand not only their nature, but the manner in which they were so rapidly and deeply absorbed by Republican Rome, it is necessary to trace, albeit briefly, Rome's increasing political involvement both with Magna Graecia and eventually with Greece itself.

Initially, relations were more commercial than political. Rome's increasing interest in trade with the Greek cities was marked first by a treaty with Carthage (in 348 BC) guaranteeing her Sicilian commerce, and then in 306 and 303 with the Rhodians and the Tarentines respectively. The fact that meantime she had captured the Greek colony of Neapolis in 326 BC, far from souring her new friendships in Magna Graecia only strengthened them. The colony of Cumae had fallen to the Samnites in 421 BC, and Poseidonia to the Lucanians about twenty years later; Rome's capture of Neapolis was seen as providing the Greek population and their trading interests with protection from the hill-tribes of southern-central Italy. When Rome did eventually fall out with one of the Greek colonies, Tarentum, it was possibly for commercial reasons alone, the Tarentines accusing Rome of breaking their existing treaty. The Hellenistic army led by Pyrrhus of Epirus, which penetrated as far north as Praeneste in 280 BC, received scant support from the Greek cities of the peninsula and was forced to withdraw south. When, following his Sicilian adventure, Pyrrhus was defeated by the Romans in 275, Rome was seen to have assumed the role not of conqueror but protector of Magna Graecia. Her victory certainly brought her into a closer and more direct contact with Greek – or rather Hellenistic – culture than ever before, symbolically marked by the display of statuary and other works of art at the triumph which marked the capture of Tarentum.

Only ten years later her protective role, and a mixture of commercial and political considerations, led Rome a step further into the Hellenistic world as she sent an army into Sicily against the Carthaginians. The successful conclusion of the first Punic War in 241 BC left Rome with an enhanced role in the west Mediterranean and in ever closer involvement with a growing number of Greek colonies. Soon, the involvement extended to Greece itself as Rome, anxious to protect her or her allies' shipping in the Adriatic took steps to put down the troublesome Illyrian pirates. The Illyrians received the support of Macedon, which feared the long-term threat posed by Roman intervention on the east side of the Adriatic, but when Rome defeated the pirates in 229–8 it was a victory welcomed by most Greek states. Corinth, indeed, went to the unusual length of formally admitting Roman citizens to the Isthmian games. Further hostilities between Rome and the Illyrians took place in 219, and after the second Punic War broke out in 218 BC Philip V of Macedon determined to ally himself with Carthage; in turn this led Rome openly to back the Greek cities opposed to Macedon, resulting in the first Macedonian War (215–205). The second Punic War undoubtedly had a profound effect on Roman attitudes, though whether it dramatically altered her approach to Greek culture as some would claim (Grimal, 1960, 66) is less certain. But Rome emerged from the war the undisputed master of the west Mediterranean, immensely more confident of her own power, and more aware of her traditional values. She was able to brush the Macedonians aside in a second war between 200 and 196. In particular, the defeat of the Macedonians at Cynoscephalae in 197 at once destroyed any possible threat to northern Italy, secured Roman trading interests and shipping in the Adriatic, and extended Roman protection and support to the states of central and southern Greece. The defeat of Macedon and the warning handed out to Antiochus of Syria to respect the freedom of the Greek cities of Asia Minor, contrasts notably with the treatment of the Greek states. Whilst the powerful Hellenistic monarchies were met by the uncompromising face of the post-Hannibalic Rome, the Greek states were treated with great favour. So favourably in fact that when the Roman envoy to the Isthmian games of 196 announced that Rome was restoring freedom, with no tributes and no garrisons, to the states of Greece, the Greeks literally did not believe their ears and asked him to repeat the announcement. The Romans subsequently underlined their commitment to the Greeks by driving the forces of Antiochus out of Greece in 191, and by overthrowing him at the battle of Magnesia in 189. All indications are that at this point the Romans were just as anxious to support and protect the states which had been at the heart of classical Greece as they were determined to remove the threat of the Hellenistic monarchies of the east.

But as first the Aetolian and then the Achaean league proved troublesome, political disenchantment set in on both sides. A revival of Macedonian power was thwarted by a third war which saw the defeat of Macedon in 168 at Pydna, and by a fourth and final war in 149 which ended with Macedon a Roman province. Only two years later the manhandling of a Roman deputation to Corinth so incensed the Romans that the army in Macedon marched south and besieged the city. When it fell, its art treasures were removed to Rome, its citizens sold into slavery, and its finest buildings destroyed as the city was razed to the ground. It might be supposed that the symbiosis between Greece and Rome was destroyed at the same time, and yet of course that was far from true, as will be seen. Equally Rome's military and political involvement with the Greeks did not end in 146, for she continued to expand eastwards and in so doing to absorb the influential Hellenistic kingdoms of the east Mediterranean.

Initially, the hellenization of Roman Italy had expressed itself in material culture, and was achieved largely by material acquisitions. The works of art removed from Tarentum in 272 were followed by 2,000 statues carried off from Volsinii in 265, and by a veritable flood of Greek art after the capture of Syracuse in 211 (Part 9, Chapter 29). In the second century, Greece itself provided the spoils. Marcus Fulvius' Greek campaigns were celebrated by a Triumph at which 785 bronze and 250 marble statues were displayed, and by games at which Greek performers and athletes were the stars. The second and third Macedonian Wars were each followed by further large shipments of Greek art treasures to Rome, where the appetite for them seemed insatiable. Greek statues adorned the gardens and homes of the wealthy, and Greek silverware became a common feature of Roman dining tables. Yet such was the quantity available, that in 142 Mummius was able to present looted Greek art works to Roman communities not only elsewhere in Italy but in Spain too. The demand continued until the end of the Republic, and indeed beyond it, and more than once we find Cicero (pl. 3.3) writing letters begging, urgently, for still more Greek statuary to be despatched to him. Elsewhere, he notes that the town house of Chrysogonus on the Palatine is 'crammed with gold and silver vessels from Delos and Corinth' (*Pro Roscio*, xiv, 33). Surveying both the historical and the artefactual evidence for the wholesale looting of Greek art treasures first from Magna Graecia and then from Greece itself, it would indeed be easy to come to the conclusion that the 'hellenization' of Rome was no more than a thin cultural veneer, with no lasting significance for, or impact on, either Roman history or Roman society. Such a view cannot, of course, be sustained.

Even in the field of art itself, the Romans borrowed and imitated, and in time adapted, modified and transformed Greek ideas, styles and techniques. Some of their earliest borrowings may have been in paintings and relief sculptures rather than sculpture in the round. The painted battle scenes recording the victories over Carthage in 264 and 202, and against Antiochus in 189, are thought to have owed their inspiration to the work of Aristides of Thebes, a painter much admired by Romans and quite possibly the painter of the famous scene of Alexander at the Battle of Issus, surviving in the form of a mosaic copy from Pompeii. One of the first Roman battle reliefs, standing ancestral to those which later recorded imperial campaigns, was set up not in Rome but at Delphi by L. Aemilius Paulus in 168 BC; significantly, as Wheeler notes (1964, 174) the relief is 'an essentially conventional battle scene in the Greek heroic tradition'. Again, it is to Hellenistic Greece, and more particularly the kingdom of Pergamum, that Wheeler looks for the intermediate inspiration for the 'continuous style' of relief sculpture which was subsequently moulded by imperial sculptors into such a potent propaganda technique for Trajan. Certainly, as Hellenistic sculptors moved increasingly away from the classical search for the ideal and towards a greater realism (pl. 3.4), so they came closer to Roman preferences. Inevitably, Pergamene and other sculptors followed in the wake of the shiploads of sculptures, vases and metalwork and were employed by Roman patrons to produce new masterpieces in Rome itself. At the same time, the demand for the works of classical sculptors reached such heights that the 'free copies' of the second century BC were replaced in the early first century by accurate copies produced by the pointing process, which allowed reproductions to be produced in greater numbers at greater speed. The Greek influences on Roman art were thus a conflicting mixture of classical and Hellenistic, to which were added the impulses still received from indigenous Italic art and late Etruscan sculpture. From this melting-pot of ideals and styles there emerged in the first century BC the new Roman school of portraiture in which realism was the dominant theme. It is impossible realistically to assess the relative value and importance of the various influences and styles which contributed to the development of Roman portraiture. The importance of the Etruscan input is often emphasized, yet it is difficult to deny a significant Hellenistic contribution. Indeed, Scullard (1959, 198) has made the important point that many of these portraits were actually sculpted by Greek artists, coming from a Hellenistic tradition which had already embraced verism, and he concludes that Roman portraiture 'may have arisen from Greek sculptors responding to the demand for realistic portraits from their Roman patrons'. If the Greek contribution is as significant as Scullard suggests, then the ultimate force of Greek influences in Roman art was formidable, and the ultimate product – Roman portraiture – was one of just and lasting renown.

The architectural environments for which the sculptures, reliefs, mosaics and paintings were created, whether private homes or public buildings, were similarly the products of the interplay between Greek invention and elegance, and Roman application and monumental vision. Sharing with the Greeks the concept of the city as the political and social focus of their civilization, the Romans founded new cities in Italy and in the provinces. The orthogonal planning of the Greek colonies was noted and adapted, and indeed the new towns were laid out by surveyors who if not Greek themselves used the methods and techniques of the Greeks, and equipment of Ionian and Alexandrian origin. Within the towns, old and new, rose buildings which truly represent a symbiosis of Greek and Roman genius. Hellenistic architects had invented the timber truss, but had used it only sparingly; they had experimented with barrel vaults and arches, but on a limited scale (Brown, 1968, 19). The Romans took both, and together with their development of concrete, they used and exploited these inventions to the full. Enthusiastically adopting the Hellenistic colonnade, they were able to create by a visionary blend of all these elements, monumental buildings such as the forums and basilicas, the great baths, the theatres, circuses and amphitheatres which were the hallmark of Roman civilization in towns and cities throughout the Empire. In both form and concept most of these structures were themselves of Greek origin – the theatre, the forum (*agora*), the basilica, the stadium and the temple were all to be found in classical and Hellenistic Greece. The Romans modified their form, inflated their scale, and embellished their facades, all through the imaginative use of the truss, the vault, the arch, the colonnade and, of course, concrete. They thus devised grandiose and formalized stage-sets for public and state spectacles which firmly embedded 'the spectacle' as an institution in the Roman way of life. The inspiration for developing public spectacles may have come from the Hellenistic kingdoms of the east Mediterranean, where they were both popular and famous, certainly it was not to be found in classical Greece. Yet far removed as Roman spectacle may have been from the vision of the Greek architects and engineers who pioneered the forms and devices so boldly adopted and employed by the Romans, the Greek contribution to imperial Roman architecture can hardly be ignored.

Just as, in adopting the Greek theatre building, the Romans modified it, so in absorbing Greek drama they gradually transformed first its content and then its form. Until the mid-third century, Greek drama had been known to the Romans only at a distance and largely through the tantalizing 'snapshots' seen on Campanian vases of the fourth century. The campaigns in Magna Graecia brought Romans into direct contact with theatres and drama, and at the Roman Festival of 240 BC Latin versions of a Greek tragedy and a Greek comedy (pl. 3.5) were performed. Their author, Livius

Andronicus, was himself a freedman of Greek origin, and we know that he wrote several tragedies, all inspired by the drama of classical Greece. His contemporary, Naevius, was already seeking to change the content of the plays, writing comedies on Roman subjects as well as providing Latin versions of Greek plays. A generation later, Plautus promoted the 'New Comedy', developed in fourth-century Athens, and in a series of brilliant comedies popularized a form of drama in which the comparative laxity of Greek morality was paraded before Roman audiences. Following in his footsteps, Terence, in the mid-second century, was both more ambitious in his objectives and more Hellenized in his style and presentation. Yet contemporary with Terence's successes there developed a new, patently Italian genre, the *togata*, in which, despite an obvious debt to New Comedy, the settings, the costumes and the character were Roman rather than Greek. More significantly, the moral tone of some of these plays was more nearly in tune with the traditional values of Roman society. Paradoxically, the development and popularity of the *togata* was balanced in the last years of the Republic by the growing popularity of two other forms of theatre, the one indigenous, the other borrowed originally from the Greeks, both of which showed scant respect for dignity, tradition or morality. The Atellane farces, originating under Greek influence in Campania, was popular by reason of its stock 'characters' and its flirtations with obscenity. Mime, immensely popular in the Greek cities of southern Italy, increasingly appealed to Roman audiences and together with Atellane farce retained its popular following throughout the imperial period. Though both forms owed their roots to Greek theatre, by the end of the Republic they were the least Greek, and most popular, of all Roman drama; those forms of Roman theatre which owed most to the Greek tradition found an equally appreciative but much smaller audience in imperial Rome.

It was this same audience which enjoyed Greek poetry and provided the readership for the great Latin poets of the late Republican era. Like Greek drama, Homer was first translated into Latin in the third century BC by Livius Andronicus. Both he, and his fellow playwright and poet Naevius, wrote in the old Italian measure known as Saturnian. It was left to Ennius, in the early second century, to revolutionize Latin poetry by adopting Greek hexameter to replace the Saturnian measure. Henceforth all Latin poetry was clearly greatly indebted to Greek, but important as the adoption of hexameter was, it was only a part of the total Greek influence which can be clearly detected in the work of the late Republican and early imperial poets. The 116 extant poems of Catullus betray the inspiration of both Sappho and of Alexandrian poetry; the poetry of Lucretius was dominated by the philosophy of Epicurus (pl. 3.6). Horace, too, was an Epicurean who found in the Aeolian poets, the inspiration to create a new Latin genre – lyric poetry. As for Virgil, the greatest of the Latin poets, in each of his periods of poetic development he revealed his indebtedness to Greece. His *Eclogues* was modelled on the *Idylls* of the Sicilian Greek, Theocritus; his *Georgics* was influenced by Hesiod, and his great epic, the *Aeneid*, was of course inspired by Homer. To trace the Greek influence in the work of these four great poets is not to deny or lessen their Latin genius, but rather to identify the stimuli which brought the genius to its fruition.

The Epicureanism which Lucretius promoted and which flavoured the works of both Horace and Virgil, was in conflict with the other dominant Hellenistic philosophy – Stoicism – during the late Republic. Cicero complained that Epicureanism had the whole of Italy in its grip, and certainly it found favour with influential politicians such as Cassius and Caesar as well as amongst the readers of Lucretius and Horace. But Cicero himself was successful in popularizing a modified Stoicism, the appeal of which survived into the age of Marcus Aurelius, and which was certainly flourishing in the first century BC. The rival philosophies had taken hold in Rome in the second century BC, when they were still relatively new and evolving themselves. Epicurus had died in 271 and Zeno, the founder of Stoicism, probably in 261 BC. Epicureanism, with its belief in individualism and self-expression and its firm materialism, inevitably appealed to some elements in a second-century Rome where old traditions and values were being abandoned and new horizons of pleasure were being explored. In such an environment it was equally certain that Stoicism's exhortations to virtue and temperance would find favour with those, led by the elder Cato (pl. 3.8), who sought to protect Roman traditions. The cause of Stoicism was revived and popularized in the later second century by the tempered teachings of Panaetius of Rhodes. A close associate of the younger Scipio, with whom he lived for two years, Panaetius taught that each man should recognize and fulfil his own potential; as for virtue, it was sufficient that a man should seek progress towards it. These modifications to the philosophy of Zeno (pl. 3.7) enabled Stoicism to compete successfully with Epicureanism in the days of the late Republic, with important political and social consequences. In the absence of any significant Roman contribution to philosophy, it was inevitable that these dominant schools in Greek thought should exercise such sway in late Republican Rome. Yet it should also be recognized that the political importance of these – and other – schools of Greek philosophy was not that they *changed* the political views of the Romans who adopted them, but rather that they bolstered and sustained those views.

The widespread adoption of Greek philosophy, as well as Greek literature, theatre, and the arts, was much encouraged and stimulated by the changing pattern of Roman education, which was itself heavily influenced by Greek practice. From the third century BC onwards, it was normal for the children of senatorial families not only to learn the Greek language but to read Greek literature as a major part of their secondary education. Greek teachers and philosophers found ready patronage in second-century Rome. A School of Greek declamation was established there in 161, and Aemilius Paullus and Tiberius Gracchus were but two of Rome's leading figures who employed Greeks to teach their children. It is particularly significant that after his victory at Pydna in 168, Paullus took no booty, save the 20,000 volumes in the library of the royal palace of Macedon, intended for his sons. It was shortly after this that the visit to Rome of the three Hellenistic philosophers Carneades, Diogenes and Critolaus, fired Rome with a passion for rhetoric. In time rhetoric joined philosophy as one of the two principal ingredients in the final stages of Roman education. It could be learnt in Rome, but such Roman schools of rhetoric as existed, were but imitations of those found in Hellenistic Greece and the east. It became increasingly common for young Romans to spend a year in Athens, for example, to conclude their formal education. Caesar and Cicero both studied rhetoric in Rhodes, and by the end of the Republic rhetoric was regarded not only as a respectable, but as an essential, education for any Roman intending to enter public life. 'Not until the invention of radio was oratory to have such scope as in the Roman republic' (Wilkinson, 1975, 19). Yet for a time, in the mid-second century BC, both the teaching of rhetoric and some other aspects of Greek education had met vigorous opposition from some elements of Roman society. The elder Cato (pl. 3.8) led a campaign against the rhetoricians and Epicureans, and Scipio the younger was appalled by the popularity of Greek-inspired schools of singing and dancing.

The crusade against the Hellenization of Rome headed by Cato was fired by a genuine, and not entirely misplaced, concern for the effect which the influx of things Greek would have on Roman society. Livy records how Cato railed against the flood of imported art works as early as 195 BC:

> I fear that those things will capture us rather than we them. Like a hostile army were statues brought from Syracuse to this city. Already I hear too many people praising and admiring the artistry of Corinth and Athens, and laughing at the traditional terracottas of our Roman temples.

Under his leadership there was certainly a reaction to the excesses of second-century philhellenism. The persecution of the Bacchanalians (inspired by the Dionysiac cult) in 186 was both widespread and harsh, and it was followed in 182 and 161 by senate-imposed restrictions on first the size and then the cost of private drinking parties. Meanwhile, as censor in 184, Cato had imposed taxes on imported luxuries (Wilkinson, 1975, 52). The attacks on the more obvious physical excesses were followed by attempts to silence, or at least diminish the influence of, the Hellenistic philosophers and rhetoricians. In 173 and 161 they were expelled from Rome, and when Carneades and Diogenes arrived in 155, Cato ensured they were moved on as quickly as their popularity allowed. There was too a determination in some quarters to prevent the Greek language from gradually usurping the role of Latin as the language of public affairs. Valerius Maximus records that, in the second century, Roman magistrates made a point of answering Greeks only in Latin, though the rule was not always adhered to, and insisted that even in Asia and Greece itself, submissions made in Greek should be translated into Latin (Salmon, 1982, 121). The resistance to the hellenization of Rome abated in the late Republic, though the censors issued an edict expressing disapproval of Latin rhetoricians and their 'new kind of education' in 92 BC, and as late as the second century AD, Juvenal was complaining of Rome 'I cannot bear this city gone Greek'. As Latin literature and drama, albeit Greek influenced, came into its own and produced its own geniuses, and as monumental and indisputably *Roman* architecture rose to dominate the centre of Rome, so the threat posed by Hellenism to Roman values and the traditional Roman way of life may seem to have receded.

In fact, some of the most fundamental and far-reaching effects of the hellenization of Rome, for both good and ill, were only just beginning to make their real impact. Cato and the younger Scipio had been alarmed by the increasing greed, scepticism, and moral laxity of Rome's ruling classes. There is no reason to think that the erosion of traditional values was halted in the earlier first century BC, rather the opposite. Polybius had already noted the decline in the morality of the governing class, and the use of wealth to buy success in urban elections was a disturbing development, which in time would lead naturally enough to the purchase of the army's loyalty and to providing the populace of Rome with extravagant spectacles. It was the followers of Stoicism and most notably Cicero, whose eclectic views embraced Stoicism, who led the struggle in the first century BC to preserve both political virtue and the Republic. In this sense Stoicism became a political philosophy, in contrast to Epicureanism which, as Scullard has observed (1959, 211) had a negative influence on public life 'in that it withdrew men from politics'. After the establishment of the Principate it was again the Stoics – L. Cornutus, Musonius Rufus, Seneca and A. Percius Flaccus – who spoke, or wrote, against the extravagancies, vices and corruption of Rome in general and the principate in particular. Stoicism became involved in the dangerous day-to-day politics of imperial Rome; it 'was the creed of many of the men who joined Piso in his attempt to kill Nero' (Scullard, 1959, 371). But by this time the tide of events had of course become far too strong to be resisted by the force of philosophy alone.

The emergence of the Principate was a lengthy and complex process, but some of its roots can be plausibly traced to Hellenistic influences in Republican Rome. Barrow, for example, was convinced that it was Latin translations of the Iliad and Odyssey, and performances of Greek drama, which brought home to ambitious Romans the opportunities which existed for men of flair, imagination, character, and perhaps daring, to mould the affairs of state (Barrow, 1949, 62); this seems unlikely. A far more potent factor was that as Rome became more directly involved in Greece and the Hellenistic east, so Romans found themselves holding office in provinces where the luxuries and adulation previously lavished on Hellenistic monarchs were theirs for the taking. The opportunities to exploit the rich resources of these provinces for their own political and personal ends were often too great to resist and were instead shamelessly embraced. Here, too, they came into closer contact with the legendary figure of Alexander, a man who by personal charisma and command of an army, had replaced democracies and oligarchies alike with a single authoritarian regime. It was Alexander too who had created, for the first time, a European empire which dominated much of the eastern Mediterranean and the Near East. As the wealth of the Hellenistic provinces came within reach of the Roman state in the later second and early first centuries BC, so the Roman attitude to the provinces became increasingly avaricious. It would be too much to claim that the idea of empire, and beyond that of an emperor, were simply borrowed directly from the Hellenistic world, but Rome's dealings with that world increasingly led her in that direction. They also helped to provide her with some of the means by which to build and hold an empire. The earliest such acquisition, but one of the most fundamental to the success of building an empire in the Mediterranean, was a fleet, and of course the skills with which to use it. From the time of the first Punic War, Roman naval techniques had relied heavily on Greek practices. In the second century Rome depended increasingly on her Greek allies, and later her Greek subjects, for both ships and sailors. As these ships and men were gradually absorbed into the Roman fleets, so their Greek methods grew more influential than ever in the development of Roman naval warfare (Starr, 1960). Hellenistic influence on the growth of the Roman army was less wide-ranging and fundamental, but it was significant in one important area, that of siege warfare and war machines. It was the Hellenistic Greeks who developed the various forms of catapult which the Romans adopted and used with great effect from one end of their expanding empire to the other. It was they, too, who taught the Romans the principal methods and techniques of siege warfare, in which the war machines played a vital role.

But winning and holding an empire was not achieved solely by developing highly trained and well-equipped forces. Greek history, with which the Romans were well acquainted, and their own involvement with the Greeks of both southern Italy and Greece, taught the Romans the invaluable lesson of divide and conquer. Rome rejected loose alliances, associations of equals, and federal solutions to political problems; after an initial reluctance to annexe new territory she imposed her rule directly over an ever-growing area, and she often did so by encouraging dissension amongst her opponents. From the later second century BC onwards, having seized new territories, Rome followed Alexander's example by planting new cities, usually as military colonies, in the conquered area. Cities were as central to Rome's plans to Romanize their empire, as they were to Hellenize Alexander's. The success of urbanization in turn depended on the successful development of commerce and markets. Greek traders and Greek shipping played a vital role in that development, and even more fundamental to its success was the Roman adoption of silver coinage based on the Greek. Such coinage enabled conquered peoples, and especially their craftsmen and traders, to be rapidly absorbed into the Roman economic system. This was to be of particular importance in the stimulation and intensification of economic activity in Rome's northern and western provinces in the later first century BC and the first century AD.

The development of overseas commerce in which foreigners played an important part in turn led the Romans to modify their civil law. To the Romans, Hellenistic commercial law was unacceptably flexible and pragmatic, but they recognized the necessity to afford legal protection to foreign traders. Thus they appointed a 'foreign praetor' to look after their interests, and developed the concept of *ius gentium* (very broadly, international law). Many scholars would argue that there were few other significant Hellenistic influences on Roman law, and, given the Roman distaste for the abstract and theoretical thinking which characterized much Greek legal practice, that would seem likely (Wilkinson, 1975, 69). But Kunkel has forcefully rejected such a view (1966, 94):

> The inner structure [of Roman law], the methods and forms of juristic activity, underwent a thorough-going transformation in the last century of the Republic. The impulse was provided by contact with Greek learning, above all with the disciplines of rhetoric and philosophy.

He points to the Greek influences on the great Republican jurists, Q. Mucius Scaevola and Servius Sulpicius Rufus; the work of both men continued to be influential into the imperial age. Their contemporary, Cicero, in whom rhetoric and Stoicism was most effectively combined, also exercised a profound influence on the practical application of Roman law. In time, the *iurisprudentes*, most of whom were heavily influenced by Stoicism, became a recognized and influential body of opinion, the views of which were carefully studied by Roman magistrates. Through their writings and their pronouncements they contributed to the formulation of Roman law for more than two centuries. Yet it remains true that in the main Greek influence on Roman law was exercised not so much on the content of that law, but rather on its practical implementation and interpretation. Kunkel has rightly claimed that in the final analysis it was the alliance of Roman tradition and sobriety with Greek logic and clarity, which improved both the methods and form of Roman law (1966, 94).

It is indeed difficult to deny that, in general, the Greek influence on Rome and Roman culture as a whole was beneficial. Even those Romans who sought to minimize the impact of Hellenism on Rome were unable completely to ignore or resist the influence of Greek culture. Cato, after all, spoke Greek, was well-acquainted with Greek literature, and betrayed considerable Greek influence in both his *Origins* and his *On Agriculture*. He had a Greek tutor for his children and it was he who erected the first Greek-style basilica (the Basilica Porcia) in Rome. But it was not *Greek* language, literature, or education that Cato resisted so vehemently, but rather *Hellenistic* culture. Most Romans professed to scorn the Hellenistic Greeks and admire the Greeks of the classical age. There is some truth in Barrow's assertion that Hellenistic culture 'lacked spontaneity and vigour, it was sophisticated and self-conscious, apathetic and disillusioned' (1949, 37). Yet, paradoxically, it was the culture of Hellenistic Greece which, in practice, the Romans so enthusiastically embraced; their acquaintance with classical culture was largely second-hand and at a distance, apart from the original vases and sculptures they managed to acquire. It was the teachings of the Hellenistic philosophers (Zeno and Epicurus) which were most widely adopted and which had the most significant effects on Roman law, poetry and politics. It was the stimulus of Hellenistic sculptors, not least those of the Pergamene school, which contributed most to the development of Roman sculpture, whether portrait, relief, or 'continuous style'. Again, it was the Hellenistic navies and military engineers who taught Rome most about warfare, and the founder of the Hellenistic world, Alexander, who gave Rome the model of empire. On balance these Hellenistic contributions far outweighed the detrimental influences exerted by the huge influx of Hellenistic wealth in the second century BC, by the moral laxity of some Hellenistic cults, and by the potential dangers inherent in the Roman passion for Greek rhetoric. In the long term 'it was primarily her willingness to respond to Hellenism that made Rome normative, largely for good, in Western civilisation' (Wilkinson, 1975, 75).

3.1   Sculptured Etruscan sarcophagus

3.2   The François Vase, Florence Museum

3.3 Bust of Cicero

3.4 The 'Boxer' of Apollonios

3.5   Greek comedy illustrated on a relief from Pompeii

3.6   Bust of Epicurus

3.7   Bust of Zeno

3.8 Statue of Cato

CHAPTER 4

·THE·LEGACY·OF·THE· ·REPUBLIC·

David C. Braund

The Roman Republic is traditionally conceived as the long period beginning with the expulsion of the last king of Rome, Tarquinius Superbus, in 509 BC and ending with the advent of the first emperor, Augustus, victor at the Battle of Actium in 31 BC. With Augustus came the Principate. The history of the Roman Republic, over this period of almost half a millennium, is the history of the growth of a small and rather insignificant city-state into an imperial power which ruled the whole Mediterranean basin and stretched beyond. It is the history of the social, political and economic pressures and tensions entailed in this expansion. The aim of this essay is to explore the pressures and tensions of the Republic so as better to understand the Principate. Selectivity of the highest order is demanded by limitations of space: matters covered in depth elsewhere in this collection, e.g. provincial government (Part 6, Chapter 15), will be deliberately neglected here. Change dominates history – creates it, ultimately – but there is also continuity. Continuity was far more important in Roman ideology. Roman society was little concerned with progress and the future: tradition (*mos maiorum*) and the past were all-powerful and all pervasive. Change for the good was essentially the restoration of tradition and the past. Innovation was dangerous: it threatened decline. Of course there was change but that change was structured, conceived and justified in terms of the restoration of the past (see North, 1976, on conservatism and change in Roman religion).

The overwhelming importance of tradition in Roman society is a warning for the historian tempted to consider Roman history in terms of turning points and separate periods. Persistent obsession with tradition fosters continuity even within a broad framework of change. In other words, while the terms 'Republic' and 'Principate' suggest separation and change, we should expect continuity, mitigating and to an extent denying this change. It is not only that the Republic conditioned the Principate: it also continued into the Principate.

The early history of the Republic and of the Regal Period which preceded it is largely a matter of myth and legend. These legends were constructed in part by learned Greeks concerned to trace and explain the genesis of this great non-Greek power in terms of Greek mythology; also by Romans concerned to establish their genealogy and, thus, their nobility and identity. The result was a confused and inconsistent history of early Rome: we know of some thirty significantly different accounts of the foundation of Rome (Cornell, 1975; cf. Wiseman, 1979).

The aftermath of the monarchy was a period of turmoil for some 150 years as the social and political structure of the Republic evolved. Society remained divided between the polarities of rich landowners and landless poor. Political power was in the hands of the rich. The Senate was the administrative centre of the political structure; its members were drawn from the elite and its members were those who held high political office. The highest political office, the consulship, was dominated by a small circle within that landowning aristocracy. Lower magistrates, praetors, aediles and quaestors, were drawn from a small circle which was hardly less exclusive. Of course, there were elections, held in Assemblies of the people, but these too were dominated by the élite which used its wealth and patronage, and the advantages which it enjoyed as a result of a voting system unbalanced in favour of the propertied (Staveley, 1972, Part 2). Religion further reinforced the dominance of the élite which also provided the priests. Law was constructed by the élite for the élite. Justice was conceived in proportion to status: natural justice was conceived as the dominance of the élite – the dominance which Roman law reinforced both *de iure* and *de facto* (Finley, 1983, 7). The Roman economy remained fundamentally and overwhelmingly agrarian. Possession of land was therefore possession of the means of production as well as a source of prestige and a particularly safe investment (Finley, 1973).

But the élite was not a monolith. For all its common interests the élite was fragmented into groupings of families and individuals. Within the peer group constituted by the élite, there was an ever-present struggle for elevation and, ultimately, supremacy. Of course, there was no resemblance to political parties. Alliances were readily formed on a temporary, *ad hoc* basis and readily dissolved again: the historian has to search hard for anything resembling the political programmes and policies of the modern world. But struggles might be fierce; they were the embryonic forms of the civil wars which produced the Principate. Family connections, extended and confirmed by marriages, and patronage, variously expressed in terms of clientage (*clientela*) and friendship (*amicitia*), founded upon the exchange of goods and services, were the most important cohesive forces within these groupings; patronage bound members of the élite to each other – conventionally as friends – and bound poorer dependants – conventionally known as clients – to the more wealthy and powerful (Saller, 1982, is more subtle, rightly).

Peer group in-fighting accelerated most sharply towards outright civil warfare in the course of the second century BC. Then Rome was engaged in almost permanent foreign wars as she expanded within the Mediterranean world; there were major wars in Spain, Gaul, North Africa, Greece and Asia Minor, sometimes fought simultaneously in different theatres. To the wealthy who commanded Rome's armies imperialism provided the military glory (*gloria*) so prized by the élite and so central to its militaristic ideology (Harris, 1979, Chapter 1). It also provided vast amounts of booty. The élite used this booty as it had always used its wealth: principally, to buy property, especially land. Land brought with it social status and was considered appropriate to that status. At the same time, land was a secure investment which involved minimal risk for the investor and brought him a reasonable return. In this way, imperialism increased pressure on land as the élite sought to invest its windfalls of wealth in the traditional manner.

The lower ranks of the legions were drawn in the second century from the smallholders, men with land, but not much. They were conscripts who were required to serve for the duration of a campaign, often several years spent far from their homesteads. While they were absent on campaign, their families were deprived of their labour. Some families might cope but others would not. Imperialism therefore made smallholdings more vulnerable to the rich who, also as a result of imperialism, had increased sums to invest in land. In this way imperialism encouraged the elite to become owners of vast acreages of land, though often fragmented into geographically distinct units. On these estates, usually described as *latifundia*, slaves were used more extensively than on the smallholdings. Imperialism made slave-owning on a large scale more attractive and more possible: vast numbers of Rome's defeated enemies were enslaved and the price of slaves was reduced accordingly. Moreover, slaves, unlike peasants, could not be taken off the land by recruitment into the army. The labour of the peasantry was in part replaced by the labour of slaves, though free casual labour was still important even on large estates, particularly at harvest time when a temporarily large labour force was required to cope with the extra work involved on a short-term basis. Moreover, many peasant smallholders survived. The degree to which slaves replaced peasants in the second century BC has often been exaggerated (Rich, 1983, 296). Precise measurement is impossible.

The Hannibalic war which dominated the last two decades of the third century BC had made its own particular contribution to the development of *latifundia*; war had raged up and down Italy creating disorder. After the war, wealthy men who had made loans to the state to finance the war were repaid with lands leased to them by the state at peppercorn rents (Brunt, 1971, 269–77 and 358–60; Hopkins, 1978, Chapters 1–2).

But the Roman army depended upon the peasant smallholders who filled its ranks. How could recruitment be maintained at a time when the number of peasant smallholders was in decline as a result of the very imperialism which made recruitment necessary? A possible solution was legislation on landholding designed to make the required land available to the peasantry. But that would be to take land from the élite which would be revolution. When in 133 BC Tiberius Gracchus introduced modest measures to make

RARITAN VALLEY COMMUNITY COLLEGE
EVELYN S. FIELD LIBRARY

some public land, occupied by the wealthy, available to the poor, he was first opposed by 'legal' means and then clubbed to death by a mob of senators and their retainers; Gracchus' measures seem to have achieved a little, but not much. Subsequent attempts at land reform in the late Republic were similarly greeted (Badian, 1972b).

Another solution was to put to one side the problems of the peasantry and to recruit into the army those who had no property. In 107 BC Marius did just this: under pressure to recruit soldiers to fight in North Africa, he by-passed the traditional system of conscription of the propertied and enrolled volunteers, with no property qualification. But Marius' army reform, as it is called, was by no means revolutionary. The minimum property qualification is thought to have been reduced progressively from the Hannibalic War onwards in order to meet the needs of recruitment. If the figures are correct, the minimum property qualification could hardly be reduced further with any impact. Abolition was the next step, no longer very great and not without particular precedents: Marius took that step (Gabba, 1976, Chapters 1–2). Conscription, however, remained important (Brunt, 1971, 10). Indeed, scholars are now undertaking a thorough reassessment of the place of Marius' action in the history of the later Republic. Rich, in particular, has successfully raised important doubts about the reliability of the standard interpretation of the second century set out above: he argues with much justice that there may *not* have been a serious shortage of propertied recruits in that century after all (Rich, 1983). The fragility of any interpretation of the second century is becoming ever more apparent, born as it is of the paucity and poor quality of our sources for the latter half of that century in particular.

Yet the effects of this change were far-reaching, even if its impact was not immediate (Rich, 1983, 323–30). The army was not only under the command of its general; it was also dependent upon his patronage, which permeated Roman society. Its role in politics has been observed; it had long had a military face, but now the landless soldier depended upon his general for provision on his discharge. The provision of land for veterans immediately became, and remained, a focus of political in-fighting in the late Republic. The crucial point is that the general now commanded an army which was not only a Roman army but also, and ever more importantly, his own army. The political battles of the past, already prone to violence as in the case of the Gracchi (Lintott, 1968), were now poised to become civil wars. In 88 BC a Roman general, Sulla, marched on Rome for the first time. Roman expansion had therefore generated problems which in turn generated the civil wars that brought about the Principate.

War in Italy had only just subsided: from 91 to 89 BC Rome's Italian allies were in revolt, the so-called Social War. Their aims are unclear; Roman citizenship was a primary aim, but there was also talk of Italian independence (Brunt, 1965; Gabba, 1976, Chapter 3). Again, Roman expansion seems to have precipitated this conflict. Roman recruiting problems had led to an increased use of Italian troops, a situation which persisted even after 107 (Brunt, 1971, 677–86). Italian aspirations seem to have increased proportionately. It is worth remembering that Rome's dominance in Italy was ultimately founded upon her military superiority over the Italians, who might indeed seek an improved position as their military importance grew *vis-à-vis* that of Rome. But, again, the weakness of the evidence must be acknowledged (Rich, 1983, 323).

The Italians lost the war but won the citizenship. The granting of Roman citizenship to individuals and communities continued until Caracalla's grant of citizenship to all the free of the empire in AD 212 (Sherwin-White, 1973, 380ff.). The Italian families who received the citizenship as a result of the Social War were to provide some of the leading figures of the Augustan regime (Wiseman, 1971, 10). Provincials were soon to follow them into the Senate (Braund, 1984, 173). Of course, these men were members of the Italian and provincial elites (cf. Wilson, 1966), and they were easily absorbed into the Senate, despite the sneers of some of the established senatorial aristocracy; their concerns and attitudes were essentially the same.

Sulla's march on Rome created a civil war which he finally won after a second march on the capital in 83 BC. Many died, not only in actual fighting but also in the proscriptions instituted both by Sulla and by his leading opponents, Marius, Cinna and Carbo. Sulla became dictator in 82. Technically, he was awarded the office quite properly under a *lex Valeria*; he showed a marked concern to act within elite traditions (today often glorified as 'the constitution') as far as possible in the circumstances.

Sulla put through a programme of legislation designed to restore the old dominance of the Senate – in other words of the ruling, élite peer-group, now somewhat widened – which had been undermined by pressure for agrarian reform and by the internal pressures which had generated Sulla's dictatorship. To that end, the Senate was approximately doubled in size; the new senators seem to have included Italians who had remained loyal in the Social War. Henceforth, twenty men gained the office of quaestor each year and with it entry into the Senate. But that in itself was to create a problem for the future: each year twenty quaestors climbed on to the bottom rung of the political ladder, but only two reached the top of that ladder: the consulship. Therefore, in very simple terms, every year, the eighteen men who failed to achieve the consulship were political casualties (Badian, 1970). These failures might very well have been plunged deep into debt as a result of electoral expenses which they had hoped to recoup through provincial office in the event of success. The savagery of Roman law on debt exacerbated their plight (Frederiksen, 1966). These were the pressures which drove Catiline to revolution in 63 BC.

Sulla tinkered with the 'constitution' but had not dealt with the source of the problems he perceived. If it is accepted that the source was the structure and ideology of Roman society itself, together with the imperialism that had sprung from that very source, it may seem that Sulla could only have succeeded with a radical alternative. The most obvious one for him was doubtless the retention of his dominance, but he preferred the less radical course of retirement.

When Sulla retired in 79 BC, the inadequacy of his arrangements became immediately apparent, for one of the consuls of 78, Marcus Aemilius Lepidus, soon sought to emulate him. Lepidus was swiftly dealt with, but at a price. Pompey, a lieutenant of Sulla, was given an extraordinary command for the purpose. His rise to power through such commands (after Lepidus, against Marian remnants in Spain under Sertorius and against the pirates who infested the Mediterranean) culminated in his conquest of the East and triumphant return to Rome in 62 BC (Seager, 1979). Pompey was preeminent, but he needed political friends in order to achieve his ends against strong opposition from within the senatorial oligarchy. He therefore joined in an informal alliance with the senior Crassus and Julius Caesar, a rising star in 60 BC; both had their own short-term reasons for joining Pompey in this informal alliance, conventionally and misleadingly known as the First Triumvirate. Caesar gained the consulship of 59 BC and passed legislation so that Crassus obtained the revision of the Asian tax contracts (Badian, 1972a, 100ff.) while Pompey received land for his veterans and the confirmation of his acts in the east. The three dominated politics at Rome, though still against opposition from an entrenched oligarchy in the Senate. By now the letter of Sulla's legislation had to a large extent been rescinded while its spirit had been totally subverted.

After his consulship Caesar left for the north and Gaul where he campaigned till 49 BC. Pompey stayed at Rome, where he was drawn gradually closer to the senatorial oligarchy and away from Caesar. Crassus died in the east fighting the Parthians in 53 BC and in 49 BC Caesar crossed the Rubicon and started the civil war against Pompey, and those who placed themselves behind him. It was not totally extinguished, despite Pompey's death in 48 BC, before Caesar's assassination in 44 BC, though the last serious fighting took place at Munda in Spain in spring 45 BC.

The background to Caesar's crossing of the Rubicon is complex, but his main stimulus is clear enough. The entrenched oligarchy in the Senate was bent on removing Caesar from his Gallic command and from all political office. Caesar could not allow this, for, once out of office, he would be vulnerable to political, judicial and quite probably physical attack. Caesar had little choice but to fight.

Victory presented Caesar with problems. Quite apart from the damage caused by the war itself, Caesar had to find a position for himself within the state. An obvious model was Sulla, who had held the dictatorship for a short period. Caesar was first made dictator, and ultimately dictator for life, early in 44 BC. Caesar's watchword was clemency; he pardoned even his greatest enemies. Clemency was particularly desirable for him, as he might otherwise have been compared with the bloody Marius and Sulla; the former through their personal connection, notably the fact that Marius' wife Julia was also Caesar's aunt, and the latter if only because Sulla had been the last Roman dictator.

But traditionally the dictatorship was an essentially temporary office: perpetual dictatorship was quite contrary to Roman tradition. There were rumours that Caesar intended to become king, even a god. Both were totally unacceptable to this tradition. Provincials had paid divine honours to Romans abroad since the third century BC at least, but worship by Romans in Rome was quite another matter, despite the headway that Hellenistic culture had made at Rome over previous centuries (Taylor, 1931). The more plausible charge that Caesar was aiming at kingship was hardly less serious. The Roman attitude to kings was somewhat ambivalent; although they were regarded as exotic, even charismatic, creatures, they were also dangerous, untrustworthy, capricious and usually tyrannical. The legendary history of early Rome reinforced this attitude, which may well have created that history; Roman kings had included relatively admirable kings like Numa but ultimately a tyrant in Tarquinius Superbus.

Historians, plagued by the particular inadequacy of the sources on these accusations, still debate their validity (Weinstock, 1971 with North, 1975 and Rawson, 1975). But whether Caesar had aimed at becoming king or not, there was little practical difference between a perpetual dictator and a king. Both were quite contrary to the traditions of the Republic. Caesar had not fashioned for himself a viable position within the state. Neither had he evolved a satisfactory relationship with those he had defeated; he proffered clemency but he left the élite to fear the loss of its traditional authority and prestige. Paradoxically the very fact that Caesar had the power to act with clemency made its own contribution to this fear.

Caesar's legislation is often admired today because it addressed some fundamental problems. But this very admiration should be a warning; restoration at Rome was more valued than reform. Reforms of the law on debt and the method of tax collection, in Asia at least, could only excite opposition from the elite which had not only a love of tradition but also its own vested interests (Frederiksen, 1966; Badian, 1972a with Braund, 1983). Even his reform of the calendar, for all its utility, was susceptible to a sinister interpretation, for the calendar was profoundly religious and had first been drawn up, it was believed, by a king, Numa. Who was Caesar to tamper with it? What did he mean by it? And what of his appointment of Caninius Rebilus as consul for less than a day? Was this not an insult to senatorial tradition and a symptom of Caesar's broader unconcern for the outraged sensibilities of the elite? (Gelzer, 1968, Chapter 6.)

The motives of the conspirators who murdered Caesar in 44 are impenetrable in detail, but the removal of the quasi-monarchical domination of Caesar and the restoration of the Republic seems to have been their principal aim; it was certainly their claim. These champions of 'liberty' (*libertas*) had nothing to offer but the removal of Caesar. The dynamic that had given rise to Caesar remained unchanged. As Caesar had followed Sulla so someone would follow Caesar. Sulla had set the example and Caesar had confirmed it.

The principal conflict for power soon came to lie between Antony, Caesar's lieutenant, and Octavian, Caesar's nephew by birth, but adopted as Caesar's son in his will. In 43 BC Antony and Octavian formed the so-called Second Triumvirate together with the noble Lepidus who never became a serious contender for sole power in his own right. This triumvirate, unlike its predecessor, was formal and official; its brief was to 'constitute the state'. Proscriptions followed; Cicero was one of their many victims. At Philippi in 42 BC the cause of the conspirators was finally finished with the defeat of Brutus and Cassius by the triumvirs.

In 31 BC Octavian defeated Antony at the battle of Actium; the next year Antony died in Alexandria where Octavian had pursued him. The previous decade or so had been a period of uneasy peace between the two principal contenders punctuated by fraught negotiations and finally erupting into the war that had long threatened. In the meantime, lesser men had suffered.

After Philippi, the triumvirs had allotted the west to Octavian, the east to Antony and Africa to Lepidus. At the same time, they disbanded most of their legions; Octavian was left with the problem of settling some 100,000 veterans. His solution was simple; the expropriation of many of those who had land and the installation of veterans in their place. Actual fighting followed as relatives of Antony in Italy moved against Octavian, but without success; the sufferings of the masses were doubtless only increased.

There was also Sextus Pompey, the surviving son of Caesar's enemy. Exploiting his father's name and the discontent and disruption caused principally by the proscriptions and expropriations, he was temporarily successful (Hadas, 1930). His was a war of attrition. Based on Sicily and Sardinia, his ships won him a place at the conference table by obstructing the sea-borne imports of grain upon which Rome depended. But in 36 Octavian and Lepidus finally succeeded in smashing Sextus on Sicily; having fled to the east he was killed by Antony's men. Meanwhile, on Sicily, Lepidus had claimed the island for himself but had been deserted by his troops. Octavian gave Lepidus his life and allowed him to remain *pontifex maximus*, but deprived him of his position as triumvir.

The positive and negative propaganda produced on all sides in the period from 44 BC down to Actium and beyond dominates the history of these years. Each contender for power sought to represent himself as the champion of everything Roman, of Roman traditional values, of the Roman *res publica*. The figure of Cleopatra stands out in this propaganda; Octavian's supporters before and after his victory painted her as a 'deadly monster' in Horace's words. As a queen she was fundamentally suspect. We have observed Roman hostility towards kings; a queen, a monarch and a woman, was even more dangerous than a king to the Roman mind, to which women in official positions of power were at best an anomaly and usually an anathema. She could also be viewed as a despised Egyptian, though she was in fact of Macedonian descent and may even have been granted Roman citizenship by Caesar or Antony (Braund, 1984, 179).

Octavian's propaganda stressed Antony's relationship with the strange, foreign queen; it claimed that she had infatuated and corrupted a noble Roman and that through him she constituted a terrible threat to the Roman state and its traditions. Octavian was thus presented, not as the leader of a faction in civil war bent on establishing himself in power, but as the champion of the *res publica* against a fearful foreign foe. Dionysiac ritual at the Ptolemaic court, as elsewhere in the east, lent substance to Octavian's allegations of 'foreign ways' (see Griffin, 1977).

Antony hit back, for example, with the claim that Octavian was planning to marry a Thracian princess and to marry off his own daughter to her royal Thracian father. Had Antony won at Actium this Thracian princess might possibly have become known as a more famous temptress even than Cleopatra. But it was Octavian who won and thus his perspective; we do not even know the name of that princess. Antony escaped relatively lightly; Sextus Pompey was branded a pirate and a slur on the name of his father, who had done so much to rid the Mediterranean of that breed.

Upon his victory Octavian was faced with problems markedly similar to those that had faced Julius Caesar; on the one hand, the aftermath of a civil war that had involved all the Mediterranean world and damaged much of it, and, on the other, the need to find himself a place within the traditions which we misleadingly describe as 'the constitution', the *mos maiorum*.

Conspiracy was an ever-present threat for Octavian and for the emperors who followed him. Potential opponents could be killed; Octavian killed Antony's eldest son by Fulvia, and Ptolemy Caesar, more familiar under his nickname Caesarion, whom Antony and Cleopatra declared to be Cleopatra's son by Caesar; Caesar's heir could not risk such rivals. But widespread killing created at least as many enemies as it removed, for in such circumstances all feared for their lives and might be driven to opposition by their fear as well as by motives of vengeance for the dead; killing was the mark of the tyrant-king. Octavian wisely avoided widespread killing and proclaimed his clemency, following the example of Julius Caesar.

Octavian returned to Rome in 29 BC after appointing men he thought reliable to key provincial governorships in the east, though the most important local kings of Antony's regime were retained (Bowersock, 1965). In Rome he celebrated three triumphs for his victories in the war in Illyricum, a war of conquest waged in the previous decade, the war of Actium and the war of Alexandria: of course all were projected as wars against foreign foes. These were followed by the triumphs of Octavian's most prominent supporters (Syme, 1939, 303). The triumph was the ultimate achievement of the Roman noble, but it was soon to become the sole prerogative of members of the imperial family (Versnel, 1970). Octavian and his successors were concerned to obtain and maintain superior military prestige. This dynamic was central to much of the military activity of the Principate: a conspicuous example is Claudius' invasion of Britain in AD 43 which had little point but to provide the emperor with military prestige (Millar, 1982).

But military glory alone was not enough: Caesar had had military glory in plenty but had soon been killed nevertheless. To avoid a similar fate, Octavian needed to come to an accommodation with the rest of the élite. By 23 BC his constitutional position had largely been evolved, built around tribunician power; other options had been mooted and continued to be advanced even after 23 BC (Brunt and Moore, 1967, 8–16). The emperor thus received legal powers defined and structured in terms of the Republican magistracies. Fundamentally, the Roman emperor was a magistrate and a senator: his occasional holding of the consulship and his regular presence at and involvement in senatorial debates reinforced the fact (Millar, 1977, 216). Like a Republican magistrate he also held religious office. After the death of the incumbent, the ex-triumvir Lepidus, in 12 BC, the emperor became, in addition to his other religious offices, *pontifex maximus*, chief priest of the Roman state under the Republic. Henceforth, the *pontifex maximus* was always the emperor.

The emperor was also Augustus. Octavian, who was usually called Caesar, had been awarded the name in 27 BC, and he was thus transformed into Augustus. This name evoked the religious charisma and authority which was expressed in more direct and extreme form in the provinces despite the attempts of some emperors to curb such expressions (Brunt and Moore, 1967, 77–8; Taylor, 1931 with Price, 1980). It was also compared to the *cognomina* boasted by the old nobility, names like Africanus and Numantinus; though similar, the religious associations of the name Augustus made it superior. At the same time his use of the title *imperator* ('general') as a forename declared to all his military prowess and achievements (on Augustus' nomenclature, Syme, 1939, 361–77).

The 'virtues' of Augustus, his courage, clemency, justice and piety, were affirmed by an inscription on a gold shield placed in the Senate House (Wallace-Hadrill, 1981). The door posts of his own house were clothed in laurel in celebration of his victory. Above the door was placed a civic crown of oak leaves, the award traditionally made to a soldier for valour in saving the life of a fellow citizen. Augustus had saved citizens by defeating the 'foreign foe' and by exercising clemency thereafter; the civic crown was to become the particular symbol of imperial clemency (Griffin, 1976, 146). Clemency was itself to be associated with the role of the emperor as 'Father of his Country' (*pater patriae*); Augustus was awarded the title in 2 BC. There was some Republican precedent (Brunt and Moore, 1967, 80, also indicating the connection between this and the cult of the Genius Augusti, itself rooted in Republican tradition: cf. Liebeschuetz, 1979). After Augustus, the title *pater patriae* also became a regular feature of the emperor's nomenclature, though not a matter of course. It expressed the paternalism exercised by the emperor which was itself part of his broader patronage.

We have observed the importance of patronage in Roman society. With the Principate was created one supreme patron in the person of the emperor. Of course, he was by no means the only patron: patronage still pervaded Roman society in every sphere and at every level (Saller, 1982). But no patron could match the emperor. In his own account of his achievements, the *Res Gestae*, Augustus sets out in detail the sums spent on the plebs and on the soldiers, particularly in their settlement, for which he bought the land required (*Res Gestae* 15–16: the confiscations of Octavian seem to be omitted deliberately; cf. *Res Gestae* 3.3). All this was in addition to sums spent on public spectacles, reminiscent of the expenditures of Republican magistrates (Millar, 1977, 135–9). There was also his strenuous and expensive building activity, again reminiscent of the building activity of the Republican elite, but on a far greater scale. It enhanced his prestige together with that of Rome (the association should be noted) and at the same time provided work for the plebs (Brunt, 1980).

But the emperor also exercised his patronage over the elite. Increasingly, from Augustus on, the ambitious depended on the patronage of the emperor for social and political advancement (Millar, 1977, 278; Syme, 1979, 209). The emperor regularly financed some senators to allow them to retain their positions (Millar, 1977, 297–9). He could only do so because of the massive wealth he had accumulated and continued to accumulate from booty, inheritances and other income, which was so great that the emperor soon subsidized the state treasury. It becomes very difficult from now on to draw distinctions between imperial wealth and state wealth, though some were drawn in antiquity (Millar, 1977, 133–201, esp. 189–201).

Augustus' position was further reinforced by his concern to establish and exhibit his respect for tradition. Nothing displays this concern more clearly than the *Res Gestae* wherein Augustus repeatedly insists upon his concern to champion tradition. Socially, he set about the restoration of ancient, therefore better, *mores*, most strikingly in his legislation on the family and on the manumission of slaves (Jones, 1970, 131–43). There was also religion; some saw the civil wars as the result of the neglect of the gods (Syme, 1939, 215). Augustus, with all his own charisma, restored lapsed priesthoods and ceremonies, restored old temples and built new ones. In particular he celebrated in grand style the beginning of a new *saeculum*, a golden age that was to be characterized by prosperity and the peace which Augustus had established within the state (of course foreign wars were quite acceptable). The descendant of Aeneas was an appropriate usher (Jones, 1970, 144–52).

Politically, Augustus expressed his concern for tradition by displaying a marked respect for 'the Senate and People of Rome' not least, once more, in his *Res Gestae*. In the Early Empire, in particular, the 'good' emperor was one who allowed the Senate as much of its traditional prestige as possible. To this end, the emperor, like Claudius, might actually need to demand that the Senate debate issues and reach its own decision (Momigliano, 1961, 39–40). *Libertas*, freedom, was this exercise of traditional functions, especially traditional senatorial functions, within the imperial framework; it was not republicanism (Wirszubski, 1950). The 'good' emperor was not an emperor at all. He was *princeps*, the leading man in the state, just as under the Republic there had been a number of *principes* in the senatorial elite. The *princeps* was a senator and a citizen, a *civis*, like any Roman; he was expected to behave as such (Wallace-Hadrill, 1982). The *princeps* relied upon his *auctoritas*, 'influence', much as Republican *principes* had done. Augustus himself makes the point in his *Res Gestae*: 'I excelled (sc. from 27 BC) all in influence (*auctoritas*), although I possessed no more official power (*potestas*) than others who were my colleagues in the several magistracies' (*Res Gestae* 34.1 and 34.3: translated Brunt and Moore).

The subtlety of the symbiosis of *princeps* and Senate has often been misunderstood. There was no dyarchy and no façade: the Principate was neither an equal partnership between emperor and Senate nor a massive confidence trick perpetrated by the emperor upon the Senate. Rather the *princeps'* dominance was quite apparent: it was significant that unlike Republican magistrates he did not need senatorial ratification of his actions and decisions. But for all that, he did not flaunt his dominance as Caesar had tended to do. He took great care to allow the Senate its old prestige, though, directly and indirectly, he controlled its composition and the careers of its members (Syme, 1939, 369ff.). The advantage for the *princeps* was clear. Allowed their traditional prestige senators had less stimulus to revolt against him; even erstwhile opponents would support his regime, as most senators did throughout the Principate. By behaving as *princeps* the emperor, as we call him, gained a great measure of security. Indeed, the *princeps*, steeped in traditional values, might actually conceive himself as the champion of senatorial traditions in particular and of Roman *mos maiorum* in general. How many tyrants conceive themselves as tyrants?

The *princeps* might even look back upon the Republic with nostalgia. Pompey was something of a hero under the Principate. So too was Cato, the best known figure in the entrenched senatorial oligarchy which had precipitated war in 49 BC, who had committed suicide after the Pompeian defeat at the battle of Thapsus in North Africa in 46 BC. Even Brutus and Cassius, Caesar's murderers, could be viewed with a degree of sympathy, even favour. That such stalwarts of Republican *libertas* also came to be associated with opposition to particular emperors does not change the fact (Syme, 1939, 213–16, cf. Wirszubski, 1950). By contrast, Caesar was something of an embarrassment. Augustus had derived prestige and charisma from being the son of the deified Caesar, *divi filius*. But Caesar was associated with kingship, domination and anti-republicanism (Syme, 1939, 317ff.). Though Caesar, after Sulla (and to an extent Pompey), had paved the way, it was Augustus who became the paradigm, the Republican *princeps*.

The strength of tradition had told against change; the political form had changed, but élite ideology, shared by the *princeps*, remained essentially the same. In other words, institutions had changed to a limited extent and were to change still further. But, on the whole, society and, in particular, the economy which supported these institutions, had been relatively little affected. The Principate was neither a new beginning for Rome nor a descent into the abyss; it was a political modification, which was to change greatly after Augustus, as the *princeps* evolved into an emperor proper.

Augustus had 'restored the Republic' (Millar, 1973, provides a useful perspective). But *res publica*, literally 'the public thing', did not mean 'Republic' in the modern sense: it meant something much nearer 'the state'. Augustus' 'restoration' of the *res publica*, the state, was not just political; it was also, and more fundamentally, social, moral, religious and, less directly, economic. The Roman state was to flourish in the peaceful conditions established by and dependent upon Augustus. Rome was born again, a literal renaissance celebrated in the Secular Games of 17 BC. This rebirth had been celebrated in poetry as early as the triumviral period when Vergil wrote his *Fourth Eclogue*. Contemporary concern with rebirth doubtless accounts for the proliferation of children in Augustan iconography, as in the reliefs on the Altar of Peace, completed in 9 BC (Walker and Burnett, 1980).

The advent of Augustus has been seen as an occasion of great innovation. To some extent it was. But the innovation, the change, was overwhelmed by the long-dominant Roman past and its traditions. The advent of Augustus was change within and through tradition, as he is at pains to point out in his *Res Gestae*. There, as elsewhere, he is presented as something new, remarkable and unusual and, to that extent, as an innovator and an innovation. But he is new by virtue of brilliant success and achievements which are of the traditional kind. He is an innovation by virtue of his greatness, applied to and achieved through his protection of the *res publica* and tradition, not through their subversion. In the *Res Gestae* Augustus projects himself as a Republican noble writ large. That is, after all, precisely what he was.

From Augustus onwards, the changing relationship between the emperor (the noble writ large) and the rest of the elite in the Senate is central to the history of the Principate. Significantly, restoration of the Republic as we understand the term, by the removal of the emperor and a return to the dominance of the Senate, was seldom even mooted. The concern of the élite was principally to maintain its traditional prestige: this, not Republicanism, was *libertas*. Those emperors who threatened that prestige have come to be considered as 'bad' emperors, for so our sources portray them. For the emperor to threaten senatorial prestige, most directly by having senators executed and seizing their property, was to breed conspiracy. Usually, of course, a conspiracy to instal a new emperor, not to put an end to the Principate.

But the emperor was in a most delicate position, for his very existence tended to threaten senatorial prestige. Hence the wise emperor's concern to play down his autocracy and to present himself not so much as emperor but as the most prominent senator, as a noble writ large. Succession was therefore a particular problem. While it might be agreed that the emperor was the most prominent senator, it need not follow, even in the context of an aristocratic ideology, that his son would be so in turn. Inheritance of the imperial position was therefore potentially inimical to the senatorial prestige upon which that position depended.

In the change from Republic to Principate continuity and tradition had exerted so strong an influence that the new emperor is, in important respects, hardly distinguishable from the most prominent figures of the Republic. Perhaps the experience of lengthy civil warfare had endowed tradition and the past with special attractions at this juncture. But no such particular explanation is necessary. The past had always dominated Rome, obstructing and conditioning change. It did so in the rise of Augustus and it continued to do so thereafter.

·BIBLIOGRAPHY·FOR·PART·2·

Allen, D. F. (1944), 'The Belgic dynasties of Britain and their Coins', *Archaeologia*, 90, 1–46.

Allen, D. F. (1980), *The Coins of the Ancient Celts*, Edinburgh.

Badian, E. (1970), *Sulla the Deadly Reformer*, Sydney.

Badian, E. (1972a), *Publicans and Sinners*, Oxford.

Badian, E. (1972b), 'Tiberius Gracchus and the beginning of the Roman revolution', in A. Temporini (ed.), *Aufstieg und Niedergang des römischen Welt*, I, 1, 668–731.

Barrow, R. H. (1949), *The Romans*, Harmondsworth.

Bowersock, G. W. (1965), *Augustus and the Greek World*, Oxford.

Braund, D. C. (1983), 'Caesar, Gabinius and the *publicani* of Judaea', *Klio*, lxv, 241–4.

Braund, D. C. (1984), *Rome and the Friendly King*, London.

Brown, F. (1961), *Roman Architecture*, New York.

Brunt, P. A. (1965), 'Italian aims at the time of the Social War', *Journal of Roman Studies*, LV, 90–109.

Brunt, P. A. (1971), *Italian Manpower, 225 BC–AD 14*, Oxford.

Brunt, P. A. (1980), 'Free labour and public works at Rome', *Journal of Roman Studies*, LXX, 81–100.

Brunt, P. A. and Moore, J. M. (1967), *Res Gestae Divi Augusti*, Oxford.

Collis, J. R. (1977), 'Pre-Roman burial rites in north-western Europe', in R. Reece (ed.), *Burial in the Roman World*, Council for British Archaeology Research Report 22, London, 1–13.

Collis, J. R. (1981), 'A theoretical study of hill-forts', in G. Guilbert (ed.), *Hill-fort Studies: papers presented to Dr A. H. A. Hogg*, 66–76, Leicester.

Collis, J. R. (1984a), *The European Iron Age*, London.

Collis, J. R. (1984b), *Oppida: earliest towns north of the Alps*, Sheffield.

Cornell, T. J. (1975), 'Aeneas and the Twins: the development of the Roman foundation legend', *Proceedings of the Cambridge Philological Society*, xxi, 1–32.

Cunliffe, B. W. (1978), *Iron Age Communities in Britain*, revised edition, London.

Cunliffe, B. W. (1983), *Danebury: anatomy of an Iron Age hill-fort*, London.

Cunliffe, B. W. (1984), *Danebury: an Iron Age hill-fort in Hampshire, Vol. I, The excavations 1969–1978*, Council for British Archaeology Research Report No. 52, London.

Dent, J. (1983), 'The impact of Roman rule on native society in the territory of the Parisi', *Britannia*, XIV, 35–44.

Finley, M. I. (1973), *The Ancient Economy*, London.

Finley, M. I. (1983), *Politics in the Ancient World*, Cambridge.

Frederiksen, M. W. (1966), 'Caesar, Cicero and the problem of debt', *Journal of Roman Studies*, LVI, 128–41.

Gabba, E. (1976), *Republican Rome, the Army and the Allies*, Oxford.

Gelzer, M. (1968), *Caesar: politician and statesman*, Oxford.

Griffin, J. (1977), 'Propertius and Antony', *Journal of Roman Studies*, LXVII, 17–26.

Griffin, M. T. (1976), *Seneca: a philosopher in politics*, Oxford.

Grimal, P. (1960), *La Civilisation romaine*, Paris.

Hadas, M. (1930), *Sextus Pompey*, New York.

Harris, W. V. (1979), *War and Imperialism in Republican Rome, 327–70 BC*, Cambridge.

Haselgrove, C. C. and Turnbull, P. (1984), *Stanwick: excavation and fieldwork, interim report 1981–83*, University of Durham, Department of Archaeology, Occasional Paper No. 4, Durham.

Hopkins, K. (1978), *Conquerors and Slaves*, Cambridge.

Jones, A. H. M. (1970), *Augustus*, London.

Kunkel, W. (1966), *An Introduction to Roman Legal and Constitutional History*, Oxford.

Liebeschuetz, W. (1979), *Continuity and Change in Roman Religion*, Oxford.

Lintott, A. W. (1968), *Violence in Republican Rome*, Oxford.

Lorenz, G. (1978), 'Totenbrauchtum und Tracht: Untersuchungen zur regionalen Gliederung in der frühen Latenezeit', *Bericht der Römisch-Germanischen Kommission*, 59, 1–380.

Millar, F. (1973), 'Triumvirate and principate', *Journal of Roman Studies*, LXIII, 50–67.

Millar, F. (1977), *The Emperor in the Roman World*, London.

Millar, F. (1982), 'Emperors, frontiers and foreign relations', *Britannia*, XII, 1–23.

Momigliano, A. (1961), *Claudius*, Oxford.

North, J. A. (1975), Review of Weinstock (1971), *Journal of Roman Studies*, LXV, 171–7.

North, J. A. (1976), 'Conservatism and change in Roman religion', *Proceedings of the British School at Rome*, xxx, 1–12.

Potter, T. W. (1979), *The Changing Landscape of South Etruria*, London.

Price, S. R. F. (1980), 'Between man and god: sacrifice in the Roman imperial cult', *Journal of Roman Studies*, LXV, 28–43.

Rawson, E. (1975), 'Caesar's heritage: hellenistic kings and their Roman equals', *Journal of Roman Studies,* LXV, 148–59.

Rich, J. W. (1983), 'The supposed Roman manpower shortage of the later second century BC', *Historia*, xxxii, 287–331.

Saller, R. P. (1982), *Personal Patronage under the Early Empire*, Cambridge.

Salmon, E. T. (1982), *The Making of Roman Italy*, London.

Scullard, H. H. (1959), *From the Gracchi to Nero*, London.

Seager, R. (1979), *Pompey: a political biography*, Oxford.

Sherwin-White, A. N. (1973), *The Roman Citizenship,* second edition, Oxford.

Starr, C. G. (1960), *The Roman Imperial Navy*, Cambridge.

Staveley, E. S. (1972), *Greek and Roman Voting and Elections*, London.

Syme, R. (1979), *The Roman Revolution*, Oxford.

Taylor, L. R. (1931), *The Divinity of the Roman Emperor*, Middletown, Conn., U.S.A.

Versnel, H. S. (1970), *Triumphus*, Leiden.

Walker, S. and Burnett, A. (1980), *The Image of Augustus*, London.

Wallace-Hadrill, A. (1981), 'The emperor and his virtues', *Historia*, xxx, 298–323.

Wallace-Hadrill, A. (1982), 'Civilis princeps: between citizen and king', *Journal of Roman Studies*, LXXII, 32–48.

Weinstock. S. (1971), *Divus Julius*, Oxford.

Wheeler, R. E. M. (1964), *Roman Art and Architecture*, London.

Wilkinson, L. P. (1975), *The Roman Experience*, London.

Wilson, A. J. N. (1966), *Emigration from Italy in the Republican Age of Rome*, Manchester.

Wirszubski, C. (1950), *Libertas as a Political Idea at Rome*, Cambridge.

Wiseman, T. P. (1971), *New Men in the Roman Senate 139 BC–14 AD*, Oxford.

Wiseman, T. P. (1979), *Clio's Cosmetics*, Leicester.

PART 3

·THE·ARMY·

CHAPTER 5

·THE·ARMY·OF·
·THE·REPUBLIC·

G. R. Watson

The early period

The earliest Republican armies were naturally a continuation of the armies of the regal period, and, in particular, the army under the Etruscan kings, especially the two Tarquins, who may really have been one. The 'Romulean' army comprised traditionally 3,000 *pedites* and 300 *celeres*, provided by the three original Roman tribes, and presumably organized as a legion. It was most likely a purely patrician force. The influx of new settlers from the neighbouring hills and their organization into new tribes changed the army into a predominantly plebeian one, at the same time increasing its size. This reorganization was traditionally ascribed not to the Tarquins but to Servius Tullius, who was believed to have ruled between them. There are strong grounds, however, for ascribing 'the Servian constitution' not to the regal period, but to the middle of the fifth century BC (Dion. Hal. IV 16–21 and Livy I 42–8; Scullard, 1980, 74–).

This new arrangement, the *comitia centuriata*, was intended to preserve political and military power for the more prosperous sections of the Roman population. This was achieved by the division of the people into five classes, though those citizens above the highest class were mounted and composed the *equites*. The first class, with property rated at more than 100,000 *asses*, contained eighty centuries, the second, third and fourth, with proportionately smaller property, twenty centuries each, the fifth class, with about 11,000 *asses*, thirty centuries, although these figures have been disputed. In addition, at one extreme there were eighteen centuries of wealthy men, the *equites*, and at the other five centuries of unarmed men, who had too little property, but served as armourers, smiths and trumpeters. This made a total of 193 centuries. The number of men in each century can hardly have been uniform, since the proletariat, who were *capite censi*, i.e. registered by heads, not by property, were the largest class, yet with only five centuries. This discrimination was intended: the *equites* and the first class, with a total of ninety-eight centuries and the privilege of voting first, had a built-in majority.

In each class half the centuries were made up of *seniores* (men aged 47 to 60), and half of *iuniores* (men aged 17 to 46). The junior centuries of the first three classes, sixty in all, probably formed the infantry when the army had only one legion. Sixty is the traditional number of centuries in a legion, and the Roman army was conservative to the core. Even in the developed legion of the imperial period with fifty-nine centuries, there were still sixty centurions; then the senior centurion, the *primus pilus iterum*, served not in the legion itself but at army headquarters.

In all classes, the seniors were intended for home guard service, the juniors for service in the field. The differences of wealth between the classes were reflected in their arms and equipment. The men of the first class were required to equip themselves with helmet, round shield, greaves, breastplate, sword and spear. In other words, they were hoplites. The second class had similar arms and armour, except that the long shield eliminated the need for round shield and breastplate. The third class was armed like the second, but with the omission of greaves. The fourth class had only spears and javelins, the fifth class only slings and stones. The remainder, those *capite censi* or *infra classem*, were exempt from service under arms, though they formed the bulk of the population. The advantage of the system from the military point of view was that the whole of the propertied citizenry was placed on a war footing, with the officers drawn from the wealthiest group, the *equites*. According to Livy the state helped the cavalry with their expenses:

> For the purchase of horses they were allowed 10,000 *asses* each from the state treasury, and for the maintenance of these horses unmarried women were designated, who had to pay 2,000 *asses* each, every year.

These arrangements were, of course, practicable only when the campaigning season was limited to the summer, in the period between sowing and harvest. When campaigning became protracted, and lasted into the winter, or much longer, as in the siege of Veii (traditionally 406–396 BC) different arrangements had to be made. For the first time payment was made to the men. This was the first halting step towards the ultimate professionalization of the army. The amount of the pay at this date is not known. Presumably, however, as in the time of Polybius, it was based upon a daily rate.

This army of the early period was organized on the model of the Greek phalanx. The phalanx had, in the fourth century BC, proved almost invincible; long after its day had passed the Greek military writers continued to write as if the phalanx was the only conceivable method of military organization. Yet what Alexander found suited to the plains of Asia, or Pyrrhus to the plains of Southern Italy was not at all appropriate to the hill country of central Italy. The fullest description of the new organization is by Livy (VIII 8):

In the beginning the Romans used the small round shield (*clipeus*); later, after they began to receive pay for military service, the oblong shield (*scutum*) was adopted. The original phalanx formation, which was like the Macedonian one, became afterwards a line of battle formed by maniples, the rear being formed by a number of different troops. The front line was filled by the *hastati*, with fifteen maniples arranged at close intervals. Each maniple had twenty light-armed soldiers, with the remainder equipped with oblong shields: the light-armed had only a spear (*hasta*) and javelins. The front line consisted of the flower of the young men who were ripe for military service. Behind them were posted a like number of maniples of the *principes*, who were older men, who all carried oblong shields and had the better weapons. This body of thirty maniples in all were called the *antepilani* because behind the standards there were fifteen other battle-lines (*ordines*), each of which was divided into three parts, the first of each being called the *pilus* (a closed rank). Each of these lines consisted of three *vexilla*. A *vexillum* had sixty men, two centurions and one *vexillarius* (colour-sergeant). The line therefore numbered 186 men. The first *vexillum* had the *triarii*, experienced veterans; the second the *rorarii*, younger and less experienced men; the third the *accensi*, who were raw and therefore posted to the rear.

After the army had been drawn up in this fashion, the *hastati* were the first to engage the enemy. If the *hastati* were not successful in repulsing them, they would gradually withdraw through the intervals between the maniples of the *principes*, who were the next to take up the fight, with the *hastati* now in their rear. In the meantime the *triarii* had been kneeling beneath their standards with the left leg advanced, their shields against their shoulders, and their spears fixed in the ground with their points obliquely forwards, as if the line of battle were protected by a bristling palisade. If the *principes* were equally without success, they gradually retired through the *triarii* (hence the proverbial expression for when people are in trouble 'matters have now come down to the *triarii*'). After the *triarii* had let the *hastati* and *principes* through spaces between their *vexilla*, they stood up and closing their ranks at once, they blocked the routes, as it were, and in one dense mass they fell upon the enemy, for there were no reserves left behind them. The enemy, who as if they were victorious had been pursuing the others, saw to their consternation a new line suddenly spring up with even greater numbers. Generally, four legions were enrolled, each of 5,000 men, with 300 cavalry assigned to each legion.

Later the cavalry were generally supplied by the Roman allies, or *socii*.

The *hastati*, therefore, were organized in fifteen maniples of sixty-two men, 930 in all, the *principes* in another fifteen maniples of sixty-two men, a further 930; the third rank consisted of fifteen *ordines*, or lines of battle, each consisting of three *vexilla*

(= maniples) of sixty-two men, i.e. a further 2,790 men. This gives a legionary total of 4,650: when the 300 cavalry are added, the resultant figure, 4,950, is close enough to Livy's 5,000.

The early and middle Republic

It was traditionally during the siege of Veii that the men first began to be paid. Though this probably was not then intended as a permanent feature, it was inevitable that as warfare ceased to be an annual summer event and became frequently continuous, payment should become normal. At about the same time, or shortly afterwards, the army was improved by the adoption of new weapons and internal reorganization. For defence the *scutum*, which had already been adopted by the men of the second class became general in place of the *clipeus*, while the *hasta* was superseded by a new offensive weapon, the *pilum*. The *pilum* may have been borrowed from Rome's antagonists – the Romans were traditionally quick to imitate, but slow to invent – or it may have emerged from a development of the native Roman *verutum*. Thanks to the introduction of the *pilum* the Romans were able to abandon the traditional Greek method of hoplite fighting and make the Macedonian phalanx obsolete. Parker believes that this was a gradual process, and that in the organization of the army described in Livy VIII the first two lines, the *hastati* and *principes*, were armed with the *pilum* and organized in maniples, the third line continuing as a phalanx armed with the *hasta*. If Parker is right it is curious that the *hastati* were so called in spite of not being armed with the *hasta*.

By this time the Roman army in most years consisted of four legions, divided into two armies, of which each was commanded by a consul. There were twenty-four military tribunes, six to each legion, fourteen of whom according to Polybius (VI 19, 2–5) had seen five years' service and ten as much as ten years. He writes:

A cavalry soldier has to serve ten years in all and an infantry soldier sixteen years before reaching the age of forty-six, with the exception of those whose census is below 400 drachmas, all of whom are employed in naval service. In cases of emergency, twenty years' service is required from the infantry. No one may hold any political office before he has completed ten years' service.

The navy, which always remained very much the junior service, was essentially a creation of the Punic Wars.

Polybius (VI 19,8; 21,3; VI 21, 6–25) also describes a most elaborate method of appointing military tribunes and selecting the men, which, as Parker says, 'resembled picking up sides for a game':

The four tribunes named first are posted to the first legion, the next three to the second, the following four to the third, and the last three to the fourth. The first two of the senior tribunes are posted to the first legion, the next three to the second, the next two to the third, and the last three to the fourth. After the distribution and posting of officers has been made so that each legion has the same number of officers, those of each legion take their seats in separate groups, and they draw lots for the tribes, and summon them individually in the order of the draw. From each tribe they first select four young men of more or less the same age and build. When these are brought forward the officers of the first legion have the first choice, those of the second the second choice, those of the third next choice, and those of the fourth take the last. Another batch of four is then brought forward, and this time the officers of the second legion have the first choice and so on, those of the first now being the last to choose. A third group is now brought forward and this time the tribunes of the third legion choose first, and those of the second last. By continuing in this way to give each legion first choice in turn, each legion gets men of the same quality. When they have chosen the number decided upon – that is when the strength of each legion is brought up to 4,200 or in times of special danger to 5,000 – the former practice was to choose the cavalry after the 4,200 infantry, but now they choose them first, the censor selecting them according to their wealth, and 300 are posted to each legion.

When the enrolment has been made in this way, those of the tribunes responsible for this task in each legion assemble the newly enrolled soldiers, and selecting from them all one single man, the one whom they think the most suitable, they make him take the oath that he will obey his officers and execute their orders as far as lies in his power. Then the others come forward and each in his turn takes the oath, swearing that he will do the same as the first man.

Not content with this time-consuming procedure, the tribunes are as long-winded in mobilizing the army:

The tribunes in Rome, once they have administered the oath, appoint for each legion a day and a place at which the men are to present themselves without arms, and then dismiss them. When they arrive at the appointed place, they choose the youngest and least wealthy to form the *velites*, or light-armed troops; those next to them are appointed *hastati*. Men who are at the peak of their powers are made *principes*, and the oldest soldiers *triarii*. (These are the titles used by the Romans for the four classes in each legion, which all differ in age and equipment.) They divide them up so that the senior men known as *triarii* number 600, the *principes* 1,200, the *hastati* 1,200, all the rest, who are the youngest, being *velites* (1,200). If the legion consists of more than 4,000 men, they divide them up in the same proportions, apart from the *triarii*, the number of whom is always the same.

The youngest soldiers, the *velites*, have to carry a sword, light javelins, and a light shield (*parma*). The shield is circular, stoutly made, and three feet in diameter, and thus large enough to afford protection. They also have a plain helmet, which is sometimes covered with a wolf's skin, or something like it, both to give more protection and to make it more easy for their officers to recognize them. The wooden shaft of the javelin (*hasta velitaris*) is about two cubits long, and a finger's breadth in thickness; its head is a span in length, beaten out and sharpened to a fine point, so that it is inevitably bent by the first impact, and the enemy is unable to return it. Otherwise the same weapon would be available for both sides.

The next group in seniority, the *hastati*, have to wear complete armour. Their equipment consists of a shield (*scutum*) with a convex surface, measuring two and a half feet in width and four feet in length, with a thickness at the rim of a palm's breadth. It is made of two pieces of wood glued together. The outer surface is covered with canvas and has calfskin on top. It has a reinforcement at top and bottom consisting of an iron edging, which has a dual function – it protects the shield from sword blows from above, and also from damage from the ground. In the centre is an iron boss (*umbo*) which turns aside stones and blows from pikes and heavy missiles. In addition to the shield they wear a sword on the right thigh. This they call a Spanish sword. This sword is both effective for thrusting and has two first-class cutting edges, as the blade is both strong and firm. The *hastati* also carry two heavy javelins (*pila*), a bronze helmet, and greaves. The *pila* are of two kinds, heavy and light. Some of the heavy *pila* are round and three cubits long, and a palm in diameter, others are a palm square. The light *pila* are like reasonably sized hunting spears, the length of the shaft being the same three cubits. They are all fitted with an iron head as long as the shaft. This is attached so firmly to the shaft, being halfway let into the shaft, and fastened with numerous rivets, that in action the iron will break sooner than become separated, though its thickness at the bottom where it meets the wood is about one and a half fingers; so careful are they to attach it firmly. Finally they wear as a decoration on top of the helmet a circle of feathers, with three upright black or purple feathers about a cubit in height. These mounted above their other arms make every man look twice his real height, and give him a striking appearance, and help to strike terror into the enemy. The ordinary soldiers also wear a breastplate of bronze about nine inches square, which they place in front of the heart and call the heart-protector (*pectorale*), thus completing their armament. Those whose census is above 10,000 drachmas wear instead a coat of mail (*lorica*). The *principes* and *triarii* are similarly armed, except that instead of *pila* the *triarii* carry long spears (*hastae*).

From each of the classes except the most junior they select ten centurions on merit, and then select a second ten. These are all called centurions, but only those selected first have a seat on the military council. The centurions then appoint an equal number of deputies (*optiones*). Next, together with the centurions, they divide each class into ten centuries, except the *velites*, and assign to each maniple two centurions and two *optiones* from among the elected officers. The *velites* are divided equally among all the companies; these companies are called *ordines* or *manipuli* or *vexilla*, and their officers are called centurions or *ordinum ductores*. Finally, the centurions appoint from the ranks two of the best and bravest soldiers to be standard-bearers (*signiferi*) in each maniple. It is reasonable that they appoint two commanders for each maniple; for it is uncertain what an officer may do or what may happen to him, and since warfare does not admit of excuses, they desire the maniple never to be without a leader. When both centurions are available, the senior centurion (*centurio prior*) commands the right half of the maniple and the junior (*centurio posterior*) the left, but if only one is present he commands the whole. Centurions are expected to be not so much adventurers as dependable and sound leaders, who will not so much initiate attacks and begin the fighting, as hold their ground when under difficulties and be prepared to die at their posts.

In the same way they divide the cavalry into ten squadrons (*turmae*), and from each they select three officers (*decuriones*), who themselves appoint three deputies (*optiones*). The senior decurion (the one first chosen) commands the whole squadron, and the two others also have the rank of decurion. If the senior decurion is not present, the next in line commands the squadron. The cavalry are now armed like those of Greece, but in former times they had no cuirasses, but only light undergarments; they were thus able to mount and dismount with great ease and dexterity, but were also exposed to great danger in combat, as they were all but naked. Their lances also were unsuitable in two respects. In the first place, they were so light and pliant that it was hardly possible to take a steady aim, and before the iron tip became fixed in anything, the shaking due to the motion of the horse caused most of them to break. Secondly, since they were without spikes at the butt-end, they could only deliver the initial stroke with the point, and if they broke they were unfit for further service. Their shields were made of ox-hide, of an appearance similar to the round cakes used at sacrifices. They were of no use for attacking for they were not firm enough, and when the leather covering peeled off, rotted by the rain, though they were hardly serviceable before, they were entirely unserviceable then. Since their arms did not stand the test, they began to make them in the Greek fashion, which requires that the first stroke of the lance be well aimed and forceful, since the lance is made to be steady and strong, and also can be effectively used by reversing it and striking with the point at the butt-end. The same applies to the Greek shields, which being both solid and strong, are serviceable both against attack from a distance and assault at close quarters.

Polybius proceeds to describe the system of mobilization; each consul appoints a separate meeting place, for he had his own share of the allies and two Roman legions. The allies are commanded by officers appointed by the consuls, who are called *praefecti sociorum* and are twelve in number. These officers select from the entire force of allies the best of the cavalrymen and infantrymen, called *extraordinarii*. The number of allied infantry is normally equal to that of the legions, whereas the cavalry are three times as many. About a third of the cavalry and a fifth of the infantry are in the *extraordinarii*, the select corps; the rest are divided into two bodies, the right wing and the left wing.

Polybius goes on to describe the construction of a Roman camp, or more strictly, the half of a four-legion camp. In his day, the two-legion camp of a single consular army must have been normal, though no doubt the handbooks of castrametation still concerned themselves with the four-legion camp of an army commanded by both consuls. His description of the contemporary Roman camp has given rise to a vast literature from the fifteenth century onwards. Walbank believes that the most satisfactory explanation so far is that of P. Fraccaro who suggests that Polybius had before him a Roman vade-mecum containing a plan of a camp, and that such a work would naturally give the typical form. The 'typical' camp would still be the four-legion camp; but Polybius describes only one half of it. The other half is then made identical, but back to back, with only the base line in common. Polybius writes:

> When both consuls with all their four legions are united in one camp, we need only imagine two camps like the one described placed back to back. The *extraordinarii* infantry of each camp we have described as being at the rearward *agger* of the camp. These then form the junction, and the camp is now oblong, its area being double what it had been, and the circumference half as much again.

The *praetorium*, the commander's tent, was the first to be erected, with the tribunes' tents forming a single line in front of the *praetorium*, fifty feet from it and facing it. The maniples were arranged in blocks behind the tribunes' tents, with in each maniple the end tent being occupied by the centurions. The areas to right and left of the *praetorium* were used for the market on one side and the office of the *quaestor* (quartermaster) on the other.

In general, it is remarkable how similar the Polybian camp was to the later imperial one. This is a further instance of Roman conservatism. The major difference is that whereas the imperial camp was the familiar playing-card shape, Polybius describes the camp of his day as a square. In practice it may have been nearer to a rectangle.

Polybius next outlines the arrangements for guard duties. Each tribune has two guards, one stationed in front of his tent and the other in the rear, with each guard consisting of four men. Guard duties for the infantry were undertaken by the *hastati* and *principes*. Since each tribune had command of four maniples, the incidence of guard duty cannot have been heavy. Guards for the cavalry were supplied by the *triarii*. Finally, each maniple in turn provided the guard for the general's tent.

Elaborate precautions were made for the security of the password. One man was selected from the tenth maniple of each class of infantry and cavalry, and was relieved from all other guard duty; instead, he attended every day at sunset at his tribune's tent, and received from him the watchword, the *tessera*. This was a wooden tablet, almost certainly waxed. The guard handed the tablet to the commander of the next maniple, who in turn passed it to the one next to him. This was repeated until the password reached the first maniples, i.e. those whose tents were near to the tent of the tribune. Before dark the password had to be handed back to the tribune. Therefore, if all the tablets issued were returned, the tribune knew that the password had been given to all the maniples. If any one was missing, an inquiry began and whoever was responsible was appropriately punished. The procedure in the imperial army was simpler, in so far as the responsibility was entrusted to one man in each century who was given the rank of *tesserarius*. By that date he received, probably, pay and a half.

The *velites* had the duty of guarding the perimeter. They were posted every day along the *vallum*, and ten of them were on guard at each entrance. Visiting rounds was the responsibility of the legionary cavalry. The decurion of the first *turma* in each legion had to give orders early in the day to one of his *optiones* to arrange for four men to visit rounds. This was repeated next day by the decurion of the second *turma* and so on. The four men chosen each day drew lots for their respective watches and went to the tribune on duty to obtain written orders which specified those stations they were to visit, and at what time. They then positioned themselves near the first maniple of the *triarii*, for the beginning of each watch was announced by a bugle-call from their guard station. When his time came, the man responsible for visiting rounds made it accompanied by friends as witnesses. He visited all the posts mentioned in his orders. If he found the guards on the first watch awake, he received their *tessera*; if not, or if he found that a sentry had left his post, he asked those with him to witness the fact, and proceeded on his rounds. All those who visited rounds brought back the *tesserae* to the tribune on duty at daybreak. If there were fewer *tesserae* than the number of posts visited, the tribune examined the *tesserae* to see which one was missing, and then summoned the centurion of the maniple concerned, and held a confrontation of the men on sentry duty with the pickets visiting rounds. If a sentry was found guilty he was condemned to the *fustuarium*; that is, he was cudgelled by men from his own unit and usually killed. If not, he was given a discharge with ignominy, and would not find life easy thereafter. The same punishment was inflicted on the *optio* and the decurion of the *turma*, if they did not give out the proper orders at the right time, or pass them on to the next *turma*. Since the penalty was both immediate and severe, the watches were normally well kept.

Punishments were not limited to individual soldiers. A tribune, or in the cases of the allies a *praefectus*, had the power to inflict fines, demand sureties, and to flog. The *fustuarium* was also the punishment for stealing anything from the camp, or for giving false evidence. It was imposed on men for gross immorality, and on anyone who had already been punished three times for the same offence. These offences were treated as crimes; other offences were considered as equally serious, as when a man boasted falsely of his own courage in order to win a distinction, when men left in a covering force abandoned their station through fear, or when a man through panic threw away his weapons in battle. So men in covering forces preferred death to dishonour, and in battle men who lost a shield or sword often hurled themselves into the midst of the enemy, in the hope either of recovering what they had lost or of escaping through death inevitable disgrace. If an entire unit deserted its post, the *fustuarium* was not imposed on them all but an equally terrible punishment instead. One tenth of the offenders were selected by lot to undergo *fustuarium*; the remainder were made to receive rations of barley instead of wheat, and to encamp outside the camp in an unprotected area. This sometimes continued over a long period.

Besides punishments, there were, of course, incentives. It was required of every man that in battle he should fight to the best of his ability, but in skirmishes or minor engagements, where there was no necessity for engaging in single combat, some men performed actions beyond the sphere of duty. The usual reward for bravery was to award a man who had wounded an enemy, a spear, the *hasta pura*: to one who had killed and stripped an enemy, a decoration if he was an infantryman, horse trappings if a cavalryman. The first man to climb the wall of a city under siege received a *corona muralis*, or crown of gold, a soldier who saved the life of a fellow-citizen (Polybius includes allies) might receive a *corona civica*, or crown of oak-leaves.

Pay

Polybius next states the daily pay for soldiers at this period (probably his own time): two obols a day for the infantryman, twice as much for a centurion, and a *drachma* for a cavalryman. Since there were normally six obols to the *drachma*, it would appear that the cavalryman's pay included the cost of keeping his horse; otherwise he would have been receiving three times the pay of an infantryman, and half as much again as a centurion. But what did Polybius mean by a *drachma*? It is usually taken to be the equivalent of a *denarius*, but that involves difficulties. One problem is that the soldier would then receive one third of a *denarius* a day. At this date there were ten sextantal *asses* to the *denarius*, which would leave the infantryman with three and a third *asses* a day. A daily rate should be one easily reckoned and this is a most unlikely number. The alternative is to adopt the suggestion first made by H. Mattingly (*JRS* 1937, 102) that two obols represented two libral *asses*, i.e. two *sestertii* (the *denarius* then being the equivalent of four *sestertii* or ten sextantal *asses*). His solution would provide for the infantryman five *asses*, for the centurion one *denarius*, and for the cavalryman one and a half *denarii* daily. It is usual for this period to assume a 360-day year. So long as ten *asses* were reckoned to the *denarius* it meant that the pay on an annual basis would be for the infantryman 180 *denarii*, for the centurion 360 *denarii*, and for the cavalryman 540 *denarii*. This is borne out by the allies' pay, which was the same for the infantry as for the Romans: in the case of the cavalry the pay seems to have been the same as that of the infantry, but with the addition of a free allowance of one and a third *medimni* of wheat (= about a bushel) and five *medimni* of barley (about four bushels). When the *as* was retariffed at sixteen to the *denarius*, the basic legionary pay would fall to $112\frac{1}{2}$ *denarii*; when Caesar doubled the pay the annual rate became 225 *denarii*, and it remained at this level until the time of Domitian. This theory has the advantage of accounting for the few pieces of clear evidence that we possess: (i) that the rate in the time of Polybius was two obols a day; (ii) that the *as* was later retariffed at sixteen to the *denarius*; (iii) that Caesar doubled the pay; (iv) that in the time of Augustus the annual rate was 225 *denarii*. The retariffing of the *as* would at first sight imply a severe reduction in the living standards of the soldier until the later increase by Caesar. Whether this was the case or not depends really on the net total remaining after all compulsory deductions had been made. Polybius tells us that the *quaestor* deducted the price fixed for the men's corn and clothes and any additional arms they may have required. These deductions may have been substantial; Parker believes that they could have amounted to more than half the man's gross pay, although the position might have been mitigated by a *lex militaris* of C. Gracchus, which allowed for a free issue of clothing.

In spite of the award of pay, the Roman legions were as yet by no means a professional army, but continued as legions enrolled each year with no doubt numerous changes in personnel and still in theory a citizen militia of peasant smallholders.

The Marian reforms

The aftermath of the Punic and Macedonian wars left the Roman economy divided between wealthy landlords, with cheap and plentiful slave labour, and a body of smallholders who found it increasingly difficult to compete and who, driven by necessity, migrated to Rome to join the urban poor. Fewer and fewer men now had the property still required for service in the legions, and gradually the rules were relaxed or ignored. One solution would have been to extend the franchise to the allies, but to this the senate was opposed. The Gracchi did attempt to secure agrarian reform, but their defeat left the impoverished smallholders and the Roman poor in as bad a position as before.

Marius is credited with changing the system, but though his efforts were undoubtedly decisive, they did no more than accelerate, and make final, army reforms that were already beginning. The first and most important is that he opened recruitment to the *capite censi*, thus at one stroke ending the class-division of the legions. At the same time, recruits were now enrolled for a definite period of service; the army was now becoming professional (see Parker, 1928, 24; but also Smith, 1958, 29, note 1). This not unnaturally raised the army to a much higher level of efficiency. The other side of the coin was that by changing the rules and enlisting men on his own initiative Marius established a precedent which ambitious senators were quick to imitate, and which was partly responsible for the civil wars of the first century BC. The army before Marius had been a national army, now it became a succession of armies which owed loyalty, not to the state, but each to its own army commander. This was exacerbated by the extraordinary commands given to Pompey and Caesar.

The second reform ascribed to Marius is one of tactics. The army of the second century BC had been based upon the maniple, and the arrangement had proved highly successful against the Macedonian phalanx. The Cimbri and the Teutones, who attacked with a strong assault at the start of the battle, proved to be too strong for the manipular system. Since between each maniple in the first line there was a gap as wide as the maniple itself, the Cimbri went straight through the gaps, and attacked the second line in the first onslaught. Marius, therefore, decided to strengthen his front line by increasing the size of the tactical units from maniples to cohorts, and reducing the gaps between them. Henceforward the cohort of six centuries became the tactical unit, and the maniple became obsolete. Organization by cohorts was not entirely new; Polybius mentions them in his account of P. Scipio's campaign against Indibilis, but he omits them from his description of the organization of the legion. It seems likely, therefore, that it was Scipio who experimented with the cohortal formation, but Marius who adopted it.

One result of the change from maniples to cohorts was that the division into *hastati, principes* and *triarii* became obsolete. The names were now used for distinguishing the various centurions, with *triarii* being omitted, and replaced by its equivalent, *pilani*. Since the *pilani* had been the most experienced men, their name was now used for the senior centurions in each cohort, while the *hastati*, who had been the youngest troops, were designated the junior. The *principes* gave their name to those in between. The ranking of centurions was now, in order of seniority in each cohort from II to X, *pilus prior, princeps prior, hastatus prior, pilus posterior, princeps posterior, hastatus posterior*. The titles of centurions in the first cohort, who now became called the *primi ordines*, were slightly different: *primus pilus, princeps, hastatus, princeps posterior, hastatus posterior*. It is not clear whether at this date the first cohort had five centurions, as in the empire, or six (i.e. two *primi pili*). The reduction to five was probably due to the *primus pilus bis* (i.e. for the second time) being too useful as a staff officer.

The third of Marius' innovations was to make each legion a recognizable unit, with its own identity, and one for which its members might feel more esprit de corps. From now on each legion had its *aquila*, or eagle, which was kept in a little chapel, and honoured as the *numen legionis*.

Other reforms of Marius were the disappearance of the *velites*, and the abolition of the legionary cavalry. Both were natural consequences of the abolition of the class divisions within the legions. The task of the *velites* could be done more effectively by foreign mercenaries, such as Balearic slingers. Roman cavalry had never been outstanding, and here again non-Romans proved more useful. It is noteworthy that Caesar used exclusively *equites* from Gaul, Spain and Germany, and this practice continued in the imperial army. There were still *equites* within the legion, perhaps 120 in all, but they were no longer organized as a tactical unit.

In weaponry the *hasta* was finally replaced by the *pilum*, so that there was uniform equipment throughout the legion, and the last traces of the phalanx organization were eliminated. *Hastati* nevertheless remained as one of the titles for centurions, in accordance with Roman traditionalism. Modifications were, however, made to the *pilum*. In the time of Polybius the shank was driven halfway into the handle and fixed with numerous rivets, so that it would break sooner than become separated. Sometime between Polybius and Marius the number of rivets was reduced to two. Marius substituted for one of the iron rivets a wooden one. The object was to ensure that when the *pilum* struck an enemy shield the wooden pin would break and the weapon be bent so that it would be difficult to remove it from the shield. Caesar improved upon this by leaving the metal of the shank beneath the head of the *pilum* untempered, so that the metal itself would bend, and make it impossible for the *pilum* to be withdrawn from the shield. In addition, Marius is reported to have devised a scheme whereby a soldier was able to remove his pack without taking off his armour. In spite of this, the nickname '*muli Mariani*' (Marius' mules) was adopted by the troops to describe the burdensome nature of carrying the pack. Finally, as a result of the Social War, the grant of citizenship to Italians meant the elimination of the *Socii*, and the extension of the legionary recruiting area to all Italy south of the Po. The Roman army was thereafter composed of legions and *auxilia* (Part 3, Chapter 3), who as non-Romans were of lower status.

The Civil Wars

The Civil Wars had the effect of multiplying the number of legions considerably. It was still normal practice to reserve numbers one to four for the consular legions, but each of the war-lords then began his own enumeration. Finally, at Actium, Antony had thirty-one legions, of which nineteen were in the land army, eight in the fleet, and four left behind in Egypt. Octavian had between forty and forty-five. So after the victory Octavian had an army consisting of more than sixty legions. He gradually reduced the number to twenty-eight by 16 BC, and it was further reduced by the loss of legions XVII, XVIII, XIX in the Varian disaster, which meant a total of twenty-five legions at the death of Augustus.

The great problem left by the reforms of Marius had been that with the lessening of the importance of the consuls, and the increasing power of the great commanders, the soldiers tended to look towards their generals rather than the state for donations and land grants on demobilization. Since each army owed its allegiance to its commander, the great commanders tended to act as war-lords, each with his own sphere of influence. The Civil Wars were therefore inevitable.

CHAPTER 6

·THE·IMPERIAL·ARMY·

Alistair Scott Anderson

The military superiority that had won Rome vast overseas territories by the late Republic was the result of a long evolution, noticeably accelerated during the Augustan age. Working upon the foundations so ably laid by Gaius Marius and Julius Caesar, Augustus set about organizing a new army that could fulfil the requirements of an expanded Roman world and support the new imperial system. In this, two objectives were paramount: the defence of the Empire and the security of his own position. His arrangements, a model for numerous successors, took due account of worthy tradition yet for the most part showed an originality that was to be both successful and lasting, and produced a professional organization that remained almost unaltered for two centuries.

After Actium (31 BC) Augustus (then Octavian) inherited parts of sixty to seventy legions. Casualties incurred in the civil wars meant that most of these legions were not at full strength but they still represented an army of over a quarter of a million men. Some had formed Augustus' own army but many had supported his opponents. It was a legacy of decades of intermittent military and political unrest and the victorious Augustus quickly reduced the size of the army to twenty-five, or -six, legions (to be raised to twenty-eight by 25 BC) in an effort to create a standing force of manageable size. This new legionary force comprised somewhat more than 150,000 men. The number of legionaries, although seemingly small when considered in relation to the expanse of the empire that they were to defend, was based upon calculations of what was both militarily and politically sound. The army had to be large enough to protect the empire yet not so big that it presented a security risk to the emperor himself; too many soldiers in a single province offered a tempting prize to any usurper willing to take up arms against Augustus. Another consideration was the flow of manpower into the legions in peacetime. By admitting *proletarii* into the legions the reforms of Gaius Marius had been instrumental in the replacement of the conscript militia by a volunteer army and, although conscription remained an alternative in times of emergency, Augustus realized the advantages of a professional volunteer army. A volunteer was much less likely to join in sedition against the emperor, a desirable objective, yet Augustus foresaw that without the incentive of additional income from campaign booty the number of volunteers in peacetime might not meet the requirements of a larger military establishment. Finally, the logistics of maintaining a standing army had to be judged against both the capability of the primitive agricultural system of the empire to feed the troops, and the limits of fiscal wealth to pay them.

Augustus realized that ultimately the position of any emperor relied on the support of the army and the safety of his empire could only be guaranteed by an efficient military presence. Accordingly he introduced several measures to regularize service conditions, to provide recruitment incentives and to bind the loyalty of the army to his own person. It was, he hoped, to be a lifelong loyalty, for he:

> standardized the pay and allowances of the entire army – at the same time fixing the period of service and the bounty due on its completion – according to military rank; this would discourage them from revolting, when back in civil life, on the excuse that they were either too old or had insufficient capital to earn an honest living (Suetonius, *Augustus*, 49).

During the later Republic it had become standard practice to give legionary veterans allotments of land on discharge. Such practice was unpopular with the Senate as it meant either the wholesale confiscation of land or enormous expenditure to purchase it. Consequently it was often left to individual generals to find land, or money for purchase, for their men. This practice, so crucial in the erosion of senatorial power in the late Republic, as it encouraged the troops in loyalty to their commander rather than to the state, was avidly pursued by Augustus. In the years immediately following Actium, Augustus demobilized more than one hundred thousand veterans, settling them in a series of new or older established colonies in Italy and the provinces. Most of the finance for this came from Augustus' own personal fortune, confiscated from the Egyptian state treasury in 30 BC, and he claimed to have spent 600,000,000 *sesterces* in Italy and 260,000,000 in the provinces on land purchases for the colonists (*Res Gestae*, 16). In addition to land grants, the veterans received other advantages, for even in the provinces many of the *coloniae* were granted the *ius Italicum* which exempted the *coloni* from land-tax (*tributum soli*) and poll-tax (*tributum capitis*) (Part 6, Chapter 15).

Such measures undoubtedly gained Augustus the loyalty he desired as the future of each soldier, in his retirement, was bound to the emperor's generosity. Land allotments also maintained recruitment since each soldier knew what to expect as a reward for his service. The legal right to a discharge award was further formalized in 13 BC when land grants were abandoned in favour of a cash gratuity which by AD 5 had been fixed at a total of 3,000 *denarii* per legionary. Many of Augustus' veteran settlements had been a direct result of the post-civil war demobilizations and an attempt to forget such unhappy times, coupled with difficulties in administration and a shortage of land, may have prompted this change in practice.

After carrying such a vast financial burden on his own shoulders for so many years, in AD 6 he transferred the responsibility for soldiers' discharge awards to the state. This was accomplished by the creation of a new military treasury (*aerarium militare*). To start it Augustus made a personal contribution of 170,000,000 *sesterces* and to provide for its continuing revenue he instituted a 5 per cent tax on inheritances and a 1 per cent tax on auction sales. Cash grants must have been welcomed by urban recruits who did not possess agricultural backgrounds but several first-century emperors saw the advantages of *coloniae* as bastions of Roman civilization in the provinces and the reversion to colonial land allotments for veterans was a common occurrence. Even as early as AD 14 soldiers were complaining of being given allotments on unsuitable land in remote countries. For the settlers in the Claudian *colonia* at Camulodunum, the Boudiccan rebellion proved conditions there to be even more unfavourable.

Augustus' financial arrangements in this sphere were not confined to the regularization of discharge benefits. Another important measure which made army life more inviting awarded each soldier control over his individual property, his *peculium castrense*; under normal Roman law the head of the family (*paterfamilias*) was the sole legal person able, not only to own property, but also to dispose of it.

Many of Augustus' military reforms were directed towards service in the legions but his total military establishment involved more than this traditional infantry force. To provide military strength in areas where trouble could most be expected and in an effort to lessen the outward display of his military power in Rome, where republican sympathies ran high, the legions were stationed mainly in the frontier provinces. This left the defence of Italy to other forces.

The navy fulfilled part of this role, based at Misenum on the Bay of Naples and on the Adriatic coast at Ravenna. Other fleets were based at Seleucia Pieria in Syria, Alexandria in Egypt, Fréjus in southern France and on the Rhine and Danube. However more important for the security of the peninsula was the Praetorian Guard, which became one of the most esteemed and influential branches of the army, especially in the field of imperial politics, until it was finally abolished by Constantine some three and a half centuries later.

The Praetorian Guard, made up of Roman citizens, formed the imperial bodyguard and was based on the personal escorts of late Republican generals such as Marius, Caesar and Antony. Augustus' guard was made up of nine cohorts each comprised of six centuries. In order to prevent danger to himself and, because the stationing of such a large body of troops in the capital would have been decidedly un-republican, only three cohorts were based in Rome with the other six stationed in nearby Italian towns. At first each cohort was under the command of a tribune with Augustus himself as overall commander. But from 2 BC command of the guard was entrusted to two *praefecti praetorio* of equestrian rank and on most occasions this duality of command was maintained. The praetorians were specially picked and enjoyed numerous privileges in terms of pay and promotions, for example to legionary centurionates. In 13 BC their length of service was fixed at twelve years which was increased to sixteen years in 5 BC. Originally their pay appears to have been 375 *denarii* a year, but by the end of Augustus' reign it had risen to 750 and then to 1,000 under Domitian. This was much more than legionary pay, as was their retirement gratuity, which Augustus fixed at 5,000 *denarii*. In his will he left the praetorians 250 *denarii* each against the legionaries' 75 per man.

The praetorians protected the emperor in Rome and accompanied him or members of the imperial family on campaign and occasionally formed additional reserves for important military expeditions. Their presence in Rome also gave them a unique influence in the choice of future emperors. Gaius raised the number of praetorian cohorts to twelve and, in AD 69, because of their support for Otho, Vitellius cashiered the members of the guards and replaced them with sixteen cohorts taken from the German legions. Vespasian reduced the number to nine although, probably in the reign of Domitian, this was increased to ten. The guard was disbanded in 312.

An important innovation in the establishment of Augustus' new army was the creation of numerous auxiliary units. The use of non-citizen allied forces to supplement Rome's own armies had a long tradition and became commonplace during the civil war. They provided specialist troops, such as archers and cavalry, areas in which legionary strength was deficient. Augustus viewed these forces in a different light to his predecessors, envisaging a role which was to give them a permanent place in his new military establishment. Accordingly the number of these auxiliaries was increased to about 150,000, similar to the legionary strength. However, unlike the legions, these soldiers were organized into units each approximately five hundred men strong. Several units were assigned to each legion and some provinces were garrisoned entirely by these *auxilia*. Indeed, to many provincials it was these non-citizen auxiliaries who became the public face of Rome, as they were gradually stationed in a series of small garrison forts throughout the empire. However, in the early imperial period, in terms of pay, status and overall military planning, for those outside the Praetorian Guard, the legions remained the most important branch of the services.

The Augustan legions were numbered from I to XXII and each bore a title, which helped differentiate it from others with the same number. Presumably Augustus retained legions that had belonged to his former colleagues in the triumvirate, Mark Antony and Marcus Aemilius Lepidus; the army of the latter transferred its loyalty to Octavian in 36 BC, and four numbers are duplicated: *IV Macedonica* and *IV Sythica*, *V Alaudae* and *V Macedonica*, *VI Ferrata* and *VI Victrix*, and *X Gemina* and *X Fretensis* and one is triplicated: *III Augusta*, *III Cyrenaica* and *III Gallica*. Some of these titles, such as

'Augusta', were undoubtedly official in origin but others like that of the *IX Hispana* were presumably acquired from the name of a province where the unit served with distinction. In some cases a nickname sufficed, an example being the *cognomen* of the *V Alaudae* (the larks), a legion raised by Julius Caesar. Later emperors raised legions either to replace those lost in battle or to add to legionary strength, usually before a specific campaign or to counter some new threat. The nomenclature of these new creations can be indicative of origin, for example, *I Italica* was raised by Nero from Italian-born recruits and *I, II* and *III Parthica* were raised by Septimius Severus for his campaigns in the east. The raising of *XXX Ulpia victrix* by Trajan suggests that at the time of its formation, twenty-nine other legions were in existence. In fact, over the first two hundred years of empire the number of legions remained relatively stable, usually numbering around the twenty-eight originally envisaged by Augustus.

The rewards due to legionaries on their discharge must have seemed more than generous to new recruits but to qualify for a land grant or a cash payment the legionary had first to fulfil his term of service. In 13 BC Augustus fixed the length of service at sixteen years – the usual obligation of a citizen in the Republic. However, even after this period of service many legionaries were to be kept in the legions for a further four years as *evocati*, exempted from routine duties, in a special cohort under its own commander, the *curator veteranorum*. Later by AD 6, this length of service was extended to twenty years *sub aquila*, as a normal soldier and five years in a veteran corps. In the Flavian period the veteran corps was abolished and twenty-five years became the standard legionary service requirement.

The Augustan legionary received pay of 225 *denarii* a year from which deductions were made for food, clothing and arms. Domitian increased this to 300 *denarii* per annum and it remained at this level until a further increase under Septimius Severus. This was the basic pay and was occasionally supplemented by special bonuses or donatives, such as the 75 *denarii* left to each legionary in Augustus' will. From the time of Claudius each emperor paid the army a donative at the time of his accession. Of course there were also different pay grades within the legion with, even in Augustus' time, centurions' pay ranging from about 3,750 to 15,000 *denarii* per annum depending upon the grade of the centurion.

In addition to a retirement grant and regular pay, the legionary also received medical care and the opportunity to learn various trades. For those from the lower levels of society, service with the legions provided a career security unknown in civilian life and such attractions resulted in a high level of voluntary recruitment into the legions serving in the west. In the Augustan period Italy still provided most of their recruits, with Cisalpine Gaul being a particularly important recruiting area. However, even at this time a significant number came from southern Gaul and some from southern Spain, both areas containing large numbers of Roman citizens, to whom legionary service was restricted. As the century wore on and the franchise spread, fewer and fewer Italians enlisted, as service and eventual settlement in the distant frontier provinces became less attractive. Their place was eagerly filled by citizens born outside Italy. Probably as many as half the legionaries in the Claudian army which invaded Britain in AD 43 were of Italian origin, yet by the Antonine period the provincialization of the western legions was complete, with Italians forming only a small minority.

In contrast the legions in the eastern provinces were recruited from the local populations, even in the Augustan period. Conscription was often used rather than voluntary recruitment and when necessary Roman citizenship was awarded on recruitment to comply with legal requirements for enlistment. Even here, though, not all rules could be bent to suit the requirements of military manpower. Legionaries were supposed to be freeborn Roman citizens. Citizenship could be awarded but the status of the freeborn could not, as is obvious from the correspondence between Trajan and Pliny, his governor in Bithynia. In a letter to the emperor Pliny complains that two slaves have been discovered among a batch of legionary recruits and asks Trajan for his advice on the procedure for dealing with the problem. Trajan's reply illustrates the magnitude of the problem:

> If they are conscripts, then the blame falls on the recruiting officer; if substitutes, then those who offered them as such are guilty; but if they volunteered for service, well aware of their status then they will have to be executed. (Pliny, *Letters*, X, 29–30)

The organization of the legions in the early imperial period owed much to the reforms of Gaius Marius, with a legion being composed of ten cohorts. Of these, cohorts II to X were each made up of six centuries (totalling 480 men per cohort) while from early in the imperial period cohort I appears to have been organized on a different basis with, according to Hyginus, twice the strength of the others. Including officers, administrative staff and a detachment of 120 men who acted as mounted despatch riders, each legion had a total establishment of about 6,000.

Under Augustus and his successors the command structure of the army was noticeably different from its republican counterpart. The consular and proconsular armies of earlier times now came under the direct control of the princeps and an early Augustan reform was the installation of a single commander over each legion, replacing the authority of the *tribuni militum* of whom there had been six to a legion, commanding in pairs for periods of two months at a time. This new commander was known as the *legatus legionis*. Caesar had sometimes used *legati* to command individual legions but it was under Augustus that the position of *legatus legionis* became established; they came from men trusted by the emperor and at first from the ranks of ex-quaestors or ex-praetors, but, towards the late first century, usually only from the latter. Such men, if they served the emperor well, could look forward to becoming consul and a provincial governor later in their careers.

The six tribunates in each legion still existed but were now subordinate to the *legatus legionis* and only one was manned by a potential senator, the other five going to equestrians. The former, the second in command of the legion and known as the *tribunus laticlavius*, was a young man in his early twenties who served a short term in a legion prior to entering the senate as a quaestor. This experience of army life was to train him for later command of a legion in a career that would span both civil and military positions. His equestrian colleagues, the *tribuni angusticlavii* were concerned largely with administrative duties. These men, usually in their thirties came from municipal magistracies or had commanded auxiliary cohorts. For those lucky or able enough the praefecture of an *ala* would follow.

Third in command was the *praefectus castrorum*. Normally a man of considerable military experience who had previously held the office of *primus pilus* (chief centurion), he was the senior professional officer in the legion. His responsibilities included building work, munitions and stores; yet he commanded the legion in the absence of the *legatus* and senior tribune. Below the *praefectus castrorum* and the equestrian tribunes were the centurions and other ranks.

The principal professional soldiers in the Roman army were the centurions, each of whom commanded a century numbering eighty men. The centurions of each cohort, other than the first, were named in order of seniority (see p. 80 above). As in the army of the Republic, each centurion had an *optio* who, when accepted for promotion to the centurionate, but while waiting for a vacancy, bore the title *optio ad spem ordinis*.

Below the centurionate can be seen three main groups of soldiers in each century: *principales, immunes* and *milites*. Whether these groups were recognized as such before the early second century is doubtful but most of the positions held by men within each group date to much earlier times. Basically *principales* were non-commissioned officers receiving double the pay of a legionary (a *duplicarius*) or pay-and-a-half (a *sesquiplicarius*). *Immunes* were soldiers who received no more than basic pay but who were exempt from fatigues because they fulfilled special duties. *Milites* were the common legionaries available for general duties.

Within each century the *principales* consisted of the *signifer*, the *optio* and the *tesserarius*. The holding of one or all of these ranks was a normal step towards promotion into the centurionate. The *signifer* was the standard-bearer and also recorded and safeguarded the men's savings; the *optio* as recorded above deputized for the centurion when he was away and assisted him in military matters and the *tesserarius* acted as an orderly sergeant, being responsible for guard duties and the daily 'watchword'.

Many legionaries had special skills or were trained in particular crafts. Among these *immunes* were surveyors, architects, medical orderlies, smiths, roof-tile-makers, plumbers, stonecutters and woodcutters. Indeed much of the equipment used by each legion could be provided by its own resources. Apart from the manufacture and repair of weapons one of the main tasks involving *immunes* was the production of building materials. In the early stages of the conquest of a province, when legions were being moved from one fortress site to another, as frontiers moved forward and areas were pacified, timber formed the main building material. But from the mid-first century, with the recognition of certain sites as permanent military bases, brick, tile and stone were used in increasing quantities for building projects. Bricks and tiles bearing legionary name stamps are known from several provinces; the earliest true name stamps appeared on tiles of *Legio IV Macedonica c.* AD 45–65, at Mainz.

A number of military tileries have been discovered, with the best known examples being the works depot of *Legio XX* at Holt some 15 km (9.5 miles) upstream from Chester and that of *Legio X* at Holdeurn, near Nijmegen in Holland. Unlike most civilian establishments, both sites are characterized by long banks of tile kilns rather than isolated examples. Production was presumably on a large scale to meet the heavy demands. It is a matter of conjecture as to who did most of the work at such depots – whether mainly soldiers or perhaps civilians supervised by small numbers of military personnel. Nevertheless at Holt a bath house and barrack blocks suggest staffing by soldiers and an inscription mentioning a master clay-worker, from Dobreta in Dacia, records him as being in charge of sixty soldiers. Clearly *immunes* were gainfully employed in the production of tiles and, in some instances, pottery. But what evidence there is suggests that most military tile production took place between June and October and it is probable that outside this period those whose expertise was in tile-making returned to normal duties or took up some other specialist occupation. For the *miles gregarius*, the common soldier who did not enjoy the benefits of an *immunis*, the daily routine could include guard duty, patrolling local roads, working in the baths or general fatigues.

Of overall importance was the staff of the legionary headquarters, the *tabularium legionis*; the *librarii* (clerks) and *exacti* (accountants) who formed this body were under the charge of the *cornicularius*. Most of these men were *immunes* and each was attached to one or other of a series of *officia*, of which within the legionary organization there were several, ranging from those of the equestrian tribunes through those increasingly larger of the *praefectus castrorum*, the *tribunus laticlavius* and the *legatus legionis*. Within each *officium* were the *beneficiarii* or personal orderlies who took their seniority from that of the officer they served. Associated with the headquarters staff but outside the *officia* was the *aquilifer*, who carried the eagle and ranked next to a centurion, and also the *imaginiferi* who carried the *imagines*, standards bearing representations of the reigning and past deified emperors.

The legions were basically heavy infantry regiments who fought in close order and with rigid discipline. Their equipment reflects this function. Over a short-sleeved, knee-length woollen tunic each legionary wore a cuirass of metal strips and plates (the *lorica segmentata*) which protected the upper part of the body. The narrow strips, which enclosed the rib-cage and the plates which covered the upper parts of the chest and back were hinged at the rear and tied and buckled with leather thongs and straps at the front; further narrow strips covered the shoulders. To assist articulation the strips seem to have been fastened to one another by leather 'webbing'. Numerous examples of the *lorica segmentata* appear on Trajan's Column but it is not certain when this type of armour was first introduced. The discovery of characteristic examples of the hinges, on military sites associated with the early conquest period in Britain, suggests that it was in extensive use by the 40s. For head protection the legionary wore a bronze helmet with an iron skull plate inside for added strength. The issue of a new helmet type was also taking place in the middle of the first century AD, with the style of the helmet being improved to give greater protection to the neck, ears and cheeks. On their feet, legionaries wore heavy leather sandals made up of several thicknesses of sole studded with hobnails.

The legionaries main long-range offensive weapon was the *pilum* (Chapter 5) or javelin, of which each man carried two. Below the hardened point of the *pilum* was an untempered iron shank, fitted into a heavy wooden stock. On contact with an adversary the soft shank bent and it could not be thrown back. When the *pilum* pierced a shield it was almost impossible to remove and the shield had to be discarded leaving the enemy unprotected. For close-quarters fighting the legionary was equipped with the *gladius*, a short sword, used mainly for thrusting, which was worn on the right side. This position was necessary as the left side of each man was masked by a large, curving rectangular shield, the *scutum*, which afforded maximum protection to the body.

Constant weapons training and manoeuvres made the Roman army proficient in the use of its equipment and encouraged military skills. As Josephus says: 'Their battle-drills are no different from the real thing; every man works as hard at his daily training as if he was on active service.' On both peacetime exercises and on campaign the building of defence works was of paramount importance for:

> The Romans never lay themselves open to a surprise attack; for, whatever hostile territory they may invade, they engage in no battle until they have fortified their camp . . . if the ground is uneven, it is first levelled; a site for the camp is then measured out in the form of a square.
>
> The interior of the camp is divided into rows of tents. The exterior circuit presents the appearance of a wall and is furnished with towers at regular intervals; and on the spaces between the towers are placed 'quick-firers', catapults, 'stone-throwers', and every variety of artillery engines, all ready for use. In this surrounding wall are set four gates, one on each side, spacious enough for beasts of burden to enter without difficulty and wide enough for sallies of troops in emergencies. The camp is intersected by streets symmetrically laid out; in the middle are the tents of the officers, and precisely in the centre the headquarters of the commander-in-chief, resembling a small temple. . . . In case of need, the camp is further surrounded by a ditch four cubits deep and of equal breadth.

This description, written by Josephus in the first century, clearly illustrates how similar the temporary camp of the early imperial period was to its late Republican counterpart as described by Polybius writing in the middle of the second century BC (Chapter 5). However, there were minor differences, largely caused by organizational changes within the army itself, and the camp that impressed Josephus would have had more in common with the type described in the treatise *De munitionibus castrorum*, attributed (falsely) to Hyginus the *gromaticus* (land surveyor) and dated variously from the first to the third century AD (Frere, 1980). The Hyginian camp (Fig. 6.1), based more probably on theory than practice, was designed to hold a force of approximately 40,000 men comprised of three legions, praetorians, auxiliary cavalry and infantry, scouts and a camel corps. Unlike the square Polybian camp, that of Hyginus was rectangular in shape with rounded corners, the sides measuring 2,320 by 1,620 Roman feet. It had a rampart of earth, turf or stone some eight Roman feet wide and six feet high and was surrounded by a ditch. Inside, two main streets, running parallel to one another across the shorter axis of the camp, divided it up into three main sections.

The first of these two streets, the *via principalis* extended across the width of the camp with a gate at either end, the *porta principalis sinistra* and the *porta principalis dextra*. Two other gates set centrally in the shorter sides of the camp were the *porta praetoria*, the main gate at the front of the camp and the *porta decumana* at the rear. The *via principalis*

Figure 6.1   Plan of a Hyginian camp (*after Richmond*)

separated the central section of the camp, the *latera praetorii*, from the front part, the *praetentura*, while the other main street, the *via quintana*, separated the centre from the rear part of the fort, the *retentura*. A further road, the *via praetoria* ran from the front gate to form a T-junction with the *via principalis* while running round the entire camp inside the rampart was the *via sagularis*, giving easy access to the defences.

In the very centre of the camp, facing the *porta praetoria*, was the headquarters, the *praetorium* surrounded by the tents of the general's personal staff, praetorian troops and legionaries of the first cohort of one of the legions in garrison. In the *praetentura* were the tents of the legionary legates and tribunes together with a hospital (*valetudinarium*), a *veterinarium* for sick animals, a workshop (*fabrica*) and accommodation for legionaries and auxiliaries. The *retentura* housed the *quaestorium* of the camp prefect where the spoils of war were kept and yet more accommodation for legionary and auxiliary soldiers.

This plan, described by Hyginus as a temporary camp, was the basis for the design and organization of legionary bases when these became permanent. The army of the Republic had fought many of its campaigns in the summer months, utilizing temporary camps (*castra aestiva*), with the troops returning to their homes at the end of each season. But as these wars increasingly involved overseas conquests it became necessary for the troops to stay on to consolidate their gains. Therefore the temporary summer camps had to be supplemented by winter quarters (*hiberna*), built in territory securely under Roman control. These *hiberna* provided more substantial accommodation, especially with regard to store buildings, but still lacked the permanency associated with the fortresses of the imperial period. The change to the latter came about under Augustus, largely as a result of campaigns against the Germans across the Rhine. Between 12 BC and AD 16 the Roman army fought a series of campaigns in Germany under first Drusus then Tiberius and finally Germanicus. The size of the field of operations and the cold mid-European winters resulted in the construction of a series of substantial semi-permanent supply depots and winter bases. This trend was further strengthened in AD 9 when the general Varus was defeated in the Teutoburg forest with the loss of three legions. So profound was the shock caused by this event that Augustus advised his successor Tiberius not to extend the limits of the empire any further and so by the end of his reign the Rhine and Danube had effectively become the northern frontiers of the Roman world. As a result permanent legionary bases and auxiliary forts were established along the Rhine. By the middle of the century the distinction between the permanent base and the *hiberna* was clearly established.

Some of these early legionary bases housed two legions, as at Xanten (Vetera) in lower Germany, but usually only one. The fortresses, designed to house a single legion of 5–6,000 men were usually rectangular in shape and covered an area of approximately 20 ha (50 acres). Inside the overall effect was reminiscent of the Hyginian temporary camp, displaying a tripartite plan with the headquarters building (*principia*), now separated from the legate's house (*praetorium*), positioned at the junction of the *via principalis* and the *via praetoria*. Although sites such as Carnuntum in Austria offer an interesting exception to the general rectangular plan, a comparison of the fortress plans of Caerleon and Inchtuthil in Britain, Lambaesis in north Africa, and Neuss (Novaesium) in Lower Germany, illustrates the overall similarity of fortress design.

In frontier provinces each legion and its attendant auxiliary regiments controlled a particular military area. On the Rhine and Danube, legionary fortresses were placed close to the frontier while in Britain the eventual permanent fortresses at Caerleon, Chester and York were at some distance from the northern limits of the empire. But in both instances the legions acted as strategic reserves available as support for the more localized peace-keeping duties of the *auxilia* and capable of undertaking major punitive campaigns into hostile territory when necessary.

Augustus organized his auxiliary forces into three types of unit: the *cohors peditata*, the *cohors equitata* and the *ala*. In this early period all these units were about 500 men strong, the number in each regiment being based on that of a legionary cohort. Later in the first century AD some larger regiments of each type were created; normally 1,000 strong, these units were designated *milliaria* to differentiate them from the smaller units, henceforth called *quingenaria*. This change probably occurred in the reign of Vespasian, a view supported by the earliest epigraphic record of a milliary regiment although Josephus records the presence of such units among Vespasian's infantry in the Jewish War as early as AD 67.

The *auxilia* supplemented the legions, providing light infantry, cavalry and specialist units such archers. Much of our knowledge concerning the standard size of these regiments comes from Hyginus (*De munitionibus castrorum*), although it appears that minor variations in unit strength could occur and that numbers were not always kept up. Basically quingenary infantry units, each commanded by a *praefectus cohortis* consisted of six centuries of eighty men with an internal hierarchy similar to that in a legion. Milliary units had ten centuries. The *cohors equitata* was a unit composed of both horsemen and infantry supposedly with 380 infantry and 120 *equites* in the smaller sized unit and 760 infantry and 240 mounted men in the larger. The *ala* was a cavalry regiment and the most important of the different types of auxiliary unit; a quingenary *ala* was made up of sixteen troops (*turmae*) each thirty-two men strong and under a troop commander (*decurio*). A *praefectus alae* was the commanding officer of the regiment. The *ala milliaria*, having twenty-four *turmae*, perhaps of larger size, was much less common with no more than ten such regiments stationed throughout the empire by the second century.

In the early part of the first century some of these auxiliary cavalry regiments were officered by local chieftains from the areas where the units were raised but this was a temporary stage and soon all auxiliary units were under the command of officers from either Italy itself or the more romanized parts of southern Gaul and Spain. They were of equestrian rank and, like their senatorial counterparts, were usually following a well-defined career structure, in this case known as the *tres militae*, holding a succession of three main posts: *praefectus cohortis, tribunus militum* in a legion and finally *praefectus equitum* in charge of an *ala*. With the right patronage and a record of capable service these men might continue up the promotional ladder to become an imperial procurator, the equestrian governor of Egypt, or a praetorian prefect in charge of the emperor's bodyguard.

Conversely, the rank and file in the *auxilia* were not usually Italians and only rarely were they Roman citizens. Membership of the *auxilia* was open to any freeborn man within the Empire, providing he satisfied army requirements. The pay and conditions of service were somewhat less attractive than in the legions or the Praetorian Guard and so Roman citizens usually chose to serve in the two latter. However, even the *auxilia* provided regular pay and certain other benefits not available in civilian life and although conscription was often used, there must usually have been a steady stream of non-citizen recruits into the *cohortes* and *alae*.

In the Julio-Claudian period many of these units were raised in Gaul, Spain and Thrace. They bear a variety of titles which are usually of tribal or national origin, but may occasionally include the name of an early commander, or be of an entirely honorific nature. For example, the *ala Gallorum Indiana*, a unit raised in Gallia Lugdunensis, was named after Julius Indus who was instrumental in putting down the revolt of Julius Sacrovir in AD 21. An interesting episode concerning auxiliary recruitment in Thrace in AD 26 is recalled by Tacitus. Thrace was not finally annexed by Rome until AD 46 but had the status of a client kingdom before this and Thracian regiments seem to have served in the Roman army as early as the reign of Augustus. Tacitus records the award of an honorary triumph to Gaius Poppaeus Sabinus for suppressing Thracian mountain tribesmen who had rebelled he tells us because of 'their uncivilized and intractable temperaments, and their refusal of the conscription system which drafted their best men into our forces'. Apparently previous levies had only served in a fairly local capacity and then under their own chieftains but now they had heard that the conscripts were to be transported to other provinces. The rebels were convincingly beaten and immediately after the revolt two *alae* and seven cohorts of Thracians were dispatched to the Rhine.

This account is informative as to the character of many auxiliary regiments and Roman policy towards them. While many units were immediately 'regularized' under an equestrian commander, as late as the 60s the Rhineland Batavi were supplying troops, in lieu of tribute, to serve in units commanded by their own nobles. As with some of the early Thracian units, many of these men were stationed close to home in the lower Rhineland, but, after their involvement in the revolt of Julius Civilis, in AD 69–70, the arrangement was altered and the Batavi were organized into more standardized units, under equestrian officers, and posted to the Danube.

Both examples illustrate the gradual development in Roman thinking away from the use of 'allied forces' and towards Roman 'auxiliary regiments'. At the time of inception each unit had its own unique ethnic character, but as units were transferred from one end of the empire to the other local recruitment from the area where the unit was stationed gradually replaced that from the home area. An early example of this situation is Sextus Valerius Genialis who served and died at Cirencester (Glos.) in the pre-Flavian period. He was a trooper in a Thracian *ala* but was himself a Frisian tribesman, recruited when the unit was stationed in the Rhineland. From the time of Hadrian most recruits will have been obtained locally, and only specialist units, such as regiments of Syrian archers, seem to have made any attempt to maintain contact with the home region. Eventually, each unit, whatever its origin, will have possessed the same organization and used the same standard uniform and equipment, even though local differences in conditions will always have produced slight variations in character.

Compared with service in the legions, auxiliaries in the Augustan period received few benefits other than regular meals, pay and medical care. Augustus seems to have set no fixed term of years for service in the *auxilia*, in contrast to the legions and Praetorian Guard. Indeed, during the reign of Tiberius it was common for men to have served between thirty and forty years. One man, Tiberius Julius Rufus, serving with the *ala Scubulorum*, had been in the army for fifty years when he was discharged, probably early in the reign of Claudius.

Disturbances such as those caused by the Numidian chieftain Tacfarinas, who, Tacitus tells us, had deserted from service as a Roman auxiliary, and in Thrace, both in the reign of Tiberius, suggests that some kind of reward for service in the *auxilia* was necessary. Perhaps in response to this need, from the reign of Tiberius can be found the first large scale awards of Roman citizenship to long serving auxiliaries. Whether or not this type of award followed an Augustan precedent is difficult to ascertain due to the shortage of epigraphic evidence for the period and the move may have been prompted solely by such episodes as those above.

The much prized award of citizenship was ultimately given to most auxiliaries who had served loyally for twenty-five years or more. Even then, not all auxiliaries received the citizenship and of those who did, many had to serve well over the twenty-five year period, until Claudius regulated the length of service at thirty years and in addition fixed the number of years service needed to qualify for the award of citizenship at twenty-five. Henceforth, at the end of his term of service an auxiliary who was given an honourable discharge (*honesta missio*) received a diploma, comprising two inscribed bronze plates, which recorded his grant of citizenship and also *conubium*, the right of marriage and the legitimization of any children. The award was given to serving soldiers after twenty-five years, until the overall length of service was reduced to this term in the Flavian period, when citizenship and discharge became simultaneous. The lure of citizenship after a fixed number of years must have proved an irresistible incentive to many a potential peregrine recruit and the children of these auxiliaries, being citizens, provided the empire with further recruits for the legions.

The main purpose of the *auxilia* in battle was to provide the flexibility of action and mobility that was impossible for the heavily armed legionary infantry. Trajan's Column illustrates the dress and equipment of auxiliaries of the early second century. Many appear to wear a mail cuirass, leather trousers and a helmet. The infantry carry swords and oval shields. For the cavalry, a better idea of their appearance can be gained from the study of the series of fine first-century tombstones with sculpted rider reliefs which occur in Britain and the Rhineland (Anderson, 1984). On the tombstones of Vonatorix, a trooper of the *ala Longiniana*, at Bonn, and of Longinus, a *duplicarius* of the *ala prima Thracum*, at Colchester, both men are shown wearing scale armour cuirasses (*lorica squamata*), that of Longinus stretching down as far as his thighs. On many of these stones the troopers are shown wielding a cavalry lance and wear a long sword (*spatha*) on the right side. On the left side they carry an oval or hexagonal shield. Their equipment is usually completed by a helmet somewhat more extravagant in its design than those worn by legionaries, although those depicted may have been for use only on ceremonial parades.

There were considerable differences in the appearance of soldiers from one regiment to the next, either because of the ethnic character of some units or local climatic conditions, or because of the differing status and pay levels of the three main types of regiment. Such differences as existed between men in an *ala*, a *cohors equitata* and a *cohors peditata* is revealed quite graphically in an address by the Emperor Hadrian to the army of Numidia on the occasion of his visit to Lambaesis in AD 128. In his speech to the horsemen of *cohors VI Commagenorum equitata* he says:

'It is difficult for the cavalry of the cohorts to make a good impression even by themselves, and still harder for them not to give dissatisfaction after the exercise of the auxiliary cavalry. They have larger ground coverage, a larger number of men throwing javelins; their right wheeling is in close array, their Cantabrian manoeuvre closely knit; the beauty of their horses and the elegance of their equipment is in keeping with their level of pay. Nevertheless, and despite the heat, you avoided being tedious by doing promptly what had to be done. In addition you hurled stones from slings and fought with missiles. Your mounting was everywhere brisk.'

The possibility of a display by a *cohors equitata* being 'tedious' to Hadrian when compared to the superior abilities of the *ala* can leave no doubt as to the relative status to each other of these two types of regiment. Although evidence for auxiliary pay scales is notoriously sparse, Watson has conjectured that during the period from Domitian to Septimius Severus a trooper in an *ala* was paid 200 *denarii* per annum, his mounted counterpart in a *cohors equitata* was paid 150 *denarii*, while *pedites* received 100 *denarii*.

In battle and on the march the auxiliaries supported the legions. An example of this concord is illustrated by Josephus when he describes the progress of Vespasian and his army from Ptolemais to Galilee:

> The auxiliary light-armed troops and archers were sent in advance, to repel any sudden incursions of the enemy and to explore suspected woodland suited for the concealment of ambushes. Next came a contingent of heavy-armed Roman soldiers, infantry and cavalry. They were followed by a detachment composed of ten men from each century, carrying their own equipment and the instruments for marking out the camp; after these came the road makers to straighten the curves on the road. Behind these Vespasian posted his personal baggage and that of his legates, with a strong escort of cavalry to protect them. He himself rode behind with the pick of the infantry and cavalry and his guard of lancers. Then came the cavalry units of the legions; . . . These were followed by the mules carrying the siege towers and the other machines. Then came the legates, the prefects of the cohorts, and the tribunes, with an escort of picked troops. Next the standards surrounding the eagle . . . followed by the trumpeters, and behind them came the solid column, marching six abreast. Behind the infantry the servants attached to each legion followed in a body, conducting the mules and other beasts of burden which carried the soldiers' baggage. At the end of the column came the crowd of mercenaries, and last of all for security a rearguard composed of light and heavy infantry and a considerable body of cavalry.

Although the *auxilia* supported the legions in battle, guarding their flanks, providing cavalry charges and pursuing the beaten enemy in their flight, they were quite capable of fighting sizeable actions without legionary assistance. The battle of Mons Graupius in AD 84, the climax of Julius Agricola's campaigns in Scotland, was fought entirely by auxiliaries, with the legions lined up in front of the rampart of the Roman camp as little more than spectators.

Auxiliary regiments that displayed particular bravery in action were rewarded with certain honours. As part of a general reorganization of the army following the civil war of 68–69, Vespasian appears to have instituted the practice of awarding block grants of citizenship to auxiliary regiments who showed outstanding valour in battle. Only men who were serving in the regiment at the time of the award received citizenship by this method; subsequent recruits still had to serve for twenty-five years to qualify as before, but henceforth the unit retained the grant as a battle honour in its official title by using the suffix c.R. (*civium Romanorum*). Such awards continued into the second century. With this and other awards for bravery auxiliary units could accumulate an impressive series of titles, such as exemplified by the *ala Augusta Gallorum Petriana Milliaria* c.R. *bis torquata* which in addition to a grant of citizenship had also been awarded ceremonial torques on two occasions.

In peacetime the roles of the legions and the *auxilia* were somewhat different. Whereas the overall jurisdiction of a legion covered an extensive area, that of the auxiliary regiment was much more localized. The main roles of the auxilia involved patrolling and policing the communications routes, roads and river crossings and controlling any civil unrest which could threaten internal security.

Newly conquered territories were covered with a network of auxiliary forts situated usually along principal communication routes and often watching over centres of the indigenous population. These forts, usually built originally of turf and timber and later of stone, each housed a single regiment, although some exceptions are known. The internal area of these forts varied in size according to the garrison. A *cohors quingenaria peditata* usually required about one hectare (2.5 acres) while five (12 acres) to five and a half (13 acres) sufficed for an *ala milliaria* (Hassall, 1983). By the Flavian period most new forts were built to a standard plan, rectangular and with rounded corners, resembling a playing card. The plan was essentially a development from the temporary camp as described by Hyginus. The buildings inside conformed to a tripartite arrangement with the central range situated between the *viae principalis* and *quintana*. It contained the *principia* in the centre, flanked on one side by the *praetorium* and the other by granaries (*horrea*) and possibly a workshop (*fabrica*) or hospital (*valetudinarium*). In the *praetentura* and the *retentura* were barracks, stables and store buildings. Despite the overall standardization, no two forts were exactly the same.

The *auxilia* had originally been organized as specialized provincial troops to complement legionary functions, yet by the end of the first century AD the *alae* and *cohortes* had become so integrated into the regular army that some of their flexibility of action was diminished and particular ethnic fighting skills fell victim to standardized training methods and the lack of specialist recruits from each unit's home area. In response, new irregular units of native soldiers were recruited from the frontier zones. These units of infantry (*numeri*) and cavalry (*cunei*) were despatched to other frontier zones to provide support for auxiliary garrisons. In the early second century several *numeri* of Britons were sent to Upper Germany to man signal towers and outpost forts such as that at Hesselbach, a 0.4 ha (1.2 acres) fort containing four barrack blocks and storebuildings. Presumably the garrison here was organized into four centuries but in general little is known of the size and character of *numeri* and there may have been considerable variation in the numbers of men serving in each unit.

Conclusion

Trajan's Dacian wars brought Rome her last great haul of war booty and also marked the last successful campaign of conquest fought by the empire. Subsequent acquisitions were small-scale, short-lived and rarely viable in economic and manpower terms.

Trajan's vast new territories in the east, so easily conquered in AD 114 and 115 proved untenable and when the emperor died in August 117, his successor Hadrian immediately abandoned these Parthian territories. The expansionism that characterized Rome's rise to empire was all but finished.

To Hadrian, establishing Rome's frontiers and defending the Empire within was more important than further conquest. Not only were frontiers established but Hadrian also intended that in many areas they should be permanent and marked by substantial linear barriers, the best known of which is Hadrian's Wall in northern Britain (Part 4).

Units now stationed along these linear barriers became permanent frontier guards. Both the legions and *auxilia* were now so entrenched in their respective fortresses and forts that regiments were only rarely moved, in contrast to the practice in the first century when it was commonplace for whole legions and their auxiliary regiments to be moved from one end of the empire to the other in response to a particular crisis. Now legionary and auxiliary detachments, rather than complete units, were despatched to deal with trouble and these were supposed to return to their parent regiments when the problem had been dealt with.

In practice this brought about a virtual split in the army itself, creating a static frontier garrison on one hand and a succession of ad hoc mobile field armies on the other. As yet, this division was temporary and borne out of circumstance but that the arrangement should become permanent and formalized in the later empire was now inevitable.

CHAPTER 7

·THE·ARMY·OF·THE·LATE· ·EMPIRE·

R. S. O. Tomlin

The late-Roman army was shaped, like all the institutions of the Late Empire, by the reforms of Diocletian and Constantine; but they only completed a process that began in the second century, when the unwarlike Marcus Aurelius was forced to take personal command, to improvise field armies and promote able officers unconventionally, and to raise two new legions, because of the crisis on the frontiers. The first soldiers' emperor, Septimius Severus, despite having seen no active service until his proclamation by the Danubian legions, had a clear grasp of military needs and realities. Soldiers' marriages were legally recognized, their pay and privileges were increased, promotion was made easier into posts traditionally held by the upper classes. Severus also increased the legionary army by one-tenth, by raising three *Parthica* legions commanded, not by senatorial legates, but like the Egyptian legion by experienced officers who had already twice been a legion's leading centurion. One of these legions, the Second, was not committed to frontier defence, but was stationed near Rome, where the old Praetorian Guard was replaced by ten new cohorts of double strength recruited from legionaries. These elite forces, equivalent to three legions, with the help of cavalry that included Moors and guardsmen seconded from provincial *alae*, were the ancestors of the fourth-century *comitatenses*: a strategic reserve with which the emperor could reinforce the frontier armies – or curb them if they rebelled.

Despite the five legions added by Marcus and Severus, the Roman army lost the initiative to its new enemies. In Germany the tribes coalesced into two confederacies, the Franks on the Lower Rhine, and the Alamanns beyond the fortifications which linked the middle Rhine and upper Danube. East German peoples like the Goths and Vandals migrated southward, pressing other tribes against the Danube frontier, and threatening Dacia and the Balkans. In the east a new Persian dynasty displaced the Parthians and set about regaining Roman Mesopotamia and Syria. This war on several fronts divided the Empire's resources. In half a century, from 235 to 284, there were almost twenty emperors who could claim to be 'legitimate' by controlling Rome, not to mention all their rivals and colleagues, but somehow the Empire survived. Due credit has not always been given to Gallienus, in whose reign the Persians took Antioch and were only driven out by the initiative of a Roman protectorate, the caravan city of Palmyra, and the western provinces proclaimed their own 'Gallic' emperor. However, despite controlling little more than Italy and Africa, Gallienus, by his ill-documented reforms, forged the weapons with which his 'Illyrian' successors achieved a military renaissance. A medieval source credits him with being the first to form cavalry units, 'the Roman army having been previously largely infantry'. This is an exaggeration as independent cavalry forces had contributed to the victories of Trajan and Severus, but a cavalry army is now heard of under a single commander; and gold coins were struck at Milan to honour, and no doubt repay, 'the loyalty of the Cavalry'. These *equites* included 'Dalmatians' and 'Moors'. It is surely no coincidence that units of 'Illyrian' *equites Dalmatae* and *equites Mauri* are systematically distributed among the fourth-century frontier armies on the Danube and in the East, together with *equites Promoti* and *equites Scutarii*, also described as 'Illyrian'. They must all derive from an 'Illyrian' (i.e. Danubian) cavalry army recruited from Dalmatians, Moors, *promoti* (detached legionary cavalry) and *scutarii* (presumably they used the *scutum* shield). Mounted archers and *equites Stablesiani* (perhaps the mounted legionaries serving as governors' bodyguards) are found similarly distributed. Infantry for a field army was found by Gallienus in the usual way, by withdrawing detachments (*vexillationes*) from frontier legions, of the sort attested in north-west Macedonia (*II Parthica* and the African legion *III Augusta*) and at key points in Pannonia, the British and German legions 'with their *auxilia*' at Sremska Mitrovica (Sirmium), and at Ptuj (Poetovio) the pair from Dacia Ripensis. These detachments became virtually independent of their parent units. Base silver coins struck by Gallienus in 259–60 honoured the Praetorian Guard, the *II Parthica*, and legions on the Rhine and Danube, with the civil-war title *pia fidelis*. These coins, however, are not found on the frontiers, which Gallienus did not then control, but in northern Italy and its north-eastern approaches; they were surely paid to legionary detachments which remained loyal after their parent units proclaimed usurpers.

'Senatorial' writers are hostile to Gallienus, because a scapegoat was needed, and probably because from *c.* 260 he replaced the old legionary legates with professional officers, equestrian prefects like those of the *Parthica* legions with the title of 'acting legates'. Officers of the field army, Praetorian tribunes and even a centurion in one of the legionary detachments now received a new title, '*protector* of the Emperor'. The word *protector* is found earlier (of legionaries serving as bodyguards), but, as a result of Gallienus' innovation, would later mark an important institution of the Late Empire. However, this mark of distinction for the officer corps did not save Gallienus from a conspiracy among them which involved his successors Claudius Gothicus and

Aurelian. They and their fellow-'Illyrian' Probus were the leaders of a virtual junta of officers from the Danubian provinces where much of the army was recruited; between them they restored the empire's unity by defeating the Goths and other invaders, annexing Palmyra, and terminating the 'Gallic' empire. Roman prestige in the east was restored by the sack of the Persian capital Ctesiphon. But Aurelian, after defeating a German invasion of Italy, began to build the walls which still surround Rome: an admission that even the heart of the Empire was no longer safe from sudden attack.

Military and political stability was finally restored by Diocletian, an administrative genius who made a system out of half a century's improvisation. As his colleagues he chose better generals than himself, his fellow-'Illyrians' Maximian, Constantius and Galerius, whose loyalty and determination are embodied in a famous statue-group: the 'Tetrarchs' are carved in porphyry, one hand on another's shoulder, the other hand clutching a sword hilt (pl. 7.1). The restless energy which suppressed revolts and restored the old frontiers is echoed in the record of his travels inscribed by one of their veterans on his wife's tombstone: Aurelius Gaius, a legionary cavalryman who rose to be an *optio* in the imperial entourage, never visited Rome or Italy, but crossed the Rhine and Danube repeatedly, and served in 'India' (upper Egypt) and almost every province from Mesopotamia to Mauretania. He was also a Christian.

A Christian critic accuses Diocletian of 'quadrupling' the army – an allusion to his three colleagues; the truth seems to be that most of Severus' thirty-three legions survived, a total more or less doubled by Diocletian. Most of them were posted in the traditional pairs, but probably under strength, to the provincial armies; they were accompanied by cavalry detachments drawn apparently from the field army of Gallienus and his successors. These cavalry *vexillationes*, as they are confusingly called, even outranked the legions, let alone the surviving *alae* and cohorts, in frontier armies which were increasingly commanded by professional soldiers, *duces*, instead of provincial governors. This tendency was completed by Constantine, who made almost all posts exclusively military or civilian. However, the nucleus of a mobile army was retained. Diocletian attached two of his new legions, the *Ioviani* and *Herculiani*, originally Danubian legionaries armed with the characteristic late-Roman weighted dart (*martiobarbulus*), to his entourage, the *sacer comitatus* which 'accompanied' him. Soldiers now speak of their service 'in the *comitatus*', from which the word *comitatenses* derives. To them should be added other elite legions, like the *Solenses* and *Martenses*, named after the patron gods of Diocletian's two junior colleagues, and the *Lanciarii* (among them Aurelius Gaius), apparently picked Praetorians and legionaries armed with lances. The most senior of the fourth-century cavalry units, the *equites Promoti* and the *equites Comites*, and the first Guards units (*scholae*), seem also to have been organized by Diocletian. Nevertheless, the permanent field forces of the Tetrarchy were small by later standards, and were supplemented as required from the frontier armies. Thus an Egyptian papyrus of 295 records the issue of fodder not only to the *Comites*, but also to as many as ten pairs of legionary detachments, probably including that from Dacia Ripensis. The same two 'legions' are later found as the garrison of Diocletian's new Egyptian province of Herculea, and were presumably detachments posted there by him; the implication is that Diocletian, perhaps unlike Gallienus, did not regard legionary detachments as permanent, and returned them to garrison duties when convenient.

Diocletian also reformed the army's logistics. During the last half-century the currency had collapsed, and with it the old system of taxation; the army had requisitioned what it needed at a 'fair' price, or at none at all. Diocletian ingeniously resolved this complex of problems by levying foodstuffs, raw materials, manufactured goods (clothing, for example), in the form of taxes calculated as a percentage of the empire's estimated production. In Egypt a sullen population was urged to obey a system devised for its own benefit, without waiting for compulsion, where, according to Ammianus Marcellinus, the retired officer whose *History* is a major source of information about the fourth-century army, a tax defaulter was ashamed of himself if he did not have scars to prove it. There are vivid glimpses of the army's provisioning in two surviving fragments from the files of the deputy governor (*strategus*) at Panopolis in Egypt. The first consists of copies of letters sent out by him in September 298, many of them relating to preparations for 'the auspiciously impending visit of Our Lord the Emperor Diocletian', but also others authorizing the issue of military rations. Thus officials are ordered to pay an *ala* two months' rations of barley and wheat; the totals are given, and it is possible to calculate that the unit numbered only 116 men and their horses. The second fragment consists of copies of letters received from the *procurator* of the Lower Thebaid, many of them authorizing cash payments to military units in early 300; thus on 30 January the *procurator* wrote to the *strategus*, who received his letter on 9 February, ordering him to pay the *ala I Hiberorum* 73,500 *denarii* (pay) and 23,600 *denarii* (in lieu of rations) for the last four months of 299. The mills ground slow, but exceeding fine: the *strategus* even acknowledges a requisition for hides to repair a cavalry fort's gates, and informs the bearer that it has been 'nibbled by mice and mutilated'.

The great Diocletian abdicated in 305 and retired to a fortified palace on the Adriatic. He had dominated his colleagues, but his arrangements were upset by an usurper in Britain, Constantius' son Constantine, who in 306 emerged from 'the lands of the setting sun', as he described them later, to become sole emperor in 324 after a series of civil wars. A blitzkrieg in 312 eliminated one of his rivals, Maximian's son Maxentius, who had held Italy even against Galerius. Constantine, who had used only a fraction of his available forces, gave the credit to his new patron, the God of the Christians. More prosaically, he monopolized a new infantry unit, the *auxilium*, which was to provide the shock troops of the late-Roman army. The first *auxilia* were probably raised by his father or Maximian, the *Cornuti* or 'horned men' who seem to be depicted on his Arch at Rome (pl. 7.2), and the 'armlet wearers', the *Bracchiati*. Later we find them and another crack *auxilium* pair, the *Iovii* and *Victores*, raising a Germanic war cry before they charge. There is good reason to suppose that the formidable new *auxilia* were raised and recruited from Rhine-Germans, whether volunteers or prisoners-of-war, or young men from the *laeti* settlements of submissive Germans established by Diocletian and his colleagues on derelict land in Gaul.

Constantine also raised new legions, but a more important source of new 'mobile' units were the existing frontier legions and the garrisons of other strategic points. Legionary detachments were withdrawn for good: some of them kept their old name, like the *Quinta Macedonica*, the longest-lived of all legions (it was still part of Justinian's army in the sixth century); others took numerical names, like *Primani* or *Undecimani*, or names from a previous station, like the *Divitenses*, which had been a detachment of *II Italica* stationed at the Cologne bridgehead of Divitia. 'Paired' with them are the *Tungrecani*, which had presumably been the garrison of Tongres (Tungri). The old Praetorian Guard was disbanded, no doubt because it had fought for Maxentius, but also because it was now obsolete: there was a new mobile army. The role of imperial guards was now filled by the *scholae*, crack cavalry units 500-strong (at least in the sixth century), of which there were a dozen by the end of the fourth century. They were followed by cavalry *vexillationes* like the elite *Comites* and *Promoti*, others drawn from the same sources as the new infantry (*equites Cornuti*, etc.), and many with titles also found in the frontier armies (*Dalmatae, Scutarii*, etc.) which recall the cavalry army of Gallienus. Some of the latter belong to numbered sequences, like the well-paid trooper of *VI Stablesiani* who disappeared with his silver helmet (pl. 7.3) into a Dutch swamp in *c.* 320, or carry titles which recall a time in garrison (*equites Dalmatae Passerentiaci*). The likeliest explanation is that these are frontier units taken from Gallienus' cavalry army, which were withdrawn once more by Constantine to swell a mobile army.

The converse of these *comitatenses* were the *limitanei*, so called because they garrisoned forts and fortified towns in the frontier zone (*limes*). They consisted of old-style legions, *alae* and cohorts, and new-style units of *equites* (sometimes reduced to *cunei* on the Danube) and infantry mostly called *auxiliares* or *milites*. The evidence is still being accumulated, but they seem to have been much smaller, as well as differently equipped, than their counterparts in the early Empire. They were grouped administratively into armies covering one or more provinces, commanded by a *dux*, except in most of Africa, where the frontier sectors, chiefly mountain massifs or semi-desert tracts, were allotted to *praepositi* supervised by a *comes* with a powerful mobile army (Part 4, Chapter 10). The fourth-century 'order of battle' on the frontiers can be recovered from the enigmatic *Notitia Dignitatum*, an illustrated handbook of high offices dating from *c.* 395, which survives in several later copies (pls 7.4 and 7.5); unfortunately its interpretation presents many problems; thus the garrison of Hadrian's Wall seems to have survived almost intact from the early third century, whereas that of the Mainz sector cannot be earlier than *c.* 368. The *Notitia*'s purpose is also disputed, but an attractive idea is that it was compiled in its present form for the convenience of the staff of the western commander-in-chief (*magister peditum praesentalis*) which levied fees for issuing officers with their commissions. Among the entries is *ala V Praelectorum, Dionisiada*, the command of a cavalry unit at Dionysias in the Egyptian Fayûm. This was a typically massive Diocletianic fort with projecting towers and walls four metres thick: since any external threat was remote, its strength suggests a defensive mentality and a ruthless application of general principles. The commandant in the 340s, Flavius Abinnaeus, is better known to us than to most of his contemporaries, since by happy chance his papers have survived. The first is a draft petition to the eastern emperor, Constantine's son Constantius II, in which he complains that when he presented his 'sacred letter' of appointment, he was told that similar letters had already been presented by other men. Theirs had been obtained illicitly, whereas Abinnaeus had been appointed after an audience with the emperor; fortunately he was confirmed in his appointment (*c.* 342). The letters he received contain vivid glimpses of the 'police' duties of *limitanei*. 'Your valiance, my lord *praepositus*, is wont to restrain the robberies and usurpations committed in the localities by the more influential men', writes one petitioner. (Abinnaeus, a soldier of some 40 years' experience, who also owned house rents in Alexandria and farm stock of his own, is clearly one of the ubiquitous 'patrons' of late-Roman society.) He receives appeals from the victims of burglaries, from people who have had sheep or pigs stolen. One of his own men is alleged to have been drunken and violent; another to have led a gang which stole the wool off eleven sheep's backs and drove off six pigs. A clergyman intercedes for a soldier who has deserted; Abinnaeus should exercise his Christian duty of forgiveness. Another clergyman asks for a loan of the nets kept at headquarters, to catch gazelles which have been eating the crops. Official letters require Abinnaeus to provide escorts for tax collectors, to look after two craftsmen cutting timber for a cavalry *vexillatio*, to help control the illicit trade in soda. These intriguing documents illustrate the integration of a garrison with the local community, not the old-fashioned idea that *limitanei* were only hereditary peasant militias. This is amply refuted by Ammianus' eye-witness account of the siege of Amida (359): the frontier-legions trapped by the Persians in a fortified town on the Tigris fought with skill and tenacity. Four years later, *limitanei* from the neighbouring province of Osrhoene shared in the Emperor Julian's invasion of Persia, and shortly afterwards units like the *I* and *II Armeniaca* legions, made redundant by surrender of territory beyond the Tigris, were incorporated in the mobile army of the east under the cumbersome title of *legiones pseudocomitatenses*.

The essential difference between *limitanei* and *comitatenses* was that the latter, though they might have families, did not have fixed stations. If they were not on active service, they were billeted in towns, where they were entitled to one-third of available accommodation, an arrangement that caused friction with their civilian 'hosts'. We hear, however, of one saving his guest's life in a mutiny, and of another who was bequeathed his guest's property. *Comitatenses*, as their name implied, were ideally at the emperor's immediate disposal. A commentary on the 119th Psalm takes the route march as a metaphor of the text, 'Teach me, O Lord, the way of thy statutes; and I shall keep it to the end.' The men marched to a prescribed itinerary, with food and lodging arranged in advance, and regular rest-days, 'until they reach the imperial capital of the moment, where the weary armies find rest'. Constantine reorganized the high command by transferring the Praetorian Prefect's military authority to a Master of Cavalry (*magister equitum*) and a Master of Infantry (*magister peditum*) attached to his court, the Prefect remaining responsible for provision and supply. In practice the command of *comitatenses* could not be so centralized. We soon find regional mobile armies, the most important being those of Gaul, the Danubian provinces, and the east, based on Antioch, each of them commanded by its own Master of Cavalry. Smaller mobile forces were detached as required, usually under the command of a count (*comes*), like the four units sent to Britain in 367 when the frontiers collapsed. Africa seems always to have had its own mobile army, strong in cavalry as one would expect, and by the time of the *Notitia* there were others in Britain, Spain and Thrace. Theodosius I grouped the eastern forces into five armies, two of them at his immediate disposal, and all of them commanded by a Master of Soldiers (*magister militum*). He thus avoided what happened in the west from the 380s, where a single commander-in-chief, notably Stilicho during 395–408, dominated the government.

By using the *Notitia* lists, many of whose units can be roughly dated, and a variety of other sources, we can make some rough guesses about the strength of the late-Roman army. Valentinian I at his accession may have divided about 150 mobile units with his brother Valens, if we ignore the African army. By the end of the century, this total seems to have doubled; about one-third were cavalry. Unfortunately these are paper figures. The Spanish army, for example, numbers sixteen units, all infantry, strangely enough; yet we hear nothing of it when there was fighting there in 407 and later. Worse still, we know very little about unit strengths. The Diocletianic *ala* of 116 men has already been mentioned; the same source suggests that there were 77 troopers in a legion's *equites promoti*, 121 in a unit of *equites sagittarii*, 164 men in the *cohors XI Chamavorum*, and about 1,000 in each of two legions. In 359 two Danubian cavalry units on service in Mesopotamia totalled 700 men; but in Libya in the early fifth century a cavalry unit of 'Unnigardae' numbered only 40. Ammianus twice mentions detachments of 300 men from unspecified mobile units, once 500 from 'legions'. The emperor Honorius is said to have withdrawn five units from Dalmatia which totalled 6,000 men; six infantry units, however, sent to his aid from the east, totalled only 4,000. The impression one gains from these and other scraps of evidence is that mobile infantry units may have been between 500 and 1,000 men strong, and cavalry units well below 500. Careful study of their forts may tell us something of the strength of frontier units. The legions at least were only shadows; *III Italica*, for example, garrisoned four forts and its old fortress, as well as providing a 'legion' for the nearest mobile army. This impression of small-sized units is reinforced by Julian's self-congratulation at taking 1,000

German prisoners 'in two battles and a siege'; in the siege, which lasted two months, 600 Franks were starved out of their refuge in two derelict forts, and sent to Constantius II for service in the eastern army. Julian's army in 357 numbered only 13,000 men; in 363, with the whole Empire to draw upon, and no other commitments, his two armies for the invasion of Persia totalled only 65,000 men. These are figures for first-rate troops, of course, and represent a fraction only of the paper strength; we get some idea of this from two sixth-century figures, one for Diocletian's army at an unspecified date of 389,704, and an estimate for 'the old empire' of 645,000.

Paper strengths were just that, and no more, when it came to fighting; but multiplied by pay and rations, they represent the cost of the army to the civil population. Late-Roman soldiers did not have to pay for their arms and equipment and uniforms, which were mostly manufactured in state factories. They were also issued with rations which increased as they rose in rank: it was suggested to Valentinian and Valens that it might be worth retiring men who had achieved quintuple rations, to save expense and encourage recruitment. This payment in kind was supplemented by the regular salary (*stipendium*) paid in the bronze small change minted in vast quantities during the fourth century, and by donatives paid by the emperor on accession and at five-year intervals. The accession donative became standardized in 360 as a pound of silver and five gold pieces (*solidi*) (pl. 7.6), and five *solidi* thereafter. Imperial gifts to officers were also manufactured: inscribed silver plate (pl. 7.7), gold and silver 'medallions', gold and silver belt-fittings and brooches as marks of rank.

These terms were generous in an Empire where most of the population lived at subsistence level, yet there was some difficulty in finding enough recruits. Diocletian enforced the tradition that sons followed their fathers into the army, and in addition levied recruits from landowners as a kind of tax. Valentinian reduced the height qualification from 5 ft 10 in (Roman) to 5 ft 7 in; he found some men liable to military service were mutilating themselves, while others were harboured by his own soldiers under the guise of 'relatives' or 'servants'. Among Abinnaeus' correspondence is a clergyman's plea for his brother-in-law, the son of a deceased soldier and the sole support of his widowed mother, who has been conscripted: release him, or at least 'safeguard him from going abroad with the draft for the *comitatus*, and may God reward you for your charity'. It was the charity of Christians that made a convert of the future monk Pachomius, when he was a young conscript on his way to the *comitatus* in 324: he and his fellows were locked up every night for fear they deserted. Not surprisingly, therefore, the army also recruited non-Romans, mostly Germans. Some were prisoners-of-war like Julian's 600 Franks, but many were volunteers attracted by a much higher standard of living. They might even rise to high rank: one of Valens' generals was an Alamann king who had been kidnapped at a dinner party by order of Julian; the great Stilicho himself was the son of a Vandal cavalry officer. Frankish-born officers at the court of Constantius II in 355 protested that they were 'men devoted to the Empire', and it is noteworthy that we almost never hear of treachery by German-born soldiers. They seem to have been assimilated with fair success, something that changed after the defeat of Adrianople (378), when a desperate shortage of fighting men forced the Roman government to enlist barbarian contingents (*federati*) under their own chieftains. These did not have the same feeling of 'belonging', and after 395 became increasingly aware of their political and military power, which they used to extort subsidies and land from their reluctant hosts.

A recruit rose slowly, by seniority within his unit. A Christian writer uses the non-commissioned ranks as a metaphor of the gulf between a demon and an angel: recruit, trooper (*eques*), *circitor, biarchus, centenarius, ducenarius, senator, primicerius*, commanding officer (*tribunus*). A late-Roman cemetery at Concordia in north-east Italy contained the expensive stone coffins of about thirty non-commissioned officers and privates from the mobile army: they include a *biarchus* of twenty years' service, a *centenarius* (twenty-two), two *ducenarii* (twenty and twenty-three), two *senatores* aged forty and sixty, and the drill-master (*campidoctor*) of the *Batavi seniores*, who died after thirty-five years' service at the age of sixty. Abinnaeus was a *ducenarius* of thirty-three years' service in a cavalry *vexillatio* before a special mission took him to court, where he 'adored the Sacred Purple'. By kissing the hem of Constantius' garment, he automatically became a *protector domesticus*: the *protectores* from the reign of Diocletian were a kind of staff college in which senior NCOs prepared for regimental commands. After three years Abinnaeus became the prefect of an *ala*, when he found his competitors had used influence to take a short-cut. Thus the senior member (*primicerius*) of the *protectores* in 363 was the future emperor Jovian, at the age of thirty-two – it can be no coincidence that his father was a senior general, the *comes domesticorum*. Ammianus himself, who was a *protector* in his early twenties, must also have had connections. By contrast, Flavius Memorius, the *comes* of the Tangiers army, had served twenty-eight years in the *Ioviani* before he became a *protector*. The future emperor Valentinian, however, was already commanding a mobile *vexillatio* at the age of thirty-six, and the future emperor Theodosius was a *dux* at the age of about twenty-eight. Both were the sons of generals: Valentinian's father Gratianus, like Memorius, is one of the few private soldiers to achieve the rank of *comes*.

Gratianus also achieved a country estate, but most recruits, if they survived twenty to twenty-five years' service, received much less than a legionary of the early Empire. Veterans were encouraged to cultivate derelict land, for which they received a small grant. They also received some tax concessions, including a limited exemption from the five-yearly tax on commerce which was used to pay the donatives of their old comrades-in-arms. Some veterans were men of substance: one, described as a 'land-owner', asks Abinnaeus to arrest some local officials, so as to make them produce persons guilty of house-breaking; a veteran's daughter, another 'landowner', requests action against a debtor who has beaten her up with the help of the village policeman when she demanded the money he owed her; a veteran promises to reimburse Abinnaeus for any money he may have to spend at court to secure the promotion of his son within the local *ala*.

Constantine, in a speech to a restive gathering of his 'fellow veterans', promised them undisturbed leisure after their labours. Intelligent emperors advertised their closeness to their men. Julian, the 'sport' of the Constantinian dynasty, who repudiated his uncle's religious faith, none the less swallowed porridge 'even a common soldier would have despised'. Stories were told of both Constantius II and Theodosius begging a crust of bread in a moment of crisis. The dour Valentinian, leading a flying column somewhere near modern Frankfurt, slept in the open under a blanket. His son Gratian, however, lost touch with his army by a passion for hunting and favouritism for a particular unit; his men abandoned him for Magnus Maximus, the general in Britain, whose first coins, struck in London to pay his first supporters, pointedly imitated the coin portrait of Valentinian. The survival of the sons of Theodosius, therefore, Arcadius and Honorius, is all the more surprising, since they reigned as figureheads without military ability or interest; a critic compares Arcadius in the eunuch-haunted depths of his palace with a deep-sea mollusc. The army was the ultimate, though not the only, source of political power and public security. This was symbolized in the accession ceremonies. Valentinian, for example, after being chosen in conclave by the generals and ministers of state, was presented to the army: he was clothed in purple, crowned, and acclaimed as *Augustus*; lifted on a shield, he was about to speak when the army interrupted him with a demand for a joint-emperor; Valentinian reprimanded them, delivered his prepared speech, and left for his palace 'hedged in by eagles and standards, already an object of fear'. Ammianus gives a splendid picture of Constantius II, a conscientious but ungifted general with the reputation of winning civil wars and losing foreign ones, making his state entry into Rome. He rode by himself in a golden carriage glittering with jewels, with purple silk snake standards (pl. 7.8) hissing in the breeze overhead. Armoured infantry and *clibanarii*, cavalry that looked like moving statues, marched either side. Amidst a storm of applause Constantius gazed stonily in front of him, moving his head only to bow as the carriage passed under an arch. The emperor in his full robes or battledress, flanked by his guards, was a favourite motif in late-Roman art, found on silver dishes, reliefs and mosaics, and in illuminated books. More than eighty years before Constantius' entry into Rome (357), Aurelian overawed a German delegation by receiving it on a platform with his army drawn up in a crescent on either side; his generals rode their horses, and behind them were the imperial standards, 'golden eagles, pictures of the emperor, the names of regiments picked out in gilt letters, all of them on silver-plated lances'.

The fourth-century army on campaign tried to live up to the standards of the early empire. Ammianus makes rhetorical complaints about its indiscipline – Valentinian's flying column gave itself away by looting and raising fires – but on the whole this is belied by his narrative. The *comitatenses*, given good leadership, would fight tenaciously and usually with success against odds. What we hear of the maintenance of discipline may not be typical. The antiquarian-minded Julian distributed wreaths after a victory at the gates of Ctesiphon; he also 'decimated' a cavalry unit, a punishment he may have misunderstood, since he selected ten victims, not a tenth. Valentinian revived another ancient punishment, according to an unreliable source, by making the *Batavi* encamp outside the fortifications. His general Theodosius, father of the emperor, treated disloyal African units very harshly; cavalry officers had their hands lopped off, the survivors of a legion were clubbed to death 'in the ancient fashion', deserters were burnt alive or lost their hands. Ammianus, who normally condemns cruelty when he finds it, seems embarrassed at having to defend this 'salutary vigour', and quotes a criticism of these 'savage innovations'. Late-Roman legislation, it is true, is full of such threats, but trained *comitatenses* were too valuable to be treated with indiscriminate brutality. Reading Ammianus, one is struck by their esprit de corps and the survival of old skills. They still entrenched themselves in marching camps with palisades and built permanent forts in stone. They were expected to carry twenty days' rations. They bridged the Rhine, Danube and Euphrates by pontoon bridges, and handled small boats skilfully enough to make night-landings in Alamannia or to hunt down Sarmatians in the Danube marshes. Julian mustered 500 men 'who from early childhood were taught in their native lands to cross the greatest of all rivers', like the Batavians of the early Empire; after they had secured a bridgehead across the Tigris, the rest of the army followed on rafts, or by using the local method of inflated animal skins.

The *comitatenses* were thus at least comparable with the auxiliaries of the early empire, the soldiers who defeated the Caledonians at Mons Graupius. In 357 Julian, with an army of only 13,000, confronted an Alamann host of 35,000 near Strasbourg, but his men and their generals were confident of winning. The Roman cavalry was massed on the right wing, opposed by Alamann cavalry stiffened by light infantry, a tactic which Caesar had learnt from their ancestors the Suebi. When the armies met, a tribune of armoured cavalry (*catafracti*) was wounded, and the Roman cavalry fell back upon the infantry in disorder. (After the battle Julian is said to have humiliated the unit concerned by parading it in female clothing.) The Alamann infantry now made a series of charges, culminating in one by 'a fiery band of tribal nobility including kings', which cut its way to the *Primani*; but this legion stood its ground like the infantry 'wall' recommended by the military theorist Vegetius, and the Alamanns faltered and gave way, suffering heavy loss in their retreat to the Rhine. There was something ominous about this Roman victory – the poor showing of the cavalry. This is a striking feature of Julian's Persian campaign, even though the *Notitia* and other sources make it clear that cavalry was regarded as the senior service. In the advance to Ctesiphon, Julian twice punished cavalry units which had broken when caught by surprise, the first by 'decimation', the second by reducing them to infantry, 'which is more laborious and lower in rank'. Shortly afterwards the infantry actually complained of the *Tertiaci*, which had given way as the infantry was penetrating the Persian line: they were made to march with the camp followers, and four other cavalry tribunes were cashiered.

The battle of Adrianople (9 August 378), the Black Day of the late-Roman army, has been seen as a victory of cavalry over infantry and a revolution in warfare. Limited offensives had failed to contain the Goths who had overrun the Balkans, so the Eastern Emperor Valens decided to mobilize his full force and to assume active command. Unfortunately he decided to fight before his nephew Gratian arrived with the western army, perhaps because he was jealous of him, or because faulty intelligence had underestimated Gothic numbers. As at Strasbourg, the Roman army made a long march in the heat of the day and arrived, hungry and thirsty, within sight of the Gothic wagon circle. There was a delay while the Goths renewed negotiations, if only to gain time for the return of their cavalry which was out foraging. Meanwhile the Roman army advanced in column, its right wing almost engaged, the left wing still coming up as fast as it could. A truce was being negotiated, when some Roman cavalry, presumably on the right wing, made an insubordinate attack which collapsed. Fighting became general, and at this moment the Gothic cavalry arrived. Ammianus, whose narrative ekes out some vital facts with masses of 'colour', unfortunately does not say where its first blow fell, only that the Roman left wing had now reached the wagons, when 'it was deserted by the rest of the cavalry, overwhelmed by weight of numbers like a collapsing rampart, and thrown back, leaving the infantry exposed'. Thus outflanked, the Roman infantry was enveloped, 'they looked round and saw no means of escape', its line was broken in a bloody mêlée, and the survivors were pursued until darkness fell. Two-thirds of the army was killed. The losses were equalled only by Cannae (216 BC), Ammianus comments. Here too the Roman cavalry had been driven from the field, and the legions enveloped and crushed. The prime cause of disaster at Adrianople would seem to have been the decision to assault a field fortification, which is what the wagon circle virtually was, while the enemy's powerful cavalry was uncommitted. This 'decision' was forced upon Valens by the undisciplined and incompetent cavalry on his right wing. The left wing, advancing hastily, was caught unprepared by a devastating charge on its flank or even from behind, leaving the infantry, already deployed in a crescent round the wagon circle and fighting hand-to-hand, trapped. We know that there were post-mortems after the disaster, and that cowardice or lack of training was held responsible. This would seem to be a fair comment – on the Roman cavalry which lost the battle.

The trained infantry lost at Adrianople could not be replaced. The new emperor Theodosius, whose descendants were figurehead emperors of east and west until the mid-fifth century, was forced to settle the Goths in the Danubian provinces under their own chieftains. When he died in 395, they were soon on the move again – westward, against an empire already weakened by civil wars. For a time Stilicho (pl. 7.9), one of Theodosius' generals and the guardian of his son Honorius the new western emperor, kept them in check, but he was fatally discredited by the collapse of the Rhine frontier at the end of 406, when east German peoples, followed by the Alamanns and Franks, flooded across Gaul and Spain. Surviving garrisons were incorporated in the mobile army, a desperate expedient. The Visigoths invaded Italy; when their demands were ignored by Honorius, they sacked Rome (410). Effective power was in the hands of the western commanders-in-chief, notably Constantius, Aetius and Ricimer, who tried to retain Italy and a few footholds by playing one barbarian people off against another, but the last real hope of recovery disappeared in 429, when the Vandals crossed the Straits of Gibraltar, to pursue an orgy of conquest across the last intact western provinces. In 444 Valentinian III, the grandson of Theodosius, admitted economic and military bankruptcy; the taxpayers were exhausted, and could no longer provide the army with food and clothing:

> Unless the soldiers should be supported by trading, which is unworthy and shameful for an armed man, they can scarcely be vindicated from the peril of hunger or from the destruction of cold ... [yet] if we require these expenses from the landowner, in addition to the expenses which he furnishes, such an exaction of taxes would extinguish his last tenuous resources.

When Valentinian was murdered in 455, the Vandals descended on Rome and sacked it again. The eastern Empire survived the fifth-century crisis: it was economically stronger, and its territory except in Europe was almost free of invasion. It even intervened from time to time in the west, but without lasting effect. The western Empire, however, was bleeding to death as it lost the territory which alone could support a regular army, and was forced to rely more and more upon barbarian *federati*. Not long before the now-barbarian army of Italy deposed the last western emperor (476), we catch a glimpse of the last *limitanei* on the upper Danube. The *cohors IX Batavorum*, the garrison of Passau, sent some men to draw back-pay for the unit. No more was heard of them, until their bodies came floating down the river. When Abinnaeus' old fort was evacuated, the last troops even closed the gate behind them; but the *Batavi* simply melted into the civilian population. 'While the Roman Empire still stood,' our source comments, 'soldiers were maintained with public pay in many towns for the defence of the frontier, but when that custom lapsed the military units were abolished with the frontier.'

A pagan critic of Constantine accuses him of reversing the strategy of Diocletian, which had made the frontiers impregnable: most of the army was withdrawn from the frontiers and stationed in cities which did not need a garrison, a burden for the cities concerned, and demoralizing for the men themselves. This is a wilful misunderstanding of the strategy of the late-Roman Empire. It was impossible to hold the frontier line against all attack, since external enemies retained the initiative and could always concentrate superior forces locally. Instead, the screen of garrisons in the frontier zone would, at least in theory, check minor incursions, and hinder major invasions by holding fortified towns and supply-bases, and strongpoints of all kinds along the lines of communication. This would protect the civil population (tax-payers, if nothing else), deny food to the enemy, and gain time to concentrate mobile forces for counter-attack. The invaders would either be forced to disperse over the countryside to forage, where they could be hunted down piecemeal by small mobile detachments; or if they massed together, they could be brought to battle, when the Roman mobile army, better armed and disciplined and regularly provisioned, had a good chance of winning against numerical odds. Once defeated in the field, invaders could be pursued into their homeland, and reprisals would follow until they made peace. For the emperor himself, this strategy had an important side-effect: he could retain personal control of the Empire's best troops and insure himself against usurpers. The strategy also had its weaknesses. Much depended, as always in Roman imperial history, on the emperor's ability and the loyalty it commanded. Slowness of communications – no army, however 'mobile', could move faster than its infantry could march – led to the multiplication of mobile armies; this shortened the Empire's reaction time, but divided its strength and increased the risk of an usurpation. Despite the premium on mobility, the Romans still failed, as they had always done, to achieve a decisive superiority over their enemies in cavalry. Inactive troops, whether they were *limitanei* or *comitatenses* in reserve, were always liable to deteriorate. For a complex of reasons, such as the number and variety of its enemies, the aspects of its social system that we loosely call 'corruption', and the economic burden of filling so many 'idle mouths', the late-Roman Empire lacked the reserves to recover, as the Republic had done after Cannae, from a major defeat. But even if we overlook the survival of East Rome, we must credit Diocletian, Constantine and Valentinian with achieving a military equilibrium that might once have seemed beyond hope.

7.1 Diocletian and his colleagues. A porphyry statue group now standing outside St Mark's Cathedral, Venice. They wear generals' cloaks over battle-dress, the 'Pannonian' undress leather cap of the late-Roman army, and are armed with swords carrying imperial eagles' heads on the handles

7.2 Arch of Galerius, Thessalonika. Galerius is in general's uniform and addresses armoured cavalrymen (*catafracti*) wearing scale armour and conical helmets; a lion (now lost) and an eagle appear on two shields; flags (*vexilla*) and snake (*draco*) battle-standards fly overhead

7.3 Cavalry helmet, *c.* 320, of iron and silver-gilt, belonging to a trooper of the *equites VI Stablesiani*. Found near Deurne, Holland, together with other clothing and equipment and 37 Constantinian coins

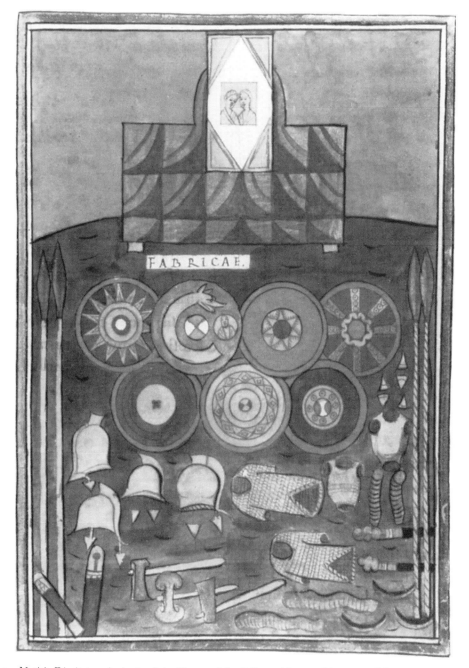

7.4 *Notitia Dignitatum*: insignia of the Master of the Offices. After 390 his responsibilities included the arms factories (*fabricae*); hence the decorated shields, lances, helmets, and armour

7.5 *Notitia Dignitatum*: insignia of the Count of the Sacred Largesses. His responsibilities included the mints, whose workmen evidently also produced gold belt-fittings (buckles, plates, strap-ends), palm-branches and silver donative dishes

7.6 The accession donative of five *solidi* of Valens, Valentinian I and Gratian, and a pound of silver

7.7 Silver and silver-gilt dish of Constantius II, weighing two pounds. Victory offers a wreath and palm-branch. The bodyguard carries a shield bearing a Chi-Rho. The emperor wears the diadem and a belted tunic, but no cloak; he is armed with a sword and lance

7.8 Snake (*draco*) battle-standard, of gilded bronze, 30 cm (12 in.) long, found at the German *limes* fort at Niederbieber. The windsock was attached at the end

7.9 Ivory diptych, *c.* 396, of Stilicho in uniform as *magister peditum praesentalis*, with his wife and son. His general's cloak is pinned with a 'crossbow' brooch; his shield carries miniature busts of the emperors

7.10 Glass beaker from Cologne, engraved with four late-Roman soldiers, each armed with two lances and a decorated oval shield

7.11 Fourth–fifth-century Christian cemetery at Concordia. The sarcophagi, as excavated in 1893, comprise the largest known collection of epitaphs of late-Roman soldiers

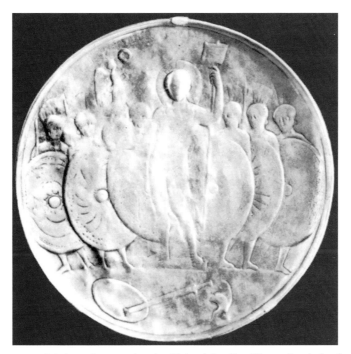

7.12 Silver donative dish from Geneva, showing Valentinian (I or II) standing in battle-dress holding the *labarum* and an orb with Victory, flanked by guardsmen holding oval shields: the shield designs, especially the opposed animal heads, resemble those in the *Notitia Dignitatum*

7.13 Letter-book from Panopolis. File-copies of letters sent out by the *procurator* of the Lower Thebaid, *c.* 300, directing payment of donatives to a legionary vexillation and the *equites promoti* of *Legio II Traiana*

7.14 Silver donative dish of Theodosius I, dated to 388; his son and colleague Arcadius, with two Germanic guardsman, wearing torques and carrying decorated shields, are illustrated

7.15 Honorius in battle-dress on an ivory diptych dated to 406. The timid emperor wears a muscle cuirass and is armed with an imperial eagle's head-handled sword. He holds the *labarum* and is attended by Victory

7.16 Part of the tombstone from Phrygia on which a retired NCO of Diocletian's mobile army recorded his travels from one end of the Empire to the other

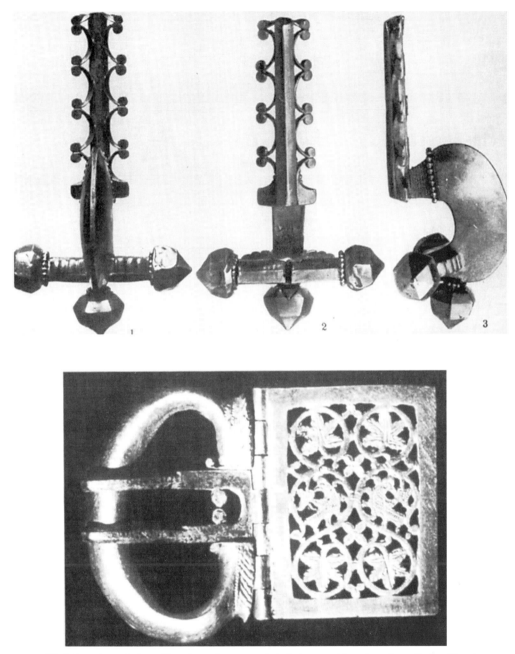

7.17 Ténès hoard consisting of four brooches, seven belt fittings, and four bracelets, all of gold and worn by an officer, from Cartenna, Mauritania Caesariensis: (a) gold crossbow brooch like that worn by Stilicho and his son; (b) gold belt-buckle like that in the insignia of the Count of the Sacred Largesses

·BIBLIOGRAPHY·FOR·PART·3·

Anderson, A. S. (1984), *Roman Military Tombstones*, Prince's Risborough.

Bell, H. I. *et al.* (1962), *The Abinnaeus Archive*, Oxford.

Birley, E. (1966), 'Alae and cohortes milliariae', in *Corolla Memoriae Eric Swoboda dedicata*, Graz.

Breeze, D. (1971), 'Pay grades and ranks below the centurionate', *Journal of Roman Studies*, LXI, 134, note 52.

Duncan-Jones, R. P. (1978), Analysis of T. C. Skeat (ed.), *Papyri from Panopolis*, 1964, in *Chiron*, 8.

Frere, S. S. (1980), 'Hyginus and the First Cohort', *Britannia*, XI, 51–60.

Gabba, E. (1949), 'Le origini dell'esercito professionále in Roma: i proletari e la reforma di Mario', *Athenaeum*, XXVII, 173–209.

Gabba, E. (1951), 'Richerche sull'esercito professionále da Mario ad Augusto', *Athenaeum*, XXIX, 171–272.

Goodburn, R. and Bartholomew, P. (eds) (1976), *Aspects of the Notitia Dignitatum*, British Archaeological Reports, S75, Oxford.

Grimes, W. F. (1930), 'The works depot of the XXth Legion at Holt', *Y Cymmrodor*, 41.

Grosse, R. (1920), *Römische Militärgeschichte von Gallienus bis zum Beginn der byzantinischen Themenverfassung*, Berlin.

Harmand, J. (1967), *L'armée et le soldat à Rome de 107 à 50 avant notre ère*, Paris.

Hassall, M. (1983), 'The internal planning of Roman auxiliary forts' in B. Hartley and J. S. Wacher (eds), *Rome and her Northern Frontiers*, Gloucester.

Heurgon, J. (1973), *The Rise of Rome to 246 B.C.*, London.

Hoffmann, D. (1969/70), *Das Spätrömische Bewegungsheer*, Dusseldorf.

Holder, P. A. (1980), *The Auxilia from Augustus to Trajan*, Oxford.

Holwerda, J. H. and Breat, W. C. (1946), *De Holdeurn bij Berg en Dal: centrum van pappenbakkernj en aardswerkindustrie in den Romeinschen tijd*, Nijmegen.

Ireland, R. and Hassall, M. W. C. (eds) (1979), *de Rebus Bellicis*, British Archaeological Reports, S63, Parts I and II, Oxford.

Johnson, S. (1983), *Late Roman Fortifications*, London.

Jones, A. H. M. (1964), *The Later Roman Empire, 284–602*, Cambridge.

Lammert, F. (1937), In *Realencyclopädie* XVII s.v. *Ocreae* col. 1778.

Lewis, N. and Reinhold, M. (1966), *Roman Civilisation,* II, No. 153, New York.

Luttwak, E. N. (1976), *The Grand Strategy of the Roman Empire*, Baltimore/London.

MacMullen, R. (1963), *Soldier and Civilian in the Later Roman Empire*, Harvard/Oxford.

Macrae, M. (1947), 'Note au sujet des briqueteries en Dacie', *Dacia*, 11–12, 275–80.

Mattingly, H. (1937), 'The property qualifications of the Roman classes', *Journal of Roman Studies*, 99ff.

Parker, H. M. D. (1928), *The Roman Legions*, Oxford (reprinted 1958).

Robinson, H. R. (1975), *Armour of Imperial Rome*, London.

Robinson, H. R. (1976), *What the Soldiers wore on Hadrian's Wall*, Newcastle-upon-Tyne.

Saddington, D. B. (1982), *The Development of the Roman Auxiliary Forces from Caesar to Vespasian (49 B.C.–A.D. 79)*, *Proceedings of the African Classical Association*, XV, 20–58.

Scullard, A. A. (1980), *A History of the Roman World 753 to 146 B.C.*, fourth edition, 30f, London.

Scullard, A. A. (1982), *From the Gracchi to Nero*, London.

Skeat, T. C. (ed.) (1964), *Papyri from Panopolis*, London.

Smith, R. E. (1958), *Service in the Post-Marian Roman Army*, Manchester.

Veith, G. (1928), *Meerwesen und Kriegführung der Griechen und Romer*, ed. Kromayer-Veith, 320–1, Munich.

Walbank, F. W. (1967), *A Historical Commentary on Polybius*, vol. 1, 698, Oxford.

Watson, G. R. (1958), 'The pay of the Roman army', in *Historia* VII, 113–20.

Watson, G. R. (1959), 'The pay of the Roman army', in *Historia* VIII, 372–8.

Watson, G. R. (1969), *The Roman Soldier*, London.

Watson, G. R. (1970), 'Crowns and wreaths', in *OCD*, second edition, Oxford.

Webster, G. (1969), *The Roman Imperial Army*, London.

Webster, G. (1980), *The Roman Invasion of Britain*, London.

PART 4

·THE·FRONTIERS·

CHAPTER 8

·MAINLAND·EUROPE·

Valerie A. Maxfield

The backbone of the frontiers of mainland Europe was formed by the two great rivers, Rhine and Danube. That this is so was not a matter of policy, of ambition successfully achieved; it came about by default. The Roman vision in the early days of the empire was for conquest of the entire world as it was then known, and this is what Augustus, the first *princeps*, the first general with supreme power to operate 'world-wide', set out to achieve, campaigning eastwards from the Rhine and planning a major expedition beyond the Danube. But this vision of *imperium sine fine*, of world domination, came up against the realities of geography, in Europe the existence of a vast and inhospitable landmass across which tribes moved, the trend of whose advance was in a southerly and westerly direction, the direction of Rome. In retrospect it is possible to see that the turning point in Europe lay very early in the imperial period, well within the reign of Augustus himself, when his plans for conquest beyond Rhine and Danube were shattered by the Illyrian revolt of AD 6 and the Varus disaster of AD 9; the emperor lost his nerve and Rome lost the initiative. Though subsequent emperors would campaign beyond the two great rivers and incorporate new lands into the Empire the advances made were of no great size; nor were they very long lived. Their major significance lay in the improved communications they brought about between east and west, the Danubian and the Rhineland provinces. For much of their length and for most of the period the two rivers formed the boundary of Rome's European provinces, marking the limit of empire; but rivers do not make good frontiers. They may be bureaucratically convenient, providing clear lines of demarcation as long as the peoples on both sides agree to observe them, but they are lines which are difficult to enforce, they are militarily weak; they are highways which unite, not barriers which divide.

The distance as the crow flies from the mouth of the Rhine in modern Holland to the Danube delta in south-east Romania is in excess of 2,000 km (1,250 miles); follow-

139

ing the winding contours of the two rivers and such provincial territory as lay beyond, that distance more than doubles. By the mid-second century AD control of this extensive line was divided among the eleven governors whose provinces it bordered – Lower and Upper Germany, Raetia and Noricum, Upper and Lower Pannonia, Upper and Lower Moesia and the three Dacias (fig. 8.1). Each governor held his command direct from the emperor; there was no concept of an overall frontier command, though provincial commands might from time to time be united in response to military requirements, so that although the general frontier policies of individual emperors may be detected, the execution of those policies in detail varied from province to province.

For convenience of discussion the European frontiers have been divided into two broad sectors. Any division is arbitrary, since it has no contemporary reality, but a reasonably sensible break may be made on the borders of Raetia and Noricum. Raetia and the headwaters of the Danube best belong with the Rhineland: the remainder of the Danubian lands belong together.

The Germanies and Raetia

The boundary of Caesar's conquests in Gaul extended from Mare Nostrum to Oceanus, from sea to sea, the Mediterranean to the Channel. But in the north and east no such natural boundary was reached. It is clear from Caesar's commentaries that the *de facto*, if temporary, limit of land under direct Roman jurisdiction was regarded, by Roman and by barbarian, as the Rhine (cf. Caesar, *De Bello Gallico* 4.4; 4.16). So it was to remain for the next forty years until the time of Augustus, for Caesar, preoccupied with more pressing concerns, launched no serious offensive across the Rhine. The river was adopted as a geographically convenient, though arbitrary, divide, which corresponded to no existing cultural distinctions. It attracted none of the paraphernalia of frontier control characteristic of later periods. The army which ensured the security of the newly-won Gallic territory lay back within the province itself, though few of its bases have been positively identified. The threat which this army constituted was, for the most part, sufficient to maintain Gaul's eastern frontier, though tribes did, from time to time, raid across the Rhine into Roman territory. Indeed in 38 BC Vipsanius Agrippa, as governor of Gaul, permitted the philo-Roman Ubii to retain lands on the left bank of the river, to which they had moved from their homeland on the right bank (Tacitus, *Germania*, 28).

From the outset it was Augustus' clear intention to take up where Caesar had left off in Gaul – to resume the thrust east beyond the Rhine. However a necessary prelude to the campaigns into Germany, as also to activity in Illyricum, was the conquest of the Alpine regions in order to gain control of the essential mountain passes north from Italy. In 25 BC the Salassi of the Val d'Aosta, who controlled the Great and Little St Bernard Passes, submitted to Terentius Varro. Beyond them and south of the Hochrhein

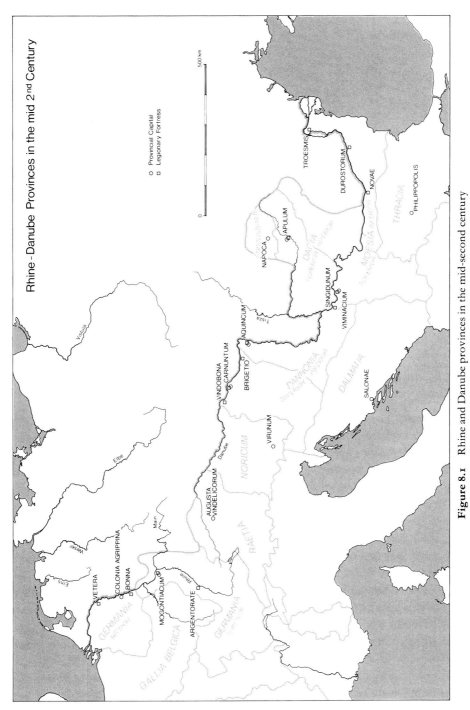

Figure 8.1 Rhine and Danube provinces in the mid-second century

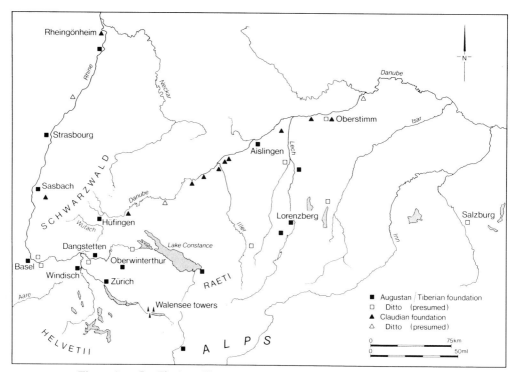

Figure 8.2 Pre-Flavian military sites in the upper Rhine and Danube regions

lay the Helvetii through whose territory then ran the highway to the north. Absorption of this region was the natural corollary to the opening up of the passes to the south, and it is at about this time that the presence of Roman troops is first archaeologically attested in Helvetian territory on the Lindenhof in Zürich and, perhaps slightly later, at Basel, at Windisch (Vindonissa) and Oberwinterthur (fig. 8.2). A series of stone-built watch-towers (three are known) along the Walensee above Lake Zürich, seems designed to oversee movement from the east, the territory of the Raeti, by water up the Walensee and via the river Limmat to Lake Zürich. Another site belonging to the period of the Alpine campaigns is that of Dangstetten which lies to the north of the Hochrhein near the entrance to the Wutach valley which gives access to the headwaters of the Danube from the important Rhine crossing at Zurzach. It is perhaps to be linked with Tiberius' activity in this area in 15 BC. Conquest of the Alpine tribes was vigorously promoted. In 15 BC Drusus and Tiberius took command and by 14 the Alps and Voralpenland were in Roman control. The way was now clear to launch the offensive beyond the Rhine.

Completion of the conquest of Spain in 19 BC had released the necessary troops and it is in the early years of the second decade BC that the first military bases appear

on the Rhine itself, sites such as Vechten, Nijmegen, Xanten, Neuss and Mainz (fig. 8.3).
In 16 BC the legate of Gaul, M. Lollius, had suffered a defeat at the hands of the Sugambri
who had invaded Gaul: a legion was lost. Augustus hastened to Gaul where he remained
until 13 BC supervising preparations for the war. In 12 BC Drusus assumed command,
launching the campaigns across the Rhine which he led until his death in 9 BC. Three
main invasion routes were used. A sea-borne attack was launched in 12 BC from the
area of Vechten around the Frisian coast to the mouths of the Ems, Weser and Elbe.
A second line of attack led eastwards up the valley of the Lippe which flowed into
the Rhine just upstream from the site of Xanten where an early military base lay on
the Fürstenberg below the later, Claudio-Neronian, fortress. The large, 54 ha (133 acres)
fortress of Oberaden, already abandoned by c. 9 BC, must belong to Drusus' activity
here. The most southerly of the three routes originated from Mainz, whence the valleys
of Main and Wetter gave access north and east towards the Elbe. Testimony of Drusus'
activity in this area is provided by the short-lived supply-base at Rödgen in the Wetterau.

By 9 BC the Elbe had been reached. Drusus died and his brother Tiberius, appointed in his stead, campaigned to consolidate the gains. This vast expanse of land – the
distance from Rhine to Elbe direct is 340 km (210 miles) – was to be reduced to the
form of a province and one at least of the legions was moved forward from its base
behind the Rhine to a newly-built 20 ha (50 acres) fortress site at Haltern. But within
less than two decades Haltern and the new province were abandoned. In AD 6 Augustus
was planning an attack on Maroboduus of Bohemia, a two-pronged attack north and
west from Pannonia, eastwards from Germany and Raetia. Troops were withdrawn from
the Rhineland for the campaign and control there left in the hands of P. Quinctilius
Varus, a senator described by Paterculus as 'a man mild of nature and peaceable in
his behaviour'. Clearly no trouble was anticipated. The Bohemian invasion was thwarted,
first by a serious and prolonged rebellion in Illyricum (p. 174 below); no sooner had
this been suppressed than in AD 9 the Germans, under the leadership of the Cheruscan
prince Arminius, rebelled, attacked and massacred Varus and the three legions that were
with him (XVII, XVIII, and XIX). The Romans were driven out of the lands they
had held a mere twenty years. 'The result of this disaster was that the Empire, which
had not stopped on the shores of the Ocean, was checked on the banks of the Rhine'
(Florus, *Epitome of Roman History*, 2.30.39). Punitive campaigns followed, led first by
Tiberius, later, after the death of Augustus in AD 14, by Germanicus. Despite the far-
reaching nature of Germanicus' campaigns – he claimed to have conquered all the tribes
between the Rhine and the Elbe – the erstwhile province was not restored. Germanicus
was recalled. Troops were pulled back to the left bank of the Rhine; two legions were
based at Cologne in the territory of the Ubii, two at Xanten, two at Mainz and, further
south, one each at Strasbourg and Windisch. Auxiliaries were stationed in their vicinity.
Although the Rhine became once more the effective limit of the Roman provinces some
supervision was maintained over the right bank. Forts were occupied in the Main-Wetter

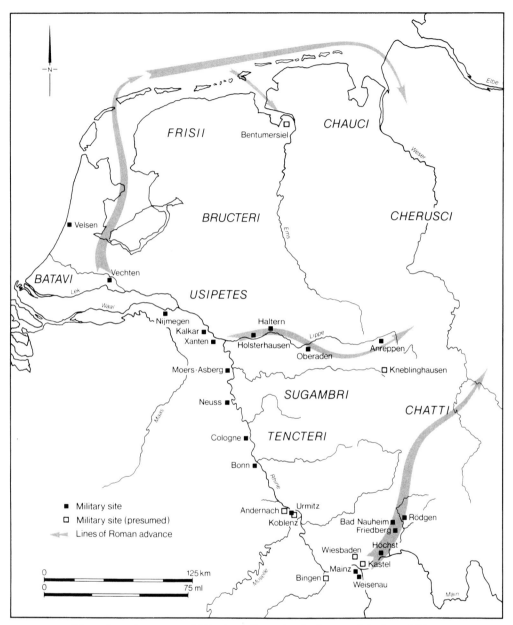

Figure 8.3 Augustan and Tiberian military sites in the area of the lower Rhine

area and, further north, beyond the Rhine mouth, the site of Velsen, established in connection with one of Germanicus' campaigns, remained in use into the Claudian period. The tribute imposed on the Frisii by Drusus in *c.* 12 BC was still being collected by Rome in AD 28 when the officer in charge of the collection provoked a rebellion during which a Roman fort in Frisian territory (Velsen ?) was attacked. It was not until AD 47 that Roman garrisons were finally withdrawn from this area. In that year the Chauci, northern neighbours of the Frisii, took advantage of the death of the commander of the lower German army to revolt and plunder the wealthy Gallic coasts. The new commander, the celebrated disciplinarian, Domitius Corbulo, took the situation firmly in hand; he settled the Frisii, hostile since the events of AD 28, constructed a fort on their lands to ensure obedience, and started to reduce them to the status of a province: at this point he was ordered by Claudius to desist and to withdraw all garrisons behind the Rhine (Tacitus, *Annals*, 11.19). Claudius, militarily committed in Britain at this time, did not wish to embark on further territorial expansion.

It was then, under Claudius, that the river bank in the area of the Rhine mouth first takes on the appearance of a controlled frontier line. Forts were disposed in a linear fashion at an average of 7 to 8 km (4.5 to 5 miles) distance from one another, along the river from the North Sea coast to the junction of Rhine and Waal (fig. 8.4). Where their garrisons are known all were occupied by cohorts, though not all these forts were large enough to hold a complete unit. Though no troops were then stationed beyond the Rhine north of the Wetterau some general Roman supervision continued to be exercised over the area and control was maintained over access across the river to the Roman province. In AD 58, for example, the Frisii and the landless Ampsivarii were refused permission to settle on territory 'set apart for military purposes', land intended for grazing horses and pack-animals but left idle. However from then on the Rhine, from its mouth to just south of Remagen, was to remain a frontier line; no subsequent attempt was made in this area to reconquer the lands beyond. Increasingly the lower Rhine was transformed from a base-line for attack into a controlled frontier line. The two-legion bases, relics of a campaigning army waiting to resume campaign, were broken up. In AD 35 the fortress of Cologne was abandoned; one of its legions, *legio XX*, moved north to Neuss, the other, *legio I*, moved south to Bonn. The double fortress at Xanten survived until 69 when it was devastated in the Batavian rebellion in which so many of the Rhineland sites were destroyed. A new single-legion fortress was built on a nearby site and another fortress constructed on the site of the old Augustan base at Nijmegen. In the reorganization following the Batavian revolt several new forts were constructed and the auxiliary troops, originally grouped quite close to the legions, came to be spread out in linear fashion in the manner so clearly foreshadowed by the Claudian arrangements in the Rhine mouth area. A couple of fortlets and an observation tower are also known along the lower German frontier; on present evidence they do not appear to have been part of a regular sequence of such structures, but rather to have performed some localized function.

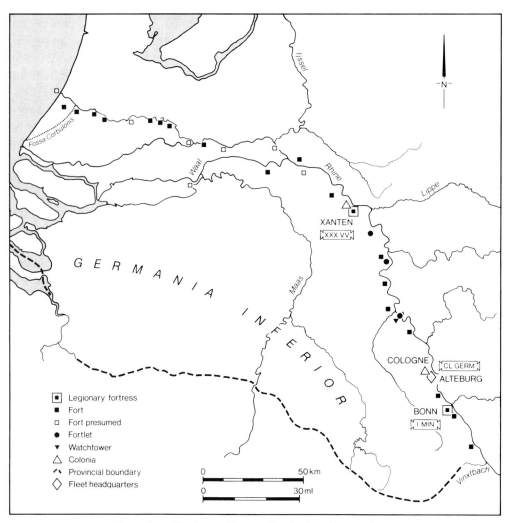

Figure 8.4 The Lower German *limes* in the mid-second century

These military installations were linked by a road along the west bank, and major routes led back into the interior of Gaul, to the coast at Boulogne, to Lyon, to Trier, whence supplies might be brought up to the troops. The river too would be used for purposes of supply, a fact which highlights one of the problems of the European river frontiers: both served as highways for civil and military traffic as well as marking the divide between Roman and barbarian. The bridges which spanned the river were guarded by forts from which troops could patrol the lands on the far bank. The waterway itself will presumably have been patrolled by the fleet, the *classis Germanica*, which had its base 3 km (1.8 miles) south of Cologne, at the Alteburg, Köln-Bayental, a site which it occupied from the period of Tiberius down to the middle of the third century. The distribution of the fleet's stamped bricks suggests the existence of several subsidiary bases, including Neuss and Xanten, but all confined to lower Germany where the river formed the provincial boundary.

The Danube wars of Domitian and Trajan caused some depletion in the size of the lower Rhineland army. By the early second century the legionary garrison had been reduced to two (based at Xanten and Bonn), but apart from these troop movements nothing occurred until the latter part of the third century to alter in any fundamental way the overall frontier arrangements as they had developed by the Flavian period. The picture in Upper Germany is, however, very different. With the exception of the bases of the Hochrhein area associated with the Alpine campaigns, and the Wetterau sites built, or rebuilt, after the Varus disaster, few military sites had been founded in Upper Germany by the death of Augustus. The rearward position of the upper Rhine, dominated in front by the thickly forested and sparsely populated area of the Schwarzwald, meant that it played no part in Augustus' German adventures. In the Tiberian period, in the wake of the withdrawal from Germany beyond the Rhine, two new legionary fortresses were established, one at Strasbourg on the left bank of the Rhine opposite the Kinzig valley, the other at Windisch on the plateau site occupied by the earlier Augustan base above the confluence of the Aare, the Reuss and the Limmat, a strategic crossroads at the foot of a pass over the Jura and controlling access to the Rhine, 15 km (9 miles) to the north up the Limmat valley. Forts were constructed at nodal points along the main communication links in the upper Rhine–Danube area (fig. 8.2). On the main routes east from Lake Constance and northwards towards the Danube, military posts appear at the major river crossings, many in dominant hill-top positions (pl. 8.1), and it may be as early as the late Tiberian period that the first forts were sited forward on the Danube itself, at Hüfingen, for example, at the exit of the Wutach valley, at Aislingen where a major route of prehistoric origin reached and crossed the river, and conceivably also in the area of Oberstimm, an important Danube crossing adjacent to the Celtic oppidum of Manching (fig. 8.2). All territory up to the Danube was under Roman control, but the only forts to be placed in a forward position were those which guarded the crossing points. This is a situation which can be paralleled at this same period in the middle and lower Danube provinces (p. 175 below).

The pattern changed under Claudius. Then at latest Raetia was formally constituted a province; its northern boundary, the Danube, was fortified with a line of forts which lay along the south bank at varying distances apart, their detailed siting determined by the local topography. The forts were linked by a road which, at its western end, cut across the Rhine–Danube re-entrant to join the Rhine at Sasbach. Communication between the upper Rhineland, Raetia and provinces eastwards was thus improved. This redistribution of troops within the upper Rhine–Danube area indicates a concern with the maintenance of security and improvement of communications within an area already under Roman control. Although Roman supervision was no doubt maintained over the right bank of the upper Rhine area no forts were moved forward into this region until the time of Vespasian when direct Roman control was extended over the upper Rhine–Neckar region as a whole. In AD 70 a legion was brought back to Strasbourg, which had had only an auxiliary garrison since the departure of *legio II Augusta* to Britain in AD 43, and shortly afterwards Vespasian's legate in upper Germany, Cn. Pinarius Cornelius Clemens, won triumphal ornaments 'for successful exploits in Germany' (*CIL* XI, 5271). A milestone of AD 74, bearing Clemens' name, has been found at Offenburg, just east of the Rhine, and attests the laying out of 'a direct route from Strasbourg into Raetia' (*CIL* XIII, 9082). The first of a series of forts at Rottweil (Arae Flaviae) on the upper Neckar was founded, and a line of forts installed along the Strasbourg–Raetia road (fig. 8.5). Further north the first military bases appeared east of the Rhine at Gross Gerau, at Ladenburg and Heidelberg-Neuenheim along a north–south route which was to link the legionary fortress at Mainz with the strategic route network of the Upper Danube and with the Raetian provincial capital at Augsburg. Meanwhile the left bank forts were abandoned.

The effect of the Flavian campaigns was to bring into the Empire land, much of which was of no great value in itself, heavily forest-covered and sparsely populated, but which brought about an improvement in the communication link between Germany and Raetia, between Rhine and Danube, cutting across the awkward re-entrant angle between the headwaters of the two rivers. Whether Vespasian had more extensive plans is not known. His short-lived successor, Titus, promoted no further campaigning here, but is attested building a fort at Kösching on the Danube, which lies, significantly perhaps, north of the river.

In AD 83 Domitian launched a campaign against the Chatti, north of the Wetterau: he took the title *Germanicus* in commemoration of his success in late summer of that year, and subsequently celebrated a triumph. The reality of the Domitianic war is, unfortunately, masked by the hostility of the historians who recorded it. In terms of new territory acquired the archaeological evidence points to little that had not already been absorbed by the time of Vespasian or earlier. A frontier line was drawn which lay short of the heartland of the Chatti, north of the Wetterau. The achievement seems to have fallen short of the aim which led Domitian to amass an expeditionary force composed of troops drawn from both the upper and lower German armies as well as from Britain. Perhaps it was the first stirrings of trouble in the Danube lands which led him to abandon greater schemes; whatever the reason the last opportunity for a major military initiative in Germany was lost.

In AD 89 the commander of the Upper German army, Antonius Saturninus, took advantage of the Emperor's absence from Rome to raise a rebellion in which he was joined by the neighbouring Germanic tribes. The revolt was quickly put down by the Lower German army, but in its aftermath and consequent on the need for further troops on the Danube, the Upper German army was depleted in numbers: Mainz, the last of the German legionary bases to retain a two-legion establishment, was now reduced to one. The redistribution of troops and the new frontier arrangements made in the face of this loss of initiative are indicative of the intention to control lands held rather than to aim for further advance. The advent of trouble on the middle and lower Danube meant that the focus of military activity had now shifted east. The Rhineland was left with only such resources of manpower as were necessary to secure what was already in Roman hands.

It was some time during the 80s, and no doubt as a result of the wars of those years, that the two provinces of Upper and Lower Germany were formally constituted from the territories of the upper and lower German armies: an acknowledgment of the fact that greater Germany was not to be conquered. The provincial reorganization occurred some time between September 82 and October 90, with the territories being carved out of the Gauls. The lower province had its capital at Cologne, the upper province at Mainz where legionary fortress and provincial capital were to develop side by side. The border between the two lay on the Vinxtbach, a small stream which flows into the Rhine south of Remagen. Here a dedication to the deities which preside over ends, *Finibus*, has been found, and altars to the spirits of the place, erected by soldiers of both the Upper and Lower German armies.

It is probably to the situation in the Taunus–Wetterau area of the frontier that Frontinus alluded when he wrote in his *Strategmata* (1.13.10):

> When the Germans in their usual manner kept emerging from their clearings and hiding-places to attack our troops, finding a safe place in the depths of the forest, the Emperor Domitian, by advancing the *limites* through 120 miles not only changed the character of the war but brought the enemy under control by exposing their hiding-places.

The line of the Domitianic *limes* is indicated on fig. 8.5b. Swinging south-eastwards from the Rhine it skirts the Neuwied basin before cutting across the ridge of the Taunus mountains which it follows eastwards and northwards to encircle the fertile valley of the Wetter. Along this line a road or cleared strip was laid out through the forest, with observation towers placed at 500–600 m (550–650 yard) intervals (more or less according to visibility) along it. These towers were simple four-post structures 2.5–3 metres square (8–10 ft), each surrounded by a ditch, normally circular, occasionally square. A number of small earth and timber fortlets have been identified in association with this line, for example to the east of the later fort of the Saalburg (fig. 8.6) at Ockstadt (fig. 8.7) and at Kemel. Their siting would appear to be associated with routes which cross the frontier line. The troops which manned these installations were presumably provided by the forts which already lay to the south in the Wetterau. This line, road, watchtowers and

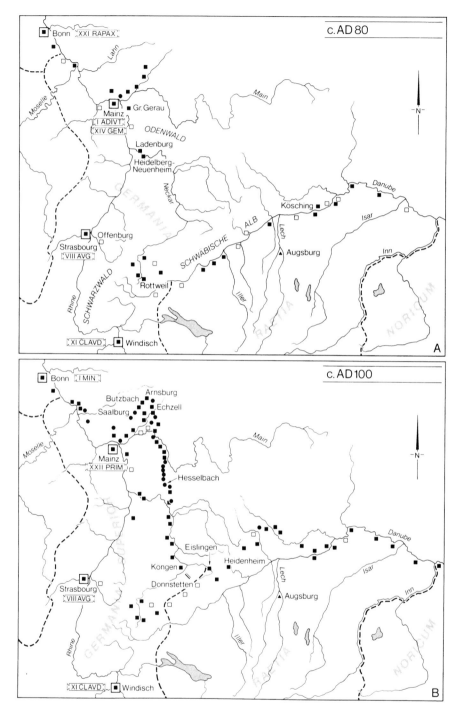

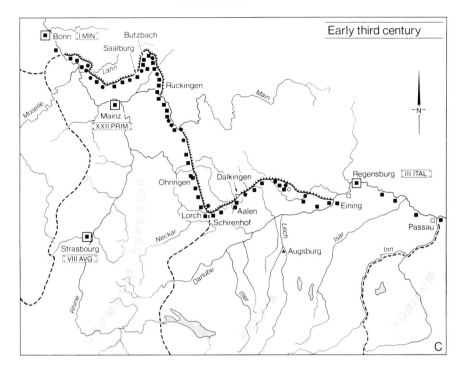

Figure 8.5 The development of the Upper German–Raetian *limes*: (a) *c.* AD 80; (b) *c.* AD 100; (c) early third century

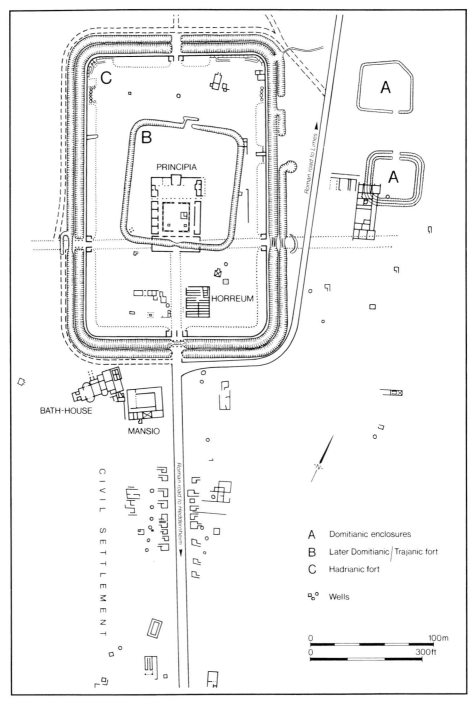

Figure 8.6   Saalburg: forts, fortlets and civil settlement

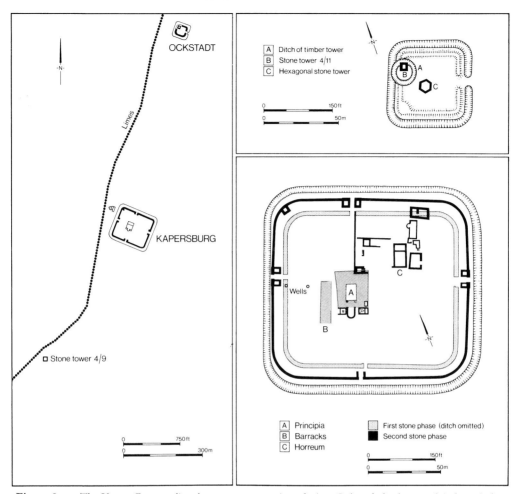

Figure 8.7 The Upper German *limes* between towers 4/9 and 4/11: Ockstadt fortlet, overlain by a timber and stone watchtowers, replaced by the *numerus* fort of Kapersburg: the two-phase stone fort overlies an earth and timber fort (not shown)

small military posts, is analogous to the arrangements on the Gask Ridge in Britain (p. 201 below) and will have served a similar function – observation and control of movement into the province.

The construction of these frontier works, road, watch-towers and fortlets, is conventionally dated to the early to mid-80s, in the aftermath of the Chattan war; however, a recent reconsideration of the dating evidence (specifically the samian pottery) from the fortlets on the frontier line suggests that their occupation begins no earlier than *c.* 90, rather than *c.* 83/4. Viewed in historical terms it would thus appear that these early developments of the frontier in the Taunus-Wetterau area came about in the wake of,

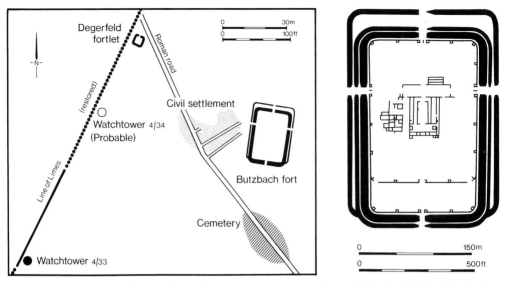

Figure 8.8 Left: upper German *limes* in the area of towers 4/33 and 4/34. Right: detail of the Butzbach fort

and no doubt as a response to, the events surrounding the Saturninus revolt in AD 89, and were not, perhaps, unconnected with the growing problems of the Danube frontier.

The paraphernalia of frontier control gradually developed in the later first and early second centuries as Domitian, Trajan and then Hadrian eschewed further advance in Germany. Late in the first century a small fort was built at the Saalburg to the west of the earlier fortlets and below the later fort (fig. 8.6). Some auxiliary forts were now added to the forward line, for example at Butzbach, a major crossing-point of the frontier in the western Wetterau where a road from Mainz came northwards via Friedberg towards free Germany (fig. 8.8). At Arnsberg, close by the point where the Wetter is crossed by the *limes* a fort guarded another frontier crossing, and some 12 km (7½ miles) to the south a 5.2 ha (13 acre) fort, one of the largest on the whole of the German *limes*, was built at Echzell, whence the frontier line ran south to reach the river Main at Gross Krotzenburg.

To the south and east, in the province of Raetia, a number of forts had been advanced, during the Flavian period, northwards from the Danube to the Swabian Alb. Epigraphic evidence points to this having begun under Titus at Kösching, while excavations at Heidenheim suggest a date *c.* 90 for the establishment of this large fort designed to accommodate the *ala II Flavia milliaria*, the only milliary *ala* attested on the German–Raetian *limes*.

These frontier arrangements continued to evolve under Trajan who showed no

Figure 8.9 Odenwald *limes*: timber tower on a dry-stone base

interest in further advance in Germany, whose campaigning ambitions lay further east, and whose policy in the Rhineland and upper Danube, in so far as one can be determined, continued that of Domitian's later years, with a gradual tightening up of frontier control. Indeed, in the absence of epigraphic evidence it is often difficult to tell in detail which of the frontier constructions belong in the latter part of Domitian's principate and which to that of Trajan. Further forts were built on the frontier line itself and more fortlets to house the troops charged with the task of patrolling its line, as for example at Degerfeld, guarding the *limes* crossing adjacent to the fort site at Butzbach (fig. 8.8). It was under Trajan, too, that the link in the frontier between Main and Neckar was established. This link, the so-called Odenwald *limes* runs roughly north-south across country between the river Main by Wörth and the middle Neckar at Wimpfen. It consists of a military road watched over by observation towers of dry-stone and timber construction (fig. 8.9) and controlled by troops based in the ten small forts (average size 0.6 ha or $1\frac{1}{2}$ acres) and intervening fortlets irregularly spaced along the 70 km ($53\frac{1}{2}$ miles) of its length. The positioning of these sites appears to be determined by topography, for they lie where natural routeways penetrate the line of the frontier. Excavation of one of these small forts, Hesselbach (fig. 8.10), showed that it was designed for a complete, if small, unit, for it contained a headquarters building and an officer's house in addition to accom-

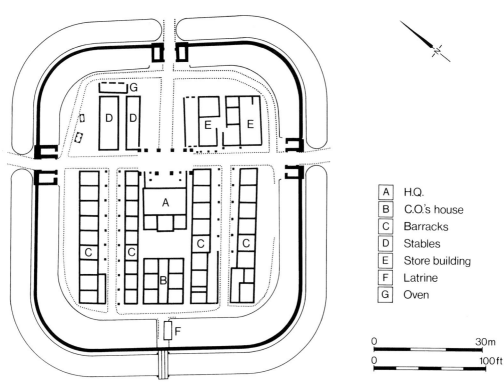

Figure 8.10 The *numerus* fort at Hesselbach

A	H.Q.
B	C.O.'s house
C	Barracks
D	Stables
E	Store building
F	Latrine
G	Oven

modation for an estimated 150 men. It is known from inscriptions that in the mid-second century Hesselbach and the other Odenwald forts (with the exception of Oberschiedental and the west fort at Neckarburken) were occupied by *numeri*, irregular units, and it is probable that this was so from their foundation.

When the frontier line reached the middle Neckar by Wimpfen, the *limes* road followed the course of the river southwards, running sometimes to its east, sometimes to its west, taking the course of greatest convenience. *Numerus* forts gave way to auxiliary sites, six in a 70 km (43½ mile) stretch, and no further watchtowers and fortlets were provided. From Köngen, the most southerly of the Neckar *limes* forts, the road turned east into Raetia.

It was probably in the early second rather than the late first century that a line of timber watch-towers comparable to those on the Taunus–Wetterau–Odenwald *limes* was begun in Raetia across the open land of the Alb *limes*, though the sequence appears never to have been completed at its western end. Moving the *auxilia* on to the frontier line led to the abandonment of forts in its hinterland, sites such as Wiesbaden and Heddernheim, which were now handed over to the civil authorities and *civitates* established. Eventually, with the exception of Friedberg in the Wetterau, all forts in the rear were given up and military control was limited to the long narrow strip of the frontier itself; the position contrasts markedly with that in Britain (Chapter 9) where a deep band of military sites continued throughout the occupation behind both the frontier walls. This contrast does not however represent any fundamental difference in approach to frontier control; it is simply a function of geography, for the mainland European frontiers were of such length in proportion to the overall size and garrison strength of the provinces they fronted that all available troops could be comfortably disposed along them. Here too, perhaps, lies the reason for the extensive use in Germany of *numeri* in frontier control. *Numerus* forts appear, not only on the Odenwald *limes*, to the virtual exclusion of auxiliary sites, but are interspersed with the *auxilia* (largely equitate cohorts) along the Taunus and Wetterau. The very length and lack of depth of the military zone was to prove a fundamental weakness when the frontier came under attack.

The Hadrianic contribution to the German–Raetian frontier was consolidation of the *status quo*. In 121–2 the emperor visited Germany and it was then no doubt that he instigated the construction of the artificial linear frontier work which demarcated the edges of the province. Hadrian's biographer states that:

> at this time and on frequent other occasions in many places where the barbarians were divided off not by rivers but by *limites*, he separated them from us with large stakes sunk deep into the ground and fastened together in the manner of a palisade. (*Historia Augusta, vita Hadriani,* 12.6).

No province is mentioned by name in connection with this passage, but the frontier work described matches perfectly what has been found in Germany and Raetia. Hadrian's frontier work here was a palisade, a substantial wooden fence. It was constructed of large oak timbers, roughly 0.3 m (*c.* 12 in.) in diameter, set side by side in a trench sunk a metre or more (over 3 ft) into the ground (fig. 8.11). The timber uprights were in places wedged in position with stones, while the fastenings alluded to by the biographer are attested by the presence of nails. In places where it runs through waterlogged ground its timbers have survived. The palisade may be conjectured to have stood to a height of about 3 m (10 ft) above ground. The purpose of such a palisade would appear to be administrative rather than military; to mark the line of the frontier, the edge of the empire, where no alternative linear demarcation existed. This is apparent from the fact that the palisade exists only where there is no river frontier. Lower Germany has no palisade. It begins where the Upper German *limes* diverges from the Rhine, runs through the Taunus and Wetterau and ceases on the Main. It resumes in the Odenwald, ceases on the Neckar and resumes again on the Alb *limes* where it continues to the point where the frontier meets the Danube at Eining.

Meanwhile the programme of fort building and restoration continued. The fort at Butzbach was redesigned for a new unit with its defences and main buildings construc-

Profile   Restored profile   Restored plan

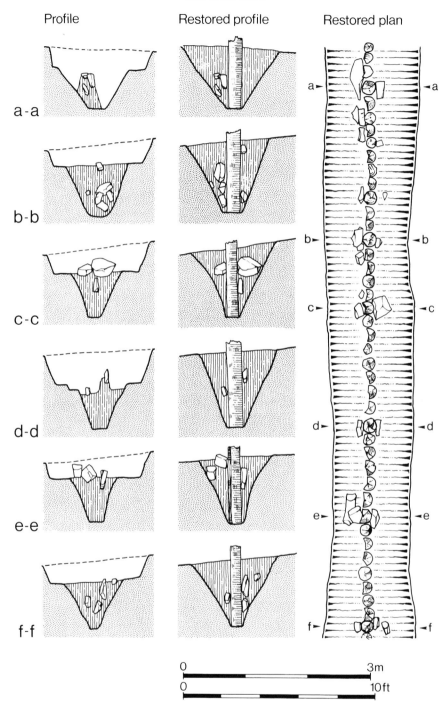

Figure 8.11   Profiles of the Upper German palisade trench between towers 3/66 and 3/67 (*after ORL*)

ted in stone; its erstwhile garrison, *cohors II Raetorum*, was moved to the Saalburg where the small Domitianic fort had been levelled and a new 3.2 ha (8 acres) fort constructed over its remains (fig. 8.6). The *numerus* fort at Hesselbach and other sites which had stood for the three and more decades since their Domitianic foundation, were rebuilt in stone.

The Hadrianic palisade does not represent the very earliest use of a linear earthwork on the German frontier. There exists in the exposed northern part of the Wetterau, running about 90 m (100 yards) in front of the road and towers, a stretch of ditch which had upright timbers planted in its bottom. It is overlain in places by the Hadrianic palisade. Recently aerial reconnaissance has revealed traces of two parallel ditches with a palisade behind running across country from the middle Neckar at Köngen, south-east in the direction of Donnstetten, the so-called Sibyllenspur (fig 8.12). Limited excavation of this earthwork and an associated fortlet at Dettingen-unter-Teck suggest a date in the very late first or early second century. These pre-Hadrianic features are however localized in appearance and function, designed in some way to give extra protection to the frontier sectors in which they lie. They contrast with the overall Hadrianic conception.

The German–Raetian *limes* underwent a continuous development from Domitian to Hadrian; at first nothing fundamental changed under Pius. Many of the timber towers, decaying now no doubt, were replaced in stone on sites adjacent to their timber predecessors (figs 8.13 and 8.14). Some had already been replaced under Hadrian. The majority of these new towers were square, with an external measurement of 4 to 5 metres (13–16 feet); a few were hexagonal. The foundations were nearly a metre (3 ft) deep and the walls not far short of a metre thick at their base. Inscriptions indicate that this work was under way in 145–6. Yet, before his death in AD 161, Pius had instigated a significant change, abandoning the Odenwald–Neckar line in favour of a forward position, the outer *limes*, no more than 30 km ($18\frac{1}{2}$ miles) to the east (fig. 8.5c). The reason for the

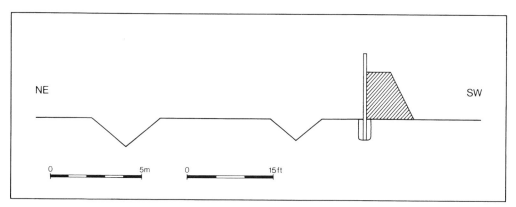

Figure 8.12 Restored profile of the Sibyllenspur; the rampart is hypothetical

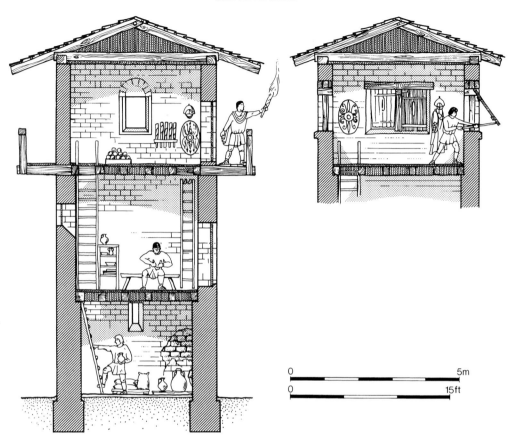

Figure 8.13 Hypothetical section through a stone tower. Alternative restorations for the upper floor show (left) a projecting outer gallery or (right) large windows for observation (*after Baatz*)

advance would appear to be economic rather than military. It involved no substantial campaign; it received, as far as is known, no mention from the historians and Pius took no imperial salutation because of it. The land embraced within the new frontier is no doubt territory over which Rome already exercised some supervision; indeed it is probable that the west fort at Öhringen (the Burgkastell) was already held as an outpost from the Odenwald–Neckar *limes*. The territory now taken within the Empire was good agricultural land; the new frontier lay on the western edge of the keuper sandstone which bore heavy pine forests. The frontier works of the inner *limes* were repeated on the outer line. A new palisade and stone towers were built (there are no timber towers on the outer *limes*), and fort garrisons, *auxilia* and *numeri*, advanced to new stations. As on the inner *limes*, the forts were interspersed with fortlets, not on the rigid system imposed on Hadrian's Wall but according to the dictates of local conditions. An equivalent adjustment necessarily occurred at the western end of the Raetian *limes* where,

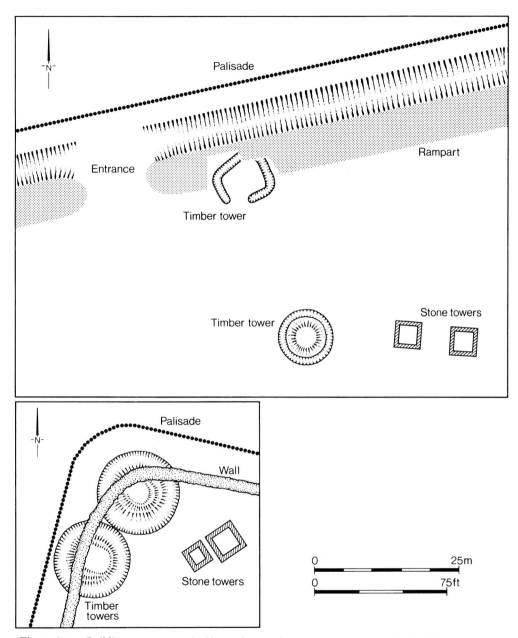

Figure 8.14 Building sequence on the Upper German *limes*: watchposts 1/59 and 3/61. The palisade was added after the two successive timber towers. A stone tower later replaced the timber. Finally, a rampart (1/59) or a wall (3/61) was added (*after ORL*)

among others, the *ala II Flavia milliaria* moved forward from its earlier base at Heiden-heim to a new fort at Aalen. The date of this move can be defined no closer than between 148, the date of two inscriptions from Böckingen on the Neckar, and 161, the latest possible date of a fragmentary text from Jagsthausen on the outer *limes*. A likely can-didate for the governor in charge of the move in Upper Germany is C. Popilius Carus Pedo who is recorded as a legate of Pius 'in the province of upper Germany and of the army stationed therein' in *c.* 152–155. The area between the two frontiers was demilitarized. The land was handed over to the civil authorities and a *civitas* set up.

The Antonine advance was the last forward move of the German–Raetian *limes*; the frontier maintained this position for just another hundred years. During this time it underwent one major structural modification, of no tactical significance whatever. In the province of Upper Germany the palisade in the Taunus–Wetterau area and on the outer *limes* was supplemented by the construction of a rampart and ditch, the so-called Pfahlgraben, behind the palisade line, the timbers of which were perhaps by now in a state of disrepair (figs 8.15 and 8.16). The ditch was V-shaped, 6 to 7 metres (19 to 22 ft) wide and about 2 metres ($6\frac{1}{2}$ ft) deep. The upcast from it was heaped, in an appar-ently unrevetted mound, behind its inner lip with no berm between the two (pl. 8.2). There is no evidence of any palisade along the top of the rampart or of any obstacles being planted in the ditch. In a few short sectors in the Taunus a dry-stone wall was substituted for the bank and ditch, presumably because of the difficulties of ditch-digging through the rocky ground (fig. 8.14). The earthwork is not absolutely continuous. East of the fort of Holzhausen in the western Taunus there is an inexplicable gap of 6.4 km (4 miles). Short gaps occur on swampy ground in the eastern Wetterau and on some very steep slopes. A row of massive timbers continued the line of the palisade bank and ditch for 150 m (165 yards) across the wet ground of the Doppelbiersumpf south of Rückingen. The *limes* road was here constructed of a corduroy of timbers. There were also, of course, small gaps through bank and ditch at other points as, for example, where roads crossed the frontier line, points which were commonly guarded by watch-towers if not by forts or fortlets (figs 8.8 and 8.14).

The date of the Pfahlgraben is uncertain. It clearly post-dates the move to the outer *limes* for it is not found in the Odenwald; hence there is a *terminus post quem* of AD 148. The single piece of specific dating evidence comes from the *limes* crossing north of the Saalburg where a coin of AD 194 was retrieved from a burnt deposit which underlay the body of the rampart. Whether this date should be transferred to the entire Pfahl-graben is doubtful for it has been suggested that repairs may have been made to the earthwork at this point. An earlier date is suggested by evidence from the Zugmantel area; one sector here, which was subsequently realigned, appears to have had no stone towers associated with it. All are of the timber and dry-stone construction characteristic of early Trajanic work on the Odenwald *limes*. It is doubtful if such towers would have stood for nearly a hundred years. A late second rather than an early third century date

Figure 8.15 Upper German *limes*: final form showing palisade, pfahlgraben, and stone watchtower

for the initial construction of the bank and ditch would seem better to accommodate the evidence.

In Raetia a stone wall, commonly known as the Teufelsmauer (the Devil's Wall) replaced the palisade (fig. 8.17). This was 1.2 m (4 ft) wide, constructed of roughly coursed masonry on shallow foundations (fig. 8.18); where it ran across swampy ground it was founded on a bed of pile-driven logs. Its original height may have been some 3 to 4 m (10 to 13 ft). It was continuous except where it crossed streams or was cut by roads. There is a gap of some 4 km (2½ miles) between the end of the Pfahlgraben and the start of the Teufelsmauer which began, at its western end, on the slope leading down to the Rotenbach, between the forts of Lorch and Schirenhof. A fortlet sits close by its terminus. At its eastern end it runs right down to the Danube downstream from Eining.

The Raetian wall is as poorly dated as the Pfahlgraben. It post-dates the construction of the earliest stone towers for it characteristically butts up to the sides of them. Evidence from excavation of the *limes* crossing at Dalkingen (fig. 8.19) suggests a date in the latter part of the second century. In places the structural sequence in Raetia is complicated by the existence of a third linear barrier, the Flechtwerkzaun, a type of wattle fencing. This post-dates the palisade but pre-dates the stone wall which overlies it in places;

163

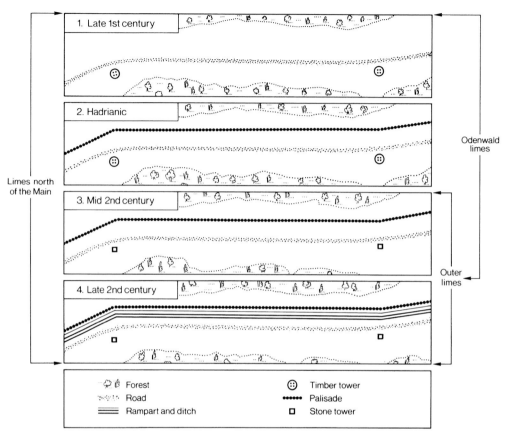

Figure 8.16 The four building phases of the Upper German *limes*

it pre-dates some stone towers, post-dates others (fig. 8.20). It would appear to be a local replacement for the timber palisade where it was in a state of decay.

The German–Raetian frontier, thus strengthened, stood until the 260s, but was subject to increasingly frequent barbarian attack. During the reign of Marcus Aurelius the Chatti invaded, causing damage in the Taunus–Wetterau–upper Main area, including some destruction within the *civitas* of Heddernheim. The Raetian frontier appears to have escaped relatively unscathed from the Marcomannic wars (166–175; 178–180) whose effects were felt most strongly further to the east in Pannonia. One effect of these wars was, however, to bring a legion (*III Italica*) back to Raetia, to a new fortress at Regensburg, while some redeployment of troops in Upper Germany is attested by building work at Niederbieber, Butzbach and Osterburken. These movements, localized as they are, can be seen as a constant refining of frontier control in the face of increasing unrest. In 213 the Alamanni make their first appearance; Caracalla is recorded as campaigning against them and it is to this period that the construction of the Pfahlgraben

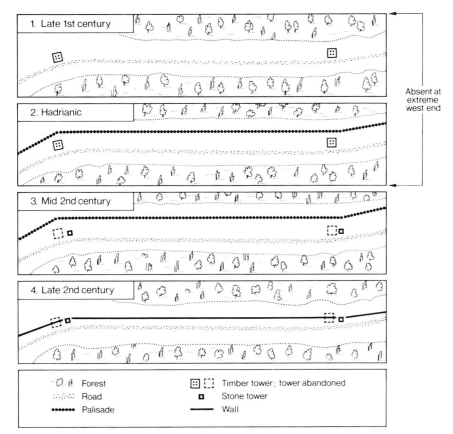

Figure 8.17 The four building phases of the Raetian *limes*

and Teufelsmauer are commonly attributed, though as indicated above, an earlier context would now seem more likely.

The growing insecurity of life in the frontier area is reflected in an increase in the number of coin hoards buried and never retrieved. In 233, in the time of Severus Alexander, a major Alamannic invasion was directed at Upper Germany and Raetia. There was widespread destruction, the effects of which have been noted in numerous forts and their *vici* the length of the frontier. A counter-offensive was launched and the frontier restored by Severus Alexander's successor, Maximinus Thrax. Forts were rebuilt, with the exception of Pfünz which was now abandoned; the immediate crisis was past but the situation was not fully retrieved. Pressure from the Alamanni continued. The, by now, static Roman frontier garrisons, strung out thinly along the *limites*, were not competent to meet such a challenge and there was no mobile reserve.

In or about AD 260 all lands east of the Rhine and north of the Danube were evacuated. The Verona list states that during the reign of Gallienus (253–268) 'the *civitates*

Figure 8.18 The Raetian *limes*: final form showing the stone wall and a stone watchtower

across the Rhine were occupied by barbarians'; the archaeological evidence is consistent with this statement. The army withdrew to behind Rhine and Danube, reoccupying many of the positions which they had held in the Julio-Claudian period before the Flavian offensive was launched. The defences of the long-abandoned legionary fortress of Windisch were restored by order of a governor of Upper Germany (*CIL* XIII, 5203), while an example of local self-help in time of crisis is provided by the hill-top site at the Wittnauerhorn, about 20 km (12 miles) to the west, where an Iron Age fortification was recommissioned at about this time as a civilian refuge.

One of the major problems arising from the loss of territory beyond the rivers was the control of the re-entrant angle between their upper reaches, where valleys led south into the diminished province. The route from Italy across the Alps via Helvetia to the Hochrhein, militarily crucial in terms of the Augustan advance, now acquired a new and sinister significance as a possible route of penetration by invaders into Italy, as indeed occurred in 270. Following further incursions by Alamanni, Burgundians, Goths and Vandals in 277 and 278 into the upper Rhine and Danube region, and their

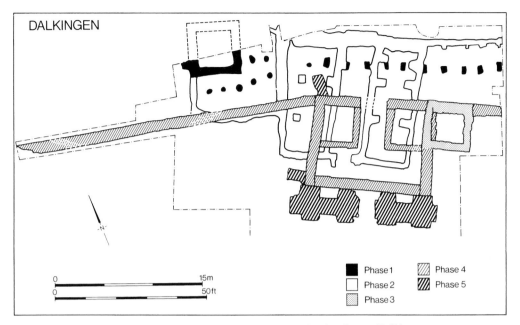

DALKINGEN

■ Phase 1	▨	Phase 4
□ Phase 2	▨	Phase 5
▦ Phase 3		

0   15m

0   50ft

Figure 8.19   The crossing through the Raetian *limes* at Dalkingen

successful expulsion, Probus, who is recorded on an inscription of AD 281 from Augsburg as 'restorer of the province' (of Raetia), began the first systematic fortification of the area, along the upper course of Rhine and Danube with a link between the two major rivers being established along the valley of the Iller, the most westerly of the main south–north flowing Danube tributaries (fig. 8.21). The work begun by Probus was continued by Diocletian. A series of strongpoints was set up along the Hochrhein from Basel on the river bend to Burg at the western end of Lake Constance, around the south side of the lake to Bregenz, from there to Kempten on the Iller and thence via Kellmunz to the Iller–Danube junction and eastwards along the Danube. At Eining, for example, a small *castellum* was constructed in one corner of the earlier fort. Sites along the routes into the interior were also fortified either at this time or in the fourth century when, in the wake of renewed Alamannic attacks in the early 350s and again in the 370s, the emperor Valentinian strengthened and augmented the frontier arrangements, adding a string of close-spaced stone watchtowers along the Rhine–Iller link, and building bridgehead fortifications across the Rhine at Basel, at Whylen opposite Kaiseraugst and at Rheinheim opposite Zurzach.

These upper Rhine defences were designed to protect not just the immediate province which they flanked but lands which lay well behind, above all Italy. No less vulnerable was Gaul, whose unwalled cities and affluent countryside lay open to attack, once the frontier had been breached, by the Alamanni from the south and east and the Frankish confederation in the north beyond the lower German *limes*.

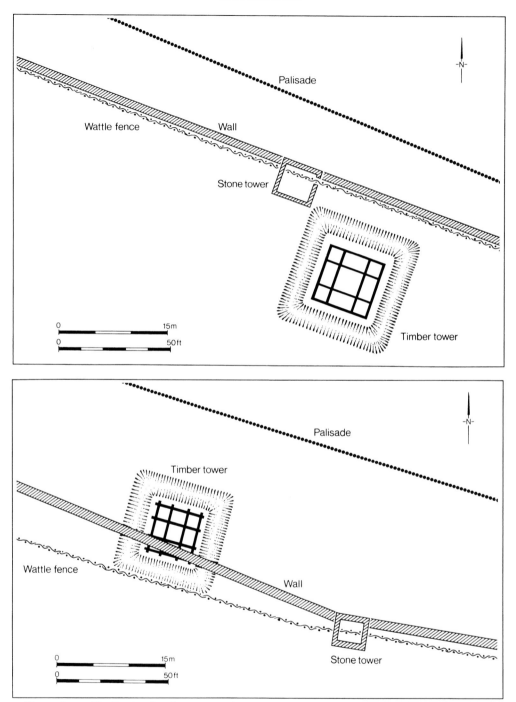

Figure 8.20   The Raetian *limes* by towers 14/15 (top) and 14/17 (bottom). The structural sequence is: timber tower with the addition of palisade; palisade replaced by wattle fence; timber tower replaced by stone tower; stone wall replaces wattle fence (*after ORL*)

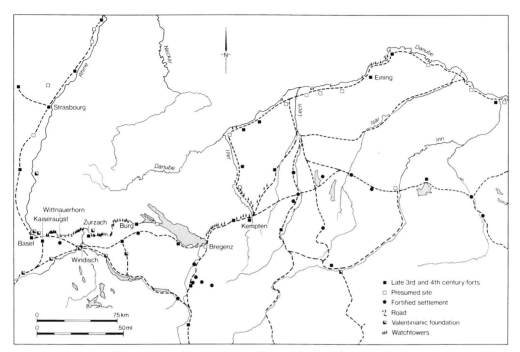

Figure 8.21 The late-Roman *limes* on the Danube–Iller–Rhine

In 256 both attacked. The Franks crossed the lower Rhine and penetrated deep into the province. Counter-measures were taken, first by Gallienus who is credited with the title *restitutor Galliarum* (restorer of the Gauls), and subsequently by the Gallic usurpers, Postumus and Victorinus. In the aftermath of these incursions, in or soon after 260, the most northerly sector of the lower German *limes* was abandoned (fig. 8.22). No fort from the Rhine mouth to south of the Waal confluence can be shown to have been occupied after that date, and the occupation of Zwammerdum ended in destruction. The land abandoned by Rome was soon settled by the Franks, and the outer edge of the province retreated to the south bank of the Waal. Along this line and its continuation up the lower and middle Rhine, an extensive programme of building and updating of defences in the new heavily defensive style of architecture was undertaken in the late third and fourth centuries. At Xanten, for example, a fortified enclosure with thick walls and projecting semi-circular towers, some 16 ha (39½ acres) in size, was constructed in *c.* 310 in the middle of the *colonia* site, and at Cologne a new bridgehead fortification with narrow defensible gates and projecting circular towers was built on the right bank of the river at Deutz, immediately opposite the main east-facing gate into the city.

The events of the 250s and the renewed devastating invasions of 275 and 276 had shown how vulnerable Gaul was once the frontier was breached. The excellent road system which linked the frontier garrisons with the interior of the province led the

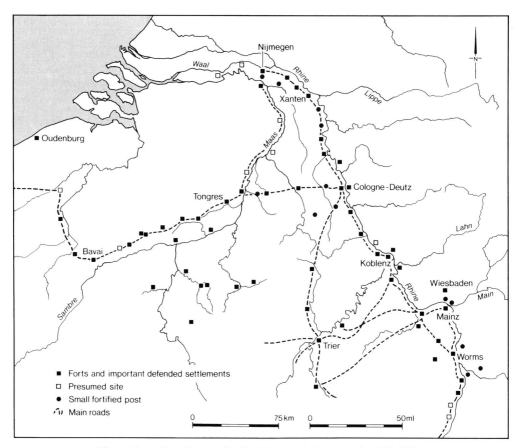

Figure 8.22 Late-Roman fortifications on the lower and middle Rhine

invading barbarians direct to the unwalled towns. One result of this was a massive programme of civic walling. Every urban settlement of any size acquired walls, not to protect the whole community, for large areas, often including major civic buildings, were
left outside the walls, but creating a citadel, a defensible strongpoint where refuge might
be sought (by the army? by those in authority?) in times of crisis. Such a measure is
a gesture of despair, not a planned policy of defence in depth as it has been described.
Another development which occurred was the construction of fortified posts at regular
intervals along all major roads, especially the vital trunk routes which led from the
coast to the frontiers and from the frontiers to the interior of the province, the vital
supply lines for the army. Measures such as these and, it should be added, the fortification
of the coasts against sea-borne invaders, though they might delay, could not prevent
the end.

   Behind its renewed defences Gaul enjoyed a period of relative calm until the middle of the fourth century. During the period of civil strife which followed the usurpation of Magnentius in 350 the Alamanni began once again to infiltrate the province. The victor in the civil war, Constantius II, entrusted the Gallic command to the able Julian who in 357 defeated the Alamanni and in 358 came to terms with the Franks who had taken advantage of Julian's preoccupation with the Alamanni to infiltrate the area south of the Maas. Julian's accession as Augustus in 360 took him away from Gaul, but as long as he remained alive the barbarians were quiescent. News of his death in 363 was the signal for renewed invasion. However the new emperor, Valentinian, paid particular attention to the Rhineland frontier. He resided in Gaul from 365 until 375 and put in hand measures for strengthening the frontier defences, including the construction of watchtowers along the Rhine–Iller–Danube *limes*. Valentinianic work is the latest detectable phase in the fortification of many of the frontier sites. Given the men to support them the frontiers could have held, but these they were denied as the troops were needed elsewhere. In 401 Stilicho withdrew troops from the Rhineland for his offensive against the hordes of the Visigothic king Alaric who had invaded Italy. On the last day of December 406 Vandals, Suebi, Burgundians and Alans swept across the Rhine and devastated Gaul. No longer could the integrity of the frontiers be maintained by the static troops (such as still remained) strung out along them. Their survival depended on the ability of the mobile field army to drive out such invaders as breached their line. Some of the invaders were allowed to stay with federate status: Burgundians settled on the left bank of the middle Rhine, Visigoths in Aquitania. Increasingly Rome's armies were manned by these federates: the frontiers no longer separated Roman and barbarian: the barbarians were in the Empire.

The Danube frontier

It was in 146 BC, following the defeat of Perseus and the collapse of the Macedonian dynasty that Rome established her first province in the lands beyond the Adriatic, Macedonia, and acquired a foothold in Illyricum. It was over a century later that Roman arms were first carried as far as the Danube, and not until the principate of Augustus that the bulk of the lands between Adriatic and Danube came under direct Roman control. Thenceforward, although indirect Roman suzerainty would be exercised by diplomatic means well beyond the banks of the river, the Danube itself, for the greater part of its length would serve as the imperial frontier, a clear and unmistakable line around this edge of the empire, but a line, like that of the Rhine, which was not easily defensible.

The Danube flows over a distance of 2,800 km (1,740 miles) from its origins on the south-eastern slopes of the Black Forest to its delta on the Black Sea. The country through which it flows changes considerably and frequently between its Alpine origins and its flat and marshy termination. There are spectacular, scenic sectors where the river flows through steep-sided gorges, as in western Noricum from Passau down to Linz, in Pannonia in the Waizen Gorge where the river changes the direction of its flow from west–east to north–south to cross the Hungarian Plain, and in Moesia where the river cuts through between the Balkan mountains and the southern Carpathians, entering a steep and dangerous defile where rocks, rapids and whirlpools make navigation hazardous (pl. 8.3). The most serious obstacle to navigation is the Iron Gate, the Prigrada, a ledge of rock which juts out from the left and almost reaches across to the right bank of the river. The current here, before the engineering works of the last decade, which raised the water level, was in excess of three metres (10 ft) a second. Communication above and below the Iron Gate was impossible until this obstacle could be by-passed. By contrast the outer bank of the river is utterly open and exposed in the stretch south of Budapest (Aquincum), where the loess cliffs of the right bank look out over the flat expanse of the Great Hungarian Plain, and to the south of the Wallachian plain where the river flows in a channel 1 to 2 kilometres ($\frac{1}{2}$–$1\frac{1}{4}$ miles) wide towards its delta, an area of vast swamps and freshwater lakes. The severity of the climate is such that the middle and lower Danube used to be ice-bound almost every winter: in such conditions its value as a deterrent to movement is nil.

The province of Macedonia, once annexed, had to be defended from Thracian aggression to the north; an overland route through Illyricum to the west was clearly desirable, and yet it was not until the establishment of the Principate that a concerted attempt could be made to confront the area's problems. Thrace and Illyricum were the scenes of sporadic but unco-ordinated campaigns by republican generals to protect existing interests and, in the harsh conditions of the mountainous Balkan terrain, to harden up armies. Military glory was hard-won in this formidable area, progress inevitably slow, and these campaigns did not result in annexation and direct control of further territory.

In 35 BC Octavian Caesar embarked upon a limited campaign against the Iapudes and Pannonians; he captured Sisak (Siscia) in the valley of the Sava and established there a garrison of twenty-five cohorts. In 34–33 he tackled the Delmatae. In 29–28 Licinius Crassus was given command of the army of Macedonia to launch a punitive campaign against the Dacians and the Bastarnae from beyond the Danube and the Moesi from north of the Stara Planina (the Balkan mountains) who were harassing the Thracian peoples who were in a treaty relationship with Rome, and threatening Macedonia itself. Crassus won a major victory, asserting Roman control over that area south of the lower Danube which was to become the province of Moesia, some time before AD 6. For the time being Thrace south of the Stara Planina was left as an independent kingdom.

Augustus' first priorities after his acquisition of power were the problems in Spain and the east. Thereafter he turned his attention to Illyricum and in a series of concerted campaigns between 14 and 9 BC, led down the Sava and Drava and northwards from Macedonia, Roman control was established over an area from the Adriatic to the

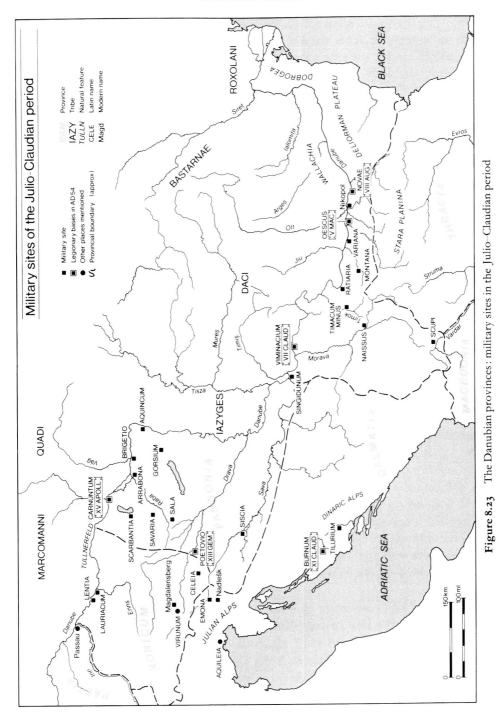

Figure 8.23 The Danubian provinces: military sites in the Julio–Claudian period

Danube. The Illyrican command, hitherto a senatorial appointment, now passed into the gift of the emperor, for it was a significant military post. In AD 6 a major expedition was launched against the menacing Maroboduus, king of the German Marcomanni, whose power centre lay north of the central Danube in Bohemia. This initiative was thwarted when Illyricum rebelled, a massive and widespread rebellion which was four years in the suppression. No sooner was it put down than the Varus disaster occurred in Germany (p. 143 above). Augustus changed from ambitious expansionism to cautious conservation of the status quo. Plans for conquest beyond Rhine and Danube were abandoned. The Illyrican command was split; Dalmatia to the south and west, Pannonia to the north and east. Beyond Pannonia lay Moesia, and between Moesia and Macedonia the kingdom of Thrace, still independent of direct Roman control, in reality a Roman puppet state, a situation which survived down to AD 46 when an uprising of the Thracian tribes led Claudius to annex the kingdom. The conquest of the Balkan area was thus complete. The kingdom of Noricum which lay west of Pannonia had been peaceably absorbed in the second decade BC. Roman control extended as far as the Danube from its source to its mouth.

While the general trend of the Augustan campaigns is known the positions of the military bases are, for the most part, no more than conjectural (fig. 8.23). After the suppression of the Illyrican rebellion seven legions remained in the Balkan area. As far as is known their bases all lay back in the heart of the region, not on its fringes, at important road and river junctions ready to deploy wherever they might be needed, be it against external or internal enemies. *Legio IX Hispana*, for example, probably lay at Sisak (Siscia) on the Sava, on the main east–west trunk route through the Balkans, while *VIII Augusta* was at Ptuj (Poetovio) where the so-called Amber Road (the great prehistoric Baltic–Italy trade route) crossed the Drava. The location of the third Pannonian legion is in doubt but a strong candidate, prior to its foundation as a veteran colony in AD 14, is Ljubljana (Emona) which controls entry to the pass over the Julian Alps, the major direct land link between the Balkans and Italy. The two Dalmatian legions both lay on the lateral road down the coastal side of the Dinaric Alps, in the territory of the hitherto troublesome Delmatae. The original stations of the two legions allocated to Moesia are not known. Possible sites lie at Niš (Naissus) and Skopje (Scupi) on the strategic overland link between Italy and the Aegean, the one commanding the valley of the Morava, the other on the upper Vardar in the Dardanian area important for its mines.

No further major campaigning took place in the Balkan area until the end of Nero's reign. Meanwhile the task of engineering a communications network was a priority and the army is early attested building roads. In Moesia the two legions undertook the construction of a towpath through the upper part of the Danube gorge, essential for the navigation of that part of the river. Some redeployment of the army took place during these generally peaceful years (fig. 8.23). A few units were moved from the interior to points where major routes crossed the Danube. Late under Tiberius or early in the reign of Claudius a legionary fortress was built at Petronell – Deutsch Alteburg (Carnuntum) where the Amber Road met the river. At much the same time an auxiliary unit was posted about 100 km (62 miles) to the south-east to Szöny (Brigetio) where a route led northwards up the Vág valley into the territory of the Quadi, and another to Budapest (Aquincum) where a diagonal road across Pannonia meets the Danube at a major crossing point, which gives access to the west–east route across the north of the Great Hungarian Plain. To east and west of Pannonia, in Moesia and Noricum, the pattern recurs. It is under Claudius that legionary bases appear on the Danube in Moesia. Kostolac (Viminacium) was founded at the head of the route up the Morava, close by the Danube crossing at Palanka (Lederata), the western route north into Dacia. Gigen (Oescus) lay opposite the entrance to the Olt valley, and, 80 km (50 miles) to the east, Stuklen (Novae) was sited on a river crossing and at the exit of the Shipka pass over the Balkan mountains from Thrace which had, at this same time, been made into a Roman province. To the west, in Noricum, the bulk of the small occupying force still lay in the interior of the province, with only two sites, a mere 18 km (11 miles) apart, occupied on the river front, Linz (Lentia) and Enns-Lorch (Lauriacum), both on routes from the north, the latter at the terminus of the trans-Alpine road from the Adriatic via Virunum, the provincial capital, to the Danube.

The army thus lay poised at nodal points on the route network, concerned with both the maintenance of internal security and supervision of tribes beyond the provincial limits. Some troop movements in the northern area of Pannonia will have been connected with the downfall, in AD 50, of the Quadian king, Vannius, a Roman nominee to the kingdom of the Suebi. Tacitus records that Claudius, while declining to interfere directly in this dispute, ordered the governor of Pannonia 'to station a legion with a picked body of auxiliaries on the bank of the Danube' in order to protect the losers and deter the victorious barbarians lest they be tempted to invade the province. Vannius' forces included cavalry recruited from the Sarmatian Iazyges, a tribe of whom more will be heard. In AD 62 *legio V Macedonica* was moved to the east from its base at Oescus. Only two legions were now available for the defence of Moesia, with its 1,000 km (600 miles) of river frontier. The garrison of the Balkan area as a whole was a small one; proportionally far more troops lay in the Rhineland at this time. It was the advent of serious troubles on the Danube in the Flavian period which brought about a reversal of this situation.

In the first half of the first century AD there moved into the region north of the Danube, east and west of the Dacian kingdom, the Sarmatians, nomadic Iranian horse-men driven westwards from the steppes of Kazakhstan by the Huns. They were a people who, in the words of the historian Florus, did not know the meaning of peace. They first appeared on the lower Danube late in Augustus' reign; by mid-century the Sarmatian Roxolani were established to the east of the Dacian kingdom beyond the

Danube delta, the Iazyges in the Great Hungarian Plain, sandwiched between Pannonia to the west and Dacia to the east, whence they had perhaps been moved with Roman connivance, to form a bulwark between the Roman province and the predatory Dacians, and to prevent any alliance between Dacia and the Germanic Quadi and Marcomanni. Soon after their arrival on the Danube the Sarmatians impinged upon the fortunes of the Roman provinces: the Iazyges first appear in a broadly pro-Roman stance, providing cavalry for the client king Vannius (p. 175 above). Some years later the Roxolani feature among the trans-Danubian peoples with whom the governor of Moesia, Ti. Plautius Silvanus Aelianus, came to terms, having, in the words of a laudatory inscription set up in his honour, 'crushed a rising of the Sarmatians at its outset'. The extent of the threat at this time is not known, but in the winter of 67–68 the Roxolani struck in earnest, crossing the Danube and massacring two cohorts. The following year with the Empire embroiled in civil war and the Moesian legions departed to fight for the Flavian cause, the Dacians attacked. A temporary reprieve was effected by Mucianus, marching west with reinforcements for Vespasian. Late in 69 a new governor, Fonteius Agrippa, brought three legions to Moesia; the one assigned to the Sarmatian front was insufficient to prevent renewed invasion and devastation in the spring of 70. The luckless governor was killed; his replacement, Rubrius Gallus, brought in another legion and succeeded in expelling the invader. As a result of the experiences of these years the military arrangements on the Danubian *limes* were reviewed:

> Having brought the war to this conclusion the governor (Rubrius Gallus) took precautions for future security by stationing more numerous and stronger garrisons throughout the area, so as to make it impossible for the barbarians to cross the river again. (Josephus, *Bellum Iudaicum*, 7.94)

A line of forts was constructed along the Danube banks, not just on the Dacian and Sarmatian front but further west where Pannonia and Noricum faced the Quadi and Marcomanni (fig. 8.24). Fort spacing and siting was related to topography. In Noricum, for example, relatively few forts lay in the stretch between Passau and the Wachau; for much of this length the river flows in a narrow steep-sided valley. The area north of the river was heavily forested and sparsely populated. Further east, between the Wachau and the Wienerwald, the *limes* fronts the Tullnerfeld, thickly populated and menaced by the Marcomanni, the most vulnerable sector of the Norican *limes*. Here five forts lay in a 50-km (31-mile) stretch. Topography too dictated that in the Danube gorge area in Moesia few forts could be accommodated on the steep approaches to the river; instead closer spaced fortlets provided the necessary troop accommodation.

It is probably at this time that the Danube watchtowers, illustrated on Trajan's Column and therefore certainly in existence by the beginning of the second century, make their first appearance. These early towers, timber or stone (the Column would

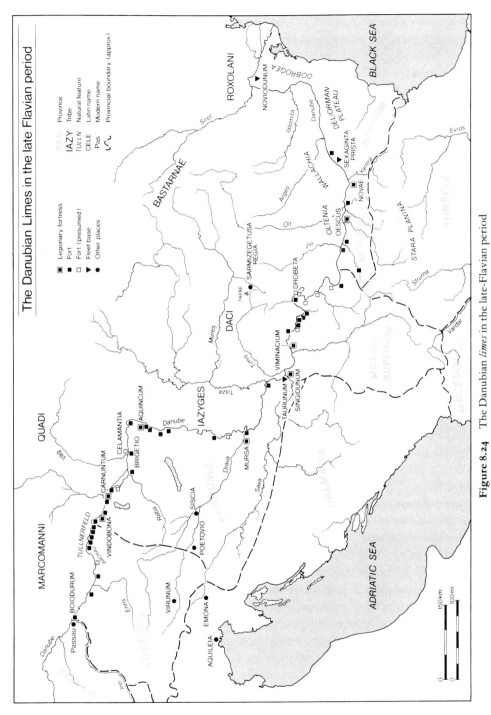

Figure 8.24 The Danubian *limes* in the late-Flavian period

appear to show stonework, pl. 8.4), have proved elusive on the ground. None has been found in the Moesian sector, and the first two have only recently been identified in northern Pannonia, just west of the Danube knee. Such examples as have been identified in Noricum appear to date to the second rather than the late first century.

The auxiliary establishment of Pannonia and Moesia increased substantially during the Flavian period, as the focus of military activity in the west swung away from the Rhine towards the Dacian–Sarmatian front. The Norican frontier, that much further west, remained quiet until the middle years of the second century. The two Danube fleets were reorganized, and it is perhaps then that new bases were built for the *classis Moesica* at Sexaginta Prisca (literally 'Sixty Ships') and at Noviodunum in the northern Dobrogea, close to the Danube delta. No auxiliary forts yet lay this far east, for the land which lay south of the river, the Deliorman plateau (the name means 'wild wood') was an ill-watered heavily forested region which supported but a sparse population.

In AD 85, despite these new measures, crisis returned to the Danube. The Dacians, whose power had been in eclipse since the death of their great king Burebista in the mid-first century BC, were once again strong and reunited under another powerful ruler, Decebalus. The heartland of the Dacian kingdom lay within the mountain amphitheatre of the Carpathians, with their major hill-top citadels lying in the Transylvanian Alps, no great distance north of the Moesian frontier. In 85 they crossed the Danube, killing the governor of Moesia and destroying part of his army: a legion, *V Alaudae*, was lost. In the Dacian war that ensued and which brought the emperor himself to the area, Rome suffered a further major defeat when the praetorian prefect, Cornelius Fuscus, was killed. Eventually in 88 a Roman victory was achieved at Tapae on the western approaches to Dacia. Perhaps because trouble had broken out in the Rhineland with the revolt of Saturninus and renewed hostilities with the Chatti, remarkably lenient terms were given to the Dacian king. He received subsidies and retained his power, though nominally as a Roman client, while Domitian warred against his vassal states, the German Marcomanni and Quadi and the Sarmatian Iazyges, because they had failed to support him against Decebalus.

In the course of the Dacian war the Moesian command had been divided; two legions now lay in each of Moesia Superior and Moesia Inferior, the last remaining Dalmatian legion, *IV Flavia*, being brought into a new legionary base at Beograd (Singidunum). With the transfer of *XIII Gemina* from Ptuj (Poetovio) on the Drava crossing of the Amber Road, the whole of the Danubian legionary strength lay on, or very close to, the river (fig. 8.24). None remained in the interior. As a result of the Dacian and Sarmatian threats the Pannonian legionary establishment had doubled from two to four units. A legionary fortress replaced the earlier cavalry fort at Budapest (Aquincum), the gateway to the territory of the Iazyges, while *II Adiutrix*, transferred from Britain to take part in the Dacian war, was based in the extreme south-east of the province at Osijek (Mursa) on the Drava, some 20 km ($12\frac{1}{2}$ miles) from its confluence with the Danube and at a major road junction whence routes led west, north and south-east into Moesia. The work of constructing auxiliary forts along the river bank, begun under Vespasian, continued under Domitian and into the reign of Trajan; such military sites as remained in the interior were largely abandoned as the army moved up to the frontier. In addition to the bases on the right bank, bridgehead fortifications were constructed on the left bank at several of the major crossing points, opposite Carnuntum and Aquincum, for example, and at Celamantia opposite Brigetio. Roman control will have extended well beyond the river itself, with patrols operating over the whole of the area north and east of the frontier line.

The treaty arrangement with Dacia, negotiated by Domitian, was rejected by Trajan. It is clear that from the outset he planned the absorption of the Dacian kingdom, and preparations for the campaign can be seen in the completion of the towpath through the Danube gorge. Access through the upper gorge had been achieved as early as the 30s, but it is only now that the road was extended through the steep and narrow defile of the Kazan in the lower gorge, a remarkable rock-cut road with a cantilevered timber superstructure whose execution is commemorated on an inscription, the *Tabula Traiana*, carved into the rock face in AD 100. The river link between Upper and Lower Moesia was completed by the digging of a 5 km (3 mile) long canal to by-pass the Iron Gate; an inscription set up in AD 101 records that Trajan 'having by-passed the river on account of the dangerous cataracts, has made safe the entire passage of the Danube' (Šašel, 1973; fig. 8.25). There now existed effective land and river links between the armies of the two provinces.

In the course of two campaigns, 101–2 and 105–6, Trajan defeated the Dacians, driving Decebalus to suicide, and took possession of his kingdom. The province of Dacia which he created comprised the territory which lay within the amphitheatre of the Carpathians, the region of the Banat bounded on the north by the river Mureş and on the west by the Tisza, and western Oltenia as far as the area of the river Jiu (fig. 8.26). Two legions were stationed here: *IV Flavia* lay on the western approach, first at Haţeg – later to become the *colonia* Ulpia Traiana Sarmizegethusa – and subsequently a little to the west along this same route at Reşiţa (Berzobis). The other legion, *XIII Gemina*, was stationed at Alba Iulia (Apulum) in the valley of the Mureş. Auxiliary units were disposed along the main routes into the province, that which led north and east from the Lederata crossing via Tibiscum to Ulpia Traiana, and on the route north from the Pontes-Drobeta crossing where Trajan had built his new bridge (the Bridge of Apollodorus), via the upper waters of the river Jiu. A third grouping of forts lay in the exposed north-west corner of the province where a gap in the mountain chain allowed easy access to and from the territory of the Iazyges. There was also a group of forts, briefly occupied, in the region of the Dacian citadels.

On the eastern flank of the new province the area of the Wallachian Plain and southern Moldavia as far as the Siret, came under the control of the governor of Lower

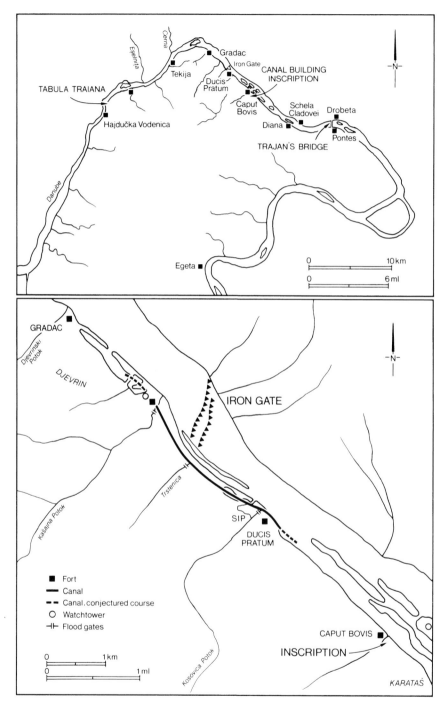

Figure 8.25 Trajan's canal at the Iron Gate

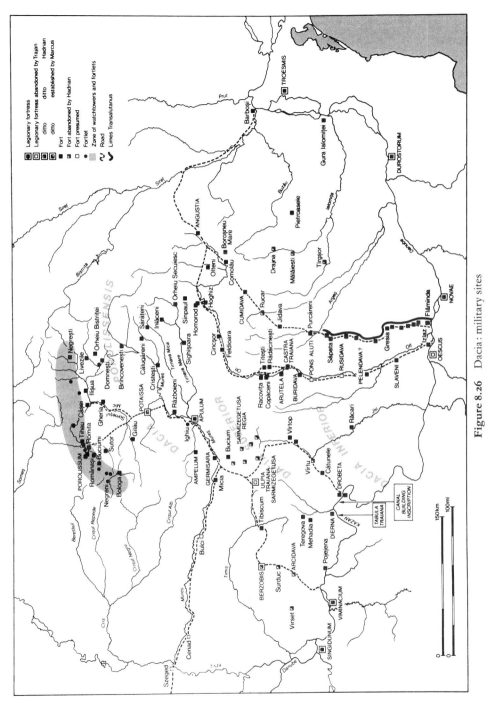

Figure 8.26 Dacia: military sites

Moesia, with units being stationed on the roads leading up to the mountain passes, in the valleys of the Olt, Ialomiţa and Siret. It is under Trajan that units were first stationed on the Danube itself east of the Yantra, the result perhaps of experience gained in the first Dacian War when Sarmatian Roxolani had invaded the province. Two new legionary bases were established, at Silistra (Durostorum) and at Igliţa (Troesmis) in the north-west corner of the Dobrogea, garrisoned by the legion from Oescus which now became a veteran colony. Further reorganization at this period involved the Pannonian command which was split into two, Pannonia Superior to the west with its three legions at Vindobona, Carnuntum and Brigetio, Pannonia Inferior in the east, with one legion at Aquincum and a substantial auxiliary garrison ranged along the Danube looking out over the Great Hungarian Plain.

The first governor of Pannonia Inferior, the future emperor Hadrian, had to deal with trouble from Sarmatians, presumably the Iazyges, and a decade later, almost immediately upon his accession to the imperial throne in 117, he launched a punitive campaign against them after they, in concert with the Roxolani, had invaded Roman territory, killing the governor of Dacia. The Roxolani complained that the subsidy due them from Rome (and presumably negotiated with Trajan in the wake of the Dacian wars) had been reduced. The peace subsequently negotiated by Hadrian in 118 lasted for half a century. The government of Roman territory north of the Danube was totally reorganized. The province of Dacia was split into three separate commands. Dacia Superior, with its one legion at Apulum (*legio IV Flavia* had departed from the province) occupied the central regions: the position of its south-western frontier is uncertain, lying either on the river Tisza or further east in the region of the line from Lederata to Tibiscum or Dierna to Tibiscum. If the latter hypothesis is correct it means that the Banat no longer formed part of the province, and had presumably been handed over to the Iazyges, now in a treaty relationship with Rome. Two large forts at Micia and Tibiscum, each capable of holding more than a single auxiliary unit, controlled access to the province, one on the road along the valley of the Mureş, the other on the route from the south. North of the Mureş the mountains of Bihar afforded some protection. The north-western area became the province of Dacia Porolissensis which contained no legion but had a major concentration of auxiliary troops, notably at Porolissum whose two forts, Pomet and Citera, were together capable of holding a force equivalent in size to almost half a legion. This north-western *limes* guarded a gap in Dacia's natural defence, access via the valleys of Criş and Someş. Fieldwork still in progress is showing this to be the most complex of the Dacian frontier sectors (fig. 8.27); it is as yet incompletely known and therefore incompletely understood. Structural evidence indicates that it is of more than one build, but its development and dating are uncertain. There are several short, discontinuous sectors of linear barrier, part earthwork (bank and ditch), part stone. In the area of Porolissum the barrier runs for a distance of about 4 km (2½ miles), and for a stretch of 225 m (246 yd) is double, the two elements

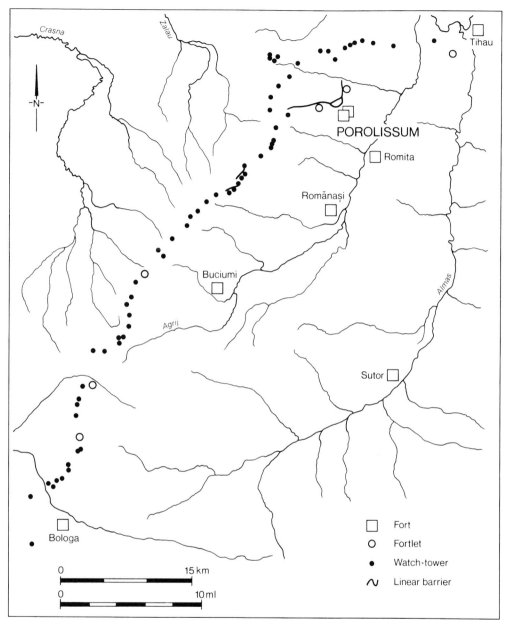

Figure 8.27 The *limes Porolissensis*

running about 18 m (19½ yd) apart (fig. 8.28). Attached to this barrier just east of the forts are two earth and timber fortlets, and two further fortlets lie to the west (fig. 8.29). Observation over this frontier area was maintained from a complex of stone-built towers, mostly square, some circular, sited at irregular intervals on high ground as dictated by local topography, which extends around the north-west and north sides of the province. This complex of installations is designed to control movement into the province via the main north-west gateway through the Meseş mountains. It indicates a continuing concern with the mobile Iazyges beyond, who, despite their client status, were not to be wholly trusted.

The third province, Dacia Inferior, lay to the south and east, between the Carpathians and the Danube. That part of southern Moldavia and the Wallachian Plain occupied by Trajan was evacuated by Roman troops, the result of the treaty arranged between Hadrian and the Roxolani. The eastern frontier lay to the east of the river Olt, troops being deployed in two north–south lines along the two roads which linked Moesia and Dacia; one ran up the valley of the Olt from the Danube crossing at Izlaz by the colony and erstwhile fortress of Oescus to the Red Tower Pass through the Carpathians (the so-called *limes Alutanus*), the other an advanced line to the east from Flaminda north and east through the Bran Pass (the *limes Transalutanus*). Just in front of this road, on its eastern flank a linear earthwork was constructed, an earth and timber rampart, but with no ditch in front, with two building phases, the first showing signs of having been destroyed by fire. The bank itself is undated and the interpretation of it depends on an understanding of the role of the forts which lie in its vicinity. The once popular theory that the line of forts on the Olt represents the original Hadrianic frontier line which was replaced later in the second century by the so-called *limes Transalutanus*, an interpretation heavily influenced by the British frontier sequence, does not accord with the available, albeit meagre, evidence on the dating of the forts on the outer road. Further, the very fact that the outer, and eastern, bank of the Olt stands higher than the inner would have made it a very difficult frontier to control. It is more likely that the earthwork here marks the eastern boundary of the province of Dacia Inferior as instituted by Hadrian when he evacuated the military sites further east in the Wallachian Plain.

One effect of the occupation of Dacia was to transform the Danubian line, in the middle reaches of its course through Moesia, from an external to an internal frontier. The evidence on the point is not totally clear but such as there is suggests that this zone was not completely demilitarized, though there was some redeployment of troops. The legion was withdrawn from Oescus, for example, and transferred to the more vulnerable frontier sector near the Danube mouth. Some forts were needed to watch the major routes and river crossings from Moesia into Dacia.

Beyond the frontiers treaties were made with the peoples who bordered the Empire and peace maintained by diplomatic means for nearly half a century. Rome's power

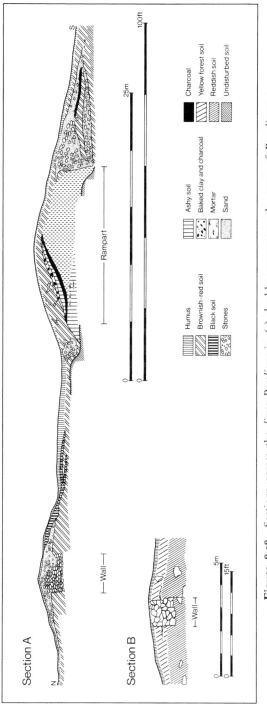

Figure 8.28 Sections across the *limes Porolissensis*: (a) double rampart to the west of Porolissum; (b) mortared stone wall (*after Macrae* et al.)

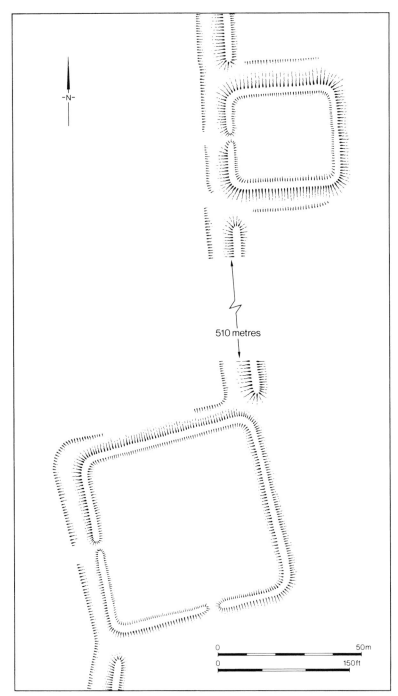

Figure 8.29 The fortlets at Brebi on the *limes Porolissensis* north-east of Porolissum (*after Macrae* et al.)

and influence extended well beyond the confines of her frontiers and she is found, for example, during the reign of Pius, intervening in the dynastic troubles of the Quadi. It was not until the 160s that serious trouble resumed, involving the area of the middle Danube, the Germanic Quadi and Marcomanni as well as the Sarmatian Iazyges. In 166 the Germans attacked and crossed the frontier, destroying many forts and civil settlements. In a renewed onslaught in 170–1 against the frontiers of Pannonia and Noricum the enemy penetrated southwards across the Alps and into northern Italy. It was some years before they were finally expelled from the Empire. During the course of and in the aftermath of these troubles, the military arrangements on the middle Danube were reviewed. In the early 170s, in the wake of the barbarian penetration into Italy, *legio II Italica* was stationed at Ločica in south-east Noricum, guarding the route from Pannonia into Italy over the Julian Alps. On conclusion of the hostilities the unit moved forward to the frontier line, first to Albing and very soon thereafter to the adjacent site of Lauriacum, a critical frontier crossing. Another legion, *III Italica*, was posted to Regensburg in Raetia (p. 164 above). Dacia now acquired a second legion, *V Macedonica* at Turda (Potaissa) in Dacia Porolissensis, stationed within easy reach of the vulnerable north-west frontier sector. Terms were once again imposed upon the peoples beyond the frontiers, limiting their access to the Danube, establishing a neutral zone along the frontier and stipulating conditions under which they might assemble and trade. Once again diplomacy was preferred to outright conquest. The seemingly logical solution of incorporating the Sarmatian Iazyges into the Empire, thereby considerably shortening the length of frontier which had to be controlled, was eschewed in favour of indirect control by treaty. The Sarmatians continued to be all but surrounded by Roman troops, hedged in by Roman restrictions, but to remain independent kingdoms against whom Rome had to be constantly on the alert.

In lower Pannonia a series of inscriptions attests the construction in AD 184 of a line of watchtowers and garrisons along the Danube front designed to prevent 'the secret infiltration of the province by brigands'. Some new units of mounted archers, equipped to deal with the threat posed by the highly mobile Sarmatians, were raised. The rebuilding of forts and fortresses in stone, begun earlier in the century, continued, but in all its essentials the frontier arrangements did not change until change was forced upon it by the disastrous invasions of the third century. One significant development which then occurred was the establishment of an overall military command for the Danubian region, with its base at Sirmium. This post was created in 247 or 248 by Philippus after he had personally participated in war on the Danube, against the Carpi. In the 240s the Gothic incursions across the lower Danube began, which led to the destruction of forts and fortresses and to the devastation of Thrace and lower Moesia, and which culminated in the death of the emperor Trajan Decius and his son in 251 at Abritus. The Gothic attacks were renewed in 267–270. The middle and upper Danube meanwhile suffered from invasions by Marcomanni, Quadi and Sarmatae (258–60). The buffer zone beyond the Danube no longer cushioned the provinces from attack, for Rome's clients, unable to resist the pressure from hostile tribes beyond, Goths, Gepids, Vandals and Carpi, were precipitated into the empire. Further west, the Norican frontier, particularly its exposed north-west corner, had been under sporadic attack from the Alamanni throughout the third century. The north of the province suffered periodic devastation. In 270, when the Alamanni and Juthungi invaded through Raetia into Italy, Noricum, on the eastern flank of the attack, did not escape unscathed, and on this occasion the destruction spread well to the south, a region which, because of its natural Alpine defences, generally suffered much less severely than the north. The following year, AD 271, Dacia was abandoned, the first entire established province to be evacuated in the face of enemy pressure. The Danube became once again the frontier. Dacia's two legions were transferred to the south bank of the river where the new province of Dacia Ripensis was carved out of what had been Moesian territory. There is little evidence for immediate reorganization of the frontier sites, but a couple of decades later, during the Tetrarchy, a complete overhaul of the imperial defences was undertaken (fig. 8.30). In addition to the administrative reforms which included major provincial reorganization (eight separate provinces now fronted the Danube), the division of civil and military responsibility and the creation of separate frontier commands (Part 3, Chapter 7), Diocletian instituted a massive programme of building on the frontiers. Existing forts were remodelled in the new overtly defensive architectural styles, with projecting towers and few, narrow and heavily guarded gateways, and new forts, fortlets and towers were added, thickening up the cordon of defence. Bridgehead forts were constructed, or reconstructed, on the left bank. Drobeta, for example, originally built as a Trajanic bridgehead at the northern end of his new Danube bridge, was redesigned and refortified; its gateways were blocked and bastions added. It lay north of the Danube gorge, an area which, with Dacia gone, had once again become a frontier sector. Numerous close-spaced posts were built along this stretch (about 90 in 30 km or 19 miles), mostly small in size because of the restrictions imposed by topography. Barrier walls were erected across some of the valleys, closing off access south into the interior (fig. 8.31).

But, however great the proliferation of forts, fortlets and towers along the frontier line, however strongly it might be manned by static limitanean troops, once it was breached Italy lay exposed and undefended, as had been demonstrated so clearly by the Quadi and Marcomanni in 170 and the Alamanni and Juthungi a century later. The solution was sought in the creation of a mobile field army (Part 3, Chapter 7), and also in the provision of an inner ring of defences. An attempt was made to shield the vulnerable corridor from Illyricum into Italy over the Julian Alps by constructing a series of short lengths of dry-stone wall with associated forts and fortlets, in an arc from Tarsatica in the south-east to Cividale del Friuli (Forum Iulii) in the north-west. These defences, the detail of whose development is unclear, are known as the *claustra Alpium Iuliarum* (fig. 8.32). Some time during the fourth century these defences came under

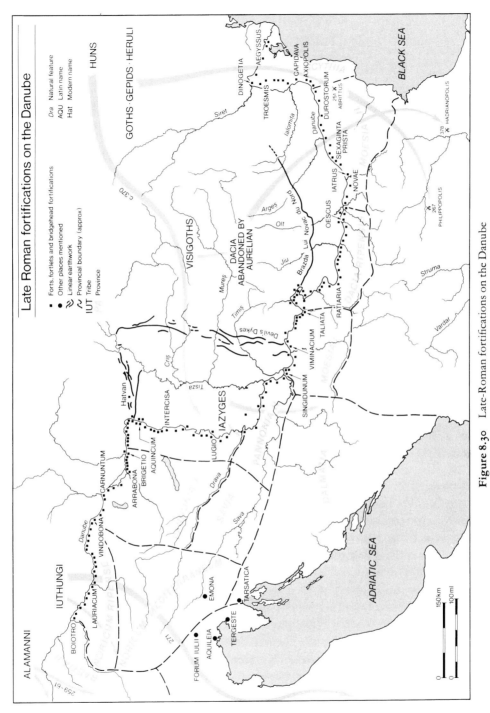

Figure 8.30 Late-Roman fortifications on the Danube

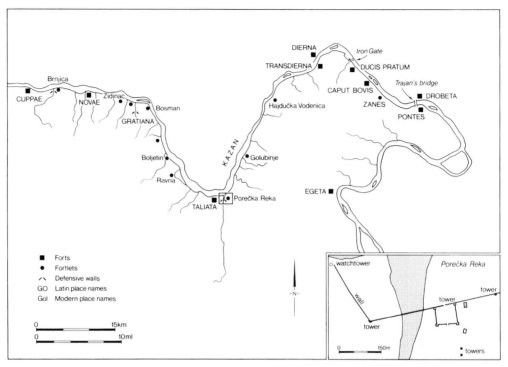

Figure 8.31   Detail of the late-Roman defensive wall at Porečka Reka

the overall command of the *comes Italiae*, whose insignia of office as illustrated in the *Notitia Dignitatum* shows a fortified city at the foot of mountains guarded by barrier walls (pl. 8.5).

The programme of frontier refortification begun during the Tetrarchy, was continued through the reigns of Constantine and his successor. Their work included the provision of outer earthworks, constructed beyond the Danube, in an attempt to relieve pressure on the frontier itself. One of these boundary earthworks, the Brazda lui Novac du Nord, runs for 300 km (190 miles) north of the Danube (but south of the Carpathians), through Oltenia into Wallachia (fig. 8.30). At the time of its construction, perhaps after the Gothic wars of the 330s, a number of military posts were in occupation in this area north of the Danube and their troops will presumably have had responsibility for enforcing this outer controlled zone. Another of these zones was created around the area of the Great Hungarian Plain, the homeland of the Sarmatians who were under great pressure from the Goths and Gepids beyond; indeed in 322 the Sarmatians had fled west across the Danube in order to escape the depredations of the enemy in their rear. In order to afford some protection to the Sarmatians the Devil's Dyke was constructed, a series of earthen ramparts running eastwards from the Danube knee then turning

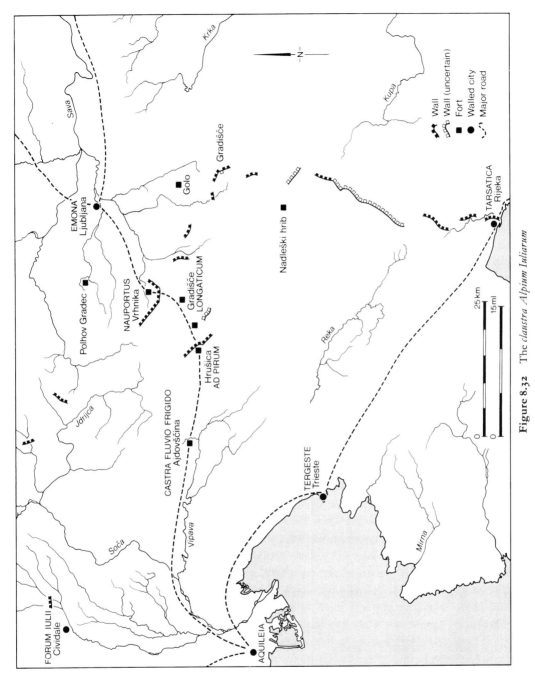

Figure 8.32 The *claustra Alpium Iuliarum*

south to rejoin the river by the fortress of Viminacium (fig. 8.30). A new fort, Visegrad, was constructed on the heights overlooking the Danube bend. In practice the Sarmatian problem remained and by the middle of the century some were being allowed to settle in the Empire.

A final period of fortification of the Norican and Pannonian *limites* took place under Valentinian I. Further watchtowers were set up in vulnerable sectors, around Brigetio where the Vág valley led straight to the frontier and on the Danube knee by the junction of the *limes* and the Devil's Dyke. Another new fort was established just west of the bend of the river, and a military post set up in Sarmatian territory 60 km (37 miles) beyond the Danube on the northern stretch of the earth wall, at Hatvan Gombospuszta. In the Moesian provinces inscriptions record the construction of fortifications following a victory by Valens over the Goths in 369. The victory was short-lived. In the 370s the Goths, driven by the Hunnic peoples who had appeared in the steppes north of the Danube delta, sought again to enter the Empire, crossed the Danube and thrust south through Thrace in the direction of Constantinople. Valens was killed in 378 at the battle of Adrianople. The Goths dispersed through the Danube provinces where some settled as federates in Pannonia and in what had been Lower Moesia north of the Stara Planina. Their role as federates was to help repel further enemies from without, but their depredations were to turn them into enemies within.

The frontier of Pannonia did not long survive. By the end of the century many forts had been abandoned: some were reduced in size, watchtowers were no longer manned. The army ceased to be paid: coin ceased to circulate. In 395 the Pannonian Danube was crossed by Goths and Alans. Many of the inhabitants of the frontier provinces fled south to the relative security of Dalmatia or further, into Italy. Such life as remained on the middle Danubian frontier was finally extinguished by the Huns in 433.

To the west, Noricum lost a substantial part of its defending garrison when Gratian took it east, never to return, in 378. After the end of the century the pay of those that remained ceased to arrive regularly. The reduced garrison was totally unable to cope with the regular raids which came from beyond the frontiers, westwards from Pannonia and eastwards from the Vindelician Plain. By the time St Severin arrived in *c.* 460 and rallied a temporary resistance movement, there was no regular army to speak of. In the late 470s the western flank of the *limes* was lost, in 488 the whole of northern Noricum was abandoned. The south of the province, protected by the Alps, survived longer, its population fleeing to mountain refuges when the barbarians swept through, emerging once more when danger was past. It survived as a Roman enclave in a seething sea of barbarity, a province without a frontier.

To the east, the history of the Lower Moesian frontier may be traced well into the Byzantine era, for its proximity to Constantinople ensured that it received imperial attention. First it was battered by the Huns. In 447, in an onslaught led by Attila, the frontier forts were sacked, the Balkans devastated. The defences were restored, the raids continued unremittingly. The Huns were followed in the sixth century by the Slavs, the Bulgars and then the Avars. Constantinople survived constant onslaught from the Balkan lands by the strength of its own defences; despite repeated attempts at refortification the frontiers themselves had long since ceased to keep the enemy at bay.

8.1   Aerial view of the Lorenzberg

8.2 View along the *limes* in the Taunus region of Upper Germany, showing the bank and ditch

8.3 The Danube at the Kazan Gorge

8.4 Trajan's column: towers on the bank of the Danube

8.5   The insignia of the *comes Italiae* from the *Notitia Dignitatum*

CHAPTER 9

·BRITAIN·

David J. Breeze

The successful landing of a force of four legions with support troops, probably 40,000 men in all, on the south coast of England in AD 43 marked the start of the conquest of Britain. There is no surviving Roman statement detailing the long-term intentions of the expedition, though the order given by Claudius to the governor Aulus Plautius, to conquer 'the rest', coupled with the general expansionism of the Empire at the time, strongly suggest that the aim was to subdue the whole island. The Romans certainly knew Britain to be an island, and that Ireland lay to one side; the invasion of Ireland was even considered at one point. It was to be forty years before Roman arms reached their greatest extent in Britain (fig. 9.1) but the famous victory at Mons Graupius in 83 or 84 was almost immediately followed by retrenchment and the abandonment of some territory. Ironically, it was during the campaigns which led to Mons Graupius that the first suggestion that the Romans might stop short of the conquest of the whole island appears.

The conquest of Britain during the forty years from 43 was not a smooth process. Much depended on the interest or involvement of the emperor. But throughout this period no frontiers were established in Britain. The army's purpose was to control the newly-conquered tribes and to protect them from external aggression. The province (and other friendly tribes) was guarded, not by the creation of an elaborate series of frontier works, which in any case were not part of the army's repertoire at the time, but by the strategic location of the main vehicles of defence, the legions. One legion was at first situated at Colchester, capital of the newly-conquered main enemy, while the other three were carefully placed for attack and defence in the frontier zone. The position of the auxiliary regiments is uncertain: it is not clear whether they were grouped around the legions, which had been the norm elsewhere to date, dispersed across the province, or placed near to the provincial boundary, as was to become the pattern in later years. In any case their forts would be little more than winter quarters, probably fairly lightly built structures of limited life occupied for only a winter or two, and often placed where supplies could be readily assured. In time, a road network was created linking these military stations and facilitating the movement of troops. It has been suggested that the Fosse Way, the road running south-west to north-east through the English Midlands, served as a frontier to the province (first made by Collingwood, 1924). However, this road was merely one part of the network established by the army and it had no special military significance beyond providing a line of communication along the frontier zone.

The provincial boundary presumably lay along the borders of the relevant frontier tribes, though it cannot be compared to that existing between two sovereign countries today: forts might be established by the Romans beyond the frontier, in the territory of either friendly or hostile tribes, if advantageous to them. As the boundary moved forward, and new tribes were taken into the province, so the army moved forward, abandoning its forts in the territory of pacified tribes and establishing new bases to protect and control the newly-conquered peoples. A major shift in the military dispositions occurred in the 70s and 80s when Wales and northern Britain up to the Scottish Highland massif were incorporated into the province. The legions were advanced to new strategic positions: Caerleon in south Wales, Chester and York. In Wales and north Britain lay a network of auxiliary forts, usually ranging in size from 1.2 to 2.4 ha (3 to 6 acres), placed about a day's march apart – 22 to 32 km (14 to 20 miles) – and connected by roads (Nash-Williams, 1969; Breeze and Dobson, 1985). This was not a rigid pattern for it was varied to suit local conditions. It was also essentially a winter pattern for in the summer the army would be on campaign (fig. 9.1).

It was during the advance north in the governorship of Agricola from 77 or 78 to 83, 84 or 85 that there is the first suggestion that the Roman army might stop short of the conquest of the whole island. In discussing the events of Agricola's fourth season (80 or 81) Tacitus, the governor's biographer and son-in-law, remarks that 'if the courage of the army and the glory of the Roman name had allowed it, an end might have been found within Britain' and the Forth–Clyde isthmus was protected by garrisons. As it happened, this line was not to be held long, for two years later Agricola pushed northwards towards his victory over the Caledonians at Mons Graupius.

Agricola's Forth–Clyde frontier – it presumably merits use of that term – remains the most shadowy of all the Roman frontiers in Britain. One fort on the isthmus, Camelon overlooking the Forth, had probably already been established before the decision to garrison this neck of land (Maxfield, 1981). Forty-eight kilometres (30 miles) to the west the fort at Barochan sits on the plateau above the southern bank of the Clyde: the date of its foundation within the Flavian period is not known. In between only one certain Flavian fort is known, the small fort or fortlet at Mollins, though other military installations have been postulated on the basis of the discovery of coins and

Figure 9.1   Military dispositions in Britain under Agricola

other artefacts of the right date. The nature of Agricola's frontier dispositions, fragmentary, unfinished and of brief duration as they might have been, remains uncertain.

If the establishment of garrisons on the Forth–Clyde isthmus marks a change in policy, then the northward advance resumed two years later reflects a return to the aims of earlier years, the conquest of the whole island: these changes in policy may reflect changes in emperors (Dobson, 1981, 7–8). It seems probable that Agricola considered that he had achieved that aim at Mons Graupius where he defeated the main enemy in northern Scotland (fig. 9.1). However, events elsewhere prevented his successor from following up that victory and securing the Roman grip on the north. Whatever intention there might have been to occupy the Highlands was first abandoned, then the outermost forts of the northern dispositions, then all forts beyond the Forth, and finally all forts north of the Tyne–Solway isthmus (Breeze and Dobson, 1976, 128–34).

The rapid changes of policy at this time, combined with our uncertainty of Roman intentions and the fragmentary state of the archaeological record, now render the events of these years and the reasons behind the establishment of certain forts difficult to comprehend. Nowhere is the problem more acute than in trying to determine the purpose of the forts constructed along the edge of the Highlands soon after Mons Graupius.

These forts run in a line from the Clyde nearly to the North Sea, from Barochan to Stracathro a little to the north-west of the Montrose Basin. Each fort effectively controls a route into, or out of, the Highlands. It has been suggested that their aim was to prevent the tribes of the Highlands using these glens to attack the Roman province (Richmond, 1939, 152; Frere, 1981, 91) and that they were the bases for further advance (Mann, 1968, 307–8). It is impossible now to be sure which interpretation is correct. However, the forts cannot be taken in isolation for also in eastern Scotland was constructed the legionary fortress at Inchtuthil (Pitts and St Joseph, 1985). This fortress in fact lies very far north, with only two known forts beyond it. But again difficulties of interpretation crowd in: was the legion in the front line, as were many such units in the first century, or was it brought up north to be the base for further conquests, becoming, in time, the support for troops further north and west? Again it is not possible to answer this question, though the position of the fortress on the north bank of the river Tay may point to an offensive rather than a supportive role.

Inchtuthil had a very short life, being abandoned unfinished in 86 or soon after. At the same time, it seems probable that the forts to the north and also those along the edge of the Highlands were abandoned, leaving the northernmost forts those along the road to the Tay. Along this road, between Ardoch and the river, a number of timber towers have been recognized and it seems probable that they date to this time (Robertson, 1974, 28; Breeze and Dobson, 1976, 129–31).

Fifteen towers have been found to date (fig. 9.2). Those between the fort at Ardoch (pl. 9.8) and the fortlet at Kaims Castle were regularly spaced at intervals of 900 m (1,000

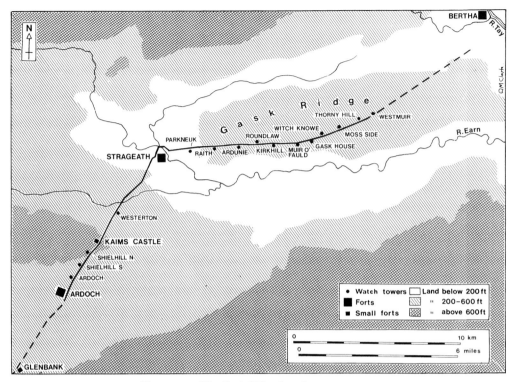

Figure 9.2 The Gask Ridge frontier arrangements

yards), but elsewhere the distance between each post varies between 0.8 to 1.6 km ($\frac{1}{2}$ to 1 mile. Except where there are obvious gaps all the towers are intervisible. Each station consisted of a twelve foot square timber tower formed of four large posts linked by walls of wattle-and-daub and surrounded by a bank and one or two ditches (fig. 9.3). A causeway led across the ditch towards the road. The fortlet at Kaims Castle, 4.8 km (3 miles) north of Ardoch, was complemented in 1983 by the discovery of a second fortlet an equivalent distance to the south at Glenbank; neither are dated but their relative positions suggest that both probably formed part of the same system as the towers.

The towers are too close together to have been used for signalling. Rather, their spacing suggests that they were elevated observation platforms enabling the soldiers stationed there to keep better watch on the cleared strip of ground between the posts and ensure that no unauthorized person entered the province. Strict regulations governed access to a Roman province: people from beyond the Empire normally could only enter if they were unarmed and they were then permitted to proceed to recognized market places, but only under military escort. Also customs duties were chargeable, either at the frontier or at the market. Presumably the purpose of the towers was to ensure that these regulations were enforced while helping to keep in check small-scale

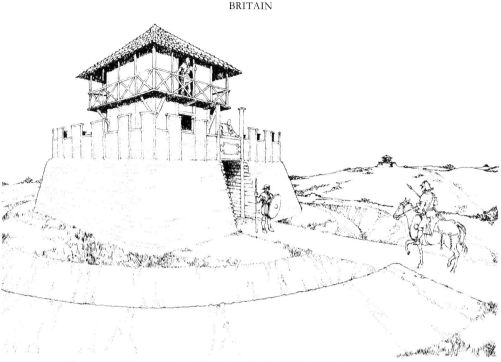

Figure 9.3 Reconstruction drawing of a Gask Ridge watchtower (*M. J. Moore*)

frontier raiding and brigandage. Together with the contemporary watchtowers in Germany (p. 153 above) they mark the first step to establish patrolled and guarded frontiers.

The exact date of construction of the Gask frontier watchtowers is not known. Two have produced late first-century pottery, but within that period further refinement of date has to be on historical and logical grounds. It seems unlikely that the towers would have been constructed in the years of advance before Mons Graupius, while their position, to the south of Inchtuthil, suggests that they were not contemporary with the legionary fortress. A date between the abandonment of the fortress in or soon after 86 and the withdrawal from all forts north of the Forth–Clyde isthmus in about 90 would seem most appropriate. In that case the Gask frontier formed one of the temporary positions held between Mons Graupius and the establishment of the Tyne–Solway line in the early second century.

The reasons for the progressive withdrawal from the forts north of the Tyne–Solway isthmus are not clear, and may have been varied. The transfer of a legion from Britain to the continent in or soon after 86 was the occasion for the abandonment of the fortress at Inchtuthil and presumably simultaneously the other forts along the edge of the Highlands; the legion may have taken some auxiliary regiments with it to the Danube (Birley, 1953, 21). It has been suggested that the final stage in the move south, to the Tyne–Solway line, was in the face of pressure from the northern barbarians (Frere,

1978, 143–4), and certainly at least two forts were damaged by fire at this time (Corbridge and Newstead). However, renewed campaigning on the Danube, in this case Trajan's Dacian wars, may have led to the transfer of further auxiliary units from Britain to the continent, and thus the need to abandon some forts on the frontier (cf. Manning, 1972, 243–6 for the suggestion that Newstead was abandoned peacefully). Whatever the cause, the northernmost forts of the province lay across the Tyne–Solway isthmus, probably by about 105 or soon after.

This line had never previously formed the frontier of the province, though it roughly coincided with the northern boundary of a major tribe, the Brigantes, which had been in treaty relationship with Rome before its incorporation into the province. In the valleys of the Tyne to the east and the Eden to the west, where the roads north crossed the rivers, important forts had been established in the late first century, almost certainly by Agricola. These forts, Corbridge and Carlisle, were linked by a road, the Stanegate, and the distance between them was broken by intermediate stations. During the first twenty years of the second century this line was gradually strengthened by the construction of new forts, fortlets and watchtowers, until in the 120s all were replaced by the construction of a new form of frontier control, a linear barrier. The details of the process are unclear, the scale of the operations uncertain and the order of works obscure, but some points may be made (cf. Breeze and Dobson, 1978, 20–6). The line between Corbridge and Carlisle seems to have been strengthened by the construction of at least one new fort and two fortlets or small forts: it seems unlikely that these two sites stood alone, but other similar installations have yet to be found. West of Carlisle a fort already existed at Kirkbride, but it seems probable that it was only then that a fort was built east of Corbridge: a fort, apparently of two phases, has been discovered from the air on the south bank of the Tyne at Washing Well, Whickham, but it has not been excavated and is therefore not dated (McCord and Jobey, 1971, 120).

It may have been as late as the early years of Hadrian that other developments took place on the isthmus. Some isolated watchtowers appear to date to this time (Breeze, 1982, 69), while the most interesting innovations took place west of Carlisle. Here, in addition to timber watchtowers, lines of ditches have been traced and it has been suggested that their purpose was to help control the fording points over the Solway (Jones, 1980; 1982, 285), though a Roman date for their excavation has yet to be proved. One tower was succeeded by a fort at Burgh-by-Sands but it seems possible that this belongs to the first phase of the Wall.

The construction of the small forts and towers on the Tyne–Solway isthmus was presumably to aid frontier control, but there seems to have been no attempt to emulate the Gask frontier by the erection of closely-spaced towers. Whatever success the 'Stanegate frontier' may have had at frontier control, the most effective aid to control, short of the conquest of the whole island, was the erection of a linear barrier. It may have been that consideration, coupled with the intention to call a halt to the expansion of the empire, which led Hadrian to order the building of a wall to separate the barbarians and the Romans (*Historia Augusta, Life of Hadrian* 11, 2).

Hadrian's Wall (pl. 9.3; fig. 9.4) was planned to run from sea to sea, from Newcastle, beside a new bridge over the Tyne, to Bowness on the Solway (Breeze and Dobson, 1978; Daniels, 1978). The eastern 45 Roman miles were built of stone and the western 31 miles of turf. The reason for this difference in treatment is not known, though it may be noted that the construction of a frontier wall in mortared stone is more unusual than building in turf. It may be that Hadrian, a great builder, simply conceived of his wall on a massive scale and ordered its construction in durable stone wherever possible.

The Wall was not an impenetrable barrier and at intervals of one Roman mile single portal gateways, protected by a small fortlet or milecastle (pl. 9.1; fig. 9.5), were provided. In between each milecastle were two watchtowers or turrets (pl. 9.2; fig. 9.5) and regularity of spacing of towers was ensured by the placing of a tower over the north gate of each milecastle. The towers were stone all the way along the Wall, whether it was built of stone or turf, but the milecastles were of stone on the stone wall and turf and timber on the turf wall. Small barrack-blocks were provided at the milecastles but it is not known whether the soldiers stationed there were also charged with the maintenance of watch at the adjacent turrets. Nor is it known where the soldiers on the Wall came from: were they a separate force, or were they drawn from auxiliary units in the area? On balance the latter seems to be the most likely.

The system of milecastles and turrets continued down the Cumbrian coast for at least 42 km (26 miles) beyond the end of the Wall at Bowness, revealing a preoccupation with raiding and unauthorized access from across the Solway estuary (Bellhouse, 1970, 40–7). Recent work has demonstrated that this was not a simple line of milefortlets and towers. The complication is the discovery of ditches (each usually recut at least twice) and a palisade in the first 13 km (8 miles) west of Bowness (Jones, 1982). In one place two parallel ditches have been found, then a single ditch a little further on, and then one ditch and a palisade. There a road also appears, while the palisade was of two phases: a third phase was represented by a stone tower, possibly preceded by one of timber, which overlay the ditch. Where the evidence survives, the milefortlets sit between the ditches, front and rear gates allowing movement across the linear features (Jones, 1976; Bellhouse, 1981). These slight remains – ditches and palisades – have come to light through aerial photography followed by selective excavation. Dating evidence is minimal, though they appear to belong to the very earliest phases of Hadrian's Wall, being modified and then abandoned apparently still within Hadrian's reign (Jones, 1976, 242–3). It is to be hoped that further reconnaissance and excavation will reveal more details concerning their date and development.

In the first plan for Hadrian's Wall the army units remained behind the Wall on the Stanegate and elsewhere in northern England, thus emphasizing that the soldiers in the milecastles and turrets on the Wall served a different function from those in the

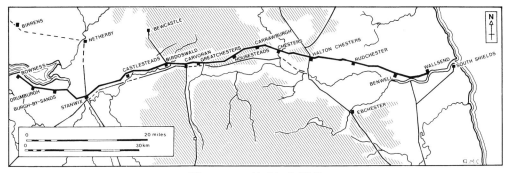

Figure 9.4 Hadrian's Wall

forts of the frontier area. The former were concerned with frontier control, including the supervision of movement across the frontier, the prevention of petty raiding and the like, while the army units were charged with the defence of the province. The existence of the Wall would hinder raiding and brigandage but it could not, and did not, stop a major invasion: that could only be done by the concerted action of the regiments of the north combining together and moving out to meet the enemy in the field. Here the army was paramount: the Roman army was not equipped to fight defensively and did not use Hadrian's Wall as a medieval castle wall. The very size of Hadrian's Wall – the stone wall was 10 Roman feet wide and the turf wall 20 Roman feet wide at its base, but perhaps only 6 feet wide at the top – has led to the general supposition that the wall top was patrolled. There is no evidence for this however, and indeed it would have been impossible to patrol the top of those frontiers where the barrier was merely a timber fence (p. 157 above).

The first scheme for Hadrian's Wall was never completed. During building work a major change in plan took place; it was decided to abandon the forts immediately behind the Wall and construct new forts on the Wall itself. Many of the soldiers building the Wall were moved on to fort building, but some remained behind to complete the construction of the milecastles, turrets and the Wall itself. After some of this work had been done it was decided to reduce the thickness of the stone wall from the initial 10 Roman feet to 8 feet or less.

The decision to move the forts on to the Wall was not taken lightly for it involved the abandonment of sixteen forts, some only recently built or rebuilt, and the construction of an equal number of new stations. Why was it taken? In the initial plan the Wall lay between the army units and the enemy and it seems probable that the barrier obstructed flexible troop movements. While the provision of gates at mile intervals was generous for civilian traffic it was restrictive for the army with only one single-portal gate at each crossing point. Thus when the forts were moved they were actually built astride the Wall with three main gates north of the Wall, providing the equivalent of six single-portal gates, while the sole southern gate was supported by the addition of two single-

Figure 9.5 Reconstruction drawing of a turret and milecastle on Hadrian's Wall (*M. J. Moore*)

portal gates at the ends of the *via quintana*. In this way freedom of movement was provided: indeed there appears to have been overprovision, for many gates north of the
Wall show little sign of use while the later forts on the Wall were built wholly south
of the barrier, though still attached to it.

The construction of the forts on the Wall was accompanied by the digging of a
new earthwork, known since the time of the Venerable Bede as the Vallum (pl. 9.3).
This earthwork extended the whole length of the Wall and consisted of a central ditch
with a mound set back on either side. The Vallum offered no advantage to either side

and its main purpose seems to have been to mark the southern limit of the military zone: it was the Roman equivalent of barbed wire! Gaps through the Vallum were provided, but only at forts and presumably also at the main roads north through the Wall. Thus the number of crossing points through the military zone was reduced from an original seventy-eight or thereabouts to about sixteen. This strengthened military control, though the reason for this change in plan is not certain. It could be that the soldiers guarding the milecastles had been too lax, and it was decided to increase supervision by placing the crossing points under the immediate control of the regimental officers.

The construction of forts on the Wall itself led to a blurring of the separate functions of frontier control and military defence. However, the functions remained separate. The construction of the Wall also blurred a further distinction, that between the military dispositions and the boundary of the province. Hadrian's Wall was not necessarily the provincial boundary. It lay close to the northern limit of Brigantian territory but the two boundaries were not necessarily coincidental. At the west end of the Wall three forts were built north of the barrier and it seems possible that these sites were intended not to act as early warning stations, as such work would have been done by mobile army patrols, but to protect provincials living beyond the barrier.

The construction of Hadrian's Wall led in time to the growth of civil settlements outside many forts (pl. 9.4) and it has been suggested that one purpose of the Wall was to allow the peaceful economic exploitation of the province unhindered by disturbance from the north. Indeed it has been proposed that Hadrian's view was that peace could only be maintained by an ambitious policy of economic development along the frontier, backed up by the intelligent deployment of the army (Birley, 1956; Birley, 1974, 18). It is difficult now, though, to determine the balance between officially encouraged economic development and the natural growth of villages and towns outside forts, settlers being attracted by the existence of a regular source of money.

The building of Hadrian's Wall probably started soon after the visit of the emperor to the province in 122. It was still being modified when the emperor died sixteen years later. The Wall had been extended 6.4 km (4 miles) down the Tyne to Wallsend and the fort at Carvoran had been rebuilt in stone while in the last years of the reign a start had been made on rebuilding the turf wall in stone. Nevertheless, within months of Hadrian's death in July 138, his successor, Antoninus Pius, ordered the abandonment of Hadrian's Wall, a move northwards into southern Scotland and the construction of a new Wall, the Antonine Wall (pl. 9.5; fig. 9.6). The reasons for this change in policy are still a matter of debate. It has been suggested that Hadrian's Wall was out of touch with the main centres of resistance to Rome in Caledonia (Gillam, 1958, 66–7), that the tribes of the Scottish Lowlands had been troublesome and needed to be brought within more immediate Roman control (Frere, 1978, 173–4), and that the expansion of the province had no connection with the local situation but was a response to the

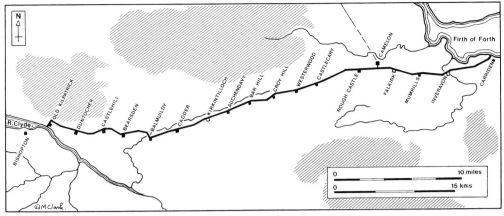

Figure 9.6 The Antonine Wall

accession of a new emperor (Birley, 1974, 17–18; Breeze, 1976, 74–8). Antoninus Pius was not Hadrian's first choice as his successor and there were other people in Rome who considered that they had a better claim to the throne. In such circumstances a brief and successful foreign war, bringing military prestige to an emperor who had never commanded an army, would help secure his peaceful accession: almost exactly a hundred years before, Claudius had invaded Britain, according to the historian Suetonius, to obtain a triumph. It is certainly interesting that at a time when the army could have moved forward to the conquest of the whole island relatively easily there was only a limited expansion of the province.

The new Wall, the building of which commenced under the direction of the new governor of Britain, Lollius Urbicus (pl. 9.5), crossed the Forth–Clyde isthmus from Bo'ness to Old Kilpatrick and was only half the length of its predecessor (Hanson and Maxwell, 1983a; Keppie, 1982). It was not built of stone, but of turf placed on a stone base 15 Roman feet wide. As on Hadrian's Wall a wide and deep ditch lay in front. Forts were placed at an average distance of 13 km (8 miles) apart: owing to the length of the Antonine Wall there were only six forts and they were a little more widely spaced than those on Hadrian's Wall. Recent discoveries have suggested that at each mile interval between these forts lay a fortlet (fig. 9.7), each the same size as a milecastle or mile-fortlet on the southern frontier (Gillam, 1976; Keppie and Walker, 1981).

No turrets have yet been found on the Antonine Wall, though they exist on contemporary continental frontiers (p. 160 above); however, different structures appear. At three points pairs of turf platforms were attached to the rear of the Wall (Steer, 1957). It has been suggested that these were the bases for signal fires (fig. 9.7), and indeed two pairs face north towards the outpost forts while the third pair looks up the Clyde valley to the fort at Bothwellhaugh. The other type of structure is rather different. In one short stretch of the Wall three small enclosures, each measuring about

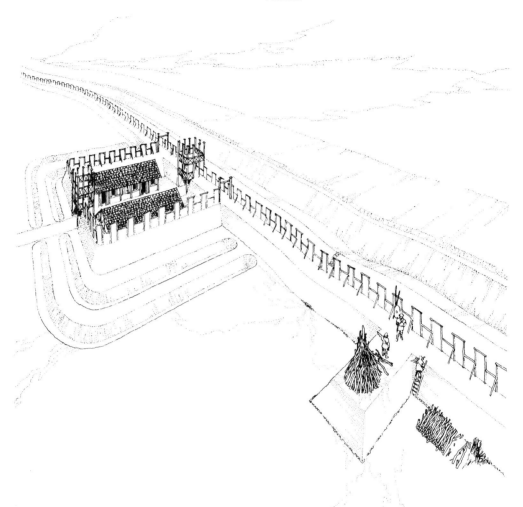

Figure 9.7   Reconstruction drawing of a fortlet and 'beacon platform' on the Antonine Wall (*M. J. Moore*)

11 m by 8 m (36 by 26 ft), lie within a small ditch, together with an intervening fortlet, about 300 m (330 yard) apart. Excavation of one site has failed to reveal any evidence for its function.

One distinctive feature of Hadrian's Wall was lacking on its northern successor: the Vallum. However, a road seems to have formed part of the earliest plans for the Antonine Wall. No road had been provided on Hadrian's Wall, presumably because of the proximity of the Stanegate, though it seems that in places a path led along the north berm of the Vallum. The lack of any earlier road across the Forth–Clyde isthmus presumably led to the realization of the need for one.

The Antonine Wall in its essentials was thus very similar to Hadrian's Wall, but different in its details. The provision of a linear barrier, the spacing and size of the forts and the milefortlets, were all based on Hadrian's Wall. The road, the 'beacon plat-forms' and the small enclosures were additions to the repertoire of the frontier builders. In another way too the Antonine Wall moved forward from Hadrian's Wall. The construction of the forts on Hadrian's Wall was an afterthought. The forts, at first built astride the Wall wherever possible, were clearly only placed on the barrier for convenience and their planning ignored the Wall. On the Antonine Wall, on the other hand, the forts all lay behind the Wall, though usually still attached to it, while their planning related them closely to the barrier. Nevertheless this is not to say that fighting tactics had changed. Both Walls probably operated in broadly the same fashion and the military issue would still be decided in the field, not from behind ramparts and ditches.

There is one other similarity between Hadrian's Wall and the Antonine Wall: a change in plan during the building operations. On the northern Wall this took the form of the construction of new forts on the barrier. In the western two-thirds of the Wall, that is west of the Forth–Clyde watershed at Castlecary, eight new forts were added, reducing the distance between any two forts to a little over 3 km (2 miles). It seems possible that this spacing was not repeated in the eastern sector, perhaps only two or three forts being built rather than the five which would have been required to reproduce the same pattern. Many of these new forts were smaller than the first series of Wall forts, only being able to hold a detachment rather than a full unit. Thus, although the number of forts was trebled, the number of men on the Wall was probably only doubled (Breeze and Dobson, 1978, 96).

The density of structures on the Wall reflected a close spacing of forts and fortlets in southern Scotland, which cluster especially close in the south-west, where timber towers have also been recorded between certain forts and fortlets (Breeze, 1974; Maxwell, 1977). These military dispositions may reflect a preoccupation with local control, new views on the best distribution of military units, or perhaps a determination that no local disturbance should damage the prestige gained by Antoninus Pius through the successful move north.

No line of milefortlets and towers is known on either flank of the Antonine Wall, though a fort and two fortlets situated on the plateau above the south bank of the Clyde overlooked the estuary of that river, while two forts lay beyond the east end of the Wall on the southern shore of the Forth. Forts also lay in advance of the eastern end of the Wall along the road to the Tay (pl. 9.8). These outposts may have been concerned to protect friendly tribes, or new provincials, in Fife rather than provide advance warning of attack, though the positioning of the forts on the route south from Caledonia is suggestive.

The Antonine Wall as completed, perhaps in the late 140s, was the most strongly garrisoned frontier in Britain. Thereafter there was a swing away from this emphasis on the frontier line when the network was reorganized later in the reign of Antoninus Pius; it seems then that one fort on the Wall was abandoned while the garrisons of at least two others were reduced. Some forts and fortlets in southern Scotland were abandoned at the same time, while the size of one of the outpost forts was reduced. The Antonine Wall and its attendant forts were abandoned about 163, for reasons which are unclear, and Hadrian's Wall recommissioned (Hartley, 1972, 36–42; Gillam, 1973, 55–6; Breeze, 1976). Over the next twenty years or so that Wall was in turn modified, perhaps in part in the light of experience gained on the Antonine Wall.

At first Hadrian's Wall seems to have been restored to its earlier condition when abandoned in the 140s, with the exception of the turf wall, where rebuilding in stone was carried through to completion, the construction of a road along the frontier, and the retention of more outpost forts than under Hadrian, presumably to allow the army to maintain better surveillance over the former provincial territory (Breeze and Dobson, 1978, 124–8). Elsewhere milecastles and turrets were repaired, forts reoccupied by similar-sized garrisons to those which had marched out twenty years before, and even the ditch of the Vallum was cleaned out. However, further changes were gradually introduced. Some turrets, especially in the central Crags sector, were abandoned while some milecastle gates were narrowed so that they were only usable by pedestrian traffic. Few of these changes can be closely dated, nor is it known what effect the invasion of the province by the northern tribes in the early 180s and the unrest at the end of the century had on the frontier. It appears, though, that in these years the garrisons of many forts on the Wall were strengthened while new large units were introduced into a reduced number of outpost forts to the north. In addition, extra units of scouts and irregulars are attested at several forts in the third century and it is possible that these units were in garrison from the final years of the preceding century. The main burden of these changes was not only to move the main theatre of action even further from the Wall than before, but also to emphasize the essentially bureaucratic role of the linear barrier, the position of which was irrelevant to the disposition of the army units. Almost in recognition of the reduced importance of the Wall, or so it seems, the Vallum was abandoned as a demarcation line and civilians were allowed to encroach on the once-enclosed space, and even build their houses and shops immediately outside the forts. It is not known how large an area was kept under surveillance by the thousand-strong regiments based in the outpost forts but the land up to the abandoned Antonine Wall, perhaps even to the Tay, would not have been too extensive for them to patrol.

The construction of Hadrian's Wall and the occupation of southern Scotland had led to the abandonment of many forts in Wales (Davies, 1980, 264–9) and northern England (Breeze and Dobson, 1985): the primary purpose of many of the remaining garrisons in Wales was probably supervision of the mines (Hanson, 1986). The return south in the 160s brought a requirement to find homes for at least twenty units. Wherever possible former stations were repaired or rebuilt but as some sites were no longer available at least two new forts had to be constructed while several forts, relinquished as long as forty years before, were recommissioned. The reoccupation of northern England does not carry with it the implication that this area was troublesome and that the tribes needed controlling, or that the army was adopting a policy of defence in depth: it was merely that regiments, whose presence was necessary for the proper defence of the province, needed a home somewhere and there was a limit to the number of units which could be placed on, or in the vicinity of, the Wall (Dobson, 1970, 34).

Disturbances are recorded in Britain on several occasions in the second century, and many appear to have concerned the northern frontier. As a result the province welcomed a series of highly qualified governors throughout the century (Birley, 1981a, 395). The most serious warfare took place in the 180s and 190s. On the former occasion the northern tribes crossed the Wall and killed a general and his army before being defeated. Towards the end of the century, immediately following the end of the civil war in 197, the governor had to purchase peace from the northern tribes who were threatening the frontier. Ten years later, partially as a result of further trouble on the frontier according to one historian, Herodian, Septimius Severus came to Britain with the intention of finishing the imperial task and completing the conquest of the island. His death at York in February 211 brought that operation to a premature end; his conquests were abandoned and the troops withdrawn from the newly constructed base at Carpow on the Tay. The situation reverted to the *status quo* (Leach and Wilkes, 1977).

While no doubt the army continued to maintain watch and ward over the northern marches through the third century, the soldiers also paid increasing attention to their forts, rebuilding and repairing when necessary, but also adding new amenities like aqueducts. This activity continued into the 240s, but thereafter little is attested (Mann, 1971, nos 160–183). Coin series frequently end in the 270s. When this evidence is combined with the arrival of new units at many of the northern forts in the fourth century (Mann, 1974), it may be suggested that the second half of the third century saw an abandonment of some forts as their garrisons were transferred elsewhere, or perhaps disbanded. On the Wall several forts had their garrisons reduced, though none appears to have been completely abandoned.

It may not be coincidental that a new local government unit is first attested in northern England at this time. This was the *civitas Carvetiorum*, in the Eden valley, now presumably charged with the administration of part of the area abandoned by the military authorities (Birley, 1967, 11–13). The only other *civitas* known in the area, that of the Brigantes in Yorkshire, had probably been constituted under Hadrian (Hartley, 1966, 19). The rarity of such local government authorities in the north is probably a reflection of the continuing military presence over much of the area (Mann, 1974, 38–9). The growth of villas and other substantial rural establishments may also have been discouraged by the military presence (Higham, 1986, 177). However, the presence of such a large garrison should have led to major demands on the local economy (Manning, 1974; Breeze, 1984), though this is not reflected in the generally small quantity of Roman material found on native sites in the north.

Trade across the frontier might also be expected to have taken place, for military contact was only one aspect of the relationship between Rome and the tribes beyond the Empire. Analogies with other frontiers suggest that the Romans will have striven to establish treaties with these tribes and certainly, in the late second and early third centuries, treaties are recorded with the Caledonians and the Maeatae. These treaties may have restricted the movement of natives in the vicinity of the frontier, as was certainly the case on the Danube in the late second century. The payment of bribes was another frequently-used branch of diplomacy and is recorded for Britain. Some of the coin hoards found beyond the frontier may have originated in subsidies (Robertson, 1978, 192). Other high-class goods, such as glass vessels, found in northern Scotland (Robertson, 1970) may also have been bribes, or perhaps imports by local chieftains. However, the level of contact between Roman and barbarian, as measured by the discovery of Roman artefacts beyond the frontier, does not seem to have been great. This may reflect lack of trade, though the almost equal paucity of Roman material from native settlements south of the frontier in northern England may suggest that this is too simplistic an hypothesis. The one site which stands out from the rest is Traprain Law, the hill-fort considered to have been the capital of the Votadini. Not only did this town maintain its defences throughout the Roman period, and continue to receive exports from the Empire, but in the second century it manufactured goods for the provincial market.

While the northern frontier was enjoying a quiescent phase in its life in the late third century, defences along the more southerly coasts of England were being strengthened (fig. 9.8). A total of ten forts were built in the third and fourth centuries along the coast from the Wash to the Solent (pl. 9.9): nine of these are named in the late fourth-century army list, the *Notitia Dignitatum* (Occ. 28), as forming the command of the Count of the Saxon Shore (Johnson, 1976). New forts and other installations were also built along the west coast in the fourth century, while at the very end of the century a series of towers were erected along the cliffs of east Yorkshire.

These forts, fortlets and towers were not built as part of a single coherent project, but piecemeal over perhaps 150 years. The *Notitia* records the garrisons of nine forts and in each case it was a normal army unit, not a naval force. However, many sites were isolated from the road network and therefore best approached by sea. Archaeological investigation of several forts has not been successful in revealing details of the internal arrangements which might help in determining their function and role. In short, it is impossible now to know how these installations worked, though it is clear that their intention was to protect the British provinces from raids by pirates and tribes beyond the empire: Picts, Scots, Saxons, Franks and Attacotti.

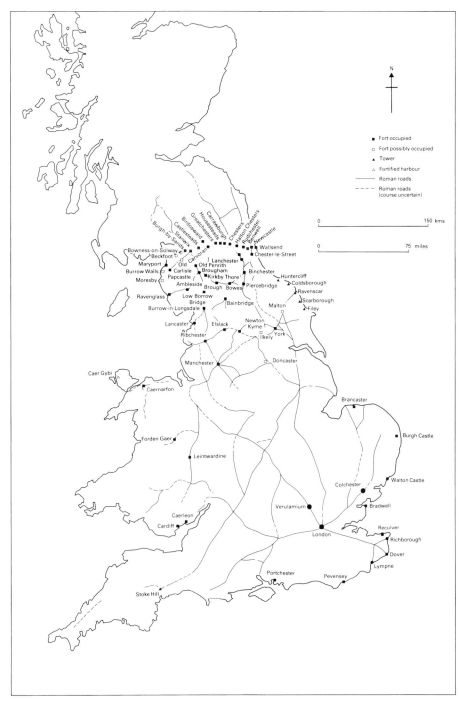

Figure 9.8 Saxon Shore forts and other fourth-century defences in Britain

The raids of these tribes increased in ferocity and frequency during the fourth century. The new enemies are first recorded in the late third century. The Franks and Saxons, from their homelands in present-day north-west Germany, sailed across the North Sea and attacked the eastern and southern coasts of Britain. In the north, the Picts are first recorded in 297 and the Romans campaigned against them in the early fourth century; the creation of the Pictish kingdom was probably a reaction, albeit subconscious, to the strong Roman presence in the southern part of Britain (Mann, 1974, 40–1). The Scots, who still lived in Ireland, do not come on to the scene until later in the fourth century; they seem to have played a part in the events of 342–3 which led Constans to visit Britain in winter. The home of the Attacotti is not known.

The Romans responded to the new threat in two ways: by fighting and by the improvement of the defences of the island, such as by the construction of the coastal forts. Much of our evidence for fighting depends upon the involvement of the emperor or a member of the imperial family and therefore it may be that these sources are seriously distorted. Specific literary references to raiding on the west coast of Britain (as opposed to general references to raiding by the Scots) are, for example, non-existent, yet the construction of new forts on the west coast goes some way to indicating the thrust of such raids. On the northern frontier it is difficult to relate the archaeological and documentary evidence for the improvement of the frontier defences to particular historical events. Too much may even be read into the statement that the frontier defences were restored following the 'Barbarian Conspiracy' of 367, for Theodosius, the general credited with the work, was the father of the emperor at the time when the events of those years were recorded.

Archaeology attests the revitalization of the northern frontier in the fourth century following the rundown of the defences which began in the later third century (Breeze and Dobson, 1978, 207–29). Some forts were repaired, others rebuilt in part or whole after long abandonment. Where dating evidence exists most points to this activity taking place in the later part of the fourth century and much has traditionally been associated with the restoration of the frontier following the invasions of 367. However, some rebuilding took place earlier. At several forts new-style barrack-blocks have been recognized. Instead of a single building divided into ten or so rooms, now the same space was apportioned into rather fewer separate little buildings termed 'chalets' (Wilkes, 1966, 128–37). It is not known how many men occupied each 'chalet'; it has been proposed that each one was the home of a soldier and his family (Daniels, 1980). However, while this cannot be substantiated, it is interesting that army units in the fourth century seem to be much smaller than their predecessors (Duncan-Jones, 1978) while some civil settlements outside forts seem to have been abandoned by the late fourth century (Salway, 1965, 14).

The *Notitia Dignitatum* records the existence of thirteen or fourteen new-style units in northern Britain in the late fourth century. Unfortunately, the document is mute on the date of the introduction of these regiments into the island. Frequently, too, their location is obscure as the Roman place names cannot now be identified. It has been postulated that these units reflect the provision of defence in depth (Jones, 1978, 140–2), but it seems equally likely that their purpose was the same as their predecessors: to provide additional support for the units on the Wall. This would be especially necessary now that the outpost forts had been abandoned. It is not certain when the forces were withdrawn from these forts, though recent work has suggested that they were taken out of Britain by Constantine in 314 (Casey and Savage, 1980); the scouts, however, seem to have survived until 367. Thereafter small buffer states may have been established by the Romans north of Hadrian's Wall, though the evidence for this is contentious (Mann, 1974, 42).

One other addition to the military forces in Britain emphasizes the pressure on the army. Throughout most of the fourth century the Empire could only respond to a major attack on the island by sending an army across from the continent. Towards the end of the century a small field army was established in Britain: the location of this force is not known.

Barbarian raids and invasions continued to plague Britain into the fifth century. At the same time successive usurpers milked the island's army in their attempts to win the empire. Nevertheless the army continued to maintain its role and no barbarian tribes secured a foothold inside the frontiers until the Saxons were invited later in the fifth century. It is not known how the life of the frontier installations in Britain ended. Possibly when the pay chests ceased to arrive the soldiers drifted off elsewhere to seek a living, or settled down with their families to a life of farming. The discovery of certain objects within some forts has led to the supposition that the soldiers' families moved inside, but whether the date of this move was within the Roman period, or after the end of Roman Britain in 410, is uncertain. Perhaps there was no sudden end, rather a gradual decline and a dawning realization that the rule of Rome in Britain had ended.

9.1   Milecastle 42 (Cawfields) on Hadrian's Wall. The north and south gates are visible; nothing is known of the internal accommodation

9.2   Turret 48a (Willowford east) on Hadrian's Wall

9.3 Aerial view of Hadrian's Wall looking east. The Wall snakes along the crags while the Vallum crosses the lower grounds to the south

9.4 The fort at Housesteads on Hadrian's Wall from the air. The Wall comes up to the northern corners of the fort. Within can be seen the headquarters building in the centre, flanked by the commanding officer's house and two granaries, and with the hospital behind; only one group of barrack-blocks has been exposed

9.5 Aerial view of the Antonine Wall at Croy Hill looking east. The Wall zigzags over the landscape, following the crest of the hill in the foreground

9.6　Aerial view of the fort at Rough Castle on the Antonine Wall looking north. The Antonine Wall crosses diagonally and to the south the two ditches defending the fort can be seen. To the east lies the annexe, protected by one ditch to the south and three to the east

9.7　The Bridgeness Distance Slab from the eastern end of the Antonine Wall recording the construction of nearly 4⅔ miles by soldiers of *legio II Augusta*. To the left, a Roman soldier rides down a group of four barbarians, while to the right, the successful conclusion of the campaign is celebrated by the sacrifice of a pig, sheep and bull

9.8 The Roman fort at Ardoch from the air. The surviving earthworks reveal a complicated history. In the second century, the fort served as an outpost for the Antonine Wall, and was surrounded by as many as five ditches to the north and east

9.9 The Saxon Shore fort at Portchester from the air. The high walls, external bastions and small gates reveal a preoccupation with defence not found in the earlier forts on Hadrian's Wall and the Antonine Wall

CHAPTER 10

·AFRICA·

Charles Daniels

> Africa is, as the others show (and indeed as Gnaeus Piso, who was once the governor of that country, told me) like a leopard's skin; for it is spotted with inhabited places that are surrounded by waterless and desert land. The Egyptians call such inhabited places 'oases'. (Strabo, *Geography* 2.5.33)

This section sets out to describe the frontiers of Roman North Africa, but, as no frontier exists in a vacuum, the terrain, climate and native populations are discussed when necessary, and an historical framework is given, as well as some account of the provincial armies.

Of the three land frontiers of the Empire, the northern, the eastern and the southern, the last was by far the longest. From Rabat to Tunis, and thence via Cairo to the Red Sea at Suez, measures as the crow flies almost 4,000 km (2,500 miles), or further than the distance from London to Timbuctoo. But the Roman frontier lay, for the first three centuries of this era, some 1,000 km (620 miles) south of Cairo, and its course from there to the Atlantic was in no way a simple straight line. The terrain it crossed varied considerably, as did the vegetation (or lack of it) and the culture and way of life of the local peoples. To the east were Egypt and Cyrenaica, in the centre Tripolitania, proconsular Africa, Numidia and Mauretania Caesariensis, while far to the west Tingitana lay isolated from the rest by the Riff and Atlas ranges, so that at times its links with Spain were stronger than those with Africa.

Egypt and Cyrenaica

Egypt (fig. 10.1), it is normally claimed, is no more than the valley of the Nile, a narrow strip of cultivation (less than 4 per cent of the country) which owes its fertility to annual

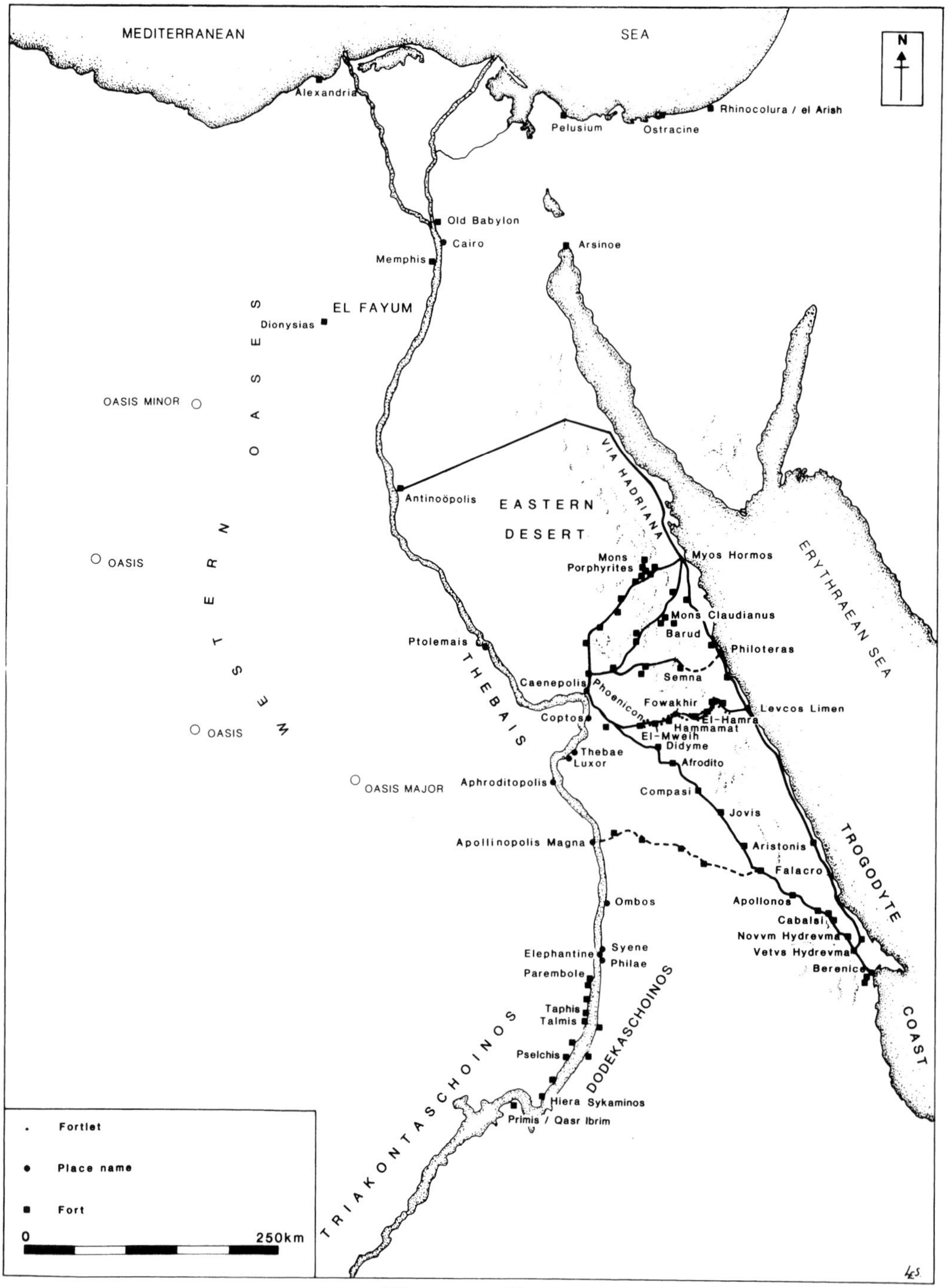

Figure 10.1 Egypt

inundation and the deposition of riverine silt. This truth is obvious when the absolute contrast between green river bank and stark bordering bluffs of striated rock, barren gravel and occasional sand, is seen from the air. Apart from the Delta, only in the Fayum, and a handful of Western-Desert oases, is agriculture possible outside the valley.

The western frontier of such a land is of necessity the western river-bank road, with predictable outpost forts in the nearer oases; the southern frontier can only be an arbitrary line drawn across the Nile valley at some chosen point. Only to the east is there an exception. The severely desiccated highlands of the Eastern Desert present a rugged and barren wilderness, with the Red Sea hills, at their highest some 2,000 m (6,600 ft), running like a north-south spine parallel with the coast. Here, because of the presence of gold, emeralds, much-prized granite and imperial porphyry, mining and quarrying settlements had existed since Pharaonic times, or were planted by the Romans. At the same time a growing trade in spices and luxuries via the Erythraean Sea from Aethiopia, southern Arabia, India and the east meant that a handful of ports had been established on the barren Red Sea coast in Ptolemaic times, with cleared tracks, provided with cisterns, connecting them with the Nile. Under the Romans these became regulated roads with forts and garrisons, and provision for teams of draft animals in the quarry areas.

That Egypt managed to evade the clutches of Rome during the late Republic was largely luck; it was certainly not the result of good management, for the later Ptolemies were both weak and incompetent, and Sulla and Crassus each had plans to seize the land. But it was not until after the defeat and death of Cleopatra in 30 BC that Octavian was able to take possession of Egypt and its wealth. Cornelius Gallus, his first prefect, easily defeated both Egyptians and Meroïtic Nubians to establish the earliest frontier at Aswan (Syene), with a client Nubia to the south. The northern portion of that, the so-called Triakontaschoinos, extending 320 km (200 miles) from Philae almost to Wadi Halfa, was under an appointed *tyrannus* (*CIL*, III, 14147). However, a Nubian uprising occurred in 25 BC which saw the destruction of Syene and other frontier forts, after which Gaius Petronius, Gallus' successor, marched over 600 km (370 miles) south to destroy the northern Nubian capital of Gebel Barkal (Napata) and plant a Roman garrison in the hill-top fortress of Qasr Ibrim (Primis), some 200 km (120 miles) south of Syene. A short time later, after further trouble, Augustus took in the so-called Dodekaschoinos by pushing the frontier 130 km (80 miles) south to Maharraqa (Hiera Sykaminos). Simultaneously, he relinquished both Roman control of the area south and further tribute, in return for a secure peace.

Although historical sources state that Primis (fig. 10.11B) was only held for something like two years, archaeological finds suggest that it continued as an outpost until the end of the first century AD, if not longer. Maspero has claimed that one of the buildings there was definitely to be attributed to Severus, while the prefect and other senior officers of *legio II Traiana fortis* are mentioned in a letter written from there some time not very long before AD 247 (Kirwan, 1977).

Once established at Hiera Sykaminos, the frontier remained static until the reign of Diocletian, in spite of a possible plan for expansion under Nero, when an expedition visited Meroë and continued as far as the *Sudd*, south of Malakal. This unbroken peace with Meroë produced such stability and prosperity that, as Adams (1977) states, the area as far south as the second cataract, which was previously a wilderness, became one of the most fertile, prosperous and populous in the entire kingdom.

The *Pax Romana* was kept by the army. Initially this was large; Strabo records three legions, three *alae* and nine cohorts, disposed: one legion and three cohorts at Alexandria, the other legions probably at Old Babylon and either Coptos or Thebes, three cohorts at Syene, with the remaining three cohorts and three *alae* situated strategically about the country. Until AD 106, Egypt had a north-eastern frontier with the Nabataean kingdom, therefore it is possible that troops were stationed at Pelusium in the eastern Delta, or Arsinoë (near Suez), as well as at Ostracine or el Arish (Rhinocolara) on the frontier itself.

As peace continued there were reductions in the garrison, until by the middle of Hadrian's reign, or soon after, only a single legion remained, *legio II Traiana* at Alexandria. Lesquier thought there was a corresponding drop in the auxiliary units, but recently this has been questioned. Nevertheless, the overall size of the army of Egypt fell from an initial *c.* 23,000, to half that strength or less, by the middle of the third century, and at the same time it was gradually spread more evenly about the country. In the Dodekaschoinos, the southern frontier region, Lesquier gives ample evidence for legionary troops and auxiliary units, or detachments in garrison during the first, second and early third centuries at such forts as Syene, Kalabsha (Talmis), Dakka (Pselchis) and Hiera Sykaminos. Of structural remains little has been recorded, and all is now below Lake Nasser, although Monneret de Villard published what looks like part of a marching camp with *clavicula* at Philae, and parts of the fort at Pselchis were excavated by Firth in 1909.

It has been argued that neither the Eastern Desert roads and forts, nor the southern Nile forts, constituted a frontier (*limes*), as both lacked the *sine qua non* of any frontier: a hostile people beyond it. The evidence suggests quite the opposite. The growth of trade in the Red Sea produced an increase in Arabian piracy, until imperial retribution dealt with it. On land, the settled Meroïtic town dwellers and farmers of the Nile were very different from the mobile tribes of the south-eastern and south-western deserts, whose principal tribal groupings are known under the names of Blemmyes (modern Beja), between the Red Sea hills and the river, Trogodytes along the coast, and Nobades (Nubae, Nobatae and Noba) to the west. Strabo dismissed them all as most unwarlike, but it is clear that they soon realized the benefits of cross-frontier raiding and pillage. A Milan papyrus of late first-century date describes a fight between Roman cavalry and a mixed band of Aethiopians and Trogodytes, who were driven off, while a fragmentary inscription of Hadrianic date records that after a two-day pursuit a certain Serenus disposed of a body of Agriophages and recovered booty on camel-back. These people, from well south of the border, had been raiding deep into the Thebaïd. Amongst the disturbances of Pius' reign, Aristides lists trouble from people dwelling along the Red Sea coast, clearly Trogodytes. All suggests that during the first to third centuries the Nile defences and Eastern Desert system constituted a *limes*, with its garrisons experiencing all the normal cut-and-thrust of frontier life.

The Eastern Desert network consisted of a series of roads running from the Nile to the coast. One, starting from Qena, soon forked, one branch going north-east by Mons Porphyrites to Myos Hormos, the other to Mons Claudianus, with a further branch probably running on to Philoteras. These roads were provided with regular garrison posts (fig. 10.1) each including a cistern, external animal lines and sometimes further enclosures. The port of Myos Hormos was a Ptolemaic foundation, but the most conspicuous remains there are the Roman fort (fig. 10.2B), the building of which, or its predecessor, is recorded on a fragmentary inscription of Augustan-Tiberian date from Coptos (*CIL*, III, 6627). Later, projecting circular angle towers were added and the interior altered. When compared with the ample evidence from the northern route, the Philoteras road does not seem to have been used by the Romans beyond the quarries at Semna.

Further south another road ran from Coptos to Phoenicon, where it split, one branch continuing to Leucos Limen, the other running south-east for 257–8 Roman miles to Berenice, which lay on Foul Bay opposite Philae on the Nile. The Leucos Limen road is not mentioned in any ancient source and, having far fewer quarries and mines along its length, it lacks animal lines. Garrisons, however, have left records at several sites (el Mweth, Hammamat and Fowakhir). Posts noted by Lesquier are small by any standard: 30 by 30 m (98 by 98 ft), 31 by 37 m (100 by 110 ft) and 30 by 50 m (98 by 164 ft). A slightly larger post at el Homra (58 by 83 m, 190 by 272 ft), is recorded as having an isolated building in its centre, a feature perhaps more commonly found in later rather than earlier military forts. But the most remarkable feature of this road is the frequency of inter-visible signal towers in its central sector, placed on heights along the twisting ravines (Meredith, 1953). This has been interpreted as evidence for a valuable traffic, but the system could equally well be interpreted as a *limes*, although of what date is not known.

The southernmost road, to Berenice, is the best documented, being recorded along with its stations in Pliny, the Antonine Itinerary and the Peutinger Table. The route, as also the post of Berenice, was the creation of Ptolemy Philadelphus and originally started at Idfu (Apollinopolis) on the Nile. In Roman times the road was taken instead to Coptos and the Idfu track abandoned. This road was undoubtedly a frontier road, with forts and garrisons in addition to the older cisterns. The Augustan–Tiberian inscription already mentioned records work at Berenice and the stations of Compasi and Apol-

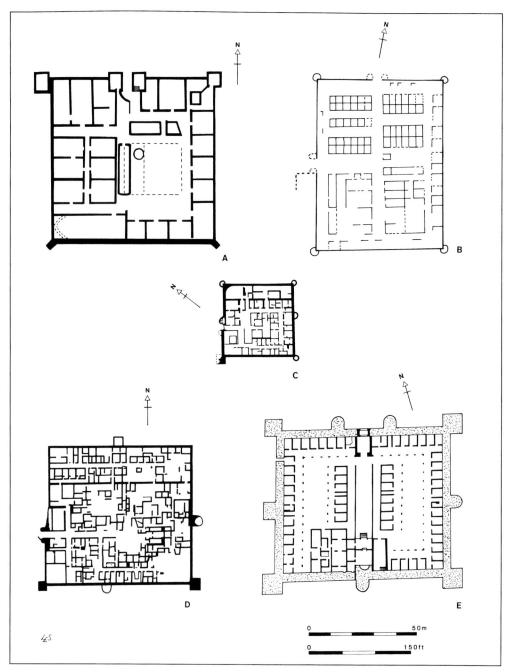

Figure 10.2 Late Roman forts in Egypt: (A) Der el-'Atrash (*after Barren and Hume*); (B) Myos Hormos (*after Scaife*); (C) Barud (*after Tregenza*); (D) Mons Claudianus (*after Scaife*); (E) Castra Dionysias (*after Carrie*)

lonos, where cisterns were constructed and dedicated; it also states that the workforce of legionaries and auxiliaries built and reconstructed forts.

Under Domitian a *praesidium* was built at an additional site, Afrodito. Pliny relates that goods were carried by camel. Sea captains, naval carpenters and sailors, and the wives of soldiers at Berenice, are all mentioned in assorted texts, as well as officers of mounted Palmyrene archers escorting caravans for protection against robbers and desert raiders (text of AD 216).

Hadrian attempted to alter the Eastern Desert routes radically, by replacing the Berenice road by a new one, the Via Hadriana. This ran from Antinoöpolis, on the Nile north of Qena, across the desert to the coast where it turned south 'through secure and level places beside the Erythraean Sea' to link Myos Hormos with the other ports and minor anchorages as far south as Berenice. The purpose of this new road may perhaps have been to provide greater security, for it was provided with plentiful watering points (cisterns), posting-stations and forts along its length. The whole work is recorded on an inscription from Antinoöpolis dated 25 February AD 137 (*IRG* I.1142). However, it is doubtful if the road was much used after Hadrian's death; certainly it provided no permanent replacement, or even rival, to the Berenice road, as many records of the later second and third centuries prove.

The supervision of the whole area between Coptos and the Red Sea, including all roads, forts and troops, the caravan trade and the quarrying and mining of stone and metals, was under the control of the Prefect of Berenice (or Mount Berenice). This command is paralleled in Augustan times by similar ones in physically wild, military regions where romanization had hardly begun. Clearly, this was a military prefecture in a true frontier region, and not surprisingly at least two legionary tribunes are known to have held it.

During the disorders of the third century tribal raiding became chronic: Blemmyes in the east and Nubians in the west (Nobades and various Noba tribes) struck deeper and deeper into Upper Egypt; in AD 249, 253, 261 and 265 we know of raids or Roman counter-attacks. Later, the Blemmyes sided with the Palmyrenes during their invasion of Egypt in 270, and although defeated more than once, they occupied Coptos and Ptolemais in 280. All these attacks, together with a series of major revolts, caused considerable destruction to the country and so, Procopius relates, in *c.* 297 Diocletian decided to withdraw the frontier again to Syene, inviting the Nobades to fill the resultant vacuum, on condition that they kept the Blemmyes out. But Kirwan (1966) has observed that Pselchis and Shellal (Teleleos) were still occupied in the reign of Constantine, and that mid and late fourth-century coins from Talmis show that there, too, close contact was still kept with Roman Egypt (fig. 10.18).

Diocletian's reforms included an increase in the size of the army: if Jones is correct the number of *limitanei*, frontier troops, in the three provinces of the Thebaïd (Upper Egypt), (Lower) Egypt, and Libya (Marmarica and Cyrenaica) was raised to some 64,000.

They were placed in towns and cities in the Delta, the Suez–Pelusium–Rhinocorara region, the western oases and along the length of the Nile to Philae, where the island, with its shrines, was fortified and garrisoned by *legio I Maximiana*. Other new forts included Dionysias in the Fayum and a fort enclosing the temple of Luxor, where a detachment of *legio III Diocletiana* was stationed (fig. 10.9B).

It is uncertain how late the Eastern Desert ports continued to be held. Coins of Constantius II have been found at Berenice, and Murray (1967) described the forts along the Berenice road as quadrangular with rounded towers at their corners and gates. That nearest to Berenice, Vetus Hydreuma, has no less than five separate walled enclosures, one with towers, the rest without. This suggests that the road stations were rebuilt in the style of the late empire, and held during the reign of Constantine, at least.

By the early fifth century certain sites on the Nile and in the desert were definitely in the hands of the Blemmyes. It is possible that there was a withdrawal from the south, while the northern quarries and Myos Hormos continued to be held, with a frontier running along the Leucos Limen road. The road has already been referred to; several sites in the Claudianus–Porphyrites area have yielded mid or late fourth-century coins and the published plans (fig. 10.2) of a number of forts show (added?) projecting towers and gate-towers in the style of the late empire.

Three posts in the Duke of the Thebaïd's command could be Eastern Desert sites: an *ala* of Palmyrenes is placed at Foenicionis (= Phoenicon), echoing the earlier mounted-archer guards on the Berenice road, a cohort is *in castris Lapidariorum*, which is presumably a reference to the northern quarry sites, as by the time of the *Notitia* the Blemmyes were moving into the southern area, if they had not already taken it over and a detachment of *legio III Diocletiana* is placed at a site called Praesentia. This is usually amended to read Praesidio: *ostraca* from Fowakhir on the Leucos Limen road (Roman, but not closely datable) show that the troops there were in regular contact with a place called Praesidium. Could it be that the *Notitia* detachment was either situated in, or had connections with the Eastern Desert? Of these definite or possible sites, however, none is further south than the Leucos Limen road.

Whereas Diocletian increased the army and built new defences, Constantine turned to diplomacy in his dealings with the Blemmyes and Nubians. Flavius Abinnaeus, who commanded the garrison at Dionysias, described how he escorted a Blemmye delegation, led by no less a person than Senecio, *Comes Limitis*, into the Imperial presence at Constantinople *c.* AD 336–7, after which Abinnaeus spent three years with the tribe as a Roman ambassador or agent. In spite of this, at some time before 346 the tribe once more struck, and again in 378, 399 and 406. Another ambassador extraordinary, Olympiodorus, visited important sites *c.* 420–1 at Talmis, Taphis and Primis on the Nile and Phoinokon and Chiris in the Eastern Desert, all in Blemmye hands. At a slightly earlier date the tribe also had a settlement at Elephantine. These settlements, and the way that some of the Blemmyes had access to important Roman officials, have even prompted Kirwan

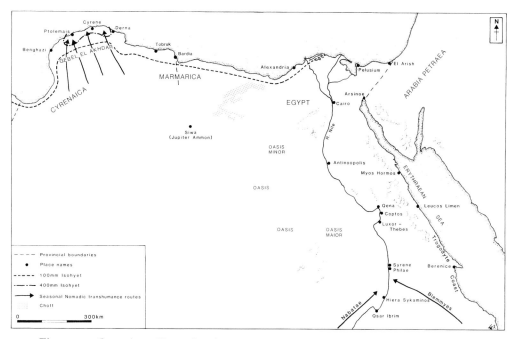

Figure 10.3 Cyrenaica to Egypt. Provinces, principal sites, regions, geographical features, and transhumance routes

(1982) to conclude that some at least of the tribe must have been Roman federates employed in frontier defence.

In the mid-fifth century the Blemmyes and Nobatae united in their devastation of Upper Egypt, until, finally, retribution came at the hands of two Roman commanders, Maximinus and Florus, each of whom inflicted a heavy defeat. The tribes were forced to accept a solemn treaty, signed in the precincts of the great temple of Isis at Philae, the 'National Shrine' of the pagan Nubians. A century's peace apparently followed.

West of the Delta, and Alexandria, the vegetation soon stops (fig. 10.3). The desert approaches the shore and only an occasional settlement along the coast road, or random variations of terrain (Halfaya pass or the cliffs at Bardia), break the monotony for nearly 800 km (500 miles), until the Cyrenaican plateau is reached. Here, roughly between Derna and Benghazi, a limestone tableland rises in two steps from the sea, to a height of 1,000 m (3,280 ft). This is sufficient to produce an annual rainfall well in excess of 400 mm (16 in.) on the lower plateau, and above 600 mm (24 in.) on the summit, ensuring the permanent cover of evergreen shrubs which gives the area its name, Gebel el Akhdar, the Green Mountain. To the south the plateau falls away gently to the desert and precipitation rapidly decreases.

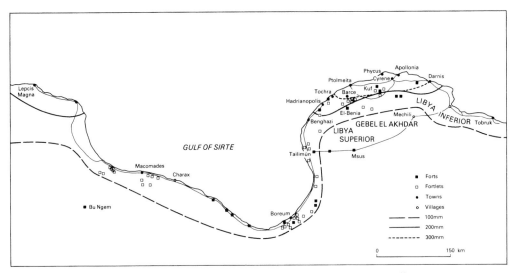

Figure 10.4 Cyrenaica to Tripolitania: sites, roads and rainfall

Attracted by its fertility, the Greeks colonized the area from the seventh century BC and established the five cities which gave it its name of Pentapolis. In 96 BC Ptolemy Apion bequeathed it to Rome, and in 74 the first *quaestor* arrived.

Augustus joined Cyrenaica with Crete, across the Libyan Sea, to form a single province under a senatorial proconsul. The early history of the province was mostly uneventful, and like Egypt it saw no major revision of its frontier; indeed, whether it ever possessed a true *limes* or, until the time of Diocletian, a proper provincial garrison, can be questioned.

The occasional, early, small military post may have existed and Goodchild thought that Bir Umm el-Garanigh, in the Syrtica, had been occupied in the first century, although there was no real frontier road, then or later, either along the coast or around the southern approaches to the Gebel. This may have been because the principal cities had been so thoroughly fortified in hellenistic times, with impressive stone walls, that they were more than adequately protected.

Early troubles with the Marmaridae (Augustan date) and the Nasamones (under Domitian) were dealt with successfully by troops from outside the province, and peace was maintained. It was, however, rudely shattered not by invasion, but by the Jewish uprising of AD 115–16, which produced appalling slaughter and damage, especially in Cyrene. Again, external forces were necessary to restore order; but even then it was not thought necessary to increase the garrison from a single equitate quingenary cohort.

There was no external threat to the safety of the province until the middle of the third century. In 268–9 Probus, then governor of Egypt, was called in to defeat the Marmaridae. Shortly after, *c.* AD 284 Diocletian carried out extensive reforms: two new provinces, Libya Superior (or Pentapolis) and Libya Inferior (or Sicca, Dry Libya) were created, and the garrison of the whole region was very greatly increased, although unfortunately, details of its composition are unknown as the appropriate page of the *Notitia* is missing. But something is known of the late defences themselves. A line of fortified posts was constructed from the coast, south of Benghazi, via Tailimun (fig. 10.19L) as far as Msus, and in time a whole series of small, late blockhouses, many of Byzantine date, sprang up in the coastal region between Benghazi and Ptolemais. Inland, south and south-east of Barce, forts were established on the plateau, including Benia (fig. 10.19M). In the Kuf region, the very broken country between Barce and Cyrene, which is intersected by a complex series of deep ravines, numerous fortified buildings were constructed. East again, Cyrene itself was protected by a screen of posts running from the coastal area near Derna to the Kuf system just mentioned.

The southern edge of the plateau more or less coincides with the 200 mm (8 in.) isohyet, but south of this the rainfall soon drops well below 100 mm (4 in.), creating predesert conditions, cultivatable only by the most careful husbanding of water. Here, actual military posts were very few: at Msus a simple watchtower existed, within an outer enclosure. Whether there was anything at Mekili, a similar site, is not known. The inland wadis are strewn with a liberal scatter of so-called 'fortified farms', which continue to the east across the equally arid terrain of southern Libya Sicca. Away to the south-east, the outlying oasis of Siwa, Jupiter Ammon, was certainly included within the province, but details of the garrison are not now known.

From AD 390 onwards the Libyas had little respite from barbarian raiding; the Austuriani struck in 395–410 and again in 449. The troubles of the time and the problems of defence are well described by Synesius of Cyrene, Bishop of Ptolemais, who suffered them both.

West from the Pentapolis the desert again sweeps to the shore around the desolate reaches of Greater Syrtes. Some 900 km (560 miles) of sub-desert steppe, here and there interrupted by a road post or occasional small town, separate Benghazi from Lepcis Magna. The Antonine Itinerary records the distance as 568 Roman miles, with twenty-two intermediate stages.

Africa, Numidia and the Mauretanias

From the Atlantic to the Syrtica most of the coastal region of North Africa, the Tell, lies within the Mediterranean domain, which means that in Roman times the cultivation of cereals in the valleys and plains, and vines and olives on the hillsides, was possible without irrigation, while many of the higher mountain slopes were covered with timber. The southern limit of this region (fig. 10.5) is usually taken to follow the 400 mm (16 in.)

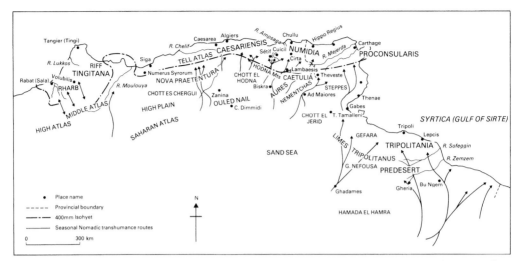

Figure 10.5   Tripolitania to Tingitana: provinces, principal sites, regions, geographical features and transhumance routes

isohyet. Between the Tell and the desert lies an intermediate zone, usually called pre-Saharan. This ranges from mountains to steppe-land where, dependent on soil, climate and rainfall variations, cultivation of olives and some cereals is possible if water is carefully used, and the natural vegetation provides grazing for part of the year. The zone includes some of north-west Morocco, and all of the High Plains of Algeria and the Steppes of Tunisia. Its southern limit is usually described as the 100 mm (4 in.) isohyet, which follows the Anti and High Atlas, the Saharan Atlas, the Aurès and Nementchas, and the Jebels Matmata, Ouderna and Nefousa.

The relationship between this last zone and the Roman frontier will become clear in what follows. South lies the Sahara, but even here, north of the Chott el Jerid, south and south-west of the Aurès and in the predesert wadis of Tripolitania, ancient cultivation was practised in areas where today the rainfall is sometimes less than 25 mm (1 in.).

The Tell is traditionally the region of sedentary agriculture and the pre-Saharan steppe, the home of pastoralism linked to a nomadic way of life. These two have usually been portrayed as continually in conflict, but a considerable body of recent work has shown that this is far too simplistic a view. The relationship between the two ways of life was complex and at the same time both hostile and symbiotic, for the pastoralists needed the farmers with whom they could exchange animal produce in return for grain, and the farmers needed the source of extra, harvest labour which the nomads provided. In addition, much of what has been called nomadism was, in fact, semi-nomadism, that is seasonal transhumance from definite areas of winter settlement, as grazing died off, along well-established routes running mostly north and north-east into the Tell. Later in the year these routes were again followed back to the southern tribal territory. Only in some of the mountainous areas is the pattern occasionally different. Although such a way of life initially brought the tribes into conflict with Rome, there is much evidence to show that in Roman times the frontier was developed as a porous and even discontinuous membrane, designed to allow north–south movement to continue, but in a more orderly, regulated fashion. The viability of such a system is shown by the steady increase of agriculture and population which occurred in the steppe-lands, particularly in the second and early third centuries AD (Lawless, 1972 and Whittaker, 1978, with detailed discussion and full references to earlier sources).

Roman expansion in Africa was slow, and this has led some to believe that there was considerable, continuing and effective hostility to it. But when compared with other regions of the Empire there is no convincing evidence that opposition in Africa was stronger than elsewhere. Why then was the conquest so slow? The reasons can perhaps be glimpsed in contemporary accounts of the remoteness, wildness and inaccessibility of inland Africa. Strabo states that the interior afforded only a wretched subsistence as it was a rocky and sandy desert, all accounts of which were untrustworthy and incomplete. Pliny records that Rabat (Sala), on the very edge of the desert, was beset by elephants, that Mount Atlas lay in a region which was at noontide silent with the terrifying silence of the desert and by night filled with the wanton gambols of Goat-Pans and Satyrs, that some parts were forests filled with wild beasts while others were deserts abandoned to swarming serpents, that the Trogodytes had no voices, the Blemmyes no heads, their mouths and eyes being attached to their chests. . . .

More seriously perhaps, it is clear that for long periods of time there was very little driving force behind the acquisition of further territory in Africa, which can only mean that once Carthage had been defeated Africa never presented a real threat or danger to Rome. Separated by the sea and vast distances of desert, isolated by its legends of remoteness, the African frontier was normally one of low priority.

As for opposition, the ease with which Caesar and the generals of Claudius, Trajan and Severus conquered additional territory, when a forward policy was in operation, shows that there was little serious military resistance. This is borne out when the size of the army is considered. First, the conquest: with the exception of Caesar, who was fighting a civil war and not just Juba I, the advancement of the frontier was achieved by a single legion, occasionally augmented, and a handful of cohorts and *alae*. Only during the revolt of Tacfarinas, the conquest of Mauretania and the Moorish War of Pius, were sizeable reinforcements brought in, and even then the resultant total force contrasts sharply with, for instance, Agricola's army in Britain (four legions and up to 50,000 auxiliaries), Trajan's Dacian and Parthian expeditionary forces, or even the 40,000 troops quartered by Marcus across the Danube amongst the Quadi and Sarmatians. Second, the size of the army of Africa. For ease of comparison the figures given by A. R. Birley (1981b) are taken, as they present a uniform assessment for the whole Empire: west of the Syrtica the mid second-century garrison of Tingitana,

Caesariensis, proconsular Africa and the Numidian command has been calculated at one legion and some 24,500 auxiliaries, or a total of 30,500 men. This should be compared with the single provinces of Syria, 33,620, and Britain, 53,180 or the Rhineland–Raetian frontier, with 56,000. It is almost laughable to contrast Brigantia and lowland Scotland at the beginning of Marcus' reign, which were held, according to Frere, and excluding legionary troops, by an auxiliary force of 30,750 and had an actual frontier on the Antonine Wall of 54 km (37 miles).

Overall, in the middle of the second century the whole southern frontier of the Empire, from Rabat to Aswan, had an army of two legions and *c.* 33,000 auxiliaries, or a little over 45,000 men. At the same time the eastern frontier had 85,000, Britain and the Germanies 91,000 and the Danube 126,000. In the light of these figures it is a complete myth to suggest that the conquest of Africa was slow because of fierce resistance, that the African frontier was difficult to maintain or that the African provinces were thought to present problems of security or continual resistance.

The defeat of Carthage in 146 BC brought Rome her first territory in Africa. The actual area was kept small, some 12,800 sq. km (5,000 sq. miles) it has been calculated, and the Numidian kings were confirmed in possession of the considerable amount of Carthaginian territory that Masinissa had annexed. No doubt mindful of that continual encroachment, the boundary of the province was defined by a ditch, the Fossa Regia, marked out under Scipio Aemilianus' supervision from near Tabarka in the north to Thenae in the south-east (fig. 10.6).

Relations with the Numidian kings were peaceful until 112 BC, when in the course of seizing Cirta, Jugurtha slaughtered Roman traders. A messy war followed. But even after Jugurtha's defeat and death very little new territory was acquired, and the Fossa Regia remained the boundary.

It was not until a century after the fall of Carthage that the first real change occurred: after his decisive victory at Thapsus in 46, Caesar annexed Numidia. The area around Cirta he gave as an independent fief to P. Sittius, his ally in war, the rest he turned into a new province (Africa Nova) to run with the older one, thereafter known as Africa Vetus. A garrison of three legions, in contrast to one in the old province, suggests that not only was the occupation to be permanent, but that Caesar entertained the possibility of further expansion. Although the civil war, and divided loyalties in Africa after Caesar's death, prevented that, triumphs were later celebrated *ex Africa* by Statilius Taurus in 34, L. Cornificius in 33 and Autronius Paetus in 28, showing that Caesar's forward policy was not totally abandoned by the more forceful proconsuls.

Among the list of provinces which took an oath to Octavian in 32 BC, were the Gauls, the Spains, but only one Africa. Some have interpreted this to mean that Numidia had been given back as a client kingdom to young Juba, the son of the old King; others that the two Africas had already been made a single province.

In 33 King Bocchus of Mauretania, the friend of Sittius and Caesar, died, and his huge kingdom was annexed. In the next few years Octavian planted a string of veteran colonies along its Mediterranean coast, with a further three beyond the Pillars of Hercules, of which two were in the Atlantic-facing Rharb plain of Morocco.

In 27 BC the situation was formalized by Augustus (as he now was): Vetus and

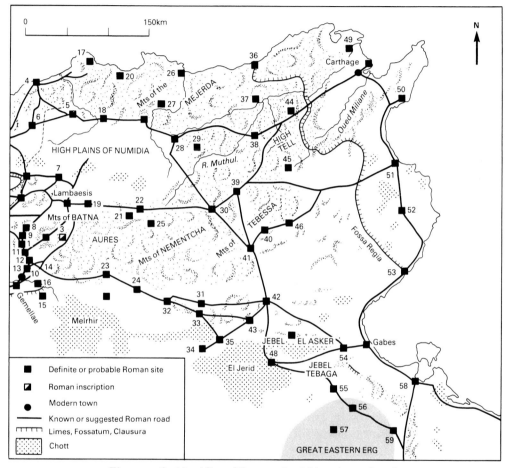

Figure 10.6 Numidia and Proconsular Africa: sites and roads

1 Oumach; 2 Tunis; 3 Tighanimine; 4 Igilgili; 5 Milev; 6 Cuicul; 7 Diana; 8 Calceus Herculis; 9 Burgus Speculatorius; 10 Aquae Herculis; 11 Mesarfelta; 12 Vescera; 13 Biskra; 14 Thabudeos; 15 Bir Djefeir; 16 Bourada; 17 Chullu; 18 Cirta; 19 Timgad; 20 Rusicada; 21 Aquae Flavianae; 22 Mascula; 23 Badias; 24 Ad Medias; 25 Vazaïvi; 26 Hippo Regius; 27 Calama; 28 Thubursicu Numidarum; 29 Madauros; 30 Theveste; 31 Ad Turres; 32 Ad Maiores; 33 Speculum; 34 Nepte; 35 Aquae; 36 Tabarka; 37 Bulla Regia; 38 Sicca Veneria; 39 Ammaedara; 40 Cillium; 41 Thelepte; 42 Gafsa; 43 Thiges; 44 Dugga; 45 Mactar; 46 Sufetula; 47 Bir Oum Ali; 48 Turris Tamalleni; 49 Utica; 50 Neapolis; 51 Hadrumetum; 52 Thysdrus; 53 Thenae; 54 Aquae Tacapitanae; 55 Vezereos; 56 C. Tibubuci; 57 Tisavar; 58 Gigthis; 59 Talalati

Nova became a single proconsular province, but because the Gaetulian tribes of the south were still independent, a legion and a handful of auxiliaries were quite exceptionally placed under the proconsul. So began the long association of *legio III Augusta* with Africa and, incidentally, an anomaly which in one form or another continued until the creation of a separate Numidian province by Severus.

The fact that the new African province was given to the senate shows that Augustus did not consider it to be either a strong or a problematic province, for such he kept for himself. Triumphs continued, with Sempronius Atratinus in 21 BC and Cornelius Balbus in 19. But whether any real territorial acquisition was made is uncertain, for Tacitus states that the army continued to winter in the old province, and the activities of the proconsuls were hardly intended to rival the expeditions of Augustus' own generals. Even Balbus' spectacular conquest of the distant Garamantes received no mention in the *Res Gestae*, unlike the Aethiopian and Arabian campaigns.

At the same time Mauretania was given by national gift of the Roman People to Juba II, as a client kingdom. Thus, the old frontier on the Ampsaga, which before Masinissa's time was not only the physical boundary between Numidia and Mauretania but also a cultural frontier of considerable antiquity, was once again restored and the limits of Africa returned to what they had been in Caesar's day. To the east, the Tripolitanian emporia had passed to Rome with the rest of old Juba's lands. The hinterland of the cities, however, does not appear to have been garrisoned, beyond, possibly, a token force. Here, as in Cyrenaica, security must have been exercised by treaty relations with the coastal and hinterland tribes.

Dio tells us that Juba was given part of Gaetulia. As the Gaetuli occupied southern Numidia, it looks as if the king and not the proconsul was responsible for the southern area of the old kingdom. When a revolt broke out there Roman intervention followed, with eventual success, but no annexation occurred. At Augustus' death a road was being driven by the legion, south from its winter quarters to Gabes. De Pachterre (1916) considered the fortress to have lain at Haïdra (Ammaedara), a view which is still generally held. But Tacitus remarks that it was not until the winter of 22–23 that the army stopped wintering in the old province, and so poses a problem, for Ammaedara was not in the old province. Perhaps the fortress had been planned, but at Augustus' death the idea was dropped by Tiberius.

Trouble with the Gaetuli continued intermittently until AD 17, when the revolt of Tacfarinas broke out. In spite of its small size, the proconsular army was at first successful, until the initiative was lost to the rebels and the revolt spread. It was not until Tiberius himself appointed a commander, and temporarily transferred *legio IX Hispana* from Pannonia, that the rebels were defeated. The permanent size of the African army, however, was not altered. The cause of the war was apparently the loss of land, or curtailment of land use, suffered by the Musulamii, and is usually linked to the movement of *legio III Augusta*. But, as noted above, the legion first wintered in the area only during this war, and so its transfer may well have been a result and not a cause of the war.

In AD 37 Gaius removed the army from the control of the proconsul by appointing one of his own legates as the commander of the legion. Thereafter, the whole frontier zone of the province was directly under the emperor. But far from improving things, Tacitus says that confusion over responsibilities led to violent rivalry between proconsul and legate. Gaius next contrived the death of Juba's son and successor Ptolemy, in AD 40, and annexed Mauretania. A revolt ensued which was apparently suppressed before Gaius' own assassination occurred. A year later the Moors again rose and a longer war followed, during which first Suetonius Paullinus and then Hosidius Geta distinguished themselves, Paullinus crossing the High Atlas and Geta driving the Moors into the desert. But at this time Claudius must have been increasingly concerned with his plans for invading Britain, and his Moorish victory received little attention. It is not even known what troops were used in the conquest of Mauretania, although epigraphic evidence suggests that detachments from two legions in Spain at the time, *legio IV Macedonica* and *legio X Gemina*, may have taken part (Cagnat, 1913). Both successful generals may later have joined Claudius in Britain, along with their successor, M. Licinius Crassus Frugi, who received honours for a victory in Mauretania in 44.

About this time Mauretania was divided into two provinces, Tingitana in the west and Caesariensis in the east. Since both were placed under equestrian procurators it seems that neither was considered to be of particular military importance; a contrast with contemporary events in Britain. Next to nothing is known of the early years of either province, or their early garrisons, but legionary troops presumably remained for a short time at least, as the governor of Tingitana in AD 44–5 held his command *pro legato*. During the civil war Lucceius Albinus, who was given control of both provinces by Galba, had a total force of five *alae* and nineteen cohorts, or roughly the same as Raetia and Noricum together, at a slightly later date.

In Tingitana effective Roman control was limited to the area about the straits, the Atlantic coastal plain, or Rharb, as far south as Rabat, and the fertile Tell area north of the Middle Atlas, as far east as Volubilis (fig. 10.7). The Atlas ranges themselves were never held, nor was much of the equally mountainous Riff to the north and east, and except in exceptional circumstances there was no land communication with Caesariensis. Much discussion of this question has taken place, but it is clear that the only route, the Taza corridor and lower Moulouya valley, was totally free from Roman posts (Euzennat, 1978, for full discussion).

In Caesariensis the century between Bocchus' death and Nero's assassination saw very little advance (fig. 10.8). As first established, the province remained essentially the coastal plain with its cities. The rugged, densely-forested and thinly-populated Dahra, Mitidjien and Kabylie massifs, with their heavy rainfall and high humidity, did not appeal and very few inland settlements were founded. The only direction in which any real

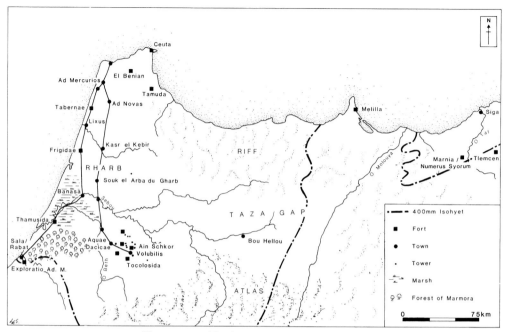

Figure 10.7 Tingitana: sites, roads and rainfall

inland advances did take place was south of Tipasa, where in addition to the early foundations of Zucchabar and Aquae Calidae, Oppidum Novum was planted under Claudius
in the attractive and fertile Chélif valley.

In a comparable period of time, from the establishment of proconsular Africa to
the early years of Vespasian, proconsular Africa had hardly grown either. The legion
had moved to Ammaedara and the Musulamii had been controlled, but beyond
Ammaedara, and south of Madauros and Cirta, the Gaetulian tribes were still free to
range. In contrast, the half century of Flavian and Trajanic rule saw a new departure:
the steady advance of the frontier. About AD 75 the legion was again moved, this time
to Tébessa (Theveste), a significant advance which gave it direct access to the Tell region
north of the Aurès. Military posts were quickly established at Mascula, Aquae Flavianae
and Vazaïvi, and in 81 a detachment of the legion built the first fort at Lambaesis
(fig. 10.9A). In 75 Banasa chose as patron Sextius Sentius Caecilianus, who had been
made responsible by Vespasian for redefining boundaries in Africa, and then for setting
in order both provinces of Mauretania (*leg. Aug. pro pr. ordinandae utriusq. Mauretaniae*),
after the shortcomings of Vitellius' administration. A little later Velius Rufus is recorded
as *dux* of the African and Mauretanian armies, implying synchronized activity by the
two forces. The wording *ad nationes quae sunt in Mauretania conprimendas* (in order that
tribes in Mauretania should be kept in check) suggests that he was concerned with
regulating the free-ranging movement of peoples on the Mauretanian–African boun-

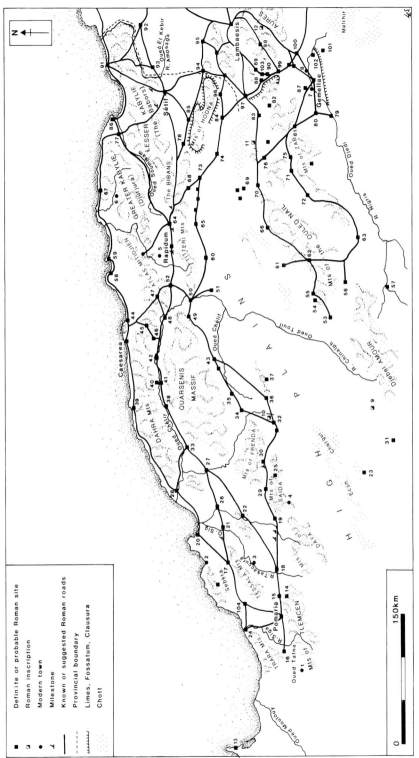

Figure 10.8 Caesariensis: sites and roads

1 Oujda; 2 Oran; 3 Sidi Bel Abbes; 4 Saïda; 5 Beni-Slimane; 6 Tizi Ouzou; 7 Ourella; 8 Oumach; 9 Agneb; 10 Oppidum; 11 Zireg; 12 Tighanimine; 13 Rusaddir; 14 Aïn Bent Soltane; 15 Altava; 16 Numerus Syrorum; 17 Regiae; 18 Kaputtasaccura; 19 Lucu; 20 Portus Magnus; 21 Tasaccura; 22 Aquae Sirenses; 23 El Khadra; 24 Siga; 25 Aïn Balloul; 26 Castra Nova; 27 Mina; 28 Quiza; 29 Ala Miliaria; 30 Cohors Breucorum; 31 El Bayadh; 32 Aioun Sbiba; 33 Gadaum Castra; 34 Tiaret; 35 Columnata; 36 Temardjanet; 37 Aïn Benia; 38 Castellum Tingitanum; 39 Cartennas; 40 Tigava; 41 Tigava Castra; 42 Oppidum Novum; 43 Aïn Toukria; 44 Tipasa; 45 Aquae Calidae; 46 Zucchabar; 47 Lambdia; 48 Sufasar; 49 Hiberna Alae Sebastenae; 50 Boghar; 51 Boughezoul; 52 Thanaramusa Castra; 53 Zenina; 54 Charef; 55 Aïn El Hammam; 56 Tadmit; 57 Laghouat; 58 Icosium, Algiers; 59 Rusguniae; 60 Aïn Touta; 61 Korirein; 62 Djelfa; 63 Castellum Dimmidi; 64 Auzia; 65 Aïn Grimidi; 66 Medjedel; 67 Rusuccuru; 68 Tatilti; 69 El Guelaa; 70 Bou Saada; 71 El Gahra; 72 Aïn Rich; 73 Aras; 74 Zabi; 75 Bou Mellal; 76 Aïn Mekrenza; 77 Tubusuctu; 78 Equizeto; 79 Ouled Djellal; 80 Doucen; 81 Ausum, Sadouri; 82 Centenarium Aqua Viva; 83 Zebaret; 84 Macri; 85 Thamallula; 86 Saldae; 87 Tolga; 88 Seba Mgata; 89 Calceus Herculis; 90 Aquae Herculis; 91 Igilgili; 92 Milev; 93 Cuicul; 94 Zaraï; 95 Diana; 96 Cellas; 97 Thubunae; 98 Menaa; 99 Mesarfelta; 100 Thabudeos; 101 Bir Djefeïr; 102 Bourada; 103 Burgus Speculatorius; 104 Aïn-Temouchent

dary, where an extremely important transhumance route is known to have lain.

Under Trajan the trunk road north of the Aurès was developed. Theveste became a colony, showing that the legion was again moved, although when and where is by no means certain (p. 248 below), and a further colony was planted at Timgad, 150 km (93 miles) further west. *Municipia* were established at Mascula and Diana. To the south, a road from Gabes was driven west along the flanks of the Aurès at least as far as Ad Maiores (AD 104–5, fig. 10.11). It has been argued that as part of this exercise lengths of *clausura* were constructed across gaps in Jebel el Asker, north of the Chott el Jerid, on the grounds of their similarity to such works as Hadrian's Wall in Britain (Trousset, 1974). On the other hand, such features are highly uncharacteristic of Trajanic thinking elsewhere and it is perhaps rash to suggest such a date, since they would fit the mentality of Hadrian, or a later age, much better.

How far was the road taken beyond Ad Maiores? Cagnat (1913), long ago, suggested that it carried on to Vescera, Calceus Herculis and Thubunae. This would be a considerable advance, and at a time when the German and British frontiers had virtually been closed down in favour of advances in Dacia and the east. The only alternative, however, is to attribute it to Hadrian, whose frontier works run from Thubunae to Mesarfelta, and south of Gemellae. Yet such an advance, of about 200 km (124 miles), would be totally at variance with Hadrianic policy on every other frontier of the Empire. To Trajan, then, must go the credit for taking the African–Numidian frontier to its logical conclusion. This had the advantage of not only controlling the Biskra gap, through the Saharan Atlas, but also of reaching the actual edge of the desert. The frontier had reached its logical limit in the south. To the west, however, it had not yet found a matching limit, and was forced to take an arbitrary line, cutting across the grain of the country and the seasonal movement of tribes from the Hodna to the Plains of Constantine.

The same argument must hold for Caesariensis as holds for Africa. By the death of Trajan the frontier had been pushed south of Oued Soummam and the Beni-Slimane plain, to Auzia and the skirts of the Titteri range, thence via Sufasar to the Chélif Valley. Further west Trajanic foundations are known at Tasaccura and Regiae, linking the Chélif line with Siga at the mouth of Oued Tafna. Here no natural division is exploited, as the southern limit of the Tell had not yet been reached, but the line took advantage of the Chélif and the Plain of Oran, while remaining clear of the Tell Atlas.

Hadrian's reign marks a decisive change of pace on the African frontier, as elsewhere, with the introduction of running barriers (figs 10.8 and 10.10). But Hadrian also constructed a number of new forts, which probably transformed the comparatively scattered Trajanic outpost-network into a regular frontier system. The most easterly running barrier was for long thought to be some 70 km (44 miles) of ditch constructed from east to west of Speculum (east of Ad Maiores). But Trousset (1980a) has recently studied part of it and come to the convincing conclusion that it was, in fact, a road.

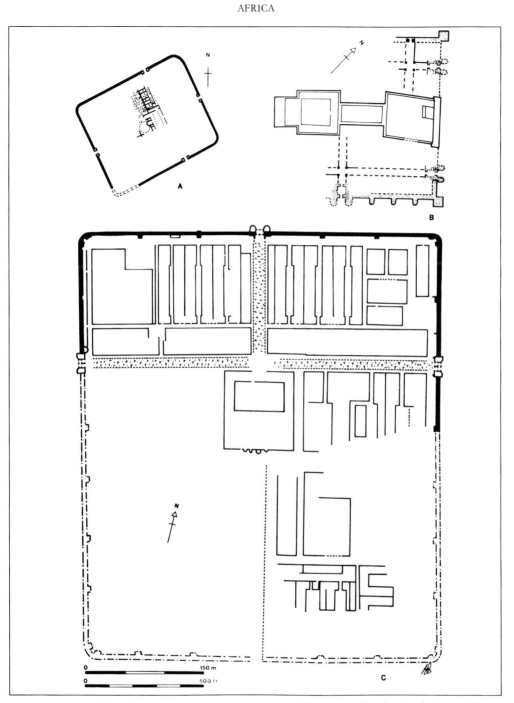

Figure 10.9 Legionary fortresses: (A) Lambaesis 'East' (*after Janon*); (B) the late fortress at Luxor; (C) Lambaesis (*after Cagnat*)

Whether free-standing towers existed in this sector is not known, although Baradez suggested that they might yet be found.

The sector which has received the most attention is that which is known locally as the Seguia bent el Krass (fig. 10.10A,G). This was a ditch fronting what had been a mud-brick wall, running for 60 km (37 miles) through an area of sparse winter grazing south of Oued Djedi. Baradez suggested that there had been a regular system of gateways at mile intervals, with a single tower placed midway between each pair of gates. The example of a gateway which he published (fig. 10.10) was a simple passageway between two guardchambers, with doors front and back, and a causeway across the ditch. Although Guey (1938) thought the whole system to have been of fourth-century date, Baradez' finds of pottery and coins proved the gates and towers to be Hadrianic foundations. The regularity of the system, however, is not so certain, for the gateways are difficult to see on the ground and there are considerably more towers than Baradez' account suggests, some on or very close to the wall, others, sometimes in groups, a short distance from it. Baradez' 'blueprint' may not have been so regular, and was definitely modified with the passage of time. Behind the line lay a scatter of small posts and isolated buildings, mostly late when they are datable, and the major fort of Gemellae, situated on the banks of Oued Djedi. This was a large fort, 2.9 ha ($7\frac{1}{4}$ acres) in size (fig. 10.11C) and built of mud bricks in the same style as the wall. Inscriptions date its first garrison, an equitate cohort, to AD 125–6.

The purpose of this barrier must have been to cover what today is a region of comparatively abundant water sources and palm groves lying around Ourella and Oumach and stretching from west of Tolga as far east as Biskra. That the *limes* was for regulation, and not total exclusion, is borne out by its gateways and the absence of any continuous rearward barrier similar to the British Vallum, with its very limited, heavily controlled crossing points. To the east the Seguia ends on the Oued Djedi, with Thabudeos covering the gap between it and the Aurès. To the west the gap between the end of the barrier and the next sector, at Mesarfelta, could have been covered by posts at Ouled Djellal (Baradez, 1949, 124) and Doucen, where Baradez records a total of four separate forts. Such a system would easily control the limited number of watering points on the western approach to Tolga, and as far north as the Zab mountains. The area north of Djebel ben Rhezal would have been watched from Mesarfelta itself.

The Mesarfelta sector (fig. 10.10B,C,D,F) consists of *c.* 45 km (28 miles) of either mound or wall, with a ditch and numerous towers. These last, and the duplication of the barrier itself at Mesarfelta, must indicate changes of plan or alterations during a long life. This sector provides a control where the frontier crosses the broken spurs of the Saharan Atlas and it would be easy to slip past unnoticed to Calceus. Baradez' published sections show a narrowish wall with ditch, of varying overall widths. Towers and gateways similar to those just described occur here, too.

North of Djebel Metlili the *fossatum* runs out into the plain and appears to end

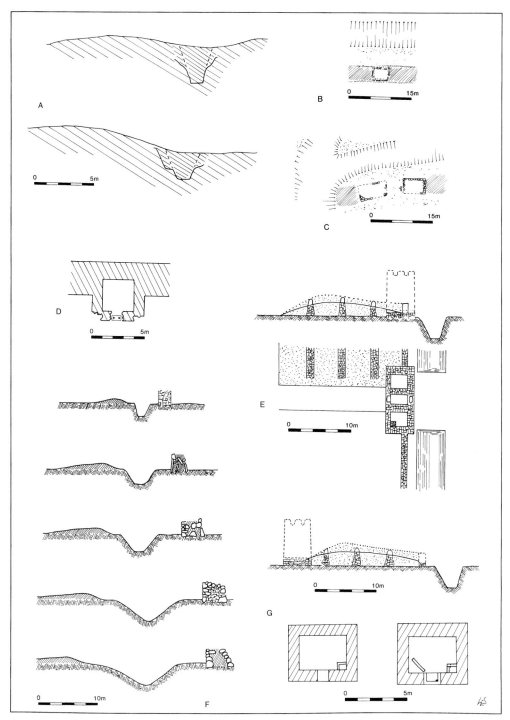

Figure 10.10 Frontier works: (A) Gemellae sector ditch (*after Guey*); (B,C,D) Mesarfelta sector, *limes*, towers and (?) gate (*after Jones and Mattingly, and Baradez*); (E) Gemellae sector gate (*after Baradez*); (F) Mesarfelta sector wall and ditch (*after Baradez*); (G) Gemellae sector rear towers (*after Baradez*)

close to Tobna (Thubunae), the plain itself continuing as far north as the Hodna mountains. Any movement of people in this area could easily be seen and controlled from Thubunae, Cellas and Macri, or from Zaraï, where the well-known customs tariff was found (*CIL*, VIII, 4508).

The third sector of *fossatum* is some 140 km (87 miles) long and all but encircles a portion of the Hodna Mountains. This length has been least studied of all and begs more questions than any of the others. If Baradez' map (1959) is to be believed it is a single-period construction running around and through the mountains, and apparently blocking off the approaches to Sétif from the south.

Seen together these lengths of *fossatum* were clearly never designed to form a preclusive frontier, but rather to control and channel north-east south-west seasonal transhumance from the Hodna area to the Plains of Constantine (Berthier, 1968).

The Hodna sector just described lies in Caesariensis. Elsewhere in that province the frontier was an open road running via Auzia to the Chélif. As suggested above, this line had been created in Trajanic times, but under Hadrian further forts were added, including Praesidium Sufative at Albulae, in AD 119, and Rapidum (fig. 10.11G) and Thanaramusa Castra, in 122. Towers may have been constructed along part of the road, for later in the century 'old towers' were rebuilt when new ones were added, in the Auzia-Rapidum sector. The original structures may have been as early as Hadrian.

Trouble occurred in the province, which is usually dated to the early part of Hadrian's reign, when the Baquates attacked Cartennas. Thereafter, the tribe is found along the Middle Atlas in Tingitana, where it might already have been situated at the time of its sally into central Caesariensis.

Conditions in Tingitana appear to have been peaceful. A whole series of inscriptions from Volubilis records solemn treaties with the Baquates, from the time of Marcus onwards, preceded by a simple dedication set up to Pius by one Aelius Tuccuda, *princeps* of the tribe. His name suggests a grant of citizenship under Hadrian. Since before the end of the first century Volubilis itself had been spreading far beyond its walls, but as new defences were not provided until AD 168, it is clear that there was no feeling of insecurity: the fort of Aïn Schkor, 3 km (2 miles) to the north, must have provided sufficient protection. On the other hand, diplomas suggest that the garrison of the province was increased between 109 and 122 by the addition of six extra auxiliary regiments, perhaps indicating that Trajan or Hadrian considered the long open frontier between Sala and Volubilis, and especially between Volubilis and Tingi, needed further protection. No sign of a regular series of forts or towers has been found, so treaty relations with the local tribes were probably an important part of frontier peace and security.

On 1 July AD 128 Hadrian reviewed the army of Africa at Lambaesis, to which the legion had recently been moved (fig. 10.9C). Parts of his address have survived (*CIL*, VIII, 2532 and 18042), carved on the base of a monument which stood in the centre of the so-called camp of the auxiliaries, to the west of the legionary fortress (fig. 10.11D).

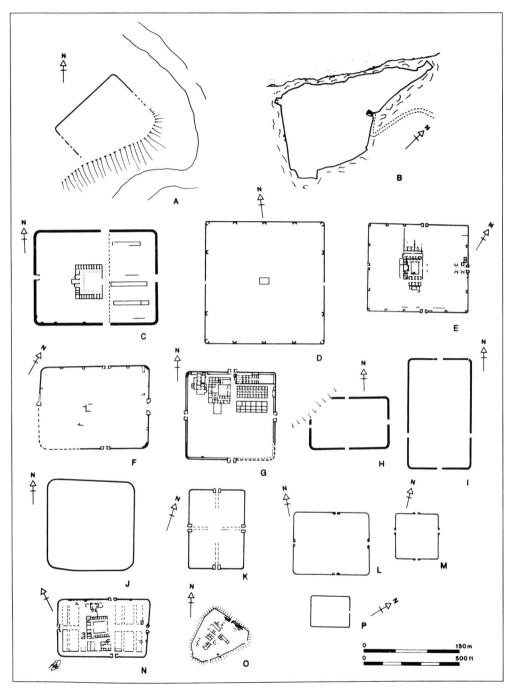

Figure 10.11 Auxiliary forts: (A) Aïn el Hammam (*after Jones*); (B) Primis, Qasr Ibrim (*after Adams et al.*); (C) Gemellae (*after Fentress*); (D) Lambaesis, 'Camp of the auxiliaries' (*after le Bohec*); (E) Thamusida (*after Rebuffat*); (F) Gheria el Garbia (*after Jones*); (G) Rapidum (*after Christofle*); (H) Djebel Mellah (*after Fentress*); (I) Ad Maiores (*after Fentress*); (J) Tocolosida (*after Euzennat*); (K) Ausum; (L) Remada (*after Euzennat*); (M) Ras el Aïn (*after Euzennat*); (N) Bu Ngem (*after Rebuffat*); (O) Dimmidi (*after Picard*); (P) Vezereos (*after Euzennat*)

The legion, Hadrian tells us, had in his own memory moved twice and built a fortress on each occasion. Since the second move was obviously to Lambaesis, a short time before 128, the first move must have been some time in the reign of Trajan, and Syme has suggested earlier rather than later. No fortress of that date has yet been found and the legion may have been split, for Hadrian noted that many widely scattered posts kept it separated. One cohort of the legion was also, by annual rote, on duty with the proconsul, and two years earlier a cohort and four men from each century had been sent to a sister *legio III*. In spite of the scattered state of the legion, and the African army, it was still felt to be strong enough to release a detachment for service in the east.

The reign of Pius was dominated in Africa by the Moorish War, when, according to Pausanias, independent nomadic tribes began an unprovoked attack, and were in return driven from their country and forced to flee as far as Mount Atlas. This must have called for extraordinary measures, and it has been suggested that the senatorial governor Uttedius Honoratus was given charge of both Mauretanias at the same time. Such a command would certainly have facilitated the defeat of the insurgents, but it is not actually attested in any source. We do know of the transfer into Caesariensis and Tingitana of legionary and auxiliary vexillations from Spain, and several northern provinces; but when the war was over these returned, leaving the provincial armies much as they had been before the war began; and not too long afterwards troops from Africa were sent to assist in Dacia.

Minor increases in defence did occur: in Tingitana Sala received walls, but Volubilis remained as before, largely unprotected. In Caesariensis the walls of Tipasa are dated to AD 146–7, on the strength of a fragmentary inscription from a minor gateway. A fort was built near Tigava at the same date, or perhaps a little earlier, but there is little sign of any change along the frontier of the province, or of any departure from the *limes*.

In Africa, on the other hand, there was a conspicuous change. The famous inscription of a detachment of *legio VI Ferrata*, road building at Tighanimine in the central Aurès defile in AD 145, shows that there was no trouble there during the Moorish War. Then, in 148–9, a fort was constructed near Medjedel, on the northern slopes of the Ouled Naïl mountains, some 150 km (93 miles) beyond the *limes* and about 115 km (72 miles) south of Auzia and the frontier of Caesariensis. The fact that such a fort could not have been placed there in splendid isolation is obvious: what is not known is where its companions lay. Doucen has already been mentioned, but is still far too distant, and although Baradez (1949) talks of forts lying between Doucen and Sadouri (Ausum) he gives no further information. El Gahra is 65 km (40 miles) further on, but still 75 km (47 miles) from Medjedel, and nothing is known about it in Antonine times. Zabi, too, is 100 km (62 miles) away; so the question remains unanswered. What is of major importance, however, is that this advance marks the first departure from the Hadrianic system.

In the reign of Marcus Aurelius a further innovation occurred. An inscription (*CIL*,

VIII, 21567), dated to AD 174, was set up by a mixed force of cavalry at Agneb, or Agueneb, on the northern edge of Djebel Amour, some 400 km (250 miles) beyond the African frontier. No trace of a fort has yet been found, although the troops were there long enough for a decurion to receive notice of promotion. The stone must indicate a mobile column patrolling tribal territory well down the Saharan Atlas (fig. 10.8, 9). This control, far beyond the *limes*, recalls the *loca* which Marcus imposed on the Marcomanni and Sarmatians beyond the Danube. These were places where tribal congregation and markets were licensed on fixed days, under regular Roman supervision. The *loca* which the *Ravenna Cosmography* lists in northern Britain are usually attributed to a later period, but there is no reason why they, too, could not have been instituted by Marcus, as an effective way of controlling the tribes beyond the frontier after the withdrawal from lowland Scotland. Seen in this light, the Agneb patrol indicates effective tribal regulation by supervision of the southern Atlas as well as the northern Tell ranges.

In Tingitana, the policy of tribal alliances was continued by means of a treaty between the Macenites and Baquates, and the emperor's procurator. Further north, a similar relationship with a local tribe is suggested by the granting of citizenship in AD 168 and 177 to two important members of the Zegrenses, as recorded at Banasa. However, some possible indications of insecurity are also to be found. In 168–9 Volubilis, at last, received a magnificent new circuit of walls, complete with towers and elaborate gates, while some 4.5 km ($2\frac{3}{4}$ miles) to the south, at Tocolosida (fig. 10.11 J), a fort was built on the site of a small settlement destroyed about the middle of the century. To the north of Volubilis the fort of Aïn Schkor was also destroyed 'about the middle of the century' and a new one built on the site. Volubilis itself, however, has produced no signs of damage.

As the century progressed, a network of forts and towers was developed in the vicinity of Volubilis and Aquae Dacicae, until a regular 7 to 9 Roman-mile mesh stretched from Oued Beth as far east as Volubilis. To the north, Thamusida (figs 10.7 and 10.11 E) received a fort and, shortly before the start of the third century, a garrison was placed at Banasa. On the coast Sala, already walled, was reinforced with a fort, while 6 km ($3\frac{3}{4}$ miles) to the south a ditch was dug for some 11 km ($6\frac{3}{4}$ miles), from the Atlantic to Oued Bou Regreg, completely shutting off the city. The ditch was complemented here and there by a wall (fig. 10.12 A,B), but its date is still no more closely assignable than to the second century (Euzennat, 1977a). Such was the southern defence of the province (fig. 10.7).

To the east no comparable works are known, although forts have been identified at Souk el Arba du Gharb, Tamuda and possibly at Kasr el Kebir. The Riff mountains remained almost totally unpenetrated and, under Marcus, sufficiently hostile for their inhabitants to cross the straits and devastate considerable areas of Spain, either in the late AD 160s or 172–3. Marcus restored order, but Commodus, too, is attributed with further action against the Moors, and the reference in the *Historia Augusta* makes best sense if it is taken to mean Moors outside the province. At the same time another reference could be interpreted as referring to successful military action in the mountains on the African side of the Mediterranean. To the south, the Baquates had a new chief, Aurelius Canartha, installed as a client ruler by the *procurator*.

In Caesariensis, Commodus reinforced the security of the province, early in his reign, by the provision of towers along the frontier road, both in the vicinity of Aïn Temouchent (Albulae) and at the other end of the province, between Auzia and Rapidum, where old towers were repaired and new ones added.

During the first and second centuries areas of the provinces, which in Tacitus' words were *solitudines Africae*, became populous and agriculturally prosperous. Hadrianic frontier policy had been to encourage development right up to the actual *limes*. As a result population and prosperity had so increased that it was now necessary to reinforce the policing of both the frontier itself and the land behind, particularly on account of the extremely porous nature of the African *limes*. Hence the provision of new watchtowers, which were designed for latitudinal observation along the line of the frontier and the regulation of those crossing it. Hence also the establishment of a *burgus speculatorius*, a police post for maintaining order and security between two roads (*inter duas vias ad salutem commeantium nova tutela constitui*), on the track between Calceus and Mesarfelta.

East again, in Tripolitania (fig. 10.13), a new fort was built on the escarpment road at Vezereos, some 80 km (50 miles) south-east of Turris Tamalleni, and another in the same sector, at Tisavar. Both these fortlets were far too small to be considered anything other than police posts (0.32 and 0.12 ha, $\frac{3}{4}$ and $\frac{1}{4}$ acres), but Tisavar is unusual in that it lay beyond the frontier line, a rarity amongst Commodan-date foundations. Elsewhere in the Empire, similar control of frontiers by the building or rebuilding of forts and *burgi* against robbers and no-goods (*latrunculi*), is recorded under Commodus, providing 'supervision and regulation of traffic across the border' (Mócsy), rather than the fortification of the frontier against increasing barbarian attacks. So seen, Commodus was clearly not the innovator of a new frontier policy which some have thought him to have been, but rather a conformer to the Hadrianic concept.

This concept was dramatically reversed by the African emperor Septimius Severus, under whom a considerable territorial advance was made. At the same time it is clear that a fuller understanding of the requirements for effective frontier control is to be seen in his system.

In Tripolitania, agricultural development of the Gebel escarpment and the predesert wadi systems of the Sofeggin and Zemzem, had gone on apace since the mid-first century AD. The production of olives, cereals and stock was developed by a steadily growing population, which has traditionally been interpreted as Roman settler exploitation of the land. However, as far as can be seen, neither here nor elsewhere on the African

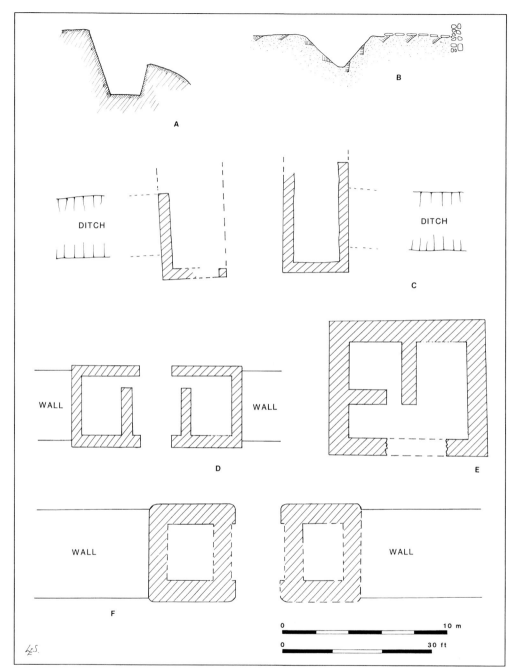

Figure 10.12 Frontier works: (A,B) Sala sector ditch (*after Rowland-Mareschal and Euzennat*); (C) Jebel Tebaga clausura gate (*after Trousset*); (D) *limes Tripolitanus* gate at Oued Skiffa (*after Blanchet*); (E,F) Hadd Hajar clausura watchtower and gate (*after Brogan*)

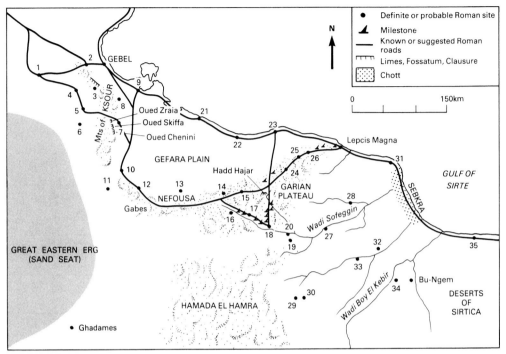

Figure 10.13 Tripolitania: sites and roads

1 Turris Tamalleni; 2 Aquae Tacapitanae; 3 Henchir Bel Aid; 4 Vezereos; 5 C. Tibubuci; 6 Tisavar; 7 Talalati; 8 Henchir Gueciret; 9 Gigthis; 10 Tillibar Remada; 11 Si-Aoun; 12 Dehibat; 13 Gasr Tigi; 14 Tentheos; 15 Auru; 16 Gasr Duib; 17 Gasr Uames; 18 Mizda; 19 Bir ed-Dreder; 20 Schedewa; 21 Pisida; 22 Sabratha; 23 Oea, Tripoli; 24 Thenadassa (Aïn Wif); 25 Tarhuna; 26 Mesphe; 27 Schmeck; 28 Gasr Bularkan; 29 Gherial-Gharbia; 30 Gherial Schergia; 31 Tubactis; 32 Faschia; 33 Ghirza; 34 Gasr Zerzi; 35 Sirte

frontier can it be shown to have been predominantly Roman colonists (traditionally '*limitanei*' or soldier-farmers) who carried this out. On the contrary, it increasingly appears to have been the local native population. The Tripolitanian zone of agriculture was now given some protection by the building of a screen of forts, placed on the main routes south (fig. 10.13). The major oases of Bu Ngem and Gheria el Gharbia received forts for detachments of *legio III Augusta*. Minor posts were placed at Gasr Zerzi and Gheria es Schergia on by-pass routes. These effectively controlled the south and south-eastern approaches to the area, the absolutely waterless Hamada el Hamra securing the south-west, beyond which the even more remote oasis of Ghadames also received a fort. Bu Ngem (AD 201, fig. 10.11N), certainly, and Gheria (fig. 10.11F), most likely, can be attributed to Quintus Anicius Faustus, who was given command of the legion in AD 197–201. Ghadames very likely dates to the same legate. North of these forts, on the escarpment road, an additional small outpost was placed at Si Aoun in AD 198,

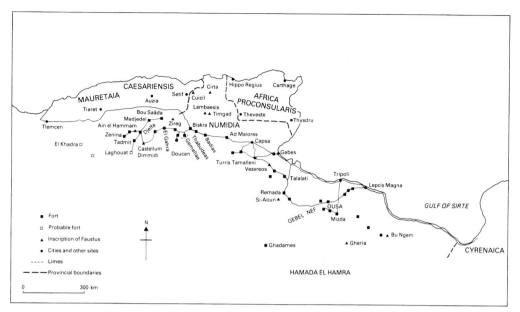

Figure 10.14 Numidia and the frontier command of Anicius Faustus

while Vezereos was virtually rebuilt in 201. Well to the east, the road station of Aïn Wif (Thenadassa) was also manned by the legion.

West of the Gemellae and Mesarfelta *limes* sectors, the Antonine 'outpost' zone was now hugely advanced by a network of forts, some small in size, extending by way of el Gahra and Aïn Rich to Castellum Dimmidi (AD 198, fig. 10.11O), and by way of Medjedel to Aïn el Hammam (fig. 10.11A), where a fragmentary inscription could be of Severan date. Other parts of the same system, but not closely datable, lie at Bou Saada, el Guelaa, Korirein, Djelfa, Tadmit and Zenina. The whole may even have extended west of Agneb, for Roman remains have been recorded at el Bayadh (ex Géryville) and el Khadra. This network ensured a permanent control of the Saharan Atlas along the southern edge of the High Plains (figs 10.5 and 14).

The smallness of garrisons (handfuls of legionaries and vexillations of *numeri*), the mixture of troops (legionaries and auxiliaries, infantry and cavalry) and the distances between posts (sometimes well over 50 km, 30 miles) stand out, and stress the same points: considerable Roman self-confidence, and little tribal opposition. The command of Faustus must have been stretched to its limits; in fact a detachment of *legio III Gallica* collaborated with *legio III Augusta*, reversing the Hadrianic situation, and long ago Carcopino (1925) pointed out the increased use of Syrian units. The overall distances Faustus had to control are staggering: from Bu Ngem via Ghadames, Tisavar and Gemellae to Dimmidi, by the straightest course, is over 1500 km (nearly 1,000 miles), the distance from the Cyrenaican frontier to el Khadra, measured the same way, is something like

2200 km (1,360 miles). These are direct distances; the army had a considerably greater area to control. By comparison, the Danube frontier, at about the same overall length, comprised six provinces and had a garrison of ten legions at this time. There was nothing like Faustus' command anywhere in the Empire, and even when Severus raised Numidia to the rank of a full province, most probably with Faustus as its first governor, there was no real change in the situation, nor increase in the size of the army.

The other half of Severus' policy was an advance in Caesariensis (fig. 10.8). This took the frontier to the southern edge of the Tell, with the creation of a new frontier line (*Nova Praetentura*) beyond the Titteri-Bibans ranges in the east, and the Ouarsenis and Frenda mountains in the west. Some control was exercised over the Saïda mountains, but the Daya and Tlemcen ranges seem to have been excluded. In AD 198, under the *procurator* Gaius Octavius Pudens, the eastern advanced posts of Tatilti, Grimidi and the road to Boghar were built, as well as a road from Sétif to Auzia. In 201 Publius Aelius Peregrinus added Aras and the winter quarters of the *ala Sebastena* in the south-west Ouarsenis, as well as the length of road, with its forts, from Cohors Breucorum to Kaputtasaccura, or possibly Altava. Four milestones actually refer to this as a *Nova Praetentura*. Other posts of Severan date fill the gaps, extending the road as far west as Maghnia (Lalla Marnia, Numerus Syrorum) on the Oued Tafna. Aïn Balloul, Aïn Benia and Ferme Romanette have been interpreted as outposts in the plains although the published plans of these sites raise serious questions as to their real nature (Benseddik, 1979?). This new line represents the advance of the old porous frontier, already discussed above (p. 244), not the institution of a new, preclusive barrier, as Gsell thought, and recently Rachet and Benabou have again claimed.

The function of a 'double frontier' of this sort has only slowly been recognized (Picard, 1947). The area between the *limes* of Caesariensis and the advance posts in the Saharan Atlas is what Despois

> calls the 'Waiting Zone' for nomadic and semi-nomadic movements between early summer, when there is sufficient grazing in the zone to support flocks while harvest labour filters northwards, and June to August, when it becomes essential to get the flocks and herds northwards to pasture on the stubble . . . the prime function of the inner line was to control the pastoralists in the 'Waiting Zone' and regulate the very important matter of the timing of their entrance and exits from the zone – not too early (especially in bad years) to trample the crops with their herds, but early enough to provide the harvest labour that was hired in the southern marches of the province (Whittaker, 1978, 349–50).

To the east the older, Hadrianic *limes* served the same function of a rear line, and recently Trousset (1974) has argued for the same arrangement in southern Tunisia. In Tripolitania, by contrast, there is less evidence for similarly large-scale seasonal movement, and as the predesert there is too arid to provide a comparable waiting zone, and no Tell lay to the north, the same system does not seem to have existed.

There is little indication of any contemporary advance in Tingitana. The existing system of forts and posts continued to protect the cities, especially Volubilis which was the seat of some at least of the procurators. To have attempted to advance to the limits of the Tell would have meant taking in extensive areas of the Middle Atlas and pushing into the Riff. Neither was practical and neither was attempted.

One area which has only been mentioned in passing is the 360 km (220 miles) of territory between Volubilis and Numerus Syrorum (fig. 10.5). Under Severus it appears that there may have been serious consideration given to annexing it. The procurators Haius Diadumenianus (AD 202–5) and Sallustius Macrinianus (probably his immediate successor) are attested as holding command in both provinces at the same time, an exceptional state of affairs. Only during the civil war after Nero's death, and under Vespasian, is it known for certain of others holding a similar command. Now, after the work of Faustus in Numidia and Pudens and Peregrinus in Caesariensis, was just the moment when the emperor could have decided to close the gap between the two Mauretanias. But the terrain and the low rainfall of the Moulouya valley, not to mention the independence of the Riff tribes, must have counselled against it. A proclamation of Roman Victory, however, was set up on a monument near Bou Hellou, 90 km (56 miles) east of Volubilis, and fragments of what was possibly another such inscription have been found at Numerus Syrorum in Caesariensis.

The generally peaceful state of the Sahara, which had existed during the reign of Severus, continued under his immediate successors. Under Caracalla milestones indicate work on the Caesariensis road and another *burgus speculatorius* was built south of el Kantara. For the first time, in the Antonine Itinerary, the escarpment or Gebel road (fig. 10.13) is described as following the *limes* of Tripolitania. Its course is given from Gabes via Turris Tamalleni to Lepcis, with the road stations listed, eighteen of which lie between Turris and Lepcis. Additionally, milestones of Caracalla record that another road ran from Tripoli to Mizda, beyond the *limes*, where it was met by a branch from the *limes* road running along the upper Sofeggin. Here too, milestones record Caracalla.

In Tingitana peaceful treaty relations with the Baquates continued. It has been observed that under Severus Alexander the increasing use of Syrian and other Eastern troops reached a peak with the augmentation or replacement of legionary garrisons by Palmyrenes (Picard, 1947). Another innovation which has been attributed to the same emperor was the introduction of veteran soldier-settlers (*limitanei*) into the farms and settlements of the frontier zone, in return for their service as frontier guards (Cagnat, 1913). Baradez and Goodchild were strong exponents of this view, which is still found, for example, in Rachet. But van Berchem and, overwhelmingly, Jones (1973) have questioned it, convincingly showing that the *limitanei* were no other than the normal, late, frontier troops, and not a peasant militia. The *Historia Augusta*'s account is a fabrication.

The settlements around frontier and rearward forts, on the other hand, had certainly been prospering, and as a whole continued to do so during the third and fourth centuries (Daniels, 1983). Figures 10.15 and 10.16 compare the size of successful *vici* with other settlements.

It has been suggested that a subtle change occurred after the succession of Severus Alexander. E. Birley (1950) pointed out that from his time onwards the status of the Numidian command dropped, so that only second-raters were appointed to the post. The importance of the legion, too, seems to have diminished with the increase in eastern troops. Having reached its peak under the African Severus, Numidia appears to have lost status under his Syrian successors.

The real crisis came shortly after the assassination of Severus Alexander in AD 235. Maximinus Thrax restored the status of the legion, and some at least of the frontier forts received legionaries again. But this uncouth and ruthless soldier was not popular with the Senate, the supporters of Alexander, or the class of landowners on whom his extortions fell most heavily and a revolt occurred at Thysdrus, in 238, which raised Gordian I to the purple. However, Capellianus, the governor of Numidia, easily destroyed the rebels with the aid of the legion and some provincial cavalry, and sacked various cities, including Carthage. Thrax himself was killed by his own troops shortly after, and the youngest Gordian became emperor. Perhaps in a bid to win favour Maximinus' name was removed from various inscriptions by the legion, but it was not enough. The legion was disbanded.

The strain on manpower must now have become acute, and it has been suggested that all forts beyond el Gahra had to be abandoned, while those still held were again garrisoned by Palmyrenes. Carcopino noted that only Palmyrenes are recorded on inscriptions between AD 238 and 253. The name of the legion was everywhere obliterated. But, as actual evidence for abandonment has so far been recovered from only one site, Castellum Dimmidi, it is perhaps a little premature to see wholesale withdrawal. To the rear, a new fort was built at Doucen in AD 242, and another at Ausum in 247, unless the latter was the rebuilding of a Severan foundation (fig. 10.11K). At least part of the Severan system was permanently retained along a line from Oued Djedi through Doucen, Ausum, el Gahra and Medjedel (fig. 10.8).

In Tripolitania the loss of the legion was crucial, and a new system was introduced under the next emperor, Philip. At Gasr Duib (fig. 10.17H) a small post, 16 m square ($52\frac{1}{2}$ ft sq), was built or rebuilt in AD 244–6. It is recorded on an inscription as a new *centenarium* constructed to close the region of the *limes [Ten]theitanus* and its road to barbarian invasion. The existence of a similar building at Gasr Uames, between Gasr Duib and Mizda, suggests that the *limes* may now have been split into a number of separate zones, perhaps in the manner implied by the *Notitia*. The use of the rank *praepositus limitis* occurs for the first time, but, as a new inscription from Bu Ngem suggests, it probably refers to the senior officer responsible for the whole Tripolitanian frontier, and not just one of a series of local sector commanders.

Within a few years of the disbanding of the legion, a new frontier arrangement had been introduced into Tripolitania. Whether this system was created at a single sweep along the whole *limes*, is not certain, but is likely. At Kasr Tarcine (fig. 10.17G) an inscription of 297–303 records the building of *Centenarium Tibubuci*, and to the east, near Tarhuna, one possible and one certain centenarium inscription have been found. The last two, however, may well have been late private buildings imitating official ones (p. 264), and the military road down the Sofeggin may mark the real line of the *limes*, via Schedewa (fig. 10.17) and Schmeck, which has produced yet another *centenarium* stone. Beyond, at Bu Ngem, an auxiliary vexillation held the fort until after the return of the legion.

How Caesariensis was affected is not clear. The legion had always been available for intervention in that province if necessary: now Numidia itself needed assistance. Certainly the *Nova Praetentura* continued to be held, but troops appear to have been sent east and it might be suspected that areas behind the frontier were stripped of their police force and such units as local *numeri*. A vexillation of Mauri from Caesariensis is recorded at Lambaesis.

The forty years, or so, between the death of Gordian III and the emergence of Diocletian saw the nadir of the High Empire, and its extinction. Barbarian pressure on the European and eastern frontiers, and Roman defeats and civil war, produced a breakaway Gallic Imperium in AD 259. A year later, after the capture of Valerian by the Persians, the eastern provinces were handed over to Palmyra. It is not surprising that there was also trouble in Africa and the scenario is not difficult to envisage: an increase of population during the long, predominantly peaceful years, reductions of police and security forces, increased taxation and ever-growing demands on the agricultural produce of the Tell, including, if Whittaker (1983) is correct, dependency on the same area by the tribes beyond the frontier, the gradual breakdown of central authority and mounting strain on officialdom. All led to outbreaks of lawlessness on both sides of the frontier.

In AD 253 Valerian restored *legio III Augusta* by sending a task force from Raetia and Noricum, perhaps containing troops who, after fifteen years' banishment, now wished to return home. In the middle 250s the governor Veturius Veturianus boasted of successful campaigning against barbarians, and military action near Auzia is known. In the following years several commanders recorded successful campaigning against Bavares, Babari Transtagnenses, Quinquegentanei and Fraxinenses, over an area from Sétif to Auzia, and about the same time Rapidum was destroyed. It appears that the removal of a portion of the outer frontier had enabled the external tribes to cross the *limes* and join rebellious internal factions, against all of whom a further governor, Macrinius Decianus, claimed three successful engagements. But the insecurity continued and it is significant that both Decianus and Veturianus were downgraded, for all their

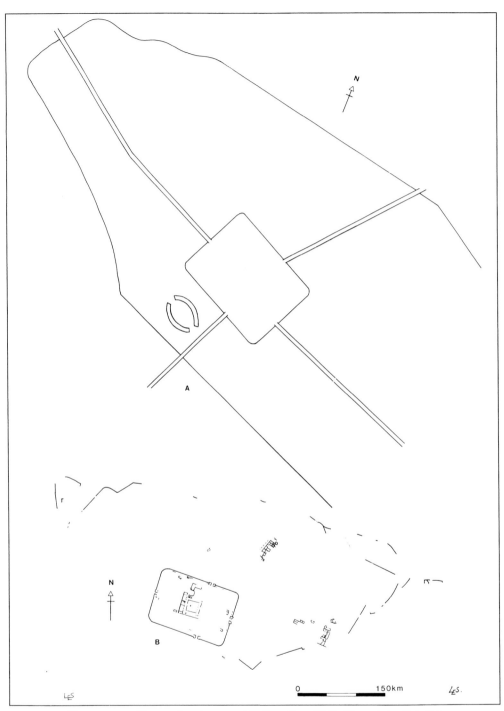

Figure 10.15 Forts and settlements: (A) Gemellae; (B) Bu Ngem (*after Rebuffat*)

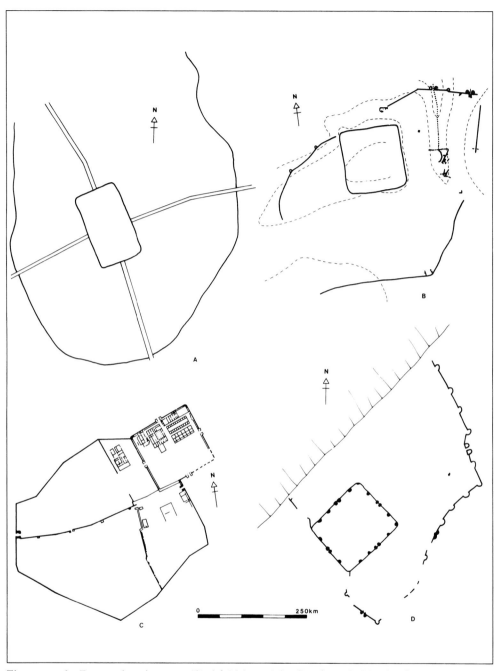

Figure 10.16 Forts and settlements: (A) Ad Maiores (*after Baradez*); (B) Tocolosida (*after Euzennat*); (C) Rapidum; (D) Thamusida

claims of success (E. Birley, 1979). It was not until Cornelius Octavianus, a tried and experienced officer, was made *Dux per Africam Numidiam Mauretaniamque* that a major victory was won in, or soon after, AD 260 and commemorated by a monument at Sétif.

A further outbreak by Bavares and Quinquegentanei occurred, to be countered by the governor Aurelius Litua in AD 289 to 292–3. Again, a greater effort was required and in 296 the co-emperor Maximianus arrived from Spain and swept the whole length of North Africa, finally restoring peace. On 10 March 298 he made a triumphal entry into Carthage.

Such a protracted period of disaster called for the sort of general reorganization which Diocletian was being forced to carry out in other regions of the Empire (fig. 10.18). The old provinces were split, a reform which had been begun before Maximianus' expedition with the separation of Sitifensis from the rest of Caesariensis and Byzacina from the rest of Proconsularis. This continued with the establishment of Tripolitania as a separate province and the division of Numidia into Cirtensis and Militana. But only in Tingitana was an area of territory given up. The whole south of the province, including Volubilis and Thamusida, was abandoned at some date after AD 280 (the last recorded treaty with the Baquates). The new frontier ran from Frigidae to the river Lukkos and then to Tamuda, although to the south Sala was certainly held until well into the fourth century and it is just possible that Banasa, too, was kept, for it may appear in the *Notitia* under the name of Castra Bariensis. The reduced province was placed under the vicar of Spain, in the Gallic Prefecture, thus finalizing the split with the rest of Africa.

Courtois (1955) argued that western Caesariensis was also abandoned late in the third century, but Salama's study of the evidence (1966) showed that this was not the case. When compared with the extensive abandoned areas of Germany, Raetia and the whole of Dacia, the comparatively minor loss of territory along the southern frontier of the empire, after such a strife-torn half century, is noteworthy.

Under Diocletian frontiers were generally strengthened. In addition to the small, tower-like *centenarium* constructed in AD 297–303 at Tibubuci (fig. 10.17G), the very much larger *centenarium* of Aqua Viva (fig. 10.19D) was built at M'doukal, west of the Mesarfelta sector of the *fossatum*. Rectangular forts with projecting angle and interval towers and with their garrison buildings placed against the rear face of the fort walls, are standard types to be seen at many early and mid fourth-century sites. Zebaret et Tir (fig. 10.19A), between Aqua Viva and the Chott el Hodna, is similar, but has a freestanding headquarters building in the centre. Aquae Herculis and Seba Mgata (figs. 10.19H, I) lie behind the Mesarfelta sector of *fossatum*. Further south the 'Castellum Schneider' of Baradez (fig. 10.19G) at Doucen and Guey's Bourada (fig. 10.19C), are akin to Zebaret, if smaller in size. These new constructions must be seen as reinforcing the existing frontier line, which still ran from Oued Djedi to Doucen, el Gahra and Medjedel. A matching site can be seen in northern Tingitana at Tamuda (fig. 10.19B).

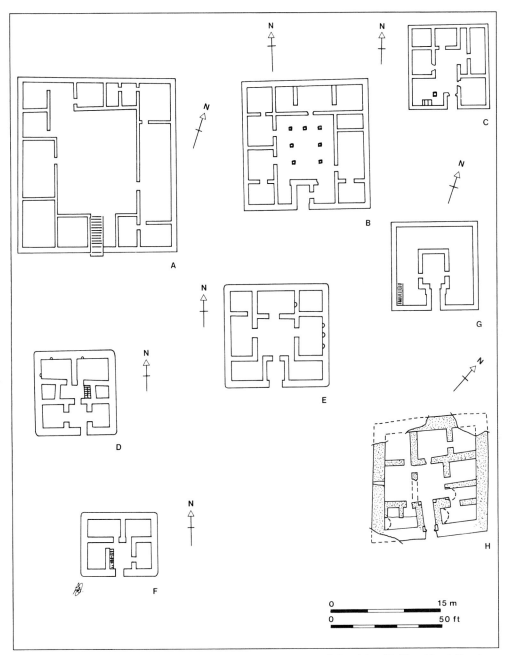

Figure 10.17 Small *centenaria, burgi* and towers: (A) Ras el Oued Gordab; (B) Henchir el Gueciret; (C) Henchir Remtia (*after Euzennat*); (D,E,F,) Gasr Bir Scedewa (*after Goodchild*); (G) Tibubuci (*after Euzenat*); (H) Gasr Duib (*after Goodchild*)

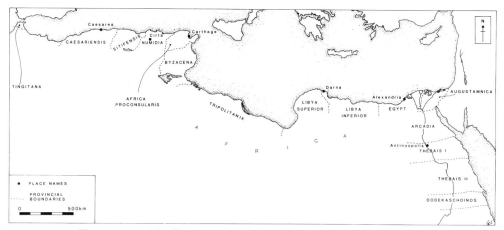

Figure 10.18 The dioceses and provinces of north Africa in the late Empire

There, however, the fort was an earlier structure, to which projecting angle and interval towers were added and the gates remodelled.

Now, at last, the army of Africa was enlarged to seven legions, with another in Tingitana, not to mention cavalry and frontier troops. It also underwent further alterations during the fourth century, including changes in the status and grouping of units, both *limitanei* (frontier troops) and *comitatenses* (the field army). In the *Notitia* the *limitanei* are divided between the Comes Africae, the Dux Tripolitaniae and the Dux Mauretaniae, where they are listed under the command of more than thirty *praepositi limitum* (regional commanders), each with a geographical location as a name. Some of these can be identified, including sites on the *limes Tripolitanus* road, the old Numidian frontier from Turris Tamalleni to the Hodna and at Columnata, but others cause problems, especially those which appear to be duplicated in both the dukes' commands and the count's. In addition, the count also commanded a body of *comitatenses* amounting to some 21,000 men. All this has caused Jones to suggest that the command originated as a limitanean duke who was raised to the rank of count when the comitatensian field-force became a permanent addition.

The composition of these frontier forces is revealed by a law of Honorius, dated AD 409, which states that land in Africa had been granted to *gentiles* for the care and maintenance of the frontier and *fossatum* (*munitionemque limites atque fossati*), which is usually interpreted as meaning that the frontier areas were entrusted to barbarian tribesmen (*gentiles*) under the supervision of army officers (*praepositi*). But Goodchild (1950) pointed out that the officers themselves, or at any rate the tribunes buried at Bir ed-Dreder just south of the Wadi Sofeggin, were not culturally very far removed from the barbarians they commanded. At last a limitanean soldier-farmer peasant army can be seen holding the frontier. But it appears to comprise natives (*gentiles*) occupying the lands

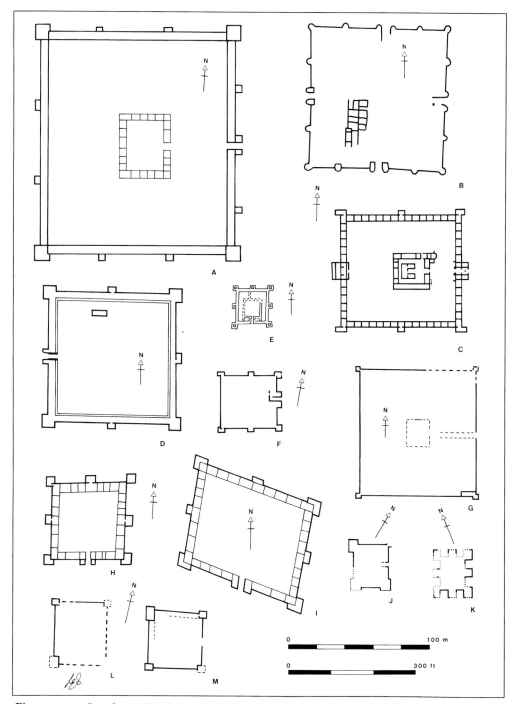

Figure 10.19   Late forts: (A) Zebaret et Tir (*after Baradez*); (B) Tamuda (*after Johnson*); (C) Bourada (*after Guey*); (D) Centenarium Aqua Viva (*after Leschi*); (E) Mselletin (*after Haynes*); (F) Benia bel Recheb (*after Euzennat*); (G) Doucen (*after Jones* et al.); (H) Aquae Herculis (*after Baradez*); (I) Seba Mgata (*after Fentress*); (J) Henchir Temassine (*after Euzennat*); (K) Henchir Rjijila (*after Euzennat*); (L) Tailimun (*after Goodchild*); (M) el-Benia, Gasr el-Geballa (*after Goodchild*)

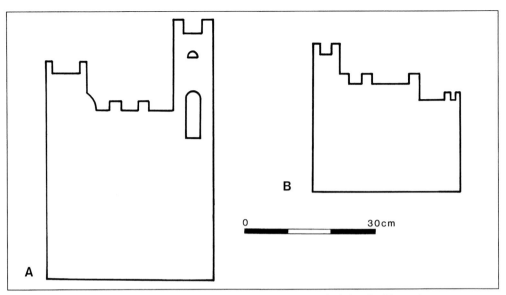

Figure 10.20   Sketch of two fortified structures; to the left (*after Trousset*)

on both sides of the old *limes*, and not the Roman, colonist soldier-farmer force it has traditionally been claimed to have been. In the light of this the barbaric inscriptions of the *centenaria* at Schmeck and near Tarhuna take on a new aspect. These buildings, and the small fort at Gasr Bularkan (fig. 10.19E), described by Goodchild as a police post, are very much the sort of structures which the *gentiles* of the frontiers could be expected to have built themselves. Together with such private *gsur* as Henchir Gueciret in the Jebel Matmata of Tunisia (fig. 10.20 for a graffito thought to be the profile of this sort of building), they follow in the long-lived Berber tradition of towers, described by such earlier writers as Diodorus Siculus, Sallust and Caesar. Perhaps the sizeable settlement of Ghirza, to the south of Wadi Zemzem, should be seen in the same context.

The law of Honorius mentions the frontier and the *fossatum* in a way which suggests that they are closely connected. Jones and Mattingley (1980) published a coin of AD 353–5 from a gateway of the Mesarfelta sector, showing that it was still in use at that date. Lengths of *clausura* are known which block access through Jebel Tebaga and the Oueds Zraïa, Skiffa and Chenini, all in the Matmata region (fig. 10.12C,D). Trousset (1974) argues their function to have been the control of nomads, and couples the names of Flavius Archontius Nilus (Comes and Praeses of Tripolitania in 355–60) and Flavius Nepotianus, specifically, with this sort of control. To the east, not far from Asabaa in the Gebel Garian, Lady Brogan recently found a 6-kilometre length ($3\frac{3}{4}$ miles) of *clausura* at Hadd Hajar, complete with gate (fig. 10.12F), all very much in the same style as those near Matmata. In spite of its superior-quality construction the shut-off wall with gateway at Bir oum Ali, south-east of Gafsa, and others across adjacent valleys in Jebel el Asker, would surely fit better into this period than Trajanic times, as has already been suggested.

Historically, the fourth century saw raiding and revolts continuing. In the 360s Tripolitania suffered from attacks by the fierce nomadic Austuriani. The demands of Count Romanus for large quantities of supplies and 4,000 camels, before he would act to save Lepcis, are well-known and finally bring our attention to the beast which is generally considered to be the indispensable tool of desert control. In reality, various studies have made it quite clear that the use of the camel at an early date was very rare west of the Nile, other than for agriculture (Gasr Tigi reliefs) or as a beast of burden (Bu Ngem *ostraca*). Although *dromadarii*, camel scouts, are recorded at Luxor in AD 156, there is so far only one possible matching reference from further west, before the fourth century. Antonine long-range patrols and Severan advances were carried out by equestrian cavalry, as was the Arab conquest.

The revolts of Firmus and Gildo, although they involved the army and general security, do not primarily concern the frontier; the pro and anti-Roman alliances of this family were more reminiscent of the vicious squabbles of the descendants of Masinissa or the opportunist alliances and betrayals of the Mauretanian and Numidian dynasties in the days of Carthage and the Roman Republic.

The next event was the Vandal invasion, followed by the fall of Carthage in AD 439 and the demolition of many town and city walls. Roman Africa had still over two centuries to run before the Arab invasions of the seventh century, but the *limes* system, as it has been seen, now ceased to function, if in fact it had not already ceased some time before.

When successful invasion occurred it was not from the south. The Vandals and Byzantines came from the sea, as had Rome's invasion of Carthage, and the Arabs from the east, through Syria. In short, the desert frontier was successfully held, over immense distances and by the smallest of regional armies, for something over half a millennium. Unlike the Rhine and Danube lines and the eastern frontier, all of which finally broke under barbarian attack, the special nature of the African *limes*, with its policy of regulation rather than preclusion, proved to be the most successful of all.

CHAPTER 11

·THE·EAST·

David Kennedy

And I saw, and behold a white horse; and he that sat on him had a bow; and a crown was given unto him; and he went forth conquering and to conquer. . . . And there went out another horse that was red; and power was given to him that sat thereon to take peace from the earth, and that they should kill one another: and there was given unto him a great sword. (*Revelations*, 6.1–6)

When, in 1071, Emperor Romanus IV Diogenes and his army were destroyed on the fateful battlefield of Manzikert in eastern Anatolia, it brought to an end over eleven and a half centuries of Roman military activity on the Euphrates, dating back to 92 BC when the commander in Cilicia, L. Cornelius Sulla, led the first Roman force there and made the first official contact with Parthia. The Parthian envoy came with offers of friendship and alliance; however, the cordiality of this first meeting soon evaporated. Within less than a generation Lucullus is found (69–7) campaigning east of the river in Armenia and allegedly contemplating an attack on Parthia; in 53 Crassus paid the price at Carrhae for his unprovoked attack on the Parthian empire and Roman Syria, stripped of many of its defenders by the disaster, was open to Parthian invasion. This first meeting did, however, establish the Euphrates as the limit of power and influence for each empire and it is notable that the amicable initiative came from Parthia. Notable, too, that even then the Roman general sought to emphasize Rome's pre-eminence: the envoy was afterwards executed for allowing Sulla to seat himself between the Great King's representative and the king of Cappadocia, as if interviewing vassals.

For almost seven centuries after Carrhae, Rome seems continually at war with first Parthia, then her Sasanian Persian successor, in a struggle along and beyond the Euphrates from its headwaters to the Palmyrene desert. Ultimately, and almost simultaneously, in AD 636, the two great protagonists, mutually debilitated by their final protracted and bloody war, were each crushingly defeated in battle by the ragged but inspired armies of Islam which on the one hand overthrew Sasanian Persia and on the other deprived Rome of her Syrian and North African provinces. At a stroke, the seemingly interminable struggle was ended, and a new Muslim Arab Empire united the lands on both sides of the former southern Euphrates frontier. The menace on the upper Euphrates was to return with the Turks but, for the moment, the danger was on the south-east.

In any examination of Rome's eastern frontier, it is inevitable that the discussion will centre on the relationship between Rome and her great neighbour. It was only in the east, after all, that she faced another great power, comparable in size and strength to herself. Moreover, the surviving literary sources for the eastern frontier are dominated by the tensions, crises and wars of the 'super powers' of classical antiquity. These same sources, overwhelmingly Roman, especially in the Parthian period, saw the struggle through the eyes of an aristocracy who were not only steeped in the Greek and Hellenistic accounts of earlier struggles with oriental powers, but also the inheritors of these same states, now the provinces of Achaea and Macedonia, which had, respectively, withstood Darius and Xerxes and overthrown the first Persian empire. Crassus and Trajan were not alone in believing that the military might and resources of the Roman Empire should have made them capable of emulating Alexander. In short, Rome could not accept equality with a state she believed she should dominate if not actually destroy. From the outset, both in attitude and in behaviour, Rome is the more aggressive. Parthia seldom struck at Roman territory or vassals west of the Euphrates, being usually on the defensive, responding to Roman intervention amongst her vassals or satraps. Indeed, even by the time of Augustus, Parthia had begun a slow decline, remaining without territorial ambitions beyond her Euphrates frontier.

Lucullus initiated Roman intervention beyond the Euphrates and although it was subsequently accepted as a boundary, Rome is soon found involved again to its east. For long the bone of contention was the large kingdom of Armenia; later principally Mesopotamia. Strategically, however, both were firmly linked. Parthia could never acquiesce easily to a Roman vassal in Armenia outflanking and dominating her own wealthy vassals in northern Mesopotamia; a Roman Mesopotamia, however, was no better, making a Parthian vassaldom in Armenia untenable. Inevitably early Roman efforts to dominate Armenia led on to intervention in Mesopotamia. What began for Republican Rome as simply the centuries-old momentum of expansion became, to some extent, in the early Principate, an actual military need to secure her north-eastern frontier by control of the southern Caucasus states – Iberia, Colchis, Albania and Armenia. The awareness of the threat from the Transcaucasian Sarmatians made it desirable at least to influence the states which controlled the southern exits of the handful of passes, as well as Armenia, which was the lynch-pin of the region. Preferably they should control these passes themselves: mountains, as Napoleon knew, make much better frontiers than rivers. The same considerations of security affected Parthia and Persia – indeed affected them more acutely since they were the first to bear the brunt of a Sarmatian invasion, but like Rome, they were unwilling to allow the key to their security in this area to be in the hands of a potential foe. Despite the blood spilled in the wars, it is ironic – and instructive – that by the end of the fourth century no more had been achieved than a partition of Armenia and Mesopotamia, the lion's share going to Persia: pathetically small gains when one thinks back to the promise of great success implicit in Lucullus' capture of the new Armenian capital Tigranocerta in 69 BC and the temporary vassaldom of Osrhoene in the last generation of the Republic.

Despite the dramatic imagery of the Revelation, invoked already by Mommsen and Wheeler, outright war was in fact infrequent in the Parthian period. Nor was it in practice a misfortune for either protagonist that two of the three great empires of the ancient world should have been juxtaposed, rather than remote and isolated as China. Despite mutual suspicion and the potential menace of the huge military resources on either side, throughout much of their history each in fact represented the sole element of reliable stability amongst the many peoples on their respective frontiers. The glory-seeking, or aggressive opportunism, or urgings of destiny which motivated Trajan, the early Severi, Ardashir and the first two Sapors, were the exception; most rulers, Roman Emperor or Great King, saw their major and long-term frontier threat, the challenge to their civilization itself, amongst the numerous, unpredictable, and often more volatile barbarian neighbours along the Central European and Central Asian frontiers, rather than from one another. As a rule, each had more to lose by defeat than they could realistically hope to gain by success in war with one another. The danger posed to Rome by her eastern neighbour may be judged by the crude comparison of army sizes in the mid-second century (fig. 11.1).

The European frontier is of course something like twice the length of the eastern and, not surprisingly, had twice the garrison. The eastern total, however, includes a large figure (*c.* 17,000) for the internal garrisoning of Palaestina (p. 277 below); without that element the eastern frontier has only some 10,000 more troops than the single province of Britain. In terms of manpower, the eastern frontier was garrisoned very economically: a reflection, in part at least, of the underlying stability and reliability of the relationship with Parthia; in part, of the means employed to defend and control the frontier provinces. The development of Roman control west of the Euphrates and the changed condition in her eastern neighbour help to explain the growth in size, changed character and re-organized deployment of her forces (p. 279 below).

A point which must be stressed is that for all the aggressiveness of successive Rome dynasts and emperors, the size of the Roman forces in the east could not of itself be a reason for constant disquiet for either Parthia or Persia. In every offensive war against the neighbouring empire, Rome had to concentrate not only much of the forces along the entire eastern frontier, but also to draft in substantial reinforcements from distant

Figure 11.1 Distribution of Frontier Forces *c.* 150

Region	Legions Number	Men	Auxilia Units	%	Men	%	Strength Men	%
Britain	3	15,000	60	15.6	35,180	15.7	50,180	13.8
Rhine & Danube	14	70,000	173	44.8	99,900	44.7	169,900	46.7
East	8	40,000	65	16.8	37,940	17.0	77,940	21.4
Africa	2	10,000	60	15.5	33,170	14.8	43,170	11.9
(Other)	1	5,000	28	7.3	17,500	7.8	22,500	6.2
Totals	28	140,000	386	100.0	223,690	100.0	363,690	100.0

(Adapted from Birley, 198b, 40–2)

provinces; wars could be seen in the making for months, indeed years, before hostilities began. Conversely, the frontier garrisons and provincial armies were only just adequate for internal security and defence: sufficient certainly to give an opponent pause, to delay if not repulse him while a major field force was prepared. For their part, Parthia and Persia both relied on a small royal army supplemented in war by the nobility and their retainers. It is noteworthy that in the long struggle between the predominating heavy infantry of Rome and the aristocratic horsemen and mounted archers of Parthia, it was the former which rebalanced her forces to give pride of place to cavalry; both empires adopted the mailed cavalry of their common Sarmatian enemy.

A concern with one another was not the sole military preoccupation of either empire. The Islamic armies of the seventh century were the outcome of a lengthy process of development among the Arabs of the steppe and desert from Mesopotamia to the Arabian peninsula. Moreover, in practical terms, especially as the client-states were absorbed, an increasingly large part of the eastern garrison was unconcerned with the single threat from Parthia or Persia, being deployed rather to police the growing power and ambitions of these nomads on or beyond the frontier zones.

Finally, there was the threat from the Transcaucasian Sarmatians mentioned above. The forceful arrival of the Sarmatian Iazyges and Roxolani on the lower Danube in the time of Nero emphasized the need to check the advance of many other Sarmatian tribes to the east of the Black Sea. In practice, the coastal route through Colchis was in Roman control first through a client-king, later through the forts described by Arrian (fig. 11.12a–e). Iberia and Albania each controlled a vital mountain route, the Darial Pass/Caucasian Gates and Derbend Pass/Caspian Gates respectively, control of which prevented access to either empire. It is probably these two passes which became from at least 244 the object of subventions from Rome for the maintenance of mutually beneficial Persian garrisons.

The frontier region

The anchor points of the eastern frontier lay at Trapezus and Aila, respectively on the Black and Red Seas; appropriately, each the base of a legion in the fourth century (fig. 11.2). The direct distance of almost 1,400 km (870 miles), impressive enough in itself, is misleading in that it hides the enormous difficulties presented by the terrain – mountain, river, steppe and desert, and ignores outposts and salients. Nor does it tell the whole story: the eastern army was responsible both for the Sinai Peninsula, and the Hisma and even, at one time, the Hedjaz; in the north, the frontier was extended through a chain of forts around the eastern end of the Black Sea to Sebastopolis. All told, the marching distance by the shortest route from Sebastopolis to Hegra was well over 3,000 km (1,860 miles), stretching today across nine modern countries (fig. 11.3).

One may divide the entire zone into two sectors: the mountain and riverine frontier in eastern Anatolia, and the steppe or desert, at times mountainous, from Mesopotamia to the Hedjaz. Along the former were to be found substantial populations involved in agriculture and pastoralism, those in the north able to exploit the lucrative minerals and extensive forests of the Pontic Alps. The major viable routes are few: that along the coastal lands past Trapezus; a caravan route from Armenia passing westwards from Satala to Ancyra and the Hellespont; also from Armenia a road through Melitene to Ancyra again or to the cities and ports of Ionia. This last, and that which reached Samosata (pl. 11.1) were the major crossing points of the northern Euphrates in an east–west direction. All, naturally, had both strategic and economic importance. Between Samosata and Satala the Euphrates itself suggested the longitudinal route, while in the final northern stretch the road to Trapezus had to negotiate the Pontic Alps through the vital Zigana Pass. The mountainous lands of eastern Anatolia present a tortured landscape, harsh winters being succeeded by very hot summers. It is also a dangerous earthquake zone.

South of Commagene one reaches the steppe of Mesopotamia and Syria, lands quite thinly populated until recently but clearly intensely settled in antiquity. In the Syrian Desert itself the main military zone runs through desert to Palmyra, then along the mountain chain of the Jebel esh-Sharqi towards Damascus. The fertile volcanic zone of the southern Hauran extends the zone eastwards once more before it proceeds south-south-west along the desert's edge in Jordan to the Hedjaz coast of the Red Sea.

Archaeological and epigraphic evidence

The archaeological evidence for the location, character and development of the eastern frontier is patchy, and often confusing. The basic evidence for much of the region remains even now the maps of Poidebard and Stein from before the Second World

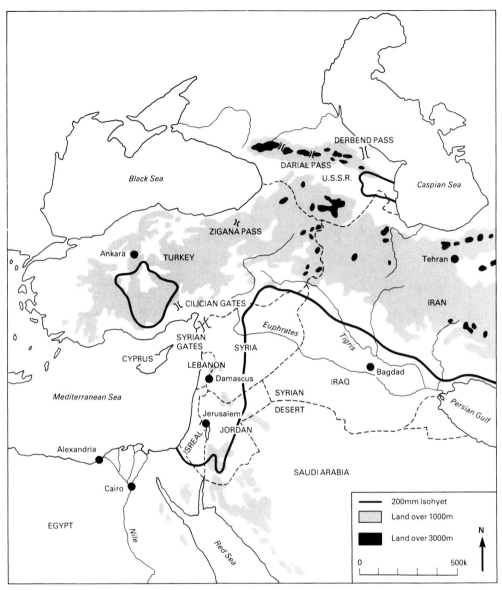

Figure 11.2 The physical geography of the eastern frontier region

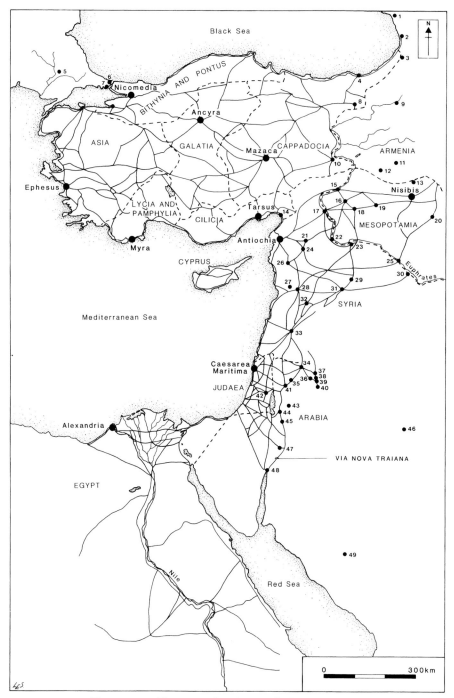

Figure 11.3 The eastern frontier area the Roman Empire

1 Sebastopolis; 2 Phasis; 3 Colchis; 4 Trapezus; 5 Adrianople; 6 Constantinople; 7 Byzantium; 8 Satala;
9 Elegeia; 10 Melitene; 11 Tigranocerta; 12 Amida; 13 Bezabde; 14 Issus; 15 Samosata; 16 Edessa;
17 Zeugma; 18 Carrhae; 19 Resaina; 20 Singara; 21 Beroea; 22 Barbalissis; 23 Sura; 24 Chalcis;
25 Circesium; 26 Apamea; 27 Raphanaea; 28 Emesa; 29 Oriza; 30 Dura–Europos; 31 Palmyra; 32 Danaba;
33 Damascus; 34 Bostra; 35 Qasr el-Hallabat; 36 Qottein; 37 Imtan; 38 Deir-el Kahf 39 Basiena; 40 Azraq;
41 Philadelphia; 42 Jerusalem; 43 Qasr Bshir; 44 Lejjun; 45 Quweira; 46 Jauf; 47 Petra; 48 Aila;
49 Medain Salih

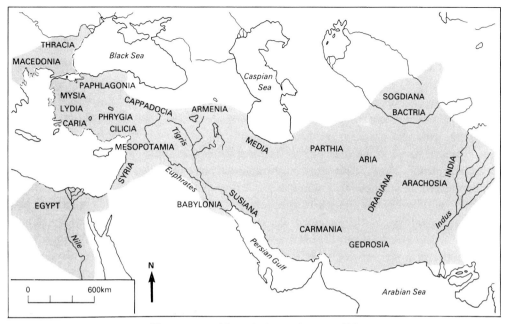

Figure 11.4 Alexander's Empire, *c.* 323 BC

War. It has long been recognized that these present a palimpsest of several centuries of occupation and, indeed, include a number of non-Roman sites. At all times, field work has varied considerably in quality and intensity from area to area; nor, even at its best, has it been on the scale one is familiar with in Britain – thus, in Arabia, a relatively well-explored province, new work has produced four new forts in the last three years. A major problem of course is that in the early Empire many regiments were simply billeted in the great towns of the east, where, even if they had their own camp, it is likely to have been long since obliterated by centuries of continuous occupation; likewise, those sites not in towns but still in the fertile lands on the edge of the steppe and intensively farmed since antiquity. Thus, we get a very unbalanced picture reflecting patterns and intensity of later settlement, modern research, and the division between the heavily urbanized regions in which garrisons lay in the early Empire, from which little evidence is available, and the steppe and desert with marvellously well-preserved late fortifications. For the early Empire, fortunately, inscriptions go some way to remedying the lack of physical evidence. Some military diplomas, naming and locating units (pl. 11.2) give wonderful pictures of part at least of the auxiliary garrison on the given date. Only at the end of our period, with the important information of the *Notitia Dignitatum*, is it possible precisely to locate a large number of units at specific places which can be equated with known forts (e.g. fig. 11.14).

Development and character of the frontier

In 30 BC, despite the huge manpower surplus available to him, Augustus elected not to take up Caesar's planned eastern war to avenge Crassus and the subsequent Parthian invasions of Syria and Asia Minor. Instead, Roman prestige for these and the more recent failure of Antony's Parthian War (36–4 BC), as well as regional objectives, was to be regained by military pressure and diplomacy. Rightly so, throughout his long reign, the principal military preoccupations of Augustus were in Europe. Moreover, much needed to be done west of the Euphrates before further major advances could be contemplated. Thus, although a considerable degree of order had been imposed on the haphazard acquisition and alliances of Rome in the east by Pompey's settlement (63 BC), two civil wars, Parthian invasions and two Roman assaults on Parthia and her vassals had, by 30 BC, renewed the need for a reassessment and reorganization. For all that he avoided war with his major neighbour, Augustus was every bit as much the imperialist in the east as he was in the west. Reorganization for Augustus meant an advance of Rome's directly administered territories; as in Pompey's scheme, however, a chain of petty kings, recognized as vassals, was retained (fig. 11.6). To the west of the Euphrates, Parthia accepted that Rome might arrange matters as she saw fit; Armenia to the east, however, was a different matter. The Augustan policy, pursued by his successors for almost a century, sought to turn Armenia into a Roman buffer state. In practice this called for the installation of a king approved by Rome and, if necessary, placed there by force of arms. It was a policy which was resisted from time to time not only by the Parthians but by factions among the Armenians themselves. The resulting turbulence is reflected in the rapid changes of ruler and repeated interventions by Roman or Parthian forces. Nevertheless, the prestige of Augustan Rome and the quiescence of Parthia in this period enabled the policy to work well enough, as symbolized by the diplomatic coup in 20 BC when Phraates IV returned the lost Roman eagles taken from the legions of Crassus and Antony, recognized Roman suzerainty over Armenia and subsequently accepted the installation of a Roman nominee by Tiberius. Roman pre-eminence was again recognized in AD 2 when Phraates V negotiated a peace with Gaius Caesar and conceded his right to proceed to install another Roman candidate by force. It is a measure of Augustus' prestige and perseverance that he was able to pursue this policy for so long despite the recurrent upheavals in Armenia and the rejection or death of so many of his nominees.

Within the acknowledged Roman sphere of power and influence west of the Euphrates, the policy was much easier to implement and more successful: others came and went but in AD 14 Pontus, Armenia Minor, Cappadocia, Commagene, Cilicia, Emesa, Chalcis, Ituraea, Galilee and Nabataea all had client-kings and there were varying degrees of restraint on the rulers of Iberia, Colchis and Albania, and Palmyra had been brought under Roman control. In the distant south one can see the Augustan imperialist

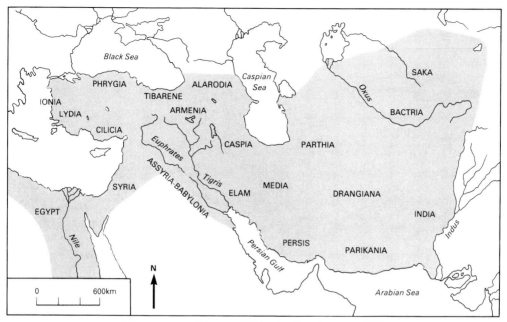

Figure 11.5 Achaemenid Empire (fourth century BC)

policy very clearly at work: in *c.* 26 BC, Aelius Gallus, the Prefect of Egypt, was sent on an expedition down the coast of Arabia 'into the territory of the Sabaeans to the town of Mariba'. Less than a generation later Augustus may well have briefly annexed the Nabataean kingdom, not to restore it until AD 1 and the *expeditio Arabica* of Gaius Caesar to the Gulf of Aqaba (Bowersock, 1983, 54–7).

The numerous client-states in the east, and in general their reliability, explain both the relatively small scale of the Roman forces and their distribution in the early Principate. The poor quality of the evidence for most of the Julio–Claudian period cannot be the sole explanation for the mere handful of auxiliary units attested. Rather, as when Aelius Gallus called upon Herod of Judaea and the Nabataean king to supply 500 and 1,000 troops respectively for his Arabian expedition or, most graphically of all, the 7,000 archers and 3,000 cavalry supplied by the client-kings of Emesa, Commagene, Ituraea and Nabataea, for the Jewish War of Vespasian and Titus, Rome supplemented her heavy legionaries principally from the armies of her royal clients. At the death of Augustus, there were apparently only four legions for the entire region, all, moreover, concentrated in northern Syria from Cyrrhus to Raphanaea, screening the major cities at the terminus of the most obvious Parthian invasion route as well as securing their large populations.

Locating the Roman army in the Augustan period is almost impossible. Literary evidence leaves little doubt that the legions were based near, if not in, the great cities

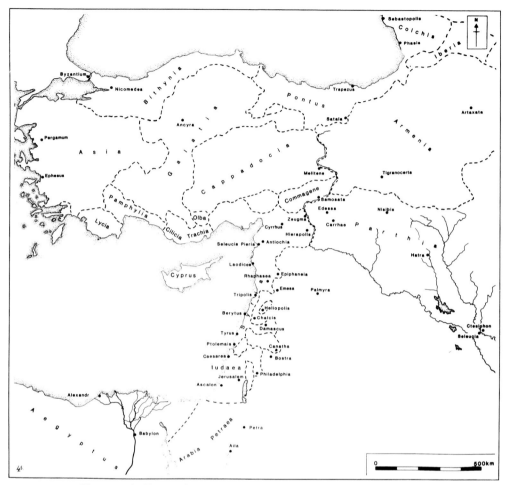

Figure 11.6 Eastern frontier provinces at the death of Augustus (AD 14)

of northern Syria. One may suppose the same to be true of many, perhaps most, auxiliary units; it was certainly the case a little later in Judaea as Josephus and the New Testament makes clear. In short, the soldiers were deployed, partly to be readily assembled for war, partly for securing a substantial and considerably urbanized population, and partly to ease the burden on the provincials of their supply. We do not know what these 'urban forts' were like: since the Praetorian Guard in Rome remained billeted in houses until the reign of Tiberius there is no reason to believe otherwise for the east too in this period or later. Perhaps, like the Guard, which acquired two-storeyed barracks in the Castra Praetoria, the eastern soldiers too, when and if they received purpose-built quarters, constructed barracks more like the high density housing of the cities than the style one is so familiar with in the west.

The development of the eastern frontier after Augustus looks logical and inevitable if it is viewed again from the situation under Antoninus Pius. By then most of the Augustan client-states had gone. Some (Pontus Polemoniacus, Armenia Minor, Commagene) were absorbed into existing provinces; others (Cappadocia, Nabataea) were themselves the core of new frontier provinces. Direct Roman control has been advanced to the Colchian coast up to the Euphrates and out into the steppe and desert of Syria and Arabia. The buffer-states and their armies now gone, the Roman army is inevitably both larger and more evenly distributed.

Two legions, at Satala (*XV Apollinaris*) and Melitene (*XII Fulminata*), and a small fleet at Trapezus are at the disposal of the consular governor of Cappadocia (fig. 11.7A, D). In the south, the annexation of the Nabataean kingdom in 106 soon led to a legion (*III Cyrenaica*) being stationed in the provincial capital, Bostra. Palaestina (formerly Judaea), though not a frontier province, had legions at Caparcotna (*VI Ferrata*) and Jerusalem (*X Fretensis*). With the extent of his military jurisdiction so much reduced, it is no surprise to find only three legions under the governor of Syria: one at Raphanaea (*III Gallica*) and two on the Euphrates at Samosata (*XVI Flavia*; pl. 11.1) and Zeugma (*IV Scythica*). Relative to his reduced responsibilities, his army was, however, stronger than a century earlier. Scattered inscriptions and, in particular, military diplomas, now suggest a powerful auxiliary presence in the same provinces: *c.* 32,000 (Cappadocia = *c.* 8,000; Syria = *c.* 14,500; Palaestina = *c.* 4,500; Arabia = *c.* 5,000). Thus, between Augustus and the mid-second century, the Roman forces had been at least doubled in numbers; the majority (except in Palaestina), advanced into the frontier zone itself. Of the *auxilia*, about one quarter were cavalry units, and most of the infantry units had a mounted element (*cohortes equitatae*).

This comparison, however, disguises a complex history. The annexation of the client-states and the shouldering of direct responsibility for relations with Parthia or her vassals, was begun on a large scale soon after Augustus' death, then reversed, only to begin again with Nero and Vespasian. Three major wars were fought with Parthia, involving an abandonment of the Augustan policy towards Armenia after the first, its restoration after the second, and the vigorous pursuit of dominance over both Armenia and north-west Mesopotamia initiated in the second, achieved in the third, to be finally consolidated and extended to the Tigris by Septimius Severus a generation later still.

Tiberius' absorption of Commagene into Syria and the appointing of a procurator to govern Cappadocia, his subsequent annexation of Pontus Polemoniacus and probably of Armenia Minor, were not in themselves unusual. Augustus had removed more petty kings in his reign; only the scale in so short a period is perhaps surprising. However, the attempt to explain Gaius' restoration not only of Commagene but of Pontus and Armenia Minor as characteristic of the unbalanced behaviour of a man seeking to enhance his own exalted position by the personal attendance of the client-kings of his empire, is too simplistic. It is significant that Claudius made no attempt to re-possess

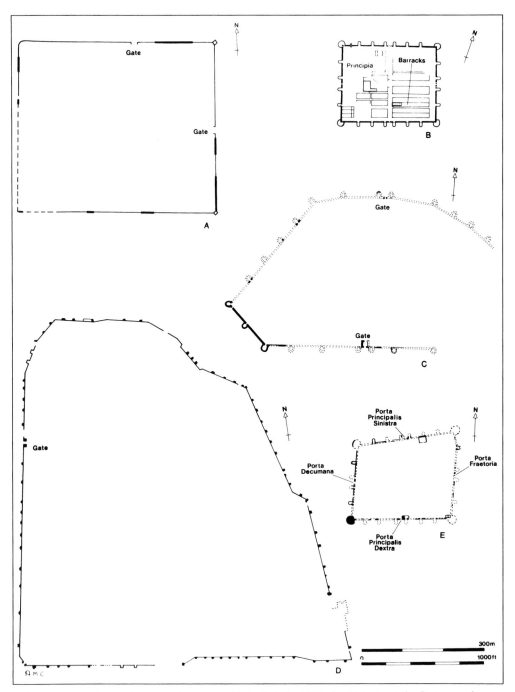

Figure 11.7 Eastern legionary fortresses: (A) Satala (*after Mitford*); (B) Lejjun (*after Brünnow and von Domaszewski*); (C) Singara (*after Oates*); (D) Melitene (*after Mitford*); (E) Udruh (*after Killick*)

these territories, but rather returned these kings to their realms; even under Nero in 64 only Pontus Polemoniacus was annexed. The explanation surely lies in the consequences of annexation of these Euphrates states. We know little of Tiberius' arrangements for their security after annexation; they seem to have been given few if any troops, even auxiliaries. Tiberius was fortunate: his largely undefended river frontier faced an Armenia enjoying a rare period of peace from AD 18–34 under its widely popular King Artaxias III. The latter's death and the brief rule of an Arsacid prince before an Iberian princeling could be installed must surely have been sufficient to indicate that the instability and insecurity of Augustan times were the more predictable state of affairs and that the upper Euphrates must be either returned to the care of native rulers and their forces or provided with a substantial garrison.

In Armenia itself, Claudius not only sent the Iberian Mithridates back from Rome to his kingdom, but bolstered his position with a detachment of Roman soldiers who, for over a decade, were stationed at Gorneae, a few miles from Artaxata. When annexation was again undertaken, it was complemented by the securing of the new territory. Thus, Agrippa II, in a speech set in 66, but possibly anachronistic, mentioned 3,000 legionaries and forty warships in Pontus and Colchis. Certainly, part at least of the royal army was retained in service in Pontus where it is found in 69.

Under Vespasian, matters were taken vigorously in hand. Commagene was again annexed in 72 and given a legionary garrison at Samosata (pl. 11.1); the rather dubious pretext – a fear that its king was about to allow the Parthians over the river at the vital crossing at Samosata – reveals both the recognition of the strategic importance of the kingdom and the desire to secure the river line. The immediate aftermath of the civil wars and the end of the Jewish Revolt saw Cappadocia transformed into a new important military province with two legions, one of them at Satala in Armenia Minor, re-annexed in 71. The half century from Vespasian to the death of Trajan saw the implementation of the same policy of annexation and provincial reorganization in the south, as petty rulers in Emesa, Ituraea and Nabataea were removed or not replaced.

The quickened pace of activity on the upper Euphrates from the last years of Nero onwards was not, however, stimulated by the belief that Armenia would always be an unstable vassal. Rather, they reflect the changed circumstances which were the outcome of Corbulo's campaigns under Nero. Claudius' military support for Mithridates of Armenia did not protect the latter from the unforeseen ambitions of his murderous Iberian nephew Radamistus. The fluctuating fortunes in the Romano–Parthian War which developed in the wake of this upheaval in Armenia left both parties ready to accept a new compromise. Thus, in 66, Rome was treated to the dramatic public spectacle of the Arsacid prince Tiridates being crowned by Nero as ruler of Armenia. Despite the impression of this brother of the Great King at Nero's feet, and despite Corbulo's restoration of Roman military prestige after the humiliating capitulation of L. Caesennius Paetus and his army in 62, the new arrangement was a considerable retreat from the policy initiated by Augustus. The half century from 66 until Trajan deposed Parthamasiris in 114 saw a succession of Arsacid kings in Armenia, each nominally vassals of the Roman emperor to whom they owed their crowning and recognition. In fact, they were as much an appanage of the Parthian Empire as Osrhoene. Whatever the public declarations of the imperial government, privately they knew that the arrangement was a face-saving formula at the end of an inconclusive war. Thus, even before the coronation of Tiridates, steps were being taken to secure the new Armenian frontier with the removal of the king of Pontus. His territory included the important Zigana Pass over the Pontic Alps and that, prior to the building of the great highways to Satala and Melitene in the Flavian period, was the major artery for supplying an army in Armenia from the royal port of Trapezus. The reorganization by Vespasian completed the securing of the upper Euphrates. Trajan's Parthian War put a Roman nominee back on the Armenian throne. The dramatic initial successes, the annexation of Armenia, Mesopotamia and Assyria, and the enthroning of a Parthian puppet ruler in Ctesiphon by the Roman emperor himself, should not obscure the fundamental foolishness of the enterprise. Just as Cassius Dio was to note over a century later in connection with Severus' new province of Mesopotamia (pl. 11.5), so too with the even more extensive new territories of Trajan: they were too distant, their peoples alien, their control a constant drain on Roman resources. For Rome, a Mesopotamian, Armenian or Assyrian province not only stretched military resources but presented immense difficulties of communications: from Antioch, the forces on the Tigris were twice or three times the distance again as formerly the units on the bend of the Euphrates. Hadrian wisely abandoned the new provinces.

The new legionary camps of the period are better known. Satala and Melitene (fig. 11.14) have both been planned and, though of a late design, probably preserve the shape of the Flavian construction. Located away from the great cities of the region both could be purpose-built and are comparable to the better known examples from the west. The same would not be true of Samosata and Seleucia/Zeugma where, significantly, nothing is known of the plans, nor at Jerusalem and Bostra (though the latter may now have been found). Auxiliary units were certainly thrust out into the desert though, with the exception of Azraq (pl. 11.9; fig. 11.8C), Hallabat (pl. 11.10; fig. 11.8E – without towers) and Qreiye (fig. 11.8A), locations are only really known from epigraphic finds.

Hadrian's rapid abandonment of territory beyond the Euphrates did little to assuage the humiliated Parthians; nor, in fact, did it restore the *status quo ante*. The 'scare' of *c.* 123 which set reinforcements marching and brought Hadrian to Syria to negotiate continued peace (pl. 11.8), and the two crises under Antoninus, emphasize how much the settlement of 117 had been to Rome's advantage. Not only had Armenia returned to Rome vassaldom but now the kings of Osrhoene too were again dependent on Rome. The spectacular explosion of Parthian frustration and rage when it came in 162 took

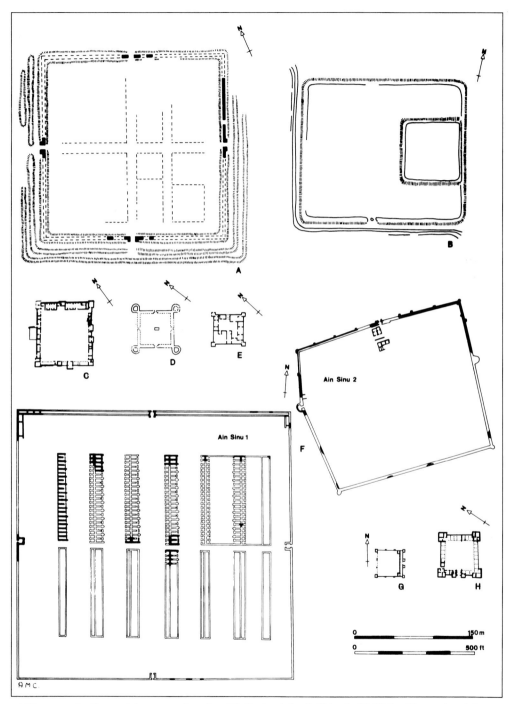

Figure 11.8 Forts of the eastern frontier: (A) Qreiye (*after Poidebard*); (B) Hirbet Hassan Aga (*after Poidebard*); (C) Qasr el-Azraq (*after Kennedy*); (D) Han al-Abyad (*after Poidebard*); (E) Qasr-el-Hallabat (*after Kennedy*); (F) Aïn Sinu 1 and 2 (*after Oates*); (G) Eski Hissar (*after Wagner*); (H) Qasr Bshir (*after Brünnow and von Domaszewski*)

one army into Syria, while another destroyed the governor of Cappadocia and a legion at Elegeia in Armenia.

The efficiency of the Roman response, essentially a repeat of Trajan's strategy, was impressive, perhaps because the threat raised recently under Antoninus Pius (*ILS*, 1076) had pushed Rome to formulate a plan. Large reinforcements, some from as far as the lower Rhine, were collected, and the inexperienced L. Verus provided with able field-commanders: Statius Priscus (called from his governorship in Britain), Avidius Cassius, P. Martius Verus and M. Claudius Fronto. In 163–4 Priscus subjugated Armenia, destroyed Artaxata and elements at least of the German *legio I Minervia* seem to have crossed the Darial Pass from Iberia (*CIL*, XIII, 8213). In 165 Edessa and Nisibis were seized and the following year Cassius destroyed Seleucia and Ctesiphon. Also in 166, and possibly for the second time in the war, Roman forces penetrated Media Atropatene.

Far from shifting the balance in Parthia's favour, the war consolidated, even extended, Rome's pre-eminence in the region: the Emesene prince Sohaemus, an ex-consul, became king of Armenia with a supporting Roman force in his new capital, Eçmiadzin (Kainepolis); a pro-Roman king was installed in Osrhoene and, apparently (p. 283 below), Roman garrisons established along the Khabur river to his east; Hatra and Adiabene may have accepted Roman overlordship; and on the Euphrates the frontier was thrust forward to the fortress city of Dura Europus (pl. 11.7).

For almost a decade after 166 this major reorganization involving the entire eastern frontier was supervised by the Syrian, Avidius Cassius, as governor of Syria until at least 171 and then as *rector totius Orientis*. Whether the Roman support of Sohaemus had been withdrawn or proved too weak, he was expelled in 172. However, an inscription (*ILS*, 9117) records vexillations of both Cappadocian legions under the tribune of a milliary cohort in garrison, in 175, at Kainepolis, which the Cappadocian governor, Martius Verus, is said to have made 'the foremost city of Armenia'. At least one of the vexillations was still there as late as 184–5 (*ILS*, 394), and, perhaps again under Commodus, a road link back to Satala was being built, or rebuilt (*CIL*, III, 13627A).

The Jewish Revolt of 66–70 (pl. 11.2) wrought important changes in the military dispositions in the east. In 70 a new and undoubtedly larger auxiliary force had to be found for the province and X Fretensis became the first legionary garrison. Fortunately Corbulo had raised new units for the recent Parthian War and the end of the civil wars allowed *IV Scythica* and a new legion, *XVI Flavia*, to be based in the east. The absorption of the armies of client-states also provided an injection of new manpower for use there. The Flavian distribution of forces from Satala to Jerusalem, transformed the Julio-Claudian legions, all in northern Syria, and still a relatively mobile field force, into a defensively oriented garrison.

Fortunately for Rome, Parthia chose not to exploit Rome's preoccupation with either the revolt or the civil war. Indeed, in 70, Vologeses I offered Vespasian the use of 40,000 cavalry. Five years later, he made the remarkable proposal that they should mount a joint expedition against the Sarmatian Alans north of the Caucasus. Previously, it was Parthia alone which had experienced their ravages: in 35, when Iberia, at Rome's suggestion, invited them southwards to attack Media, and in 72 when they raided southwards from east of the Caspian and returned home over the Caucasus. Nevertheless, the apparent concern underlying Nero's planned Caucasian expedition persisted in the Flavian period and precautions were taken: some of the forts on the Colchis coast are probably Flavian in origin; in 75 Roman troops were helping the king of Iberia fortify his major stronghold at Harmozica which controlled the southward egress from the Caucasian Gates/Darial Pass (*SEG*, XX (1964), 122); under Domitian, a centurion of *XII Fulminata* cut an inscription (*AE* (1951) 263) on a rock face at a point overlooking the Caspian and controlling the exit of the Caspian Gates/Derbend Pass. Not least, perhaps, because of these measures, Rome did not have any clash with the Alans until *c.* 134 when, returning from another raid into Parthia, they were repulsed by the governor of Cappadocia, Flavius Arrianus, who has left his account in his 'Battle Order Against the Alans'.

As in so many other areas, the policies of Septimius Severus in the east can be traced back to Marcus Aurelius. The first of his two Parthian Wars, in 195, may have been cut short by the need to return westwards to confront the usurper Clodius Albinus; certainly the victory titles – Parthicus Arabicus, Parthicus Adiabenicus – imply war against former Parthian vassals alone. While the war may have been seen as an opportunity for welding together recent civil war opponents, and for restoring the morale of an eastern army recently decimated – 20,000 of them are said to have been killed at the final battle of Issus – but with many new recruits, it was also required to restore Roman dominance in Mesopotamia. According to Cassius Dio, taking advantage of the civil war, the Osrhoeni and Adiabeni 'revolted' and laid siege to Nisibis. Although this is the first indication of the extent of Roman pre-eminence in northern Mesopotamia and even of garrisons, they probably date back to 166 or at least to Marcus Aurelius' own visit and final reorganization after the short-lived usurpation of Avidius Cassius in 175. It seems likely that north-west Mesopotamia, like Armenia, was subjected by Marcus to what Dilleman has called 'occupation sans annexion'.

Until very recently, scholars were divided about the treatment of Osrhoene. A province of Osrhoene is soon heard of (*ILS*, 1353) but equally, the monarchy persisted or was restored to be heard of under Severus' successor. Wagner's discovery of remarkable new texts resolves the problem: one, for 195, is a boundary stone set up by the procurator C. Julius Pacatianus 'between the province of Osrhoene and the kingdom of Abgar'. The rump kingdom seems to have consisted of no more than Edessa and its territory, the province probably being garrisoned by a new *legio (III?) Parthica*, perhaps at Nisibis.

The Second Parthian War (197–8) was aimed at Parthia itself. Ctesiphon was sacked but Severus was twice frustrated in his attempts to capture Hatra. This second war

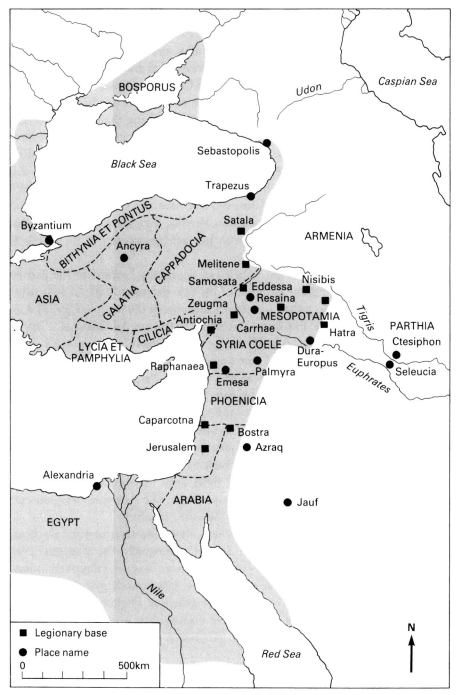

Figure 11.9   Eastern frontier provinces at the death of Severus (AD 211)

and the return of troops withdrawn to face Albinus, provided the opportunity for a major reorganization. Beyond the Euphrates, Osrhoene was complemented by a new military province, Mesopotamia, established, probably in 197, and unexpectedly placed under an equestrian prefect with two newly formed legions at his disposal (pl. 11.5). The whereabouts of *I* and *III Parthicae* under Severus, is not clear: Singara (fig. 11.7C) and Nisibis are likely, but, at a later date, coins of Resaina name *III Parthica* (Castelin, 1946). After the second war, Osrhoene would no longer have needed its own legion: in 197 it is *IV Scythica* which is found building a fort there at Eski Hissar on the road linking Zeugma and Samosata (pl. 11.1 and fig. 11.10); and in 205, a road was built

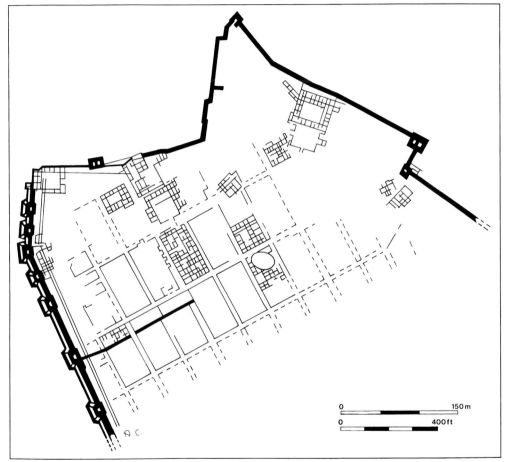

Figure 11.10 Dura-Europus, Syria, was occupied by Roman forces during the Parthian campaigns of Lucius Verus; it retained a large and growing garrison, including legionary vexillations, until its loss to Sapor in the 250s. The army was quartered in the northern end of the city, cut off from the town by a wall, and utilizing some existing buildings, for military purposes. until it was formalized to some extent after AD 210. Such must have been the practice in many eastern towns from the Republic onwards, purpose-built camps being rare or only a late development (*after Perkins*)

'from the Euphrates as far as the boundaries of the kingdom of Septimus Abgar' (Wagner, 1983, 115).

The repercussions of the wars and the new provinces were bound to be considerable. No longer the major frontier province, Syria was divided into Coele with two legions and Phoenice with one; part of the latter was soon detached and added to Arabia. The rationale for legions at Samosata and Zeugma no longer existed and, though we do not know when they moved, it is notable that detachments of both were in garrison far to the south-east at Dura already under Severus (fig. 11.10). New auxiliary units for Mesopotamia, probably including *Cohors IX Maurorum* and *XII Palaestinorum*, are likely. From Dura too comes the remarkable letter of *c.* 208 from the governor, advising the garrison commander to prepare to receive a Parthian envoy through the city and its dependent outposts. A tantalizing and all too rare insight into the mechanism of the largely unknown but presumably regular contacts between the two empires.

Inscriptions show Severus active elsewhere along the eastern frontier, the best attested being in north-east Arabia. There, just as was happening in Numidia and Tripolitania in the same reign (Chapter 10), garrisons were thrust out into the desert, in this case to seize the important Azraq oasis and possibly even that at Jauf 400 km (250 miles) to the south-east at the end of the great Wadi Sirhan route. At the former a fort and outposts were built and a road constructed linking the oasis back to the Syrian *limes* (fig. 11.9).

The eastern aims of Severus' half-Syrian successor Caracalla are unclear. The known details suggest a vigorous pursuit of his father's policy. In the north there was a short-lived attempt to annex Armenia, where the client-kingship was restored by the next emperor, Macrinus. The rump of Osrhoene was annexed in 215 and Edessa, just as Singara, Nisibis and Resaina had been under his father, declared a *colonia*. When Caracalla was assassinated before it was fully under way his apparently unprovoked Parthian expedition had to be terminated after a reverse and on unfavourable terms by Macrinus.

The early Severan period saw the climax of Roman military power in the east (fig. 11.9, 11.18 and pl. 11.5). To be sure, victories followed in the succeeding generations and new territories were acquired, but crisis and disaster soon followed in the third century and Rome's dominance in the area was never again as clear as it must have seemed in 217 when Caracalla had proposed an Alexander-like fusion of Roman and Iranian, himself to marry the Great King's daughter. The explanation is not hard to find: the Arsacids of Parthia were no longer the thrusting successful dynasty of two centuries before, and now successive humiliations at the hands of Roman armies, together with internal division, left them weak and vulnerable. The crisis reached a head in the later Severan period when a rising, begun some years before in the province of Persia, led to the Arsacids' downfall *c.* 224 and the establishment of a neo-Persian dynasty, the Sasanians (fig. 11.11).

The weakness of Arsacid Parthia explains in large part the relative ease of Severus'

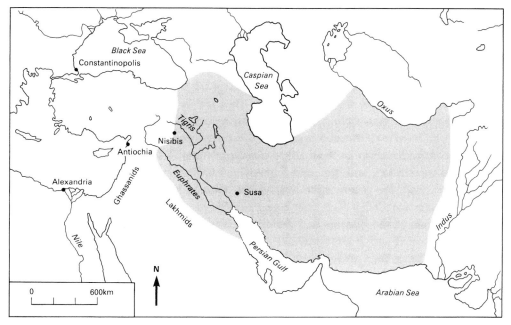

Figure 11.11   Sasanian Empire

victories. The early Sasanian rulers, vigorous and able men, motivated by religious zeal and national pride to strengthen their empire and recover the lands of Achaemenid Persia (figs 11.5 and 11.11) overthrown by Alexander the Great, were a tough opponent. Ironically, and unfortunately for Rome, Ardashir, the first of the new dynasty, faced not Septimius Severus or even the militaristic Caracalla, but the weak and inexperienced Severus Alexander, last of his dynasty. Sapor I, a greater threat still, could exploit not only the growing internal strife of the Roman world and its preoccupations on its European frontiers, but easily outclassed the emperors pitted against him: the nineteen-year-old Gordian III, in 244 after the untimely death of his able father-in-law and praetorian prefect, Timesitheus, and later the ageing, vacillating and ineffectual Valerian.

From the moment of the first Persian invasion of Mesopotamia in 230 until the invasion of Babylonia by Carus in 283, Rome was on the defensive, the military situation rapidly deteriorating. The course of the campaigns waged by Severus Alexander were, at best, mixed, one of the three divisions of his army apparently being defeated. They achieved enough, however, to eject the Persians, restore peace and free the European reinforcements, together now with detachments from the east, for the more critical threat then posed closer to Italy by the tribes on the Rhine. That minor raids at least continued in the east, may be inferred from the happy discovery at Dura Europus of the tombstone of the tribune Julius Terentius (Welles, 1941), recording his death in the course of one such skirmish in 239. By that date, Alexander's short-lived successor, Maximinus Thrax, was heavily involved on the Rhine. In 242, a new emperor Gordian III took the field in person against a renewed Persian attack. Under the guidance of Timesitheus, the Persians were thrown back in battles at Resaina and Nisibis, but the prefect's death left affairs in the hands of Gordian at the moment when the Roman offensive was about to begin. For the events which follow, for once we do not have to rely on Roman sources alone. The remarkable trilingual inscription, '*Res gestae divi Saporis*' throws fascinating light on both this and Sapor's two subsequent wars with Rome. In the Great King's account, the claim to have killed Gordian in a major battle in 244 at a site just inside Persian territory and renamed Perosapor (='Victory of Sapor') may be closer to the truth than the commonest Roman tradition which placed the blame on the emperor's successor Philip. Certainly Sapor's claim, not reported elsewhere and indicative of the scale of the disaster and the changed fortunes, to have received a ransom of half a million *denarii* from Philip for prisoners, cannot be invented. Although the war seems to have been ended without territorial loss, Sprengling may be correct in view of the sequel in suggesting that Philip was forced to concede Sapor a free hand in Armenia against its Arsacid kings. Certainly, at some time between 244 and 253, perhaps in 252, Armenia came under Persian control.

The year 253 was undoubtedly one of the blackest in Roman military history. There was civil war in Europe, Trebonianus Gallus and his brief successor Aemilius Aemilianus were both overthrown, Valerian and Gallienus proclaimed emperor, all against a back-cloth of Gothic invasions of Thrace and Moesia, incursions into Asia Minor and catastrophe in Syria. The pretext for Sapor's second war, an alleged 'wrong' done to Armenia by 'Caesar', may allude to a Roman refuge for the Armenian pretender Tiridates and possibly their failure to pay the subsidy for the defence of the Caucasian passes. The Persian attack was dramatic and astonishingly successful: 'And we made an attack upon the Roman's Empire and slaughtered the Roman's force, 60,000, at Barbalissus.' Then follow the names of thirty-six 'castles and cities' taken then or in the subsequent campaigns of this same war. Antioch itself is listed, its loss proven by the break in minting there at that time; the captive population of the greatest city of the east after Alexandria, carried off into Persia to inhabit Sapor's new city Veh Antiok Shapur/ Gundeshapur: 'Sapor (has made it) Better than Antioch.' The other names are largely a roll-call of the major cities of Syria: Beroea, Apamea, Zeugma, Seleucia, Cyrrhus, Alexandria, Hama. . . .

Undoubtedly a severe defeat for the army of Syria, it must nevertheless be supposed that many of the forts, and possibly their garrisons, escaped in 253 when the invasion followed the south, more lightly guarded, bank of the Euphrates. However, to the fortress at Zeugma lost in that campaign (if still garrisoned) the next three years added many more losses: Dura, perhaps lost briefly in 253 (pl. 11.7 and fig. 11.10), was destroyed in 256/7 and never re-occupied; Circesium was captured and, in a raid into

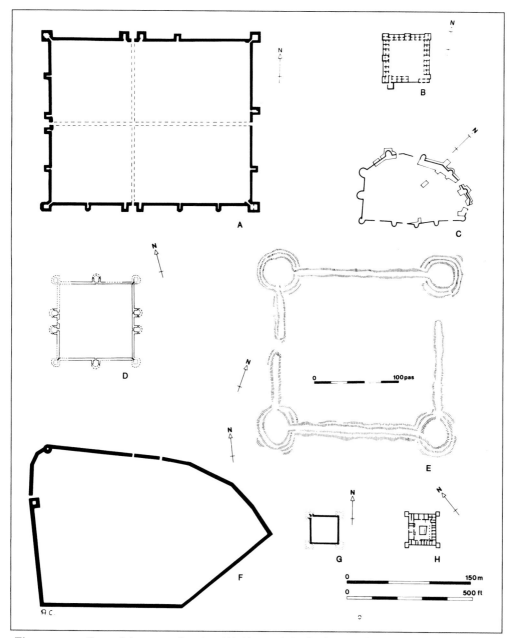

Figure 11.12 Forts of the eastern frontier: (A) Absarus *(after Levkinaze)*; (B) Deir el-Kahf *(after Butler)*;
(C) Pagnik Öreni *(after Harper)*; (D) Han al-Manqoura *(after Poidebard)*; (E) Phasis *(after Dubois de Montpéreux)*; (F) Çit Harabe *(after Mitford)*; (G) Qasr el-Quweira *(after Alt)*; (H) Tamara *(after Gichon)*.
All are to the same scale except Phasis, where the only record refers to distance in *pas*. No English
equivalent can be found for this Russian measurement

Cappadocia, Satala, together with some frontier forts, was taken. At the same time as these disasters, the Borani, a tribe settled north of the Black Sea, having been repulsed at Pityus *c.* 253–4 in an attempt to invade Pontus through Colchis, returned *c.* 255–6 with stunning results: Pityus fell and Trapezus, massively reinforced by perhaps as many as 10,000 men, was sacked.

Sapor initiated one further war *c.* 259–60 culminating in the humiliating seizure of Valerian and the possible defeat of his army, said by the inscription to be 70,000 strong, near Edessa:

> And Valerian Caesar himself with (our) own hand(s) (we) made captive. And the rest, the praetorian prefect, (and) senators, and generals, (and) whoever of that force were officers, all (these) we made captive, and away to the Persis we led. And Syria, Cilicia and Cappadocia (we) burned with fire, laid waste and led captive. And we took in that war from the Romans' Empire . . . altogether cities with their surroundings on all sides 36. And people who are of the Romans' Empire, non-Aryans, captive we led away; in the Aryans' Empire, in Persis, Parthia, Khuzistan, Assyria and others, land by land, where our own and our father's and our grandfathers' and our forebears' foundations were, there we settled (them).

Although Sapor lived on until 270, this expedition, with its capture of Valerian, a second sack of Antioch, and the subsequent penetration of his forces into Galatia marked the high point of his achievements against Rome. The glorious campaign was soon overshadowed by two of Valerian's generals, Callistus and Macrianus, who defeated elements of the Persian army in Cilicia and, as his army retired, the Palmyrene noble, Odaenathus mounted a successful attack on it near the Euphrates. Tragically, the Roman generals proclaimed the sons of Macrianus – Macrianus and Quietus – in opposition to Gallienus and, after the latter's defeat of the Macriani in Thrace, Odaenathus, still loyal to the legitimate emperor, destroyed Callistus and Quietus in Syria. Unable to act himself, Gallienus was content to appoint the Palmyrene, now self-proclaimed 'King of kings' (possibly a calculated insult to Sapor), as *dux* and *corrector totius Orientis* to oversee reorganization and pursue the Persian War. Before his murder in 267, Odaenathus had not only recovered much of Mesopotamia but advanced to Ctesiphon. His widow Zenobia, acting for their son Vaballathus, was much less ready to accept her inferior role as appointed client-ruler and, after Gallienus had apparently sent an unsuccessful force under Heraclianus to remove her, she extended her control over all of the Roman garrisons from Egypt to Asia Minor. The later assumption of the titles Augusta and Augustus for mother and son were a direct challenge to Gallienus' successors in the west but one which had to be overlooked until Aurelian, in 272, could bring an army to the east. Although swiftly overthrown, the episode of Zenobia's brief empire and the final battles further decimated the Roman forces, which had survived

Sapor and the revolt of Macrianus. Indeed, the queen boasted that Aurelian's early victories in the east cost no Palmyrene blood, only the demoralized Roman troops of the area being employed. After its brief rebellion in 273, Aurelian garrisoned the shattered Palmyra, placing there a new legion, *I Illyricorum* (pl. 11.8).

The rise and fall of Palmyra, however, had other consequences. In the deserts of southern Syria a tribal confederation now appeared. These tribes, the Tanukh, had recently migrated north-west to the Roman frontier under their leader Jadhima. The latter is said by early Islamic writers to have been humiliated and killed by Zenobia and it is his successor, Amr ibn Adi, whom they credited with the overthrow of Palmyra. That these tribes, jealous and fearful of Palmyrene power, assisted Aurelian, is likely and borne out by the exaggerated claims of the Arab tradition. More important in the longer term was the political realignment of the tribes in this region. The Palmyrene episode not only revealed the potential of an Arab confederation but underscored the group security of closer alliances. Under Amr ibn Adi and his son Imru' lqais, the Tanukh was apparently converted into the great tribal confederation based at al-Hira west of the lower Euphrates under the powerful Lakhmid dynasty. The extent and power of this confederation may be judged from the famous tombstone inscription of Imru'lqais who died in 328 and was buried at Nemara, a former Roman fort in the Hauran (MacAdam, 1980). He is described there as 'King of all the Arabs' and his empire is seen to extend across the entire desert from the Hauran to the lower Euphrates and south into the Arabian peninsula. While the origin of his royal title is unknown and his relationship to and independence of Rome and Persia are much in debate, it is tempting to link his rise and role with the Diocletianic overhaul of the frontier.

The ancient sources are unanimous in attributing the major reorganization of the eastern defences to Diocletian. Certainly Diocletian's work can be seen extensively all around the Empire, developed, supplemented or modified by Constantine, the two long reigns providing the political stability necessary. An important factor in their success was the very changed condition of Persia and her declining fortunes in war. The long reigns of Ardashir and Sapor I gave way to six monarchs in the thirty-nine years between 270 and 309, followed by the long minority of Sapor II from 309. Moreover, there is a suggestion that Aurelian already in 272 may have defeated a Persian force sent to help Zenobia; certainly Probus was confident enough to refuse gifts sent by Vahram II; in 283 Carus sacked both Seleucia and Ctesiphon; in 288 Diocletian restored the Arsacid Tiridates III to Armenia and obliged Vahram to renounce his claim to Mesopotamia, perhaps even to Armenia; finally, in 297, after an initial disaster, the Caesar Galerius crushed the new Great King Narses, receiving by the subsequent treaty, recognition that Mesopotamia was Roman, Armenia a Roman vassal, and acquiring five small Persian satrapies across the Tigris. Only in 334 was the peace seriously broken again.

The respite was employed to good effect. The great *strata Diocletiana* running from Sura on the Euphrates via Palmyra to Damascus linked on to the *via nova Traiana* in

Arabia, and broadly marking the crust of new and rebuilt forts from Circesium to Aila. A branch ran further east of the Hauran through Imtan to the Azraq oasis which seems to have been strongly held for some half a century from Diocletian's time (pl. 11.9). The great frequency and strength of the new posts provided enhanced security for the garrisons and a tighter control of the frontier zone (pl. 11.9, 11.11 and 11.12; fig. 11.9).

Little enough is known from contemporary evidence for the army on the eastern frontier in the early fourth century. There are no auxiliary diplomas after the late second century and military inscriptions, comparatively rare in the eastern provinces in earlier times became even scarcer. New legions were introduced: *I Pontica* at Trapezus (*ILS*, 639), and the recent Tetrarchic date from the excavations at Lejjun/Betthoro (pl. 11.11) in Arabia, supports the Diocletianic origin for *IV Martia* (Parker, 1982). Then, if not before, legions were moved forward on to the frontier, usually in pairs in new smaller provinces. Thus, while the two early imperial legions remained at Satala and Melitene, *XVI Flavia* and *IV Scythica* moved forward to Sura (pl. 11.3) and Orisa, *III Gallica* at Danaba was the pair of *I Illyricorum* at Palmyra, *III Cyrenaica* and *IV Martia* lay in Arabia, and *X Fretensis* was removed from Jerusalem to Aila, to become the only legion in the new Palestina Salutaris.

While some of the legionary movements of Diocletian's time can be deduced from their later locations as given in the *Notitia Dignitatum*, one can be far less confident for the many non-legionary forces recorded there, most known only from that document. One can certainly find an origin for some new auxiliary units from their names. The large numbers of units of *equites* are more difficult, perhaps going back as far as Aurelian both in origin and their settlement in the east. Cavalry of all kinds, lancers, dragoons and horse archers, gradually became more important in the third century. Thus, the *dux Syriae et Euphratensis* in the *Notitia* had ten units of *equites*, two legions, two *alae* and four cohorts under his command on the frontier. Only the two legions and the *cohors I Ulpia Dacorum* can be traced back to before Caracalla, the bulk of the inferable losses almost certainly attributable to the third century chaos.

The renewed warfare with Persia in Armenia at the end of Constantine's reign began auspiciously enough for Rome with the appointment of the emperor's nephew, Hannibalianus, as king of Armenia, and his victory in 336 over the Persians who had removed the legitimate king and occupied the country. The major warfare took place further south, however, where the Caesar Constantius had been sent in 334, and it was on him as Augustus that the brunt of Sapor II's (309–79) aggressive thrusts fell.

In contrast to those of many of his predecessors and even to that of his successor Julian, the Persian War of Constantius, recorded by Ammianus Marcellinus, who served there under both Constantius and Julian, appears an inglorious, uninspiring period in Roman military history, culminating soon after his death in the disaster and death of Julian and the shameful peace concluded by Jovian in 363. Apart from a bloody and ultimately drawn battle at Singara-Hileia (fig. 11.7C), the wars were largely campaigns

Figure 11.13 Dioceses and provinces according to the *Notitia Dignitatum*

of sieges and varying fortunes. In part the explanation is certainly that the admittedly cautious Constantius, with only the resources of his own sector of the Empire at his disposal for so long, was unable or unwilling to risk too much in a set battle or an over-ambitions invasion of Persian territory. In part, it is a reflection of the changed character of the frontier provinces where heavily defended fortresses (pl. 11.12) and forts had sprung up and where each side struggled to seize strategic border posts such as Nisibis, Amida and Bezabde, the field armies seldom coming into collision. After his third siege of Nisibis the war abated for a time in 350 as Sapor withdrew from Roman Mesopotamia to confront an invasion by barbarians of his northern frontier. Free again in 358, Sapor began with a demand for Armenia and Mesopotamia, followed in 359 with the capture of Amida. With it went some 6,000 men of its garrison but Sapor's own considerable losses forced his withdrawal. Nevertheless, the frontier was vulnerable as the Persian seizure of Bezabde and Singara in 360 emphasized; indeed, it was Constantius' urgent demand for Julian to send him reinforcements from Gaul which led to the latter's usurpation.

The invasion of Persia by Julian in 363 and his assault on Ctesiphon, recall the glorious campaigns of earlier emperors. What he hoped to achieve is unknown; his death in the war and the decimation of his retreating army proved a disaster. In the same year, his successor Jovian, to salvage something from the war, concluded a Thirty Years Peace which signed away the overlordship of Armenia, Mesopotamia beyond the Khabur, four of the Transtigritane satrapies and even Nisibis: Sapor II gained from Jovian what his namesake had not from his victorious invasions of Syria and Mesopotamia and his capture of a Roman emperor.

Sapor soon began to assert his claim to the overlordship of Armenia and even ejected Sauromaces, the Roman client-king of Iberia. Neither act, whatever the terms of Jovian's peace, could be countenanced by Rome and in 373 Valens' generals defeated a Persian army at Vagobanta. While tension remained high, serious warfare was past. Fortunately Sapor II himself died the year after Valens and his army were destroyed at Adrianople (378).

Ammianus Marcellinus on several occasions mentions the military role of the Saracens, a people whom he located as living in the lands between the Assyrians and the Nile. In 363, soon after setting off downstream from Callinicum, Julian received the offer of aid from 'the princes of the Saracens' which he was glad to accept 'since they were adapted for guerilla warfare'. At subsequent points we hear of Saracens active both on his behalf and against his forces. The retreating army suffered considerably from their raids and it is clear that both sides used and valued their services as scouts and skirmishers. It has recently been argued that these people, whom Ammianus specifically says were those formerly called Scenitae, were now renamed from their own term for confederation, Sirkat (Graf and O'Connor, 1977), thus emphasizing the new political groupings in the desert and explaining the enhanced power of the nomads. A few years later, under Valens, perhaps in 378 when he left Antioch to confront the Goths in Thrace, Mavia, described as Queen of the Saracens, broke her treaty relationship, invaded Phoenicia and Palestine, and ravaged the provinces as far as the Nile. The curious episode was short-lived as she soon sent troops to help defend Constantinople from the Goths in 378. The contingent is described by Ammianus:

> the Saracens are a people 'more adapted to stealthy raiding expeditions than to pitched battles. . . . One of their number, . . . a man with long hair and naked except for a loin-cloth, uttering hoarse and dismal cries, with drawn dagger rushed into the thick of the Gothic army, and after killing a man, applied his lips to his throat and sucked the blood that poured out.'

As for the Goths, in 376 Valens had sent large numbers of those who had been allowed to settle south of the Danube to the east to be formed into new units. To avoid disorder in 378, the *magister militum per Orientum* had them all massacred simultaneously. It was not their first employment in the east; Speidel (1978, 712) has recently argued that *Gothi gentiles* were stationed in the southern Hauran at Imtan by 208 and regularly served in Roman armies thereafter. The loss of so much of the army of the east at Adrianople ensured that Valens' successor, Theodosius, could not do without Goths. After 378, units were withdrawn from the eastern frontier for service in the Balkans and some of the new Theodosian units replacing them may well have been Gothic (Jones, 1973, 1430). The eastern frontier was mercifully quiescent under Theodosius, not just during the major Gothic crisis at the outset of his reign but throughout. Indeed, in 387 occurred an event which might have seemed to resolve finally one of the areas of contention with Persia: Armenia was formally divided, by agreement, between the two powers. Rome received about one fifth which she chose to administer through its existing Armenian satraps as vassals.

In 395 on Theodosius' death, the empire was permanently divided. It is this division which is preserved in the *Notitia Dignitatum*, probably compiled under Arcadius (fig. 11.13). Its lists for the east, unlike the west, probably preserve a close picture of the Roman army as reorganized by Diocletian but with later additions and an unknown number of subsequent losses. It is, consequently, an invaluable document not only for the order of battle on the eastern frontier at the end of the fourth century, but even as a guide to the Diocletianic reform and the extent of the losses of the third century.

For the extent of the disaster in the mid-third century, the tables tell the story (figs 11.15 and 11.16). Of some 65 auxiliary units on the eastern frontier in the late Antonine period, fewer than half (31) survive in the *Notitia*. More telling still, 80 per cent of these survivors, 24 of 31 units, are in Armenia (44 per cent), Palaestina (20 per cent) and Arabia (16 per cent). In the central sector of the frontier, the principal area of Sasanian activity, there are only five survivors in total in Syria and Osrhoene

Figure 11.14 Eastern frontier provinces at the death of Arcadius (AD 408). The inset shows the early Muslim Empire

Figure 11.15 Pre-Severan survivals in the *Notitia Dignitatum*

Region	Pre-Severan units I II III	Survivals I+II %
Britain	21 + 0 + 0*	30.00
Rhine & Danube	4 + 2 + 7	8.6
East	15 + 10 + 6	35.7
Africa	11 + 5 + 10	22.85
(Other)	2 + 0 + 3	2.85
Totals	53 + 17 + 26	100.00

(Adapted from Roxan, 1976, 73–7)
* Units divided as 'certain', 'probable' and 'possible'.

Figure 11.16 Pre-Severan survivals in the east

Region	I Certain	II Probable	III Possible	Total	% I+II	% Empire-wide I+II	c. **150**
Armenia	10	1	0	11	44.00	15.71	18
Osrhoene	1	2	0	3	12.00	4.29	
Mesopotamia	0	0	0	0	0	0	
Syria	1	0	1	2	4.00	1.42	27
Phoenice	0	1	1	2	4.00	1.42	
Palaestina	2	3	3	8	20.00	7.14	13
Arabia	1	3	1	5	16.00	5.72	6*
Total	15	10	6	31	100.00	35.70	64†
(Empire-wide)	53	17	26	96			

(Adapted from Roxan, 1976, 73–7, and Birley, 198b, 40–2)
* Probably too low – 9 or 10 is more likely (cf. Speidel, 1978, 700).
† Excluding one unit in Bithynia.

Province	Septimius Severus		Notitia Dignitatum	
	Legions	*Bases*	*Legions*	*Bases*
Pontus			I Pontica	Trapezus
Cappadocia/ Armenia	XV Apollinaris XII Fulminata	Satala Melitene	XV Apollinaris XII Fulminata	Satala Melitene
Isauria			II Isaura III Isaura	Not given Not given
Mesopotamia	I Parthica III Parthica	Nisibis ? and Singara ?	I Parthica II Parthica	Constantina Cefa
Osrhoene			(III Parthica IV Parthica	Apatna) Circesium
Syria	XVI Flavia IV Scythica	Samosata Zeugma	XVI Flavia IV Scythica	Sura Orisa
Phoenice	III Gallica	Raphanaea ?	III Gallica I Illyricorum	Danaba Palmyra
Arabia	III Cyrenaica	Bostra	III Cyrenaica IV Martia	Bostra Betthoro
Palaestina	X Fretensis VI Ferrata	Jerusalem Caparcotna	X Fretensis	Aila

Figure 11.17 Comparison of legionary distribution from Severus to the *Notitia Dignitatum*

(8 per cent and 12 per cent respectively). This appallingly high loss has to be placed in context, however. In *c.* 175 there were some 386 auxiliary units in the empire; the *Notitia*, however, records only 96 which may be, or are, pre-Severan in origin – about one quarter. Of these, however, a third are on the eastern frontier which gives it in fact the highest survival rate of the four frontier regions under discussion and compares well, for example, with the Rhine–Danube where the survivors are not quite 9 per cent of the empire-wide survival, less than 1 per cent of the late Antonine figure. In short, although the central Euphrates region suffered very badly, the east fared better in terms of continuity of early empire units than any other frontier. When looking at the legions on the eastern frontier the picture is more remarkable still. Only one legion of the early empire – *VI Ferrata* – is missing from the *Notitia* (fig. 11.17).

The new non-legionary units are very instructive. Every province had regiments of *equites Illyriciani*, which may have been introduced by Aurelian or, more probably, Diocletian. Many local units had been formed: thus there were several regiments of *equites sagittarii indigenae* and the *cohortes XIV Valeria Zabdenorum* and *XV Flavia Carduenorum* point to recruitment in Diocletian's new Transtigritane satrapies.

Province	Augustus	Vespasian	Hadrian	Severus	N.D.
Pontus					1
Cappadocia	[1/2 Galatia?]	2	2	2	2
Isauria					2
Mesopotamia				2	2
Osrhoene					2
Syria	3/4	3	3	2	2
Phoenice				1	2
Arabia			1	1	2
Palaestina		1	2	2	1
Total	4/6	6	8	10	16

Figure 11.18   Legions on the eastern frontier

The overall size of the eastern army in the *Notitia* is more difficult to gauge. Jones (1973, 1450) calculated 120,500 for the *limitanei*, assuming legions of 3,000 and other units of 500 and 1,000. Even for the time of Diocletian it seems dubious that old auxiliary units and the new units of *equites* should have been so large; certainly, all units must have been much smaller by the end of the century. Nevertheless, the Diocletianic army on the eastern frontier seems certain to have been much larger than that in the late Antonine period.

For almost two and a half centuries more, wars continued between Rome and Persia, only the early fifth century being relatively quiet. Neither Sapor I nor Sapor II achieved the Sasanian ambition of recovering the empire of the Achaemenids; finally, in the early seventh century, Khusrau II did just that, occupying the eastern provinces from Egypt to the Bosphorus. It was too late however; within less than a generation Heraclius had inflicted crushing defeats on Persia and restored the situation only to see many of the same provinces seized by the armies of Islam which then astonishingly went on to conquer Persia itself (fig. 11.18).

For centuries the eastern frontier had presented Rome with a serious and ever growing problem. Dynasts and emperors sought glory there through the humiliation if not overthrow of a worthy opponent. For some, like Mark Antony, it proved the graveyard of their military reputation; for others – Crassus, Gordian III, Valerian and Julian – it saw their death. The account which can be presented of the history and development of the eastern frontier from the literary sources will change only slowly in the years to come; new inscriptions, however, are constantly modifying the picture, while the 'bones of the red and the white horses', as Wheeler put it, now being unearthed from the Caucasus to the Hedjaz by a number of scholars offer the greatest scope for a fuller understanding in the future.

11.1 Aerial view of the Euphrates at Samosata, looking east. This strategic crossing point became the
site of a legionary fortress in AD 72 and was occupied by *legio XVI Flavia firma*
in the second and early third century

A

B

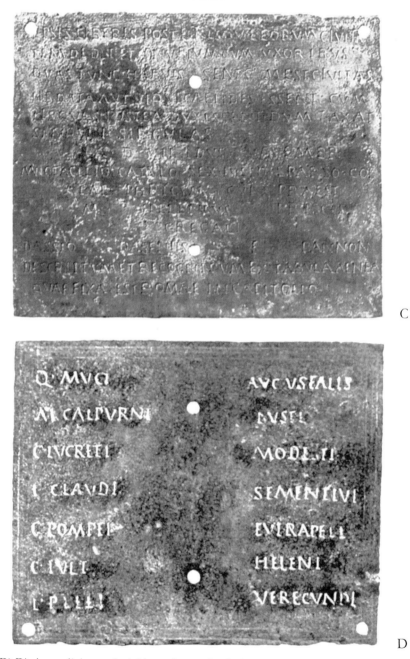

II.2 (A–D) Discharge diploma of 7th November, 88 for Syria. Together with the complementary list in another diploma of the same date, they give a list of what must be virtually the entire auxiliary garrison of the province at that time: eight *alae* and nineteen cohorts

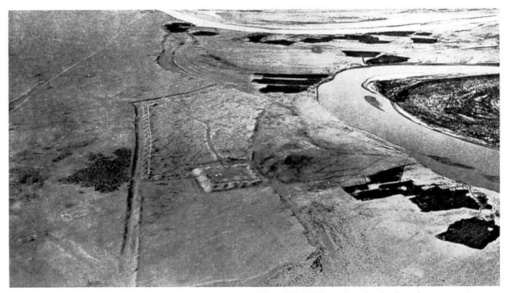

11.3   Aerial view of Sura, Syria, the fortress of *legio XVI Flavia firma* in the fourth century
and later rebuilt by Justinian

11.4   A dedication to Good Fortune set up by Ti. Claudius Subatianus Aquila, who was the first prefect
of the new province of Mesopotamia, created by Severus *c.* 198

11.5 Wall and road (?) apparently of Roman origin at Zairwan, Iraq, along the northern slopes of the Jebel Sinjar. It dates presumably either to the time of Trajan, or to the occupation from Severus to Jovian

11.6 Aerial view of Hatra. The earth and stone wall of the circumvallation, 8 km (5 miles) long, presumably belongs to one of the four sieges mounted by Roman or Persian forces. Sacked by Ardashir in 240, it was 'long since abandoned' when Julian passed the site in 363

11.7   Aerial view of Dura-Europus, Syria, a Seleucid military colony of *c.* 300 BC and later a Parthian stronghold. It was the site of a battle in the first Parthian War of AD 165 and the seat of the *dux ripae* until its fall to Sapor I in his second war. Its best-known garrison was the *cohors XX Palmyrenorum*

11.8   Aerial view of Palmyra, Syria. It is the largest oasis of the Syrian desert, situated half way between Emesa and the Euphrates. The 'Camp of Diocletian' is in the rear right at the foot of the hills beyond the triumphal arch

11.9 Aerial view of Qasr el-Azraq, Jordan. The site commanded a major oasis and controlled seasonal movements of bedouin and caravan traffic along the Wadi Sirhan from the Persian Gulf. A characteristic *tetrapyrgium* is set within the earlier fort of traditional outline. Occupations ranged from AD 208 to 333

11.10 Qasr el-Hallabat, Jordan. The two storeys of the north-west range of rooms as they were in 1929; an inscription refers to the construction of a *castellum novum* under Caracalla; another to reconstruction in 529

307

II.II Aerial view of Lejjun, Jordan. The fortress at *c.* 4.6 ha (15 acres) is only about a quarter of the size of earlier fortresses and suggests accommodation for 1500. With construction dated to *c.* AD 300, it probably housed the *legio IV Martia*, perhaps formed by Diocletian, and, together with a network of smaller forts and watch-towers, barred passage from the desert. It was abandoned in the mid-sixth century

II.I2 El Ula Oasis, ancient Dedan in the Hedjaz, Saudi Arabia. The site is just a few kilometres south of Medain Salih, ancient Hegra, where graffiti record the presence of Roman soldiers of *ala I Gaetulorum* and of *ala dromedariorum* at what had been an important Nabataean site later become, apparently, a Roman frontier post at the entrance to the narrow steep-sided valley

·BIBLIOGRAPHY·FOR·PART·4·

Adams, W. Y. (1977), *Nubia, Corridor to Africa*, London.

Adams, W. Y., Alexander, J. A. and Allen, R. (1983), 'Qasr Ibrim 1980 and 1982', *Journal of Egyptian Archaeology*, 69, 43–60.

Admiralty War Staff Intelligence Division (1915), *Handbook of the River Danube*, London.

Albertini, E. (1934), 'À propos des Numeri syriens de Numidie', *Revue Africaine*, 75, 23–42.

Alföldy, G. (1974), *Noricum*, London.

Altheim, F. and Stiehle, R. (1964–9), *Die Araber in der alten Welt*, Berlin.

Baatz, D. (1964), 'Zu den älteren Bauphason des Odenwald-Limes', *Limes Congress*, 6, 86–9, Köln.

Baatz, D. (1973), 'Kastell Hesselbach und andere Forschungen am Odenwald-Limes', *Limes Congress*, 12, Berlin.

Baatz, D. (1974), *Der römische Limes*, Berlin.

Baatz, D. (1976), *Die Wachttürme am Limes*, Stuttgart.

Baatz, D. and Herrmann, F.-R. (1982), *Die Römer in Hessen*, Stuttgart.

Baradez, J. (1949), *Fossatum Africae*, Paris.

Baradez, J. (1954), 'Les nouvelles fouilles de Tipasa et les opérations d'Antonin le Pieux en Maurétanie', *Libyca*, 2, 89–142.

Baradez, J. (1959), 'Réseau routier de commandement, d'administration et d'exploitation de la zone arrière du Limes de Numidie', *Limes Congress*, 3, 19–33, Basel.

Baradez, J. (1967), 'Compléments inédits au *Fossatum Africae*', *Limes Congress*, 6, 200–10, Köln.

Bellhouse, R. L. (1970), 'Roman sites on the Cumberland coast 1968–1969', *Transactions of the Cumberland and Westmorland Antiquarian and Archaeological Society*, 70, 9–47.

Bellhouse, R. L. (1981), 'Roman sites on the Cumberland coast: Milefortlet 20 Low

Mire', *Transactions of the Cumberland and Westmorland Antiquarian and Archaeological Society*, 81, 7–13.

Bellhouse, R. L. and Richardson, G. G. S. (1982), 'The Trajanic fort at Kirkbride: the terminus of the Stanegate frontier', *Transactions of the Cumberland and Westmorland Antiquarian and Archaeological Society*, 82, 35–50.

Bellinger, A. R. (1949), *The Excavations at Dura-Europus, Final Report, VI: The Coins*, New Haven.

Benabou, M. (1976), *La Résistance Africaine à la Romanisation*, Paris.

Benseddik, K. (1979?), *Les Troupes auxiliaires de l'armée romaine en Maurétanie Césarienne sous le Haut Empire*, Alger.

Berchem, D. van (1952), *L'Armée de Dioclétien et la réforme Constantinienne*, Paris.

Berchem, D. van (1971), 'L'occupation militaire de la Haute Egypte sous Dioclétien', *Limes Congress*, 7, 123–7, Tel Aviv.

Berciu, D. (1967), *Romania*, London.

Berciu, D. (1981), 'The Dacians in the First Century', in F. Millar (ed.), *The Roman Empire and its Neighbours*, second edition, 270–80, London.

Berthier, A. (1968), 'Nicibes ou suburbures: nomades ou sédentaires', *Bulletin d'Archéologie Algerienne*, 3, 293–300.

Berthier, A. (1981), *La Numidie, Rome et le Maghreb*, Paris.

Biernecka-Lubanska, M. (1982), *The Roman and Early Byzantine Fortifications of Lower Moesia and Northern Thrace*, Warsaw.

Birley, A. R. (1974), 'Roman frontiers and Roman frontier policy: Some reflections on Roman imperialism', *Transactions of the Archaeological and Architectural Society of Durham and Northumberland*, 3, 13–25.

Birley, A. R. (1975), 'Agricola, the Flavian Dynasty, and Tacitus', in B. Levick (ed.), *The Ancient Historian and his Materials*, 139–54, Farnborough.

Birley, A. R. (1976), 'The date of Mons Graupius', *Liverpool Classical Monthly*, 1, no. 2, 11–14.

Birley, A. R. (1981a), *The Fasti of Roman Britain*, Oxford.

Birley, A. R. (1981b), 'The economic effects of Roman frontier policy', in A. King and M. Henig (eds), *The Roman West in the Third Century*, British Archaeological Reports S109, 39–53, Oxford.

Birley, E. (1950), 'The governors of Numidia, A.D. 193–268', *Journal of Roman Studies*, XL, 60–8.

Birley, E. (1953), *Roman Britain and the Roman Army*, Kendal.

Birley, E. (1956), 'Hadrianic Frontier Policy', in E. Swoboda (ed.), *Limes Congress*, 2, 25–33, Köln.

Birley, E. (1962), Review of B. Thomasson (1960), *Die Statthalter römischer Provinzen Nordafrikas von Augustus bis Diokletianus*, in *Journal of Roman Studies*, LII, 219–27.

Birley, E. (1967), 'Hadrian's Wall and its neighbourhood', *Limes Congress*, 6, 6–14, Köln.

Birley, E. (1979), 'Inscriptions indicative of impending or recent movements', *Chiron*, 9, 495–505.

Bivar, A. D. H. (1972), 'Cavalry equipment and tactics on the Euphrates frontier', *Dumbarton Oaks Papers*, 26, 271–91 pls 1–30.

Blois, L. de (1975), 'Odaenathus and the Roman–Persian War of 252–64 A.D.', *Talanta*, VI, 7–23.

Bogaers, J. E. and Rüger, C. B. (1974), *Der niedergermanische Limes*, Köln.

Bogdan Cătăniciu, I. (1981), *Evolution of the System of Defence Works in Roman Dacia*, Oxford.

Bogdan Căatăniciu, I. (forthcoming), 'The Frontiers of Dacia', in D. J. Breeze (ed.), *The Frontiers of the Roman Empire*, London.

Bosworth, A. R. (1976), 'Vespasian's reorganisation of the North–East frontier', *Antichthon*, X, 63–78.

Bosworth, A. B. (1977), 'Arrian and the Alani', *Harvard Studies in Classical Philology*, 81, 217–55.

Bowersock, G. W. (1971), 'A report on Arabia Provincia', *Journal of Roman Studies*, LXI, 219–42.

Bowersock, G. W. (1976), 'Limes Arabicus', *Harvard Studies in Classical Philology*, 80, 219–29.

Bowersock, G. W. (1983), *Roman Arabia*, Cambridge, Mass.

Braásch, O. (1983), *Luftbild-archäologie in Süddeutschland*, Stuttgart.

Bradford, J. (1957), *Ancient Landscapes*, London.

Braund, D. (1983), *Rome and the Friendly King*, London.

Breeze, D. J. (1974), 'The Roman fortlet at Barburgh Mill, Dumfriesshire', *Britannia*, V, 130–62.

Breeze, D. J. (1976), 'The abandonment of the Antonine Wall: its date and implications', *Scottish Archaeological Forum*, 7, Edinburgh, 67–80.

Breeze, D. J. (1982), *The Northern Frontiers of Roman Britain*, London.

Breeze, D. J. (1984), 'Demand and supply on the Northern Frontier', in R. Miket and C. Burgess (eds), *Between and Beyond the Walls*, Edinburgh, 264–86.

Breeze, D. J. (ed.) (1986), *The Frontiers of the Roman Empire*, London.

Breeze, D. J. and Dobson, B. (1976), 'A view of Roman Scotland in 1975', *Glasgow Archaeological Journal*, 4, 124–43.

Breeze, D. J. and Dobson, B. (1978), *Hadrian's Wall*, revised edition, Harmondsworth.

Breeze, D. J. and Dobson, B. (1985), 'Roman military deployment in Northern England', *Britannia*, XVI, 1–19.

Brogan, O. (1936), 'The Roman Limes in Germany', *Archaeological Journal* 92, 1–41.

Brogan, O. (1980), 'Hadd Hajar, a clausura in the Tripolitanian Gebel Garian south of Asabaa', *Libyan Studies*, 11, 45–52.

Brogan, O. and Reynolds, J. (1960), 'Seven new inscriptions from Tripolitania', *Papers of the British School at Rome*, 28, 51–4.

Brogan, O. and Smith, D. J. (1957), 'The Roman frontier settlement at Ghirza: an interim report', *Journal of Roman Studies*, XLVII, 173–84.

Brunk, G. (1980), 'A hoard from Syria countermarked by the Roman legions', *American Numismatic Society Monographs and Notes*, 25, 63–76.

Brünnow, R. E. and von Domaszewski, A. (1904–9), *Die Provincia Arabia*, Strasbourg.

Butler, H. C., Garrett, R., Littmann, E. and Prentice, W. K. (1903–14), *The Publications of an American Archaeological Expedition to Syria, 1899–1900*, New York.

Butler, H. C., Littmann, E. and Prentice, W. K. (1907–21), *The Publications of the Princeton University Archaeological Expeditions to Syria in 1904–5 and 1909*, Leiden.

Cagnat, R. (1913), *L'Armée romaine d'Afrique*, Paris.

Cagnat, R (1932–39), *CAH*, IX–XII.

Cagnat, R. (1983), *The Cambridge History of Iran*, III, Cambridge.

Cagnat, R. (1924), *CMH*, second edition.

Carcopino, J. (1925), 'Le *Limes* de Numidie et sa garde syrienne d'après des inscriptions récemment découvertes', Parts 1 and 2, *Syria*, 6, 30–57; 118–49.

Carrie, J.-M. (1974), 'Les *Castra Dionysidos* et l'évolution de l'architecture militaire romaine tardive', *Mélanges de l'École Française de Rome*, 86(1), 819–50.

Casey, P. J. and Savage, M. (1980), 'The coins from the excavations at High Rochester, in 1852 and 1855', *Archaeologia Aeliana*, fifth series, 8, 75–87.

Castelin, K. O. (1946), 'The coinage of Rhesaena in Mesopotamia', *Numismatic Notes and Chronicles*, no. 108, The American Numismatic Society.

Christofle, M. (1938), *Rapport sur les travaux de fouilles et consolidations éffectuées en 1933, 1934, 1935, 1936 par le service de monuments historiques de l'Algérie*, Alger, 273–93.

Collingwood, R. G. (1924), 'The Fosse', *Journal of Roman Studies*, XIV, 252–6.

Condurachi, E. and Daicoviciu, C. (1971), *The Ancient Civilisation of Romania*, London.

Courtois, C. (1955), *Les Vandales et l'Afrique*, Paris.

Crow, J. and French, D. (1980), 'New research on the Euphrates frontier in Turkey', *Limes Congress*, 12, 903–12.

Cumont, F. (1907), 'Inscriptiones latines des armées de l'Euphrate', *Bulletin de l'Académie royale de Belgique*, 55–78.

Cumont, F. (1926), *Fouilles de Doura-Europos*, Paris.

Dabrowa, E. (1979), 'Les troupes auxiliaires de l'Armée Romaine en Syrie au 1er s. de notre ère', *Dialogue d'Histoire Ancienne*, 5, 233–54.

Dabrowa, E. (1980a), 'Le limes anatolien et la frontière caucasienne au temps des Flaviens', *Klio*, 62, 379–88.

Dabrowa, E. (1980b), 'Quelques remarques sur le limes romain en Anatolie et en Syrie à l'époque du Haut Empire', *Folia Orientalia*, 21, 245–52.

Daniels, C. M. (ed.) (1978), *Handbook to the Roman Wall*, thirteenth edition, Newcastle-upon-Tyne.

Daniels, C. M. (1980), 'Excavations at Wallsend and the fourth-century barracks on

Hadrian's Wall', *Limes Congress*, 12, 173–93, Oxford.

Daniels, C. M. (1983), 'Town defences in Roman Africa: a tentative historical survey', in J. Maloney and B. Hobley (eds), *Roman Urban Defences in the West*, Council for British Archaeology Research Report, 51, 5–19, London.

Davies, J. L. (1980), 'Roman military deployment in Wales and the Marches from Claudius to the Antonines', *Limes Congress*, 12, 255–77, Oxford.

Debevoise, M. C. (1938), *A Political History of Parthia*, Chicago.

Desanges, J. (1964), 'Les territoires Gétules de Juba II', *Revue des Études Anciennes*, 66, 33–47.

D'Escurac-Doisy, H. (1953), 'M. Cornelius Octavianus et les révoltes indigènes du troisième siècle d'après une inscription de Caesarea', *Libyca*, 1, 181–7.

Dillemann, L. (1962), *Haute-Mésopotamie Orientale et Pays Adjacents*, Paris.

Dobson, B. (1970), 'Roman Durham', *Transactions of the Archaeological and Architectural Society of Durham and Northumberland*, 1, 31–43.

Dobson, B. (1981), 'Agricola's life and career': *Agricola's campaigns in Scotland, Scottish Archaeological Forum*, 12, 1–13, Edinburgh.

Drijvers, H. J. W. (1978), 'Hatra, Palmyra und Edessa', in H. Temporini (ed.), *Aufstieg und Niedergang der römischen Welt*, II, 8, 799–906, Berlin – New York.

Dumitrescu, S. (1969), 'Contribuţii la cunoaşterea graniţei de vest a Daciei Romane', *Acta Musei Napocensis*, 6, 483–91.

Duncan-Jones, R. P. (1978), 'Pay and numbers in Diocletian's army', *Chiron*, 8, 541–60.

Dussaud, R. (1955), *La Pénétration des Arabes en Syrie avant l'Islam*, Paris.

Eadie, J. W. (1967), 'The development of Roman mailed cavalry', *Journal of Roman Studies*, LVII, 161–73.

Euzennat, M. (1957), 'L'Archéologie Marocaine de 1955 et 1957', *Bulletin d'Archéologie Marocaine*, 2, 199–239.

Euzennat, M. (1960), 'Annoceur (Kasba des Aït Khalifa) faux poste romain dans le moyen Atlas', *Bulletin d'Archéologie Marocaine*, 4, 381–404.

Euzennat, M. (1967), 'Le Limes de Volubilis', *Limes Congress*, 6, 194–9, Köln.

Euzennat, M. (1972), 'Quatre années de recherches sur la frontière romaine en Tunisie meridionale', *Académie des Inscriptions et Belles-Lettres. Comptes Rendus des séances de l'année 1972*, 7–27.

Euzennat, M. (1973), 'Le Castellum Thigensium', *Bulletin Archéologique du Comité des Travaux Historiques et Scientifiques*, new series 7, année 1971, 229–39.

Euzennat, M. (1977a), 'Recherches récentes sur la frontière d'Afrique 1964–74', *Limes Congress*, 10, 429–43, Köln.

Euzennat, M. (1977b), 'Les récherches sur la frontière romaine d'Afrique, 1974–6', *Limes Congress*, 11, 533–43, Budapest.

Euzennat, M. (1978), 'Les ruines antiques du Bou Hillou (Maroc)', *Actes du 101ᵉ Congrès National des Sociétés Savants, Lille, 1976: Archéologie Militaire*, 295–329.

Fentress, E. W. B. (1979), *Numidia and the Roman Army: Social, Military and Economic Aspects of the Frontier Zone*, British Archaeological Reports S53, Oxford.

Ferenczi, St. (1967), 'Die Erforschung des römischen Limes auf den Höhen des Meseşgebirges', *Dacia*, 11, 143–62.

Ferenczi, St. (1968), 'Observaţii cu privire la sistemul şi caracterul aşa-zisului "Limes Dacicus",' *Acta Musei Napocensis* 5, 75–98 (with French summary).

Ferenczi, St. (1974), 'Die Nordstrecke des dakischen Limes von Crisul Repede bis zu den Ostkarpaten', *Limes Congress*, 9, 201–5, Bucarest.

Février, P.-A. (1981), 'Á propos des troubles de Maurétanie (villes et conflits du IIIe siècle)', *Zeitschrift für Papyrologie und Epigraphik*, 43, 143–8.

Filtzinger, P. *et al.* (1976), *Die Römer in Baden Württemberg*, Stuttgart.

Fishwick, D. (1971), 'The annexation of Mauretania', *Historia*, 20, 467–87.

Fishwick, D. and Shaw, B. D. (1976), 'Ptolemy of Mauretania and the conspiracy of Gaetulicus', *Historia*, 25, 491–4.

Fishwick, D. and Shaw, B. D. (1977), 'The formation of Africa Proconsularis', *Hermes*, 105, 369–80.

Frere, S. S. (1978), *Britannia*, revised edition, London.

Frere, S. S. (1981), 'The Flavian frontier in Scotland', *Agricola's Campaigns in Scotland, Scottish Archaeological Forum*, 12, 85–97, Edinburgh.

Frézouls, E. (1957), 'Les Baquates et la province romaine de Tingitane', *Bulletin d' Archéologie Marocaine*, 2, 65–116.

Gabler, D. (1980), 'The structure of the Pannonian frontier on the Danube in the Antonine period: some problems', *Limes Congress*, 12, 729–44, Oxford.

Gabler, D. and Lörincz, B. (forthcoming), 'The frontier of Pannonia and Upper Moesia', in Breeze, D. J. (ed.), *The Frontiers of the Roman Empire*, London.

Gajewska, H. (1974), *Topographie des fortifications romaines en Dobroudja*, Wrocklaw.

Garbsch, J. (1970), *Der spätrömische Donau-Iller-Rhein-Limes*, Stuttgart.

Gautier, E. F. (1937), *Le Passé de l' Afrique du Nord*, Paris.

Gechter, M. (1979), 'Die Anfang des niedergermanisches Limes', *Bonner Jahrbücher*, 179, 1–138.

Gichon, M. (1971), 'Das Kastell en Boqeq', *Bonner Jahrbücher*, 171, 386–406.

Gichon, M. (1976), 'Excavations at Mezad Tamar', *Saalburg Jahrbuch*, 33, 80–94.

Gichon, M. (1980), 'New research on the Limes Palaestinae: A stocktaking', *Limes Congress*, 12, 843–64, Oxford.

Gillam, J. P. (1958), 'Roman and native, AD 122–97', in I. A. Richmond (ed.), *Roman and Native in North Britain*, 60–90, Edinburgh.

Gillam, J. P. (1973), 'Sources of pottery found on northern military sites', in A. Detsicas (ed.), *Current Research in Romano–British Coarse Pottery*, Council for British Archaeology Research Report, 10, 53–65, London.

Gillam, J. P. (1976), 'Possible changes in plan in the course of the construction of the

Antonine Wall', *Scottish Archaeological Forum*, 7, 51–6, Edinburgh.

Goodchild, R. G. (1950), 'The Limes Tripolitanus II', *Journal of Roman Studies*, XL, 30–8.

Goodchild, R. G. (1953), 'The Roman and Byzantine *Limes* in Cyrenaica', *Journal of Roman Studies*, XLIII, 65–76.

Goodchild, R. G. (1954), 'Oasis forts of Legio III Augusta on the routes to the Fezzan', *Papers of the British School at Rome*, 22, 56–58.

Goodchild, R. G. and Ward-Perkins, J. B. (1949), 'The *Limes Tripolitanus* in the light of recent discoveries', *Journal of Roman studies*, XXXIX, 81–95.

Gracey, M. H. (1983), 'The Roman Army in Syria, Palestine and Arabia', unpublished M. Litt. thesis, University of Oxford.

Graf, D. (1978), 'Saracens and the defence of the Arabian frontier', *Bulletin of the American Schools of Oriental Research*, 229, 1–26.

Graf, D. and O'Connor, M. (1977), 'The origin of the term Saracen and the Rawwafa inscriptions', *Byzantine Studies*, 4, 52–66.

Gray, E. W. (1973), 'The Roman eastern *limes* from Constantine to Justinian: Perspectives and problems', *Proceedings of the African Classical Associations*, XII, 24–40.

Gregory, S. and Kennedy, D. L. (eds) (1985), *Sir Aurel Stein's Limes Report*, British Archaeological Reports, S272, Oxford.

Gsell, S. (1926), 'La Tripolitaine et le Sahara au IIIe siècle de notre ère', *Mémoires de l'Académie des Inscriptions et Belles-Lettres*, 43, 149–66.

Gudea, N. (1979), 'The defensive system of Roman Dacia', *Britannia*, X, 63–87.

Guey, J. (1938), 'Note sur le *Limes* romain de Numidie, et le Sahara au IVe siècle', *Mélanges d'Archéologie et de'Histoire de l'École Française de Rome*, 55, 178–248.

Haberl, J. and Hawkes, C. (1973), 'The last of Roman Noricum', in C. and S. Hawkes (eds), *Greeks, Celts and Romans. Studies in Venture and Resistance*, 97–149, London.

Hammond, M. (1934), 'Corbulo and Nero's eastern policy', *Harvard Studies in Classical Philology*, 45, 81–104.

Hammond, N. (1967), 'The Limes Tripolitanus: a Roman road in North Africa', *Journal of the British Archaeological Association*, third series, 30, 1–18.

Hanson, W. S. (1981), 'Agricola on the Forth-Clyde isthmus', *Agricola's Campaigns in Scotland, Scottish Archaeological Forum* 12, 55–68, Edinburgh.

Hanson, W. S. (1986), 'Rome, the Cornovii and the Ordovices', *Limes Congress*, 13, Stuttgart.

Hanson, W. S. and Maxwell, G. S. (1980), 'An Agricolan *Praesidium* on the Forth-Clyde isthmus (Mollins, Strathclyde)', *Britannia*, XI, 43–9.

Hanson, W. S. and Maxwell, G. S. (1983a), *Rome's North-West Frontier: The Antonine Wall*, Edinburgh.

Hanson, W. S. and Maxwell, G. S. (1983b), 'Minor enclosures on the Antonine Wall at Wilderness Plantation', *Britannia*, XIV, 227–43.

Harper, R. P. (1977), 'Two excavations on the Euphrates frontier 1968–1974: Pagnik Öreni (Eastern Turkey) 1968–1971 and Dibsi Faraj (Northern Syria) 1972–74', *Limes Congress*, 10, 453–60, Köln.

Hartley, B. R. (1966), 'Some problems of the Roman military occupation of the north of England', *Northern History*, 1, 7–20.

Hartley, B. R. (1972), 'The Roman occupation of Scotland: the evidence of samian ware', *Britannia*, III, 1–55.

Haynes, D. E. L. (1965), *An Archaeological and Historical Guide to the pre-Islamic Antiquities of Tripolitania*, Tripoli.

Hellenkemper, H. (1977), 'Der limes in Nordsyrischen Euphrat', *Limes Congress*, 10, 461–71, Köln.

Higham, N. R. (1986), *The Northern Counties to AD 1000*, London.

Hind, J. G. F. (1971), 'The Middle Years of Nero's Reign', *Historia*, 20, 488–505.

Hoddinott, R. F. (1975), *Bulgaria in Antiquity: and Archaeological Introduction*, London.

Hoffman, D. (1969), *Das spätrömische Bewegungsheer und die Notitia Dignitatum (= Epigraphische Studien*, 7), Dusseldorf.

Hopkins, C. (1979), *The Discovery of Dura Europos*, Yale.

Jameson, S. (1968), 'Chronology of the campaigns of Aelius Gallus and C. Petronius', *Journal of Roman Studies*, LVIII, 71–84.

Janon, M. (1973), 'Recherches à Lambèse', *Antiquités Africaines*, 7, 193–254.

Johnson, S. (1976), *The Roman Forts of the Saxon Shore*, London.

Johnson, S. (1982), *Late Roman Fortifications*, London.

Jones, A. H. M. (1973), *The Later Roman Empire 284–602*, two volumes, Oxford.

Jones, G. D. B. (1976), 'The western extension of Hadrian's Wall: Bowness to Cardurnock', *Britannia*, VII, 236–43.

Jones, G. D. B. (1978), 'Concept and development in Roman frontiers', *Bulletin of the John Rylands Library of Manchester*, 61, No. 1 (Autumn), 115–44.

Jones, G. D. B. (1980), 'The hidden frontier', *Popular Archaeology* 2, no. 1, (July), 14–17.

Jones, G. D. B. (1982), 'The Solway Frontier: Interim Report 1976–81', *Britannia*, XIII, 283–97.

Jones, G. D. B. and Mattingley, D. (1980), 'Fourth-century manning of the *Fossatum Africae*', *Britannia*, XI, 323–6.

Keaveney, A. (1981), 'Roman treaties with Parthia c. 95–c. 64 BC', *American Journal of Philology*, 102, 195–212.

Keaveney, A. (1982), 'The king and the war lords: Romano–Parthian relations c. 64–53 BC', *American Journal of Philology*, 103, 412–28.

Kennedy, D. L. (1979), 'Ti. Claudius Subatianus Aquila. "First Prefect of Mesopotamia"', *Zeitschrift für Papyrologie und Epigraphik*, 36, 255–62.

Kennedy, D. L. (1980), 'The frontier policy of Septimius Severus: New evidence from Arabia', *Limes Congress*, 12, 879–88, Oxford.

Kennedy, D. L. (1980), '*Legio VI Ferrata*: The annexation and early garrison of Arabia', *Harvard Studies in Classical Philology*, 84, 283–309.

Kennedy, D. L. (1982), *Archaeological Explorations on the Roman Frontier in North East Jordan*, British Archaeological Reports, S134, Oxford.

Kennedy, D. L. (1983), 'C. Velius Rufus', *Britannia*, XIV, 183–96.

Kennedy, D. L. (1983), 'Military cohorts: The evidence of Josephus, BJ III. 4.2. (67) and of Epigraphy', *Zeitschrift für Papyrologie und Epigraphik*, 50, 253–63.

Kennedy, D. L. (forthcoming), 'The Eastern Frontier', in D. J. Breeze (ed.), *The Frontiers of the Roman Empire*, London.

Kennedy, D. L. and Macadam, H. I. (1985), 'Some Latin inscriptions from the Azraq Oasis, Jordan', *Zeitschrift für Papyrologie und Epigraphik*, 60, 97–107.

Keppie, L. J. F. (1982), 'The Antonine Wall 1960–1980', *Britannia*, XIII, 91–111.

Keppie, L. J. F. and Walker, J. J. (1981), 'Fortlets on the Antonine Wall at Seabegs Wood, Kinneil and Cleddans', *Britannia*, XII, 143–62.

Kettenhofen, E. (1983), 'The Persian campaign of Gordian III and the inscription of Sahpuhr I at the Ka^cBe-Ye Zartost', in S. Mitchell (ed.), *Armies and Frontiers in Roman and Byzantine Anatolia*, British Archaeological Reports S156, 151–72, Oxford.

Killick, A. (1983), 'Udruh – The frontier of an Empire: 1980 and 1981 seasons, a preliminary report', *Levant*, XV, 110–31.

Kindler, A. (1975), 'Two coins of the Third Legion Cyrenaica struck under Antoninus Pius', *Israel Exploration Journal*, 25, 144–7.

Kirwan, L. P. (1957), 'Rome beyond the southern Egyptian frontier', *Geographical Journal*, 123, 13–19.

Kirwan, L. P. (1966), 'Prelude to Nubian Christianity', *Mélanges offerts à K. Michalowski*, 121–8, Warsaw.

Kirwan, L. P. (1974), 'Nubia and Nubian Origins', *Geographical Journal* 140, 43–51.

Kirwan, L. P. (1977), 'Rome beyond the southern Egyptian frontier', *Proceedings of the British Academy*, 63, 13–31.

Kirwan, L. P. (1982), 'The X-group problem', *Meroitic Studies, Meroitica*, 6, 191–210.

La Chapelle, F. de (1934), 'L'expédition de Suetonius Paulinus dans le sud-est de Maroc', *Hespéris*, 19, 107–24.

Lander, J. (1984), *Roman Stone Fortifications*, British Archaeological Report S206, Oxford.

Lassère, J.-M. (1982), 'Un conflit routier: observations sur les causes de la guerre de Tacfarinas', *Antiquités Africaines*, 18, 11–25.

Lawless, R. I. (1972), 'The concept of *tell* and *Sahara* in the Maghreb: a reappraisal', *Transactions of the Institute of British Geographers*, 57, 125–37.

Lawless, R. I. (1973), 'Population, resource appraisal and environment in the pre-Saharan zone of the Maghreb', *Maghreb et Sahara: études géographiques offertes à Jean Despois*, 229–37, Paris.

Leach, J. D. and Wilkes, J. J. (1977), 'The Roman military base at Carpow, Perthshire, Scotland: summary of recent investigations (1964–71, 1975)', *Limes Congress*, 11, 47–62, Budapest.

Le Bohec, Y. (1979), *Archeologie militaire de l'Afrique du Nord, Bibliographie Analytique 1913–1977: Armée Romaine et Provinces*, II, Paris.

Lengyel, A. and Radan, G. (ed.) (1980), *The Archaeology of Roman Pannonia*, Kentucky – Budapest.

Lepper, F. (1948), *Trajan's Parthian War*, Oxford.

Leschi, L. (1957), *Études d'Épigraphie, d'Archéologie et d'Histoire Africaine*, Paris.

Lesquier, M. J. (1918), *L'Armée romaine d'Egypte d'Auguste à Dioclétien*, Paris.

Limes Congress (1952–), *The Proceedings of the International Congress of Roman Frontier Studies* as follows:

1. Durham, 1949, Eric Birley (ed.), Durham, 1952.
2. Carnuntum, 1955, Eric Swoboda (ed.), Graz-Köln, 1956.
3. Basle, 1957, R. Laur-Belart (ed.), Basel, 1959.
4. Durham, 1959, unpublished.
5. Yugoslavia, 1963, Grga Novak (ed.), Zagreb, 1964.
6. Süddeutschland, 1964, H. Schönberger (ed.), Köln, Graz, 1967.
7. Tel Aviv, 1967, S. Appelbaum (ed.), Tel Aviv, 1971.
8. Cardiff, 1969, Eric Birley, Brian Dobson and Michael Jarrett (eds), Cardiff, 1974.
9. Mamaia, 1972, D. M. Pippidi (ed.), Bucarest, 1974.
10. Lower Germany, 1974, Dorothea Haupt and Heinz Günther Horn (eds), Köln, 1977.
11. Székesfehévár, 1976, J. Fitz (ed.), Budapest, 1977.
12. Stirling, 1979, W. S. Hanson and L. J. F. Keppie (eds), Oxford, 1980.
13. Aalen, 1983, D. Planck and C. Unz (eds), Stuttgart, forthcoming.

Luttwak, E. N. (1976), *The Grand Strategy of the Roman Empire. From the First Century A.D. to the Third*, London.

MacAdam, H. I. (1980), 'The Nemara inscription: some historical considerations', *'Al Abhath*, 28, 31–46.

Macrae, M. (1967), 'L'organisation de la province de Dacie', *Dacia*, 11, 121–41.

Macrae, M. *et al.* (1962), 'Santierul arheologic Porolissum', *Materiale si Cercetari Arheologice* 8, 485–504 (with Russian and French summaries).

Magie, D. (1950), *Roman Rule in Asia Minor*, Princeton.

Mann, J. C. (1968), Review of R. M. Ogilvie and I. A. Richmond (eds), *Cornelii Taciti, de vita Agricolae*, Oxford, 1967, in *Archaeologia Aeliana*, fourth series, 46, 306–8.

Mann, J. C. (1971), *The Northern Frontier in Britain from Hadrian to Honorius: Literary and Epigraphic Sources*, Newcastle upon Tyne.

Mann, J. C. (1974), 'The Frontiers of the Principate' in H. Temporini (ed.), *Aufstieg und Niedergang der römischen Welt*, II, 2, 508–33, Berlin–New York.

Mann, J. C. (1974), 'The northern frontier after AD 369', *Glasgow Archaeological Journal*, 3, 34–42.

Manning, W. H. (1972), 'Iron work hoards in Iron Age and Roman Britain', *Britannia*, III, 224–50.

Manning, W. H. (1974), 'Economic influence on land use in the military areas of the Highland Zone during the Roman period', in J. G. Evans, S. Limbrey and H. Cleere (eds), *The Effect of Man on the Landscape: the Highland Zone*, London, 112–16.

Maricq, A. (1958), 'Res Gestae Divi Saporis', *Syria*, 35, 295–360.

Matthews, J. (1976), 'Mauretania in Ammianus and the Notitia', in R. Goodburn and P. Bartholomew (eds), *Aspects of the Notitia Dignitatum*, British Archaeological Reports, S15, 157–87, Oxford.

Mattingley, D. J. (1983), 'The Laguatan: a Libyan tribal confederation in the Late Roman Empire', *Libyan Studies*, 14, 96–108.

Maxfield, V. A. (1981), 'The Flavian fort at Camelon', *Agricola's Campaigns in Scotland, Scottish Archaeological Forum*, 12, 69–78.

Maxwell, G. S. (1977), 'A linear defence-system in south-western Scotland', *Limes Congress*, 10, 23–30, Köln.

McCord, N. and Jobey, G. (1971), 'Notes on air reconnaissance in Northumberland and Durham, II', *Archaeologia Aeliana*, fourth series, 49, 119–30.

Meredith, D. (1952), 'The Roman remains in the Eastern Desert of Egypt 1', *Journal of Egyptian Archaeology*, 38, 94–111.

Meredith, D. (1953), 'The Roman remains in the Eastern Desert of Egypt 2', *Journal of Egyptian Archaeology*, 39, 95–106.

Mitchell, S. (ed.) (1983), *Armies and Frontiers in Roman and Byzantine Anatolia*, British Archaeological Reports S156, Oxford.

Mitford, T. B. (1974), 'Some inscriptions from the Cappadocian Limes', *Journal of Roman Studies*, LXIV, 160–75.

Mitford, T. B. (1980), 'Cappadocia and Armenia Minor: Historical setting of the Limes', in H. Temporini (ed.), *Aufstieg und Niedergang der Römischen Welt*, II.7.ii, 1169–1228, Berlin – New York.

Mócsy, A. (1974), *Pannonia and Upper Moesia*, London.

Monneret de Villard, U. (1914), *La Nubia Romana*, Rome.

Monneret de Villard, U. (1953), 'The Temple of the Imperial Cult at Luxor', *Archaeologia*, 95, 85–105.

Mouterde, R. and Poidebard, P. (1945), *Le limes de Chalcis*, Paris.

Murray, G. W. (1925), 'Roman roads and stations in the Eastern Desert of Egypt', *Journal of Egyptian Archaeology*, 11, 138–50.

Murray, G. W. (1967), 'Trogodytica: the Red Sea Littoral in Ptolemaic times', *Geographical Journal*, 133, 24–33.

Nash-Williams, V. E. (1955), 'Roman Africa', *Bulletin of the Board of Celtic Studies*, 16:2, 134–64.

Nash-Williams, V. E. (1969), *The Roman Frontier in Wales*, second edition, by M. G. Jarrett, Cardiff.

Naval Staff Intelligence Division (1917), *A Handbook of Bulgaria*, not stated.

Oates, D. (1955), 'A note on three Latin inscriptions from Hatra', *Sumer*, 11, 39–43.

Oates, D. (1956), 'The Roman frontier in northern Iraq', *Geographical Journal*, 122, 190–99.

Oates, D. (1968), *Studies in the Ancient History of Northern Iraq*, London.

Oldenstein-Pferdehirt, B. (1983), 'Die römischen Hilfstruppen nördlich des Mains', *Jahrbuch des Römisch-Germanischen Zentralmuseums Mainz*, 30, 303–48.

Oldenstein-Pferdehirt, B. (forthcoming), 'Archäologische Untersuchungen zur romischen Okkupations recht des Rheins', *Jahrbuch des Römische-Germanischen Zentralmuseums Mainz*.

Olmsterad, A. T. (1942), 'The mid-third century of the Christian era', *Classical Philology*, 37, 241–62; 398–420.

Overbeck, B. (1976), 'Raetien zur Prinzipatszeit', in H. Temporini (ed.), *Aufstieg und Niedergang der römischen Welt* II.5, 658–89, Berlin – New York.

Pachterre, F. de (1916), 'Les caps de la troisième légion en Afrique au premier siècle de l'Empire', *Académie des Inscriptions et Belles-Lettres: Comptes rendus des séances de l'année 1916*, 273–84.

Parker, S. T. (1976), 'Archaeological survey of the *Limes Arabicus*: A preliminary report', *Annual of the Department of Antiquities of Jordan*, 21, 19–31.

Parker, S. T. (1982), 'Preliminary report on the 1980 season of the Central Limes Arabicus Project', *Bulletin of the American Schools of Oriental Research*, 247, 1–26.

Parker, S. T. (1985), 'Preliminary report of the 1982 season of the Central Limes Aribicus Project', *Bulletin of the American Schools of Oriental Research*, Supplement 23, 1–34.

Parker, S. T. and Lander, J. (1982), 'Legio IV Martia and the Legionary Camp at el-Lejjun', *Byzantinische Forschungen*, 8, 185–210.

Petrikovits, H. v (1971), 'Fortifications in the north-western Roman Empire from the third to the fifth centuries AD', *Journal of Roman Studies*, LXI, 178–218.

Picard, G. C. (1947), *Castellum Dimmidi*, Alger/Paris.

Pigoulevskaya, N. (1960), 'Les Arabes à la frontière de Byzance au IVᵉ siècle', *Actes due XXVᵉ Congrès Internationale des Orientalistes, Moscow, 1960*, I, 443–5.

Pitts, L. and St Joseph, J. K. (1985), *Inchtuthil: The Roman Legionary Fortress*, London.

Planck, D. (1976), 'Neue Forschung zum obergermanischen und raetischen Limes', in H. Temporini (ed.), *Aufstieg und Niedergang der römischen Welt*, II.5, 406–56, Berlin – New York.

Planck, D. (1983), 'Ein neuer römischer Limes in Württemberg', *Archäologische Ausgrabungen in Baden-Württemberg 1982*, 94–9.

Planck, D. (ed.) (1983), *Führer zu römischen Militäranlagen in Süddeutschland*, Stuttgart.

Poidebard, A. (1934), *La Trace de Rome dans le désert de Syrie*, Paris.

Poulter, A. (ed.) (1983), *Ancient Bulgaria*, Nottingham.

Poulter, A. (1986), 'The Lower Danubian Limes from Augustus to Aurelian' in Breeze

D. J. (ed.), *The Frontiers of the Roman Empire*, London.

Rachet, M. (1970), 'Rome et les Berbères: un problème militaire d'Auguste à Dioclétien', *Collections Latomus*, 110, Brussels.

Raepsaet-Charlier, M.-T. and Raepset, G. (1975), 'Gallia Belgica et Germania Inferior: vingt-cinq années de recherches historiques et archéologique', in H. Temporini (ed.), *Aufstieg und Niedergang der römischen Welt* II.5, 73ff, Berlin – New York.

Raven, S. (1984), *Rome in Africa*, second edition, London.

Rebuffat, R. (1966), 'Le developpement urbain de Volubilis au second siècle de notre ère', *Bulletin Archéologique du Comité des Travaux Historiques et Scientifiques*, 231–40.

Rebuffat, R. (1972), 'Nouvelles recherches dans le sud de la Tripolitaine', *Académie des Inscriptions et Belles-Lettres, Comptes Rendus des séances de l'année 1972*, 319–39.

Rebuffat, R. (1975), 'Trois nouvelles campagnes dans le sud de la Tripolitaine', *Académie des Inscriptions et Belles-Lettres, Comptes Rendus des séances de l'année 1975*, 495–505.

Rebuffat, R. (1980), 'Le Fosse romain de Sala', *Bulletin d'Archéologie Marocaine*, 12, 237–60.

Rey-Coquais, J. P. (1978), 'Syrie romaine de Pompée à Dioclétien', *Journal of Roman Studies*, LXVIII, 44–73.

Reynolds, J. M. (ed.) (1976), *Libyan Studies: select papers of the late R. G. Goodchild*, London.

Reynolds, J. M. and Ward-Perkins, J. B. (1952), *Inscriptions of Roman Tripolitania*, Rome.

Richmond, I. A. (1939), 'The Agricolan fort at Fendoch', *Proceedings of the Society of Antiquaries of Scotland*, 73 (1938–9), 110–54.

Richmond, I. A. (1962), 'The Roman siege-works of Masada, Israel', *Journal of Roman Studies*, LII, 142–5.

Robertson, A. S. (1970), 'Roman finds from non-Roman sites in Scotland', *Britannia*, I, 198–226.

Robertson, A. S. (1974), 'Roman "signal stations" on the Gask Ridge', *Transactions of the Perthshire Society of Natural Science*, Special Issue, 14–29.

Robertson, A. S. (1978), 'The circulation of Roman coins in North Britain: the evidence of hoards and site-finds from Scotland', in R. A. G. Carson and C. Kraay (eds), *Scripta Nummaria Romana*, 186–216, London.

Rostovtzeff, M. I. (1943), 'Res Gestae Divi Saporis and Dura', *Berytus*, VIII, 17–60.

Roxan, M. (1973), 'The *auxilia* of Mauretania Tingitana', *Latomus*, 32, 838–55.

Roxan, M. (1976), 'The pre-Severan Auxilia named in the *Notitia Dignitatum*', in R. Goodburn and P. Bartholomew (eds), *Aspects of the Notitia Dignitatum*', British Archaeological Reports Series S15, 59–79, Oxford.

Salama, P. (1951), *Les Voies romaines de l'Afrique du Nord*, Alger.

Salama, P. (1953), 'Nouveaux témoignages de l'oeuvre des Sévères dans la Maurétanie Césarienne: part 1', *Libyca*, I, 231–61.

Salama, P. (1955), 'Nouveaux témoignages de l'oeuvre des Sévères dans la Maurétanie Césarienne: part 2', *Libyca* III, 330–67.

Salama, P. (1958), *Le Sahara Antique : état de la question*, Alger.

Salama, P. (1966), 'Occupation de la Maurétaine Césarienne occidentale sous le Bas-Empire romain', in R. Chevallier (ed.), *Mélanges d'Archéologie et d'Histoire offerts à Andre Piganiol*, 1291–311, Paris.

Salama, P. (1977), 'Les déplacements successifs du Limes en Maurétanie Césarienne (essai de synthèse)', *Limes Congress*, 11, 577–95, Budapest.

Salway, P. (1965), *The Frontier People of Roman Britain*, Cambridge.

Sartre, M. (1982), *Trois études sur l'Arabie Romaine et Byzantine, Collections Latomus*, 178, Brussels.

Sartre, M. (1986), *Bostra, des Origines à l'Islam*, Paris.

Săšel, J. (1973), 'Trajan's canal at the Iron Gate', *Journal of Roman Studies*, LXIII, 80–5.

Săšel, J. and Petru, P. (1971), *Claustra Alpium Iuliarum I*, Ljubljana.

Schleiermacher, W. (1954), 'Trockenmauern im Zuge des Taunus Limes', *Saalburg Jahrbuch*, 13, 74–5.

Schnurbein, S. von (1974), *Die römischen Militäranlagen bei Haltern*, Münster.

Schnurbein, S. von (1981), 'Untersuchungen zur Geschichte der römischen Militärlager an der Lippe', *Bericht der Römisch-Germanischen Kommission*, 62, 5–101.

Schönberger, H. (1969), 'The Roman frontier in Germany : an archaeological survey', *Journal of Roman Studies*, LIX, 144–97.

Seeck, O. (ed.) (1962), *Notitia Dignitatum*, Frankfurt.

Shahid, I. (1984a), 'Byzantium and the Arabs in the Fourth Century', (Dumbarton Oaks Monographs), Washington.

Sherwin-White, A. N. (1944), 'Geographical factors in Roman Algeria', *Journal of Roman Studies*, XXXIV, 1–10.

Smith, D. J. (1956), 'The Roman frontier in French Morocco', *Report of the Durham University Exploration Society's Expedition to French Morocco*, 1952, 88–166, Durham.

Soproni, S. (1978), *Der spätrömische Limes zwischen Esztergom und Szentendre*, Budapest.

Soproni, S. (1980), 'Limes' in A. Lengyel and G. T. B. Radan (eds), *The Archaeology of Roman Pannonia*, Budapest.

Sölter, W. (ed.) (1981), *Das römische Germanien aus der Luft*, Bergisch Gladbach.

Speidel, M. P. (1975), 'Africa and Rome : continuous resistance?', *Proceedings of the African Classical Association*, 13, 36–8.

Speidel, M. P. (1978), 'The Roman Army in Arabia', in H. Temporini (ed.), *Aufstieg und Niedergang der Römischen Welt*, II.8, 687–730, New York – Berlin.

Speidel, M. P. (1982), 'Legionary cohorts in Mauretania : the role of legionary cohorts in the structure of expeditionary armies', in H. Temporini (ed.), *Aufstieg und Niedergang der Römischen Welt II Principat 10.2*, 850–60, Berlin – New York.

Speidel, M. P. (1983), 'The Roman Army in Asia Minor', in S. Mitchell (ed.), *Armies and Frontiers in Roman and Byzantine Anatolia*, British Archaeological Reports S156, 7–34, Oxford.

Sprengling, M. (1953), *Third Century Iran: Sapor and Kartir*, Chicago.

Starr, C. G. (1941), *The Roman Imperial Navy*, New York.

Steer, K. A. (1957), 'The nature and purpose of the expansions on the Antonine Wall', *Proceedings of the Society of Antiquaries of Scotland*, 90 (1956–7), 161–9.

Stein, A. (1938), 'Note on the remains of the Roman *Limes* in north-western Iraq', *Geographical Journal*, 92, 62–6.

Stein, A. (1940), 'Surveys on the Roman frontier in Iraq and Trans-Jordan', *Geographical Journal*, 95, 428–38.

Stein, M. A. (1941), 'The ancient trade route past Hatra and the Roman posts', *Journal of the Royal Asiatic Society*, 9, 299–316.

Stolte, B. H. (1971), 'The Roman emperor Valerian and Sapor I, King of Persia', *Rivista Storica dell' Antichita*, I, 157–62.

St Joseph, J. K. (1973), 'Air reconnaissance in Britain, 1969–72', *Journal of Roman Studies*, LXII, 214–46.

St Joseph, J. K. (1977), 'Air reconnaissance in Roman Britain, 1973–76', *Journal of Roman Studies*, LXVII, 125–61.

Sulimirski, T. (1970), *The Sarmatians*, London.

Syme, R. (1928), 'Rhine and Danube legions under Domitian', *Journal of Roman Studies*, XVIII, 41–55.

Syme, R. (1938), 'The first garrison of Trajan's Dacia', *Laureae Aquincenses* I, 267–86.

Syme, R. (1951), 'Tacfarinas, the Musulamii and Thubursicu', in P. R. Coleman-Norton (ed.), *Studies in Roman Economic and Social History in honour of Allan Chester Johnson*, 113–30, Princeton.

Syme, R. (1959), 'The Lower Danube under Trajan', *Journal of Roman Studies*, XLIX, 26–33.

Syme, R. (1971), *Danubian Papers*, Bucarest.

Tabula Imperii Romani (1954), Sheet H.I. 33 Lepcis Magna (Map of Roman Libya: west sheet), R. G. Goodchild, London.

Tabula Imperii Romani (1954), Sheet H.I. 34, Cyrene (Map of Roman Libya: east sheet), R. G. Goodchild, London.

Tabula Imperii Romani (1958), Sheet G.36 Coptos, D. Meredith, London.

Tabula Imperii Romanii (1965), Sheet of Drobeta–Romula–Sucidava, D. Tudor, Bucarest.

Tabula Imperii Romanii (1968), Sheet L34, Aquincum–Sarmizegetusa–Sirmium; Budapest.

Tabula Imperii Romanii (1969), Sheet L35, Romula–Durostorum–Tomi; Bucarest.

Tabula Imperii Romanii (1976), Sheet K34, Naissus, Dyrrhachion–Scupi–Serdica–Thessalonike; Ljubljana.

Tabula Imperii Romanii (1983), Sheet M30–1, Condate–Glevum–Londinium–Lutetia; London.

Talbot-Rice, T. (1981), 'The Scytho-Sarmatian tribes of south-eastern Europe', in F. Miller (ed.), *The Roman Empire and its Neighbours*, second edition, 281–93, London.

Ternes, Ch.-M. (1976), 'Die Provincia Germania Superior im Bilde der jüngeren Forschung', in H. Temporini (ed.), *Aufstieg und Niedergang der römischen Welt* II.5, 721–1260, Berlin – New York.

Toynbee, J. M. C. (1972), 'Some problems of Romano–Parthian sculpture at Hatra', *Journal of Roman Studies* LXII, 106–10.

Trousset, P. (1974), *Recherches sur le Limes Tripolitanus*, Paris.

Trousset, P. (1976), 'Reconnaissances archéologiques sur la frontière saharienne de l'Empire Romain dans le sud-ouest de la Tunisie', *101e Congrès National des Sociétés Savantes, Lille, 1976, Archéologie*, 21–33.

Trousset, P. (1977), 'Le camp de Gemellae sur le Limes de Numidie d'après les fouilles du Colonel Baradez (1947–1950)', *Limes Congress*, 11, 559–75, Budapest.

Trousset, P. (1980a), 'Les milliaires de Chebika (Sud Tunisien)', *Antiquités Africaines*, 15, 135–54.

Trousset, P. (1980b), 'Signification d'une frontière: nomades et sédentaires dans la zone du Limes d'Afrique', *Limes Congress*, 12, 931–42, Oxford.

Trousset, P. (1982), 'Le franchissement des Chotts du sud-Tunisien dans l'antiquité', *Antiquités Africaines*, 18, 45–59.

Ubl, H. (1980), 'Der österreichische Abschnitt des Donaulimes. Ein Forschungsbericht (1970–1979)', (with English summary), *Limes Congress*, 12, 587–610, Oxford.

Velkov, V. (1981), 'Thrace and Lower Moesia during the Roman and Late Roman Epoch', *Klio*, 63, 473–83.

Waasdorp, J. A. (1982–3), 'Immanes Raeti: a hundred years of Roman Defensive Policy in the Alps and Voralpenland', *Talanta*, 14–15, 33–89.

Wagner, J. (1976), *Seleukeia am Euphrat/Zeugma*. Beihefte zum Tübinger Atlas des Vorderen Orients, 10, Wiesbaden.

Wagner, J. (1983), 'Provincia Osrhoenae: New archaeological finds illustrating the military organization under the Severan Dynasty', in S. Mitchell (ed.), *Armies and Frontiers in Roman and Byzantine Anatolia*, British Archaeological Reports, S156, 103–30, Oxford.

Warmington, B. H. (1954), *The North African Provinces from Diocletian to the Vandal Conquest*, Cambridge.

Warmington, B. H. (1976), 'Objectives and strategy in the Persian War of Constantius II', *Limes Congress*, 11, 509–20.

Welles, C. B. (1941), 'The Epitaph of Julius Terentius', *Harvard Theological Review*, 34, 79–102.

Welles, C. B. *et al.* (1959), *The Excavations at Dura-Europus, Final Report V: The Parchments and Papyri*. New Haven.

Wells, C. (1972), *The German Policy of Augustus*, Oxford.

Welsby, D. (1983), 'The Roman fort at Gheria el-Garbia', *Libyan Studies* 14, 57–64.

Wheeler, R. E. (1952), 'The Roman frontier in Mesopotamia'. *Limes Congress*, 1, 112–28, Durham.

Whittaker, C. R. (1978), 'Land and labour in North Africa', *Klio: Beiträge zur Alten Geschichte*, 60:1, 331–62.

Whittaker, C. R. (1983), 'Trade and frontiers of the Roman Empire', in P. Garnsey and C. R. Whittaker (eds), *Trade and Famine in Classical Antiquity*, 110–27, Cambridge.

Wightman, E. (1971), 'Some aspects of the late Roman defensive system in Gaul', *Limes Congress*, 7, 46–51, Tel Aviv.

Wilkes, J. J. (1966), 'Early fourth century rebuilding in Hadrian's Wall forts', in M. G. Jarrett and B. Dobson (eds), *Britain and Rome*, 114–38, Kendal.

Wilkes, J. J. (1969), *Dalmatia*, London.

Wilkes, J. J. (1981), 'The Illyrian provinces: external threat and internal change', in A. King and M. Henig (eds), *The Roman West in the Third Century*, British Archaeological Reports, S109, 515–24, Oxford.

Wilkes, J. J. (1983), 'Romans, Dacians and Sarmatians', in B. Hartley and J. S. Wacher (eds), *Rome and her Northern Provinces*, 255–289, Gloucester.

PART 5

·CITIES·TOWNS·AND· ·VILLAGES·

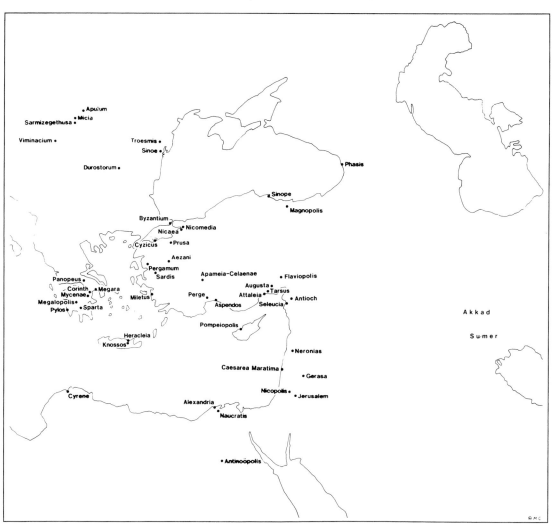

Figure 12.1 The Eastern Empire. Places mentioned in the text of Part 5

CHAPTER 12

·URBANIZATION·IN·THE· ·EASTERN·EMPIRE·

Barbara Levick

As the Romans assumed control from the Adriatic to the Euphrates, from the Black Sea to the First Cataract on the Nile, they found themselves dealing with areas organized, below the governmental level, on a tribal, clan, village, township, or city basis. City life had spread with the Greek language unevenly over the entire region. This section is intended to sketch what the Romans inherited by way of urbanization in the eastern provinces: its extent and depth, institutions, political life, and culture, and how far it was preserved and even extended and developed under their aegis as old forms responded to the demands made of them, both by the Romans and by peoples for whom city life was something new.

There had been cities in the beginning, in the east of what was to become the Roman Empire. Iran, Iraq, Syria, and Anatolia saw the phenomenon at the start; in the third millennium BC the city states of Sumer and Akkad were attaining sizes of nearly half a million hectares ($1\frac{1}{4}$ million acres) and populations estimated at more than 30,000 (Roux, 1980, 125). Further west the Aegean Bronze Age produced the palace architecture of Knossus, Mycenae, and Pylos, princely centres surrounded by mazes of houses and workshops.

These were not the cities, *poleis*, that made classical Greece, and only exceptionally, as at Athens, did they survive to develop into them. The *polis* was:

> a unit of people who a) occupied a territory containing as its central rallying point a town which held the seat of government and was itself usually clustered round a walled citadel (*acropolis*) which had originally contained the whole settlement and b) had autonomy in that government was provided by and from their own ranks, not from outside (Jeffery, 1976, 39).

The political centre of classical Athens was no longer the *acropolis* but the public buildings in the *agora* (market place). Political control likewise passed from kings to oligarchs and then to the people. Later Greek town planning, with its 'Hippodamian' grid of residential blocks incorporating the central *agora* and public buildings, canonized the change.

The architect Hippodamus was born about 500 BC at Miletus and into an area already well urbanized. Already in the tenth century Greek settlers from the mainland had come to the west coast of Asia Minor, regaining contact, as Ward-Perkins (1974, 11) indicates, with the architecture of the east. In a second wave of colonization, belonging to the seventh and sixth centuries BC, traditionally also to the eighth, the cities of mainland Greece and the west coast of Asia Minor were sending colonies to the Black Sea, the north coast of Africa, and even the western Mediterranean. Many of the foundations survived to become high-ranking cities in the Roman Empire: Sinope, a Milesian colony; Cyrene, sent from Thera; Syracuse, a Corinthian colony dated by Thucydides as early as 734; Massalia, settled by Phocians; and Byzantium, a colony of Megara.

The Greek sailors occupied coastal sites. How far they penetrated and controlled the hinterland depended on the success of the foundation, the terrain, and the attitude of the natives. In mainland Greece itself there remained regions such as Aetolia that were not urbanized and were organized on a tribal basis even in the fifth century BC (Thucydides I, 5, 3).

The conquests of Alexander gave a fresh impulse to the spread of the Greek city, whether as garrison, veteran settlement, trading centre, cultural beacon, or as an amalgam of all four. Cities named after him, including the great foundation of 332–1 BC on the Canopic mouth of the Nile, which by the first century BC was to have an estimated 300,000 free inhabitants, testify to that. Some were short-lived, but they showed how far afield, even in Afghanistan, a Greek city might be founded. The successors followed Alexander's example. Cities called after the hellenistic monarchs of Macedon, Syria, and Egypt proliferated, although the conferment of a name does not necessarily mean that the monarch responsible made any substantial real change in the community involved. Prime amongst these cities were Antioch on the Orontes, founded in 301, and Seleuceia on the Tigris, which belonged to the same period and was if anything larger than Alexandria. The fact that Antioch and Alexandria, as capital cities, enjoyed dignity beyond those of the normal *polis* under the hellenistic monarchs was to affect the behaviour of their inhabitants when they became subject to Roman rule.

Latecomers in the dramas acted out by the hellenistic monarchs before the advent of Rome at the end of the third century BC were the Attalids of western Asia Minor, but they played a leading part in the closing scenes and made their capital Pergamum into an outstanding example of the hellenistic city, its sculptures now the glory of the Staatliche Museen, Berlin. It is to Pergamum, its landscaped architecture and its sense of grandeur, that much of the monumental character of city architecture in the eastern provinces under the Principate is to be traced (Martin, 1956, 184).

The creations of classical colonists and hellenistic monarchs were not all made from scratch; villages could be developed or amalgamated (the amalgamation was called *synoecism*, joint settlement), or the constitution of one existing community might be changed: so Gerasa became Antioch on the Chrysorhoas. Nor were all the developments due to the initiative of monarchs and, later, emperors; the standing that the *polis* enjoyed throughout the Greek world roused the emulation of other communities. Wherever the Greek language penetrated it carried with it a built-in regard for the city, its amenities and institutions.

The institutional requirements of the *polis* were clear: annual magistrates, council, and people in assembly, no matter whether the magistrates were the eponymous *Stephanephorus* (Garland-wearer) and *Strategi* (Generals) or *Demiurge* (Artisan) and *Prytaneis* (Presidents), or how many sat on the council (450 at Ephesus, 500 at Athens, 600 at Marseilles (Massalia), but small cities would have been hard put to reach those figures), or how its composition and powers, and those of the assembly, were regulated. It was equally clear to Pausanias, writing in the second century AD (*Guide to Greece* 10, 4, 1), what amenities the city should possess. He was inclined to deny the title to Panopeus in Phocis, when it lacked state buildings, a training ground (*gymnasium*), theatre, *agora*, and piped water; but he had to admit that it had the organized administration to establish a boundary with its neighbours and to send delegations to the Phocian Assembly. It is this administration of a tract of country under its control that makes the city-state, and in an agricultural economy the amenities of the town are the products of the revenues from the country it administers.

Direct Roman control over the heartlands of Greek civilization, Achaea, Macedon, and western Asia Minor, dates from the third quarter of the second century BC. One by one other kingdoms and principalities fell into Rome's hands: Cyrene, bequeathed to her in 96 but not taken over until at least twenty years later; the kingdoms of Mithridates Eupator and Nicomedes, Pontus and Bithynia, annexed by Pompey in the late 60s, like the core of the Seleucid kingdom, which became the stipendiary province of Syria. The last and biggest plum hung on the bough, too big for any individual to be allowed to pick, until the very end of the Republic. Indeed its acquisition marked the beginning of Octavian's sole supremacy: Ptolemaic Egypt was finally annexed on the deaths of Antony and Cleopatra VII in 30 BC.

Only the first of Rome's acquisitions, mainland Greece and the province of Asia, were sufficiently urbanized not to present problems. Not all the territories were governed directly as provinces. Augustus allowed some of the smaller principalities to remain under their existing rulers, like Judaea under Herod the Great, or under new rulers, like the kingdom of the Amanus in Cilicia, returned in 20 BC to the son of King Tarcondimotus Philantonius, who had been loyal to his patron. Too insignificant to be dangerous, they were useful in controlling areas where, as Strabo says, a Roman governor could not always be on the spot with an army. In the absence of cities, their direct rule was a cheap alternative. But if these dependent rulers were too successful, or if they failed, or died without leaving a suitable heir, their domains might be annexed: this happened to Galatia in 25 BC after its king was killed fighting hill tribesmen, to Judaea in AD 6 when Herod's heir proved unacceptable to his subjects, to Cappadocia in AD 17, Commagene finally in AD 72, to the Nabataean kingdom in 106 when it was annexed as the province of Arabia.

The alternative was to found cities and charge them with the work of administration, with the maintenance of order at police level, and with keeping up roads and producing taxes. In the wake of his campaigns against the pirates and against Mithridates Eupator, Pompey, like Alexander and the Successors, had founded cities bearing his name or called by his title of Magnus. For reformed pirates he provided a settlement at Soli in Cilicia, restoring the town under the name Pompeiopolis. Then there were backward areas of Mithridates' kingdom, formerly administered directly by the royal officials, to be incorporated in the new province of Bithynia and Pontus. Cities, some with vast territories, were Pompey's solution. In Bithynia they were already in existence and the country could be divided between them; in the interior of Pontus Pompey had to develop three existing towns into cities, create three new cities by synoecism, and complete Mithridates' undertaking, Eupatoria, which became Magnopolis (cf. Jones, 1940, 57–8).

Caesar did not campaign extensively in the east, nor did he create new provinces there. It was the problems of Italy that brought about a new, peculiarly Roman, development in urbanization: the foundation of colonies. Laus Julia, founded in 44 BC on the site of ruined Corinth and a brilliant success, virtually guaranteed by its position (cf. Robinson's description, in the *Princeton Encyclopedia of Classical Sites*, of the development of its public buildings during the first three-quarters of a century after its foundation), was not a military settlement but was intended to provide land for dispossessed civilians and the landless poor of Rome and Italy. Exactly the same purpose was served by Octavian's colony at Knossus in Crete: dispossessed landowners of Capua were offered compensation in the colony of Julia Nobilis. Later, when Octavian had to find land for the veterans who had fought in the final civil wars of the Triumviral age, he founded military colonies, thus satisfying his troops' land hunger and at the same time setting up defences against rebels, for instance in central and southern Asia Minor, where the king of Galatia had been killed.

Colonization sometimes caused bad feeling, and an unofficial settlement of Caesar's at Heracleia in Pontus had been annihilated by natives. No such fate overtook the Augustan settlements; conditions were more stable, and the privilege of membership of the new colonies may have been extended to the original inhabitants in return for part of their land. It is a measure of the hold that the Greek language and the institutions of the *polis* had, even on comparatively unhellenized districts, that Greek began to intrude into the private and even the public inscriptions set up in the colonies and Greek games into their entertainments (cf. Levick, 1967, 130 ff.). Certainly the presence of legions and of unofficial settlements of Italian businessmen in the east had more effect on the culture and language of less hellenized areas than the foundation of military colonies, scattered as they were.

Augustus was the heir of Pompey as well as of Caesar, and a founder of Greek cities. Most famous is Nicopolis, on the site occupied by his army during the battle of Actium. Sweeping up the inhabitants of the neighbourhood, he brought them together in one *polis* which as an administrative centre replaced the Leagues of Aetolians and Acarnanians. Elsewhere in the east cities are found named Sebaste after him (Sebastus was used as the equivalent of Augustus) or incorporating the word in their titles. Permission for that would presumably be granted only if there had been some genuine, if minor, connection between emperor and city, a benefaction conferred on it by way of material aid, privilege, or exemption. Towns were also named in Augustus' honour by the dynasts, like Juliopolis on the borders of Galatia and Bithynia, the former Gordioucome (*come* means *village*), renamed by the condottiere Cleon Juliopolis; it remained insignificant, but other important foundations were made by potentates who knew what would win approval: Caesarea Maritima in Judaea, with its harbour Sebastus, founded near an old Phoenician port by Herod the Great and intended for Greeks since it contained the temples and monuments that made a Greek city and were repugnant to Jews.

In the east, then, the Romans, who had embarked on direct rule with an appalling act of vengeance, the destruction of Corinth in 146 BC and who had sacked Athens sixty years later in the course of restoring their supremacy after the retreat of Mithridates, came to be strenuous promoters of the *polis* and generous in acceding to petitions from native communities which sought advancement to that status. They lacked the means to implement a new system even if they could have devised one. Then there was their leaders' ingrained passion for glory: in the east at least Pompey, Caesar, Augustus, and all their successors were the heirs of Alexander and the hellenistic monarchs. Self-interest was enlightened by education; Roman politicians were versed in the literature that the cities, especially Athens, had produced. Two and a half centuries after the subjection of mainland Greece the younger Pliny wrote to a friend, sent there on a special mission, to remind him that he was dealing with Greeks in the truest sense and should show them respect.

With its long history of urbanization and hellenization, it is not surprising that the east could eventually show cities equal in numbers to the nine hundred of Africa, Iberia, and Italy combined (Hopkins, 1978, 70), more than three hundred of them in the province of Asia. The advance of urbanization after Augustus, leaving its traces in the nomenclature of the cities, may be charted in miniature in the hinterland of Cilicia and in Galatia on the central plateau of Anatolia (Jones, 1971, 204 and 119). In Cilicia the tribal districts that had probably been under the Tarcondimotid dynasty became the territories of three cities: Augusta, founded in AD 20, Neronia (52), and Flaviopolis, which took the family name of Vespasian in 74. Amongst the three Galatian tribes it is a change of nomenclature that Jones notices. On coins and inscriptions they began by referring to themselves by their tribal names, Tectosages, Trocmi, and Tolistobogii; then the names of the towns in their territories (old Phrygian centres; Pessinus was devoted to the cult of the Great Mother) were brought in: the coins come to be ascribed to Ancyra of the Tectosages, and so on; finally the tribal name itself could be omitted.

The developments would not have been possible without heavy capital investment in the cities, for buildings and organization, in which both emperors and provincials were involved. The part consciously played by the government both directly and indirectly is easier to distinguish than efforts made by the cities and their inhabitants on the basis of increasing prosperity in the Roman peace.

The central government could directly and materially affect the welfare of communities, if only marginally in most cases, by founding new cities, adorning existing ones, maintaining them and restoring them after disaster, as the senate in AD 17 relieved twelve cities of Asia ruined by earthquake and as Domitian in 93–4 restored a portico at Megalopolis in Arcadia after it had been destroyed by fire (McCrum and Woodhead, 1961, 436). It could also operate indirectly by conferring grants of status and privilege. It was the more important cities in a province that became assize centres and so benefited not only from the prestige which that position brought but also from the material advantages of having:

> an unnumbered throng of people, litigants, jurymen, orators, princes, attendants, slaves, pimps, muleteers, hucksters, harlots, and artisans; consequently, not only can those who have goods to sell obtain the highest prices, but nothing in the city is out of work, neither the teams nor the houses nor the women.

So Dio of Prusa on the Phrygian assize centre of Apameia-Celaenae; not surprisingly it had six well-known and nine 'inconsiderable' cities attached to it. Similar advantages accrued to a city that had been granted permission, by the emperor, to hold 'Sacred' Games ranking with those of Delphi and Olympia; the importance of its games is stressed by Strabo in his description of Nicopolis. Likewise in AD 26 there was fierce competition between eleven cities of Asia for the privilege of building a temple to the emperor and so becoming *neocorus* or temple warden as Pergamum already was, great though the capital outlay and cost of maintenance must have been. Both the position of assize centre and possession of a temple of the provincial cult were bones of contention between Tarsus and other cities of Cilicia. So Rome could exert its power and regulate the flow of wealth to some extent.

Profound peace, interrupted only by local outbreaks and lasting in the eastern provinces from the battle of Actium until the civil war between Septimius Severus and Pescennius Niger in 193–4, was the factor underlying the efflorescence of the cities. More potent, if Hopkins (1980) is to be believed, was the imposition of taxes, which helped to monetize the economy; but that would only be true where dues were not payable in kind. Certainly the conquest of new provinces such as Dacia and their opening up as markets produced more wealth for subject areas of longer standing; so too did the establishment of a stable market in the form of legions stationed on the lower Danube, on the Euphrates, and within the provinces of Syria, Judaea, and Egypt. What emperors could do was to recognize and marginally to enhance achievements that the prevailing conditions of the Empire made possible for the cities. Nero 'freed' the Greeks and was their declared friend; but he could not improve the condition of Greece.

Up to a point the Empire was an economic unit, but local conditions varied; one city might be outstripped, even swallowed up by another, as Myus was by its huge neighbour Miletus, and over whole provinces new factors, such as the placing of a garrison army or the rerouting of a main channel of communication, might have a profound effect. The depopulation of Greece was a subject of concern to Polybius in the second century BC and at the end of Augustus' reign the provinces of Achaea and Macedonia were complaining of their poverty and their inability to meet their tax obligations. Nero's speech, and Dio of Prusa's essay on Euboea paint the same picture. Remote now from the Balkan legions and unable to compete in the production of wine and oil with Italy, Asia Minor, and Spain, Greece became something of a backwater.

It was in the early part of Vespasian's reign that administrative changes were made that reflected and contributed to a gradual increase in the importance of the Danubian provinces and Bithynia-Pontus, though not necessarily at the expense of Asia. With Commagene finally annexed and Cappadocia united with Galatia in a province guarded by legions, and Dacia becoming a province in 106, there came new economic opportunities. As Pliny's correspondence with Trajan shows, the cities of Bithynia and Pontus were not able to cope with the improvement in their fortunes, and there was an outbreak of ill-considered expenditure on new and restored amenities; an aqueduct, theatre, gymnasium, and bath are mentioned within the space of two letters from the governor and Trajan's replies. Taken with the dissensions apparent from the *Discourses* of Dio of Prusa (38–50), it suggests heightened rivalry and perhaps the advance of new men; Pliny mentions the possibility of admitting the sons of commoners to the city councils.

Granted local variations, it is generally admitted that it was in the first three quarters of the second century that the eastern provinces enjoyed the time of their greatest prosperity. The century opened under a philhellene emperor, Trajan, but it was Hadrian who ended the war with Parthia and who showed his awareness of the importance of the provinces, not only by issuing a series of coins devoted to them, but also by his travels. Twice he toured the eastern provinces, offering the cities easy access to himself and the chance to put in petitions. It was Hadrian who resolved the long-standing and troublesome dispute caused at Aezani in Phrygia by the occupation of land belonging to the temple of Zeus by private squatters. His foundations in Mysia were of the traditional kind, offering the tribes of the district an opportunity of city life (Jones, 1971, 89). But the individuality of the man, and the scope it was allowed, shows in his most famous foundation, Antinoopolis in Egypt, on a site chosen for its proximity to the spot where his friend drowned in 130. That the memorial should take the form of a *polis*, one of the few in Egypt outside Alexandria, speaks loudly for the significance of the city in his mind. The settlers, 'New Hellenes', were Greeks from the other cities and veterans from the Egyptian legions, and the legal system of the city was modelled perhaps with self-conscious archaism, on that of the original Greek settlement at Naucratis. The intellectual Hadrian's special care was Athens, although he was able to help the whole of mainland Greece except Megara, and he acceded to the request of its citizens that he should draft a fresh law code modelled on those of Draco and Solon (Eusebius-Jerome, *Chronicon*, under AD 122); but besides indulging Athenian ruling circles in their nostalgia and their concern for privilege, Hadrian gave attention to practical matters. His oil law provided that olive-growers were to reserve one third of their produce for public purchase at market price, which may have been less than export price. Hadrian showed himself a traditionalist in another way when he founded a Roman colony, Aelia Capitolina, at Jerusalem (Jones, 1971, 277): like Gaius Gracchus at Carthage and Caesar at Corinth, he was replacing an enemy city that the Romans had destroyed with a Roman one. The new colony had a large territory and Jews were completely excluded from it; indeed it helped to provoke yet another Jewish uprising.

The material development of cities in which the emperor had no personal involvement illustrates the rising prosperity of Asia Minor and other areas during his reign and that of Antoninus Pius. It was under Hadrian that a new complex containing a colonnaded *agora* and *temenos* (sacred enclosure) of Zeus, with his magnificent new temple, was begun at Aezani, not only transforming the city but inspiring a whole school of masons there. Continuity of architectural development was assured by the conservatism of Greek architecture, on which Ward-Perkins insists (1974, 12–13): materials, architectural themes, and the use of established building types – temple, theatre, council building, colonnade, and, from the fourth century onwards, gymnasium – all contributed, and matched the conservatism of social and political life. But there were novelties. It was under Hadrian that Perge in Pamphylia was able to convert its central avenue into the axial colonnaded street that is noted by Ward-Perkins as being, with the *nymphaeum* or tall fountain building, one of the characteristic developments of oriental architecture under the Empire; aqueducts too were an innovation of the first and second centuries as far as the east was concerned. At Perge the street, with a central water channel, runs toward the low acropolis from the south gate (the vistas are still impressive), and the gate was adorned with a triple arch. Such monumental constructions at

the end of colonnaded streets, breaking the severity of the hellenistic plan, are characteristic of the first and second centuries AD. Perge's neighbour Attaleia was one of the
earlier cities to embark on reconstruction, with the help of the Emperor Claudius; but
it seems to have been anticipated by Sardis, where the colonnaded street is said to have
been built *c.* 20–40. Some developments took many years: those at Gerasa, begun under
Vespasian, were apparently not completed until the time of the Severi. Large-scale
schemes of reconstruction and development could involve complex negotiations with
the owners of buildings scheduled for demolition and rouse intense resentment and
jealousy, as Dio of Prusa discovered when he embarked on the construction of a portico
at Prusa some time before 101:

> One might have supposed that the Propylaea at Athens were being tampered with,
> or the Parthenon . . . instead of the disgraceful, ridiculous ruins. . . . There were
> some who were distressed to see the signs of their former poverty and ill-repute
> disappearing, who, far from being interested in the columns which were rising,
> or in the eaves of the roof, or in the shops under construction in a different quarter,
> were interested only in preventing you ever feeling superior than that crew (of
> men who bore you malice).

It required confidence to invest substantial amounts of capital in them, and substantial
capital to invest.

It was fittingly in the reign of Hadrian's successor Antoninus Pius that Aelius
Aristides delivered his Panegyric on Rome to an appreciative Roman audience. He was
able to speak of the world as 'filled' with cities, some founded by Rome, others fostered
by her; and of cities so clustered that a man could travel through two or three on the
same day, as if passing through sections of one and the same city. A more tangible
and trustworthy index of prosperity in the east than Aristides' effusion is provided by
the issues of local coinage, which provided change, supplemented the imperial coinage,
and facilitated local and regional dealings. More important perhaps it was a sign of
local autonomy and an opportunity for magnates to demonstrate generosity by supplying
the requisite metal. In Asia Minor the number of authorities coining rose from 154
under the Julio-Claudians to 246 in the period from the Flavians to the Antonines
(Broughton, in Frank, 1938–41, volume 4, 715 and 746). What for the cities was a
glorious efflorescence was for Rome the satisfyingly smooth working of an administrative device. The cities did Rome's work for her, running country districts, so that the
natives of villages were considered natives of the community to which the village was
assigned; maintaining roads, at first local, eventually arterial, and servicing the imperial
post; providing medical and educational facilities and above all collecting direct taxes.

When a governor was not available on a visit of inspection or on his judicial circuit
he could be approached by envoys armed with letters. So in time of famine under

Domitian the authorities of the colony of Antioch towards Pisidia approached the governor of Galatia for help, and he issued an edict ordering grain stocks to be declared and fixing the price to be charged for grain in the colony. The emperor too was frequently approached by embassies: diplomacy survived from the period of independence to a time when cities enjoyed only limited autonomy, and embassies to the emperor are named by Plutarch among the enterprises that still required fire and daring.

Theoretically the cities enjoyed various relations with the suzerain, according to their status. Some possessed treaties with Rome that went back to the time before Roman control over the east was known to be permanent. New treaties were still granted and Augustus even gave one to his creation of Nicopolis, but any treaty could be torn up if a city gave offence. Other communities were officially 'free', indeed whole areas could be so, as with the Lycian federation until 43. Greece had been declared free by T. Quinctius Flamininus in 196 BC after the defeat of Antiochus, and was so again in AD 67 by Nero. Freedom meant the absence of a provincial governor; it did not necessarily carry immunity from tribute, which was an additional special privilege. Without the protection of a treaty, freedom was even more vulnerable; the offence of the Lycians was the killing (murder or execution?) of Roman citizens. Cyzicus cost its freedom twice in the first century of the principate in 20 BC and again in AD 25.

These privileges, like lesser ones such as the right of giving asylum to fugitives or of housing a temple of the imperial cult, had to be pleaded for in the presence of emperor or senate. The patronage of influential Romans, or the favour of the imperial family, was of great importance for a city. The fact that Sparta was in the clientship of the Claudian family earned it special attention in the first hundred years of the principate; Ilium was lucky to find one of her Roman descendants to plead for a grant of immunity in the senate in AD 53: none other than the seventeen-year-old Nero.

For a lesser man to secure remission of tribute, the promise of a building from the emperor, or permission to add to the number of city councillors, as Dio of Prusa did for his city, was a coup that added greatly to his prestige and much easier to bring off if he enjoyed the favour of the emperor or even of the governor. Many of the links that bound cities to the ruling class of Rome were of this personal nature, but the Romans also had a consistent policy, put into practice after the struggle with the Achaeans in 146 BC, of maintaining the supremacy of the wealthy upper classes in the cities. These men were the natural allies of the Roman oligarchy, and it was easier to deal with few than with a changing many. In return for helping to maintain order, 'guarding the cities' in Aristides' words, and for superintending the performance of Rome's work, the wealthy classes were protected and kept in power; in Bithynia Pompey had arranged for membership of city councils to be permanent and to depend on adlection by an official, equivalent to the Roman censor. It was alien to Greek practice, led to the development of an hereditary curial class, and to class antagonism within the cities. The apathetic populace of Nicomedia watched private houses and two public buildings being destroyed by fire, since the governor was forbidden by Trajan to raise a fire brigade of 150 men for fear of it turning into a political organization, easy to supervise though they would have been. In times of famine, which were not infrequent in Mediterranean lands and which for inland cities like Antioch towards Pisidia could not be remedied by imports from the sea, the people roused themselves and could attack their rulers; that was what happened in Aspendus in Pamphylia under Tiberius when there was nothing on sale in the market but vetch and the rich were hoarding the grain. When Antioch on the Orontes was betrayed to the Persians in AD 253 by a city councillor, who was also leader of the lower classes in the city, decent people fled, but the masses remained behind under Persian rule.

The antagonism may be seen in terms of town and country as well as of rich and poor. In the territories for which they were responsible the cities offered amenities and prestige for those who lived in them; outside the walls it was very much a question of subsistence. It was not that land was taxed by the city, but that income derived from the land was spent in or on it. How important manufacture, commerce, and shipping were as means of amassing wealth in the ancient world is a matter of controversy (see most recently Pleket, 1983). The information provided by ancient authors and the epigraphic record is incidental and sporadic: they were not a subject for polite letters and in relatively few cities did the inhabitants make a practice of recording their occupations on the monuments. Hopkins (1978, 72) notes the insignificant city of Corycus on the coast of Cilicia as an exception, counting 100 different trades there. Manufacture was closely linked to the produce of the soil; the carpets of Hierapolis came from the backs of the sheep that abounded in Phrygia, as did the woollen garments of Laodiceia. The activities offered by Dio of Prusa as 'respectable' alternatives to linen-working at Tarsus were those of dyer, cobbler, and carpenter (34, 23).

The basic producers, even when they were free citizen peasants and not officially treated as a separate class in society or even as aliens, like the Tarsus linen-workers, belonged to what came to be officially recognized as the humbler classes; even if they were permitted to take part in the limited political life of the assemblies to the extent of having a vote in them, they were debarred by law from membership of the city councils and tenure of magistracies.

It was the city, and the wealth, culture, and political expertise it conferred, that took easterners into the Roman senate in increasing numbers. Not surprisingly, they came in the greatest strength from the cities of western Asia Minor: nearly a third of the total from the Greek east. When they entered the House they did not necessarily turn their backs on their native cities; the consular Cassius Dio eventually retired to his Bithynian estates. Local patriotism played an even larger part in the lives of men who had not embarked on imperial service, while for the poorer city-dwellers it provided an escape from their insignificance as individuals. It did not preclude resentment against the upper class and their Roman protectors, rather the reverse. Cities cultivated a long historical memory, going back to a time when many were still real democracies and when what really mattered was relations with the city on the other side of the mountains. It was natural that ancient cities like Athens and Megara should retain these feelings, so violently indeed, that it seemed to one travelling sophist, as if Athens had only just passed the decree against Megara that opened the Peloponnesian War, a decree that was half a millennium old in his time (Philostratus, *Lives of the Sophists*, 529). Newer cities such as Nicaea, founded at the end of the fourth century BC, but cultivating fantasies of an earlier and more distinguished origin, were proud too, the more so when confronted by upstarts like mid-third century Nicomedia. The rivalry between these two cities, for which they were chided by Dio at the beginning of the second century, was still alive in the middle of the fifth. Augustus had allowed the site of the provincial temple to Rome and himself to be placed at Nicomedia, Nicaea being allowed only the second prize of a shrine to Caesar, who was dead and so less helpful. There was an attempt to deal fairly in the matter of titles: Nicomedia was the metropolis, Nicaea 'first city' of the province. But Domitian also permitted Nicomedia the title 'first'. Not content with that, the Nicomedians tried at first unsuccessfully to deprive Nicaea of its title, until, in 193–4, Nicaea supported the losing claimant to the throne, Pescennius Niger, against Septimius Severus, in part because of its very rivalry with Nicomedia. Then the words 'first city' were systematically hammered out of the monumental inscriptions that bore them. Even later at the Council of Chalcedon in 451 Nicomedia and Nicaea were still at loggerheads, although the rights they were claiming had undergone a metamorphosis; Nicaea was challenging Nicomedia's sole right as a metropolis to consecrate bishops.

The disadvantages of conflict, repeatedly pointed out by sophists and philosophers, were real; energy was wasted on slanging-matches, money on embassies to governor and emperor. Vespasian limited to three the number of envoys that a city might send him. There was the cost of real fighting in time of civil war and Herodian's narrative reveals that it was not only Nicaea and Nicomedia that were involved in the struggle of 193–4, but also Tyre and Berytus, Laodiceia and Antioch in Syria. Then there was the ease with which unscrupulous governors were able to play off one side against the other for their own purposes, as Dio of Prusa warned the people of Nicomedia. The emperor too might be drawn in, together with his favourites.

But the effects of inter-city rivalry were by no means all deleterious. The cities could not normally fight, so they tried to outdo each other, not only in mere titles, but in magnificence and amenity, to the advantage of their inhabitants, often to the lowest as well as the highest. Nor did the money go only on buildings, statuary, and tips. Cultural life flourished, especially in the form of the oratory of the Second Sophistic; music filled the *odeia* that many cities possessed as well as their theatres, while athletics survived the increasing, and much deplored, taste for the gladiatorial games and wild-beast shows that formed part of the imperial cult. Moreover, athletics and literary culture, though essentially city-based and inculcated in all youths under training (*ephebes*) by masters and professors supervised by the city *gymnasiarch*, were forces for unity. Men competed as individuals, though their city of origin was what identified them, and athletes and professional musicians were members of officially recognized international guilds. Sophists, as we have seen, were among the strongest advocates of harmony; even at Megara the visiting sophist Marcus was able to persuade the assembly to let the Athenians participate in the Lesser Pythian Games. The *Homonoia* (Concord) which they advocated was sometimes attained and celebrated on the coinage. A formal treaty was not implied, and the basis might be political, cultural, or economic co-operation between the elites of the cities involved; distinguished men might become citizens of more than one city, and ties were formed by intermarriage.

Another unifying and mediating factor was the provincial assemblies that existed in one form or another throughout the east, sometimes with more than one to a province, as in Bithynia-Pontus (cf. Millar, 1977, 385 ff.). The Lycian Assembly was well-established and had a serious function, that of guiding the federation of cities that made up the League. Other associations, like that of 'The Greeks in Asia' had less clear-cut functions but were used to dealing with governors and senate. Under the principate these organizations, and others that developed, found a new and most important role in maintaining good relations with the emperor and his family through homage offered to him and to the goddess Roma. They could also organize joint prosecutions of offending governors, relieving individual members of a high proportion of the heavy cost, and mediate between members in dispute. An inscription from Cierium in Thessaly reveals that the governor of Moesia, some time before 35, referred a boundary dispute between Cierium and Metropolis to the Thessalian Assembly; at least 334 votes were cast, revealing that some members, presumably the larger cities as in the Lycian League, had more than one vote.

In sustaining their own position within the city, and their city's within the Assembly, local notables incurred heavy expenditure; they had to satisfy their fellow citizens by providing amenities such as oil for the *gymnasium* and even durable gifts like buildings, or impress the governor and perhaps the emperor, and so outdo their rivals. It was only while the upper classes could maintain themselves in comfort while continuing to meet the cost of office that the system could continue to work satisfactorily for those associated with it. In the course of the second century danger signs began to appear. First, Roman concern for the mismanagement of city finances, which was no new thing in Greek cities, but aggravated because one class was permanently in power and had to pay for the privilege. From Domitian's reign onwards the emperors began to send curators (the Greek word used means 'accountants') to the cities not as permanent officials but from time to time (cf. Burton, 1979). Then came a new office within the cities, that of the 'Twenty (or Ten) leading men', who were responsible for the production of tax dues. There must always have been individuals who preferred to keep their funds intact. But the number and universality of the measures, that began to be taken to enforce the performance of civic duties (*liturgies*) and the holding of civil office, together with, by Ulpian's time, the enforced return of runaway councillors to the cities to which they belonged (*Digest* 50, 2, 1), show the trend, as do the inscriptions that begin to treat the voluntary holding of office as a merit not a privilege.

The change coincides, as it should, with the beginnings of economic difficulty. In the second half of the second century the defence of the empire became less sure; a Scythian tribe penetrated deep into mainland Greece and was fought off by local levies. The security of the countryside within was requiring more attention and the cities were appointing officials called Irenarchs and Paraphylaces, who had bodies of mounted policemen, *Diogmitae* ('pursuers'), under their command. In the civil wars which opened the reign of Septimius Severus and which were conducted over a large area of the east, the cities suffered, and some were afterwards punished, although others benefited from the claims they had established on the emperor's generosity.

Severus' efforts at restoration and defence, including the settlement of veterans in Mesopotamia and the grant of colonial status to Tyre and other cities (Jones, 1971, 220–1), could not stem the difficulties that beset them in the third century. The invasions of Greece and Asia Minor must have ruined crops that demanded long cultivation, and the war and the secession of provinces would have disrupted trade. Above all, the burden of taxation required to support the armies became ever more crushing. The steep decline in the number of inscriptions commemorating individuals and the benefits they had conferred vividly illustrates the decline in prosperity.

But decline was uneven, as progress had been. C. Roueché has suggested that it was because of the relative advance of Caria and Phrygia that the province of Asia was partitioned in the middle of the century (1981, 103 ff.); only under separate governors would the districts involved have received the attention they demanded. The Upper Tembris valley in Phrygia abounds in documents that refer to its rural activities and produce. Yet towns were few in this area, which was partly given over to imperial estates. The inhabitants had a strong agricultural economy with little costly superstructure to support. Besides, they were away from the main routes through the peninsula and escaped the burden of supporting the armies on their way to and from the eastern frontier.

The emperors did not waver in their commitment to urbanization, and even in the fourth century were conferring city status on the deserving communities of central Asia Minor in exemplary terms; but besides these stretches of country that were only lightly touched by city life, there were whole provinces that resisted or were thought unsuitable for it. More ruthlessly and less efficiently than their predecessors the Ptolemies, the Romans exploited the natives of Egypt, over concern for the corn supply and out of inertia. Alexandria was not allowed the council of a Greek *polis* until Septimius Severus granted it; then the old *metropoleis* were also granted councils, selected from the élite members of the *gymnasia* who were to appoint city magistrates and most *nome* officials; the cities became responsible for the administration of the nomes, but the concession to Greek sentiment did not succeed in galvanizing the administration into further efforts.

In Judaea the Seleucids had met resistance to hellenization and there was hostility to towns on the part of country folk; Jesus had no time for them and Tiberias was an object of hatred at the time of its foundation by Herod Antipas. Gradually Judaea was broken up between city territories, but they were alien foundations imposed on its intractable population.

Outside the heartland of hellenization in Greece and Asia Minor lay cultures which the peace imposed by Rome allowed to burgeon into productive hybrids. Besides the developments in philosophy at Alexandria that culminated in Plotinus, there was the school of Roman law that flourished in Berytus and the development in Tiberias of the authoritative version of the Mishnah under Rabbi Judah ha-Nasi. The caravan cities of Petra, Bostra, and Palmyra on the edge of the Empire had different functions and interests from those of normal Greek cities, although they possessed some of their amenities, such as theatres. Their language was Aramaic; Palmyra's irregular city plan, the dress, nomenclature, housing, cults, and funerary monuments of its inhabitants were all alien. The direction taken by western influences can be seen in the words borrowed from Greek and Latin; twenty-five of the fifty Greek words are concerned with political life, ten with art and architecture.

But it is Ward-Perkins' description of Dura-Europus (1974, 20–1) that gives a dynamic picture of the rise and fall of the tide of Greek city life in the far east. A Seleucid foundation of about 300 BC, it had a space reserved for the *agora* at the centre of the Hippodamian plan, but although the walls and fortress were well maintained by all its occupiers, Seleucid, Parthian, and Roman, the projected public buildings were never completed; the city centre occupied only half the area allotted to it:

> The temples of the last three centuries were all traditionally Eastern buildings dedicated to oriental divinities, including for good measure a synagogue and a church, and by AD 250 the monumental buildings of the agora had been engulfed by the warren-like structures of an oriental bazaar.

In the heartlands of hellenization the late Empire saw an evening up in the distribution of cities (Jones, 1940, 89 ff.). In Thrace and Bithynia-Pontus, where the few had been made responsible for the administration of large tracts of country, new cities emerged; urbanized Greece, Macedonia, and Galatia suffered a severe decline in the number of cities, while in areas remote from invasion, like Lycia and Cilicia, the number remained stable. In the well-urbanized areas smaller cities could not maintain their councils, or guarantee imperial revenue; elsewhere what cities there were found it difficult to manage the districts for which they were responsible. It was superior resources, combined with a long urban tradition, that protected western Asia Minor from entering the Byzantine age with a net loss of no more than one-fifth on the Augustan tally of cities.

CHAPTER 13

·URBANIZATION·IN·ITALY· ·AND·THE·WESTERN· ·EMPIRE·

J. F. Drinkwater

The cities of the Roman west varied greatly in their origins, importance and material splendour. Nevertheless, they manifested a consistent family likeness, both in their layout and in the amenities which they provided (Berchem, 1977, 25). They represented an aggressively homogeneous culture which stretched from Scotland to the Sahara. The very incongruity of the remains of certain Roman cities, in surroundings which today seem utterly alien to them, serves as a dramatic reminder of the penetration of Graeco-Roman civilization into the lands around the western Mediterranean and occasionally finds an echo in the east (p. 332) (pl. 13.1).

The characteristic features of the western Roman city, alike with many in the east, comprised, first of all, a geometric, chequer-board street-grid (fig. 13.1). Within the blocks of land (*insulae*) thus formed were expensive and extensive complexes of public buildings and monuments. Chief amongst them were those which were used for administration – the law-court (*basilica*) which was also available as a general assembly-hall, and the local senate-house (*curia*). These were grouped around the *forum*, an open paved or gravelled space, bounded by porticoes as protection against rain or excessive heat (fig. 13.2). Frequently associated with the forum-complex was a temple, the focus of civic religious activity, in and around which were worshipped either Jupiter, Juno and Minerva, the 'Capitoline Triad' of Republican Rome, the reigning emperor, his family and imperial ancestors (the 'Imperial Cult'; Part 10), or some major indigenous deity in Graeco-Roman form (pl. 13.2). Other temples, for other deities, were scattered through the city, which was regarded by its inhabitants as a community of the divine, the living and the dead. The last were found in cemeteries which lined the main roads leading from the city. Their remains were interred beyond the sacred boundary (*pomerium*) of the settlement of the living, but the prominence of their tombs, often richly sculptured and inscribed, must have constantly brought them to the minds of

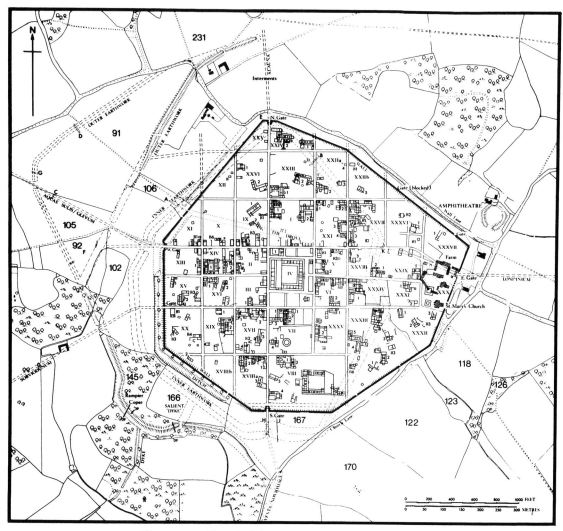

Figure 13.1 Plan of Silchester, Britain (*revised Fulford, 1984*)

their successors (pl. 13.3; Part 9, Chapter 29). Elsewhere within the *pomerium* were those lavishly equipped leisure-centres of the Graeco-Roman world, the bath-buildings, of which every self-respecting western Roman community would have had at least one, and usually several (figs 13.3 and 13.19). There were also additional centres of amusement and resort in the shape of theatres for drama, mime and perhaps even music-hall turns (Février *et al.*, 1980, 294), amphitheatres for blood-sports and combat and circuses for chariot-racing (pl. 13.4). A number of streets and public buildings were adorned with fountains and, of course, the baths too made direct use of great quantities of water.

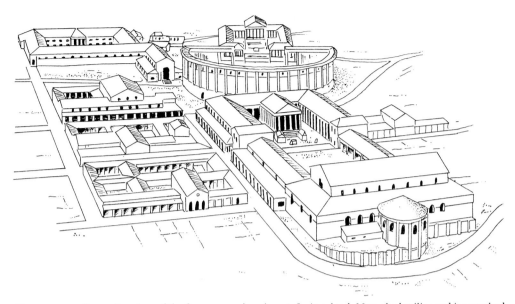

Figure 13.2 Reconstruction of the forum complex, Augst, Switzerland. Note the basilica and its attached curia in the foreground – the seat of the self-perpetuating local aristocratic oligarchy (*after Boethius and Ward-Perkins*)

The supply and disposal of this water required the construction of elaborate systems of leats, conduits, siphons, arcaded aqueducts, settling-basins, and mains, together with equally efficient networks of drains and sewers, which also made feasible the provision of large public latrines (pls 13.5 and 13.6). However, it should be stressed that, despite such facilities, much water for domestic use continued to be drawn from private wells and cisterns. The main streets were often graced by porticoes, monumental gateways and triumphal arches (pl. 13.7). Private building was at its grandest in the homes of the well-to-do, decorated with mosaics and frescoes, and built around one or more internal courtyard-gardens (fig. 13.4). The dwellings of ordinary people were much smaller and more simple – often just a range of rooms running back from the street, with business-premises at the front and workshop-facilities in a back-yard (fig. 13.5). However, the enterprising rich were not averse to letting the ground-floor fronts of their town properties as commercial and manufacturing premises (fig. 13.6). Taverns and brothels were popular businesses. More respectable professional and commercial activities, for example associated with the law, and banking, were usually accommodated within the forum-complex, and traders could sometimes find additional public space in secondary forums, or market-halls (*macella*) (fig. 13.7). Noisome or dangerous activities, such as tanning and the firing of pottery, were often confined to the fringes of the city. Most private building was single- or double-storied; high-rise accommodation, such as is heard of in Rome, and is still dramatically on view at Ostia, was very much

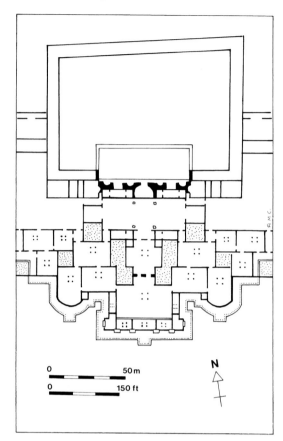

Figure 13.3 Plan of the 'Barbarathermen', Trier, Germany. The baths of this major provincial city, though simpler in design and decoration, are very similar in size to the Baths of Caracalla (*after Février*)

a metropolitan phenomenon, seldom to be found in provincial cities (fig. 13.8).

The fact that it is possible to describe the physical characteristics of the cities of the Roman west virtually according to a checklist should not induce us to suppose that they were mindlessly mass-produced according to some uniform specification. Historical, economic and political forces combined to make all settlements different in status and aspect. Rome, 'The City' par excellence, was herself unique – an immense sprawl of streets and buildings which it was impossible to recast into a more orderly shape. She outstripped every other urban centre, west and east, in the number of her inhabitants and the splendour of her public buildings. Within the Italian peninsula there were other cities whose development was also long and eventful, as exemplified in the palimpsest which was Pompeii (fig. 13.9). Beyond Italy, a city's place in the imperial hierarchy played an important part in its growth. In terms of size and magnificence it would have been impossible to have confused Silchester (fig. 13.1), the small national capital of the

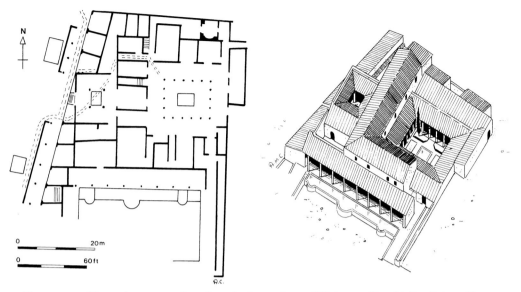

Figure 13.4   Plan and reconstruction of a peristyle-type house ('Maison au Dauphin') at Vaison, France
(after Février)

British Atrebates, with Carthage, seat of the proconsular governor of the province of Africa. Even cities of very similar ranking would have been easy to tell apart thanks to the continued exploitation of vernacular styles of building and materials. The underlying archaeological repertoire was solidly Graeco-Roman, but this did not prevent the occurrence of distinct regional variations, as exemplified in the forum-complex, with Italianate African, enclosed Gallic and military British designs (figs 13.10, 13.11 and 13.12).

However, Roman technological and administrative skills permitted the surveying and development of city-sites on a much grander scale than had earlier been practised in the west. Despite individual differences it is clear that there was a strong conception of an ideal form which went to make most western cities look generally similar. The most striking manifestation of this was the striving after an orthogonal street-system.

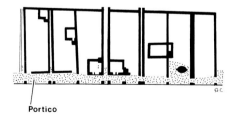

Portico

Figure 13.5   Shops, workshops and houses along a street front at Alise-Ste-Reine, France. Scale 1:100
(after Février)

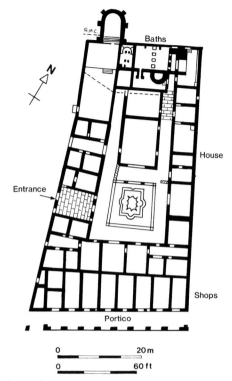

Figure 13.6   Large house fronted by shops at Volubilis, Morocco (*after Clavel and Lévêque*)

Wherever possible priority was given to creating a street-plan which was impeccably correct in two dimensions, what has been usefully termed 'perfect horizontality' (Février *et al.*, 1980, 266–7), through the levelling of ridges, the filling of hollows and the terracing of hillsides (pl. 13.8). However, such ambitions required virgin sites and suitable topographies to keep costs within reasonable bounds. These advantages rarely occurred

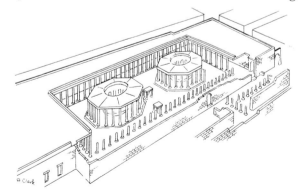

Figure 13.7   Reconstruction of the market-hall at Lepcis Magna (*after Picard*)

350

Figure 13.8   Apartment building with cookhouse on the ground floor at Ostia, Italy (*after Boethius and Ward-Perkins*)

together, so the numbing regularity of the classic gridiron is a rarity, even in many colonial settlements. Relatively few western cities were, in the end, able to display perfect horizontality, but fewer still had the courage to dispense with the ideal altogether. Most settled for a compromise, and it is this which, perhaps most of all, gives them their family likeness.

It should not be forgotten though that the fabric of the Roman city was but an expression of the cultural values of those who caused it to be built. The ubiquitous similarity of the cities of the western Empire was the mark of a strong and self-assured imperial power, ready to impose its own ideas on others. It also reflects the willingness of western peoples to co-operate in the process of their own romanization. Rome con-

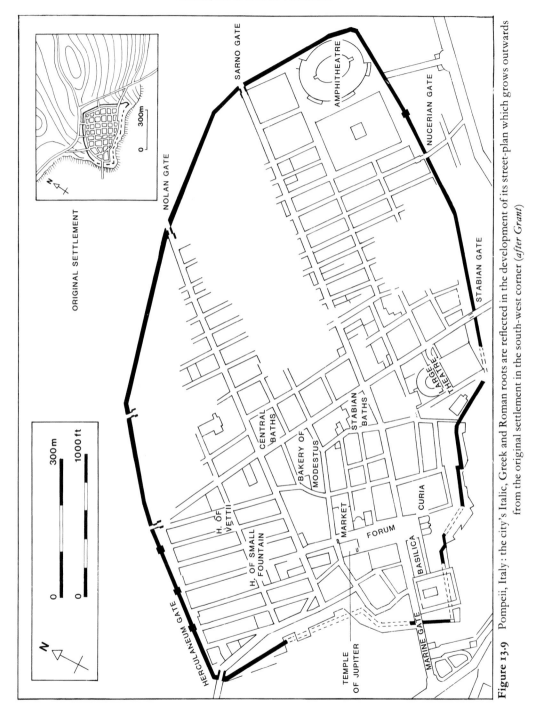

Figure 13.9 Pompeii, Italy: the city's Italic, Greek and Roman roots are reflected in the development of its street-plan which grows outwards from the original settlement in the south-west corner (*after Grant*)

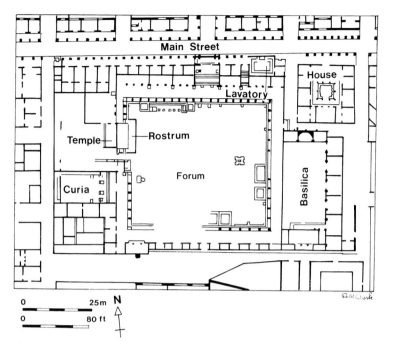

Figure 13.10   Forum complex of Timgad, Algeria: the curia, basilica and temple are independent
elements (*after Boethius and Ward-Perkins*)

sidered cities to be essential for the existence of her Empire, and its well-being. She
borrowed and developed Greek ideas on the theory of urbanization, as is seen in
Vitruvius' *De architectura* of the late first century BC, and, in practice, her ruling elite
encouraged as a matter of course the creation of cities in those parts of her Empire
which they considered to be backward in this respect as is seen in the activity of Agricola,
governor of Britain, in AD 79 (Tacitus, *Agricola* 21) (fig. 13.13). Such an attitude was
derived from an historical experience common to many cultures around the eastern and
central Mediterranean, where discrete riverine and coastal sites had encouraged the
growth of permanent human communities to no more than city-state size, thus generat-
ing the importance of the central city. Rome herself was the product of this process,
and, as her power and awareness grew, her traditional respect for the city-community
was particularly reinforced by her absorption of the ideal of the classical Greek *polis*,
and the common popular and educated opinion that this was the only acceptable location
for civilized human activity (p. 43 above). Indeed, the extent of a people's progress
towards the establishment of a city-state became Rome's standard measure for its level
of development. Thus when Rome sought to pacify the west by persuading it to enjoy
the fruits of her civilization she first sought to establish city-states there. The concrete
indication of the promotion and success of this policy was the founding and embellish-

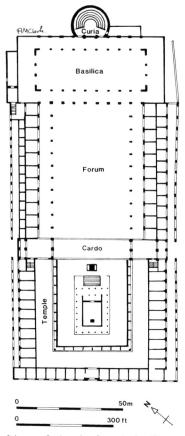

Figure 13.11 Forum complex of Augst, Switzerland: curia, basilica and temple have been brought into the same orientation (*after Duval*)

ment of the central cities in prescribed Graeco-Roman fashion. An acceptable city was hard proof of the existence of an acceptable city-state: 'The aesthetic-architectural definition was shorthand for a political and social definition' (Finley, 1973, 124). However, this is not the whole of the story because there were other motives involved in Rome's encouragement of the western cities. Above all, even when the central government of the empire was increasingly revealing itself as an autocratic monarchy, the city-state was seen as the natural unit of administration (Ward-Perkins, 1974, 29). Indeed, the Romans continued to view their possessions as an aggregate of autonomous city-states under the hegemony of the supreme city-state, which was Rome. This attitude enabled them to delegate most of the responsibility for the day-to-day administration of provincial affairs, including even the collection of imperial taxes, to the multiplicity of self-perpetuating oligarchic regimes which ran the city-states of the empire. They were, therefore, able to avoid the expense of a professional imperial civil service. Urbanization

354

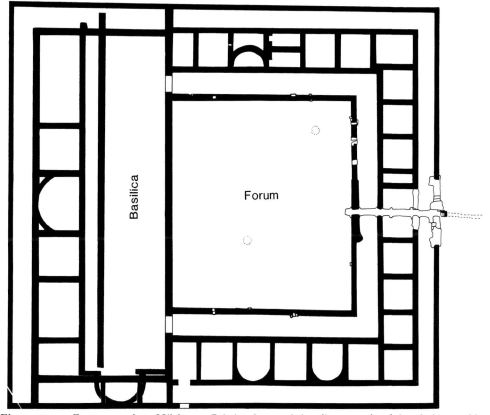

Figure 13.12   Forum complex of Silchester, Britain: the temple has disappeared and the whole resembles a legionary headquarters. Scale 1 : 800 (*after Fulford*)

was generally the post-military arm of Roman conquest, and especially so in the west, where client-kingdoms tended to be rather thin on the ground (p. 391).

The cares of local office were not, however, foisted on unwilling provincial notables. On the contrary, traditional aristocratic rivalry fused with Graeco-Roman ideals of public service to produce local leaders eager to become senators (*decuriones, curiales*) and magistrates. As in the east (p. 338) they sought these positions to advertise, confirm and increase their local standing, and to demonstrate the degree of their *romanitas*, the extent to which they conformed to the conventions of Graeco-Roman civilization. Aristocratic ambition (*aemulatio*) was also directed towards improving the legal status of the western communities within the formal hierarchy of the Empire, from simply 'foreign' to 'Latin' or even to the heights of honorary 'municipal' or 'colonial' rank, which gradually removed their juridical disabilities and eventually, through the associated acquisition of Roman citizenship, put them on an equal footing with Rome and her original settlement colonies. For their aristocratic rulers the ultimate prizes in this competition could be considerable – above all, the opportunity to proceed to win equestrian and senatorial office. A high level of architectural development of its central city greatly increased a community's chance of promotion. It was thus as part of this highly competitive process that the western cities were adorned, occasionally as a result of imperial generosity, but far more often at the private expense of their wealthy rulers, with their basilicas, temples, baths, aqueducts, libraries and the like.

Rome, therefore, played an undeniably significant role in the urbanization of the lands around the western Mediterranean. But it should not be supposed that western urbanization would not have taken place without her. On the contrary, in the last few centuries before Christ there was a spontaneous crystallization of urban life along the western Mediterranean littoral, and deep within its hinterland. Here, agriculture was moving beyond the level of bare subsistence. A food surplus both encouraged and required the evolution of more complex social systems which supported an increasing number of specialists – political, military, religious, educational, commercial and

Figure 13.13   Conjectural reconstruction of the forum inscription from Verulamium, Britain. It reflects Agricola's encouragement of urbanization in Britain (*after Frere*)

industrial – who did not themselves work the land. The natural base for such people and their dependants, the best place for them to protect, display and increase their position and status, was the town (cf. Sjoberg, 1960, 65). The stimulus to urbanize might well be external, such as the fear or admiration of outsiders, prompting the establishment of towns as specific acts of political policy. However, the potential had to be there to begin with. The western Mediterranean had long witnessed productive interplay between stimulus and potential. Punic trading-settlements had been established in Spain and north Africa as early as *c.* 1000 BC; and within three centuries Greek colonies appeared along the coasts of southern Italy, Sicily, Gaul and Spain. The newcomers influenced the native peoples in their vicinity. In Italy there was a fertile exchange of urban ideas between Greeks and Etruscans, leading to important advances in the evolution of Italian town-planning, for example at Marzabotto (Ward-Perkins, 1974, 26). These were eventually taken up by Rome and her colonies. In southern Gaul, Greek influence on a vigorous local culture produced dramatic Gallo-Greek urbanization, including orthogonal street-planning, at sites such as Ensérune, Entremont and Nages. South-eastern Spain, following both Greek and Punic examples, embarked on its own urban revolution, particularly in the region of Turdetania, around the valley of the Guadalquivir. As a result of Carthage's confrontation with Rome, direct Punic urbanization in Spain increased substantially in the third century BC culminating in the foundation of Cartagena, in 228. In Africa an extensive and close network of indigenous agglomerations had long been influenced by the Punic coastal cities, as may be seen in the early remains of Numidian Dougga (fig. 13.14). However, perhaps even more dramatic than this Mediterranean-centred urbanization was that which took place in western continental Europe. For example, a number of Celtic sites in the vicinity of the Drau (Magdalensburg), the Danube (Heuneburg; Manching), the Mosel (Titelberg) and the Rhône (Bibracte) have revealed the beginnings of proto-urbanization (by which is meant agglomerations with significant functions other than those to do with just agriculture and defence) well ahead of the arrival of Rome (figs 13.15, 13.16 and 13.17). This resulted from the interaction of considerable local economic development and Mediterranean influences: Greek, Punic, perhaps even Etruscan. When Rome arrived she did not recognize these indigenous developments as cities because, lacking overall planning and ostentatious public buildings, they did not conform to the aesthetic-architectural criteria of the established Graeco-Roman model. However, such embryonic or proto-towns, though born of loosely-linked tribal communities quite different from the *polis*, with its closely defined and extremely self-aware citizen-body, eased the way for the introduction of the Roman version of the city-state. Rome rode the wave of western urbanization, she did not create it.

Rome in fact both quickened and distorted existing processes of indigenous urbanization. Once the initial turmoil of annexation was ended Roman rule brought peace and material prosperity. Imperial taxation was not excessive under the High Empire, and in and about the frontier areas, where troops and administrators tended to be concentrated, imperial expenditure served to stimulate provincial economies, already helped by the provision of better means of communication. Urban centres, old and new, could flourish along the highways and, above all, around military bases. As they stood, however, they had no specific place within the administrative framework of the Empire; they were still 'towns'. The *cities* resulted from Rome's early and uncompromising encouragement of the city-state. In some areas, such as southern Gaul and Africa, the new states were from the start, probably because of their longer historical development, established as relatively small units, which allowed many, though not all, of the emerging towns to continue as central cities. However, it is possible to argue that elsewhere, especially in central Gaul, the pressure to establish a single centre to serve each large national area diverted aristocratic interest from other existing sites of urban development. The consequent failure of the subsidiary towns (*vici*; see Part 5, Chapter 14) to meet the standards expected of a western classical city, especially in the matter of orthogonal planning, has tempted too many scholars influenced by Graeco-Roman prejudices, to ignore them in their evaluation of the character of western Roman

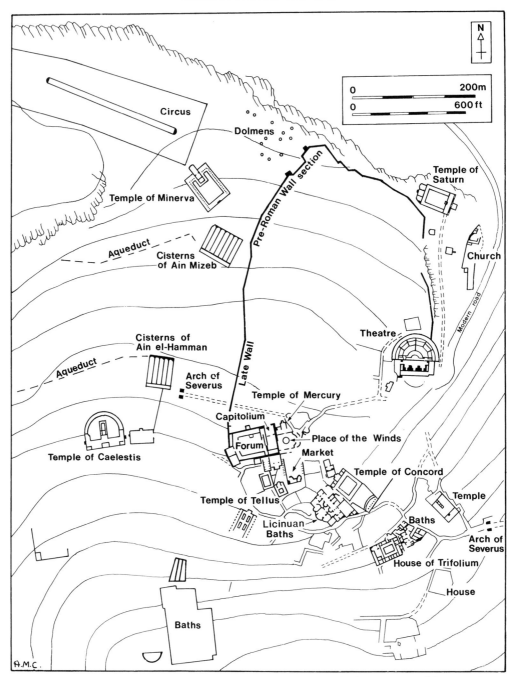

Figure 13.14 Dougga, Tunisia: 'an excellent example of the fusion of Libyan, Punic and Roman culture in North Africa' (*after Finley*)

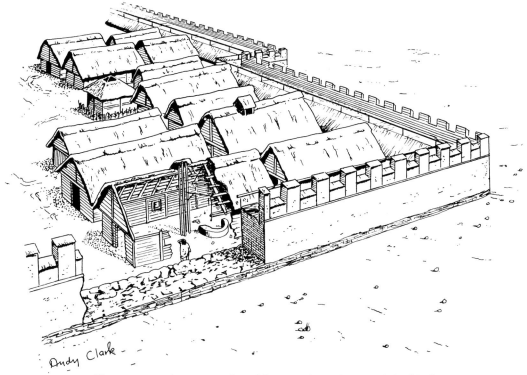

Figure 13.15   A reconstruction of the Heuneburg, Germany (*after Bittel*)

urbanization. The townships, despite their legal inferiority to the cities, continued and flourished under the High Empire, playing a significant role in the life of their communities (fig. 13.18).

The cities of the Roman west reached their monumental peak around the turn of the second and third centuries AD, following two hundred years or so of steady accumulation of the buildings and facilities appropriate to their standing. Such long-term acquisition was facilitated by the pigeon-hole nature of western orthogonal planning, which, though unsuitable for the designing of great architectural vistas, allowed communities to reserve sites for important building projects years in advance of actually beginning them. Conservative architectural traditions also minimized variation in style over long periods. A final factor in bringing the western cities to their perfection was the success and generosity of the Severan dynasty, as a result of which, for example, the imperial home-city of Lepcis Magna was splendidly rebuilt (pl. 13.9), while sea-borne trade brought prosperity to Bordeaux. In Britain, the civilian settlement which had grown up around the legionary base at York was accorded honorary colonial status. The same dynasty endowed Rome with the Baths of Caracalla (fig. 13.19).

The preceding stages are, however, difficult to describe, given the poor state of

Figure 13.16   Reconstruction of wooden houses in ordered arrangement along a street at Titelberg,
Luxembourg (*after Metzler and Weiller*)

our evidence. The process was clearly very uneven, both in time and space. Rome herself
began to exchange Graeco-Etruscan for Greek building-styles around the early-second
century BC. However, in common with other cities in the Italian peninsula, which had
earlier been important in the introduction of Greek ideas, such as Naples, Capua and
Pompeii, her congested site quickly became unsuitable for further large-scale innovation.
Hence the forcing-bed of true Graeco-Roman urbanization was located, not in the
capital, but in the plain of Lombardy, where numerous citizen-colonies had been founded
to forestall insurrection on the part of the newly-conquered Celts of the region. Here,
untrammelled by property-rights, and adopting a pronounced military look in response
to the danger of armed attack, the gridiron city of the Roman west was born, and an
architecture devised to suit its needs (Ward-Perkins, 1970, 5; 1974, 29) (fig. 13.20). But
similar settlement around the rest of the western Mediterranean basin was at first rather
slow. Spain led the way, with a fair amount of activity from the end of the Hannibalic
war, but settlements consisted mainly of mixed foundations of Romans, Italians and
natives, rather than full colonies. In Africa there was colonial settlement from the later-
second century BC, but this was much less intensive than that in Spain, and again
involved only irregular establishments. In southern Gaul there was only one full colony,
at Narbonne, established around 118 BC. The great advance in colonization came with
Caesar (pl. 13.4), and was sustained by Augustus. Both had to find land for veteran
troops and the Italian poor, and to this end both undertook the intensive colonization

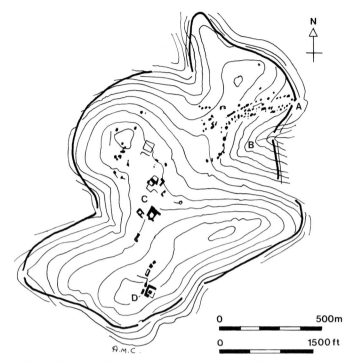

Figure 13.17 Mount Beuvray (Bibracte), France: (A) entrance; (B) artisan quarter; (C) aristocratic quarter; (D) sanctuary (*after Février*)

of Spain, southern Gaul and Africa (often on or by pre-existing native settlements). A further consideration may have been their perception of the need to create a Latin west to balance the eastern Greek half of the empire.

The role of these early settlement-colonies, both in Italy and overseas, should not be misunderstood. In the early years of the Empire there was clearly little thought of romanization through urbanization. The colonies were set up to fulfil precise military and political ends, and were individually sited to expropriate the richest lands of subject-peoples and to exploit these for the benefit of themselves and Rome. However, the settlers had to establish a *modus vivendi* with their neighbours. Rome had neither the manpower nor the technology to enable her to exterminate or permanently subject those whom she conquered. To survive, the colonists had to co-operate with the locals, and indeed, it is increasingly accepted that even the most formal colonies included from the start a proportion of the original inhabitants of the places where they were founded (Clavel and Lévêque, 1971, 218–19). With co-operation came the spontaneous spreading of Graeco-Roman ideas which was accelerated by the arrival of Italian traders whose wares and, no doubt, critical comments on the places where they did business, would have served to alert the wealthy natives to the luxuries they were missing. As local

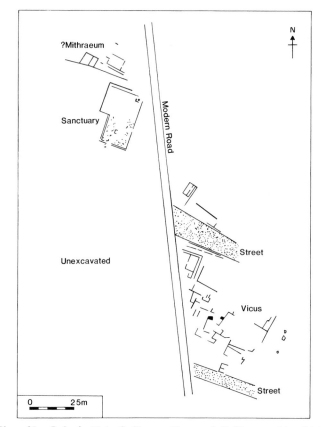

Figure 13.18 Plan of Les Bolards, Nuits St George, France. A Gallic township which developed round a sanctuary complex. It remained occupied until the fifth century (*after Groupe Recherche Archéologique de Nuiton*)

aristocratic rivalry began to work, and native communities, employing their own resources, aspired to copy the nearby colonies, the Roman urban model began its great diffusion. When Augustus, in his re-shaping of the western provinces, came to insist upon the city-state as the basic administrative cell, he would for the most part have been preaching to the converted.

Change is discernible in the archaeological record from the turn of the first centuries BC and AD, as central cities were founded and given planned and monumental aspects. It is also reflected in the generous distribution of Latin rights to those communities whose leaders had thus demonstrated their loyalty to Rome. This was especially the case in northern Italy, south-south-eastern Spain and southern Gaul. The tide of romanized urbanization was, however, running strongly elsewhere, for example in central Gaul. Here it was marked by the appearance of cities such as Autun, created by native

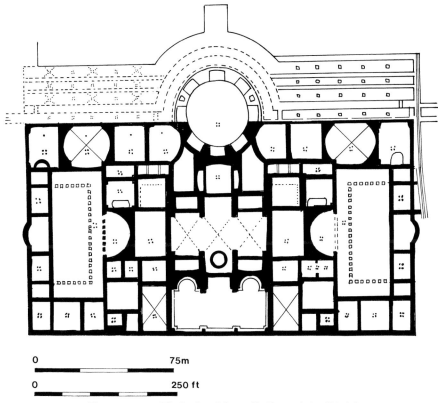

Figure 13.19 The baths of Caracalla, Rome (*after Février*)

communities on Roman lines at sites made important by the new road-system, probably often, as was later to be the case in Britain, first developed by Roman garrisons, planted to guard important junctions and other places (fig. 13.21). Indeed, the garrisoning of Roman troops within Gaul, and then, from *c.* 16 BC, their transference to the Rhine, not only provided opportunities for urbanization in the Gallic heartland, but also stimulated the urbanization of the frontier provinces. This included the foundation of two of the greatest cities of the Roman north-west, Cologne and Trier (figs 13.22 and 13.23). Unlike the east, where troops tended to be put into long-established garrison-towns, the west owed a good deal to the urbanizing power of the Roman army. In Britain, for example, military materials and expertise may even have been made available to certain native communities in the earliest days of city-building.

With the encouragement of rulers who were positively inclined directly to promote romanization through urbanization (for what began as a matter of accident became a principle of policy), western urbanization quickened and strengthened through the first century and into the second. However, it remained far from uniform. During the first

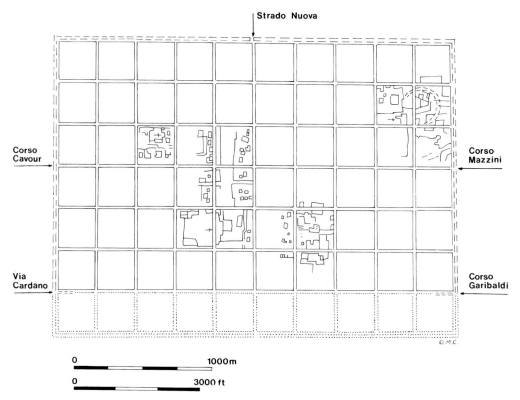

Figure 13.20 Plan of Pavia, Italy, illustrating the grid-iron cities of Lombardy (*after Chevallier*)

three-quarters of the first century the trail was blazed, ranked in order of success, by Italy, south and south-eastern Spain, southern Gaul and the province of Africa Proconsularis. Success in this field was generally rewarded with grants of higher status, although, oddly, as with Proconsularis, this was not always the case. The Flavian dynasty (AD 69–96) directed attention and approval to other areas. Although the assumption has been disputed, grants of citizen-privilege to communities in north and north-western Spain must surely suggest the existence of appreciable urbanization. There was further colonization in Proconsularis and Mauretania. Further, as has already been noted, under the Flavians, Agricola directly encouraged the urbanization of Britain, apparently still disappointing since the conquest of a generation earlier, and despite the precocious growth of St Albans (Verulamium) under Claudius and Nero (fig. 13.24). The establishment of colonies in the former legionary fortresses of Gloucester and Lincoln around the end of the dynasty would also have been useful in this respect (fig. 13.25). Under Trajan and Hadrian the cities of the African provinces enjoyed increased prosperity and renown as the last wave of direct colonization, which included the foundation of Timgad (pl. 13.1), built for veterans of the legion stationed in Africa (again underlining

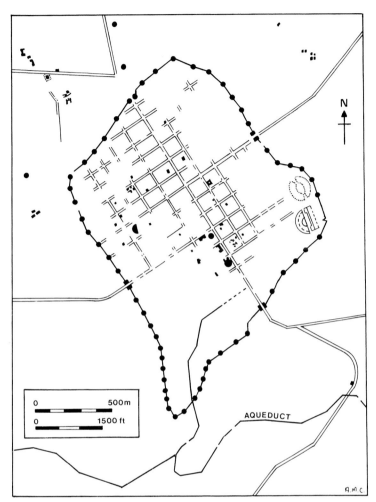

Figure 13.21 Plan of Autun, France (Augustodunum – 'Augustusville'): the Gallic interpretation of the grid-iron city is more generous than its colonial originals (*after Février*)

the significance of the army as a powerful instrument of romanization), spread the zone of urbanization further to the south. Existing settlements increased in magnificence, and at last began to be accorded honorary municipal and colonial status on a generous scale. Neighbouring Mauretania also shared in this development. These emperors were also instrumental in furthering urbanization in northern Gaul, along the German frontier, and in Britain. As the second century progressed the western cities as a whole moved increasingly together towards the Severan climax.

As has been emphasized, the Romans accepted established Greek architectural traditions, which enabled their cities to develop over a long period while maintaining a high

Figure 13.22 Plan of Cologne, Germany (*after Doppelfeld*)

degree of homogeneity. It must not, though, be assumed that Roman architects were enslaved by the past, and that they refused to experiment or change. Roman utilitarianism led to innovation and elegance. Increasing skills in the manufacture and handling of concrete, especially from the late first century AD, made feasible the construction of large and striking vaulted roofs. There was, indeed, a gradual abandonment of the restricted and angular interiors of Greek buildings and a movement towards the enveloping of space within curvilinear shells (pl. 13.10). At the same time, in the field of ornamentation and decoration, Africa was evolving her own confident and exuberant baroque.

The western Roman cities also varied in their geographical distribution. Cities were at their most frequent in north Africa, where the province of Proconsularis, in particular the region of the Bagradas valley, was probably the most highly urbanized place in the whole Empire. Proconsularis contained over 200 cities and around Dougga there were ten within a 10 km (6 miles) radius (Picard, 1959, 48). Next, in decreasing order

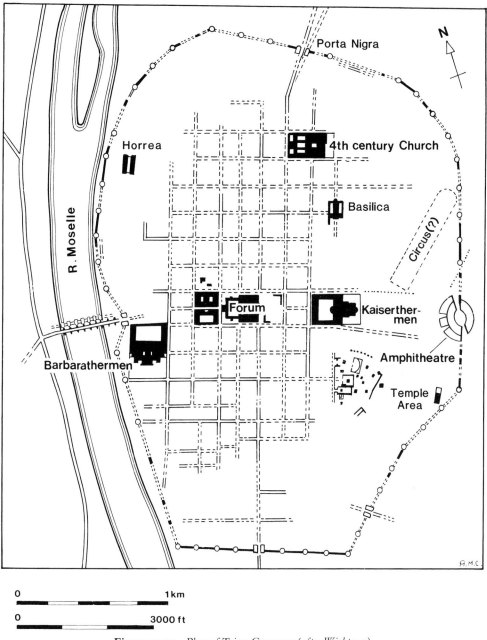

Figure 13.23 Plan of Trier, Germany (*after Wightman*)

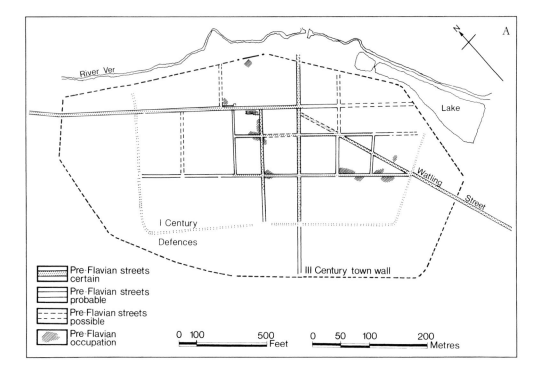

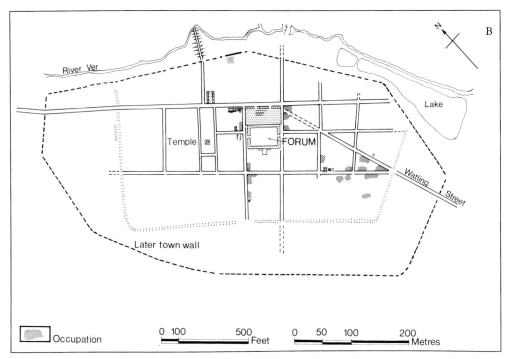

Figure 13.24 Verulamium, Britain:
(A) Julio-Claudan; (B) late-Flavian; (C) late-Antonine; (D) fourth-century (*after Frere*)

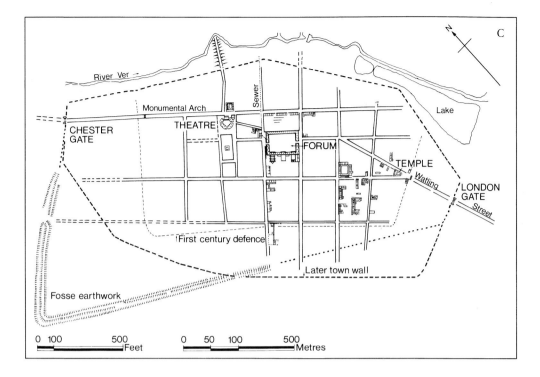

River Ver

CHESTER
GATE

Monumental Arch

Sewer

THEATRE

FORUM

TEMPLE

Watling

Street

LONDON
GATE

Lake

First century defence

Later town wall

Fosse earthwork

0 100	500
Feet	

0 50 100	500
Metres	

N

C

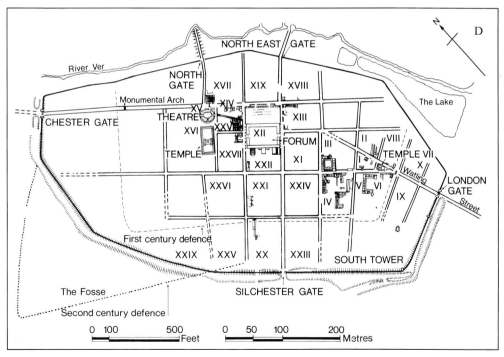

River Ver

NORTH EAST GATE

NORTH
GATE

XVII XIX XVIII

Monumental Arch

XV XIV

THEATRE

XVI

TEMPLE

XXVII

CHESTER GATE

XIII

XII

FORUM

XXII

XI

XXVI XXI XXIV

IV

II

III

VIII

TEMPLE VII

X

V VI

IX

The Lake

Watling

Street

LONDON
GATE

First century defence

XXIX XXV XX XXIII

SOUTH TOWER

The Fosse

SILCHESTER GATE

Second century defence

0 100	500
Feet	

0 50 100	200
Metres	

N

D

369

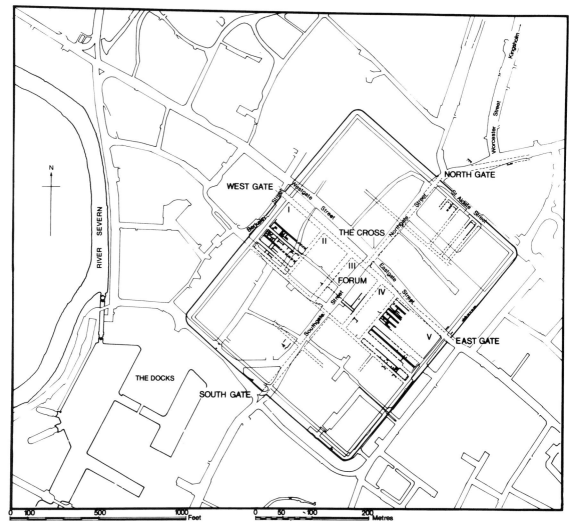

Figure 13.25 Plan of the early colony at Gloucester, Britain: the first colonists adapted the existing legionary buildings (*after Hurst*)

of city-density, came the Italian peninsula, south and south-eastern Spain, southern Gaul, northern Italy, the Rhône–Rhine corridor, south-eastern Britain and northern Gaul. However, it must be appreciated that this generalization has its problems. Above all, as has been earlier emphasized, it is too easy to concentrate on the cities, and ignore the subsidiary towns, thus virtually equating *state*-distribution with the general level of urbanization within a particular region. Scholars have been fond of comparing the hundreds of cities of Roman Africa with the meagre sixty-odd of the Three Gauls, to

370

the disparagement of the latter. This is to ignore the frequency and vigour of the subsidiary towns, which must always be included in any assessment of the intensity of Gallic urbanization. Towns were also present in southern Gaul and in Africa, again not without importance. An accurate distribution map of *all* western urban agglomerations under the Roman Empire has yet to be drawn (cf. Pounds, 1969, 155, fig. 10).

The surface areas of the western cities are easier to assess than the size of their populations, although even here calculations are not entirely straightforward. For example, it is easy to forget possible suburban expansion beyond city-walls (e.g. Timgad, cf. pl. 13.1), or to fail to appreciate that the latter, by accident or design, originally enclosed too generous an extent of land, which the city never fully occupied (e.g. Silchester, cf. fig. 13.1). As far as populations are concerned, there are very few ancient statistics, leaving us to deduce what we can from the likely productivity of the surrounding territory, the volume of piped water, the density of housing, the seating capacity of places of public entertainment, or inscriptions recording benefactions to the city-populace. None of these methods is reliable; even the last, which is probably the best, cannot, for example, distinguish between city-dwellers and non-urban citizens usually resident in the countryside. Such figures as are accepted cover an extremely wide range, from Rome, occupying *c.* 2,000 ha (5,000 acres) and accommodating a (high imperial) population of the order 500,000–1,000,000, down to places such as Caistor-by-Norwich, of just 14 ha (35 acres), and with probably no more than a few hundred permanent residents. Between lay the provincial capitals, such as Lyon and Cologne, each containing about 25,000 souls; Carthage, at 300 ha (750 acres), and a population of *c* 250,000 was exceptional. The average Italian city, for example Pompeii, may have had a population of about 20,000; the average Gallic, such as Paris, about 8,000. In addition, again, there were the towns, most of which were probably much smaller than the cities, although in certain areas, for example the Three Gauls, some particularly prosperous ones may have been larger than some minor cities. Clearly, though the western cities displayed a similar appearance, it is impossible to talk of an overall average size. This was the result of differences in the historical experience of urbanization, region by region and period by period. In this respect, to compare the colonies of northern Italy and southern Gaul, the capitals of the constituent nations of the Three Provinces and Britain, and the cities of north Africa is not to set like against like. Much more fruitful is to perceive the underlying pattern, namely the absence of smooth gradation in the figures. There were a few very large cities, and very many small ones, a hierarchy which closely resembles those of other pre-industrial societies, where the economy required at least ninety per cent of the total population at work on the land (Sjoberg, 1960, 83). Large city populations came about only when governments diverted to specific centres more resources than they could normally provide for themselves. But comparison with other societies also reminds us that the social and economic importance of the pre-industrial city does not necessarily fit with modern conceptions of size. After London, only fourteen towns in seventeenth-century England had more than 30,000 inhabitants, and most had fewer than 2,500, yet all played considerable political, social and economic roles (Laslett, 1971, 57–8).

The main role of the western Roman city was to serve as the administrative centre of its state. A wider political function lay in its usefulness in directing provincial enthusiasm and resources into public displays of romanization, thus diverting aristocrats from sedition. Indeed, the more cities a region possessed the more equestrians and senators it produced, from families experienced in local affairs now willing to proceed to give service to the empire. The cities thus provided a valuable preliminary training for imperial administrators. They also had a more straightforward educational role. It was their schools and universities, for instance at Marseille, which propagated the classical culture which was the cement of the imperial upper-classes, allowing people from different races and different backgrounds to speak to each other in the same language and with reference to a common heritage (pl. 13.11). They provided more of the same for less wealthy and literate audiences in their plethora of public monuments, which trumpeted the power and beneficence of Rome, and the names and features of the emperors who maintained her Peace (pl. 13.7). Additionally, by accommodating visitors, official and unofficial, such as administrators, soldiers, craftsmen and traders, from all over the Empire, they were important cultural melting-pots. Through the cities, as through the army, Latin became the *lingua franca* of western life; and later through the cities Christianity achieved its western foothold (Part 10, Chapter 4).

The economic function of the cities and towns remains hotly disputed (see Finley, 1977). Some communities, such as Carthage, Lyon, Cologne and London, clearly derived a substantial part of their livelihood from trading and manufacturing activities. Many, however, argue that these were exceptional, and that most cities did not add to the wealth of the economy in which they were set. Such goods and services as they produced were for city-consumption only, thus benefiting only that relatively small proportion of the population who were permanent city-dwellers, made up of the local and imperial elites and their families, together with those who served their needs. In fact, the urban centres, where they were not themselves just large agricultural villages accommodating farmers who went out each day to work the surrounding fields, a practice which may well have been common in north Africa, were parasitic on a fundamentally agrarian world in which large-scale, long-distance industrial and commercial activity played little part. City-based elites had attained a level of power which enabled them to wring more from the countryside than the original surplus which had brought them into being (Sjoberg, 1960, 118); on this depended their extravagant, essentially wasteful and economically sterile lifestyle. It has, indeed, been postulated that the dense urbanization of north Africa represented reckless and unnecessary *over*development of the land (Deman, 1975, 17f). However, it is possible to adopt a rather less negative approach. Societies vary in their assessment of their own needs, and how these should be satisfied.

In the Graeco-Roman world the city embodied the 'good life' to which all aspired. Given the way it was run, all who belonged to it had access to its facilities and could take pride in its achievements. It provided well-being for many, not luxury for a few (Thompson, 1982; Ward-Perkins, 1974, 33). All reckoned it a worth-while object for the investment of spare resources. Moreover, the cities were not insulated from their society. Whatever their prime purpose, they must have been affected by the general rise in economic activity, which reached its peak in the second and third centuries. Their own growth, necessitating a wide variety of productive human activities, both reflected and stimulated high Roman prosperity. Recently, too, the importance of long-distance trade in the Roman Empire, channelled through the cities and towns, has found new champions (Hopkins, 1978; 1980) (pls 13.12 and 13.13). In fact it seems unrealistic to deny these places a significant economic role which, though it may well have been consequent upon their administrative functions, was not thereby inferior to them – witness the spectacular commercial success of Lyon, capital of the Three Gauls. In addition, the healthy development of the towns, whose growth was much less likely to be inflated by administrative and cultural pressures, suggests positive economic forces which were elsewhere partially hidden (pl. 13.14). Certainly, one of the most dramatic social phenomena of the age was the appearance of self-aware commercial and manufacturing populations, often grouped into properly constituted trades-associations, with rules of procedure based upon the constitutions of the urban communities which gave them birth (Clavel and Lévêque, 1971, 245). Africa, simply by providing so many urban centres, allowed the most successful of such people to rise at least as high as decurial level. Even at the bottom of the social scale, the cities and towns perhaps had something to offer by providing occasional work for the rural poor, whose chronic underemployment has always been a feature of the pre-industrial society.

One function which the cities and towns of the High Empire did not perform was that of military protection. Many existing cities retained or rebuilt their walls, and some new ones were endowed with them, but this was generally a badge of status. Only very few places, in the most exposed areas, for example Cherchel, in Algeria, were defended for strategic reasons. The majority of western nucleated settlements were open – an outstanding measure of the effectiveness of Roman order.

Of course, we are still far from a fully satisfying reconstruction of western urban life under the High Empire. Archaeology, architecture, literature and inscriptions afford us only the shell of urban society: intriguing, sometimes beautiful, but generally empty. Pompeii and Herculaneum offer fascinating insights into everyday urban life, but as a whole we can only guess at, say, the endless aristocratic squabbles which split families, enlivened forum-gossip, and manifested themselves in the provision of fine buildings (p. 347 above). There is very little idea of the number, character and meaning of the pagan religious ceremonies which provided citizens with entertainment, diversion and, perhaps, some relaxation of normal social restrictions; these last were very important in a society characterized by staggering differences in wealth and status, expressed no doubt in dress, speech, even standards of health. And, for all its confidence and glitter, the western city had its seamier side. Most places must have closed down virtually completely at nightfall, leaving their pitch-dark streets to prostitutes, beggars and thieves (Sjoberg, 1960, 104; Février *et al.*, 1980, 306). When dawn came, and shop-boys took down the shutters, no doubt they whistled the popular songs of the day. It reveals much about the paucity of our evidence that there is no idea what these were.

During the late-second and early-third centuries previously unwalled cities in Britain were fortified following serious internal and external troubles. In the middle years of the third century the whole Empire was convulsed by further political and economic crisis, and by barbarian raids which both precipitated and were precipitated by these inner calamities. Towards the end of the same century Rome herself received a new defensive circuit, the first since the early-fourth century BC (fig. 13.26); and in Gaul a number of urban centres were wiped out, while several surviving Gallic cities took on the appearance of grim redoubts, defended by stout ramparts built from masonry torn from once proud buildings of the high imperial period. The Late Empire had arrived.

It has been conventionally held that the fourth century saw the final collapse of the *polis*-ideal. Indeed, it is possible to argue that even before it had spread into the west the *polis* was already out of date, having been overtaken by the hellenistic kingdoms, and imperial Rome. The city-state had continued to exist because it was still regarded as the natural unit of administration; and indeed, despite its weaknesses, it remained a great powerhouse for the maintenance and propagation of classical culture. However, from the second century AD, the significance of local patriotism grew weaker in the minds of those who mattered, namely the provincial aristocrats. They had exploited the city by using it to become fully-fledged members of the Roman world-state. Local office was increasingly regarded as an inferior and excessively expensive privilege, best to be avoided. The Empire, however, still relied upon the cities for local routine administration, therefore measures had to be taken to arrest the rot. The office of *curator rei publicae* (imperial auditor) which had developed in the second century to curb excessive enthusiasm by local magistrates, underwent a change of character, and was used increasingly by the imperial government to prop up a sagging system of city administration. However, the intrusion of central government served only further to undermine local autonomy, and could not prevent the well-to-do from neglecting their duties. By the fourth century they had entrenched themselves in rural retreats, and the burden of civic responsibility was shifted on to the shoulders of lesser aristocratic families, who could ill afford such responsibilities but who were even more bound to them by law. Much of later Roman legislation concerns itself with the problem of the shortage of provincial decurions, especially in the west. The decline of local aristocratic *aemulatio* spelled the end of the classical city-state. New priorities had anyway asserted themselves. Greater

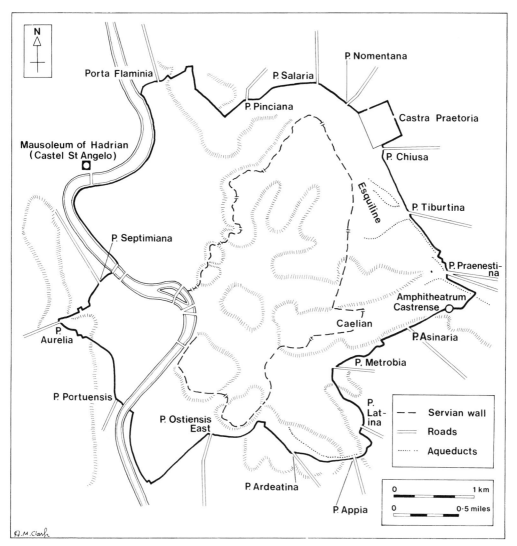

Figure 13.26   Plan of the third-century, Aurelianic circuit of Rome (*after Todd*)

and more efficient taxation caused much of the wealth which had earlier been available for local spending to be channelled into imperial projects, such as forts and palaces; and the Christian church competed extremely successfully for resources, both public and private.

However, the conventional picture of the decline of western urbanization is not immune from criticism. For example, it has long been realized that in Britain city-life remained strong into the fourth, and even the fifth, century. In recent years an even

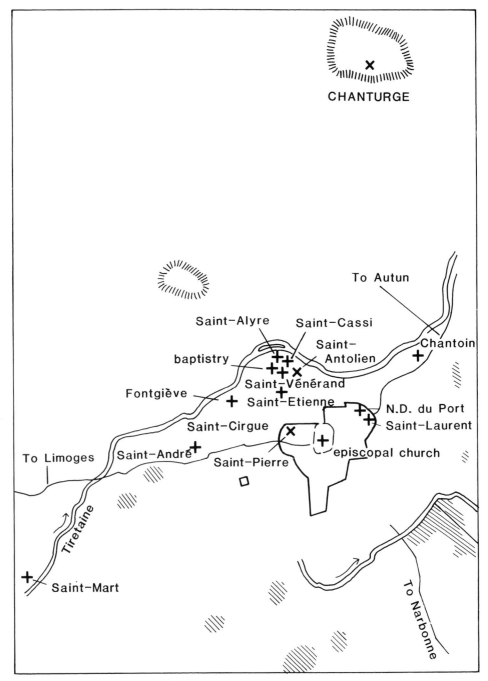

Figure 13.27 Clermont-Ferrand, France. Christian cemeteries and associated places of worship and congregation develop beyond the redoubt (*after Février*)

stronger case has been made for the continuing vitality of the north African cities until as late as the arrival of Islam in the seventh century (Kolendo and Kotula, 1977; Lepelley, 1979). Both these areas had escaped the worst horrors of the third-century crisis, but this cannot be seen as the main cause of continuing urban prosperity, since it has also been recognized in Gaul, especially in the appearance of Christian buildings inside and outside the new defences, which, as centres of religious administration and pilgrimage, must have assured constant traffic to and fro (fig. 13.27). Additionally, in Gaul, as in Italy, literary evidence testifies to the continuing importance of the cities as late as the late fourth and early fifth centuries. The cities of Spain have also of late been allowed a more prosperous later imperial history. Even the western townships do not seem to have succumbed completely to the third-century crisis and its aftermath. In Britain a number were fortified presumably because they fulfilled some important governmental function, and in Gaul, consequent upon Diocletian's thorough reorganization of provincial administration, some even won city-status.

In fact the western cities could not die. The later imperial government, more extensive and bureaucratic than its predecessor, needed them as centres of imperial administration, and as places where local members of the vastly increased imperial bureaucracy could be compelled to gather to demonstrate their loyalty to the emperor (Löhken, 1982, 93f). The imperial court had left Rome to shuttle along the threatened northern and eastern frontiers; the cities where it rested became temporary imperial headquarters and virtual sub-capitals. Provinces were divided for greater administrative efficiency; each new division required its own capital. As the government led, so the Church followed, with ecclesiastical reflecting imperial administration; and where emperors, prefects, governors and bishops, and their staffs, resided there too congregated traders and craftsmen. Indeed, the relative decline in importance of the city of Rome brought new-found wealth and splendour to provincial sub-capitals. The fourth century saw the heyday of Roman Trier (fig. 13.23). Local aristocrats were needed to operate the system, though some were plainly unwilling to perform their duties, so arousing imperial wrath. However, the unquestioning acceptance of the decline of local patriotism and autonomy has its problems. It has recently been shown that the *curatores rei publicae*, particularly after their office had been assimilated into the normal hierarchy of local administration, were hardly the ogres they have been painted (Burton, 1979). Other evidence from Gaul and, especially, from north Africa, reveals that local office was prized, and even contested, deep into the fourth century. Despite changes and pressing problems, late imperial civilization in the west was still very much an urban civilization, as is clear from the pages of St Augustine's *Confessions*, although the African Father is at pains to point out that the citizenship of an earthly city, Carthage, Milan, even Rome, is inferior to that of the City of God.

What had happened was probably just a shift in priorities. Late-Roman western society had not regressed to the point of no longer needing urban centres. Indeed, by

Figure 13.28 The Western Empire. Places mentioned in the text of Part 5

pre-industrial standards it remained strong and sophisticated, and so both required and supported cities and towns. On the other hand, it seems to have outgrown the city-state, and the architectural-aesthetic definition by which the city was deliberately and self-consciously used as a vehicle to express the totality of the values and aspirations of the community in which it was embedded. Other concerns had forced the city from the centre of the stage, to become just part of society. The great western aristocrats balanced their activity between town and country. The rate of change varied certainly much more quickly in Gaul than in Africa where the very density of cities, and the distance from the threatened frontiers kept old feelings alive for longer. Overall, however, we may perhaps even discern the re-emergence of the pre-Roman western town – less stylized, and certainly less monumentally magnificent, but much more flexible and therefore perhaps enjoying greater potential than the Graeco-Roman city. 'City-life' was becoming 'life in towns' (cf. Wacher, 1975a, 411f), which barbarian invasion, epidemic and the political upheaval which accompanied the disintegration of the western empire in the fifth century would be unable completely to destroy (fig. 13.28).

13.1 Aerial view of Timgad, Algeria. Note the forum at the intersection of the two main streets of the classic grid-iron system, the triumphal arch spanning the *decumanus* and the development of the less-regular suburban buildings

13.2   The 'Maison Carrée', Nîmes, France. The forum temple dedicated to the Augustan dynasty: 'a perfect masterpiece of Roman classicism'

13.3   Model of a rich road-side cemetery, Bonn, Germany. Note the magnificence and variety of tombs available to those who could pay

13.4 Arles, France. A Caesarian colony, endowed from an early date with both
a theatre and an amphitheatre

13.5 The *castellum divisorum*, Nîmes: the water basin built to receive and distribute the supply brought
to the city by the Pont-du-Gard aqueduct

13.6 Traces of four parallel wooden water-pipes show as dark stains in the surrounding soil at Colchester, Britain

13.7 Triumphal arch at Orange

13.8 Aerial view of Cuicul, Algeria. The original foundation of AD 96–7 to the north reflects the desire for geometric regularity, even on a steep and narrow spur. The later, less regular development can be seen to the south

13.9 Aerial view of Lepcis Magna: the city at its Severan height

13.10 The Pantheon, Rome; the classic example of Roman ability to capture space in a completely new way. The great dome is virtually a concrete eggshell

13.11   School scene from Neumagen, Germany

13.12   Heavy transport of woollen cloth by road: the Igel monument, Germany

13.13   Heavy transport of woollen cloth by river: the Igel monument, Germany

CHAPTER 14

·TOWNSHIPS·AND·VILLAGES·

Andrew Poulter

Within the Roman Empire, the distinction between cities and other types of civilian settlements was clearly defined by law, never determined simply by considerations of size, economic or social importance; it was Rome which granted the city its charter or confirmed its legal status by treaty. Excluded from the rank of city and denied the full rights of municipal autonomy, there nevertheless existed numerous settlements which were important local centres, occasionally even larger and more prosperous than many of the smaller cities of the empire. Townships grew up around the legionary and auxiliary forts and large villages played an important role in providing for the needs of their inhabitants and those of the surrounding rural population; both types of settlement possessed a variety of industrial, commercial and social functions which distinguished them from smaller agricultural hamlets which provided none of these more specialized services. Both townships and villages differed also in more than just status from the cities of the Empire; *coloniae, municipia, civitates foederatae* and the tribal centres all exhibited a general uniformity in their administrative organization, their regular provision of a grid-system of streets and similar range of public buildings; they were planned foundations and their character reflected their purpose, and often their origin, as instruments of imperial policy (Part 5, Chapter 13). The unchartered township and village often attempted to provide some of the facilities offered to urban communities. The townships shared a common origin and a certain uniformity in their economic and administrative organization. However, both villages and townships were rarely official creations. They developed their own particular character as local conditions and opportunities allowed. Some were obliged to perform duties imposed upon them by central government and by the provincial authorities but they always remained responsive to the needs of their own population. They reflected, in their development, the variety of social and economic conditions which existed in different provinces and within different regions of the Roman Empire.

The Roman armies of the Late Republic and Early Empire, even when actively campaigning, attracted camp-followers, willing to endure the hardships and not inconsiderable risks involved in selling goods to the soldiers and providing off-duty entertainment. When permanent quarters were established for the garrisons of the Empire during the course of the first century AD, townships rapidly developed around the forts and fortresses; they attracted traders, merchants and craftsmen eager to provide for the needs of the soldiers and to relieve them of their pay. The military authorities retained an ambivalent attitude towards these communities; while their usefulness to the soldiers was recognized and tolerated, their activities and the development of the civilian settlement was restricted so as not to undermine military discipline nor to interfere with the garrisons' official duties.

The townships which grew around the legionary fortresses were particularly populous; legionaries were well-paid and the large numbers of soldiers offered the prospect of substantial profits to the enterprising civilians prepared to take advantage of the opportunities of the market. By the mid-first century AD, the legionary fortresses on the Rhine had attracted considerable numbers of civilians. Outside the double legionary fortress at Xanten (Vetera), housing a garrison of more than ten thousand men, civilians built a large, sprawling township. At Mainz (Mogontiacum), the township, which already existed by the early first century AD, spread south of the legionary fortress and smaller, satellite settlements grew in size, notably on the banks of the Rhine, close to the port at 'Dimesser Ort', where goods to be supplied to the fortress could be unloaded and stored (fig. 14.1). Although the native population soon participated in the development of the extramural settlements, the dominant role was played by Romano-Gallic and Italian traders and merchants. The occupants of the township outside the fortress at Nijmegen (Noviomagus) would seem to have been immigrants for the most part and the settlement attracted few native settlers during the first half of the first century AD. As the townships increased in size and importance, so they became more attractive to veterans who, after discharge, preferred to remain close to their comrades still serving in the army and chose to invest their money in commercial or industrial enterprise. The townships also housed the families of serving soldiers; although not permitted to marry before retirement from the army, soldiers regularly formed permanent liaisons with local women who settled with their children in the extramural settlements where they could be close to their menfolk. By AD 69 the township at Vetera was so large and prosperous that it resembled a city (Tacitus, *Histories* 4. 21). Despite appearances, the settlement occupied military land and was only permitted to exist so long as the legionary commander approved of its presence. When the garrison at Vetera resisted the attack of the rebel, Civilis, the township was systematically levelled to prevent its use by the enemy as cover for an attack on the legionary fortifications. Exceptionally, measures were taken to protect the civilian community in moments of crisis; during the invasion of eastern Asia Minor by the Alans in AD 134, the governor of

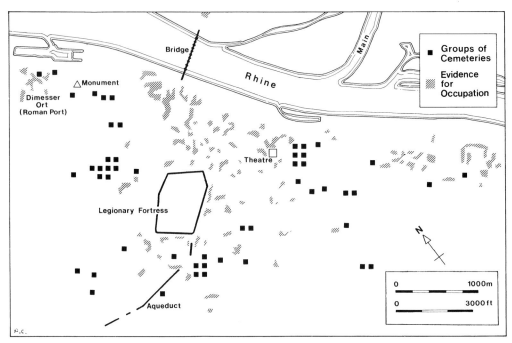

Figure 14.1 Settlements around the legionary fortress at Mainz (*after Esser*)

Bithynia and Cappadocia thoughtfully provided a walled enclosure to protect the community of traders and veterans living outside the fort of Phasis in the Caucasus (Arrian, *Periplus* 9). More often, the immediate needs of the army came first. On the Danube, Deutsch-Altenburg (Carnuntum) possessed a large extramural settlement by the second century; buildings encircled the fortress on three sides; its irregular street system spread out to serve the growing township which eventually covered some 130 ha (327 acres). However, the construction of shops and houses was carefully restricted; a 'free fire' zone was maintained for a distance of at least 100 m (109 yards) on each side of the fortress; civilian buildings were not permitted to encroach on the legion's defences. At Caerleon (Isca), shops and private dwellings had been erected on the west side of the fortress but were summarily demolished towards the middle of the second century, no doubt on the orders of the legionary legate, when it was decided to develop the site as a military parade ground.

Despite their lack of municipal autonomy and the enforcement of strict military control over their development, the townships were permitted considerable freedom to administer their own affairs. The term *canabae*, literally 'the hutted encampment', though it accurately describes the original appearance of these settlements, was also used as an official title to describe legionary townships. The *canabae* at Mogontiacum is attested by the middle of the first century AD as an administrative organization representing the interests of the Roman citizens and veterans; they formed their own corporate organization with an executive president (*curator*). By the second century, the inhabitants of the township (*canabenses*) also had an officer in charge of finances (*quaestor*), an assembly (*ordo*) to which Roman veterans, who invariably possessed Roman citizenship, and other Roman citizens could be elected, although native *peregrini*, by then certainly living within the townships, were not permitted to hold office in the administration of the *canabae*. At Szöny (Brigetio), on the Danube, the township outside the legionary fortress possessed its own corporate organization headed by a *curator* during the first century but by the second, it had its own *quaestor, ordo* and the functions of the *curator* were replaced by two executive magistrates (*magistri*). A change in title is evidenced also at Budapest (Aquincum) where, before the second century, the organization of the township was officially described as consisting of 'veterans and Roman citizens settled close to the legion' (*veterani et cives Romani consistentes ad legionem II Adiutricem*), a description which defined their status; the community occupied (*consistentes*) but did not own the land outside the legionary fortress which remained imperial property, controlled by the army. During the second century, the township adopted the shorter title of *canabae* and although Aquincum, like other townships, remained dependent upon the military it seems likely that Hadrian introduced reforms which granted the legionary townships greater freedom to administer their own affairs and acquire additional magistracies in imitation of the chartered cities (Mócsy, 1974, 142). The *canabae* at Silistra (Durostorum) was permitted to use the imperial name in its title (*canabae Aeliae*) and, at Lambaesis, the township was allowed to use the same honorary epithet for its assembly (*curia Aelia*). Of these developed, pseudo-municipal organizations, the township of the *veterani et cives Romani consistentes ad legionis V Macedonicae* near Măcin (Troesmis) was probably typical. The *canabenses* had two magistrates with executive authority, *magistri canabensium*, a *quaestor*, an officer in charge of public buildings and markets (*aedilis*) and an *ordo* whose members (*decuriones*) were probably selected for office from amongst the ex-magistrates at five-yearly intervals by the *quinquennalis canabensium*, an officer who exercised considerable authority by attaining this prestigious post; two men who were honoured with this responsibility, each gratefully donated two hundred and fifty *denarii* to the *curia canabarum*. The community of the *canabenses* erected its own religious dedications and public buildings but the *ordo* retained the right to vote for the erection of statues (*decreto suo*) in honour of provincial governors and the local legionary commanders; a suitable display of deference to the authorities who had the final say in controlling the affairs of the township.

Although the early legionary fortresses, such as Ivoševci (Burnum) and Gardun (Tilurium) in Dalmatia, were not always well-placed to attract civilian settlements (Wilkes, 1969, 110), the establishment of the legionary bases along the Rhine and Danube provided attractive markets which were easily supplied by ships, bringing all kinds of luxury goods from different parts of the Empire; Italian and Gallic fine tableware, wine and oil from Spain, high-quality bronze vessels from Campania, spices from the Far East and exotic glass-ware from Egypt. Roman citizens, traders from Cologne (*colonia Agrippinensis*) in the Rhineland, settled at Aquincum, and were joined by merchants from Thrace and the eastern provinces. Outside the fortress at Chester (Deva) in Britain, a family from Egypt settled in the *canabae* no doubt for purposes of trade. At Mogontiacum, one veteran became a merchant and specialized in selling weapons (*negotiator gladiarius*). Each of the larger commercial interests established their own associations such as that attested at Windisch (Vindonissa), comprising traders in fish-sauce and beans. Mogontiacum had its own corporation of money-lenders. Human merchandise was also for sale; an Illyrian, Dasius Breucus from Alburnus Maior in Dacia bought a young man called Apalaustus in the *canabae* of Apulum for 600 *denarii*. Local industries specialized in pottery manufacture, leather and metal working, and townships often developed trade with peoples beyond the frontiers.

The *canabae* were concentrated on the roads leading up to the legionary fortress. Houses were simple, rectangular structures, built of timber and their narrow frontages jostled for position along the major thoroughfares where the greatest traffic and the most customers offered the best chance of business. Other houses occupied winding streets and alleyways spreading out from the main roads which passed through the centre of the township. The main buildings could be as much as 50 m (55 yards) in length, the front portion often open to the street and serving as a shop which was closed off from the street by a wooden shutter at the end of the day's business. Behind, the buildings were regularly subdivided and used as living accommodation and workshops or for storage of goods for sale. Additional concentrations of settlement grew up close to the fortress. At Mogontiacum, subsidiary *vici*, wards of the *canabae*, developed in the vicinity of the fortress but away from the primary settlement around the south gate of the legionary camp (fig. 14.1). By the second century, the advancement of the imperial frontier into Germany and the development of trade beyond the Rhine encouraged the rapid development of a new area on the road leading from the fortress to the bridge across the river; its route was lined by well-built stone houses, equipped with mosaics and at least one public building decorated with its own colonnade. The second century saw a general rise in the prosperity of the townships outside the legionary camps. Deva could boast several large public buildings and Carnuntum, despite the foundation by Hadrian of a city only 2 kilometres ($1\frac{1}{4}$ miles) from the fortress, continued to prosper as late as the Severan period, its houses decorated with figure-mosaics and wall-paintings, no doubt accommodating the richer traders who preferred the commercial life of the *canabae* to that of the neighbouring city. Carnuntum also possessed an impressive public building just outside the legionary fortress. Entered through a colonnade on its north side, the visitor passed through a cross-hall, into a courtyard surrounded by storerooms or shops, then through a second forum-like court before reaching a basilical hall which probably acted as an administrative building and audience chamber. This large building,

220 m (242 yards) long and 180 m (198 yards) wide, must have functioned both as a market and administrative complex for the *canabenses*; in such a building the *ordo* of the *canabae* at Troesmis must have met to discuss the affairs of the community and vote upon proposals to erect statues in honour of its more eminent patrons.

The importance of these settlements was often acknowledged by the grant of full municipal autonomy. The *municipia* created at Carnuntum and Aquincum in the early-second century must have drawn upon the thriving townships already established outside the legionary fortresses for their citizens. The fortress of Melitene, founded as late as AD 70, already had a sufficiently populous extramural settlement for the creation of a city also by the early-second century. Sometimes, the reward of a charter was delayed. A *municipium* was created at Durostorum only in the late-second century. Mogontiacum received municipal status a century later. The creation of *municipia* close to the legionary fortresses presented problems. Not until the Severan period was a settlement outside the fortress itself granted municipal rights. Such caution is understandable; depriving the military of control of such lands by handing its administration over to a city could result in conflicts of interest. The usual expedient was to establish the new town at a respectable distance, between $1\frac{1}{2}$ and 2 kilometres ($1-1\frac{1}{4}$ miles) from the fortress, as at Lambaesis, Aquincum and Carnuntum. It has been suggested that these *municipia* established close to legionary fortresses involved the elevation of an existing village to municipal status and one located outside the territory controlled by the legion (Vittinghoff, 1968, 135–6; 1970, 346–8; Mócsy, 1974, 139–40). However, legions are known to have possessed extensive lands (*territorium legionis*), reserved for military use (Mócsy, 1972, 133–68) and it would seem most improbable that before the creation of a *municipium*, any village only 2 kilometres ($1\frac{1}{4}$ miles) from a fortress would have been any less dependent on military control than the settlement immediately outside the fortress. It seems more likely that the choice of site for a *municipium* in the vicinity of a legionary fortress was a purely practical decision. The city took over for its own use a sizable portion of the legion's former territory and its site was selected for the convenience of its citizens, while ensuring that it lay at some distance from the fortress so as to avoid any conflict between civilian and military authorities; the immediate environs of the fortress, for military reasons, had to be retained under the control of the legionary legate (Poulter, 1983, 78–82).

There may also have been another facet to the relationship between *canabae* and legion. Although the military were responsible for their own pottery kilns (*figlinae castris*) and legionaries were certainly detailed to look after cattle and horses required for military use, there is no reason to believe that the soldiers would normally engage in farming military lands. Still, the army required feeding and the extensive territories assigned to the legionary fortresses and which are known to have existed in Spain, Dalmatia and Germany, would be an obvious source of agricultural produce. As noted for Mogontiacum, the *canabae* included not only the settlement immediately outside the fortress but also subsidiary communities living at least 2 kilometres (1¼ miles) away. Also 2 kilometres (1¼ miles) north of the fortress of Strasbourg (Argentorate), at Königshofen, there was an important industrial site dependent upon the legionary township (*vicus canabarum*). It seems that the organization of the *canabae* could include a variety of settlements at a distance from the fortress but still on military land. The legion at Lambaesis took a keen interest in village settlements. Legionaries were engaged in building operations in the *vicus* of Verecunda, 2 kilometres (1¼ miles) from the fortress and the legionary legate was responsible for passing details of an imperial rescript to the *magistri* of the *vicus* of Lamiggiga, about 30 kilometres (19 miles) from the fortress of Lambaesis. Whether these settlements were on an imperial estate or within the *territorium legionis*, the army was clearly responsible for their welfare (Fentress, 1979, 134–42). The inhabitants of the township at Lambaesis itself would seem to have been engaged in agriculture and the cultivation of vines. It seems not unlikely that the military lands were farmed by communities of Roman veterans and peregrine natives settled in villages and, given the evidence for the control of settlement at a distance from a legionary fortress by the organization of the *canabae*, it may well have been through this organization that the legion at Lambaesis arranged for the collection of agricultural supplies. Such an arrangement would explain the remarkable degree of freedom permitted to townships since they performed an important role in feeding the army. It would also explain why the *canabae* at Kostolac (Viminacium) was rebuilt by the legionary garrison; the township was as useful to the legion as the legionary market and lands were important to the *canabenses*. However, the foundation of *municipia* close to legionary fortresses and the award of military land to the new city, which must have followed, may well have reduced the importance of the *canabenses* as civilian administrators of the *territorium legionis*. Although Aquincum and Carnuntum possessed flourishing townships engaged in commerce and industry after the creation of *municipia*, the case of Durostorum may well be more typical; after the foundation of the *municipium Aelium*, by Marcus Aurelius, the *canabae Aeliae* had declined to a small settlement by the early third century, its community of veterans and *peregrini* still engaged in the traditional occupations of trade and shipping but no longer possessing the status and economic importance of the Antonine township.

The soldiers stationed in auxiliary forts also attracted civilian settlements. Since, by the second century, most auxiliary forts were on the imperial frontiers, the auxiliary townships offered good prospects for trade beyond the empire. In their organization, these townships, called *vici*, resembled that of the *canabae*; they possessed their own magistrates, and assemblies. An extensive township surrounded Housesteads (Vercovicium) on Hadrian's Wall in the third century AD (pl. 9.4); the community is attested passing its own decrees (*decreto vicanorum*). At Old Carlisle (Olerica) the *magistri vicanorum* dedicated an altar to Jupiter and Vulcan for the welfare of Gordian III with money collected from the inhabitants of the *vicus*; they would seem therefore to have had their own financial organization.

The auxiliary townships attracted both auxiliary and legionary veterans. Like the *canabae*, the *vici* housed the women, who had formed unofficial relationships with serving soldiers, as well as artisans and traders, some immigrants from other provinces, such as Barates from Palmyra whose profession was selling military standards; he settled in the *vicus* of Arbeia (South Shields) with his wife, Regina, of British or possibly Gallic origin. Despite the mixed social origin of these settlements, the civilian administration was firmly in the hands of the veterans and other Roman citizens; at Adony (Vetus Salina) it was the *veterani et cives Romani* who administered the affairs of the *vicus*; native *peregrini* were excluded, even though they must often have constituted the majority of inhabitants in the townships. Also like the *canabae*, *vici* were allowed to engage in building projects; in AD 100, the *cives Romani consistentes* outside the fort of Rusé (Sexaginta Prista), made arrangements for the repair of a public building, probably a bath-house.

There is reason to suspect that the *vici* could also prove useful to the military in the administration of the lands assigned to the supervision of auxiliary units. A civilian *quinquennalis* is attested as an official administering a territory which took its name from the auxiliary fort of Capidava (*territorium Capidavensis*). The auxiliary fort at Veţel (Micia) in Dacia possessed a substantial extramural township of *veterani et cives Romani* but was also the centre of a civilian territorial organization (*pagus Miciensis*). The clearest evidence that the territory assigned to an auxiliary garrison could be directly organized from the *vicus* comes from the fort of Százhalombatta (Matrica) where the Roman citizens living in the township exercised control over the *territorium Matricensium*, which can hardly be other than the military district assigned to the auxiliary unit based at Matrica. A reasonable explanation for civilian involvement in the administration of military land, as suggested for the *canabae*, would be that it was the responsibility of the civilian organization to administer settlements on military land and to ensure that the garrison was supplied with such agricultural products which could be levied from the civilian community as a whole by direct taxation. Certainly, there is good evidence to show that the townships were not only communities of traders and manufacturers. The terraces visible today, outside the fort of Vercovicium, were used as house-platforms but those on the periphery of the settlement were used for growing crops as early as the third century AD (pl. 9.4). At Rainau-Buch finds of agricultural implements and stores of spelt, emmer and lentils, suggest that some of the inhabitants of the townships were also here engaging in farming lands close to the fort.

Despite their interests in agriculture, the primary occupation of these townships was certainly commerce and industry. Waldürm *vicus* received substantial quantities of Spanish oil amphorae which must have been imported for local distribution or trade across the German frontier. At Micia, the auxiliary fort commanded an important trading route which followed the Mureş valley east to Apulum and west to the river Tisza, Sarmatian territory, and thence to the Danube. The settlement, which was quickly established during the second century, had its own port and substantial storebuildings and workshops. There were Moors from north-west Africa and Syrians from the eastern Mediterranean. The township was a centre for salt-working and it possessed its own association of stoneworkers whose products were no doubt shipped to the neighbouring city of Sarmizegetusa. Most *vici* had their metal-workers and carters. Chesterholm (Vindolanda) had craftsmen working with leather and bone and weaving was an important domestic industry. At Rainau-Buch there were workshops producing similar goods and potteries producing domestic wares although traders also came with fine bronze and pewter vessels to sell in the markets which must have been a regular feature of these townships, such as that evidenced for the auxiliary fort of Seligenstadt. Not all commercial enterprises were legal. The *vicus* of Vercovicium had at least one forger, producing counterfeit coins. The profits must have been good; the penalty for discovery was death. Although the inhabitants of the *vici* could hope for substantial profits, life was rough and could be dangerous. Again at Vercovicium, a building, probably used as a tavern, contained two skeletons, one of a man with the point of a sword still between his ribs, the other that of a woman; both had probably been murdered and their bodies secretly buried beneath the floor of the tavern's inner room.

The townships which grew up outside the auxiliary forts resembled in their buildings and their haphazard, irregular development, the larger legionary settlements. Saalburg was typical of many such *vici* which developed outside auxiliary forts during the second to third centuries AD (fig. 14.2). For 150 years, there was an auxiliary garrison there, just south of the Roman frontier. The civilian settlement spread west and east of the fort but concentrated along the main road south; care was taken to prevent it developing too close to the fort's defences. Typically, there was an official posting station (*mansio*) for the use of travellers on imperial business. At Saalburg, the official importance of the *mansio* is emphasized by its position north of the *vicus* and within convenient reach of the bath-building situated close to the southern corner of the fort. At Vindolanda, the *mansio* was also built close to the baths although here separated from the fort by the *vicus*. Where possible the *mansio* was kept away from the civilian settlement. At Rainau-Buch, official visitors were no doubt thankful that both the bath-building and *mansio* were situated apart from the activities of traders and craftsmen; the official buildings were east of the fort whereas civilian housing was restricted to the open plateau to the south.

Relations between the townships and the military must always have been close although the conditions for the civilians, particularly during the first and early-second centuries AD, must have been spartan. Outside the auxiliary fort of Moers-Asberg (Asciburgium), a large township with timber shops and houses developed during the early-first century AD. Initially, security was a problem; the settlement was protected by its own enclosure which was levelled by the middle of the century to allow continued expansion over some 40 ha (100 acres). The inhabitants engaged in some industrial production of pottery and building tiles. However, with the departure of the garrison in

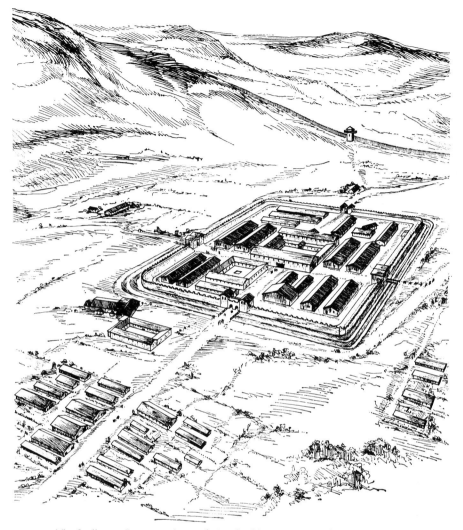

Figure 14.2 The Saalburg, Germany, fort and *vicus*, looking west towards the frontier (*by kind permission of D. Baatz*)

the Flavian period, the settlement lost its importance and no doubt its most enterprising traders and artisans, shrinking to the size and function of a small agricultural hamlet. Forts which were occupied during the second and third century AD allowed the development of prosperous communities and a more generous provision of amenities. After the military reforms of Septimius Severus allowed serving soldiers to marry, the *vici* rapidly expanded. At Rainau-Buch finds of military equipment from the *vicus* suggests that soldiers, by the middle of the third century, were allowed to cohabit with their wives outside the fort. Amenities were shared between fort and settlement. At Chesters (Cilurnum), the drains used by the garrison were shared by the extramural community. Both at Vindolanda and Rainau-Buch civilians, including women, were permitted to use the military bath-building. In Britain, the restricted area between the '*vallum*', a broad, flat-bottomed ditch, and Hadrian's wall was reserved during the second century for military use but by the third century AD civilian settlement was permitted to spread right up to the outer ditches of the fort defences (pl. 9.4). Although some of the *canabae* had already prospered and declined by the early-third century, their importance eclipsed by the foundation of cities close to the legionary fortresses, the *vici* on the frontiers of the Empire and those which had developed around the garrisons still maintained in the interior, were enjoying their greatest period of prosperity.

In the western provinces the term *vicus* (village) was usually applied to even the largest of settlements which lacked municipal authority. The term had a strict legal definition in that it was used of dependent communities which, despite limited, local autonomy, owed allegiance to a higher civilian authority, sometimes the tribe, often a neighbouring city (Festus ed. Lindsey 502 and 508; *Isid. Etym.* XV. 2, 11f.; Van Buren, 1958, 2090–1). However, the definition of a settlement as a *vicus*, in the absence of literary or epigraphic evidence presents practical difficulties (Johnson, 1975, 175–9; Wightman, 1976, 59–64), particularly since the term *vicus* is also applied to townships, as noted above, tribal capitals, wards of cities and even complexes of buildings used for official tribal religious and political gatherings without, apparently, being centres of population (Picard, 1976, 47–9). Nevertheless, there existed villages which can be defined as possessing such a range of administrative and economic functions that, although their legal status may have remained that of a *vicus*, they are clearly important settlements which often merit the description of 'small town' even though the majority never acquired municipal authority (Todd, 1970, 114–17; Rivet, 1975, 111–14). This category of settlement, for which the Greek word generally used in the Eastern Empire was *komé*, occurred most often in those parts of the Empire where there was little or no official promotion of urbanism.

In Britain, the Balkans, northern Gaul, inland Asia Minor and above all, in Egypt, where cities were few and administered extensive territories, villages assumed particular importance and performed many of the functions elsewhere reserved for chartered settlements. Even within small provinces, there could be important regional differences. In Lower Moesia, the western half of the province retained its native settlements which rarely possessed civilian magistrates but were usually administered by locally appointed officials or chiefs (*principes vicanorum*). To the east, poor quality agricultural land failed to attract large settlements whereas, to the north-east, there were numerous villages, mixed communities of Roman citizens and native immigrants from Thrace which possessed their own assemblies, passed decrees, elected *magistri* and *quaestores* and administered their own territories; these settlements were exceptional, particularly in the election of two magistrates, one of which was regularly a *peregrinus*, the other a Roman citizen; their developed and liberal administration may have resulted from imperial intervention and a planned colonization of a backward but strategically important part of the province (Poulter, 1980, 729–44). Elsewhere, there is also reason to suspect official encouragement behind the establishment of some villages. Not all townships established outside forts declined after the garrison's departure, as occurred at Asciburgium. In Gallia Belgica, prosperous roadside settlements occupied sites earlier used as military stores-bases (Mertens, 1983, 155–68). In southern Britain, many villages superseded abandoned military installations, perhaps originating as extramural settlements or as local market centres created by the military or civilian tribal administration after the departure of the garrison (Frere, 1975, 4–7). Other *vici* received no official encouragement. A number of important villages were established by Italian traders, such as the Republican settlement of Nauportus at the head of the Adriatic. Although a tribal centre, the Magdalensberg in Noricum developed as an important settlement containing large numbers of Italian traders and merchants during the late first century BC and remained an important commercial centre until the middle of the first century AD. However, in most villages, the native population constituted a majority and many of the communities themselves were already in existence before the Roman conquest. Braughing was an important late Iron Age settlement which continued to prosper during the Roman period, possibly after a short military presence. During the Roman period the village shifted its location slightly and concentrated along the Roman road which bypassed the centre of the pre-Roman settlement. Some villages, such as Baden (Aquae Helveticae) and Bath (Aquae Sulis), originated as native religious sites and derived considerable income from hot-water springs which permitted their development as spa-resorts; the sick came to take advantage of the healing properties of these springs, baths were provided for their use and temples constructed to the patron deity of the waters, to which thankful patients could make suitable recompense for successful cures. Important shrines became centres of pilgrimage and stimulated the development of settlements, catering for the needs of the visitors. Frilford, a sprawling settlement of *c.* 30 ha (74 acres), developed around an important temple. The Pachten *vicus Contiomagensium*, with some sixty to eighty houses, could boast an important shrine and its own theatre for religious gatherings, no doubt paid for by devotees of the village deity, Pritona.

Although a few villages could depend upon their specialized functions as religious centres or spas, they usually developed as market and industrial centres. Markets provided for the exchange of locally grown agricultural produce but they also attracted traders bringing imported goods both for sale to the native population and to travellers passing through the settlement on official or private business. Industry was important although usually conducted on a small scale; the smelting of ore, bronze and iron-working, tile and coarse pottery production were common occupations. Occasionally, a village might be chosen for official industries; a centurion of *Legio III Augusta* in

Africa, was dispatched to Gaul and to Brèves *vicus Briviae* to administer an imperial factory producing armour. Villages with harbour installations, on the coast or on a river, could become important trading centres; Nantes (Portus Namnetum) attracted sailors, probably merchant-traders, from northern Italy.

Mining settlements could also become important centres, accommodating the workers in the mines and a variety of traders and artisans offering services to the community. However, these settlements were regularly under direct imperial control, their affairs supervised in detail by a *procurator*. The mining settlement of Aljustrel (Vipasca), producing silver and copper, was supervised by such a *procurator*, controlling both the lessees (*conductores*) who purchased the mining rights and the traders and artisans who lived in Vipasca. There was a lessee for the baths, another for shoemaking, and one *conductor* was granted a monopoly for barbering. Any barber, other than the official lessee, found practising his trade in Vipasca or its territory, would be fined and have his razors confiscated but an exception was made for slaves attending to their master. Despite their lowly status and being subject to imperial control, some of the larger cosmopolitan mining villages, as in Moesia Superior during the late-second and early-third century AD, were granted full municipal autonomy (Mócsy, 1974, 131, 223–4).

Given the variety of types of villages, there was inevitably little conformity either in the number of their magistrates and officials or the extent of their responsibilities. Generally, villages possessed two *magistri*, like the auxiliary townships. Within the larger territories assigned to cities, villages could acquire a variety of local officials. Although responsible to the city of Vienne (Vienna), Lausanne (Lousonna) had a single executive magistrate (*curator vicanorum*), and an aedile, no doubt to supervise the village market. At Aix-les-Bains (Aquae), there was a council of elders (*decemlecti*) and two magistrates, here styled *patroni* not *magistri*. Usually, the villages, even those permitted to exercise direct control over their own affairs, were responsible to a higher authority, usually a city. Occasionally, there was an intermediate administration; the *vicus Budalia* was subject to the officials of the district (*pagus Martius*) which in turn was controlled by the *colonia* of Mitrovica (Sirmium). Cities imposed taxes and other duties upon villages within their territories and could be expected to take a more than passing interest in village affairs; a series of inscriptions erected by *IIviri* (*duoviri*) from Salzburg (Iuvavum) in the *vicus* of Seebruck (Bedaium) were probably set up during regular inspections by the city's magistrates.

Patrons, particularly wealthy and influential patrons, were a useful asset and worth cultivating. Villages had only limited financial resources; public buildings could be paid for by public subscription but villages were thankful for demonstrations of kindness from wealthy people. Individual generosity allowed for the construction and decoration of a temple for the *vicus* of Aoste (Augusta) and no doubt the legacy left by a certain Tiberius Iulius Quadratus for the *vicani* of Susa (Segusa) was put to good use. A patron who was also a member of the urban aristocracy could be particularly useful and result in the occasional windfall; the villagers of Moudon (Minnodunum) received money for a *gymnasium*, a gift from a *sevir Augustalis* of Avenches (Aventicum), for which they enthusiastically passed a decree providing land for its erection. But even if money was available, the city could still withhold planning permission; the villagers of Frascati (Angusculanum) cautiously obtained permission from Tusculum, the city to which the *vicus* belonged, before repairing a village shrine. Obtaining the good-will of neighbouring land-owners was always good policy. The villagers of Yverdun (Eburodunum) dedicated an inscription in honour of Iulia Festilla, their neighbour, as a token of thanks for her good services. The smaller villages could even be owned by wealthy individuals; Čerević (*vicus Iosista*), in the territory of Sirmium, was one such community on the estates of a large land-owner. In Africa, estates were often so large that they contained numerous villages. The *vicus Annaeus*, probably on the estate of Q. Geminius Annaeus, faithfully erected two statues in the settlement after the land-owner's death and in accordance with the terms of his will; since the villagers complied with Annaeus' wishes, relations between the village and the wealthy Roman citizen were presumably cordial. The relations between land-owner and villagers were not always to each party's satisfaction. When a boundary dispute arose between Sariurt (*vicus Buteridavensis*) and the neighbouring land-owner, Messia Pudentilla, the dispute had to be settled by the governor who sent the fleet-commander to erect boundary stones between the village lands and those of the private estate.

Villages could be required to perform a number of official functions. They might be obliged to provide accommodation for local policemen, often soldiers seconded from the governor's secretariat (*beneficiarii consulares*) or centurions from the legions who were detailed to administer a rural district (*centuriones regionarii*). The larger roadside settlements were responsible for the provision of rest-houses and for providing supplies for the use of the imperial posting service (*cursus publicus*). Guest-houses, used by officials of the imperial administration on business (*mansiones*), like those outside the auxiliary forts and legionary fortresses, offered overnight accommodation and often a change of horses or mules. At Godmanchester (Durovigutum), a central courtyard was surrounded by separate bedrooms, storerooms, a kitchen and dining accommodation; both the unusually lavish amenities and its proximity to another important facility for travellers, the bath-house, recommends an interpretation as a *mansio*. Beside the building, there were stables to house the horses and mules used by travellers. The provision and maintenance of these buildings, particularly when coupled with additional responsibilities could prove a strain on a village's resources.

Villages usually developed on or close to main roads, often at important road-junctions or river-crossings. The larger villages covered an extensive area of as much as 50 ha (124 acres) with rarely any sign of planning in the layout of streets or buildings. At Water Newton (Durobrivae), the central part of the straggling settlement extended along Ermine Street, which passed through the settlement and it was this nucleus which

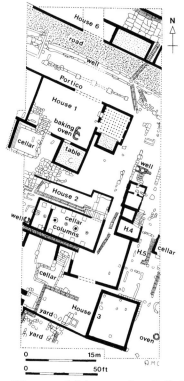

Figure 14.3 Plan of Houses 1–6, Schwarzenaker, G. D. Luxemburg (*after Kolling*)

was provided with its own fortifications, enclosing 18 ha (45 acres), by the fourth century AD (pl. 14.1). Even within this restricted area, most of the buildings would seem to have been concentrated along the main road and the adjoining sideroads which branched off, more or less at right-angles, from Ermine Street. Away from the main road, subsidiary tracks and streets meander across the site. One public building, perhaps a market or *mansio*, is visible on the aerial photographs, set back from the centre of the village (pl. 14.2). At Vervoz-Clavier, shops and taverns lined the main street and the village boasted a few public buildings: a market, a shrine and a basilical building, possibly used for village assemblies and providing offices for the *magistri vici*. There was certainly an assembly hall (*auditorium*) for Sinoe (*vicus Quintionis*) and Durovigutum possessed an aisled building which may well have performed a similar function. Occasionally, as at Dorchester and Kenchester in Britain and at Tournai in Gallia Belgica, the wealthier villagers could provide for themselves houses built of stone, even equipped with mosaics but, more usually, houses were constructed of timber or mudbrick with a simple stone foundation.

Typical of the more prosperous villages of eastern Gaul was the *vicus* of

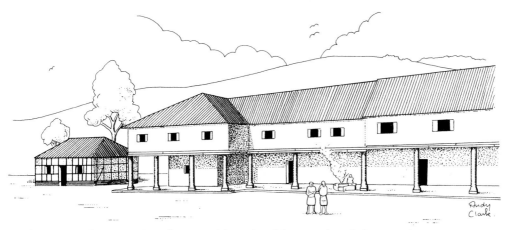

Figure 14.4 Reconstruction of a street with portico, Schwarzenaker, G. D. Luxemburg (*after Kolling*)

Schwarzenacker an der Blies. The settlement was located close to an important road-junction although its prosperity derived largely from its function as a market centre for its rich agricultural hinterland. During the first century AD, buildings were of timber but by the early third, they had been replaced by sturdy, stone built houses (pl. 14.3 and fig. 14.3). 'House 1' was a shop with living rooms for the owner provided around an interior courtyard which was used as a domestic bakery. The proprietor made enough of a profit from his trade to afford the construction of a hypocaust system to heat his living room and a large cellar to store his goods. The shop was fronted by a portico which gave the premises a tolerably distinguished appearance (fig. 14.4). Opposite the shop, there was a small inn on the street-corner and the road was paved, with its own drain flushed by the village aqueduct. The primary industrial occupations would seem to have been iron-working and pottery manufacture.

The wealthiest villages and townships were able to acquire a variety of additional amenities. The *vicus* of Brough-on-Humber (Petuaria) had a theatre and so did the *vicus* of Bitburg (Bida), the money for which was provided by L. Ammiatius Gambvio who also charged the *curatores vici* with its maintenance and the provision of entertainment every year on 30 April. Both Lousonna and Geneva (Genua) had aqueducts; Pallien (*vicus Voclanniorum*) had more mundane facilities, including a communal kitchen. More surprisingly, villages and townships could have their own public clocks, sundials or, in less clement parts of the Empire, water-clocks. C. Blaesius Gratus generously gave the villagers of Annecy (Boutae) a new timepiece and a building furnished with decorative adornments to contain it. He also thoughtfully provided additional money to pay a slave to maintain the clock. But villages were rarely allowed fortifications before the third century. Only in Britain were many permitted to erect their own fortifications of earth and timber; possibly because they wished to emulate the dignified appearance of the cities (Hartley, 1983, 84–95; see also Frere, 1984, 23), or, more probably, because defensive measures were necessary during a period of crisis in Britain, towards the end of the second century AD (Wacher, 1975b, 51–2).

In the eastern provinces, village life already possessed its own traditional institutions before the Roman conquest; although some villages increased their administrative authority or developed new institutions, the village (*komé*) generally remained unaffected by Roman practice and maintained its character as it had evolved during the hellenistic period; traditional magistracies were still used and Greek remained the language of its administration. There were concessions to Roman practice. The *cursus publicus* was extended to the eastern Empire and impositions were placed upon the *komé* as they were on the *vicus*. However, in the east, there was already a tradition of providing facilities for a public posting service; a similar system had been operated by the Persians and later, by the hellenistic kings. During the reign of Tiberius, Augustus' instructions concerning the provision of food and lodging for official travellers were implemented in the territory of the town of Sagalassus in Psidia. The system catered for the requisitioning of mules and donkeys by travelling officials, to take them to the next posting station, although payment to the villagers was made for their use (Mitchell, 1976, 106–31). As in the west, the villagers sometimes found their duties excessive, and even unfair.

Wherever few towns had been established during the hellenistic and Roman periods, villages could largely look after their own affairs, untroubled by interference from city magistrates. In Asia Minor, the village, often described simply as the 'settlement' (*katoikia*) usually had two magistrates called komarchs, an assembly of elders (*gerousia*), a village scribe (*grammateus*) and an officer in charge of the village market (*agoranomos*). Communal land could be administered by the officers of the village and funds, partly raised from contributions, partly from fines imposed by the magistrates, were used for public building projects. In central Caria, villages not only maintained their own administrative officials but also imitated the cities by uniting into religious leagues (*koina*) which even acquired a political role, electing magistrates and granting local rights of citizenship (Magie, 1950, 1024–31). In the frontier districts of Trachonitis and Auronitis in eastern Syria, villages were supervised by centurions detached from service with the legions although the communities were still allowed to evolve their own forms of local administration; whereas, during the first and second centuries AD, most villages were controlled by a single headman (*strategos*), by the third century AD, many of the larger communities possessed annually elected magistrates and village assemblies, empowered to pass decrees authorizing the construction of public baths, basilicas and *mansiones* (Jones, 1971, 284–5; Harper, 1928, 117–21). Village officials acquired a variety of different titles as each community provided for its own needs; *pistoi, pronoetai* and *epimeletai* all seem to have been involved in aspects of public administration and the provision of buildings for use by the villagers (Harper, 1928, 122).

Roman Egypt preserved the system of Ptolemaic administration largely intact within which it was the village, and not the city, which was the usual instrument of local administration. Papyri fortunately provide detailed information about the organization of the Egyptian villages. Each had its own council of elders (*presbuteroi*), often a local policeman (*phylacos*) and a village scribe (*komogrammateus*) although imperial control was more strictly enforced than in other provinces; appointments to office were made, or at least approved, by the local representative of the provincial administration, the *epistrategos* or *strategos* (Abbott and Johnson, 1926, 27–8). The *komogrammateus* was a particularly important functionary; he drew up the official tax-returns and accounts of the village which had then to be forwarded to the Roman authorities. Petaus, son of Petaus, from Karanis in the Fayum, held the important post of village scribe for three years, serving no less than five villages in the vicinity of his home. He submitted accounts, lists of goods and office-holders to the local *strategos*. Petaus was fearful lest he should make any mistakes with his documentation and was at pains to ensure his duties were carried out correctly. However, Petaus, the *komogrammateus*, had one failing which made his job particularly difficult; he could neither read nor write. By carefully practising his signature and persuading his literate brother, Theon, to check the documents prepared for him by his clerks, Petaus succeeded in keeping his guilty secret from the *strategos* whose anger he clearly feared, should his incompetence ever be discovered (Youtie, 1966, 127–43). Yet the papyri recovered from Egyptian villages demonstrate that Petaus' case was exceptional. Not only were many villagers quite able to read and write Greek, at least some of the more educated had a taste for classical literature. Letters also reveal both the high standards of literacy common in villages and provide information about the lives of ordinary villagers.

Karanis, the home of Petaus, was typical of villages in Roman Egypt. Unlike the sprawling villages common in the western provinces, the four to six thousand inhabitants of Karanis lived in comparatively cramped surroundings. Houses were constructed from sun-dried bricks and timber was used sparingly for doors, window-frames and roofs. Although houses regularly had one or two upper storeys, the available accommodation was often subdivided for separate families and personal privacy must have been minimal. Buildings were closely packed, often separated by only narrow alleyways, affording some protection from the sun's rays. Cooking, washing and the preparation of food had all to be done in the small courtyards behind the houses where domestic animals were also kept (fig. 14.5). Overcrowding, the hot climate of Egypt and the rudimentary arrangements for sanitation assisted the rapid transmission of disease; the temporary abandonment of outlying parts of the village in the later second century AD probably followed a serious outbreak of plague and the death of many of Karanis' occupants. However, the villagers' diet was remarkably varied; in addition to plentiful supplies of grain and vegetables, fish, chickens and other domestic animals, dovecotes, a regular feature of many houses in the village, provided additional reserves of fresh meat. Karanis maintained a detachment of soldiers housed in two-storeyed barracks, placed, for security, close to the state granary where supplies were kept before shipment down

Figure 14.5 Plan of the eastern quarter of the village at Karanis, Egypt: scale 1:900 (*after Husselman*)

the Nile to Alexandria. The granary itself, although built almost entirely from mud brick, was three storeys in height and contained vaulted storerooms with bins to keep the grain dry (fig. 14.6). Though by no means a wealthy community, the villagers of Karanis enjoyed most of the basic amenities and facilities found in Roman villages even though in language, economy and administration Karanis had little in common with contemporary villages in the western provinces of the Empire.

The third-century barbarian invasions proved catastrophic for the open, undefended villages and townships of the western provinces. With the collapse of the German frontier and the withdrawal to the Rhine, the townships of the 'outer limes' were either destroyed by the enemy or abandoned. At Rainau-Buch, the civilians hastily fled from their settlement *c.* AD 260, leaving hoards of metalwork and equipment in the vain hope that they would later be able to retrieve their belongings. At Mogontiacum, part of the *canabae* was protected by a wall on the south-east side of the fortress and the principal part of the settlement, north of the fortress, was provided with a larger circuit of defences and finally granted municipal status towards the end of the third century. Most communities were less fortunate. The *canabae* at Carnuntum, which had continued to prosper in the early years of the third century, was largely abandoned by the fourth.

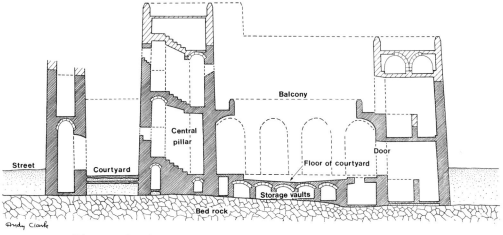

Figure 14.6 Elevation of the state granary, Karanis, Egypt (*after Husselman*)

In the interior, the small road-side villages were particularly exposed to barbarian raids. Some, like Schwarzenacker were abandoned; others, like Ernodunum, although no longer as prosperous as they had been during the peaceful years of the second century, survived as late as the fifth century AD. The most important of the villages, like Liberchies in Gallia Belgica, were provided with small fortlets which offered some protection for the residual civilian population. Sporadic, locally organized resistance in the form of *ad hoc* militias helped during particular moments of crisis (MacMullen, 1963, 137–8). A common expedient during the third and particularly the late fourth century was to construct hill-top refuges, fortifications to which the village community could retire when danger threatened. The inhabitants of Chameleux and Arlon in Gallia Belgica built fortifications for their own defence (Mertens, 1980, 423–70). On the Lower Danube, similar fortifications were constructed on steep-sided hills or overlooking precipitous river cliffs and were provided with watch-towers and enclosures to protect stock as well as the villagers who continued to live in the open settlements, though within easy reach of their strongholds (Poulter, 1983, 97–100). Britain, exceptionally, was not directly affected by the collapse of the Rhine and Danube frontiers. Braughing and Ancaster prospered in the fourth century; Water Newton and Godmanchester may even have acquired urban status.

The eastern provinces were also largely unaffected by the barbarian invasions of the third century. The village of Orcistus in Phrygia had prospered and was able to petition the emperor Constantine for a municipal charter; the request was granted, partly because of its large population and good water-supply but also because, as was duly noted, it was a useful place, being a road-junction, to support an official posting station of the *cursus publicus*. The villages of eastern Syria continued to erect their public buildings in the fourth century and preserve their local autonomy. The village of Beḥyo is typical

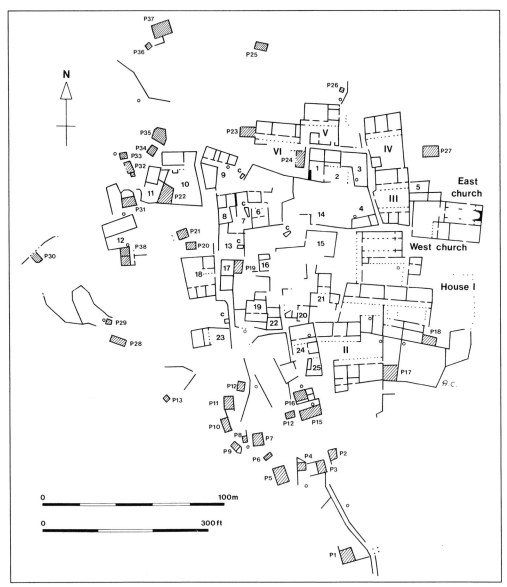

Figure 14.7 Plan of Beḥyo, Syria. I–VI, large houses; 1–25, farms and houses; P1–P38, oil presses; OC, wells (*after Tchalenko*)

of the villages of the region (fig. 14.7). The centre of the village in the fourth to fifth centuries AD was the 'West Church' and the house of a wealthy land-owner (house 1). The poorer artisans and farmers occupied small houses in the western part of the settlement. The economy of the village relied on the production of olive-oil and presses for processing olives were built both within the village and on the edge of the settlement, close to the olive-groves. The community prospered during the fifth century and expanded: new, medium-sized houses were built (houses 2–6), suggesting that, by the late fifth and sixth centuries, at least some of the villagers were deriving a modest income from trading oil with neighbouring villages and more distant cities; they also invested some of their profits in the construction of a second church (the 'East Church'). The economic development of Beḥyo in the late Roman period was typical of the villages in eastern Syria but there were new problems which were afflicting villages elsewhere in the Near East. The growth of landed estates which absorbed large numbers of villages was coupled with the spread of patronage, exercised by wealthy land-owners and soldiers who took control of villages, and denied the central government their taxes and those due to the cities, while taking the village revenues for their own use. The problem was of increasing concern to the imperial government during the fourth century, a sure indication that its development could not be arrested (Jones, 1964, 773–88; Liebeschuetz, 1972, 201–3). Some villages suffered a noticeable decline during the late Empire; in Karanis, 618 land-owners lived in the village during the late second century but there were only 140 in the early fourth century and the village was totally abandoned by the middle of the fifth; failure to maintain the irrigation channels, vital to the agricultural system, may well explain the collapse of village-life in the Fayum. However, elsewhere in Egypt, villages maintained their own local administration and would seem to have survived as late as the sixth century AD (Johnson and West, 1967, 98–9). A general picture is difficult to reconstruct although it would seem that, despite serious economic and social problems, villages in the eastern provinces continued to play an important role in the life of the late Roman Empire.

The economic and political development of villages throughout the Roman provinces was undoubtedly one of the successes of the early Empire which allowed diverse communities to establish their own, if limited, administration and even to aspire, in some cases successfully, to self-government, with the acquisition of municipal status. The disruption of rural life in the western provinces, closely reflected in the fate of many villages, may have contributed to the eventual collapse of the Roman Empire in the west whereas the villages in the east, though never to recover the prosperity of the early Empire, continued to provide the resources of manpower and money which certainly played a vital part in the survival of the eastern provinces and the Empire of Byzantium.

14.1   Aerial view of Water Newton (Durobrivae, Britain), showing the walled settlement and internal streets, with an extramural cemetery along the road to Irchester towards the bottom

14.2   Aerial view of part of the interior of Water Newton, showing the irregular pattern of streets and a large building at bottom right

14.3 Schwarzenaker from the air showing houses 1–6 (centre left) and a neighbouring *insula* (centre right); the tavern is visible at top right

·BIBLIOGRAPHY·FOR·PART·5·

Abbott, F. F. and Johnson, A. C. (1926), *Municipal Administration in the Roman Empire*, New York.

Alföldy, G. (1974), *Noricum*, London.

Baatz, D. (1972), *Die Saalburg, Eine Führer durch das römische Kastell und seine Geschichte*, Hamburg.

Bechert, T. (1980), 'The Roman military settlement of Asciburgium; topography and chronology', in *Roman Frontier Studies*, XII, 501–14.

Berchem, D. van (1977), 'Réflexions sur la dynamique du développement des villes antiques', in P.-M. Duval and E. Frézouls (eds), *Thèmes de recherche sur les villes antiques de l'Occident*, Proceedings of the 1971 Strasbourg Conference, Paris, 21–8.

Birley, R. (1977a), *Vindolanda, a Roman Frontier Post on Hadrian's Wall*, London.

Birley, R. (1977b), *The 1976 Excavations at Vindolanda*, Hexham.

Bloemers, J. H. F. (1980), 'Nijmegen: ROB excavations 1974–9 in the Roman forts, cemeteries, and canabae legionis', *Roman Frontier Studies* XII, 471–4.

Boak, A. E. R. (1955), 'The population of Roman and Byzantine Karanis', *Historia*, IV, 157–62.

Boak, A. E. R. and Peterson, E. E. (1931), *Karanis: topographical and architectural report of excavations during the seasons 1924–28*, University of Michigan Studies, Humanistic series, vol. XXV.

Böcking, W. (1974), *Die Römer am Niederrhein und in Norddeutschland*, Frankfurt.

Boon, G. C. (1972), *The Roman Legionary Fortress at Caerleon*, Cardiff.

Bowersock, G. W. (1965), *Augustus and the Greek World*, Oxford.

Bowersock, G. W. (1969), *Greek Sophists in the Roman World*, Oxford.

Bowie, E. L. (1970), 'The Greeks and their past in the second sophistre', *Past & Present*, 46, 1ff. (reprinted in M. I. Finley (ed.), *Studies in Ancient Society*, London, 166ff.).

British Museum (1872–), *Catalogue of Greek Coins in the British Museum*, London.

Broise, P. (1976a), 'L'urbanisme vicinal aux confins de la Viennoise et de la Séquanaise', in H. Temporini (ed.), *Aufstieg und Niedergang der römischen Welt*, II Principät 5.2, 602–29.

Broise, P. (1976b), 'Les vici Viennois d'après l'épigraphie lapidaire', *Caesarodunum XI*, 205–10.

Broughton, T. R. S. (1968), *The Romanisation of Africa Proconsularis*, New York.

Bruler, R. (1969), 'Essor commercial et développement économique du *vicus* des "Bons-Villers" à Liberchies', *Revue des archéologie et histoire d'art de Louvain*, II, 39–46.

Burton, G. P. (1975), 'Proconsuls, assizes and the administration of justice under the Empire', *Journal of Roman Studies*, LXV, 92ff.

Burton, G. P. (1979), 'The curator rei publicae: towards a reappraisal', *Chiron*, 9, 465–87.

Cabal, M. (1973), 'Le site archéologique d'Ardres', in *Revue du Nord*, LV. 17–28.

Cagnat, N. (1906–27), *Inscriptions graecae ad res Romanas pertinentes*, 3 volumes, Paris.

Calder, W. M. *et al.* (eds) (1926–), *Monumenta Asiae Minoris Antiqua*, Manchester.

Claes, P. (1970), 'Fouilles dans le vicus des Bons Villers a Liberchies', *Annales de la Fédération Archéologique et Historique de Belgique*, XLI, 31–43.

Clavel, M. and Lévêque, P. (1971), *Villes et structures urbaines dans l'Occident romain,* Paris.

Colledge, M. (1976), *The Art of Palmyra*, London.

Cunliffe, B. W. (1969), *Roman Bath*, Oxford.

Day, J. (1942), *An Economic History of Athens under Roman Domination*, New York.

Decker, K.-V. and Selzer, W. (1976), 'Mogontiacum: Mainz von der Zeit des Augustus bis zum Eude des römischen Herrschaft', in H. Temporini (ed.), *Aufstieg und Niedergang des römischen Welt, II, Principat 5.1, 457–559.*

Deininger, J. (1965), *Die Provinziallandtage der römischen Kaiserzeit von Augustus bis zum Ende des dritten Jahrhunderts nach Christus*, Vestigia, 6, Munich.

Deman, A. (1975), 'Matériaux et réflexions pour servir à une étude du développement et de sous-développement dans les provinces de l'Empire romain', in H. Temporini (ed.), *Aufstieg und Niedergang der römischen Welt*, II.3, Berlin/New York, 3–97.

Dittenberger, W. (1903–5), *Orientis graecae Inscriptiones selectae*, 2 vols, Leipzig.

Dittenberger, W. (1915–24), *Sylloge Inscriptionum graecarum*, third edition, Leipzig.

Downey, G. (1961), *A History of Antioch in Syria from Selencus to the Arab Conquest*, Princeton.

Drinkwater, J. F. (1985), 'Urbanisation in the Three Gauls', in B. Hobley (ed.), *Roman-British Urban Topography*, Council for British Archaeology Research Report.

Ehrenberg, V. and Jones, A. H. M. (1976), *Documents illustrating the Reigns of Augustus and Tiberius* (ed. D. L. Stockton), Oxford.

Esser, K. H. (1972), 'Mogontiacum', *Bonner Jahrbücher*, CLXXII, 212–27.

Fentress, E. W. B. (1979), *Numidia and the Roman army: social, military and economic aspects of the frontier zone*, British Archaeological Reports, International series, 53, Oxford.

Février, P.-A. (1973), 'The origin and growth of the cities of southern Gaul to the third century A.D.', *Journal of Roman Studies*, LXIII, 1–28.

Février, P.-A. (1977), 'Permanence et discontinuité dans le réseau urbain de la Gaule meridionale', in P.-M. Duval and E. Frézouls (eds), *Thèmes de recherche sur les villes antiques de l'Occident*, Proceedings of the 1971 Strasbourg Conference, Paris, 197–204.

Février, P.-A., Fixot, M., Goudineau, C. and Kruta, V. (1980), *Histoire de la France urbaine: la ville antique*, Paris.

Finley, M. I. (1973), *The Ancient Economy*, London.

Finley, M. I. (1977), 'The ancient city', *Comparative Studies in Society and History*, 19, 305–27.

Florescu, Gr. *et al.* (1958), *Capidava monografia archeologică* I, Bucharest.

Frank, T. (ed.) (1938–41), *An Economic Survey of Ancient Rome*, 5 volumes, Baltimore.

Frei-Stolba, R. (1976), 'Die römische Schweiz' in H. Temporini (ed.), *Aufstieg und Niedergang der römischen Welt*, II, Principät 5.1, 288–403.

Frend, W. H. C. (1956), 'A third-century inscription relating to Angareia in Phrygia', *Journal of Roman Studies* XLVI, 46–56.

Frere, S. S. (1975), 'The origin of small towns', in W. Rodwell and T. Rowley (eds), *Small Towns of Roman Britain*, 4–7, Oxford.

Frere, S. S. (1978), *Britannia*, second edition, London.

Frere, S. S. (1984), 'British urban defences in earthwork', *Britannia*, XV, 63–74.

Garnsey, P. (1974), 'Aspects of the decline of the urban aristocracy in the Empire', in H. Temperini (ed.), *Aufstieg und Niedergang der römischen Welt* II, 1, 229f.

Geagan, D. (1967), 'The Athenian Constitution after Sulla', *Hesperia*, supplement 12.

Graindor, H. (1927), *Athènes sous Auguste*, Cairo.

Graindor, H. (1931), *Athènes de Tibère à Trajan*, Cairo.

Graindor, H. (1934), *Athènes sous Hadrien*, Cairo.

Green, H. J. M. (1975), 'Roman Godmanchester', in W. Rodwell and T. Rowley (eds), *Small Towns of Roman Britain*, Oxford, 183–210.

Green, J. P. (1975), 'Bath and other small western towns', in W. Rodwell and T. Rowley (eds), *Small Towns of Roman Britain*, Oxford, 131–8.

Habicht, Chr. (1975), 'New evidence on the Province of Asia', *Journal of Roman Studies*, LXV, 64ff.

Halfmann, H. (1979), *Die Senatoren aus dem östlichen Teil des Imperium romanum bis zum Ende des 2 Jh. n. Chr., Hypomnemata* 59, Göttingen.

Hanfmann, G. M. A. (1983), *Sardis from Prehistory to Roman Times*, Cambridge, Mass.

Hanson, W. S. and Keppie, L. J. F. (eds), (1980), *Papers Presented to the 12th International Congress of Roman Frontier Studies*, British Archaeological Reports, International series, 71, parts i–iii, Oxford.

Harmand, L. (1970), *L'Occident romain*, Paris.

Harper, G. M. (1928), 'Village administration in the Roman province of Syria', *Yale Classical Studies*, I, 105–68.

Hartley, B. R. (1983), 'The enclosure of Romano-British towns in the second century A.D.', in B. Hartley and J. S. Wacher (eds), *Rome and her Northern Provinces: papers presented to S. S. Frere*, 84–95, Gloucester.

Head, B. V. (1911), *Historia Numorum*, second edition, Oxford.

Hingley, R. (1982), 'Recent discoveries of the Roman period at the Noah's Ark Inn, Frilford', *Britannia*, XIII, 305–9.

Hodder, I. (1974), 'Some marketing models for Roman-British coarse pottery', in *Britannia*, IV, 340–59.

Hondius, J. J. E. *et al.* (eds) (1923–   ), *Supplementum epigraphicum graecum*, Leiden.

Hopkins, K. (1978), 'Economic growth in towns in classical antiquity', in P. Abrams and E. A. Wrigley (eds), *Towns in Societies*, Cambridge, 35–78.

Hopkins, K. (1980), 'Taxes and trade in the Roman Empire', *Journal of Roman Studies*, LXX, 101–25.

Husselman, E. J. (1952), 'The granaries of Karanis', *Transactions of the American Philological Association*, LXXXIII, 56–78.

Husselman, E. M. (1979), *Karanis Excavations of the University of Michigan in Egypt 1928–35, Topography and Architecture*, Kelsey Museum of Archaeological Studies, 5, Ann Arbor.

Janon, M. (1973), 'Recherches à Lambèse', *Antiquités Africaines*, VII, 193–254.

Jeffery, L. H. (1976), *Archaic Greece*, London.

Johnson, A. C. and West, L. C. (1967), *Byzantine Egypt: economic studies*, Amsterdam.

Johnson, S. (1975), 'Vici in lowland Britain', in T. Rowley and W. Rodwell (eds), *Small Towns of Roman Britain*, 75–9, Oxford.

Jones, A. H. M. (1940), *The Greek City*, Oxford.

Jones, A. H. M. (1954), 'The cities of the Roman Empire', reproduced in *The Roman Economy*, 1–34, Oxford 1974.

Jones, A. H. M. (1955), 'The economic life of the towns of the Roman Empire', reproduced in *The Roman Economy* 1974, 35–60, Oxford.

Jones, A. H. M. (1964), *The Later Roman Empire 284–602: a social and administrative survey*, vols I–III, Oxford.

Jones, A.H. M. (1971), *Cities of the Eastern Roman Provinces*, second edition, Oxford.

Jones, C. P. (1971), *Plutarch and Rome*, Oxford.

Jones, C. P. (1978), *The Roman World of Dio Chrysostom*, Cambridge, Mass.

Kalinka, E. *et al.* (eds) (1901–), *Tituli Asiae Minoris antiquae*, Vienna.

Kolendo, J. and Kotula, T. (1977), 'Quelques problèmes de développement des villes en Afrique romaine', *Klio*, 59, 175–84.

Kolling, A. (1970), 'Schwarzenacker. Eine römische Kleinstadt zwischen Mete und Mainz', *Germania Romana* III, 70–89.

Kolling, A. (1972), 'Schwarzenacker au der Blies', *Bonner Jahrbücher* CLXXII, 238–57.

Kraeling, C. H. (ed.) (1938), *Gerasa, City of the Decapolis*, New Haven.

Kraeling, C. H. and Adams, R. M. (eds) (1960), 'The Greek and Roman Orient', in *City Invincible, a Symposium on Urbanization and Cultural Development in the ancient Near East*, 190 ff. Chicago.

Larsen, J. A. O. (1955), *Representative Government in Greek and Roman History: Sather Classical Lectures*, 28, Berkeley.

Laslett, P. (1971), *The World We Have Lost*, second edition, Cambridge.

Leday, A. (1980), *La Campagne à l'époque romaine dans le centre de la Gaule: Rural settlement in central Gaul in the Roman period*, British Archaeological Reports, International series, 71, 203–321, Oxford.

Leday, A. (1976), 'Trois vici du Cher', in *Caesarodunum*, XI, 237–41.

Lepelley, C. (1979), *Les Cités de l'Afrique romaine*, i, Paris.

Levick, B. M. (1967), *Roman Colonies in Southern Asia Minor*, Oxford.

Levick, B. M. (1979), 'Pliny in Bithynia and what happened afterwards', *Greece and Rome*, 29, 119ff.

Lewis, N. L. (1983), *Life in Egypt under Roman rule*, Oxford.

Lewis, N. and Reinhold, M. (1966), *Roman Civilization Source Book II: the Empire*. New York, 188–94.

Liebeschuetz, J. H. W. G. (1972), *Antioch: city and imperial administration in the Later Roman Empire*, Oxford.

Löhken, H. (1982), *Ordines dignitatum: Untersuchungen zur formalen Konstituierung der spätantiken Führungsschicht*, Cologne/Vienna.

McCrum and Woodhead, A. G. (1961), *Select Documents of the Principates of the Flavian Emperors, A.D. 68–96*, Cambridge.

MacMullen, R. (1963), *Soldier and Civilian in the Later Roman Empire*, London.

Macro, A. D. (1980), 'The cities of Asia Minor under the Roman Imperium', in H. Temporini (ed.), *Aufstieg und Niedergang der Römischen Welt*, II, 7, 2, 658ff.

Magie, D. (1950), *Roman Rule in Asia Minor to the End of the Third Century after Christ*, 2 volumes, Princeton.

Mansel, A. M. (1956), 'Bericht über Ausgrabungen und Untersuchungen in Pamphylien in den Jahren 1946–55', *Archäologischer Anzeiger*, 71, 34ff.

Martin, R. (1956), *L'Urbanisme dans la Grèce antique*, Paris.

Mazzolini, L. S. (1970), *The Idea of the City in Roman Thought*, London.

Mertens, J. (1968), *Le Relais romain de Chameleurs*, Brussels.

Mertens, J. (1980), 'Recherches récentes sur le limes en Gaule Belgique', *Roman Frontier Studies* XII, 423–70.

Mertens, J. (1983), 'The military origins of some Roman settlements in Belgium', in B. Hartley and J. S. Wacher (eds), *Rome and her Northern Provinces: papers presented to S. S. Frere*, 155–68.

Millar, F. G. B. (1969), 'P. Herennius Dexippus: the Greek World and the Third Century invasions', *Journal of Roman Studies*, LIX, 12ff.

Millar, F. G. B. (1971), 'Paul of Samosata, Zenobia and Aurelian: The Church, Local Culture and Political Allegiance in Third Century Syria', *Journal of Roman Studies* LXI, 1ff.

Millar, F. G. B. (1977), *The Emperor in the Roman World*, London.

Mitchell, S. (1976), 'Requisitioned transport in the Roman empire: a new inscription from Pisidia', *Journal of Roman Studies*, LXVI, 106–31.

Mitchell, S. (1983), 'The Balkans, Anatolia, and Roman Armies across Asia Minor', in S. Mitchell (ed.), *Armies and Frontiers in Roman and Byzantine Anatolia*, British Archaeological Reports, 156, 131ff, Oxford.

Mitford, T. B. (1980), 'Cappadocia and Armenia Minor', in H. Temporini (ed.), *Aufstieg und Niedergang der Römischen Welt, Principal 7.2.* 11, 86.

Mócsy, A. (1953), 'Das territorium legionis und die canabae in Pannonien', in *Acta Archeologica Hungarica* III, 184.

Mócsy, A. (1972), 'Das Problem der militärischen Territorien im Donaurum', *Acta Antiqua Hungarica* XX, 133–68.

Mócsy, A. (1974), *Pannonia and Upper Moesia*, London.

Mócsy, A. (1980), 'Zu den auxiliar vici in Pannonien', in W. Eck, H. Galsterer and H. Wolff (eds), *Studien zur auhken socialgeschichte*, Festschrift F. Vittinghoff, Vienna, 365–75.

Naumann, R. (1979), *Der Zeustempel zu Aizanoi*, Berlin.

Nörr, D. (1969), *Imperium und Polis un der hohen Prinzipatszeit*, Münchener Beiträge zur Papyrus forschungen, second edition, Munich.

Oliver, J. A. (1953), 'The Ruling Power: a study of the Roman Empire in the second century after Christ through the Roman Oration of Aelius Aristides', *Transactions of the American Philosophical Society*, new series, 43, 4, Baltimore.

Partridge, C. R. (1975), 'Braughing', in T. Rowley and W. Rodwell (eds), *Small Towns in Roman Britain*, Oxford, 139–57.

Partridge, C. R. (1981), *Skeleton Green: a late Iron Age and Romano-British site*, Britannia monograph series 2.

Passelac, M. (1970), 'Le vicus Ebruromaque', *Revue archéologique de Narbonnaise*, III, 71–101.

Petry, F. (1976), 'Observations sur les vici explorés en Alsace', *Caesarodunum*, XI, 273–95.

Picard, G. Charles (1959), *La Civilisation de l'Afrique romaine*, Paris.

Picard, G. Charles (1965), *Living Architecture: Roman*, London.

Picard, G. Charles (1976), 'Vicus et conciliabulum', *Caesarodunum* XI, 47–9.

Piccotini, G. (1977), 'Die Stadt auf dem Magdalensberg, ein spätkeltisches und frürömisches Zeutnien im südlichen Noricum', in H. Temporini (ed.), *Aufstieg und Niedergang der Römischen Welt* II, Principat 6, 263–301.

Piganiol, A. (1976), 'Actes du colloque, le vicus Gallo-Romain, Bulletin de l'institut d'études latines et du Centre de Recherches', *Caesarodunum*, XI.

Planck, D. (1983), *Das Freilichtmuseum am rätischen Limes in Ostalbkreis, Führer zu den archaeologischen Denkmätern in Baden-Württemberg*, Stuttgart, 110–66.

Pleket, H. W. (1983), 'Urban Elites and Business in the Greek Part of the Roman Empire', in P. Garnsey *et al.* (eds), *Trade in the Ancient Economy*, 131ff. London.

Poulter, A. G. (1980), 'Rural communities (vici and komai) and their role in the organisation of the limes of Moesia Inferior', *Roman Frontier Studies* XII, 729–44.

Poulter, A. G. (1983), 'Town and country in Moesia Inferior', in A. G. Poulter (ed.), *Ancient Bulgarian: Proceedings of the international symposium on the archaeology and ancient history of Bulgaria*, 74–118, Nottingham.

Pounds, N. J. G. (1969), 'The urbanization of the classical world', *Annals of the Association of American Geographers*, 59, 135–57.

Prieur, J. (1976), 'Le vicus thermal d'Aix-les-Bains', in *Caesarodunum* XI, 157–66.

Raepsaet-Charlier, M.-T. and G. (1975), 'Gallia Belgica et Germania Inferior', in H. Temporini (ed.), *Aufstieg und Niedergang des Römischen Welt* II, Principat 4, 3–299.

Ramsay, W. M. (1890), *The Historical Geography of Asia Minor*, Geographical Society Supplementary Papers, 4, London (reprinted Amsterdam, 1962).

Reynolds, J. M. (1959), 'Four Inscriptions from Roman Cyrene', *Journal of Roman Studies*, XLIX, 95ff.

Reynolds, J. M. (1982), *Aphrodisias and Rome*, London.

Richmond, I. A. (1963), 'Palmyra under the aegis of Rome', *Journal of Roman Studies*, LIII, 43ff.

Rivet, A. L. F. (1975), 'Summing-up: the classification of minor towns and related settlements', in W. Rodwell and T. Rowley (eds), *The Small Towns of Roman Britain*, British Archaeological Reports 15, 111–14, Oxford.

Rivet, A. L. F. (1977), 'The origins of cities in Roman Britain', in P.-M. Duval and E. Frézouls (eds), *Thèmes de recherche sur les villes antiques de l'Occident*, Proceedings of the 1971 Strasbourg Conference. 161–72, Paris.

Robert, J. and L. (1938–), *Bulletin épigraphique*, in *Revue des Etudes grecques*.

Robert, L. 1940–), *Hellenica*, Paris.

Robert, L. (1962), *Villes d'Asie Mineure*, second edition, Paris.

Robert, L. (1977), 'La titulature de Nicée et de Nicomédie: la Gloire et la Haine', *Harvard Studies in Classical Philology*, LXXXI, 81, 1ff.

Rodwell, W. and Rowley, T. (eds) (1975), *Small Towns of Roman Britain*, British Archaeological Reports 15, Oxford.

Rostovtzeff, M. I. (1957), *Social and Economic History of the Roman Empire*, second edition, Oxford.

Roueché, C. (1981), 'Rome, Asia and Aphrodisias in the third century', *Journal of Roman Studies*, XXI, 103ff.

Rougier, J. (1976), 'Le vicus d'Aoste', *Caesarodunum* XI, 172–84.

Roux, G. (1980), *Ancient Iraq*, Harmondsworth.

Rowley, T. (1975), 'The Roman towns of Oxfordshire', in W. Rodwell and T. Rowley (eds), *Small Towns of Roman Britain*, 115–18, Oxford.

Salway, P. (1967), *The Frontier People of Roman Britain*, second edition, Cambridge.

Schachermayr, F. and Merkelbach, R. (eds) (1972–), *Inschriften griechischen Städte aus Kleinasien*, Bonn.

Schallmayer, E. (1983), 'Kastell, Badegebände und Lagerdorf von Walldürni', *Führer zu römischen Militäranlogen in Süddeutschland*, 93–7, Stuttgart.

Schleiermacher, W. (1954), 'Nundinensis', *Germania*, XXXII, 326–8.

Sherk, R. K. (1969), *Roman Documents from the Greek East*, Baltimore.

Sjoberg, G. (1960), *The Preindustrial City*, Glencoe, Illinois.

Smallwood, E. M. (1966), *Documents Illustrating the Principates of Nerva, Trajan and Hadrian*, Cambridge.

Smallwood, E. M. (1967), *Documents Illustrating the Principates of Gaius, Claudius and Nero*, Cambridge.

Ste Croix, G. E. M. de (1981), *The Class Struggle in the Ancient Greek World*, London.

Stiglite, H., Kandler, M. and Joost, W. (1977), 'Carnuntum', in H. Temporini (ed.), *Aufstieg und Niedergang der Römischen Welt* II, Principat 6, 583–730.

Strickland, T. J. and Davey, P. J. (1978), *New Evidence for Roman Chester*, University of Liverpool, Institute of Extension Studies, 29–40.

Syme, R. (1957–60), 'The Greeks under Roman Rule', *Proceedings of the Massachusetts Historical Society*, 72, 3ff.

Tchalenko, G. (1953–8), *Villages antiques de la Syrie du Nord, le massif de Bélus a l'époque romaine*, Paris, volume I, 343–73, volume II, Plate CX.

Ternes, Ch. M. (1976), 'Le vicus d'époque gallo-romaine en pays trevire et rhénan', *Caesarodunum*, XI, 23–4.

Thompson, L. A. (1982), 'On "development" and "underdevelopment" in the early Roman Empire', *Klio*, 64, 383–401.

Todd, M. (1970), 'The small towns of Roman Britain', *Britannia* I, 114–30.

Todd, M. (1975), 'Margidunum and Ancaster', in W. Rodwell and T. Rowley (eds), *Small Towns of Roman Britain*, 215–23, Oxford.

Todd, M. (1981), *The Roman Town of Ancaster: excavations of 1955–71*, Universities of Nottingham and Exeter.

Tovar, A. and Blazquez, J. M. (1975), *Historia de la Hispania romana*, Madrid.

Tudor, D. (1968), *Orase, tîguri si sate în Dacia romana*, Bucharest.

Van Buren, A. W. (1958), 'Vicus' in *Realencyclopaedie* VIII, A2, 2090–4.

Velkov, V. (1980), 'Eine neue Inschrift über Laberius Maximum und ihre Bedeutung für die ältere Geschichte der Provinz Moesia Interior', in *Roman Cities in Bulgaria, collected studies*, 21–40, Amsterdam.

Vittinghoff, F. (1951), 'Römische Stadtrechtsformen der Kaiserzeit', *Zeitschrift für Savigny-Stiftung, römanistische Abteilung*, 68, 435–85.

Vittinghoff, F. (1968), 'Die Bedeutung der Legionslager für die Entstehung der römischer Städte an der Donau und in Dakien', *Studien zur europaischen Vor und Frühgeschichte, Festschrift H. Jankuhn*, Neumünster, 132–42.

Vittinghoff, F. (1970), 'Die Entstehung von städtischen Gemeinwesen in der Nachbarschaft römischer legionslager', *Legio VII Gemina : coloq. Inst. de Roman*, Leon, 339–52.

Von Petrikovits, H. (1963), 'Mogontiacum: das römische Mainz', *Mainzer Zeitschrift*, LVIII, 27–36.

Wacher, J. S. (1975a), *The Towns of Roman Britain*, London.

Wacher, J. S. (1975b), 'Village fortifications', in W. Rodwell and T. Rowley (eds), *Small towns of Roman Britain*, 51–2. Oxford.

Ward-Perkins, J. B. (1970), 'From Republic to Empire: reflections on the early provincial architecture of the Roman west', *Journal of Roman Studies*, LX, 1–19.

Ward-Perkins, J. B. (1974), *Cities of Ancient Greece and Italy : planning in classical antiquity*, London and New York.

Ward-Perkins, J. B. (1980), 'Nicomedia and the Marble Trade', *Papers of the British School at Rome*, 35, 23ff.

Wightman, E. (1976), 'Le vicus dans le contexte de l'administration et de la société gallo-romaine', *Caesarodunum*, XI, 59–64.

Wilkes, J. J. (1969), *Dalmatia*, London.

Willens, J. (1968), 'Les fouilles archéologiques de Clavier-Verzov', *Collections Latomus*, XXVII, 187–90.

Willens, J. (1970), 'Considérations relatives aux découvertes effectuées au vicus gallo-romain de Verzov-Clavier', *Annales de la Federation Archéologique et historique de Belgique*, XLI/2, 44–9.

Willens, J. and Lauwerijs, E. (1973), 'Le vicus Belgo-romain de Verzov à Clavier', *Helinum*, XIII, 155–74.

Wilson, D. R. (1975), 'The "small towns" of Roman Britain from the air', in W. Rodwell and T. Rowley (eds), *Small towns of Roman Britain*, 9–49, Oxford.

Wycherley, R. A. (1976), *How the Greeks Built Cities*, second edition, London.

Youtie, H. (1966), 'Pétaus, fils de Pétaus, ou le scribe qui ne savait pas écrire', *Chronique d'Egypte*, XLI, 127–43.

PART 6

·GOVERNMENT·AND·LAW·

CHAPTER 15

·GOVERNMENT·AND·THE· ·PROVINCES·

Graham Burton

Introduction

The Roman Empire stretched a thousand miles from southern Scotland to the deserts of southern Egypt. The purpose of this chapter is to describe and analyse the administrative mechanisms which served to maintain the political unity of this vast territorial expanse. The Roman government did not pursue many of the goals which, today, are conventionally associated with the exercise of political power by the state, e.g. the control or modification of economic developments, social welfare, education. Its concerns were more limited, above all the regular exaction of taxes and the maintenance of internal order. In the period from the first emperor, Augustus, up to the political and military crisis of the mid-third century, the most striking feature of Roman rule is the stability and persistence of the administrative tasks carried out by the imperial state and of the institutional mechanisms created to achieve them. For that reason this essay concentrates on *typical* practices and relationships, and eschews tangential discussion of minor variations of practice across time or by region; the governance of the province of Egypt stands as an exception to much of what is said in this chapter. To begin, the personnel of Roman government in the provinces and the internal administrative organization of the provinces are described briefly, before proceeding to examine the three main manifestations of Roman rule, taxation, jurisdiction and the supervision of the local administrative units (the cities; Part 5) of the provinces.

Governors and governed

The Roman Empire was divided for administrative purposes into a set of territorial circumscriptions called provinces. Each province was set under the authority of a Roman governor. Although the number of provinces increased during the principate, especially in the first century through imperial expansion and occasionally through the division of a single geographically large area into two, provinces remained the basic unit for all administration throughout this period. Governors of provinces were selected from the ranks of the most prestigious status-groups in the social structure of the empire, namely the senatorial and equestrian orders; most were senators. In AD 138, for example, thirty-two provinces were governed by senators; at that time, besides a small congeries of minor provinces, such as the Cottian Alps or Corsica, only five substantial areas, Egypt, Noricum, Raetia and the two Mauretanias, were governed by equestrians. Governors of senatorial rank were split, in terms of formal public law, into two categories, imperial legates and proconsuls. For example, in AD 138, twenty-two provinces were governed by imperial legates, ten by proconsuls. The only significant practical distinctions between the two categories resided in their method of appointment and their tenure of office. Imperial legates were appointed on the authority of the emperor. No fixed term of office was ever introduced, but from the late first century onwards their normal tenure was about three years. Proconsuls were selected for office by lot from the ranks of senators of appropriate seniority; their tenure was fixed by law at one year. Within each category certain posts were considered more responsible and senior than others. For example imperial legates of militarily important provinces where more than one legion was stationed (e.g. Syria or Britain) were appointed only from the ranks of senators who had held the highest civil magistracy at Rome, the consulship. In the Republic the consulship had been the highest and most powerful political office available in the state. In the principate, although shorn of most of its practical powers, it remained an important and prestigious marker in a senator's career; normally held at age about forty it gave access to the most important administrative and military posts in the empire. Similarly the proconsuls of Africa and Asia, economically prosperous and highly urbanized provinces, were always ex-consuls; the remaining proconsuls were normally more junior senators in their mid-thirties. However despite differences in title, method of appointment, length of tenure, and seniority, *all* governors of senatorial rank exercised similar powers and responsibilities over their provincial subjects. The appointment and titulature of equestrian governors was a more straightforward matter. They were all appointed by the emperor and normally carried the title of procurator with the exception of the governor of Egypt who was styled prefect; when Mesopotamia was annexed as a province in 195 it also received an equestrian governor who was styled prefect. Their length of tenure was not legally fixed, but probably averaged three years.

No large-scale corps of lower-status professional administrators linked governors to their provincial subjects. Rather governors were assisted by a small, mainly non-professional, staff who were recruited from four sources. First, in the majority of provinces, a small number of junior senators, varying according to the status and importance of the province, assisted the governor. The proconsul of Asia, for example, was assisted by three more junior senators (technically termed legates), to whom he delegated some administrative and judicial functions, and by a quaestor (the most junior rank in the senate) who had primarily financial functions. In contrast, in a number (in 138, eleven, such as Arabia or Thrace) of provinces, the governor had no senatorial assistants. Second, provincial governors, like all senatorial magistrates, were accompanied by a small group of attendants, known as *apparitores*, who acted as lictors, messengers, heralds or scribes. Third, every governor, before he set out for his province, would assemble on his own initiative a body of friends (*amici*) and advisers who served him during his tour of duty. For example, an eminent senator and sometime tutor to the future emperor Marcus Aurelius, Cornelius Fronto, reported that, as part of his preparations for becoming governor of Asia, he had:

> taken active steps to enlist the help of my friends in all that concerned the ordering of the province. Relations and friends of mine, of whose loyalty and integrity I was assured, I called from home to assist me. I wrote to my intimates at Alexandria to repair with all speed to Athens and await me there, and I deputed the management of my Greek correspondence to those most learned men. From Cilicia too I called upon eminent citizens to join me, for owing to my continual advocacy of the public and private interests of Cilicians before you, I had hosts of friends in that province. From Mauretania also I summoned to my side Julius Senex . . . in order to make use not only of his loyalty and diligence, but also of his military activity in the hunting down and suppressing of bandits.

Finally, every governor had a detachment of regular soldiers, seconded from their normal military duties, attached to his personal service. They acted as his military body-guard and performed certain executive functions such as executing condemned criminals and helping to hunt down fugitives. Together these four groups formed a mini-court to the governor and many of them would accompany him on his tour of his province. From their ranks, especially the *amici*, he would choose advisers who assisted him in his formal hearings of judicial and administrative disputes (p. 431 below).

Alongside the provincial governor stood a formally distinct set of elite officials called procurators who were normally recruited from the equestrian order and performed a variety of fiscal functions. In modern works such procurators are conventionally designated as 'fiscal procurators' to differentiate them from the small set of equestrian officials who *governed* provinces and were also called procurators (praesidial procurators; p. 424 above). In every province ruled by a senatorial governor the emperor appointed an equestrian procurator who exercised overall supervision over imperial estates and property and controlled, with the governor, the allocation and collection of the direct tax, the tribute. These fiscal procurators, also, sometimes supervised the collection of indirect taxes, although, according to a variable administrative practice, specially designated procurators were often put in charge of the collection of indirect taxes for individual provinces or groups of provinces (p. 428 below).

Given the small number of élite officials regularly sent out to the provinces and the parallel absence of a large-scale bureaucratic apparatus, the imperial state needed an intermediary institutional mechanism whereby its authority over the provincial population could be effected. This mechanism was provided by the cities of the Empire. Each province can be viewed, for present purposes, as a congeries of civic units. Each city had a territorial hinterland, its *territorium*, attached to it. Each, despite variations of title and status, possessed a common form of political organization: boards of executive magistrates and permanent deliberative councils, recruited largely from ex-magistrates. The magistrates and councils exercised routine *local* administrative and political control over their territories (p. 434 below). In addition the imperial state devolved on these local civic authorities much of the routine administrative work of collecting taxes and facilitating jurisdiction. As will be seen in more detail, in the Roman Empire the processes of taxation, jurisdiction and administration were dependent on the regular co-operation of the elite representatives (governors and procurators) of the imperial state on the one hand and of the local civic authorities on the other.

Three aspects of this brief description deserve emphasis. First, governors and procurators who possessed supreme decision-making and administrative powers in the provinces were not professional administrators. As members of the socio-political élite of the empire provincial administration formed only a part of their wider social and political role. Second, the number of elite administrators was small in comparison to the size of the Empire. In the mid-second century there were only about one hundred and fifty such administrators in the provinces to govern a population conventionally estimated at 50 to 60 million people, that is one élite administrator for about every 350,000 to 400,000 inhabitants. By comparison in southern China, in the twelfth century, with a population of a similar size, there was roughly one elite administrator for every 15,000 people. Third, the routine co-operation of the local ruling class of the provinces, the civic magistrates and councillors, was crucial to the administrative stability of the Empire.

Taxation: the material demands of the state

Roman taxation and jurisdiction were the twin symbols of Roman domination and provincial subjection. Taxation in money and kind enabled the imperial state to maintain a large standing army, to provide an elaborate network of roads for military and political communication, to pay administrators, to help feed the massive population of the Imperial City, and to underpin conspicuous consumption at the imperial court. In terms of revenue the most important tax was the tribute, which took two forms, a tax levied on land and property (*tributum soli*) and a poll-tax (*tributum capitis*). The land and population of all the provinces were subject to tribute. The only significant exceptions occurred when specific communities were granted the Italian right which exempted their territory from the imposition of tribute.

The process of levying the tribute involved three distinct stages: the census, the assessment, and collection. The census acted as the backbone of the Roman tax-system by providing the information on which assessment and collection were based. The annexation of any new territory by the imperial state (e.g. Cappadocia under Tiberius or Arabia under Trajan) was followed immediately by the taking of a census. Otherwise censuses of individual provinces or groups of provinces occurred on a regular periodic basis. Responsibility for supervising the census lay either with the provincial governor or with officials of senatorial or equestrian rank who had been especially designated for the task by the emperor. The practical work of collecting information, however, devolved on the local civic magistrates. They registered the inhabitants of their city and its territory (for the purpose of the poll-tax) and collected individual returns from owners of property in their territory for the land tax. Ownership of land had to be reported in the following manner:

> Name of each farm, in what city it is and in what district, and the two nearest neighbours; arable, how many *iugera*, which have been sown in the last ten years; vineyards, how many vines; olive yards, how many *iugera* and how many trees; meadows, how many *iugera*, which were mown in the last ten years; pasture, how many *iugera* approximately; also woods. The person who makes the declaration must estimate everything. . . . A man who has land in another city must make a declaration in the city in which the land is, since the tribute for land must be raised in that in whose territory it is occupied. (Ulpian, *on the Census*, Book III)

Once people and property had been enumerated and registered, assessment of liabilities ensued. Assessment, at least for the land-tax, was not imposed on individuals but on communities and their territories. The process of collecting the taxes devolved, again, on the local authorities. They, not imperial officials, were responsible for the physical exaction of tribute. Individual provincials were liable to their city, the city to the imperial government. The principle of communal liability explains the need for large-scale land-owners to declare in their returns separately, city by city, the location of their property, as well as the Roman government's practice of granting communal remissions of liability to cities on occasions of natural disasters or special need. Within this process of census-taking, assessment and exaction, the role of the governors and provincial procurators was supervisory and adjudicatory. They tried to ensure that each city paid its due assessment, held legal hearings when individuals were accused of providing false information for the census, and adjudicated disputes between cities, especially neighbouring ones, which arose out of the collection of tribute.

Three major indirect taxes were regularly levied in the provinces, the tax on manumissions, the inheritance tax, and a toll on goods in transit known as the *portorium*. The manumissions tax was paid by slaves on the sums they paid to their masters for their freedom. The inheritance tax was levied on the property of Roman citizens alone. This tax had been instituted by the first emperor, Augustus, to fund the special military treasury which disbursed the retirement bounties to veteran soldiers. Both these taxes were levied at a rate of 5 per cent. The toll on goods which passed across various territorial circumscriptions of the empire, not necessarily coincident with individual provinces, was levied at rates of 2 to $2\frac{1}{2}$ per cent on the value of the goods, rates which varied in different parts of the Empire. Although the full details of how these taxes were administered remain obscure, the general outline is reasonably clear. Procurators (p. 425 above), either the fiscal procurator of a province, or procurators specially appointed to the tax, assumed overall responsibility for supervising the taxes and adjudicating disputes. The process of collection was either farmed out to groups of private tax-contractors or placed in the hands of imperial slaves and freedmen. Administrative practice in this last matter appears to have varied from period to period and from area to area. One striking feature of these administrative arrangements deserves emphasis. Of all the forms of contact between the imperial state and the subject population these indirect taxes alone were not handled by the cities and the civic authorities as intermediaries. Consequently they represent a rare case where the agents of the imperial state, whether directly in guise of imperial slaves and freedmen or indirectly in the guise of tax-farmers, came routinely into direct contact with the subjects of the Empire.

Money taxes do not exhaust the catalogue of regular material demands which the imperial state made on its subjects. At any time a major military expedition or the peripatetic movements of the imperial court could make extraordinary demands, in the form of forced requisitioning, on provincials. Provincials were also routinely subject to three closely interlinked sets of material imposts (in the form either of provisions or transport or labour), namely labour and money for the maintenance of roads, *hospitium*, and the *vehiculatio*. *Hospitium* was the obligation of provincial subjects to provide shelter and hospitality, without payment, to governors and their staff and to soldiers passing through a province on official military service. *Vehiculatio* was a system whereby designated agents of the imperial state, such as governors, procurators, or imperial slaves and freedmen, or soldiers on official business, were entitled to requisition, at fixed prices, transport and supplies for their journeys. The organization of the levying of resources for the *vehiculatio* was similar to that for the collection of tribute. The local civic authorities were responsible within the territory of their own city for the maintenance of supplies and the provision of transport which they levied from the land-owners and peasants of their territory. Provincial governors and fiscal procurators laid down, and tried to enforce, rules governing access to these services, and also adjudicated disputes. Communities which were situated on or close to major highways tended to suffer most from the various claims for food, lodging and transport made by passing soldiers and officials. Throughout this period peasant communities and villages are attested petitioning governors to seek protection from the depredations caused by the excessive and abusive claims of soldiers and officials. Although we cannot quantify in monetary terms the amount of surplus extracted by the Roman government through these material imposts, there is no doubt that the inhabitants of the Empire perceived their exaction as one of the most onerous burdens imposed on them by the imperial state.

As long as political and military stability persisted in the Empire, the system of taxation, which we have described, offered clear advantage both to the Roman government and to the local elites of the provinces. The collection of the bulk of taxes in money (through the tribute and the indirect taxes) facilitated the transfer by the Roman government of resources from one end of the Empire to the other. Prosperous provinces where government expenditure was low (such as Asia) provided the revenues to fund expenditure in provinces which were economically poorer or where substantial military forces were permanently stationed. The use of the census to assess and reassess periodically the wealth of the empire helped to provide a rational and predictable framework for collecting revenue and for correlating it with expenditure. The system was also cost-effective to the Roman government since it had no need to maintain a permanent and substantial corps of official tax-collectors. The local elites who actually effected the collection of taxes also gained advantages. Their administrative and political authority, as local magistrates and councillors, was enhanced by their role as tax-collectors of the imperial state. Financially they acquired the opportunity of manipulating the allocation of taxes in their own locality to their own advantage, in their role as substantial landowners, by imposing a disproportionate share of the tax-assessment on the dependent peasantry or other politically subordinate groups.

The military crisis of the third century, however, and the associated need of the Roman government for increased financial resources severely strained the existing fiscal system. The traditional reliance on periodic censuses and on the administrative co-operation of the local elites made it administratively and politically difficult either to increase the general level of taxation or to raise money quickly when sudden crises supervened. The government, therefore, resorted to repeated debasements of the coinage (Part 8, Chapter 21). Debasement interacted with a more generalized economic crisis to produce inflation. In a vicious circle monetary inflation and economic crisis combined with political instability to undermine the unitary fiscal system based on money taxes. Increasing resort was had to exactions in kind to supply and reward the armies. When, by the end of the third century, unitary political control was restored over the Empire, taxation in kind was institutionalized as the keystone of the fiscal system which now operated within a radically altered framework of provincial organization and administration (Part 6, Chapter 17).

Jurisdiction: the maintenance of the social order

The Roman imperial state arrogated to itself the monopoly of the legitimate use of violence. In the provinces only the governor possessed the right to impose capital sentences. According to one contemporary commentator it was the duty:

> of a good and conscientious governor to see that the province he rules is peaceful and tranquil, and this result he will achieve without difficulty if he takes careful measures to ensure that the province is free from criminals and searches them out. He should search out persons guilty of sacrilege, brigands, kidnappers and thieves and punish them according to their offences; he should also repress those who harbour them, without whom a brigand cannot long be concealed. (Ulpian, 'On the Duties of a Proconsul', Bk. 7, *Digest*, 1.18.13.pr.)

Two key practices, the assize tour and the co-operation of the local authorities, shaped the way in which governors attempted to suppress crime.

First, the assize tour. No standing courts existed in the provinces. Instead governors annually toured their provinces and conducted judicial hearings at specifically designated cities, known as assize-centres. The status of assize-centre became a highly-prized privilege. Economic advantages accrued to such cities because of the influx of officials, litigants, and hangers-on, while their inhabitants gained the practical advantage of relatively easy access to the governor's tribunal.

Second, the role of the local authorities. Given the lack of a substantial executive force at the disposal of the governor, the local system of rule exercised the routine functions of apprehending and detaining criminals. Local magistrates were responsible for tracking down and arresting brigands and robbers in the territory of their city. Prisoners frequently underwent preliminary interrogation by local magistrates who, then, either sent them under escort to the governor or detained them pending the governor's arrival in the city. For example during a pogrom against Christians at Smyrna, *c.* 155, the bishop of Smyrna, Polycarp, fled the city. He was hunted down and arrested by a local magistrate, 'the warden of the peace', and his police force who held him in prison at Smyrna to await the arrival of the governor. Criminal charges of all kinds were also laid by private initiative. Injured parties, their relatives, personal enemies, or *delatores* could petition the governor for leave to bring a formal accusation. If the governor assented, either the accuser personally served a copy of the charge or the governor authorized an official summons which ordered the accused to appear at an assize.

When assize-hearings commenced, two procedures were open to the governor. First, he could mete out summary justice, especially on non-citizens, without recourse to a formal hearing. Prisoners accused of brigandage were often summarily executed on the basis of the preliminary investigations of local magistrates. Gaol clearances were also conducted in which the governor had the power to condemn on the spot those whom he considered manifestly guilty. This summary procedure, which was also used for minor crimes, was termed *de plano* justice and stood in contrast to the second procedure open to the governor, a full scale court-hearing at his tribunal (*pro tribunali*). Under this procedure litigants were represented by advocates, and written and oral evidence was taken from witnesses and interested parties. The governor presided over the trial with the help of an advisory body known as a *consilium*. A *consilium* was normally recruited from the *amici* of the governor and members of the local élite. For example, in 60 in Caesarea, when Paul appealed to be tried at Rome the governor, Festus, adjudicated this claim with the help of Agrippa II, a descendant of Herod, officers of the auxiliary troops stationed in Judaea and 'the leading men of the city'. A *consilium* was not however a jury. The governor might take its advice on matters of fact or law, but the final decisions as to guilt and any appropriate penalty were his alone.

The assize-system of peripatetic hearings and the reliance on local civic or private initiative, for the detection of criminals and for the laying of accusations, provided two structural constraints on the governor's exercise of his supreme powers of jurisdiction. In the course of the court-hearings themselves, from pre-trial preliminaries to the act of sentencing, the governor possessed a wide-ranging discretion and freedom of action which were on the one hand partially limited by rules of statute law and on the other continually shaped and restrained by the informal and formal demands of status. First to be considered is statute law. Roman criminal law presented in no way as an elaborate and sophisticated edifice of rules and procedure as Roman civil law. Some crimes (e.g. adultery, poisoning) were indeed defined by statute laws which laid down correct court procedure and prescribed appropriate penalties. Such statutes, in strict theory, only applied to Roman citizens, who also enjoyed the right of appeal from the sentence of the governor to the emperor. Non-citizens, in contrast, were always liable to undergo the summary procedure which has been described above. The scope of statute law was, however, restricted, and governors were always at liberty to define as criminal activities which were not covered by such laws. The dictum *nullum crimen sine lege* was alien to Roman practice. In Egypt, for example, causing damage to an irrigation dyke or cutting down mulberry trees, which were planted on dykes to strengthen them, were considered capital offences; they had clearly been created by the prefect of Egypt. Other offences were created which were actionable throughout the Empire. For example, no general law outlawing Christianity was ever promulgated during the first two centuries AD, but by precedent and custom all provincial governors came to treat being a Christian as a capital offence. Within the category of non-statute offences governors were originally free, in contrast to statute offences, to fix the appropriate penalties as they saw fit; so, the penalties for rustling varied between provinces. The principal legal restraint on the governor in such cases was the right of Roman citizens to appeal against conviction to the emperor. The contrast in possible treatment between citizens and non-citizens is well illustrated by an incident in the province of Pontus-Bithynia, *c.* AD 110. When certain provincial subjects were accused of being Christians, the governor accepted the charges and conducted an investigation. Of those who confessed and refused to recant, the non-citizens were summarily executed, while the citizens were transferred to Rome.

The second factor which shaped the governor's handling of criminal trials was the social status of the litigants and other interested parties. The status of defendants, especially, affected all aspects of criminal procedure. During the course of the second century AD, the advantages and privileges of high social status were codified and reformulated by a series of imperial rulings which were especially directed to the judicial activities of provincial governors. For analytical purposes the judicial process can usefully be separated into three elements: pre-trial preliminaries, the trial, and sentencing. During the preliminaries, if the defendant had been accused by private summons, the governor had to decide whether to imprison him, allow him to be given bail, or let him remain at liberty under his own recognizances. Although the governor took into consideration the seriousness and character of the alleged crime, the main criteria for his decision were the status, wealth and character of the accused. In general few rules structured the practical organization of assizes. No formal mechanisms existed to regulate the delivery of petitions by prospective litigants to the governor or to fix the order in which cases would be held at any specific assize. There was not even any assurance that all litigants who had gathered at an assize would obtain a hearing. This lack of fixed procedures helped to ensure the effective operation of the informal social influences of status and bribery. For example in 158–9, when the governor of Africa heard a charge of misuse of magical practices laid against the rhetorician Apuleius (author of the Golden Ass), the case was completed only five days after the charge had been brought. Apuleius thought that the speed with which the case was heard helped to prevent the forgery of documents by his accusers and specifically thanked the governor for the favour of hearing the case so quickly.

During a trial the influence of social status was most apparent in the evaluation of evidence. Various imperial rulings encouraged governors to attach great weight to the status and wealth of witnesses and to their general character and repute. Slaves, in contrast, were routinely subjected to torture as witnesses, a practice which was probably *de facto* extended for some purposes to freeborn provincials of low status by the end of the second century. Cognately high-status provincials could hope to promote their own interests by producing letters of recommendation, especially if written by patrons within the imperial aristocracy. Penalties on conviction, unless laid down for citizens by statute, originally lay within the discretion of the governors. During the course of the second century a series of imperial rulings were issued which created *de iure* a dual-penalty system whose main consequence was to entrench the privileges of high-status defendants. The example of capital punishments will suffice to illustrate the general picture. Low status defendants were frequently executed by public crucifixion

432

or by condemnation to the beasts at the periodic festivals and public spectacles which occurred in all provinces. Such cruel and public execution acted as a ritual demonstration of the power of the imperial state. High-status defendants, in contrast, were scarcely ever executed, instead they suffered deportation to an island or relegation from their province. Members of the local political elites (civic magistrates and councillors) were especially privileged in that any governor who wished to impose on them the sentence of deportation had automatically to write to the emperor to acquire confirmation of his decision.

The entrenchment, by way of codification, of the privileges of the provincial upper-class represented in formal terms at least an important restriction on the governor's discretionary use of his jurisdictional and coercive powers. In practice the restriction was more apparent than real, since governors had always exercised their discretion in the context of their own social values. As one eminent senator in *c.* 100 wrote to another junior senator, about to take up a second office as a governor:

> You have done splendidly – and I hope you will not rest on your laurels – in commending your administration of justice to the provincials by your great tact. This you reveal particularly in the consideration you show for the best men yet in such a way as to win the reverence of the lower orders at the same time as you hold the affection of their superiors. Many men, in their anxiety to avoid seeming to show excessive favour to men of influence, succeed only in gaining a reputation for perversity and malice. I know there is no chance of your falling prey to that vice, but in praising you for the way you tread the middle course, I cannot help sounding as if I were offering you advice: namely, that you should maintain the distinctions between ranks and degrees of dignity. Nothing could be more unequal than that equality which results when those distinctions are confused or broken down. (Pliny, *Letters*, 9.5)

If criminal jurisdiction and the maintenance of internal order in his province represented the prime judicial task of any governor, his tribunal also operated as a forum for the resolution of material and other disputes, between individuals, by his exercise of civil jurisdiction. Consequently civil litigants faced many of the same problems as litigants in criminal cases: difficulties of access to the governor's tribunal, the lack of a fixed ordering of cases, the possibilities of severe delays. *Mutatis mutandis* high-status litigants gained advantages analogous to those their peers gained in criminal hearings. Two additional factors, specific to the exercise of civil jurisdiction, also deserve emphasis. First, local courts – that is, courts controlled and organized by the local authorities of each city in a province – possessed legitimate jurisdiction in civil cases over their own subjects, unless they had become Roman citizens. Second, Roman civil law: provincials who acquired Roman citizenship by definition organized their affairs (e.g. wills) according to the tenets of Roman civil law; in principle the proper tribunal for hearing cases between Roman citizens under the aegis of Roman law was that of the governor. In many areas (e.g. property, inheritance) Roman civil law provided a highly developed and elaborate set of rules and procedures. The spread of Roman citizenship and, thus, Roman law, especially among the upper class of the provinces, offered them a rational method of adjudication in disputes and, thereby, an ordered framework for the organization of their routine material, commercial and social existence.

To sum up. The Roman government maintained internal peace and provided a regular system of adjudication, by way of the mechanisms of civil and criminal jurisdiction, through a continuous process of co-operation with the local system of rule. The specific forms of interdependence and co-operation, which were especially significant for the operation of criminal jurisdiction, served to entrench the dominant local political role of the local elites. Also the formal rules and informal practices of Roman jurisdiction offered privileges to the socially advantaged in general (Roman citizens) and, in particular, to provincials of high social status, especially local magistrates and councillors. The maintenance of internal order and the entrenchment of privilege within the social order were mutually dependent and reinforcing processes.

The supervision of local administration

Administrative structures provide the mechanism for the allocation and supervision of resources, the implementation of policies and rules, and the resolution of conflicts between interested parties; in the Roman Empire parallel central and local authorities exercised these tasks. The governor possessed an untrammelled discretionary power to intervene in the administrative affairs of the subject cities of his province. Paradoxically this power was not matched by equivalent bureaucratic resources (p. 426 above). The local authorities, consequently, maintained *de facto* a wide-ranging control over their internal administrative affairs. No clear demarcation of mutually exclusive areas of competence between the governor and the local authorities existed except in rare instances where normative rules were enacted which required the local authorities to gain the approval of governor and/or emperor for specific types of administrative decisions. For the sake of analysis it is easiest to proceed by describing first those administrative activities where the local authorities exercised a day-to-day control, subject only to the occasional possible intervention of the governor.

Local magistrates and councils exercised responsibility for the supervision of the needs and services of civic life, such as the corn and food supplies, the regulation of prices and the markets, the public baths and gymnasia, the maintenance of the streets, sewerage and the water-supply, the public record-offices, the construction and repair of public and religious buildings, the holding of customary games and festivals. The extent and diversity of these tasks varied from city to city. Great cities like Carthage, Antioch or Ephesus possessed resplendent public buildings and ruled large territorial hinterlands. Other cities were little more than villages. Despite such variety of scale the functions of the local authorities were similar: to meet the perceived needs of communal existence through the supervision of financial and physical resources earmarked for those needs.

Within this framework of effective local autonomy governors were able to intervene at their own initiative or, more likely, at the request of the local authorities. For example at Antioch in Pisidia, *c.* AD 93, the local authorities wrote to the governor to inform him that their corn supply had dried up because of the severity of the winter and to seek his help to secure a supply for sale. The governor, in reply, ordered all the inhabitants of the city and its territory to declare before the local magistrates the amount and location of all their grain. Any surplus, beyond what was needed for seeding and for the feeding of their own families, was to be made available to the city's buyers. The governor backed his edict with the threat of judicial sanctions against people who hoarded supplies of corn contrary to his orders. At Ephesus in the mid-second century the local authorities were unable to enforce their harbour regulations which were designed to protect access to the quayside. The governor of Asia, in response to their request for help, issued new rulings and announced that anybody found contravening his edict would have to render account for their disobedience before his tribunal.

Financial administration, in the sense of raising, protecting, and allocating resources, posed continuous difficulties for the local authorities, and was, therefore, the sphere of administration in which governors intervened most often. A governor, if local difficulties were deep-seated and wide-ranging, could issue detailed reformatory rulings. For example in *c.* AD 45 the governor of Asia attempted to suppress the maladministration and malversation of civic and temple funds at Ephesus. His rulings embraced, among other things, abusive auctions of the local priesthood, the borrowing of money by the city in greater amounts than could be repaid from current income, the pledging of future civic income as security for present loans, the diversion of funds bequeathed for fixed purposes to others, the payments for performers at religious festivals. Many financial problems were not so far-reaching. Cities sometimes found themselves either unable to enforce their legitimate rights over public lands in their territory or were challenged in their claim to ownership. Consequently governors were asked to intervene to help to restore public lands or to judge disputes over ownership. When, in the late second century, jurists wrote handbooks on the duties of provincial governors, they advised them that the leasing out and control of public land should be a matter of special concern.

The problems of local financial administration stemmed primarily from two causes, first, embezzlement and misappropriation of funds and second, the weakness of the local tax-base; the latter phenomenon was a direct consequence of the prior lien of the imperial state on resources through the direct tax on land, the tribute (p. 427 above). The recurrence of financial problems and of requests from cities for intervention by the governors led the imperial government to appoint special financial commissioners (*curatores*) who were attached to individual cities or, rarely, groups of cities. These commissioners are first attested in the late first century; the number of such appointments was at first very small though it increased sensibly in the late second and third centuries. They were recruited at first only from the ranks of the imperial aristocracy (senators and equestrians), later also from the upper echelons of provincial society. Their powers were restricted solely to the supervision of local financial administration. Although the appointment of *curatores* added a measure of flexibility to the Roman government's response to requests for help, this institution did not mark a radical break with past practice. For the numbers of financial commissioners appointed remained, at all periods, very small in relation to the number of civic communities in the provinces. For example in the provinces of North Africa (Mauretania, Numidia, Africa Proconsularis) between AD 196 and 270 thirty-two *curatores* are known to have been appointed; in the province of Asia, where at least 300 civic communities existed, only thirty appointments are known between AD 160 and 260.

The emergence of *curatores* was a qualitatively important phenomenon because they represented the only institutional novelty of this period which supplemented the effective powers of provincial governors, especially their capacity to meet demands made by the local authorities. Nothing suggests, however, that the appointment of *curatores* was intended to lead or ever did lead to the removal of responsibility for local financial administration from the local authorities. Once a *curator* had completed his tenure of office, responsibility, including the enforcement of any new regulations created by him, reverted to the local authorities. The overall structure of administrative authority in the provinces and the relative influence of the agents of local and central power were modified but not radically changed by the creation of *curatores*.

Two exceptions exist within the general model of a day-to-day local administrative autonomy operating under the canopy of the discretionary control of the Roman governor. These exceptions concern the questions of policy and law-making by individual cities and of their external relations. The two questions can be considered briefly in turn. Local authorities throughout our period maintained a legitimate power to pass laws of a purely local import without recourse to ratification by the Roman government. For example cities were able to create new citizens, to draw up regulations controlling the conduct of local police forces in their subject territory, to issue rules for the leasing-out and cultivation of public lands, or to regulate the activities of religious associations and cults. But, as far as financial policy was concerned, the Roman government enacted normative rules which limited the powers of local authorities to raise new taxes and to undertake large-scale new building operations which involved additional expenditure from civic funds. The prior permission of the emperor, mediated through the governor, was required before new local taxes could be raised. The standard procedure is clearly laid down in an extant letter of the joint emperors Severus and Caracalla:

> the exaction of new taxes should not be granted lightly; but if your home-state is so weak (in resources) that it needs to be helped by extraordinary aid, present to the governor of the province the facts you have gathered into this petition. That man, after careful investigation of the situation and consideration of the common interest, will report to us what he has discovered. We will then judge whether and to what extent your account should be accepted. (*Codex Justinianus* 4.62.1)

Although the exact origins of this procedure are not known, it was already in force in the first century. During the reign of Vespasian, for example, the town of Sabora in Baetica petitioned the emperor, among other matters, for the right to levy new taxes. Vespasian replied that he confirmed the taxes

> which you say you received from Augustus (the first emperor), but if you wish to introduce any new ones you should approach the governor about them, for I cannot make any decision if I have no advice on this matter.

A cognate procedure existed to control the construction of new public buildings at public expense, the commonest form of long-term major additional expenditure on which a city might embark. By the late-second century provincial governors were advised that:

> new *private* building is possible without the permission of the emperor as long as it is not of the kind done in emulation of another city, nor provides the basis for rioting (*seditio*), nor is a circus, theatre or amphitheatre. But at *public* expense new public work is not possible without the permission of the emperor. That is declared in constitutions. (*Digest* 50.10.3.pr.-1: Macer, *On the Duties of Provincial Governors*, Bk 2)

Financial motives clearly lay behind this attempted control by the Roman government. For example when, early in the second century, a governor of Pontus-Bithynia consulted the emperor Trajan, about plans for new baths at Prusa, he replied that

> if the construction of the new baths will not burden the resources of Prusa, we can grant their request; only let no special tax be levied nor let any less revenue in the future accrue to them for their necessary expenses.

Explanation of this normative control of local financial policy, which stands in contrast to the general practice of an intermittent and discretionary intervention in and control of local affairs, is not hard to seek. The economy of the empire produced only a limited surplus which had to provide, through rents, for private élite consumption and, through taxation, for the fiscal demands of the imperial state. The revenue-raising needs of the provincial cities stood in competition with private rent and imperial taxation. The imperial state, therefore, attempted to protect its own position by delimiting the fiscal powers of the authorities of the provincial cities.

Finally and briefly, the external relations of the cities must be considered. Although they could make claim, whether directly by petition or through the mediation of influential patrons, to a variety of privileged statuses (such as, e.g., first city of their province, assize-centre, centre for celebrating the imperial cult or immunity from tribute), such privileges were only in the gift of the Roman government. Similarly disputes between communities over the ownership of land or the mutual allocation of tax-burdens were always settled by the governor or specially designated mandatories of the imperial state. No other legitimate mechanisms existed for the ordering and settlement of such disputes.

To sum up. Administrative authority over the population of the provinces was exercised by two parallel, but unequal, powers, the provincial governor and the political authorities of each city. The subordination of the local authorities to the central power (normally represented by the governor) manifested itself in a variety of ways: the discretionary ability of the governor to intervene in any administrative matter he chose, the role of his tribunal to adjudicate disputes between communities, the exercise of his superior sanctions at the request of any local authority to reinforce their powers, the creation of a limited set of prescriptive rules which required the local authorities to obtain approval and ratification for specific administrative decisions and policies from the imperial power. Despite this political subordination the local authorities exercised a wide-ranging routine administrative control over the provincial population. The representatives of the imperial power exercised their authority in general in a discretionary, not a routine, fashion.

Concluding remarks

The Roman government achieved its two major administrative goals, the extraction of a regular surplus (taxation) and internal peace (jurisdiction), only through the routine co-operation of the local system of rule with the elite administrators appointed to each province. The provincial governor possessed supreme discretionary authority in his province, an authority manifested most strikingly in his powers of life and death over his provincial subjects. Governors and procurators acted as the final arbiters of all forms of dispute, whether administrative, fiscal, judicial or territorial. Most of the routine procedures of administration and jurisdiction were devolved on the local authorities. The mass of provincial subjects scarcely come into direct contact with the élite representatives of the imperial state. Instead contact was routinely mediated through the local authorities. They continued, also, to exercise legitimate authority over their subjects as far as purely local matters were concerned. Their local political authority was enhanced by their role as surrogate administrative agents of the imperial state, and they were rewarded for their service by the acquisition of judicial privileges.

Four consequences of the administrative goals and procedures of the Roman government deserve emphasis for their wider historical implications. First, the regular extraction of resources, through taxation, provided the means to finance the standing armies which protected the Empire from external attacks and invasions, while the exercise of jurisdiction ensured a level of internal peace. Internal peace and the absence of foreign invasions underpinned the political unity of the empire. Second, both the goals of Roman government, and the specific methods created to achieve them, reinforced the social and political hierarchy within the provinces and helped to integrate the local élites into the imperial system of rule. Third, continuous internal peace provided a secure framework for economic activity, especially agriculture and trade. The economically powerful, especially provincial land-owners from whom the majority of the local political élite were recruited, were enabled to maintain and reproduce, across time, their economic hegemony. Fourth, the practice of devolving much responsibility for the collection of taxes and for the execution of justice on the local authorities served continuously to entrench their local political power. In short, Roman rule was predicated on, recognized and enhanced the social and political hierarchy of the provinces.

CHAPTER 16

·LAW·AND·THE·LEGAL· ·SYSTEM·IN·THE· ·PRINCIPATE·

Elizabeth Green

A knowledge of law and of the legal system is of particular relevance for an understanding of Roman history because of the interest taken in law by the Romans, to which the abundance of juristic evidence testifies. This evidence sheds light not only on their social life and institutions but also on the workings of politics and of the Roman legal mind.

The excellence of Roman law is attested by its adoption as the basis of numerous modern legal systems. This process owes much to the great codification of Roman law authorized by the Emperor Justinian in the sixth century AD, which brought together into a convenient form both a wide range of imperial enactments and numerous excerpts from the writings of the most famous jurists. The basic pattern of Roman law and its most fundamental principles were established during the Republic, but it was under the Empire that Roman law is generally thought to have reached its peak, and thus the second century and the first half of the third century is a period designated by scholars as the Classical period of Roman law. The main characteristic of the period was the assiduous, consolidating activity among the great jurists of the time; thus most by far of the juristic excerpts preserved in Justinian's codification are taken from their works.

The imperial period is not only of interest because of the juristic literature produced. Clearly the transition from Republic to Empire raises many important and interesting questions concerning both the continuing relevance of republican legal institutions and processes and the competence of the emperor to influence the formulation and application of the law. In addition, there were many developments under the Empire which could not fail to have important legal implications, among these the changing role of political institutions, notably the Senate, the growth of a professional imperial administration and the large-scale extension of the Roman citizenship. This chapter is therefore designed to look at the effect on Roman law and the legal system of the advent of the emperor as a law-maker and as a judge.

The emperor as law-maker

It has often been said that Augustus, while establishing for himself a position of supremacy, realized the need to avoid an undisguised, blatant accumulation of personal power, and to display sensitivity towards the nostalgic regard in which republican institutions, practices and privileges were held. The masterly diplomacy with which he achieved his difficult task is well illustrated in the area of law-making. Clearly he could not achieve supremacy without gaining control over the formulation of law whether public or private, nor did he wish to cast aside the traditional republican organs and procedures of law-making within which there was technically no place for the emperor. There is, in fact, no need to assume that Augustus' reluctance to do so was based only on fear of the consequences of such an action; the way in which he manipulated existing institutions suggests that he recognized the value of the various checks and balances inherent in them. In the second and third centuries the jurists were claiming that the emperor's pronouncements had the force of law (Gaius, *Institutiones*, 1.5; Ulpian, D.1.4.1pr,1). The basis of this claim is not easy to discern, and Augustus and his immediate successors, at least, did not make such a claim, but exercised their influence within a gradually changing framework inherited from the Republic.

The fact that Augustus and his successors were able to influence the formulation of law ostensibly within this framework, is indicative of the flexibility and adaptability of these republican institutions. One of the most notable features of the republican legal system was the tendency for new practices and institutions to be introduced alongside old ones when the need for them arose, and gradually to encroach on the competence of the old without totally superseding them. It was for this reason that by the end of the Republic there were various channels through which law might be made. Thus Cicero enumerates the sources of law as statute, senatorial decrees, previous judgments, the authority of the jurists, the edicts of magistrates, custom and equity. The most important of those listed are statutes passed through the popular assemblies (that is, *leges* and *plebiscita* passed through the *comitia* and *concilium plebis* respectively), juristic interpretation, senatorial decrees and magisterial edicts.

Interpretation of the civil law was originally a privilege exercised by the priests, but was at an early stage taken over by a group of legal experts, mainly of senatorial rank, but towards the end of the Republic increasingly of equestrian rank. Since Republican magistrates and judges were not themselves legal experts, it is easy to see how necessary the role of the jurists was and how profound their influence. As for senatorial decrees (*senatusconsulta*), many scholars believe that these were strictly only advisory. Whatever their precise status, they clearly had great influence, in practice, along with the magisterial edict, in supplementing statute law. The development of magisterial law (*ius honorarium*) is perhaps the best illustration of the tendency of the Romans to improvise and to bring in new practices alongside the old. The limitations of statute law and the rigidity of the processes associated with it were, to some extent, overcome by the competence of the republican magistrates, notably the praetors, to issue edicts on entering office, laying down the circumstances in which they would grant or refuse actions at law. Thus new rules and institutions gradually grew up alongside the old *ius civile*.

None of these channels of law-making was formally abolished by Augustus. The popular assemblies continued to meet in order to pass *plebiscita* and *leges* on the proposal of magistrates; praetors, aediles and provincial governors still enjoyed the right to issue edicts; and the Senate was active in passing decrees. Yet what is known of the content of the legislation of the Augustan period strongly suggests his influence on the formulation of every enactment, however it was made law. Possession of *tribunicia potestas* enabled him actually to propose some laws, presumably to the *concilium*, and thus there are several *leges Iuliae* dated to his reign. But there is also evidence of laws which were presumably passed in the *comitia*, since they bear the names of the consuls. The evidence suggests that these *leges* belong to the latter period of the reign of Augustus, while the *leges Iuliae* attested all date to the earlier period. Whatever the reason for this, the content of the statutes suggests that they were all the work of a single legislator.

Statutes continued to be supplemented by *senatusconsulta*, and some believe that these decrees acquired strict law-making status at this time because of the association of the emperor with the Senate and its decrees (Watson, 1974, 21ff.). Certainly, by the second century AD, the jurists were attributing undisputed legal status to resolutions of the Senate. However, it is not possible to designate a specific point at which theoretical legal force was granted to them, and they seem to have enjoyed as much efficacy, at least in practice, during the Republic as under the empire. What is important here is that the Senate's activities in the legal sphere did not become obsolete, and that Augustus, in fact, aimed to enhance the prestige and self-consciousness of this body. Nevertheless the existence of a figure possessing the power and *auctoritas* of Augustus makes the formal privileges of senators appear, to a considerable degree, to have been compensation for the loss of real power which they had enjoyed during the Republic. Augustus was entitled to sit between the consuls at meetings of the Senate, but his main channel of communication with this body, and thus influence over senatorial proceedings, was a select group of friends or advisers of senatorial rank, the members of his *consilium*. As in the case of statutes, the nature of the Augustan *senatusconsulta*, for which there is evidence, strongly suggests his personal influence in this area. It seems, therefore, that as well as safeguarding senatorial *dignitas*, Augustus saw the continued enactment of *senatusconsulta* as another channel through which he could supplement his law-making activities.

Just as the Senate continued to enjoy competence in law-making, so certain magistrates retained the right to issue edicts relating to their spheres of office. This conveniently enabled Augustus to issue edicts, and there is evidence of his doing so in his capacity as proconsul of his vast province. However, he does not seem to have limited his edicts to the affairs of these areas, and the sources also attest Augustan edicts relating to issues of private law which were clearly designed to have a general application. Some associate his right to issue edicts with his supposed possession of consular *imperium*. But this would only have extended his competence to Rome and Italy. It is more likely that his *auctoritas* made it acceptable for his right to issue edicts relating to his province to develop into a more general right. At any rate, his activity in this area seems to have overshadowed that of the other magistrates, for the evidence suggests little enterprise or innovation by anyone else.

The role of the jurists under Augustus is a much debated issue. Clearly there was still a need for advice to be submitted by these experts to the magistrates and judges (including the emperor), who continued to be men without any particular legal expertise. The controversy centres on a statement made by the second-century jurist Pomponius, preserved in Justinian's *Digest* in which he attributes to Augustus a measure which gave to certain favoured jurists the right to give opinions 'by his authority'. This seems to be confirmed by Gaius who says that the answers of the jurisprudents are the decisions and opinions of those who have been authorized to lay down the law. Scholars are divided over the exact status which this gave to the opinions of jurists who either did or did not enjoy this privilege. Gaius, writing in the second century, adds that an opinion held by all the privileged jurists had the force of law. This provides an indication of the prestige associated with such jurists, which must have rendered the opinions of any others, if not valueless, at least of very limited worth. Augustus presumably wished to curtail independent activity by jurists, and to make those who were able to influence the law to some extent dependent on him. More importantly, he perhaps wished the most eminent jurists to be identified with him, so that juristic activity should be associated with his rule. The evidence suggests that the jurists whom Augustus favoured were senators, a reversal of the trend towards equestrians of the late Republic. It may be seen as part of Augustus' attempt to enhance the prestige of the senatorial order and that of juristic science, as a response to complaints expressed, for example, by Cicero, that jurisprudence had become chaotic and discredited.

Honoré has argued that one of Augustus' methods of effecting change in the law was to persuade the jurists to agree to an innovation (Honoré, 1981, 3). He cites a passage in Justinian's *Institutes* in which is described the process whereby Augustus gathered some jurists together and persuaded them to agree to a measure which would provide legal validity for codicils, informal documents sometimes appended to wills. Another passage from the *Institutes* describes the repeated order by Augustus to the consuls to use their authority to enforce trusts, which had hitherto not been legally binding. Honoré sees Augustus acting in these incidents like a republican praetor in taking on a reforming role. What, in fact, seems to emerge most forcibly from these passages of the *Institutes* is the enormous prestige enjoyed by Augustus which made any precedent set by him sufficiently influential gradually to be adopted into legal practice and accepted by lawyers.

It was this same prestige which perhaps gave to *senatusconsulta* (with which the emperor was associated) and to the opinions of the approved jurists, a higher status in the eyes of lawyers, than they had enjoyed in the Republic. It also underlies the system of rescripts (discussed below p. 446) which later emerged, whereby the advice or instructions obtained by individuals or by communities from the emperor came to be regarded as legislative by the jurists. Thus in issuing rescripts, the emperor took on the role both of republican praetor and of jurist. At the time of Augustus this system had not yet developed. He therefore exploited all the existing channels of law-making, engineering a place for himself within them and, as it were, feeling his way. At the same time, the prestige which he built up and the precedents he established, strengthened the position of the emperor within these existing channels and undermined the roles of others. Thus changes were effected, and the basis laid for the rescript system which was eventually to overshadow every other law-making channel.

The actual volume of legislation issued under Augustus was enormous, as might be expected from a long reign which was historically so crucial. It is interesting that a close examination of much of his legislation shows that it was far less traditionally republican than it at first appears. Two laws relating to marriage were complex statutes which represented intervention in the realm of family law on a scale which is not comparable to that of the republican censors. In addition, the privileges and penalties introduced by these Augustan statutes had implications for the attaining of magistracies, the rights of tutors (that is, those appointed to oversee the affairs of women and of boys under age), the powers of fathers of households (*patres familiarum*) over those descendants under their control, the rights of patrons over their freed slaves and above all for the rules of inheritance. It was clearly useful for Augustus to exercise influence in all of these areas of the law by means of statutes supposedly designed to promote traditional virtues. A similar encroachment on the rights of private individuals is to be seen in another important Augustan statute, the *lex Iulia de adulteriis coercendis*, which added to the republican standing criminal courts (*quaestiones*, p. 451 below), one for the prosecution of adultery. This involved a loss of authority for the *paterfamilias* who had previously been responsible for the punishment of acts of adultery within his *familia*. His rights and those of the husband of an adulteress were redefined, and rules were introduced regulating the prosecution and punishment of those involved in adultery.

An interesting measure often attributed to Augustus is the ban on the contracting of valid marriages by soldiers: this ban was evidently introduced in the very early Empire although there is no firm evidence which associates it with Augustus (Campbell, 1978, 153ff.). It was a rather severe restriction, especially in the light of the marriage laws, and subsequent emperors tried to alleviate the consequences for soldiers in various ways, until Septimius Severus, as is suggested by Herodian, lifted the ban. If it was indeed an Augustan measure, it would provide support for the view that the enactments of Augustus were regarded with such reverence by subsequent emperors that there was great reluctance to repeal them. The penalties associated with the marriage laws, for example, continued to be effective until AD 320 when they were repealed by Constantine, and it was around the same time that changes were made to the adultery law; the *quaestio de adulteriis* was the last of the standing courts to be abolished. Thus the characteristic Roman tendency to modify and adapt rather than formally to abolish institutions seems to have been particularly evident in the case of the laws of Augustus.

Law-making after Augustus

As the principate became more firmly established after Augustus, it is interesting to see how the traditional forms of law-making were gradually overshadowed by the pronouncements of the emperor in various different capacities. A number of popular statutes were passed under the Julio-Claudians, especially Claudius, but by the end of the first century AD the popular assemblies had died out, and the last popular statute for which there is firm evidence was a *lex Cocceia agraria* under Nerva. *Senatusconsulta*, however, did not die out, but continued to be important until the third century AD for the modification and application of rules of law. It is unlikely that any resolution of the Senate was passed without the approval of its most important member, the emperor. Not only could, and did, he propose *senatusconsulta*, but he might even have them proposed in his absence by means of an *oratio* read on his behalf in the Senate. The juristic evidence suggests that the Senate's adoption of the emperor's proposal became a mere formality, since by the later second century the jurists referred to imperial *orationes* as if they were legal enactments; references to *sca* after Hadrian are rare.

The composition of the Senate had, of course, by this time undergone considerable change. As Roman citizenship was systematically granted to people living in all the provinces of the Empire, so the urban aristocracies of the most civilized parts came to be represented in the Senate. Thus it was that men of provincial origin were able to pass through its ranks to the highest position of emperor. In spite of its changing composition, the Senate continued to be jealous of its privileges, and while the close association of the emperor with it no doubt enhanced its prestige, no less was that of the emperor enhanced by his close association with the Senate; there was mutual benefit. Nevertheless, whatever prestige and respect the Senate enjoyed, its real influence on legislation cannot fail to have been further curtailed, not only by the increasing importance of the various types of imperial enactment which involved members of an ever-growing bureaucracy, rather than the Senate, but also by the tendency for many of the emperors in the second and third centuries to spend long periods away from Rome.

Absence from Rome might prevent the emperor from making use of the traditional organs of law-making, but wherever he went he was accompanied by members of his *consilium* and of his bureaucracy; hence the increasing importance and volume of measures enacted with the co-operation of these assistants. It has already been observed that Augustus exercised the right which continued to be enjoyed by the holders of certain magistracies of issuing edicts. His activity in this area seems to have inhibited that of other competent magistrates, and the lack of innovation by the praetors, who had, in the Republic, exercised so much influence on the law, culminated in the consolidation of the praetor's edict during the reign of Hadrian. The jurist Julianus was ordered to perform this task, and the resulting codified edict provided material for a great deal of subsequent juristic commentary.

The emperors after Augustus continued to issue general edicts relating to issues of public and of private law. However, the evidence suggests that far more common imperial pronouncements were rescripts, that is, the replies of the emperor to requests for instructions, either from magistrates or official bodies, or from individuals. The emperor might be required to provide a political decision (such as a grant or refusal of certain privileges) or he might be asked for a ruling in a case of private law. Obviously some of these replies would have involved merely a restatement of the law as it stood, but in other cases a new ruling might be necessary. Similarly, the decisions of the emperor in his role as a judge (p. 451 below), known as decrees, might also involve establishing new principles.

Thus while some of the traditional forms exploited by Augustus continued to be useful, others disappeared, the gap being filled by the increasingly authoritative pronouncements of the emperor. The imperial rescript system became a complex and organized one. It was clearly necessary for the smooth and uniform running of affairs in the Empire for the emperor to provide replies to all the requests for advice and legal rulings which seem to have poured in from officials responsible for law and order in the provinces. Similarly it was important that the principle of the accessibility of the emperor be upheld by the provision of rulings on behalf of individuals who asked for them either in person, by letter or through the agency of the provincial governor. There is evidence of only a few rescripts from the reigns of the earlier emperors, but the system clearly became more common by the second century, and well over a hundred rescripts are attested from the reign of Hadrian (Gualandi, 1963, 24–57).

The number of constitutions preserved in Justinian's *Code* directed to officials in the provinces which merely state the existing law suggests considerable ignorance on the part of these men. This is not surprising, considering that, as in the republican period, most officials had no particular legal training. During the Republic, provincial governors would have consulted the legal experts on their staff. But now that legal advice independent of the emperor had been undermined, requests for advice and instructions were largely directed to him and to his staff. As far as individuals involved in law cases were concerned, a statement from the emperor on a straightforward point of law might be required not because of ignorance, but because the assertion in a rescript of a principle which favoured them would be invaluable.

One of the most controversial questions is that of the exact status of imperial rescripts. When enquiries were made by officials or by individuals involved in law-suits, it is questionable whether the emperor's ruling was strictly binding, and, if it was, whether a general principle was established by such a ruling applicable beyond the individual case concerned. There is no evidence of a specific grant being made to any emperor which would have made his replies to requests for legal rulings more than advisory. Thus the claim of the jurist Gaius that the emperor's enactments have always been regarded as having legal force is based on a rather doubtful argument. Nevertheless, an official who asked for a ruling from the emperor was hardly likely to disregard his reply. More importantly, the fact that the classical jurists attribute law-making powers to the emperor suggests that because of the prestige which he enjoyed, rescripts and decrees, known, together with edicts as imperial constitutions, gradually came to be regarded in practice as not merely advisory nor of limited relevance, but as having a general, binding application.

There were, of course, replies made by emperors which were clearly intended to have a local and limited application, such as grants made to communities of certain privileges or rights. There is also evidence to suggest a reluctance on the part of some emperors to make rulings on certain issues which would have a general application. For example, Trajan, in his correspondence with Pliny, says that he cannot make a general ruling concerning the obligation for members of local senates to make a certain pecuniary contribution. Honoré (1979, 52) argues, in addition, that in the case of petitioners involved in law-suits, a judge was not obliged to await the arrival of the emperor's reply before pronouncing sentence. Nevertheless, there can be no doubt that a favourable reply from the emperor to an enquiry made by an individual involved in a case of law, if received in time, would have greatly improved his position, virtually ensuring his success, and it is scarcely less likely that the judge involved would have felt bound by the ruling. Thus rescripts were, at least in practice, authoritative and influential. The number of references to imperial rescripts in the excerpts from the juristic commentaries preserved in Justinian's *Digest* provides a good indication of the increasing importance of these rulings in the formulation of Roman law. The evidence also suggests that the decision of an emperor was not regarded as relevant only for the duration of his reign. Clearly there must have been occasions when a ruling had to be abrogated or modified by a subsequent emperor, but there seems to have been a great reluctance to do this.

As the rescript system grew in importance as a source of law, it was clearly impossible for the emperor himself to deal with all of the work involved. Thus secretaries concerned with the various types of reply required were appointed within the administrative system. The people involved came to be largely men of equestrian status, whose main task initially must have been to provide information, no doubt by referring to precedents recorded in the archives, which would enable the emperor to make his reply.

447

As more and more constitutions were issued, so those employed in this way must have come to possess considerable expertise and responsibility.

The question thus arises as to the degree of personal involvement on the part of the emperor in the issuing of rescripts. The wording of some of them strongly suggests the emperor's personal interest in the matter in question (Ulpian, D.42.1.33, see Williams, 1976, 69). On the other hand, it has been argued that the work of secretaries can be detected in the texts of preserved rescripts. Honoré (1979, 52ff.) believes that a study of the rescripts concerning issues of private law reveals a consistency of style over certain periods which corresponds to the terms in office of certain secretaries rather than to the reigns of certain emperors. In fact, some of his arguments are not convincing, and caution is necessary in drawing conclusions regarding responsibility for composition from literary style, since allowance must be made for conformity to accepted legal phraseology. Nevertheless, the existence of a secretary and staff responsible for rescripts suggests some degree of delegation, and in cases of petitions requiring simple statements of the law on certain uncontroversial issues, the personal involvement of the emperor would hardly have been necessary. It was sufficient that his name be appended to the reply in order to make it authoritative in court for the benefit of the petitioner. The fact that there is some evidence for the employment of well-known jurists as secretaries (although Syme (1984, 1393) argues that the extent of this has been greatly exaggerated), suggests that some emperors wished to be able to leave the answering of petitions for rulings on private law issues to them. This is not to deny the diligence of many emperors which Millar (1967, 9ff.) postulates; no doubt complex or unprecedented issues of private law would occasion the personal involvement of the emperor, as would important public law decisions, and this explains the personal tone of some of the preserved rescripts.

This leads on to the issue of the exact role of the jurists after the Augustan period. If legal advice and instruction came increasingly to be given by the emperor and his staff, what place was there for the advice even of the 'approved' jurists? In fact, the wealth of legal literature produced in the second and third centuries clearly indicates that juristic activity, far from being rendered superfluous, then reached a peak, the so-called Classical period of Roman law. Since most emperors and many of the members of the administration responsible for the drawing up of rescripts lacked legal training, the jurists would have had an advisory part to play within the rescript system. They exercised influence over the law by means of their prolific writings which were, no doubt, consulted by the emperor and his staff. Some also submitted advice as members of the emperor's *consilium*.

The excerpts from the juristic commentaries preserved in Justinian's *Digest* provide some impression of the vast works produced by many jurists of the classical period. General treatises on the civil and criminal law were written, as well as commentaries on the edict and on important statutes. Some jurists composed legal textbooks, the most notable being the *Institutes* of Gaius from the second century AD, a large portion of which has been preserved. The value of Justinian's codification for the preservation of the works of the classical jurists is enormous, in spite of the extent of interpolation sometimes suspected. Justinian's codifiers were ordered to bring the chosen juristic excerpts into line with the law of the day and the consequent editorial activity has caused some scholars to view much of the content of the *Digest* and the *Code* with scepticism. But the esteem in which the classical jurists were clearly held in the time of Justinian and the prestige associated with the rescripts of deified emperors surely precludes the large-scale interpolation which some have postulated. This is not to deny that the state of some texts of the *Code* and *Digest* suggests that they have indeed been tampered with or corrupted. Perhaps more significant is the fact that the excerpts have been taken from their contexts by the codifiers and placed in the appropriate chapters of the collections; this inevitably causes problems of interpretation. But it does not affect the general view of the work of the classical jurists who are notorious for their assiduous activity and obsession with detail. Their commentaries on the interpretation and application of the law include discussion of every kind of legal case and circumstance, both real and imaginary. They also provide very specific definitions of words and phrases relevant to the law.

The jurists were by no means always in agreement; conflicting views on many issues are revealed by the *Digest* excerpts. Such conflicts are to some extent to be explained in terms of two main schools of jurists, the Proculians and Sabinians, whose existence, according to Pomponius, went back to two jurists of the Augustan period, Labeo and Capito, although it is from later jurists that the names of the schools derive. A much discussed passage of Gaius cites a rescript of Hadrian which laid down that an opinion held by all of the 'authorized' jurists should have the force of law, but that in the case of a disagreement, a judge might choose whom to follow. However, the existence of disagreements must have been a contributing factor to the stream of petitions for rulings from the emperor, and there is no doubt a link between the growth of the rescript system and the disappearance of the two schools within a century.

In spite of the astonishing volume of literature produced by the jurists of the second and third centuries, the surviving representation of this literature suggests that the contribution of these jurists was more in terms of consolidation than innovation. This is not surprising, if the complexity and sophistication of Roman law by the end of the Republic is considered. In addition, independent activity by the jurists can hardly have been encouraged by the successors of Augustus who continued his policy of maintaining a close association between the best legal minds and the emperor. This association culminated in the nature of juristic activity in the late empire which seems to have been largely confined to participation in the rescript system, now dominating the formulation and application of the law. Instead of producing treatises and commentaries, jurists collected and edited imperial constitutions. Thus there is evidence of two collections of constitutions made during the reign of Diocletian, the Gregorian and Hermogenian codes. These *Codes* are generally thought to have been unofficial collections, unlike the later Theodosian *Code* compiled in AD 429 and the famous *Code* of Justinian for which the earlier codes no doubt provided material.

The activity of the classical jurists illustrates the richness of written law in the Roman legal system which distinguishes it from every other, and which helps to explain why custom and precedent did not play a very significant part in the formulation of the law. It also explains why it has been comparatively easy for the Roman system to be adopted as the basis for so many modern systems of law.

The overall trend under the Empire, therefore, was a growing monopoly over law-making by the emperor, at least in name. The importance of the emperor's influence on the law should have been further advanced by the spread of the Roman citizenship to an increasing number of provincials, culminating as it did in the virtually universal grant of citizenship in AD 212 by the *Constitutio Antoniniana* of the Emperor Caracalla. The distinction between the *ius civile*, the law applying only to Roman citizens, and the *ius gentium*, the law applying to Romans and non-Romans, was now, in theory, obsolete, and the rules of Roman law should have been applicable to every area of the Empire and to every inhabitant. Thus rulings made by the emperor were becoming applicable to an ever-increasing number of Roman citizens. In practice, however, the application of the rules of Roman law to people in distant and culturally distinct parts of the Empire, who had become accustomed to local systems, was no simple achievement. Roman officials in the provinces could not deal with every legal case which arose, and therefore needed the co-operation of local officials who would, at least initially, have been ignorant of the Roman system. A text of Gaius provides an example of local custom being upheld in a matter of private law, and considering the chaos and uncertainty of the years between the death of Severus Alexander in AD 235 and the accession of Diocletian in 284, it is hardly likely that much progress could have been made in enforcing adherence to the rules of Roman law throughout the provinces. Some scholars believe that, following the *Constitutio Antoniniana*, the character of Roman law changed as it became infused with elements of Greek law. The examples cited in favour of this view, are, however, fairly few in number and tend to belong to the post-Diocletianic period, when the seat of the emperor had become firmly established in the eastern Empire. Under Diocletian, a reorganization of the provincial system suggests a desire for improved organization and centralization, and the content of many of his constitutions reveals a strong assertion of the traditional principles of Roman law. Clearly there were still enormous practical difficulties involved in achieving Empire-wide application of the principles of Roman law, but the enactments of the later emperors such as Diocletian must nevertheless have had a far-reaching influence. The power and prestige of the later emperors is illustrated by the fact that from the time of Constantine they no longer made rulings only in response to requests, but also began to issue *leges generales* which were more directly legislative.

There were, therefore, considerable developments in the role of the emperor as a law-maker between the Augustan period and the fourth century. Augustus may be seen to be feeling his way, exploiting all the existing channels and institutions, and establishing a place for himself within them. As a result, the traditional channels soon either became obsolete or were transformed, as the prestige of the emperors enabled them to monopolize the contribution traditionally made to the development of the law by magistrates and jurists. It is important, however, to set against this the use made by the emperors of assistants, and also the complex system of private law already established by the end of the Republic. This was not radically altered by the emperors whose rescripts so often restated traditional principles of private law.

The emperor as judge

Reference has already been made to Cicero's list of the republican sources of law in which is included that of previous judgments. There was, in fact, no established rule of precedent in Roman law, and there are few references to previous judgments in the arguments of the jurists. Nevertheless, Cicero recognized that precedent, if not binding, was influential. Thus the role of the emperor as a judge may be seen as yet another means by which he established himself firmly within the legal system and built up prestige and influence. This section is designed to trace this role and to examine its implications for the civil and criminal courts under the empire.

As in the case of the formulation of law, the history of the courts in the Republic is characterized by the tendency for institutions and processes to develop or to be supplemented as the need arose. Thus the early *legis actio* system of the civil courts, whereby a very limited number of rigidly defined actions could be granted, was gradually superseded by the formulary system whereby the praetor, or other magistrate, having made the usual preliminary enquiry into a case between two parties, would submit a set form of words (*formula*) to a judge, who would make a decision: the variety of different *formulae* which could be used made this system more flexible. This tendency may also be seen in the development of criminal jurisdiction. In the early days of the Republic, many offences which are now regarded as crimes gave rise to civil actions, and it was only very gradually that certain offenders came to be brought to law by the state rather than by the injured party. By the second century BC, magistrates, particularly the praetors, became responsible for the punishment of certain crimes committed within their jurisdiction. In the late Republic, and especially following the legislation of Sulla, there also appeared permanent jury courts (*quaestiones*) for the trial of certain, largely upper-class, crimes such as extortion by officials in the provinces, treason, bribery, embezzlement and forgery. Even at this stage, the offences of assault and theft continued to be handled by the civil courts. Any citizen, not just the injured party, could initiate a prosecution before the *quaestiones* and these were presided over by praetors.

What is interesting about the important part played by praetors in jurisdiction in the Republic is the fact that they were annual magistrates who possessed no particular legal training. The same applied to the other magistrates who were involved in presiding over courts, and to the judges appointed by these magistrates in civil cases. Against this must be set the availability to such men of the advice of jurists who were legal experts and, more importantly, the great interest that the Romans generally took in law and the courts which must have resulted in a fair degree of knowledge.

Given that Augustus was supposed to be working within the republican framework, the question arises of the basis of his right to investigate civil suits and to preside over criminal courts. He did not claim to possess the rights of a praetor, the most important judicial magistrate of the Republic. He did, however, possess *imperium* in the provinces assigned to him, and hence, just as he could issue edicts relating to the affairs of these areas, so he possessed the right (which he mostly delegated to legates) to try cases arising in them. This meant that Roman citizens dissatisfied with judgments passed by his representatives could appeal to him, just as they had appealed to an assembly of the people at Rome when dissatisfied with the judgments of magistrates during the Republic. The privilege of appeal seems also to have extended to citizens in senatorial provinces, perhaps on account of Augustus' *maius imperium*, that is, an *imperium* superior to that of other provincial governors. It is more difficult to explain the basis of his right to judge cases in Rome and Italy. Some scholars would explain this in terms of his possession of consular *imperium*, and Kunkel (1966, 68) suggests that his *tribunicia potestas* gave to him a certain competence. But apart from the uncertainty over whether or not he did possess consular *imperium*, neither the rights associated with a consul nor a tribune can explain his competence to judge criminal cases which should have come before inappellable *quaestiones*. It is equally difficult to explain his competence to investigate civil suits. The only conclusion is that there is a parallel here with the gradual extension, by virtue of his *auctoritas*, of the right of issuing edicts relating to his provinces into a more general right. He did not formally claim a general right of presiding over civil and criminal cases in Rome and Italy, nor is there evidence of such being granted to him, but the fact that he did investigate and judge at Rome suggests that he simply appropriated the right. In other words, he gradually engineered a role for himself within the courts which, like his law-making role, must have undermined the activities of others who were entitled to preside over courts as holders of magistracies.

Dio provides an anecdote which portrays Augustus sitting in judgment, and Maecenas struggling through the crowd in an attempt to prevent him from passing a series of death sentences. Suetonius also provides some glimpses of Augustus sitting as a judge, including an interesting one, which shows him presiding over a case of a forged will. If the story is to be taken seriously, not only was Augustus encroaching on the jurisdiction of the standing court responsible for such a case, but he also created a precedent of some significance by giving to the members of his court the opportunity not only of acquitting or condemning, but also of excusing those witnesses who had acted in ignorance. This action by Augustus illustrates his great interest in the procedure of the courts, and other measures attributed to him suggest that there were many ways, apart from sitting as a judge, in which he could exert influence over them.

In addition, Augustus was able to exercise influence over trials through the legates who represented him in his provinces. Not only were these men answerable to him, but they did not change every year like senatorial governors. He furthermore replaced the rather inadequate republican policing system with a highly-organized police force and fire-brigade, the *vigiles*, headed by a prefect. There was also a prefect in charge of the praetorian guard, the elite corps of soldiers stationed in the city of Rome, and a prefect of the city who was originally the emperor's deputy at Rome during his absences, and courts later grew up under the presidency of these officials. In the sphere of civil jurisdiction, there was considerable continuity. The existing courts remained, including that of the *centumviri* which was concerned with claims regarding inheritance.

What is striking about Augustus' activities relating to the courts is the extent of his interference in a system which had formerly developed in a typically haphazard and *ad hoc* manner. Thus by the end of his reign, the civil and criminal courts of Rome and the provinces had become more controlled and uniform, and the policing system at Rome had become closely associated with the emperor. It is not difficult to see parallels here with his achievements in the system of law-making and of private law.

Augustus' assumption of judicial rights created a precedent which made it easy for subsequent emperors to involve themselves in judging cases. The fact that one man could at the same time be the foremost law-maker and the foremost judge provides a reflection of a unique and fascinating characteristic of the Roman legal system. Honoré has carried out an extensive study of the activities of the individual emperors in the judicial sphere, and has concluded that the extent of their involvement depended on their own personalities; some were diligent, others lazy (Honoré, 1981, 3). The composition of the emperor's court must have varied, since he judged cases while on his travels as well as at Rome. He would always have had a large entourage wherever he happened to be, and the friends and prominent men who made up his court must have overlapped considerably with the members of his advisory *consilium*. There would, no doubt, have often been jurists in the emperor's court, and there is evidence to suggest that Hadrian added to the members of his court the secretaries concerned with the issuing of imperial constitutions. It was clearly inconceivable for the emperor to judge cases without consultation, and Suetonius describes how Nero felt the need to make a pretence of accepting the majority decision of the members of his court by asking for their opinions to be handed to him in writing and then announcing the result himself. However, the principle of consultation and collaboration was based on accepted practice, as well as on the need of the emperors for advice, rather than on a strictly legal requirement, and it was clearly the role of the emperor which was crucial.

Furthermore, it has already been observed that decrees, that is decisions made by the emperor in his role as a judge, were included in the category of imperial constitutions which the classical jurists regarded as legally binding. By means of these decrees and of rescripts issued on behalf of those involved in law-suits, the emperor was able to influence decisions made in courts other than his own. In the third century, the jurist Paul issued a collection of imperial decrees and there is a fair number of references in the *Digest* excerpts to decrees of Septimius Severus.

The court of the emperor was not the only new court to be established under the Principate. The development of the jurisdiction of the prefects has been mentioned; that of the urban prefect was criminal, while that of the praetorian prefect was military and civil. The cases tried by the senate under the presidency of the consuls seem to have mostly involved members of its own order. The existence of such courts had various results. First, it brought about a partial demise of the formulary system in civil suits; it was more convenient and appropriate for an important official, and especially for the emperor, to conduct an entire case himself rather than making an enquiry and then submitting the case to another party for judgment. Second, the trial of criminal cases in such courts led to the gradual disappearance of the *quaestiones*, the standing criminal courts. Third, the right enjoyed by those of a certain social status to be tried before a particular special court (only those of high rank, for example, would have been privileged to appear before the emperor), promoted a system of legal privilege linked with social status (see Garnsey, 1970). Fourth, those officials who presided over special courts were closely linked with the emperor. Thus, while the number of cases which he could judge personally was obviously limited, he was able to delegate to officials both at Rome and in the provinces over whom he could exercise control.

The trends which may be discerned in the first three centuries AD culminated in the fourth century (Chapter 17). Law-making and jurisdiction became more and more bureaucratized: the system of imperial constitutions continued to grow in importance and in organization, and judges became synonymous with imperial officials. In addition, the influence of Christianity can be seen in the nature of many of the imperial enactments from Constantine onwards. This may all be far removed from the situation under the Republic. However, it is important to remember that, in spite of the passage of four centuries which saw major political and social developments, many of the great and fundamental principles of Roman law which had been established under the Republic remained unchanged.

CHAPTER 17

·GOVERNMENT· ·AND·ADMINISTRATION· ·IN·THE·LATE·EMPIRE· ·(TO·AD 476)

J. H. W. G. Liebeschuetz

When Diocletian and Constantine rebuilt the structure of the Empire shattered by the events of the third century they were faced with many problems that had not existed during the Principate (Rostovtzeff, 1957; Cook, Adcock *et al.*, 1939; Walser and Pekáry, 1962; Alföldy, 1979, 139–64). The Empire was now under more or less continuous attack, often at more than one frontier at a time. The needs of defence impelled the government to make much greater and inevitably more unpopular demands on the manpower and resources of the Empire than ever before. At the same time it had lost cohesion. The army, once the great romanizer, had become regionalized, and the soldiers' concern for their native province, and often their attachment to particular generals had become stronger than their loyalty to the Empire as a whole. The economic ties linking frontier areas with the central provinces had grown weaker as the provinces had become self-sufficient in many of the items that they had previously imported from Mediterranean areas. There was thus less need for traders and shippers. The need had been further reduced by the fact that armies and civil servants had come to be paid in produce, raised and distributed by compulsory transport duties (MacMullen, 1976, 173ff.; Hopkins, 1980, 106 and 123–5). As the economy had become more localized the Roman way of life had lost some of its appeal. Even under the most favourable conditions romanization ceased to advance; in the north-western provinces it went into retreat.

From the point of view of administration the most harmful aspect was the weakening of city organization in Britain and parts of Spain and Gaul as well as the Balkan provinces. By leaving most administrative tasks to city authorities the Empire had been able to manage with a very small staff of officials of its own. This would no longer be possible after the third century. Another damaging development was that the patriotic pride of the ruling and privileged Roman nation which had once held together the empire had been diluted out of existence with the conferment of citizenship on all free inhabitants of the empire by Caracalla (AD 212). More damaging still, privilege of citizenship had been progressively replaced by privilege of class, the division of the inhabitants of the empire into *honestiores* (soldiers, decurions, equestrians and senators) and *humiliores* (everybody else, including the peasants), with the inevitable long term result that those without privilege became completely alienated from the Empire (Garnsey, 1970; de Ste Croix, 1981, 474ff.).

The circumstances required a thorough reform of the administration. Diocletian, a very great emperor, seems to have grasped the scale of the problem quite early in his reign, and the reforms introduced by him and carried further in some important respects by Constantine, succeeded in giving the Empire a second lease of life. Diocletian saw that the Empire would henceforth require more than one emperor, and that the administration would have to become much more active at provincial level. He therefore established a tetrarchy of two senior emperors (*Augusti*) and two junior partners (*Caesars*), and he subdivided almost all the provinces of the Empire, doubling their number to around a hundred. The doubling of provincial governors caused a problem of supervision, which he solved by creating an intermediate unit of administration between court and province: the diocese. The system may have been established by 293 (Barnes, 1982, 203–5, 224–5; cf also Jones, 1954 otherwise Noetlichs, 1982). The three-tiered structure of administration remained intact until the end of the Roman Empire in the West, and in the East into the seventh century.

The tetrarchic system did not last, but from the reign of Diocletian to the deposition of the last western emperor in 476 there were relatively few years when there was only one emperor. After the death of Constantine there were normally two or three. When Theodosius I died in 395 he was for practical purposes the sole ruler, but then the Empire was divided between his sons Arcadius and Honorius, never again to be united under a single monarch. Nevertheless in law, all emperors (*Augusti* and any Caesars) continued to form a college which jointly ruled an undivided Empire. Imperial constitutions were issued in the names of all emperors. One coinage circulated over the whole Empire. The inhabitants enjoyed one citizenship. For most of the fourth century there was one elite which provided officials for all the Empire. Nevertheless east and west were growing apart. The development accelerated as Constantinople grew into a second Rome, and the real capital of the east (Dagron, 1974). After 395 east and west were for practical purposes separate realms, linked but also divided by their past history.

A new feature of the fully developed system of the Late Empire was the separation of military (Part 3, Chapter 7) and civil administration. Under the Principate a senator was thought equally capable of civil government and military command, and the governorships of important provinces combined both types of administration. Not so under the Late Empire, although the transition was gradual. We hear of a number of dukes in charge of parts of frontier armies under Diocletian, but in many frontier provinces the governor was still in command of the troops (Seston, 1946, 313–19). The praetorian prefect continued to act as commander-in-chief (under the emperor), and a vicar might deputize for the prefect in his military as well as his civil capacity. The separation was completed at the earliest by Constantine. He created a permanent mobile field army commanded by a master of the infantry (*magister peditum*) and a master of the cavalry (*magister equitum*). It was probably also in his reign that the frontier units still under the control of governors were placed under dukes (van Berchem, 1952, 100–5). By the 360s the masters of the soldiers had become the superiors of the dukes of the frontier armies. The praetorian prefects had lost all military authority and the two hierarchies were united only in the person of the emperor. The two branches of the administration grew entirely distinct. The commanders had purely military careers, the governors no military experience whatsoever. Besides a growing proportion of the generals and of their troops was of barbarian origin (Demandt, 1980), with the result that some of the most important positions came to be held by men born outside the Empire. The new system had advantages. Armies were commanded by experts. A general had no authority over the departments that paid and supplied his troops, and this made rebellion more difficult. But the division also involved risk of conflict between the civil and military branches of government.

The structure of the developed system was something like this. The emperor was head of state and source of all authority. His unique position was proclaimed by increasingly elaborate protocol and ceremony. For much of the fourth century emperors travelled from crisis-spot to crisis-spot, and spent longer periods of time at large cities with easy access to frontier areas, Antioch, Nicomedia, Naissus, Serdica, Sirmium, Trier. Court and central administration travelled with the emperor. Eventually this proved intolerably inconvenient, and there was a return to a permanent capital. By 395 Constantinople was the permanent imperial residence in the east. In the west this development was never completed, but Trier, Milan and especially Ravenna came near to becoming capitals at different times.

The court (*comitatus*) consisted of the officials and attendants of the emperor's household (*sacrum cubiculum*), his advisers (*consistorium*), the confidential shorthand writers who took down the discussions and decisions of the *consistorium*, and might be sent out to see their enforcement in the provinces (*notarii*), and last but not least the principal officers of state with their office staffs. Chief of these was the praetorial prefect. Although he had lost his military command he remained responsible for the feeding and supplying of the army, and since troops, like all other imperial employees, were paid most of their wages in kind, he was in fact the principal finance-officer of the Empire. He was also the superior of all provincial governors, and had great influence over appointments. A wide range of laws concerning provincial government was addressed to him, often because the laws had been promulgated in response to the prefect's request. As deputy of the emperor the praetorian prefect exercised appellate jurisdiction over the whole

Empire. The prefect might fairly be described as the premier-minister of his part of the Empire.

Second in importance among the great officers was the *magister officiorum*, an office which was split from the praetorian prefecture by Constantine. The creation of this post was a consequence of the great numerical growth of the central administration for he was the principal administrative official – as it were the registrar – of the court. The master of the offices was head of the secretarial departments (*scrinia*) which had developed out of the offices staffed by freedmen under the early principate. He was also responsible for the public post, which he supervised by means of his own corps of inspectors the *agentes in rebus*. Through the same *agentes*, whose activities were far from secret, he received information from all over the Empire. Since *agentes in rebus* finished their career as head of the offices (*officia*) of praetorian prefects and other important officers, the *magister officiorum* was able to obtain information how these officers conducted their administration, and to pass on his knowledge to the emperor. The *magister officiorum* was in at least administrative command of the palace guards (*scholae palatinae*). The *magister officiorum* was also concerned with the reception of ambassadors, and from time to time might be sent on an embassy himself. He was often the official chosen to represent the emperor at church councils. The nature of his responsibilities made it essential that the *magister officiorum* should be a man whom the emperor, or whoever else directed policy, could trust absolutely. They were often 'new men'.

Two other officers of the *comitatus*, the *comes sacrarum largitionum*, and the *comes rei privatae*, were concerned with finance. The former was responsible for gold and silver mines, mints, and taxes levied in precious metals. In other words his sphere was the collection, production and expenditure of money. Owing to the extent of the state natural economy, controlled by the praetorian prefect, he did not have the importance of a modern chancellor of the exchequer but the *stipendium*, paid in money, and above all the donatives given on imperial anniversaries still played an essential part in maintaining morale and loyalty of the army. By depriving his Caesar Julian of a *comes sacrarum largitionum*, Constantius, the senior emperor, hoped to prevent the development of dangerously close ties between Julian and his troops. The *comes rei privatae* was responsible for the administration of the emperor's estates. His officials collected rents, and claimed properties forfeited to the emperor, as for instance the estates of men found guilty of treason. The emperor's private estates were extensive, and their income enabled an emperor to reward members of the *comitatus* and others with the generosity that was expected of him. The last of the great civil officers was the *quaestor*. He was the direct superior of the secretarial departments (*scrinia*) who were responsible for dealing with the vast mass of petitions, consultations and appeals addressed to the emperor. The *quaestor* was also responsible for the drafting of imperial constitutions. In addition to the civilian officials there were the military members of the *comitatus*, above all the *magistri militum praesentales* commanding the field army units accompanying the emperor, and the two *comites domesticorum* who were in charge of the corps of officer cadets, the *domestici et protectores*.

The great civil officers of the *comitatus* represented each of the principal concerns of a Roman emperor: the raising and spending of taxes to supply and pay army and civil service, the making of law and the administration of justice, and the answering of a vast mass of miscellaneous requests for assistance by individuals, corporations, cities and provinces. The military officers represented the fact that for most of the fourth, but not the fifth century, the emperor was active commander in chief of fighting armies and that even when he ceased to be that he had to maintain a special relationship with the officer corps, symbolized by the ceremony of the adoration of the sacred purple. Towards the end of the fourth century the total civilian strength of the court was around 3,000. The palace guards (*scholae*) amounted to as many men again. The total of 6,000 does not of course include the units of the field army attached to the emperor (*palatini*).

At diocesan level the administration was represented by vicars (the diocese of Oriens being governed by a *comes*, and Egypt by a *praefectus Augustalis*). These had at their disposal an office staff of around 300, divided between judicial and financial departments. Originally, the deputy praetorial 'prefects' might have some military function too, but from the reign of Constantine onwards their main duties were the distribution of levies and the hearing of appeals. The departments of the *sacra largitio* and the *res privata* also had officials at diocesan level. Up to a point vicars were the superiors of the provincial governors, but orders were often passed directly to governors from the *comitatus*. Provincial governors and citizens of the provinces in their turn often by-passed the vicar, to communicate with the *comitatus* directly.

The governors of eventually about 119 provinces, (de Ste Croix, 1981, 491) had *officia* around 100 strong (the proconsuls had a larger staff), of basically the same structure as those of the higher officials, being made up of three sections: judicial, financial and sub-clerical. The first two represented a governor's principal activities: jurisdiction and taxation. The governor's court had replaced local courts for most kinds of case, civil or criminal. The governor spent much of his time travelling from assizes to assizes, and much of the rest supervising the collection of taxes. He would normally take a very active role in the administration of cities. He was a busy man, and access to him was likely to be slow and expensive. Constantine authorized an alternative source of jurisdiction in civil disputes: the court of the Christian bishop (Waldstein, 1976).

The total number of active civil servants in the Late Empire has been estimated at around 30,000 (Jones, 1964, 1057). This is a very modest figure for the administration of so vast an Empire. It must however be remembered that in addition to the salaried civil service there was a large number of unpaid but nevertheless privileged supernumeraries and honorary office holders. The creation of this large army of active and inactive civil servants certainly made a very great change compared with the administration of the principate, and one which would have far-reaching consequences.

Members of administration all belonged to the legally privileged class of *honestiores* and all but the humblest had the rank of soldiers. Their service was known as *militia*. They wore the military belt (*cingulum militiae*), and like soldiers they were paid in rations (*annonae*). The military organization of the civil service (MacMullen, 1963, 162ff.) was partly a consequence of the filling of civilian office staffs with men seconded from the army (Jones, 1949), partly of the fact that civil administration as a career service for citizens had not existed during the Republic and early Empire. As it gradually came into existence it was shaped on the only available model, the army. Under the early emperors the office work of the Empire was done by imperial freedmen. In the course of time these were replaced from the top downwards by knights (*equites*) and humbler freeborn citizens. Nevertheless as late as the reign of Diocletian freedmen still seem to have played a significant role. It was left to Constantine to grant military privileges and status to departments still staffed by freedmen. In the emperor's private household freedmen of course continued to be employed, and the chamberlains (*cubicularii*), eunuchs who had originated as slaves bought in Persia, might exercise great influence without corresponding responsibility.

The administration of the Late Empire was still far from being manned entirely with career civil servants. In fact all the executive posts, magistracies and governorships of the old type as well as the headships of the central departments continued to be filled by amateurs, of high social status who in the course of their lives normally held only a small number of posts, and those only for a relatively short time (p. 461 below). But these holders of high office were assisted and served by departments staffed entirely by professionals, who were employed by the state until they formally retired like soldiers (*honesta missio*), after spending their working lives advancing slowly from grade to grade. The successful functioning of the service depended on the professional knowledge and experience of the more senior of these men. John Lydus, an official of the praetorian prefecture of the east in the reign of Justinian, has preserved the outlook of such a man in his book on the magistrates of the Roman people (*De Magistratibus Populi Romani*), which has been analysed and translated in Carney (1971). While career civil servants often found themselves in positions of power *vis-à-vis* the public, they were poorly paid, on average around 4 *solidi* a year (or its equivalent in kind) or less. In wages most of them were probably worse off than private soldiers. But there was a very wide gap between the average salary and the salaries of the highest paid heads of the various offices. Roman civil servants (particularly the senior men) were however in a position greatly to increase their earnings by charging the public for services such as access to the governor, completion of legal documents, enforcement of the orders of a court, or even the paper used in making court records. Tax collectors had to be paid fees. Earnings were highest in the central departments. Not only were the litigants that used the courts of the capital wealthy, and the amounts at stake large, but officials were also in a position to charge for imperial benefits such as commissions in the army, codicils of real or honorary rank, privileges, immunities, or laws favouring special interests which poured out from the *comitatus*. Fees (*sportulae*) were so much part of the accepted emolument that the government produced tables of the amounts that might be legally charged, and were no doubt regularly exceeded. In his first year of service in the prefecture of the east John Lydus earned 1,000 *solidi* in fees, more than thirty times his salary.

Salaries of officials were supplemented by privilege of status. As *honestiores* all holders of *militia* were immune from the more savage punishments. Members of the central departments were exempt from normal jurisdiction, and could claim to have their cases tried by their head of department (*praescriptio fori*). This privilege might also be claimed by sinecure holders of official positions. The eastern government in the fifth century attempted to limit the abuse. In ceremonial precedence even the humblest officials, the office staff of provincial governors (*cohortalini*) were at least the equals, often the superiors, of city-councillors, and they were of course exempt from the expensive and troublesome duties which city-councillors were obliged to perform. As a result service in even a provincial office might seem attractive to a decurion – if he had reason to believe that he might be able to circumvent the legislation which tied him and his children to the service of his local *curia*. Nevertheless the *cohortalini* were the humblest of officials, and their low pay and slow promotion to the posts of high pay and perquisites, and not least the expensive transport duty (*primipili pastus*) which was required of the officials who retired with the rank of *primipilaris*, made service in a provincial office unpopular with those who saw prospects of entering central departments. The government responded characteristically by making service compulsory and hereditary.

As has been shown earlier the clerks and accountants of the career civil service continued to be directed by heads of department who were amateurs as far as departmental work was concerned. These holders of *dignitates* or *honores* were appointed with codicils issued by the *primicerius notariorum*. The average term of office was less than two years, and most men only held one or two such posts in their lives. A majority seem to have been content with just one post. A small number of individuals, ambitious to reach top posts like that of praetorian prefect or master of the offices held a succession of posts. It is clear that there was tremendous pressure to obtain *honores*. It was perhaps partly a matter of pay. The fifty *annonae* and fifty *capitus* of the Augustan prefect of Egypt in the reign of Justinian will have amounted to 100 times the wages of his humble clerks, while the 100 lbs of gold of the praetorian prefect of Africa must have amounted to something like 1,800 times as much. Even so Justinian's prefect of Africa earned less than half the salary of the proconsul of Africa under the principate (1,000,000 *sesterces* = 220 lbs of gold). Salaries would of course be supplemented by perquisites of office. Not all of this was pure profit. The holder of the dignity will have paid a very large sum for it either to a patron for his support (*suffragium*), or later to the emperor himself or to another official to whom the emperor had turned over the right to make the appointment. Perhaps the greatest attraction of imperial *honores* was the rank conferred by them, which raised the ex-official above his former peers in civic society and which might, with a little luck, provide a means of avoiding curial duties not only for the man himself but also for his descendants. During the fourth century rank suffered from inflation comparable to that of the currency. More and more posts came to entitle their holder first to simple senatorial rank (*clarissimus*) and then to its higher grades (*spectabilis, illustris*). Senatorial rank also came to be awarded honorifically to men retiring from leading places in palatine offices, or to private individuals in return for miscellaneous services, or just because they had influential patrons, or because they had paid for the honour. No doubt the elaborate rules of precedence and seniority helped to oil the working of the administrative machinery. Not the least important function of rank was to integrate the otherwise completely separate hierarchies of military and civil administration. Another effect was to demonstrate on public occasions that position derived from proximity to the emperor excelled all other sources of social distinction.

The most important function of the bureaucracy was to supervise the collection of the taxes out of which soldiers and civil servants themselves were paid. The exercise through which the annual list of demands (*indictio*) was prepared was a bureaucratic operation of a size without parallel in the early Empire. Annual returns from the various departments, military and civilian, were passed up the hierarchy to the praetorian prefecture where the officials would calculate how much corn, or clothing, or whatever would be required by government employees in different areas, and would then proceed to distribute the burden as equally as practicable between dioceses and provinces. At provincial level the burden was divided between cities who were told not only how much they would have to provide but also where to transport it. In the city, administration passed out of the hands of paid civil servants into those of city councillors, who were not only unpaid, but also held collective liability for deficits, and who might be required to transport the supplies for great distances at their own cost (e.g. in Egypt from Hermopolis to Syene, 370 miles by river). Supervision of the magazines where the product of taxation was stored and the making of payments to imperial employees, whether in kind or in money equivalents, were also curial duties. The operation might be profitable, particularly if the decurions were men of influence, but it also involved the risk of extremely unpleasant consequences. A decurion who failed to collect the amount due might suffer savage corporal punishment. Alternatively – or even additionally – he might be compelled to sell his property to make up the deficit (Jones, 1964, 951–62).

Assessment of taxes was based on an empire-wide census of land and population which was revised every twelve years. According to Jones's view (Jones, 1957) the taxable value of land over most of the Empire was assessed in *iuga*. The *iugum* was a notional unit, like our rateable value, which in some provinces, e.g. Syria, took into account the quality of land and the use to which it was put, but more often did not. The corresponding unit for assessing the tax on population was the 'head' (*caput*). The total value for tax purposes of a piece of land was obtained by adding *iuga* and *capita* together. The annual tax liability was then stated as so much of each item per *iugum* or *caput*. Empire-wide uniformity was not achieved. In Asia (unlike Syria) the *iugum* took into account use – but not quality of land. In Italy the unit was the *millena*, and in Africa the *centuria*, both simple units of area. In Gaul, confusingly, a unit called *caput* seems to have been used to assess liability for land tax. The value of the *caput* too seems to have varied regionally. Some of this confusing variety of terms may be due to the coexistence of imperial units, used by the central administration, and local units used in the provinces. It may be that the annual indiction was announced in standard *iuga* and *capita* by the prefecture but that this was translated into local units when the burden was distributed at diocesan or provincial level. The above account based on Jones is almost certainly oversimplified. It has been shown that Jones's account of a single *iugatio-capitatio* tax seems to apply fully only to the diocese of Asia. In most areas a poll tax charged per head of the male population seems to have been quite separate from the land-tax (MacMullen, 1976, 129–52; Chastagnol, 1979; also 1982, 364ff.; Cerati, 1975).

The principal tax after being collected in kind, was paid out in salaries also assessed in kind, namely in rations (*annonae*) and fodder allowances (*capitus*). For employees whose salaries exceeded what they needed for immediate subsistence this system was intolerably clumsy. There is no doubt that from the beginning salary earners bargained with the curial storekeepers to draw their emolument in money rather than kind. Officials and soldiers abused their position to extort favourable prices. This led to a succession of laws forbidding or regulating commutation (*adaeratio*) in particular circumstances. But while this did not prevent a great deal of commutation, the principle that the main revenue (*annona*) should be both collected and paid out in kind remained intact for a long time. The conversion of tax payments into payments in gold was only completed in 424 in the west. In the east it was left to Anastasius to convert the bulk of the land tax (except for supplies needed to feed the army) into gold. Salaries continued to be stated (if not paid) in *annonae* and *capitus* for much longer. The fact that *adaeratio* was completed earlier in the economically weaker west shows that the natural economy of the state was maintained not because of economic weakness but because it was in the interest of the administration and its officials: the stronger administration maintained it longer.

But even while its principal revenue was in produce the government needed an income in precious metal. This was provided in part by the 'voluntary' contributions of *curiales* (*aurum coronarium*) and senators (*aurum oblativum*) on the occasions of imperial celebration or anniversaries. Silver and gold (later only gold) were also produced by the tax on shopkeepers, craftsmen and merchants (*collatio lustralis*) which caused great hardship among those liable when the tax was collected at five-yearly intervals. The *sacra largitio* also received some gold revenue from the land-tax, although its share was much smaller than the prefect's revenue in kind. In addition the *largitio* seems to have obtained gold by buying-in *solidi* with debased *denarii*. The fact that a large part of the income of the *sacra largitio* arrived in five-yearly intervals suggests that the government's need for gold was cyclical also, i.e. that its main use was to pay the five *solidi* per soldier at the accession of an emperor, and subsequently at the quinquennial anniversaries of the accession.

The administrative system has been described as if it had sprung up fully grown, and remained more or less unchanged thereafter. In fact like all human institutions it was subject to evolution. The separation of military and civil administration was a gradual process completed under Constantine. The assimilation of the great offices of the court into the same career structure as the provincial governorships and other traditional honours, and the consequent integration of the two privileged groups, the senatorial and equestrian orders, into a single hierarchically graded imperial aristocracy of office, was completed under the sons of Constantine (Vogler, 1979). Under Diocletian and Constantine there had probably been as many praetorian prefects as emperors, and each had accompanied his emperor on his travels. By the second half of the fourth century they had become heads of permanent administrative subdivisions of the Empire. This in a sense preserved the tripartite division of the Empire after the death of Constantine, the prefecture of the east corresponding to the Empire of Constantius, the prefecture of Italy, Illyricum and Africa to that of Constans and the prefecture of the Gauls, which included Britain and Spain, to the short-lived Empire of Constantine II. When the Empire was divided into eastern and western halves after the death of Jovian and again after the death of Theodosius I the prefecture of the east (*Oriens*) in effect became the Eastern Empire for which it provided the administrative substructure. After 395 the Eastern Empire included most of the Balkans which were organized as a second eastern prefecture of Illyricum. But the prefecture of *Oriens* remained the core of the administration. The fact that it was essentially based on a single prefecture, was one of the factors which gave the Eastern Empire a cohesion not possessed by the west. In the course of the fourth century there developed a tendency, natural in view of the language situation, to appoint easterners to posts in the east, and this was reinforced by the creation in the reign of Constantius of a senate at Constantinople on the model of the Roman senate. The complete hellenization of the eastern administration was delayed when Theodosius I became emperor and brought many westerners into the government of the east. After his death the development resumed, and the new aristocracy of Constantinople was determined that they would not again be subject to the west. When Stilicho the powerful western *magister peditum praesentalis* tried to become the guardian and principal adviser of the eastern emperor also, the ensuing conflict was most damaging to the empire as a whole, and particularly to its western half in its struggles with the Visigoths under Alaric.

The west was itself suffering from regional separatism. For some ten years after 368 Trier had been the residence of the praetorian prefect of the Gauls and of a western emperor almost continuously. This period saw the consolidation of a Gallic aristocracy.

The senatorial aristocracy of Gaul did not cease to think of themselves as Romans, but they did come to feel, justifiably, that the defence of Gaul was being neglected by the government in Italy, and on several occasions supported usurpers who could be expected to do more for the protection of their home country. At the same time posts in the imperial administration of Gaul came to be held almost exclusively by Gallic senators, while the administration of Italy was nearly monopolized by Italians.

The administration of the Late Empire was established in the face of terrible difficulties. It was set up rapidly in response to crisis in a society which lacked bureaucratic traditions. All action was extremely slow. An ordinary law suit might take several years. A law issued at Milan might reach Rome in twelve days but delays of three weeks are known, and six weeks are also recorded. Navigation stopped in winter and laws issued in autumn normally only reached Africa in the following spring. A law issued at Constantinople might reach any place in the east within a fortnight but the journey might take much longer, quite apart from likely bureaucratic delay. It might be many months before a communication from a province to the capital was answered. Long delay came to be expected. A court official might absent himself from his duties for six months before penalties began to be applied. A year's absence was punished with the loss of ten places of seniority, and only after he had stayed away for more than four years could the official be dismissed from the service. Soldiers were struck off the role when they had been absent for three years.

The administration, or rather the classes from which it was recruited, lacked an adequate code of public conduct. It is true that the government took an idealistic view of its duty to provide for the needs of the community, to ensure the safety and well-being of the governed, to provide justice for those who appeared in its courts. But members of the administration treated their appointments as a means to social and economic gain for themselves, and above all their friends and dependents. The city-state code of the duties which a public figure owed to his friends and dependants had not been superseded by one which proclaimed that impartiality and disinterestedness are required of a public servant. It is not therefore surprising that for men making appointments to administrative posts the problem was not to find candidates who had the right qualifications for particular responsibilities, but to find enough posts for numerous would-be officials who were socially qualified and well connected, or willing to pay for the post. The semi-legal gratuities paid to officials, shading into outright extortion, were a heavy burden on the ordinary citizen. The fact that the wealthy and influential could often obtain constitutions or other documents bearing the emperor's signature which exempted them from the scope of existing legislation amounted to a serious limitation of the rule of law. The large number of regulations by which emperors made office staff and heads of department mutually responsible for each other's conduct, and the frequency with which emperors tried to forestall anticipated legalization of illegalities, show how serious these abuses were, and how ineffective the authorities' attempts to check them. If the history of the Late Empire shows an increasing alienation of the population from the government, the conduct of an administration that appeared to exist mainly for the sake of its self-perpetuation is likely to have been a principal cause.

As it was the system could only be maintained by far-reaching regimentation to prevent individuals leaving the more unpleasant and exposed occupations to enter the more prestigious, more profitable and safer ones. Thus a large part of the population were frozen into hereditary occupations. Tenants registered on their land-lord's tax returns were forbidden to leave his farms. The duties for the feeding of Rome performed by corn-shippers (*navicularii*), bakers and butchers were attached in perpetuity to these men's land so that they would pass automatically to any purchaser. Sons of soldiers were forced to follow their fathers into the army, and of workers in government factories into the factories. Service in the offices of provincial governors was made hereditary and so was the decurions' membership of city-councils (*curiae*). The effects of this legislation are best known in the case of the decurions. It is quite clear that social mobility on their part was hampered but by no means prevented.

The inevitable movement of decurions into the civil service was one of several ways in which the growing imperial administration weakened the local government which it was supposed to supervise and direct. Since a governor now only had to supervise two or three cities in his reduced province, his intervention could become continuous. The councils ceased to be debating and policy-making assemblies, and probably no longer met for any other purpose than to elect men to perform compulsory public service. Decisions of policy were made by the governor on the advice of whomever he chose to consult. At the same time the council ceased to be composed of the natural leaders of the city. From the beginning of the fourth century the wealthiest and most enterprising decurions were drawn into imperial service. This was less serious when most of the posts involved were of equestrian rank which did not confer hereditary immunity from curial duties. But in the course of the century more and more posts were raised in status so that they came to confer senatorial rank, which was hereditary, and would deprive the councils of the service of men and property for ever. To make things worse councillors who failed to obtain imperial office might manage to get honorary rank. The government legislated again and again to keep councillors and property at the disposal of their council, evidently to little avail. One reason for the failure was the fact that information, on which enforcement of the legislation could be based, had to come from the councillors themselves, and that they, whether as a favour to friends or because they might themselves one day hope to seek imperial honours, or even because they saw opportunities of profit as leaders of a reduced council, did not provide the information. Thus a large number of decurions did succeed in getting away. Such men eventually settled either as senators at Rome or Constantinople, or in some provincial city as *honorati*, fortified with privilege of ex-officials, and with exemption from the compulsory duties of the local city-council. They would become leaders of provincial society and their patronage and opinions would be valued more highly than those of the more dutiful men who had remained councillors. Inevitably it was to them rather than to the councillors that the humbler inhabitants looked for protection. In strongly Christian areas the prestige of the councillors would be further undermined by the appearance of effective patrons of the country population in the shape of hermits or heads of monasteries.

How this development affected the administration of cities and their territories is difficult to observe as evidence for the fifth century is less than that for the fourth. Decurions continued to exist and to perform executive roles in the cities to the reign of Justinian at least, and in many places much longer. Councils became smaller and poorer, although they continued to include some men of wealth and influence (*principales*) whose status was not very different from that of members of the senatorial order of less than illustrious rank who were no longer required to live in the capital. It is likely that the administration of the city, as far as it was not in the hands of the governor and his *officium*, passed from the council to a more informal body of notables which included both *principales* and *honorati* and – a new development – the bishop and leading clergy (Jones, 1964, 758ff.; cf. also Liebeschuetz, 1973, and 1974, and Hohlweg, 1971). As early as 407 a western law transferred the election of the *defensor* to the notables. In the east it was left to Anastasius to assign to the notables the election of the *defensor, curator* (or *pater*) and corn-buyer. Anastasius' legislation, perhaps only confirming what had already been the practice for many years, may well have marked the formal end of curial administration of the cities. At any rate John Lydus in the 550s could write of curial administration as belonging to the past. Compared with decurions notables enjoyed the advantage that they would negotiate with governors and their senior officials on more or less equal terms since most notables could claim at least some privileges of official rank. There is no evidence that the authorities ever attempted to subject the notables to the hereditary compulsion to which decurions continued to be subject.

It should be noted that the decline of curial government was a consequence of the strengthening of the central administration, not of the physical decline of the cities and their population. There is evidence that cities continued to flourish in the east up to at least the first quarter of the sixth century (Foss, 1976 and 1977). In much of the west, in the Balkans, in Britain and in large parts of Gaul and Spain there was of course, in addition, a withdrawal from city-life from the third or at least the second half of the fourth century (see King and Henig, 1981: essays by Reece, Blagg, Walker, Sheldon, Keay), but where cities survived councils continued to meet, and magistrates to be elected – even if the activities for which we have evidence are notarial rather than administrative. It may even be that from the fifth century decurions were relatively more important in the shrinking cities of the west than their colleagues in the flourishing cities of the east. Documents testify to the survival of councils in Italy and Spain to the seventh and even eighth centuries (Jones, 1964, 760–1; Thompson, 1969, 118–21). In the east city councils were formally abolished by Leo the Wise (886–912) (see Ostrogorsky, 1968, 217–18; Jones, 1940, 209–10).

The history of the city councils illustrates how the strengthening of the administrative machinery for enforcing the demands of the central government set in motion other trends which would eventually make the new machinery less effective. A similar reaction happened in the area of patronages. The same officials, officers, soldiers, *honorati* who used their influence to enable decurions to escape from councils, also helped humble peasants to reduce their tax payments. The patron might physically assist his clients to resist the tax collectors. Alternatively he might use his influence when the case of the recalcitrant tax payers came to court. In the east the patron's reward seems normally to have consisted – at first at any rate – of regular payments by the client. In the west it seems to have been more usual for the peasant to hand his land over to the patron who would then resist the tax-claim as if it had been made against himself. Patrons were also used to protect tenants against their landlords. Not all patronage was voluntary. There is no doubt that powerful men often imposed their protection on unwilling peasants. The eastern government – not that of the west – legislated against patronage, but not perhaps with great success. The long-term consequence of patronage seems to have been the concentration of property in the hands of those able to offer or enforce patronage, and a reduction in the administration's ability to raise taxes.

It might therefore be said that the reforms of Diocletian and Constantine proved to some extent self-defeating. They nevertheless achieved extremely important positive results. The Empire was given a new lease of life. The frontiers were defended successfully. Usurpation became very much more difficult. In the east no usurper at all succeeded within our period, and even attempts were few and ineffective. After the death of Theodosius I stable government survived the reigns of the feeble Arcadius and the not much more effective Theodosius II. The west was less stable. Not all the provinces enjoyed continuous peace and a number of usurpations were at least temporarily successful. In spite of this the fourth century was on the whole an age of recovery.

It was only possible because the administration was able to collect the taxes required to maintain the Empire's armies or alternatively to buy off invaders. In some ways the administration was too efficient. The authorities found it easier to force money out of the tax-payer than to ensure that it was spent for the purposes for which it was collected. The level of taxation tended to rise and may well have reached crushing levels. But Jones was probably mistaken to conclude that taxation helped to bring about a reduction in the population, as rents and taxes together had not left peasants with enough income to bring up children (Jones, 1964, 1040–5). In fact the population of the east seems to have been growing through most of the fourth and fifth centuries (Patlagean, 1972, 231–5, 302–13). In the west there was a reduction in some areas which made possible the settlement of very large numbers of barbarians (de Ste Croix, 1981, 509–18). But the legislation on abandoned land is much less good evidence of depopulation than has been thought, and there seems to be evidence of actual growth of population in some areas. There is a suspicion that barbarian invasions contributed at least as much as taxation to any reduction in the rural population and abandonment of land in the west. Nevertheless taxes were resented, and when the western government eventually failed to protect the provincials in spite of the heavy taxes that they had paid to it disillusion with the Empire must have been all the more complete.

The achievement of the Late Empire was to maintain control of a civilian central administration over the provinces, and especially, because this was hardest, over the great land-owners and the army. In both crucial areas the administration of the east was more successful than that of the west. In the east it remained in clear control of its great land-owners well beyond the end of this period. In the west the senatorial aristocracy came to neutralize the provincial administration by filling a high proportion of its principal posts with its own members. In the relationship between the civilian government and the army important differences between east and west became evident when the Empire was divided between the sons of Theodosius I in 395. In the east the five commanders of field armies, the *magistri militum praesentales* and the *magistri militum* of Thrace, Illyricum and the East were all independent of each other, and each the superior of the dukes commanding frontier forts in his area. In the west the *magister peditum praesentalis* was the commander-in-chief of all armies in that half of the Empire. He was so powerful that he could only be deposed by assassination or battle. Under a weak emperor like Honorius or Valentinian III the Empire was governed by its commander-in-chief. Potentially strong emperors like Majorian and Anthemius were frustrated, and eventually destroyed, by their generals. The Western Empire came to an end when Odoacer, the *magister peditum*, deposed Romulus Augustulus, the last emperor in 476 (Croke, 1983). In the east the situation was quite different. The civilians remained in control. Under the weak Arcadius the Empire was guided by its praetorian prefects, notably Rufinus and Anthemius and for a time, Eutropius, *praepositus sacri cubiculi* and a eunuch. During the reign of Theodosius II the Empire seems to have been directed for many years by the emperor's sister Pulcheria. It was a measure of civilian supremacy in the east that the *magister officiorum* was given important duties in the supervision of the army. During all this time the Eastern Empire followed consistent, if unheroic policies when expedient, diverting threatening barbarians with large payments, so that they attacked the west instead. Thus the east weathered the storm in which the west foundered.

·BIBLIOGRAPHY·FOR·PART·6·

Abbott, F. F. and Johnson, A. C. (1926), *Municipal Administration in the Roman Empire*, Princeton.

Alföldi, A. (1934), 'Die Ausgestaltung des monarchischen Zeremoniells am römischen Kaiserhofe', *Mitteilungen des Deutschen Archäologischen Instituts*, Römische Abteilung, 49, 3–118.

Alföldi, A. (1935), 'Insignien und Tracht der römischen Kaiser', *Mitteilungen des Deutschen Archäologischen Instituts*, Römische Abteilung, 50, 3–158.

Alföldi, A. (1970), *Die monarchische Repräsentation im römischen Kaiserreiche*, Darmstadt.

Alföldy, G. (1974), 'The crisis of the third century as seen by contemporaries', *Greek, Roman and Byzantine Studies* 15, 89–111.

Alföldy, G. (1977), *Konsulat und Senatorenstand unter den Antoninen*, Bonn.

Alföldy, G. (1979), *Römische Sozialgeschichte*, Wiesbaden.

Arnheim, M. T. W. (1972), *The Senatorial Aristocracy in the Later Roman Empire*, Oxford.

Avery, W. T. (1940), 'The *adoratio purpurae* and the importance of the imperial purple in the 4th century of the Christian Era', *Memoirs of the American Academy in Rome*, 17, 66–80.

Barnes, T. D. (1981), *Constantine and Eusebius*, Cambridge, Mass.

Barnes, T. D. (1982), *The New Empire of Diocletian and Constantine*, Cambridge, Mass.

Berchem, D. van (1952), *L'Armée de Dioclétien et la réforme Constantinienne*, Paris.

Birley, E. (1953), 'Senators in the Emperor's service', *Proceedings of the British Academy*, 29, 197ff.

Birley, E. (1981), *The Fasti of Roman Britain*, Part I, Oxford.

Blagg, T. F. C. (1981), 'Architectural patronage in the western provinces of the Roman Empire in the third century', in A. King and M. Henig (eds), *The Roman West in the Third Century. Contributions from Archaeology and History*, British Archaeological Report, S109, Oxford.

Bleicken, J. (1962), *Senatsgericht und Kaisergericht*, Göttingen.

Boak, A. E. R. (1924), *The Master of the Offices in the Later Roman and Byzantine Administration*, University of Michigan Studies, Humanities Series 14, New York.

Brown, P. (1971), 'The rise and function of the holy man in late antiquity', *Journal of Roman Studies* LXI, 80–101.

Brown, P. (1978), *The Making of Late Antiquity*, Cambridge, Mass.

Brunt, P. (1966), 'Procuratorial jurisdiction', *Collections Latomus*, 25, 461ff.

Brunt, P. A. (1966), 'The fiscus and its development', *Journal of Roman Studies*, LVI, 75ff.

Brunt, P. A. (1975), 'The administration of Roman Egypt', *Journal of Roman Studies*, LXV, 124ff.

Brunt, P. A. (1981), 'The revenues of Rome', *Journal of Roman Studies*, LXXI, 161ff.

Burton, G. P. (1975), 'Proconsuls, assizes and the administration of justice under the Empire', *Journal of Roman Studies*, LXV, 92ff.

Burton, G. P. (1979), 'The curator rei publicae: towards a reappraisal', *Chiron*, 9, 465ff.

Cameron, A. (1970), *Poetry and Propaganda at the Court of Honorius*, Oxford.

Campbell, B. (1975), 'Who were the Viri Militares?', *Journal of Roman Studies*, LXV, 11ff.

Campbell, B. (1978), 'The marriage of soldiers under the empire', *Journal of Roman Studies*, LXVIII, pp. 153–66.

Carney, T. F. (1971), *Bureaucracy in Traditional Society: Romano-Byzantine bureaucracies viewed from within*, Lawrence.

Cerati, A. (1975), *Caractère annonaire et assiette de l'impôt foncier au Bas-Empire*, Paris.

Chastagnol, A. (1953), 'Le ravitaillement de Rome en viande au Ve siècle', *Revue Historique*, 77, 13.

Chastagnol, A. (1960), *La Préfecture urbaine à Rome sous le Bas-Empire*, Paris.

Chastagnol, A. (1966), 'Le sénat romaine sous le règne d'Odoacre', *Antiquitas*, Reihe 3, volume 3, Bonn.

Chastagnol, A. (1970), 'Les modes du recruitement du sénat au IVième siècle', in C. Nicolet (ed.), *Recherches sur les structures sociales dans l'Antiquité classique*, 187–211, Paris.

Chastagnol, A. (1976), *La Fin du monde antique de Stilicon à Justinien*, Paris.

Chastagnol, A. (1978), 'L'album municipal de Timgad', *Antiquitas*, Reihe 3, volume 22.

Chastagnol, A. (1979), 'Problèmes fiscaux du Bas-Empire', in *Points de vue sur la fiscalité antique*, 127, 40, Paris.

Chastagnol, A. (1982), *L'évolution politique sociale et économique du monde romain*, 248–363, Paris.

Clauss, M. (1980), *Der magister officiorum in der Spätantike (4–6 Jahrhundert)*, Munich.

Collot, C. (1965), 'La pratique de l'institution du *suffragium* au Bas-Empire', *Revue historique de droit Français et étranger*, 43, 185–22.

Cook, S. A, Adcock, F. E, Charlesworth, M. P, Baynes, N. H. (eds) (1939), *Cambridge Ancient History*, volume 12, Cambridge.

Croke, B. (1983), 'AD 476: the manufacture of a turning point', *Chiron*, 13, 81–119.

Dagron, G. (1974), *Naissance d'une capitale: Constantinople et ses institutions de 330 à 451*, Paris.

Déléage, A. (1945), *La Capitation du Bas-Empire*, Annales de l'Est, Mémoires, No. 14.

Demandt, A. (1980), 'Der spätrömische Militäradel', *Chiron*, 10, 609–36.

Demougeot, E. (1951), *De l'unité à la division de l'empire romain, 395–410*, Paris.

Dunlap, J. E. (1924), 'The office of the Grand Chamberlain in the Later Roman and Byzantine Empires', in *Two Studies in Later Roman and Byzantine Administration*, University of Michigan Studies, Humanities Series 14, New York, 161–322.

Duthoy, R. (1979), 'Curatores rei publicae en occident durant le principat', *Ancient Society*, 10, 171ff.

Eck, W. (1974), 'Beförderungskriterien innerhalb der senatorischen Laufbahn' in H. Temporini (ed.), *Aufstieg und Niedergang der römischen Welt*, 2:1, 158ff, Berlin/New York.

Eibach, D. (1977), *Untersuchungen zum spätantiken Kolonat in der kaiserlichen Gesetzgebung unter Berücksichtigung der Terminologie*, Bonn.

Fitz, J. (1983), 'L'administration des provinces pannoniennes sous le bas-empire romain', *Collection Latomus*, 181, Brussels.

Foss, C. (1976), *Byzantine and Turkish Sardis*, Cambridge, Mass.

Foss, C. (1977), 'Archaeology and the Twenty Cities of Byzantine Asia', *American Journal of Archaeology*, 81, 469–86.

Garnsey, P. D. (1968), 'The criminal jurisdiction of governors', *Journal of Roman Studies*, LVIII, 51ff.

Garnsey, P. D. (1970), *Social Status and Legal Privilege in the Roman Empire*, Oxford.

Garnsey, P. D. (1971), 'Honorarium decurionatus', *Historia*, 20, 309ff.

Garnsey, P. D. (1974), 'Aspects of the decline of the urban aristocracy in the empire', in H. Temporini (ed.), *Aufstieg und Niedergang der römischen Welt*, I, 2.1, 229ff, Berlin-New York.

Giardina, A. (1977), *Aspetti della Burocrazia nel Basso Impero*, Rome.

Goffart, W. (1974), *Caput and Colonate: Toward a History of Late Roman Taxation*, Toronto.

Goffart, W. (1980), *Barbarians and Romans*, Princeton.

Goffart, W. (1981), 'Rome Constantinople and the Barbarians', *American Historical Review*, 86, 275–306.

Gualandi, G. (1963), *Legislazione imperiale e giurisprudenza*, Milan.

Haehling, R. von (1978), *Die Religionszugehörigkeit der hohen Amsträger des römischen Reiches seit Constantins I Alleinherrschaft bis zum Ende der Theodosianischen Dynastie*, Antiquitas, 3 (23), Bonn.

Hahn, I. (1962), 'Theodoretus und die frühbyzantinische Besteuerung', *Acta Antiqua* X, 123–30.

Hahn, I. (1981), 'Das bäuerliche Patrocinium in Ost und West', *Klio* 50 (1968) 261–76, reprinted with bibliographical supplement in H. Schneider (ed.), *Social und Wirtschaftsgeschichte der römischen Kaiserzeit*, Darmstadt, 234–52.

Hirschfeld, O. (1963), *Die Kaiserlichen Verwaltungs beamten*, second edition, Berlin.

Hohlweg, A. (1971), 'Bischof und Stadtherr im frühen Byzanz', *Jahrbuch für österreichische Byzantinistik*, 20, 51–62.

Holum, K. G. (1982), *Theodosian Empresses, Women and Imperial Dominion in Late Antiquity*, Berkeley.

Honoré, A. M. (1979), 'Imperial rescripts AD 193–305: Authorship and Authenticity', *Journal of Roman Studies*, LXIX, 51–64.

Honoré, A. M. (1981), *Emperors and Lawyers*, London.

Hopkins, K. (1980), 'Taxes and trade in the Roman Empire (200 BC–AD 400)', *Journal of Roman Studies*, LXX, 101–25.

Hopkins, M. K. (1963), 'Eunuchs in politics in the later Roman Empire', *Proceedings of Cambridge Philosophical Society* 9, 62–80.

Hopkins, K. and Burton, G. P. (1983), 'Ambition and withdrawal: the senatorial aristocracy under the emperors', in K. Hopkins, *Death and Renewal*, Cambridge.

Jacques, F. (1983), 'Les curateurs des cités africaines au III siècle', in H. Temporini (ed.), *Aufstieg und Niedergang der römischen Welt*, II, 2.10, 62ff, Berlin/New York.

Johnson, A. C. and West, L. C. (1967), *Byzantine Egypt: Economic Studies*, Amsterdam.

Jolowicz, H. (1972), *Historical Introduction to the Study of Roman Law*, Cambridge.

Jones, A. H. M. (1940), *The Greek City*, Oxford.

Jones, A. H. M. (1949), 'The Roman civil service (clerical and sub-clerical grades)', *Journal of Roman Studies*, XXXIX, 38–55.

Jones, A. H. M. (1949), *The Greek City from Alexander to Justinian*, Oxford.

Jones, A. H. M. (1953), 'Census records of the Later Empire', *Journal of Roman Studies*, XLIII, 49–64.

Jones, A. H. M. (1954), 'The date and value of the Verona List', *Journal of Roman Studies*, XLIV, 21–9.

Jones, A. H. M. (1957), 'Capitatio and Jugatio', *Journal of Roman Studies*, XLVII, 88–94.

Jones, A. H. M. (1958), 'The Roman colonate', *Past and present*, 13.

Jones, A. H. M. (1959), 'Over taxation and the decline of the Roman Empire', *Antiquity*, 33, 39–43.

Jones, A. H. M. (1960), *Studies in Roman Government and Law*, Oxford.

Jones, A. H. M. (1964), *The Later Roman Empire, 284–602*, Oxford.

Jones, A. H. M. (1964), 'Collegiate prefectures', *Journal of Roman Studies*, LIV, 78–89.

Jones, A. H. M. (1968), 'The Dediticii and the *Constitutio Antoniana*', *Studies in Roman Government and Law*, 127–40, Oxford.

Jones, A. H. M. (1970), 'The caste system of the Later Roman Empire', *Eirene* 8, 79–97.

Jones, A. H. M. (1972), *The Criminal Courts of the Roman Republic and Principate*, Cambridge.

Jones, A. H. M. (1974), *The Roman Economy*, Oxford.

Jones, A. H. M., Martindale, R. and Morris, J. (1971), *The Prosopography of the Later Roman Empire (260–395)*, volume 1, Cambridge.

Jones, M. E. (1979), 'Climate, nutrition and disease, a hypothesis of Roman-British Population' in P. J. Casey (ed.), *The End of Roman Britain*, British Archaeological Reports 71, 231–5, Oxford.

Kaser, M. (1966), *Das römische Zivilprozessrecht*, Munich.

Keay, S. J. (1981), 'The Conventus Tarraconsensis in the third century A.D. Crisis and change', in A. King and M. Henig (eds), *The Roman West in the Third Century: Contributions from Archaeology and History*, British Archaeological Reports, S1099, 451–86, Oxford.

Keenan, J. K. (1975), 'Soziale Mobilität im spätrömischen Ägypten', *Zeitschrift fur Papyrologie und Epigraphie*, 17, 257ff.

Kent, J. P. C. (1961), 'The comes Sacrarum Largitionum', in E. C. Dodd, *Byzantine Silver Stamps*, 31–45, Washington.

King, A. and Henig, M. (eds) (1981), *The Roman West in the Third Century: Contributions from Archaeology and History*, British Archaeological Reports, S109, 1–2, Oxford.

Knepper, A. (1979), *Untersuchungen zur städtischen Plebs des 4 Jahrhunderts nr.Chr*, Bonn.

Koch, P. (1903), *Die byzantinischen Beamtentitel von 400 bis 700*, Jena.

Kunkel, W. (1966), *An Introduction to Roman Legal and Constitutional History*, Oxford.

Lallemand, J. (1964), *L'administration civile de l'Égypte de l'avènement de Dioclétian à la creation du diocèse (284–382)*, Académie Royale de Belgique, Classe des Lettres, Mémoires LVII, 2.

Langhamer, W. (1973), *Die rechtliche und sociale Stellung der magistratus municipales und der decuriones*, Wiesbaden.

Lepelley, C. (1979), 'Les cîtés de l'afrique romaine au bas-empire', *La Permanence d'une civilisation municipale*, volume 1, Paris.

Lepelley, W. (1981), 'Notice d'histoire municipale', *La Permanence d'une civilisation municipale*, volume 2, Paris.

Liebenam, W. (1897), 'Curator rei publicae', *Philologus*, 56, 290ff.

Liebenam, W. (1900), *Städtverwaltung im römischen Kaiserreiche*, Leipzig.

Liebeschuetz, W. (1961), 'Money economy and taxation in kind in Syria in the fourth century A.D.', *Rheinisches Museum*, 104, 242–56.

Liebeschuetz, J. H. W. G. (1972), *Antioch, City and Imperial Administration in the Later Roman Empire*, Oxford.

Liebeschuetz, J. H. W. G. (1973), 'The origin of the office of the pagarch', *Byzantinische Zeitschrift*, 66, 38–46.

Liebeschuetz, J. H. W. G. (1974), 'The pagarch: city and imperial administration in Byzantine Egypt', *Journal of Juristic Papyrology*, 18, 163–68.

MacCormack, S. G. (1981), *Art and Ceremony in Late Antiquity*, Berkeley.

MacMullen, R. (1962), 'The emperor's largesse', *Collections Latomus*, 21, 159–66.

MacMullen, R. (1963), *Soldier and Civilian in the Later Roman Empire*, Cambridge, Mass.

MacMullen, R. (1964a), 'Social mobility and the Theodosian code', *Journal of Roman Studies*, LIV, 49–53.

MacMullen, R. (1964b), 'Some pictures in Ammianus Mariellinus', *Art Bulletin*, 46, 435–55.

MacMullen, R. (1969), *Constantine*, London.

MacMullen, R. (1976), *The Roman Government's Response to Crisis, AD 235–337*, New Haven and London.

Magie, D. (1950), *Roman Rule in Asia-Minor*, Princeton.

Mann, J. C. (1976), 'What was the Notitia Dignitatum for?', in R. Goodburn and P. Bartholomew (eds), *Aspects of the Notitia Dignitatum*, British Archaeological Reports, S15, Oxford.

Marquadt, J. (1957), *Römische Staatsverwaltung*, Bände I–III, Darmstadt.

Martindale, J. R. (1980), *The Prosopography of the Later Roman Empire AD 395–527*, volume 2, Cambridge.

Matthews, J. F. (1971), 'Gallic supporters of Theodosius', *Collections Latomus*, 30, 1073–99.

Matthews, J. F. (1975), *Western Aristocracies and the Imperial Court, AD 364–425*, Oxford.

Mazzarino, S. (1951), *Aspetti Sociali del Quarto Secolo*, Rome.

Millar, F. (1967), 'The emperors at work', *Journal of Roman Studies*, LVII, 9ff.

Millar, F. (1977), *The Emperor in the Roman World*, London.

Millar, F. (1980), 'The Res Privata from Diocletian to Theodosius', in C. E. King (ed.), *Imperial Revenue and Expenditure and Monetary Policy in the 4th Century AD*, British Archaeological Reports, S76, Oxford.

Millar, F. (1981), *The Roman Empire and its Neighbours*, London.

Mitchell, S. (1976), 'Requisitioned transport in the Roman Empire', *Journal of Roman Studies*, LXVI, 106ff.

Mommsen, Th. (1899), *Römisches Strafrecht*, Leipzig.

Monks, G. R. (1951), 'The administration of the privy purse: an inquiry into official corruption and the fall of the Roman Empire', *Speculum*, 32, 748–79.

Mrozek, S. (1978), 'Munificentia Privata in den Städten Italiens während der späten Kaiserzeit', *Historia*, 27, 355–68.

Neesen, L. (1980), *Untersuchungen zu den direkten Staatsabgaben der römischen Kaiserzeit (27v. Chr.–284n. Chr.)*, Bonn.

Neesen, L. (1981), 'Die Entwicklung der Leistungen und Aemter (munera et honores) im römischen Kaiserreich des zweiten bis vierten Jahrhunderts', *Historia*, 30, 203–35.

Nellen, D. (1977), *Viri litterati, gebildetes Beamtentum und spätrömisches Reich im Westen zwischen 234 und 395 nach Christus*, Bochum.

Noetlichs, K. L. (1971), *Die gesetzgeberischen Massnahmen der christlichen Kaiser des vierten Jahrhunderts gegen Häretiker, Heiden und Juden*, Cologne.

Noetlichs, K. L. (1973), 'Materialien zum Bischofsbild aus den spätantiken Rechtsquellen', *Jahrbuch für Antike und Christentum*, 16, 28–39.

Noetlichs, K. L. (1981), *Beamtentum und Dienstvergehen zur Staatsverwaltung in der Spätantike*, Wiesbaden.

Noetlichs, K. L. (1982), 'Zur Entstehung der Diözesen als Mittelinstanz des spätrömischen Vervaltungssystems', *Historia*, XXXI, 70–81.

Nörr, D. (1969), *Imperium und Polis in der hohen Prinzipatszeit*, Munich.

Oliver, J. H. (1941), 'The sacred', *Hesperia*, Supplement 6.

Oliver, J. H. (1953a), 'The Roman governor's permission for a decree of the polis', *Hesperia*, XXXIII, 22, 163ff.

Oliver, J. H. (1953b), 'The ruling power', *Transactions of the American Philosophical Society*, new series, 43, 871ff.

Ostrogorsky, G. (1968), *History of the Byzantine State* (translated J. M. Hussey), second edition, Oxford.

Palanque, J.-R. (1933), *Essai sur la préfecture du prétoire du Bas-Empire*, Paris.

Patlagean, E. (1972), *Pauvreté économique et pauvreté sociale à Byzance 4e–7e siècles*, Paris.

Pedersen, F. S. (1976), *Late Roman Public Professionalism*, Odense Classical Studies, Volume 9, Odense.

Pekáry, T. (1968), *Untersuchungen zu den römischen Reichsstrassen*, Bonn.

Petit, P. (1955), *Libanius et la vie municipale à Antioche au IVe siècle après J-C.*, Paris.

Petri, E. and Droege, G. (1978), *Rheinische Geschichte*, volume I, Düsseldorf.

Petrikovits, H. von (1978), *Altertum*, Düsseldorf (F. Petri and G. Droeg (eds), *Rheinische Geschichte*, Volume I).

Pflaum, H. G. (1940), 'Essai sur le cursus publicus sous le haut-empire romain', *Mémoires présentés à l'Académie des Inscriptions et Belles-Lettres*, 14, 189ff.

Pflaum, H. G. (1950), *Les Procurateurs équestres sous le haut-empire romain*, Paris.

Pflaum, H. G. (1976), 'Zur Reform des Kaisers Gallienus', *Historia*, 25, 109–117.

Piganiol, A. (1947), *L'Empire chrétien (325–395)*, Paris.

Reece, R. (1981), 'The third century, crisis or change?' in A. King and M. Henig (eds), *The Roman West in the Third Century*, British Archaeological Reports, S109, 27–38, Oxford.

Rémondon, R. (1965), 'P. Hamb. 56 et P. London. 419: notes sur les finances d'Aphrodito du VIe siècle au VIIIe', *Chronique d'Égypte*, XL, 401–30.

Rouillard, G. (1928), *L'Administration civile de l'Égypte byzantine*, Paris.

Ruprecht, G. (1975), *Untersuchungen zum Dekurionenstand in den westlichen Provinzen des römischen Reiches*, Frankfurter althistorische Studien VIII, Kallmünz.

Ste Croix, G. E. M. de (1954), 'Suffragium, from vote to patronage', *British Journal of Sociology*, 5, 33–48.

Ste Croix, G. E. M. de (1981), *The Class Struggle in the Ancient World*, London.

Saller, R. P. (1980), 'Promotion and patronage in equestrian careers', *Journal of Roman Studies*, LXX , 44ff.

Saller, R. P. (1982), *Personal Patronage under the Early Empire*, Cambridge.

Salmon, P. (1974), 'Population et dépopulation dans l'empire romain', *Collections Latomus*, 137, Brussels.

Schaller, W. (1975), 'Grenzen des spätrömischen Staates, Staatspolizei und Korruption', *Zeitschrift für Papyrologie und Epigraphie*, 16, 1–17.

Seeck, O. (1876), *Notitia Dignitatum*, Frankfurt (reprinted 1962).

Seeck, O. (1919), *Regesten der Kaiser und Päpste für die Jahre 311–476 n.Chr.* Stuttgart (reprinted 1964).

Selb, W. (1967), '*Episcopalis audientia* von der Zeit Konstantins bis zu *Nov. XXXV* Valentinians III', *Zeitschrift der Savigny Stiftung*, 84, 167–217.

Seston, W. (1946), *Dioclétien et la Tétrarchie*, Paris.

Sheldon, H. (1981), 'London and south-east Britain 236–72', in A. King and M. Henig (eds), *The Roman West in the Third Century: Contributions from Archaeology and History*, British Archaeological Reports, S109, Oxford.

Sherwin-White, A. N. (1966), *The Letters of Pliny. A Historical and Social Commentary*, Oxford.

Sherwin-White, A. N. (1973), *The Roman Citizenship*, Oxford.

Sinnigen, W. C. (1957), *The Officium of the Urban Prefecture during the Later Roman Empire*, Rome.

Sinnigen, W. C. (1961), 'The Roman secret service', *Classical Journal*, 57, 65–72.

Stahl, M. (1978), *Imperiale Herrschaft und provinziale Stadt*, Göttingen.

Stein, E. (1959), *Histoire du Bas-Empire* (édition française par J. R. Palanque), Paris.

Stevenson, G. H. (1939), *Roman Provincial Administration*, Oxford.

Stroheker, K. F. (1943), *Der senatorische Adel im spätantiken Gallien*, Tübingen.

Syme, R. (1984), 'Fiction about Roman jurists' in R. Birley (ed.), *Roman Papers III*, Oxford.

Tengstrom, E. (1974), *Bread for the People: Studies in the corn-supply of Rome during the Late Empire*, Stockholm.

Thompson, E. A. (1969), *The Goths in Spain*, Oxford.

Treitinger, O. (1969), *Die oströmischen Kaiser und die Reichsidee nach ihrer Gestaltung im höfischen Zeremoniell*, Hamburg.

Vercauteren, F. (1969), 'Die spätantike Civitas im frühen Mittelalter', in J. C. Haase (ed.), *Die Stadt des Mittelalters*, I, 122–38, Darmstadt.

Veyne, P. (1981), 'Clientèle et corruption au service de l'état', *Annales économies, sociétés et civilisations*, 339–60.

Vogler, A. (1979), *Constance II et l'administration impériale*, Strasbourg.

Waldstein, W. (1976), 'Zur Stellung der Episcopalis Audientia im spätrömischen Process', in D. Medicus and H. M. Seiter, (eds), *Festschrift für Max Kaser*, 533, Munich.

Walker, S. (1981), 'The Third Century in the Lyon Region', in A. King and M. Henig (eds), *The Roman West in the Third Century: Contributions from Archaeology and History*, British Archaeological Reports, S109, Oxford.

Walser, G. and Pekáry, Th. (1962), *Die Krise des römischen Reiches*. Bericht über die Forschungen zur Geschichte des 3 Jahrhunderts, Berlin.

Watson, Alan (1974), *Law-making in the Later Roman Republic*, Oxford.

Weiss, P. B. (1975), *Consistorium und comites consistoriani Untersuchungen zur Hofbeamtenschaft des 4 Jahrhunderts n.Chr.* auf prosopographischer Grundlage, Würzburg.

Wes, M. A. (1967), 'Das Ende des Kaiseriums im Westen des römischen Reiches', *Arch. Stud. van het Nederlands Hist. Inst. te Rome*, II, s'Gravenhage.

Whittaker, C. R. (1976), 'Agri Deserti', in M. I. Finley (ed.), *Studies in Roman Property*, 137–65, Cambridge.

Williams, W. (1976), 'Individuality in the imperial constitutions, Hadrian and the Antonines', *Journal of Roman Studies*, LXVI, p. 69.

Wlassak, M. (1919), *Zum römischen Provinzialprozess*, Vienna.